A Brief Guide

Charlotte Huck's
Children's
Literature

A Brief Guide

Charlotte Huck's
Children's
Literature

Barbara Z. Kiefer
The Ohio State University

Cynthia A. Tyson
The Ohio State University

Higher Education

Boston   Burr Ridge, IL   Dubuque, IA   New York   San Francisco   St. Louis
Bangkok   Bogotá   Caracas   Kuala Lumpur   Lisbon   London   Madrid   Mexico City
Milan   Montreal   New Delhi   Santiago   Seoul   Singapore   Sydney   Taipei   Toronto

 **Higher Education**

This book is printed on acid-free paper.

1 2 3 4 5 6 7 8 9 0 DOC / DOC 0 9

ISBN: 978-0-07-340383-0
MHID: 0-07-340383-0

Editor in Chief: *Michael Ryan*
Editorial Director: *Beth Mejia*
Publisher: *David Patterson*
Sponsoring Editor: *Allison McNamara*
Developmental Editor: *Vicki Malinee, Van Brien & Associates*
Marketing Manager: *James Headley*
Media Project Manager: *Thomas Brierly*
Production Editor: *Leslie LaDow*
Manuscript Editor: *Patricia Ohlenroth*
Designers: *Cassandra Chu & Brian Salisbury*
Cover Art: *Rafael López*
Photo Research Coordinator: *Alexandra Ambrose*
Photo Researcher: *Jennifer Blankenship*
Production Supervisor: *Tandra Jorgensen*
Composition: *9.5/12 Stone Serif by Thompson Type*
Printing: *45# Pub Matte by R. R. Donnelly & Sons*

Library of Congress Cataloging-in-Publication Data

Kiefer, Barbara Zulandt, 1944–
Charlotte Huck's Children's Literature: A Brief Guide / Barbara Z. Kiefer, Cynthia A. Tyson
    p. cm.
  Includes bibliograpical references and index
  ISBN-13: 978-0-07-340383-0 (alk. paper)
  ISBN-10: 0-07-340383-0 (alk. paper)
  1. Literature—Study and teaching (Elementary)—United States. 2. Children's literature—Study and teaching (Higher)—United States. 3. Literature teachers—Training of—United States. I. Tyson, Cynthia A. II. Huck, Charlotte S. III. Title.
  LB1575.5.U5K54 2009
  372.64—dc22   2009003179

www.mhhe.com

This book is dedicated with love to our families.

Contents in Brief

Contents

Part One
Learning About Books and Children 1

Part Two
Exploring Genres in Children's Books   57

Part Three
The Literature Program Across the Curriculum   268

Preface

As the tenth edition sets to publish in the spring of 2009, *Charlotte Huck's Children's Literature* continues to be the classic, comprehensive text for those involved in all aspects of the evaluation and selection of children's literature for preK through middle-school readers. Like no other book, it not only provides the classroom teacher, librarian, administrator, and parent with a thorough understanding of children's literature, but it also—like no other book—reflects the passion for children's literature that resonated with Charlotte Huck. A true pioneer in the field, it was apparent that Charlotte's goal was not for readers to simply learn the history, concepts, and evaluation criteria necessary to understand and select children's literature—but to jump headfirst into the joy and excitement that the literature of childhood can bring, and in turn to share this enthusiasm with the children they teach. As we continue with the tenets originated by Charlotte, who passed away in 2005, we keep that goal of passion and enthusiasm at the forefront of our writing.

Approach of This New Text

As instructional programs continue to evolve and change, this allows us an ideal opportunity to present this trusted, essential material in two formats: the classic, comprehensive text for those requiring deeper instruction, and this new, briefer version that provides an introduction to the field of children's literature that addresses the needs of preservice teachers by employing a multifaceted approach to the study of children's literature:

- By focusing on the core definitions, key examples, and essential evaluation guidelines, *Charlotte Huck's Children's Literature: A Brief Guide* provides a **launching point for further exploration of actual children's books** during the course setting.

- This text not only serves as a valuable resource by providing the most current reference lists from which to select texts, but it also emphasizes the critical skills needed to search for and select literature—**researching, evaluating, and implementing quality books in the preK–8 classroom**—to give preservice teachers the tools they need to evaluate books, create curriculum, and share the love of literature.

- We have drawn from the key understandings that are found in the big book and have added **critical perspectives that face teachers in the twenty-first century.** The critical perspectives offered here, many of which explore the use of multicultural literature, are presented to the reader to assist in the process of evaluating children's literature through themes and issues of social and political nature that often find their way into today's classrooms. These discussions, along with the application of the Ten-Point Model for Teaching Controversial Issues presented in each of the genre chapters, encourage higher levels of examination and will help facilitate critical-thinking skills in even their youngest students.

- We contend that the literature and accomplishments of all groups should be part of every subject taught. Thus, **multicultural literature is infused throughout the entire text** and in each genre or subject area.

Organization

The three-part organization of this book emphasizes the triple focus of the text: the reader, the book, and teaching. Part One focuses on the values and criteria for choosing and using literature with children at various stages in their development. Part Two provides an in-depth look at the various genres of children's literature and establishes evaluative criteria for each genre. Each of these chapters has been written with children at the center and includes references and resources for involving children in exploring books across the curriculum. Part Three explores this curricular strand in-depth by focusing on the teaching, planning, and evaluating of literature-based programs.

Features

As touched on previously, this text not only provides the core material necessary to understand children's literature, but it also provides a number of unique features and presentations:

- **Full-color throughout:** In order to truly show the visual impact of children's literature, the entire text is full-color, with approximately one hundred images of covers and illustrations from children's books presented throughout the chapters.
- **The art of Rafael López:** We are very fortunate to have Rafael López involved in this new text. The multitalented and award-winning illustrator has created a vibrant and exciting look for the book, developing unique artwork for the cover and interior features.
- **Thoroughly integrated multicultural literature and diversity topics:** Examples of multicultural literature and its applications in the classroom are provided throughout the entire text, ensuring that future teachers will have the skills to choose challenging and inspiring literature for all their students. Multicultural titles are called out by a margin icon as well as printed in blue in the children's literature lists at the end of each chapter.
- **The Ten-Point Model for Teaching Controversial Issues:** A unique framework for tackling controversial topics in and out of the classroom, the Ten-Point Model for Teaching Controversial Issues is presented in Chapter 1. The subsequent genre chapters include specific examples of how to use the model. A blank format is available on the book's Web site at **www .mhhe.com/kieferbrief1e.**
- **Teaching Features:** Resource boxes throughout the text highlight the best examples of children's literature for each genre or topic.

- **Evaluating children's literature:** *Guidelines* boxes provide specific criteria and questions to consider when evaluating children's literature. Expanded forms are available on the text's Web site. These forms can be used as course activities or in practice when evaluating specific books.
- **Unique Challenging Perspectives discussions:** *Challenging Perspectives* sections appear in each genre chapter, outlining difficult or controversial social issues facing today's teacher (and children) and providing instruction on how to evaluate and select appropriate children's literature that will help address those topics. Many topics involve cultural issues, such as sensitivity to the use of color in different cultures and "slams" in poetry.
- **Applications to standards:** The *Curriculum Connections* feature at the end of each genre chapter gives examples of how to use children's literature to fulfill educational standards in a variety of course areas.
- **Children's literature selections:** Comprehensive, up-to-date lists of children's literature are provided at the end of each chapter, with more titles available in the searchable Children's Literature Database on the book's Web site at **www.mhhe.com/kieferbrief1e.**
- **Books to Read Aloud:** The endpapers serve as an introduction to the field of children's literature by providing a quick list of books to read aloud to different age groups.
- **Practical appendixes:** The book's appendixes—Children's Book Awards and Book Selection Aids—provide current resources to aid in text selection. The complete set of award winners and a comprehensive list of publishers' contact information can be found on the book's Web site at **www.mhhe.com/kieferbrief1e.**

Teaching and Learning Resources

Charlotte Huck's Children's Literature: A Brief Guide is accompanied by a number of supplemental resources and learning aids for instructors and students.

- **Online Learning Web site at www.mhhe .com/kieferbrief1e.** Visit the book's Web site to find many valuable resources. Instructors will have access to a computerized test bank, instructor's manual, and PowerPoint presentations. Student resources include quizzes with feedback, chapter objectives, annotated Web links, expanded evaluation guides, and much more.

- **Children's Literature Database.** Accessible from the Online Learning Center, this extensive children's literature database of more than five thousand titles can be searched a number of ways. The books listed have been carefully evaluated and selected as excellent books for children, including the award winners listed in Appendix A.
- **PageOut.** PageOut is a course management tool you can use to create a course Web site. This tool helps you create an interactive course syllabus through which you can post content and links, an online gradebook, lecture notes, bookmarks, and even a discussion board where students can discuss course-related topics. For more information, go to <www.pageout.net>.
- **LitLinks:** *Activities for Connected Learning in Elementary Classrooms,* **second edition,** by Dena Beeghly (ISBN 0-07-327569-7). This resource text contains guidelines and guidance for creating literature-centered lessons across the curriculum and sample lesson plans.
- *FolioLive. Folio*Live is an online portfolio tool you can use to create an electronic portfolio in three easy steps: (1) Use a template to create a homepage, (2) choose to create a custom framework or select an existing framework to structure your portfolio, and (3) add the artifacts to build your portfolio by uploading existing files (from Word to PowerPoint to video), linking to artifacts posted elsewhere on the Web, or creating an artifact through *Folio*Live embedded forms. Go to <www.foliolive.com> to learn more about this product.

Acknowledgments

As one can imagine, condensing a classic text into the essentials can be quite a daunting task. Making sure the end result is a fluid text with appropriate supporting examples, along with introducing cutting-edge, controversial issues, is a challenge, but one that we believe we successfully achieved

with the expert assistance of a number of instructors who teach this course to preservice teachers. We want to personally thank and acknowledge the contributions of those educators who participated in the review of the proposal and many drafts of this text:

Linda Alexander, *University of South Florida*
Katherine Bucher, *Old Dominion University*
Marsha Riddle Buly, *Western Washington University*
Ellen Campbell, *Fairleigh Dickinson University*
Barbara Smith Chalou, *University of Maine–Presque Isle*
Rebecca Compton, *East Central University*
Margaret Deitrich, *Austin Peay State University*
Brenda Drewett, *Columbia College-Fort Worth*
Terrance Flaherty, *Minnesota State University*
Sherry Gill, *West Texas A&M University*
Carol Greene, *Ashland Community and Technical College*
Joyce Hamon, *University of Southern Indiana*
Susan Higgins, *University of Southern Mississippi*
Deborah Ann Jensen, *Hunter College*
Susan Knell, *Pittsburgh State University*
Dianne Koehnecke, *Webster University*
Deborah Jenkins Linville, *Salem College*
Susan Monier, *Central Florida Community College*
Vanessa Morris, *Clarion University of Pennsylvania*
Ann Neely, *Vanderbilt University*
Sheryl O'Sullivan, *Azusa Pacific University*
Patricia Panitz, *Cape Cod Community College*
Kay Rayborn, *Henderson State University*
Patricia Rieman, *Northern Illinois University*
Ilene Rutten, *St. Cloud State University*
Mary Schumacher, *Wichita State University*
Wenju Shen, *Valdosta State University*
Lucille Strain, *Bowie State University*
Kathleen Tice, *University of Texas-Arlington*
Sylvia Vardell, *Texas Woman's University*
Bradford Walker, *University of North Carolina–Wilmington*
Marilyn Ward, *Carthage College*
Elizabeth Witherspoon, *Stephen F. Austin State University*

We also must thank Susan Hepler and Janet Hickman, dear friends and colleagues whose involvement in earlier editions of *Charlotte Huck's Children's Literature* has surely made its way into the content—if not the soul—of this new briefer text.

Sincere thanks also goes to Detra Price-Dennis and Caitlin Ryan for their assistance in developing the unique Curriculum Connections feature, and to Eun Hye Son for her continued support and hard work on both children's literature texts.

Finally, we hope that readers of this book will see it as a first step to understanding and appreciating the richness of offerings in children's literature and the complexity of its readership. Our desire is that as you gain insights into children's developmental needs and interests, the information provided here will simultaneously better prepare you to appropriately incorporate considerations from cultural points of view and the social contexts in which the deepest responses to literature can occur.

Barbara Z. Kiefer
Cynthia A. Tyson

Welcome to *Charlotte Huck's Children's Literature: A Brief Guide*. This text has been designed to launch your exploration of children's literature and to prepare you to evaluate and select books for your future students that will instill an interest and passion for literature.

- Approximately one hundred **full-color images** of covers and illustrations from children's books show the visual impact of children's literature.

Joseph Bruchac's warm and realistic *Eagle Song* is one of the few books for children that feature a Native American character in a contemporary setting. Cover from *Eagle Song* by Joseph Bruchac, illustrated by Dan Andreasen, copyright © 1997 by Dan Andreasen. Used by permission of Dial Books for Young Readers, a Division of Penguin Young Readers Group, a Member of Penguin Group (USA) Inc., 345 Hudson Street, New York, NY 10014. All rights reserved.

Two girls of African heritage grow up in two very different worlds in Berlie Doherty's moving *The Girl Who Saw Lions*. Jacket cover from *The Girl Who Saw Lions* by Berlie Doherty. Copyright © 2008 by Berlie Doherty. Used by permission of Roaring Brook Press, a division of Henry Holt and Company, LLC.

Popular Types of Realistic Fiction

Certain categories of realistic fiction are so popular that children ask for them by name. They want a good animal story, usually about a dog or horse; a sports book; a "funny" book; or a good mystery. Each decade seems to have a popular series, as well, that lingers on the bookshelves. From Gertrude Chandler Warner's Boxcar Children to Ann Martin's Baby-Sitters Club series, from Nancy Drew and the Hardy Boys to Patricia Reilly Giff's Kids of Polk Street School series, children read one volume of a series and demand the next. Although many of these books are not high-quality literature, they do serve the useful function of getting children hooked on books so that they will move on to better literature.[8] Children also develop fluency and reading speed as they quickly read through popular books or a series.

Chapter Seven **Contemporary Realistic Fiction** 199

---

teaching **feature 5.1**

Chronicles, Sagas, and Trilogies: Recent Fantasy Series for Children

Author	Series Title	Description	Grade Level
T. A. Barron	The Great Tree of Avalon	These stories the battle between good and evil take place in the legendary land of Avalon.	5 and up
—	The Lost Years of Merlin	These tales relate the childhood of Merlin and his rise to power.	5 and up
Ian Beck	Tom Trueheart	Tom, youngest of seven brothers all named Jack, enters the land of stories to seek happy endings.	3–6
Patrick Carman	Atherton	Edgar lives on an artificial world that has three levels strictly divided by class.	4–7
Tony DiTerlizzi and Holly Black	The Spiderwick Chronicles	Three children move into an old estate and experience new adventures with fairies and other magical creatures.	3–6
Jeanne DuPrau	The City of Ember	Lina and Doon struggle to escape their existence in a devastated future world.	4–7
Nancy Farmer	Islands of the Blessed	Jack, a young Saxon boy, enters into adventures with heroes from Celtic and Norse mythology.	5 and up
Jean Ferris	Marigold series	An amusing take on traditional fairy tales in which young Marigold is pitted against a wicked Queen.	4–7
Cornelia Funke	Inkheart	Meggie and her father can live in two worlds, their own and the world of the book.	4–7
Debi Gliori	Pure Dead	An over-the-top comedy series featuring the Strega-Borgia clan.	4–7
Erin Hunter	Warriors	The cats of the Thunder Clan face trials and tribulations.	4 and up
Brian Jacques	Redwall	A large cast of animal characters fight for right in the mythical medieval kingdom of Redwall.	4 and up
Catherine Jinks	Genius Squad	Thaddeus Roth is a young genius who is recruited into the Axis Institute for World Domination.	5 and up
William Nicholson	The Wind on Fire Trilogy	Twins Bowman and Kestral lead their people on a journey to their ancestral home.	5 and up
Jenny Nimmo	Magician Trilogy	Gwyn, a young Welsh boy, learns that he is descended from wizards and with the help of magical gifts battles villains from Wales' past.	4–7
Kenneth Oppel	Silverwing	A young bat ventures out into the wide world to save his colony and find his identity.	3–6

132 Part 2 Exploring Genres in Children's Books   www.mhhe.com/kieferbrief1e

- **Teaching Feature** resource boxes throughout the text highlight the best examples of children's literature for each genre or topic.

- **Multicultural literature** is thoroughly integrated throughout, pointed out by an icon in the text as well as printed in blue in the children's literature lists.

characters like Frankie in *The Disreputable History of Frankie Landau-Banks* by E. Lockhart, who are willing to challenge traditional role models and expectations.

Boys, too, can get beyond such beliefs as "men don't cry." Modern realistic fiction shows that everyone may cry as they grieve, as do a boy and his father following the drowning of a friend in *On My Honor* by Marion Dane Bauer. The issue of presenting multiple role models in books for boys has led to a campaign by popular author Jon Scieszka. Scieszka's Web site, called Guys Read <www.guysread.com>, has suggestions for books and activities that will appeal to boys. Scieszka has also selected various male authors to contribute to *Guys Write for Guys Read*, a collection of short stories for boys.

People with mental or physical impairments have in the past been depicted as "handicapped" or "disabled." Books such as Tracie Vaughn Zimmer's *Reaching for the Sun* or Sis Deans's *Rainy* provide more enlightened views that suggest that the person is more important than the impairment; one can be differently abled without necessarily being disabled. Older people (and other adults) in children's literature have often been dismissed as irrelevant in a young person's life, as ineffectual in contrast to the vibrancy of young spirits, or as unable to do certain things because of their age. High-quality contemporary realistic fiction stories depict adults and older people in many ways—as mentors to young people, for instance, and as having their own romances, problems, and triumphs.

Children's books have made great gains in the depiction of our changing society. However, today's books need to continue to reflect the wide ranges of occupations, education, speech patterns, lifestyles, and futures that are possible for all, regardless of race, gender, age, ability, or belief.

The title character of Sis Deans's *Rainy* is a 10-year-old girl who struggles to control her ADHD while away from her supportive family at summer camp. Cover of Rainy by Sis Deans. Cover copyright © 2005 by Henry Holt and Company, LLC. Reprinted by permission of Henry Holt and Company, LLC.

The Author's Background

The subject of an author's racial background has become another source of controversy in children's contemporary realistic fiction. Must an author be black to write about African Americans, or Native American to write about Native Americans? As Virginia Hamilton states:

It happens that I know Black people better than any other people because I am one of them and I grew up knowing what it is we are about. . . . The writer uses the most comfortable milieu in which to tell a story, which is why my characters are Black. Often being Black is significant to the story; other times, it is not. The writer will always attempt to tell stories no one else can tell.[5]

It has been generally accepted that an author should write about what he or she knows. But Ann Cameron, an Anglo-American author who has lived in Guatemala for many years, is the author of many books about children from diverse places and

192 Part 2 Exploring Genres in Children's Books   www.mhhe.com/kieferbrief1e

---

Second, teachers can expand their understanding of what it means to respond to traditional literature.[10] If the only legitimate way to respond is to discuss the literature within in its genre—plot structures, style, themes, motif and variants, and other measures used to capture many's responses to literature—then we may lose the opportunity to use traditional literature to open up a whole world of imagination, cross-cultural understanding, and pure enjoyment. Children will come to the classroom with many varied lived experiences that will be the foundation of engagement and response to literature. What happens when a teacher wants to use a traditional folktale to teach all the objectives found in a reading standard and some of the children's responses indicate they are not engaged with the text? The teacher may decide to continue with the unit and hope those students will change their attitude or the teacher may want to develop teaching strategies that will facilitate creating classroom spaces for multiple ways of responding to literature. The Ten-Point Model below (**Figure 4.1**) provides suggestions for using traditional literature to respond to the perspectives some children bring to a reading of this genre. This model provides additions to a repertoire of many successful strategies for differentiated instruction.

- A unique framework for tackling controversial topics in and out of the classroom, the **Ten-Point Model for Teaching Controversial Issues** is presented in Chapter 1 with relevant examples in each genre chapter.

figure 4.1   The Ten-Point Model for Teaching Controversial Issues
Teaching Traditional Literature

Step	Task	To Consider
1. Raise the initial question and have the children brainstorm all their initial responses.	Ask students to critically analyze traditional literature (such as folktales, myths, or legends).	For example, ask what a different perspective of the story would be. What would Red Riding Hood think or do differently if her grandmother's house was in your neighborhood?
2. Create a list of "Things to find out more about."	As children read variations of traditional literature they can compare and contrast different versions of the story, asking which is the "correct one" and why. What is the author's viewpoint? Can you detect propaganda techniques in the writing of traditional literature?	Many cultures approach "strangers" in different ways. Ask if Little Red Riding Hood grew up in your house, what would have been expected of her when she met the wolf that was a stranger? Do you think other children are taught to respond differently?
3. Assign information-gathering homework.	Children can illustrate ways to compare various tales or to note similarities and differences in the main character, setting, conflict, advice, animals, and resolution of conflict. Students should gather, evaluate, and synthesize information in a variety of ways, perhaps using multimodal approaches to information gathering and display.	Traditional literature is a powerful tool for teaching critical reading. It offers children the opportunity to actively engage with the texts while simultaneously considering ideas, values, and ethical questions. For example, ask what would Little Red Riding Hood have done to solve the conflict with the wolf if she lived a big city? Small town? Rural town?

(continued)

Chapter Four Traditional Literature 117

Light by Jane Breskin Zalben is based on a scholarly interpretation of the Old Testament creation story. From *Light* by Jane Breskin Zalben, copyright © 2007 by Jane Breskin Zalben. Used by permission of Dutton, a Division of Penguin Young Readers Group, a Member of Penguin Group (USA) Inc., 345 Hudson Street, New York, NY 10014. All rights reserved.

literature, children can form a link with the common bonds of humanity from the beginnings of recorded time, as well as form a foundation for much of their future reading.

Challenging Perspectives on Traditional Literature

An important point to consider when teaching traditional literature is that not all children will view fairy tales in predictable ways. Some children will opt not to participate in classroom activities that center on reading fairy tales, fables, or myths. Simply put, this would not be their genre of choice. Their perceptions about traditional literature present particular challenges for the classroom teacher. This can be especially challenging if fairy tales, well liked by the teacher, are used to teach across the curriculum. In that context, a student's lack of engagement and lack of response can eventually create a barrier to academic achievement.

Some educators assert that there are universals across all children's experiences and these universals are the places in discussions that reading and responding to traditional literature are best facilitated. This is not always the case. Teachers' childhood experiences and those of their students, particularly those from diverse backgrounds, may find themselves at disparate crossroads. Therefore the mediation of responses

Chapter Four Traditional Literature 115

- **Challenging Perspectives** discussions appear in each genre chapter, outlining difficult or controversial social issues and providing instruction on how to evaluate and select appropriate children's literature that will help address those topics.

- **Guidelines** boxes provide specific criteria and questions to consider when evaluating children's literature.

Guidelines

Evaluating Children's Fiction

Go to www.mhhe.com/kieferbrief1e to access an expanded version of this evaluation form.

Before Reading
- What kind of book is this?
- What does the reader anticipate from the title? Dust jacket illustration? Size of print? Illustrations? Chapter headings? Opening page?
- For what age range is this book intended?

Plot
- Does the book tell a good story?
- Will children enjoy it? Is there action?
- Does the story move?
- Is the plot original and fresh?
- Is it plausible and credible?
- Is there preparation for the events?
- Is there a logical series of happenings?
- Is there a basis of cause and effect in the happenings?
- Is there an identifiable climax? How do events build to a climax?
- Is the plot well constructed?

Setting
- Where does the story take place?
- How does the author indicate the time?
- How does the setting affect the action, characters, or theme?
- Does the story transcend the setting and have universal implications?

Theme
- Does the story have a theme?
- Is the theme worth imparting to children?
- Does the theme emerge naturally from the story, or is it stated too obviously?
- Does the theme overpower the story?
- Does it avoid moralizing?
- How does the author use motifs or symbols to intensify meaning?

Characterization
- How does the author reveal characters? Through narration? In conversation? By thoughts of others?
- Are the characters convincing and credible?
- Do we see their strengths and their weaknesses?
- Does the author avoid stereotyping?
- Is the behavior of the characters consistent with their ages and background?
- Is there any character development or growth?
- Has the author shown the causes of character behavior or development?

Style
- Is the style of writing appropriate to the subject?
- Is the style straightforward or figurative?
- Is the dialogue natural and suited to the characters?
- How did the author create a mood? Is the overall impression one of mystery? gloom? evil? joy? security?

Point of View
- Is the point of view from which the story is told appropriate to the purpose of the book? Does the point of view change?
- Does the point of view limit the reader's horizon, or enlarge it?
- Why did the author choose this particular point of view?

Additional Considerations
- Do the illustrations enhance or extend the story?
- Are the pictures aesthetically satisfying?
- How well designed is the book?
- Is the format of the book related to the text?
- What is the quality of the paper? How sturdy is the binding?
- How does the book compare with other books on the same subject?
- How does the book compare with other books written by the same author?
- How have other reviewers evaluated this book?
- What age range would most appreciate this story?

14 Part 1 Learning About Books and Children   www.mhhe.com/kieferbrief1e

Take a look inside . . .   **xvii**

- The **Curriculum Connections** feature at the end of each genre chapter gives examples of how to use children's literature to fulfill educational standards in a variety of course areas.

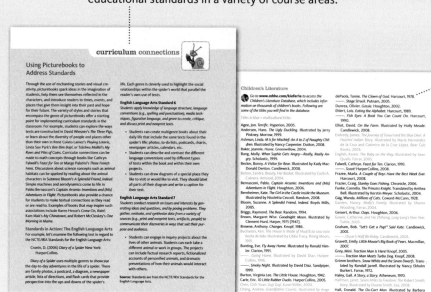

- Comprehensive, up-to-date **lists of children's literature** are provided at the end of each chapter, with multicultural titles printed in blue. More titles are available in the searchable Children's Literature Database.

- The **Online Learning Center Web site** at www.mhhe.com/kieferbrief1e provides many resources for further exploring children's literature.

- Now accessible from the Online Learning Center at **www.mhhe.com/kieferbrief1e**, the **Children's Literature Database** is a searchable database listing over 5,500 carefully selected children's books, including major award winners and the hundreds of titles referenced in this text.

In Memoriam

Charlotte S. Huck **1923–2005**

Born in Evanston, Illinois, Charlotte Huck attended Wellesley College in Massachusetts, then graduated from Northwestern University, where she earned master's and doctoral degrees. After teaching in elementary schools in Missouri and Illinois, followed by a teaching position at Northwestern. Dr. Huck joined the faculty of The Ohio State University in 1955, where she created and led the first-ever graduate program in children's literature for thirty years. She believed that stories are what motivate children to want to read, and she encouraged teachers to use children's literature in reading lessons, emphasizing her concept of "webbing," in which every subject taught to a child is supported by reading.

Charlotte Huck established an annual OSU children's literature conference that attracted thousands of teachers, librarians, and book enthusiasts from 1982 to 2004. After she retired and moved to California, she started a similar conference at the University of Redlands. She continued to write professionally and remained active in community and school-based literacy programs.

Besides authoring the classic *Children's Literature in the Elementary School* (originally published in 1961), she also wrote books for children. With Anita Lobel, she published *Princess Furball* (1994), *Toads and Diamonds* (1995), and *The Black Bull of Norroway* (2001). Those and her other books, *Secret Places* (1993) and *A Creepy Countdown* (1999), are published by Greenwillow Books.

Dr. Huck served on the Newbery and Caldecott medal committees and was a president of the National Council of Teachers of English. The numerous awards and honors she received included The Ohio State University's Distinguished Teaching Award, the Landau Award for Distinguished Service in Teaching Children's Literature, and the Arbuthnot Award, given annually by the International Reading Association to an outstanding professor of children's literature. In 1997, she was presented with the Outstanding Educator in the English Language Arts Award by the NCTE Elementary Section.

Charlotte Huck was honored in 1987 with the NCTE Distinguished Service Award for her service to the English teaching profession and to NCTE. The 1988 NCTE President Julie Jensen made the award presentation, commending Huck for her service "to The Ohio State University, to the state of Ohio, and most of all, to language learners and teachers everywhere. They are the beneficiaries of her knowledge and enthusiasm for the literature of childhood, and of her unyielding conviction that readers are made by those who have themselves discovered the joys of reading."

Charlotte Huck was considered to be one of the foremost experts on children's literature and its uses. In 1996, Ohio State University established in her name the first endowed professorship in children's literature in the United States. In her career at OSU, she mentored Ph.D. students, teachers, and library media specialists who continue her beliefs and enthusiasm as new programs in children's literature are launched across the country.

About the Authors

Barbara Z. Kiefer

Barbara Kiefer is the Charlotte S. Huck Professor of Children's Literature at The Ohio State University. She was formerly Robinson Professor of Children's Literature at Teachers College, Columbia University. Originally trained in art education, she taught grades one, two, four, and five in several regions of the United States and in overseas schools. She served as the elected chair of the year 2000 Caldecott Award Committee of the American Library Association and was a member of the 1988 Caldecott Award Committee. She has also served as chair of the Elementary Section Committee of the National Council of Teachers of English (NCTE) and as a member of the NCTE Executive Board. She is currently a co-editor of *Language Arts,* a journal of the NCTE, and a board member of NCTE's Children's Literature Assembly. She has published numerous articles and book chapters about reading and children's literature and is author of *The Potential of Picturebooks: From Visual Literacy to Aesthetic Understanding,* and the co-author of *An Integrated Language Perspective in the Elementary School: Theory into Action,* with Christine Pappas and Linda Levstik.

Cynthia A. Tyson

Dr. Cynthia A. Tyson is an associate professor in the School of Teaching and Learning at The Ohio State University. Her research and scholarship interests include teaching for social justice, early childhood social studies, and multicultural children's literature. Dr. Tyson's work is both national and internationally recognized. She has presented numerous research papers at national meetings and conferences and has published articles in many books and journals, including *Educational Researcher, Theory and Research in Social Education, International Journal of Qualitative Research in Education,* and *Reading Research Quarterly.* She recently completed the co-edited volume *Handbook of Social Studies Research.* Dr. Tyson started her career as an elementary classroom teacher and multicultural education professional development specialist. She has worked as a consultant to school districts across the United States, the United Kingdom, and Mali, West Africa, and is currently collaborating with teachers and researchers on a project in Johannesburg, South Africa.

About the Illustrator

Rafael López

The work of Rafael López is a fusion of strong graphic style and magical symbolism. López grew up in Mexico City, where he was immersed in the city's rich cultural heritage and in the native color of its street life. Influenced by Mexican surrealism, *dichos* (proverbs), and myths, he developed a style with roots in these traditions.

His many international clients include Amnesty International, Apple, Chicago Tribune, HarperCollins, IBM, Intel, Los Angeles Times, the Grammy Awards, and World Wildlife Fund. His work has been selected into multiple juried shows and his children's books have won two Americas Awards and a Pura Belpré Honor for *My Name Is Celia/Me llamo Celia: The Life of Celia Cruz/La vida de Celia Cruz* by Monica Brown. His 2008 poster "Voz Unida" was selected by the Obama/Biden campaign as an official poster at Artists for Obama. The Latino dance stamp he created for the United States Postal Services was featured on the cover of the commemorative stamp yearbook in 2006 and at a special exhibition at the Smithsonian entitled "Trendsetters." His 2007 U.S.P.S. stamp celebrated *Mendez vs. Westminster,* an important legal case in equality of education.

López envisioned and led the Urban Art Trail Project that transformed San Diego's blighted East Village with colorful murals, sculptures, and art installations that serves as a model of urban renewal that has been implemented in cities around the nation.

He divides his time between his studios in the colonial town of San Miguel de Allende, Mexico, and a loft in downtown San Diego, where he works and lives with his wife and son.

Part One

Learning About Books and Children

Chapter One

Knowing Children's Literature

Chapter Outline

A toddler's first response when introduced to the wonderful world of reading is typically an excited, "Read it again!" A three-year-old carries a copy of Martin Waddell's *Can't You Sleep, Little Bear?* for a week, hugging it as tightly and lovingly as a stuffed bear. A seven-year-old closes the cover of Jessica Scott Kerrin's *Martin Bridge: In High Gear,* saying proudly, "I read the whole book." Five 10-year-olds joyfully page through Louis Sachar's *Holes* looking for clues and connections in the intertwining stories. A 12-year-old holds up a copy of Mildred Taylor's *Roll of Thunder, Hear My Cry* and states emphatically, "This is the best book I've ever read." All of these children have had some deep and intensely personal response to a work of children's literature. Surely, it is such responses that may lead them to become lifelong lovers of literature.

Children's Literature Defined

There are many ways of defining children's literature. Our ideas about what should be included have changed over time; and definitions vary a bit from culture to culture, critic to critic, and reader to reader. In this book we think of literature as *the imaginative shaping of life and thought into the forms and structures of language.* We consider fiction as well as nonfiction, books with pictures as well as those with words, and ask how different genres work to produce an aesthetic experience. How do they help the reader perceive pattern, relationships, and feelings that produce an inner experience of art? This aesthetic experience might be a vivid reconstruction of past experience, an extension of a recent experience, or the creation of a new experience.

We all have memories of certain books that changed us in some way—by disturbing us, by affirming some emotion we knew but could never shape in words, or by revealing to us something about human nature. The province of literature is the human condition and it encompasses all such feelings and experiences. Perhaps our memories of books are strong because they help illuminate life by shaping our insights.

What Is Children's Literature?

The experience of literature always involves both the book and the reader. Try as we might to set objective criteria, judgments about the quality of literature must always be tempered by an awareness of its audience. The audience we address in this text is the group of children from birth to 14. Therefore, we will want to ask if and how children's literature is different from literature for adults. We could say that a child's book is a book a child is reading, and an adult book is a book occupying the attention of an adult. Before the nineteenth century only a few books were written specifically for the enjoyment of children. Children read books written for adults, taking from them what they could understand. Today, children continue to read some books intended for adults, such as the works of Stephen King and Mary Higgins Clark. And yet some books first written for children—such as Margery Williams's *The Velveteen Rabbit,* A. A. Milne's *Winnie the Pooh,* J. R. R. Tolkien's *The Hobbit,* and J. K. Rowling's Harry Potter stories—have been claimed as their own by adults.

Books about children might not necessarily be for them. Richard Hughes's adult classic *A High Wind in Jamaica* shows the "innocent" depravity of children in contrast to the group of pirates who had captured them. Yet in Harper Lee's novel *To Kill a Mockingbird,* also written for adults, 8-year-old Scout Finch reveals a more finely developed conscience than is common in the small Southern town in which she is raised. The presence of a child protagonist, then, does not assure that the book is for children. Obviously, the line between children's literature and adult literature is blurred.

Children today appear to be more sophisticated and knowledgeable about certain life experiences than children of any previous generation were. They spend a great deal of time within view of an operating television or other electronic media. The evening news shows them actual views of war while they eat their dinners. They have witnessed acts of terror, assassinations, and starvation. Though most modern children are separated from first-hand knowledge of birth, death, and senility, the mass media bring the daily experiences of crime, poverty, war, death, and depravity into the living rooms of virtually all American homes. In addition, today's children are exposed to violence purely in the name of entertainment. Such exposure has forced adults to reconsider what seems appropriate for children's literature. Today it is difficult to believe that Madeleine L'Engle's *Meet the Austins* was rejected by several publishers because it began with a death; or that some reviewers were shocked by a mild "damn" in *Harriet the Spy* by Louise Fitzhugh. Such publishing taboos have long since disappeared. Children's books are generally less frank than adult books, but contemporary children's literature does reflect the problems of today, the ones children read about in the newspapers, see on television and in the movies, and experience at home.

There are some limits to the content of children's literature, however. These limits are set by children's experience and understanding. Certain emotional and psychological responses seem outside the realms of childhood and are therefore unlikely in children's literature. For example, nostalgia is an adult emotion that is foreign to most boys and girls. Children seldom look back on their childhood, but always forward. Also, stories that portray children as "sweet" or that romanticize childhood, like the Holly Hobbie books that go with cards and gift products, often have more appeal for adults than for children. The late Dr. Seuss (Theodor S. Geisel) also took an adult perspective in his later books such as *Oh, the Places You'll Go*. His enduring place in children's literature rests on earlier titles such as *And to Think That I Saw It on Mulberry Street* and *The Cat in the Hat,* books that are filled with childlike imagination and joyful exuberance.

Cynicism and despair are not childlike emotions and should not figure prominently in a child's book. Even though children are quick to pick up a veneer of sophistication, of disillusionment with adults and authority, they still expect good things to happen in life. And although many children do live in desperate circumstances, few react to these with real despair. They may have endured pain, sorrow, or horror; they may be in what we would consider hopeless situations; but they are not without hope. The truth of the Russian folktale by Becky Reyher, *My Mother Is the Most Beautiful Woman in the World,* shines clear. Children see beauty where there is ugliness; they are hopeful when adults have given up. This is not to suggest that all stories for children must have happy endings; many today do not. It is only to say that when you close the door on hope, you have left the realm of childhood.

The only limitations, then, that seem binding on literature for children are those that appropriately reflect the emotions and experiences of children today. Children's books are books that have the child's eye at the center.

Writing for Children

Editor William Zinsser says:

> No kind of writing lodges itself so deeply in our memory, echoing there for the rest of our lives, as the books that we met in our childhood. . . . To enter and hold the mind of a child or a young person is one of the hardest of all writers' tasks.[1]

The skilled author does not write differently or less carefully for children just because she thinks they will not be aware of style or language. E. B. White asserts:

> Anyone who writes down to children is simply wasting his time. You have to write up, not down. . . . Some writers for children deliberately avoid using words they think a child doesn't know. This emasculates the prose and . . . bores the reader. . . . Children love words that give them a hard time, provided they are in a context that absorbs their attention.[2]

Authors of children's literature and those who write for adults should receive equal admiration. C. S. Lewis maintained that he wrote a children's story because a children's story was the best art form for what he had to say.[3] Lewis wrote for both adults and children, as have Rumer Godden, Madeleine L'Engle, Paula Fox, E. B. White, Isaac Bashevis Singer, Jill Patton Walsh, and many other well-known authors.

The uniqueness of children's literature, then, lies in the audience that it addresses. Authors of children's books are circumscribed only by the experiences of childhood, but these are vast and complex. Children think and feel; they wonder and they dream. Much is known, but little is explained.

Children are curious about life and adult activities. They live in the midst of tensions—balances of love and hate within the family and the neighborhood. The author who can bring imagination and insight to these experiences, give them literary shape and structure, and communicate them to children is writing children's literature.

Valuing Literature for Children

Because children naturally take such delight in books, we sometimes need to remind ourselves that books can do more for children than entertain them. Values inherent in sharing literature with children include personal qualities that might be difficult to measure as well as qualities that result in important educational understandings.

Personal Values

Literature should be valued in our homes and schools for the enrichment it gives to the personal lives of children, as well as for its proven educational contributions. We will consider these affective values of literature before we discuss the more obvious educational ones.

Enjoyment First and foremost, literature provides delight and enjoyment. Children need to discover delight in books before they are asked to master the skills of reading. Then learning to read makes as much sense as learning to ride a bike; they know that eventually it will be fun. Four- and 5-year-olds who have laughed out loud at Jules Feiffer's *Bark, George* can hardly wait to read it themselves. Six- and 7-year-olds giggle at the silly antics in Arnold Lobel's Frog and Toad books. Many older children revel in tales of mystery and suspense such as Blue Baillett's *The Calder Game,* Wendelin Van Draanen's *Sammy Keys and the Art of Deception,* or Siobhan Dowd's *The London Eye Mystery.* Sad books also bring

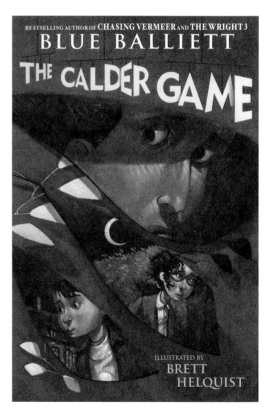

Older children are drawn to complicated stories of mystery and suspense, such as Blue Balliett's *The Calder Game.* Book cover from *The Calder Game* by Blue Balliett, jacket art by Brett Helquist. Jacket art copyright © 2008 by Brett Helquist. Reprinted by permission of Scholastic Inc.

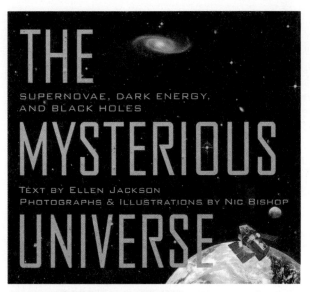

The Mysterious Universe by Ellen Jackson is among the many nonfiction titles that spark children's scientific imagination. Cover from *The Mysterious Universe* by Ellen Jackson, photographs and illustrations by Nic Bishop. Jacket art copyright © 2008 by Nic Bishop. Reprinted by permission of Houghton Mifflin Harcourt Publishing Company. All rights reserved.

a kind of enjoyment, as the children who have read *Bridge to Terabithia* by Katherine Paterson or *Stone Fox* by John Reynolds Gardiner will tell you. The list of books that children enjoy can go on and on. There are so many fine ones—and so many that children won't find unless teachers, librarians, and parents share them with children. A love of reading and a taste for literature are the finest gifts we can give to our children, for we will have started them on the path of a lifetime of pleasure with books.

Imagination Literature develops children's imagination and helps them consider people, experiences, or ideas in new ways. Books like Antoinette Portis's *Not a Stick* or Paul Fleischman's *Weslandia* celebrate characters who see the world differently and make the most of their imagination. Nonfiction books such as *Frogs* by Nic Bishop or *The Mysterious Universe* by Ellen Jackson can spark children's scientific imagination.

Today, television has made everything so explicit that children are not developing their power to visualize. Teachers need to help them see with their inner eye to develop a country of the mind. Mollie Hunter, whose books such as *A Stranger Came Ashore* and *Mermaid Summer* have this power to create the visual image in the mind of the reader and to stretch the imagination, says that the whole reward of reading is:

> to have one's imagination carried soaring on the wings of another's imagination, to be made more aware of the possibilities of one's mind . . . ; to be thrilled, amazed, amused, awed, enchanted in worlds unknown until discovered through the medium of language, and to find in those worlds one's own petty horizons growing ever wider, ever higher.[4]

Vicarious Experience Their experiences with literature give children new perspectives on the world. Good writing can transport readers to other places and other times and expand their life space. Readers feel connected to the lives of others as they enter an imagined situation with their emotions tuned to those of the story. One 10-year-old boy, sharing his love of Jean Craighead George's survival story *My Side of the Mountain,* said, "You know, I've always secretly felt I could do it myself." This boy had vicariously shared Sam Gribley's adventure of "living off the land" in his tree home in the Catskill Mountains. Sam's experiment in self-sufficiency had strengthened the conviction of a 10-year-old that he, too, could take care of himself.

Insight into Human Behavior Literature reflects life, yet no book can contain all of living. By its very organizing properties, literature has the power to shape and give coherence to human experience. It might focus on one aspect of life, one period of time in an individual's life, and so enable a reader to see and understand relationships that he had never considered. In *The Friends* by Kazumi Yumoto, three boys feed their morbid curiosity by spying on an old man, hoping to see him die. As the boys begin to know the old man, they become more and more involved in his life and put aside their misconception of the aged to find a real, vital human being. Eventually, through their intergenerational friendship, the boys discover important qualities in themselves as well as in the old man.

So much of what we teach in school is concerned with facts. Literature is concerned with feelings and the quality of life. It can educate the heart as well as the mind. As children gain increased awareness of the lives of others, as they vicariously try out other roles, they may develop a better understanding of themselves and those around them. Through wide reading as well as living, they acquire their perceptions of literature and life.

Universality of Experience Literature continues to ask universal questions about the meaning of life and our relationships with nature and other people. Every book provides a point of comparison for our own lives. Are we as courageous as the tiny mouse who must take responsibility for her family in Avi's *Poppy,* or as conflicted by peer pressure as Palmer in Jerry Spinelli's *Wringer*? Would we have the tenacity and resilience of Gim Lew in Laurence Yep's *The Dragon's Child*?

We also learn to understand the common bonds of humanity by comparing one story with another. The story of Max leaving home to go to the island in Maurice Sendak's *Where the Wild Things Are* follows the ancient pattern of Homer's *Iliad* and *Odyssey.* This pattern is repeated again and again in myth and legend and seen in such widely divergent stories as Cynthia Voigt's *Homecoming* and Jean Claude Mourlevat's *The Pull of the Ocean.* These are all stories of a journey through trials and hardship and the eventual return home. The pattern reflects everyone's journey through life.

Books can also highlight human compassion in the midst of inhumanity. *Number the Stars* by Lois Lowry and *Greater than Angels* by Carol Matas both tell of the uncommon bravery of common people to do what they can to right a wrong. Literature illumines all of life; it casts its light on all that is good, but it can also spotlight what is dark and debasing in the human experience. Literature enables us to live many lives, good and bad, and to begin to see the universality of human experience.

Educational Values

The intrinsic values of literature should be sufficient to give it a major place in the school curriculum. Happily, there is research to show that literature plays a significant role in developing oral, language, reading, and writing abilities and should play a central part in the school curriculum. Books such as *Miss Polly Has a Dolly* by Pamela Duncan Edwards engage young children in language play that can help them develop the phonological understanding so necessary to learning letter-sound relationships. The playful text in Emily Gravett's *Monkey and Me* draws the attention of young eyes to printed words. Meg Rosoff's *Jumpy Jack and Googily* or Jane O'Connor's Fancy Nancy books intrigue young children with multisyllable words. Older children will find models for writing in Doreen Cronin's *Diary of a Fly* and Lynne Rae Perkins's *Pictures from Our Vacation.* They will make personal connections to geography in *The Scrambled States of America Talent Show* by Laurie Keller or discover mathematical concepts in Bruce Goldstone's *Greater Estimations.*

Picturebooks such as Laurie Keller's *The Scrambled States of America Talent Show* entice children to learn in various content areas, such as history and geography. Cover of *The Scrambled States of America Talent Show* by Laurie Keller. Copyright © 2008 by Laurie Keller. Reprinted by permission of Henry Holt and Company, LLC.

Reviews of research found in such books as *Handbook of Early Literacy Research,* edited by Susan B. Neuman and David K. Dickinson (2006), and *On Reading Books to Children: Parents and Teachers,* edited by Anne Van Kleeck, Steven A. Stahl, and Eurydice B. Bauer (2003), summarize research conducted over the last fifty years that supports the importance of literary experiences both before and after

teaching feature 1.1

Books at the Center

In the Home

Phonological Development	Toddlers who were read to at home produced more sounds and vocalized more often than those who were not read to. (Irwin, 1960)
Syntactic Development	Three- to 4-year-olds who interact with adults around book readings have more complex sentence structure. (Cazden, 1966)
Lexical Development	Reading to young children supports their acquisition of vocabulary. (Ninio and Bruner, 1978)
Interactional Patterns	Children learn discourse patterns in the context of picturebook reading. (Snow and Goldfield, 1983)
Text Patterns	Children who are read to form understandings of how stories and characters work. (Applebee, 1978)
Correlated with Early Reading	Access to books and being read to were significant factors in children's learning to read before they came to school. (Durkin, 1966)

In the School

Correlated with Successful Reading	Reading aloud in the home was significantly associated with later reading comprehension test scores. (Wells, 1986)
Knowledge of Textual Characteristics	Children acquired understandings of text patterns and characteristics of fiction and nonfiction genres when books were shared regularly. (Pappas and Brown, 1989)
Correlated with Attitude	Sixth graders with positive attitudes toward reading had been read to as children. (Sostaritch, 1974)

children come to school. **Teaching Feature 1.1: Books at the Center** highlights classic research studies that began the support for literature across the curriculum.

Evaluating Children's Literature

What makes a good children's book? Who will read it? Why? Whose purposes will it serve? All of these are important considerations to be taken up in later sections of this chapter and throughout the book. The primary concern of evaluation, however, is a book's literary and aesthetic qualities. Children show what they think of books through their responses, but they are not born critics in the conventional sense. Teachers and librarians need to value children's own interests, interpretations, and judgments. At the same time, they need to help children discover what practiced readers look for in a well-written book. Each genre or type of literature (picturebooks, traditional literature, fantasy, poetry, contemporary realistic fiction, historical fiction, and nonfiction) has criteria that relates to that form. For example, in picturebooks it is important that the

teaching feature 1.1

(continued)

Recreational Reading   Reading outside of school was related to improved comprehension, vocabulary, and fluency scores. (Anderson, Wilson, and Fielding, 1986)

Literature Across the Curriculum   Literature positively affected understanding of written language. (Purcell, et al., 1995)
Literature positively affected science and social studies learning. (Smith, 1993)

Sources: Anderson, Richard C., Wilson, Paul T., and Fielding, Linda G. (1988). Growth in Reading and How Children Spend Their Time Outside of School. *Reading Research Quarterly, 23*, 285–303.

Applebee, Arthur (1978). *The Child's Concept of Story: Ages Two to Seventeen*. Chicago: Chicago University Press.

Cazden, Courtney (1966). Some Implications of Research on Language Development for Preschool Education. Paper presented to Social Science Research Council Conference on Preschool Education, Chicago, 7 Feb. *ERIC*, ED. 011 329.

Dickinson, David K., and Neuman, Susan B. (Eds.). (2006). *Handbook of Early Literacy Research*. New York: Guildford Press.

Durkin, Delores (1966). *Children Who Read Early*. New York: Teachers College Press.

Irwin, O. C. (1960). Infant Speech: Effect of Systematic Reading of Stories. *Journal of Speech and Hearing Research, 3*, 187–190.

Ninio, A., and Bruner, J. (1978). The Achievement and Antecedent of Labelling. *Journal of Child Language, 5*, 1–15.

Pappas, Christine C., and Brown, Elga (1989). Using Turns at Story "Reading" as Scaffolding for Learning. *Theory into Practice, 28* (2), 105–113.

Purcell, Gates, V. McIntyre, E., and Freppon, P. A. (1995). Learning Written Storybook Language in School: A Comparison of Low SES Children in Skills-Based and Whole Language Classrooms. *American Educational Research Journal, 32* (3), 659–85.

Smith, John A. (1993). Content Learning: A Third Reason for Using Literature in Teaching Reading. *Reading Research and Instruction, 32* (3), 64–71.

Snow, Catherine E., and Goldfield, Beverly (1983). Turn the Page Please: Situation Specific Language Learning. *Journal of Child Language, 10*, 551–70.

Sostarich, Judith (1974). A Study of Reading Behavior of Sixth Graders: Comparisons of Active and Other Readers [unpublished Ph.D. dissertation]. Ohio State University.

Van Kleeck, Anne, Stahl, Steven A., and Bauer, Eurydice B. (Eds.). (2003). *On Reading Books to Children: Parents and Teachers*. Mahwah, N.J.: Earlbaum.

Wells, Gordon (1986). *The Meaning Makers*. Portsmouth, N.H.: Heinemann.

verbal text and illustrations act harmoniously. Nonfiction books should be accurate and unbiased. All books need to be evaluated from a multicultural perspective. It is important for readers to identify the kind of book they are reading in order to apply the appropriate criteria for evaluation. As we discuss specific genres in Chapters 3 through 9, we will highlight criteria that apply to these particular types of literature.

Plot

Of prime importance in any work of fiction for children is the plot. Children ask first, "What happens? Is it a good story?" The plot is the plan of action; it tells what the characters do and what happens to them. It is the thread that holds the fabric of the story together and makes the reader want to continue reading.

A well-constructed plot is organic and interrelated. It grows logically and naturally from the action and the decisions of the characters in given situations. The plot should be credible and ring true rather than depend on coincidence and contrivance. It should be original and fresh rather than trite, tired, and predictable.

In books that have substance, obstacles are not easily overcome and choices are not always clear-cut. When Damien, in Frank Cottrell Boyce's *Millions*, discovers a bag of money thrown from a passing train straight into his secret hideout, the pace of the story takes off. But the compelling plot is enhanced by the ethical dilemmas with which he wrestles in dealing with this windfall and by our growing awareness of Damien's grief at his mother's death.

Setting

The structure of a story includes both the construction of the plot and its setting. The setting may be in the past, the present, or the future. The story may take place in a specific locale, or the setting may be deliberately vague to convey the universal feeling of all suburbs, all large cities, or all rural communities.

The setting for Karen Hesse's *Out of the Dust* is so well developed that readers can almost feel the grit of dirt between their teeth. Hesse's use of free verse conveys the essence of Billie Jo's terrible experiences during the Oklahoma dustbowl.

> On Sunday winds came, Bringing a red dust Like prairie fire, Hot and peppery, searing the inside of my nose, and the whites of my eyes.[5]

Just as the wind tore away layers of sod to lay bare the land, Hesse dispenses with flowery rhetoric for words and rhythms that reveal the depths of human courage and the heart of human love.

Theme

A third point in the evaluation of any story is its over-arching theme, or themes, the larger meanings that lie beneath the story's surface. Most well-written books can be read for several layers of meaning—plot, theme, or metaphor. On one level the story of *Charlotte's Web* by E. B. White is simply an absurd but amusing tale of how a spider saves the life of a pig; on another level, it reveals the meaning of loneliness and the obligations of friendship. A third layer of significance can be seen in the acceptance of death as a natural part of the cycle of life. Finally, E. B. White himself wrote that it was "an appreciative story. . . . It celebrates life, the seasons, the goodness of the barn, the beauty of the world, the glory of everything."[6]

The theme of a book reveals something of the author's purpose in writing the story and provides a dimension to the story that goes beyond the action of the plot. The theme of a book might be the acceptance of self or others, growing up, the overcoming of fear or prejudice. This theme should be worth imparting to young people and be based on justice and integrity. Sound moral and ethical principles should prevail. However, one danger in writing books for children is that the theme will override the plot. Authors might be so intent on conveying a message that they neglect story or characterization. Didacticism, the attempt by an author to preach a moral lesson, is still alive and well in the twenty-first century. However, the best books don't *teach* children, they *reach* children. Or, as Roger Sutton emphasized, "If you want to convince children of the power of books don't tell them stories are good, tell them good stories."[7]

Characterization

True characterization is another hallmark of fine writing. The people portrayed in children's books should be as convincingly real and lifelike as our next-door neighbors. Many of the animal characters in modern fantasy also have human personalities. The credibility of characters depends on the author's ability to show their true natures, their strengths, and their weaknesses.

Just as it takes time to know a new friend in all her various dimensions, so too does an author try to present the many facets of a character bit by bit. In revealing character, an author might tell about the person through narration, record the character's conversation with others, describe the thoughts of the character, show the thoughts of others about the character, or show the character in action. A character who is revealed in only one way is apt to lack depth. If a single dimension of character is presented, or one trait overemphasized, the result is likely to be stereotyped and wooden. One-dimensional characters are the norm in folk and fairy tales, where witches are prototypes of evil and youngest children are deserving and good. However, modern fiction requires multidimensional characters whose actions and feelings grow out of the circumstances of the story.

Style

An author's style of writing is simply selection and arrangement of words in presenting the story. Good writing style is appropriate to the plot, theme, and characters, both creating and reflecting the mood of the story. Most children do not enjoy a story that is too descriptive, but they can appreciate figurative language, especially when the comparisons are within their background of understanding. Natalie Babbitt's vivid prologue to *Tuck Everlasting* invites children to visualize the intense images by describing the month of August as curiously silent "with blank white dawns and glaring noons and sunsets smeared with too much color."[8]

There is no one style or set of language patterns that is more appropriate than others for a children's book. Yet children's tastes do place some demands on the writer. Because young readers tend to prefer action over description or introspection, those elements must be handled with special skill. Children crave dialogue, like readers of all ages. Masters at writing dialogue that sounds natural and amusing include Lois Lowry in *Gooney Bird Is So Absurd* and Barbara Park in *Junie B. Jones* or *Skinnybones*. Writing the dialogue for a book of contemporary realistic fiction is particularly difficult because slang and popular expressions are quickly dated. Kevin Henkes's characters in *Olive's Ocean* and *Bird Lake Moon* sound convincingly real, and Christopher Paul Curtis captures African American cultural nuances in books like *Bucking the Sarge*.

The best test of an author's style is probably oral reading. Does the story read smoothly? Does the conversation flow naturally? Does the author provide variety in sentence patterns, vocabulary, and use of stylistic devices?

Point of View

The term *point of view* is often used to indicate the author's choice of narrator(s) and the way the narrator reveals the story. Whose story is it? Who tells it? A storyteller's voice is often used in modern fiction, for books in which the author reports the comings and goings, the conversations, and the feelings of all the characters, villains as well as heroes. We say that such stories have an omniscient, or all-knowing, narrator.

Many children's books take a point of view that also uses the third person but gives the author less freedom. This limited-omniscient, or concealed, narrator view does, however, provide closer identification with a single character. The author chooses to stand behind one character, so to speak, and tell the story from over his or her shoulder. The story is then limited to what that character can see, hear, believe, feel, and understand. Katherine Paterson has told the story *The Great Gilly Hopkins* from this perspective.

The more direct narrative voice of the first person is quite common today. In contemporary realism it is almost the norm. The advantage of using first-person narrative is that it can make for easy reading. It attempts to invite its audience by taking a stance that says, "Look—we speak the same language."

At times authors counter the limitations of a single point of view by alternating the presentation of several views within the same story or changing points of view. E. L. Konigsburg's multiple narratives in *The View from Saturday* add great richness to the textual tapestry. Author Linda Sue Park provides an innovative twist on this technique in *Project Mulberry* when she intersects the first-person narrative of her main character, Julia Song, with a dialogue between herself as author and Julia as a product of her imagination.

The author's own personal and cultural experience is reflected in more subtle ways in every book's point of view. This is one reason we have included the Ten-Point Model throughout this book as a way of helping teachers and children develop a comprehensive, more critical understanding of the world they live in. For example, Shana Burg is not African American but in *A Thousand Never Evers* she has told a moving story of life in the Jim Crow South based in part on her parents' own experiences as civil rights workers. Her point of view is no substitute for those of an author who has lived those cultural experiences from birth. Mildred Taylor's *Roll of Thunder, Hear My Cry,* which is based on her own history as an African American, shows how an author of color has a unique opportunity to illuminate those nuances of culture that outsiders can never capture.

Additional Considerations

The books we think of as truly excellent have significant content and, if illustrated, fine illustrations. Their total design, from the front cover to the final end paper, creates a unified look that seems in character with the content and invites the reader to proceed. Today, we have so many picture storybooks and so many beautifully illustrated books of poetry, nonfiction, and other genres that any attempt to evaluate children's literature should consider both the role of illustration and the format of the book. We will discuss these criteria in greater depth in the subsequent genre chapters of this book. In general, however, we should consider the format of a book—its size, shape, page design, illustrations, typography, paper quality, and binding. Frequently, some small aspect of the format, such as the book jacket, will be an important factor in a child's decision to read a story. All types of books—novels, picturebooks, poetry, biography, nonfiction books—should be well designed and well made. The type should be large enough for easy reading by children at the age level for which the book is intended. At the same time, if the type is too large, children might see the book as "babyish." Space between the lines (leading) should be sufficient to make the text clear. The paper should be of high quality, heavy enough to prevent any penetration of ink. In longer works written for older children, this means off-white with a dull finish to prevent glare, although other surfaces are used for special purposes. The binding should be durable and practical, able to withstand hard use.

Guidelines: Evaluating Children's Fiction on page 14 lists criteria by which we have traditionally evaluated a work of fiction. These criteria relate to elements as plot, setting, theme, characterization, style, point of view, and format and form a foundation on which to examine each of the genres described in subsequent chapters.

Developing Sources to Help Choose Books

There are many professional resources to help teachers as they go about choosing books for their students. Book review journals such as *School Library Journal, The Horn Book Magazine, Booklist Magazine,* and reviews in other professional journals such as *Language Arts and the Reading Teacher* provide guidance and often single out titles with exceptional strengths. Book award lists are another source to help busy teachers single out books of note. Three of the most coveted awards in children's literature in the United States are the Newbery, Caldecott, and Sibert medals. Winners are chosen every year by two committees of the Association for Library Service to Children, a division of the American Library Association. The International Board on Books for Young People awards the Hans Christian Andersen Medal every two years to an artist and author for a "substantial and lasting contribution to children's literature." The Children's Book Council publishes a list called "Awards and Prizes for Children's Books," which includes over 321 awards in English. We have named a few of these awards in **Teaching Feature 1.2: Selected Book Awards for Children.** See Appendix A for recent winners of the most prominent awards.

Yuyi Morales, illustrator of Marisa Montes's *Los Gatos Black on Halloween,* has won several Pura Belpré awards for a Latino/a writer-illustrator who celebrates the Latino cultural experience. Cover of *Los Gatos Black* by Marisa Montes and Yuyi Morales. Copyright © 2008 by Marisa Montes and Yuyi Morales. Reprinted by permission of Henry Holt and Company, LLC.

Evaluating Children's Fiction

 Go to **www.mhhe.com/kieferbrief1e** *to access an expanded version of this evaluation form.*

Before Reading
- What kind of book is this?
- What does the reader anticipate from the title? Dust jacket illustration? Size of print? Illustrations? Chapter headings? Opening page?
- For what age range is this book intended?

Plot
- Does the book tell a good story?
- Will children enjoy it? Is there action?
- Does the story move?
- Is the plot original and fresh?
- Is it plausible and credible?
- Is there preparation for the events?
- Is there a logical series of happenings?
- Is there a basis of cause and effect in the happenings?
- Is there an identifiable climax? How do events build to a climax?
- Is the plot well constructed?

Setting
- Where does the story take place?
- How does the author indicate the time?
- How does the setting affect the action, characters, or theme?
- Does the story transcend the setting and have universal implications?

Theme
- Does the story have a theme?
- Is the theme worth imparting to children?
- Does the theme emerge naturally from the story, or is it stated too obviously?
- Does the theme overpower the story?
- Does it avoid moralizing?
- How does the author use motifs or symbols to intensify meaning?

Characterization
- How does the author reveal characters? Through narration? In conversation? By thoughts of others?
- Are the characters convincing and credible?
- Do we see their strengths and their weaknesses?
- Does the author avoid stereotyping?
- Is the behavior of the characters consistent with their ages and background?
- Is there any character development or growth?
- Has the author shown the causes of character behavior or development?

Style
- Is the style of writing appropriate to the subject?
- Is the style straightforward or figurative?
- Is the dialogue natural and suited to the characters?
- How did the author create a mood? Is the overall impression one of mystery? gloom? evil? joy? security?

Point of View
- Is the point of view from which the story is told appropriate to the purpose of the book? Does the point of view change?
- Does the point of view limit the reader's horizon, or enlarge it?
- Why did the author choose this particular point of view?

Additional Considerations
- Do the illustrations enhance or extend the story?
- Are the pictures aesthetically satisfying?
- How well designed is the book?
- Is the format of the book related to the text?
- What is the quality of the paper? How sturdy is the binding?
- How does the book compare with other books on the same subject?
- How does the book compare with other books written by the same author?
- How have other reviewers evaluated this book?
- What age range would most appreciate this story?

Selected Book Awards for Children

 Go to **www.mhhe.com/kieferbrief1e** *for links to the most current Web sites.*

Award	Given by	Description	More Information
Caldecott Medal	Association for Library Service to Children (ALSC)	Awarded annually to the artist of the most distinguished American picturebook for children.	www.ala.org/ala/mgrps/divs/alsc/awardsgrants/bookmedia
Newbery Medal	Association for Library Service to Children (ALSC)	Awarded annually to the author of the most distinguished contribution to American literature for children.	www.ala.org/ala/mgrps/divs/alsc/awardsgrants/bookmedia
Robert F. Sibert Informational Book Medal	Association for Library Service to Children (ALSC)	Awarded annually to the author and illustrator of the most distinguished informational book published in English.	www.ala.org/ala/mgrps/divs/alsc/awardsgrants/bookmedia
Orbis Pictus Award	National Council of Teachers of English (NCTE)	Promotes and recognizes excellence in the writing of nonfiction for children.	www.ncte.org/awards/orbispictus
Pura Belpré Medal	Association for Library Service to Children (ALSC) and REFORMA	Presented to a Latino/Latina writer and illustrator whose work best portrays, affirms, and celebrates the Latino cultural experience in a work of literature for children and youth.	www.ala.org/ala/mgrps/divs/alsc/awardsgrants/bookmedia
Mildred L. Batchelder Award	Association for Library Service to Children (ALSC)	Awarded to an American publisher for a children's book considered to be the most outstanding of those books originally published in a foreign language in a foreign country.	www.ala.org/ala/mgrps/divs/alsc/awardsgrants/bookmedia
Coretta Scott King Book Award	Ethnic Multicultural Information Exchange Round Table of the American Library Association (EMIERT)	Recognizes an African American author and illustrator of outstanding books for children and young adults.	www.ala.org/ala/mgrps/rts/cskbookawards/index.cfm
Hans Christian Andersen Award	International Board on Books for Young People	Presented every other year to a living author and illustrator of children's books whose complete works have made a lasting contribution to children's literature.	www.ibby.org

No one but the most interested follower of children's literature would want to remember all the awards that are given for children's books. And certainly no one should assume that the award winners are the only children's books worth reading. Like the coveted Oscars of the motion picture industry and the Emmys of television, the awards in children's literature focus attention not only on the winners of the year but also on the entire field of endeavor. They recognize and honor excellence and also point the way to improved writing, illustrating, and producing of worthwhile and attractive books for children.

Challenging Perspectives

"Each of the children had completed the text for their 32-page picture book on spiders. The only task left to complete was the illustrations. The children were instructed to select a medium for their art. They were familiar with the variety that they could choose from. Some chose collage, some chose pen and ink, some chose photo essay. Each of the children was also aware that a panel of fifth-grade judges would select an 'award winner' and an 'honor book.' After two days of work, Eric brought his book up to my desk saying that he had completed his task. Upon opening the book, I saw that the pages were blank. I asked Eric where his illustrations were, and he answered, 'They are right there!' When I asked where the spider was in his story, he said that as soon as you turn the page, it crawls away and you don't see it anymore. I told him that while this was a clever and different perspective, I wasn't sure if the judges would 'get it.' His response was, 'Then we need a new panel of judges!'"
—**First-grade teacher**

This teacher's story recounts a student's display of imagination, creativity, and alternative art form or expression. The challenge for the fifth-grade panel of judges would be to look at the aesthetic representation of spiders in Eric's story and use criteria to judge and later award a prize. Unfortunately, criteria for such awards often fall short when juxtaposed with new perspectives. In the picturebook world, the emergence of new and challenging perspectives in picturebook illustrations was often met by award committees as not even deserving an honorable mention. Neither did these award committees respond to the racial and cultural stereotypes found in picturebooks. Often the stereotypes were oversimplifications and generalizations about a particular group, which carried derogatory implications. Some of the stereotypes were blatant, others more subtle. These committees, historically, did little to check for depictions that demeaned or ridiculed characters because of their race, gender, age, ability, appearance, size, religion, sexual orientation, socioeconomic class, or indigenous language. For example, *Tikki Tikki Tembo*, a book that depicts an Asian protagonist, has been at the seat of controversy related to language, culture, and authenticity. Though the book has a delightful repetitive pattern that many children enjoy, the text and illustrations are inaccurate depictions of Chinese people and culture. In the text, the first and most honored son had the grand long name of "Tikki tikki tembo-no sa rembo-chari bari ruchi-pip peri pembo," which sends a false and less-than-flattering message about Chinese names.

With so few books historically with underrepresented groups as protagonists or serving as the center of picturebook illustrations, it is no wonder that when judged in a larger pool the illustrators of nonmainstream subjects often continued to be marginalized or excluded. This gave rise to the creation of new awards to bring a new lens to the artistic and sometimes alternative formats in picturebooks.

One example is the Coretta Scott King Book Award that is presented annually by the Coretta Scott King Committee of the American Library Association's Ethnic Multicultural Information Exchange Round Table (EMIERT), and is awarded to an African American author and African American illustrator for an outstandingly inspirational and educational contribution. These books should promote "understanding and appreciation of the culture of all peoples and their contribution to the realization of the American dream and commemorate the life and works of Dr. Martin Luther King, Jr. and to honor Mrs. Coretta Scott King for her courage and determination to continue the work for peace and world brotherhood."

These new awards at their inception were not seen as "the awards." The Caldecott Medal is still viewed by some as the top medal awarded for illustrations in picturebooks. However, librarians and independent bookstore owners that serve diverse constituencies use other award winners to help make selections for stocking the shelves. It is not unusual, for example, in libraries that serve patrons in predominantly Latino communities to feature the Pura Belpré Medal winners in more prominent places than the Caldecott winners.

The challenge for those of us who use award-winning lists to make decisions about books we use in classrooms or how we use our resources to purchase books for classrooms or libraries is to not depend only on the lists that make the best-seller list, but to look for lists of award winners that represent diverse children, families, and communities. Often as teachers, you will receive a list of chosen titles to support standards and objectives outlined in your curriculum. An examination will reveal many award winners from current or previous years. Seldom will these lists include books from smaller presses or from other awards that don't receive the same spotlight of recognition from the American Library Association or the *New York Times* best-seller list. This is not to suggest that award criteria, evaluation, and subsequent lists do not have a useful place in the criteria and selection of books used in classroom settings. It does suggest, however, that as diverse as our lived experiences are, so should be the list from which we select books to use in classrooms with children.

Throughout this text, we will explore the issues you will encounter as you strive to develop an effective reading curriculum for your students. Instilling a passion for reading often takes a backseat to the challenges you will face in today's sociocultural and political climate. The Ten-Point Model, introduced in the next section and featured throughout the text, has been developed and adapted to serve as a tool to help you address challenging and controversial situations and issues.

Teaching Controversial Issues: The Ten-Point Model

Everyday life is full of controversies. Children's literature is not immune to it. Issues such as censorship, gender stereotypes, the struggle for freedom and equality, cultural authenticity, ethical heroes, violence, sexuality, the partnership of classroom teacher and librarian, and the current trends in buying, selling, publishing, and using children's books all cause or contribute to controversy.

Exploring controversial issues helps children develop a comprehensive, more critical understanding of the world they live in and is an important part of helping them become critically reflective thinkers. Teaching controversial issues allows for content across the curriculum to be related in authentic ways to children's lives, providing an

portunity for children and teachers to reflect, analyze, and critically comprehend
re deeply. The goal can be summed up in a quote from Dr. Martin Luther King,
"The ultimate measure of a man is not where he stands in moments of com-
t and convenience, but where he stands at times of challenge and controversy."
ching about controversial issues related to books written for children, when it is
well planned, can help children gain the necessary confidence and skills to "take a
stand."

Teaching controversial issues is multifaceted and complex. It challenges the student's as well as the parent's personally held values, beliefs, and worldviews, and it
requires achieving a balance between taking a stance and coercion or indoctrination.
This can be confusing to students and may cause some children and their parents
and communities considerable concern.

It is important to plan thoroughly for issues-related teaching. The Ten-Point Model
for Teaching Controversial Issues,[9] developed by Susan Jones (a Boston educator and
member of Educators for Social Responsibility), is a framework for teaching controversial and difficult issues (**Figure 1.1**). In this approach, students begin by pooling
what they know and what they think they know about an issue. They also develop a
list of questions. This is followed by an information-gathering period during which
students search for answers to the questions.

Next, using information they have collected, students correct any misinformation
previously listed and develop more questions. This process continues until some type
of culminating activity emerges from the information.

This model can be easily adapted to various topics across the curriculum to assist
in teaching about controversial issues. For example, consider using the Ten-Point
Model in a discussion of global warming, a very timely topic that can elicit a variety
of responses and may be controversial. The following is a possible approach to such
a discussion:

1. **Raise the initial question and have the children brainstorm all their
   initial responses.** *Does global warming really exist?* Ground rules should be created to enable the free flow of ideas in a safe, nonthreatening environment, with
   the goal of having students think about and question their assumptions and
   listen to others' ideas.
2. **Begin a separate list of "Things about global warming to find out
   more about."** Students should create a list of what they know about the issue
   and what they want to learn about the issue.
3. **Assign information-gathering homework.** For homework, ask children
   to research information from different sides of the debate. For example, some
   believe the scientific evidence argues against the existence of a greenhouse crisis,
   or against the notion that realistic policies could achieve any meaningful climatic impact, or against the claim that we must act now if we are to reduce the
   greenhouse threat. Others believe the evidence is overwhelming and undeniable
   that global warming is real, is a serious concern, and is the result of our activities
   and not a natural occurrence. Children can use research skills to explore opposite views using children's literature, such as *The Down-to-Earth Guide to Global
   Warming,* co-authored by activists Laurie David and Cambria Gordon, and *The
   Sky's Not Falling! Why It's OK to Chill About Global Warming* by Holly Fretwell,

The Ten-Point Model for Teaching Controversial Issues provides a framework for encouraging students to question, research, share, and evaluate information related to current, controversial topics. Go to **www.mhhe.com/kieferbrief1e** for a template.

Step

1. **Raise the initial question and have the children brainstorm all their initial responses.** Write them down. Don't discuss them, and accept all contributions. The teacher only asks questions, such as "What does that mean?" "Can you say any more about that?" "Does anyone else have anything to add to that information?" and (especially for erroneous or extremely one-sided information) "Where did you learn that?" or "Is that a fact or is it someone's opinion?"

2. **Begin a separate list of "Things to find out more about"** as soon as undefined vocabulary words, vague concepts, and unanswered questions begin to emerge. These will serve as guidelines for the ongoing research, and some may even develop into separate topics to pursue later.

3. **Assign information-gathering homework.** Have children find out everything they can about the initial questions. Tell them to be prepared to share what they can in their own words. It is fine to read articles or watch the TV news, but the best source of information is interviewing parents, other relatives, or friends. Tell them not to copy down anyone else's words, but that it is a good idea to take notes.

4. **Share again responses to the initial question in a brainstorming session.** Again, children must share the information they gathered in their own words. Write down all responses. You can ask the same questions as in item 1, but offer no information and no "answers." Add to the list of "Things to find out more about" from item 2.

5. **Continue the process of gathering information.** Identify things to find out more about and continue to gather still more information for as long as the topic seems interesting. Encourage the children to listen to and learn from each other. They can begin to ask each other to explain what a new word means, to elaborate on a concept, to consider a new question, and to state their source of information. The teacher's role is an active one—facilitating, clarifying, and questioning—but the teacher doesn't impose information.

6. **If a concept emerges that sparks much interest or confusion, pose it as a new question about which to seek information.** Share and question until a satisfactory base of information has been established. More than one line of questioning can go on at the same time.

7. **Periodically give the children an individual written assignment in class to summarize their thoughts about a particular question.** The assignment can be worded as "What you know about X," "Things you don't understand about X," "Something X makes you think about," or any other way you can find to help crystallize children's individual thinking about the topic. Sharing these compositions aloud or posting them for all to read helps make all information public.

8. **As individual or group projects emerge, follow up on them.** The class may decide to write letters to a public figure; one or two children may decide to pursue a challenging research topic to report on to the group; or an outside resource may unexpectedly appear. Be flexible.

9. **Let others—parents, your colleagues, the media—know what you are doing.** Invite their participation. Encourage dialogue.

10. **End your project with something either public or permanent.** Ideas include a class presentation to the rest of the school about what they have learned, an article for the school paper or the local newspaper, a class book or individual books for the school library, or class participation in an event. It is important for children to feel that their learning is relevant and can lead to the ability to contribute to the larger world.

Source: Adapted from Kreidler, W. *Elementary Perspectives: Teaching Concepts of Peace and Conflict.* Copyright © 1990, Educators for Social Responsibility, Cambridge, MA. www.esrnational.org. Used by permission.

resource economist and a senior research fellow at the Property and Environment Research Center (PERC). The two books sharply disagree on whether humans are causing global warming.

Students could research organizations that have information representative of both sides. Following are examples of Web sites that have resources geared for students, parents, and teachers:

- *Atmospheric Radiation Measurement Program Education Center: Global Warming* <http://education.arm.gov>. Sponsored by the U.S. Department of Energy, this site offers fun activities and classroom modules for middle-school students and teachers. It includes a question archive, an option to "ask a scientist" questions about global warming, news, an extensive list of lesson plans, and "cool sites" related to climate change science.
- *EekoWorld (Environmental Education for Kids Online)* <http://pbskids.org/eekoworld>. Designed for younger children, this site features an engaging and interactive format that invites children to explore, experiment, and collaborate as they learn about conservation and the environment. Online guides for parents and teachers are also provided.
- *U.S. Environmental Protection Agency Global Warming Kids Site* <www.epa.gov/globalwarming/kids>. This site includes in-depth discussions of the major issues surrounding the climate change debate, arranged in an easy-to-understand system. Links to an internal glossary, games with global-warming themes, and links to external climate change sites for children are also provided.
- *The Why Files: Global Warming* <www.whyfiles.org/080global_warm/index.html>. Designed for teachers, students, and the lay public, this site provides a fairly detailed explanation of global-warming issues. Articles include graphs from NASA and hyperlinks to original data and articles, with additional internal links to related topics such as overpopulation, the greenhouse effect, and biodiversity.

4. **Share again responses to the initial question in a brainstorming session.** Return to the brainstorming session questions and, given the information they have gathered, have students determine if they can now answer questions raised using inquiry and information-gathering skills: searching for relevant information, determining the reliability of the source, evaluating the information.

5. **Continue the process of gathering information.** Students can use the school and local library to look for print and multimedia resources that have information about global warming. They could brainstorm lists of keywords to use in their searches to answer questions about climate, greenhouse gas emissions, extreme weather, glacier retreat, extinctions of flora and fauna, and so on.

6. **If a concept emerges that sparks much interest or confusion, pose it as a new question about which to seek information.** For example, the teacher may pose the questions, "What is the debate or dispute regarding global warming?" "What do scientists say about the causes of increased global average air temperature?" Students can then discuss the disputes concerning the estimates of climate sensitivity, predictions of additional warming, what the consequences are, and what action should be taken (if any). While differences of opinion related to global warming will arise, students can take a stand using supporting evidence from their research.

7. **Periodically give the children an individual written assignment in class to summarize their thoughts about a particular question.** As the conversations ensue, use whole-class discussion, small-group discussions, journaling, and other forms of writing to help students create outlines or other formats to summarize the information they have gathered.

8. **As individual or group projects emerge, follow up on them.** Some students may wish to contact organizations that provide guest speakers that present both sides of the issue. Students can generate a list of people from the popular media, on the policy level (local politicians and environmental protection agencies), with individuals in the community (local scientists or professors), corporations (oil or automobile manufacturers) to speak to the class. The availability of speakers may be limited to the location of the school; however, using technology, such as video conferencing (Skype, for example) may enable you to bring in speakers from outside the geographical location of the school.

9. **Let others—parents, your colleagues, the media—know what you are doing.** Parents may express their dismay or delight with the discussion of the topic depending on where they stand. If you live in an area where logging, mining, hunting, or fishing contribute significantly to the local economy or recreation, reading children's literature that highlights preservation and conservation by curtailing these activities may not be well received. Keep them informed of your goal: to create open-ended dialogue from multiple points of view and to create a space for debate and discussion, so that once students have gathered information they can make their own decisions.

10. **End your project with something either public or permanent.** Depending on where students stand, they may choose to work with organizations on either side of the issue or conduct a debate with other students to evaluate the reliability and credibility of information gathered. Students may also advocate for the inclusion of a particular book in the school library to expand the information available for other students to read, analyze, and evaluate related to this issue.

There are several benefits to the Ten-Point Model. The model starts where students are and is very respectful of children's knowledge. The process of correcting misinformation is empowering, not punitive. Because students spend time going from whole group to small group and back again, the process encourages community building and lets all students participate at their own level.

The Ten-Point Model requires that elementary students make use of some sophisticated reference and study skills. However, there can be an aimless quality to the procedure if the teacher doesn't present students with some boundaries to their explorations. Even though one purpose of the procedure is to demonstrate the open-ended nature of inquiry, the teacher often needs to structure a clear culminating activity so that the process doesn't just drift off into an anticlimactic and unsatisfying ending.

There are concerns that delving into issues that cause children to use their ethical and moral reasoning is like opening a metaphorical Pandora's box. While there is a variety of versions of the legend of Prometheus and Pandora's box, one component that finds its way into every story is that Pandora was inquisitive, curious, and a risk taker—after all, she did open the box! That being said, it is the inherent nature of what makes an issue controversial: the competing values, people strongly disagreeing with statements, the political sensitivity, the evoked strong emotions that is fodder for increased student engagement, culturally relevant teaching, service learning, authentic assessments, and ultimately children that grow up to be participants in our constitutional democracy.

In each of the genre chapters (Chapters 3 through 9), we will explore how to use the Ten-Point Model to teach controversial issues related to each chapter's content. For example, when discussing picturebooks in Chapter 3, we'll look at how culture influences our perceptions and use of color, and how to encourage children to create meaning that enhances and extends stories using their lived experiences.

Additionally, each of these chapters will also include a **Curriculum Connections** feature. This feature demonstrates how children's literature can be integrated into a variety of disciplines to accomplish meeting educational standards.

Notes

1. William Zinsser, ed., *Worlds of Childhood: The Art and Craft of Writing for Children* (Boston: Houghton Mifflin, 1990), p. 3.
2. E. B. White, "On Writing for Children," quoted in *Children and Literature: Views and Reviews*, ed. Virginia Haviland (Glenview, Ill.: Scott, Foresman, 1973), p. 140.
3. C. S. Lewis, "On Three Ways of Writing for Children," *Horn Book Magazine* 39 (October 1963): 460.
4. Mollie Hunter, *The Pied Piper Syndrome* (New York: HarperCollins, 1992), p. 92.
5. Karen Hesse, *Out of the Dust* (New York: Scholastic, 1997), p. 46.
6. Dorothy L. Guth, ed., *Letters of E. B. White* (New York: Harper & Row, 1976), p. 613.
7. Roger Sutton, "Because It's Good for You," *New York Times Book Review* 11 May 2008: 25.
8. Natalie Babbitt, *Tuck Everlasting* (New York: Farrar, Straus & Giroux, 1975), p. 62.
9. W. Kreidler, *Elementary Perspectives: Teaching Concepts of Peace and Conflict* (Cambridge: Educators for Social Responsibility, 1990).

Children's Literature

Go to **www.mhhe.com/kiefer1e** *to access the Children's Literature Database, which includes information on thousands of children's books. Following are some of the titles you will find in the database.*

Titles in blue = multicultural titles

Avi. *Poppy.* Illustrated by Brian Floca. Orchard, 1995.
Babbitt, Natalie. *Tuck Everlasting.* Farrar, 1985.
Balliett, Blue. *The Calder Game.* Scholastic, 2008.
Bishop, Nic. *Frogs.* Scholastic, 2008.
Boyce, Frank Cottrell. *Millions.* HarperCollins, 2004.
Burg, Shana. *A Thousand Never Evers.* Delacorte, 2008.
Cronin, Doreen, *Diary of a Fly.* Illustrated by Harry Bliss. HarperCollins, 2007.
Curtis, Christopher Paul. *Bucking the Sarge.* Random, 2004.
Dowd, Siobhan. *The London Eye Mystery.* Random, 2008.
Edwards, Pamela Duncan. *Miss Polly Has a Dolly.* Illustrated by Elicia Castaldi. Putnam, 2003.
Fine, Anne. *Up on Cloud Nine.* Delacorte, 2002.

Fitzhugh, Louise. *Harriet the Spy*. Harper, 1964.

Fleischman, Paul. *Weslandia*. Illustrated by Kevin Hawkes. Candlewick, 1999.

Gardiner, John Reynolds. *Stone Fox*. Illustrated by Marcia Sewall. Crowell, 1980.

George, Jean Craighead. *My Side of the Mountain*. Dutton, 1988 [1959].

Goldstone, Bruce. *Greater Estimations*. Holt, 2008.

Gravett, Emily. *Monkey and Me*. Simon, 2008.

Henkes, Kevin. *Bird Lake Moon*. Greenwillow, 2008.

——. *Olive's Ocean*. Greenwillow, 2003.

Hesse, Karen. *Out of the Dust*. Scholastic, 1997.

Hughes, Richard. *A High Wind in Jamaica*. Harper, 1989 [1929].

Hunter, Mollie. *Mermaid Summer*. Harper, 1988.

——. *A Stranger Came Ashore*. Harper, 1975.

Jackson, Ellen. *The Mysterious Universe: Supernovae, Dark Energy, and Black Holes*. Photographs by Nic Bishop. Houghton, 2008.

Keller, Laurie. *The Scrambled States of America Talent Show*. Holt, 2008.

Kerrin, Jessica Scott. *Martin Bridge: In High Gear*. Illustrated by Joseph Kelly. Kids Can, 2008.

Kleven, Elisa. *The Puddle Pail*. Dutton, 1997.

Konigsburg, E. L. *The View from Saturday*. Atheneum, 1996.

Lee, Harper. *To Kill a Mockingbird*. HarperCollins, 1995 [1960].

L'Engle, Madeleine. *Meet the Austins*. Vanguard, 1960.

Lowry, Lois. *Gooney Bird Is So Absurd*. Illustrated by Middy Thomas. Houghton, 2009.

——. *Number the Stars*. Houghton, 1989.

Matas, Carol. *Greater than Angels*. Simon, 1998.

Mosel, Arlene. *Tikki Tikki Tembo*. Illustrated by Blair Lent. Holt, 1968.

Mourlevat, Jean-Claude. *The Pull of the Ocean*. Translated by Y. Maudet. Delacorte, 2006.

O'Connor, Jane. *Fancy Nancy: Bonjour Butterfly*. Illustrated by Robin Preiss Glasser. HarperCollins, 2008.

Park, Barbara. *Junie B. Jones and the Stupid Smelly Bus*. Illustrated by Denise Brunkus. Random, 1992.

——. *Skinnybones*. Yearling, 1997.

Park, Linda Sue. *Project Mulberry*. Clarion, 2005.

Paterson, Katherine. *Bridge to Terabithia*. Illustrated by Donna Diamond. Crowell, 1977.

——. *The Great Gilly Hopkins*. Crowell, 1978

——. *The Same Stuff as Stars*. Clarion, 2002.

Perkins, Lynne Rae. *Pictures from Our Vacation*. Greenwillow, 2007.

Portis, Antoinette. *Not a Stick*. Harper, 2007.

Reyher, Becky. *My Mother Is the Most Beautiful Woman in the World*. Illustrated by Ruth Gannett. Lothrop, 1945.

Rosoff, Meg. *Jumpy Jack and Googily*. Illustrated by Sophie Blackall. Holt, 2008.

Rowling, J. K. *Harry Potter and the Deathly Hallows*. Scholastic, 2007.

Sachar, Louis. *Holes*. Farrar, 1998.

Sendak, Maurice. *Where the Wild Things Are*. HarperCollins, 1963.

Seuss, Dr. [Theodor S. Geisel]. *The Cat in the Hat*. Random, 1966 [1957].

——. *Oh, the Places You'll Go*. Random, 1990.

——. *And to Think That I Saw It on Mulberry Street*. Random, 1989 [1937].

Spinelli, Jerry. *Wringer*. HarperCollins, 1997.

Taylor, Mildred. *Roll of Thunder, Hear My Cry*. Dial, 1976.

Tolkien, J. R. R. *The Hobbit*. Houghton, 1938.

Voigt, Cynthia. *Homecoming*. Atheneum, 1981.

Waddell, Martin. *Can't You Sleep, Little Bear?* Illustrated by Barbara Firth. Candlewick, 1992.

White, E. B., *Charlotte's Web*. Illustrated by Garth Williams. Harper, 1952.

Williams, Margery. *The Velveteen Rabbit*. Illustrated by William Nicholson. Doubleday, 1969 [1922].

Yep, Laurence, with Kathleen Yep. *The Dragon's Child: A Story of Angel Island*. HarperCollins, 2008.

Yumoto, Kazumi. *The Friends*. Translated by Cathy Hirano. Farrar, 1996.

Chapter Two

Understanding Children's Responses to Literature

Chaper Outline

Following "Buddy Reading Time" in Mr. Jacobson's first-grade classroom, Rosalie and Tamika volunteer to tell the class about Katie Sciurba's *Oye Celia! A Song for Celia Cruz,* the book they have been reading together.

"It's about a girl who goes to a party and sings a song for her favorite singer," says Rosalie.

Tamika adds, "Everyone should read it. It's a really good book!"

Mr. Jacobson asks Tamika to explain. "Why do you think it's a good book, Tamika?"

"Because I liked it," replies Tamika confidently.

Meanwhile, down the hallway in a fourth-grade classroom, students studying Japan have created comparison charts of Japanese folktales and then wrote about their findings. Ten-year-old Elijah compared *The Wave* by Margaret Hodges and *The Burning Rice Fields* by Sarah Bryant, two illustrated versions of a Japanese folktale:

> "I really notice the difference in the language and the illustrations of the two books. In *The Wave,* the

language is very exquisite and very delicate—the words carefully picked one by one and in *The Burning Rice Fields*, the words are slopped on the page. The illustrations in *The Wave* are cardboard cuts carefully cutted [sic] to resemble objects in the story and in *The Burning Rice Fields* the pictures are done in a child's version of crayon drawings. Unfortunately, I like *The Burning Rice Fields* better because its [sic] in more detail."

These children are enthusiastically responding to works of literature in ways that may be affected by age, experience, gender, and ethnicity. As teachers, we hope to provide children with books that deeply engage their intellect and emotions—books that will help them to decide to become life-long readers. The phrase "response to literature" has been used in a variety of ways. Theoretically, response refers to any outward sign of that inner activity, something said or done that reveals a reader's thoughts and feelings about literature. A 6-year-old's drawing of a favorite character and a book review in the *New York Times* are both responses in this sense. Teachers or librarians who predict that a book will bring "a good response" use the term in a different way, focusing on the likelihood that children will find a book appealing and will be eager to read, talk about it, and transform it through writing and other art forms. In order to choose books that will satisfy individual readers and to plan for satisfying responses to literature in elementary classrooms, teachers may gain insight through studying research on children's reading interests and preferences, research about children's developmental patterns of growth, and research into classroom-based studies of responses to literature.

Reading Interests and Preferences

Children's desire to read is a major concern for adults in this multimedia age. Happily, the *2008 Kids and Family Reading Report* indicated that there is still great enthusiasm for reading for enjoyment, although the percentage of children who read for pleasure drops as children get older.[1] If we are to reverse this trend, teachers, librarians, parents, publishers, and booksellers who select children's books can make better choices by knowing which books are likely to have immediate appeal for many children and which ones might require introduction or encouragement along the way.

Studies of reading interests over the years have consistently identified certain topics and elements of content that have wide appeal.[2] Researchers have found that animals and humor, for instance, are generally popular across age levels. Among other elements that are frequently mentioned for reader appeal are action, suspense, and surprise. Sales figures, too, can reflect children's reading interests. Best-seller lists in

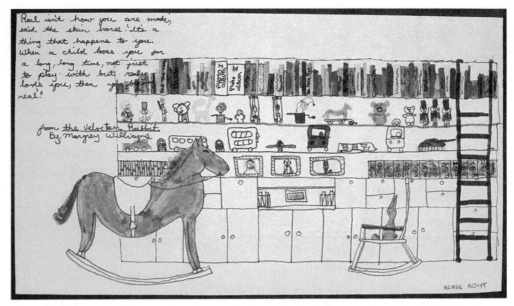

Choosing favorites and interpreting them are both a part of response to literature. Notice how the details of the modern playroom setting in this child's illustration of *The Velveteen Rabbit* provide a glimpse of her unique personal perspective on the book. Martin Luther King, Jr., Laboratory School, Evanston Public Schools, Evanston, Illinois.

Publishers Weekly magazine show that tie-ins to popular movies or television shows and series books were among the best-selling children's books. A 1998 survey by *Publishers Weekly* showed that teenagers (12- to 17-year-olds) bought fiction slightly more often than nonfiction, a figure that did not vary much with gender. Favorite topics included mysteries, science fiction/fantasy, books about celebrities and athletes, and how-to books.[3]

Even though we can identify commonly chosen topics and story features that have wide general appeal, it is still impossible to concoct a formula for books that would have unfailing popularity with all children. Teachers and librarians need to be sensitive to children's individual tastes, which often are unique and very particular. Nevertheless, the variations in interests among different groups of children seem to be linked to age, gender, and certain other influences.

Age and Gender Differences

The most obvious change in children's interest patterns occurs with age, as children take on more complex material and new areas of concern. Good book choices for first and sixth graders seldom overlap, even when the general topic is the same. Robert McCloskey's picturebook *Make Way for Ducklings* is a favorite animal story among 4- and 5-year-olds; 12-year-olds prefer their animal characters to be part of something more dramatic, as in Ann Martin's *A Dog's Life: The Autobiography of a Stray*. Seven-year-olds laugh at Peggy Parish's *Amelia Bedelia* and her literal interpretation of instructions like "Draw the drapes" and "Dress the chicken." Eleven-year-olds like "funny" books, too, but prefer a different brand of humor, such as the comic situations in Roald Dahl's *The BFG* or the deadpan humor of Louis Sachar's *Holes*.

The influence of gender differences on reading interests is not entirely clear. Previous studies have found that interests of children vary according to age and grade level and that girls read more than boys but boys had a wider interest range and read a greater variety. Girls showed an earlier interest in adult romantic fiction than boys, whereas boys tended to prefer nonfiction from an early age. Boys seldom showed preference for a "girl's" book, but girls read a "boy's" book more often.[4] A 1995 study done in England with close to eight thousand 10-, 12-, and 14-year-olds found a swing away from book reading as children grow older, particularly among 14-year-old boys. The survey found that although "boys' predilection for non-narrative remains, . . . its significance in boys' reading diet is somewhat overstated."[5] The 2005 National Literacy Trust report, also conducted in Great Britain with eight thousand primary and secondary school students, stated that when it came to reading fiction both boys' and girls' most popular topics were adventure, comedy, and horror or ghost stories. Least favorite topics for boys were poetry and romance/relationships while girls' least favorites were sports related and war/spy titles.[6] A study that looked at sixth graders' preferences for media such as magazines and comics in addition to books found that boys' and girls' top choice was scary stories. For boys, comics and sports stories were next while girls chose magazines and comics.[7]

The influence of gender on reading interests is thus not entirely clear. What we do not know about gender differences in children's choices is whether they reflect a natural interest or conformity to cultural expectations. Research that further updates preference studies in our postmodern age is certainly important. We can assume, however, that in school and home settings where traditional sexual stereotypes are downplayed, boys and girls share enthusiasm for many common favorites. It is important to give children many options for book choice so that girls and boys can have a chance to explore each other's perspectives. It is just as unfortunate for girls to miss the excellent nonfiction being published today as it is for boys to turn away from fine fiction that offers insight into human relationships.

Other Determinants of Interest

Many factors other than age and gender have been investigated in relation to children's reading interests. At one time, the influence of mental age vs. chronological age as measured by standardized tests received considerable attention. Now, however, we believe that children of varying academic abilities still are more alike than different in the character of their reading interests. It is more likely that the quantity of books involved and the rate at which interests develop will vary widely.

Illustrations, color, format, length, and type of print can also influence children's choices. It would be unwise to oversimplify the effect of these factors on children's book choices, especially because so much of the research has been done outside the context of normal reading and choosing situations. When children choose and use books in their own classrooms, their reactions to books are more complex than controlled experiments or surveys could reveal.

Social and environmental influences also affect children's book choices and reading interests. Many teachers and librarians feel that cultural and ethnic factors impact reading interests. One of the arguments for providing culturally authentic picture-books and novels about Asian, Hispanic, African American, and Native American children is that readers from a particular culture will find material drawn from their own culture more interesting. The relationship between interests and culture does not seem to be simple, and unfortunately there is not yet enough research to clarify this point.

Although interests do not seem to vary greatly according to geographical location, the impact of the immediate environment—particularly the availability and accessibility of reading materials in the home, classroom, and public and school libraries—can be very strong. Children in classrooms where books are regularly discussed, enjoyed, and given high value tend to show livelier interest in a wider range of literature than do children from situations where books are given less attention. It is hard to tell how much of this effect is due to contact with the books and how much is social. Teachers' favorite books are often mentioned by children as their own favorites, perhaps because these are the stories closest at hand or perhaps because of positive associations with the teacher.

Children frequently influence each other in their choice of books. In the culture of the classroom, a title or an author or a topic may rise to celebrity status for a time. Shel Silverstein's *Runny Babbit* might be "the book" to read in one group of third graders, or children might make their own sign-up sheets to read the classroom's only copy of the latest Dear America book. Younger children might spend time on a study of bears and long afterward point out "bear stories" to each other. Media presentations like the Reading Rainbow series from the Public Broadcasting System create demand for specific books.

Peer recommendations are especially important to middle graders in choosing what to read. Some fifth and sixth graders are very candid:

"Everyone else in the class read it, so I figured I ought to, too."
"I usually read what Tammy reads."
"Most of my friends just like the same type of book I like. So, if they find a book, I'll believe them and I'll try it."[8]

Explaining Children's Choices

How can children influence each other's book choices so readily? Part of the answer may be simply that age-mates are likely to enjoy the same kinds of stories because they share many developmental characteristics. As children grow and learn, their levels of understanding change, and so do their favorites in literature. A few thought-provoking studies have suggested that children prefer those stories that best represent their own way of looking at the world—stories that mirror their experiences, needs, fears, and desires at a given age.[9]

There are many things to consider in explaining children's book choices. One of the most important is prior experiences with literature. Some children have heard many stories read aloud at home or have been introduced by their teachers to many different authors and genres. These children are likely to have tastes and preferences that seem advanced compared with those of children their age who have had less exposure to books. Children's personal experiences influence their interests in ways that teachers and librarians might never be able to discover. And sometimes apparent interests are only the product of which books are available and which are not. We must be careful not to oversimplify the reasons for children's book choices. Even so, it is important not to underestimate a developmental perspective that takes into account both experience and growth. This is a powerful tool for predicting reading interests and for understanding other ways in which children respond.

Developmental Patterns That Influence Response

The child-development point of view begins with recognizing and accepting the uniqueness of childhood. Children are not miniature adults but individuals with their own needs, interests, and capabilities, all of which change over time and at varying rates.

In the early decades of child study, emphasis was placed on discovery of so-called normal behavior patterns for each age. Growth studies revealed similarities in patterns of physical, mental, and emotional growth. Later, longitudinal studies showed wide variations in individual rates of growth. One child's growth might be uneven, and a spurt in one aspect of development might precede a spurt in another. Age trends continue to be useful in understanding the child, but by the 1960s research began to be concerned with the interaction of biological and cultural forces with life experience. Researchers recognized that development is not simply the result of the maturation of neural cells but evolves with each new experience. Thus, the interaction of the individual with his or her environment, especially the social and cultural aspects of that environment, affects the age at which development appears.

Studies in children's cognitive and language growth, as well as in other areas of human development, can be very helpful in the choice of appropriate books and the understanding of children's responses. Although in this text we can highlight only a few findings, it should alert you to the importance of such information.

Physical Development

Children's experiences with literature can begin at a very early age. Even before they can talk, babies enjoy the sounds of the human voice reading stories and poetry. Their eyes are increasingly able to focus on color and shape, and by the time they are beginning to talk, their visual perception has developed to the point where they show fascination with small details in illustrations and often enjoy searching for specific objects in pictures.

Children's attention spans generally increase with age. In their first school experiences, some young children have trouble sitting quietly for even a twenty-minute story. It is better to have several short story times for these children than to demand their attention for longer periods and so lose their interest. Some kindergarten and primary teachers provide many opportunities for children to listen to stories in small groups of two or three by using the listening center or asking parent aides or student teachers to read to as few as one or two children.

Physical development influences children's interests as well as their attention spans. Growth in size, muscularity, and coordination is often reflected in a child's choice of a book in which characters share their own newly acquired traits or abilities. *Whistling* by Elizabeth Partridge, for example, seems most rewarding for young children who have just learned to whistle. The demand for sports books increases as girls and boys gain the skills necessary for successful participation.

Children are growing up faster, both physically and psychologically, than they ever have before. The age of onset of puberty figures prominently in an early adolescents' self-concept and influences book choices. Both physical maturity and social forces have led to the development of sexual interests at a younger age. Girls are still reading Judy Blume's *Are You There, God? It's Me, Margaret* (1970) because it reflects their own concerns about menstruation. Robie Harris's nonfiction books such as *It's Not the Stork: A Book About Girls, Boys, Babies, Bodies, Families and Friends* are popular with elementary-age children whose parents may feel squeamish about their frank discussions about physical maturation and human reproduction, while today's children seem to take such books in stride.

Cognitive Development

The work of the great Swiss psychologist Jean Piaget has had a great influence on educators' understanding of children's intellectual development.[10] Piaget proposed that intelligence develops as a result of the interaction of environment and the maturation of the child. In his view, children are active participants in their own learning. Piaget's observations led him to conclude that there are distinct stages in the development of logical thinking. According to his theory, all children go through these stages in the same progression, but not necessarily at the same age. He identified these stages as the sensory-motor period, from infancy to about 2 years of age; the preoperational period, from approximately 2 to 7 years; the concrete operational period, from about 7 to 11; and a two-phase development of formal operations, which begins around age 11 and continues throughout adult life.

In recent years, the validity of Piaget's stage theory has been called into question by many researchers who express concerns about its interpretation. Researchers have suggested that children's social and cultural backgrounds and their familiarity with a task or situation might influence their thinking.[11] Some psychologists feel that stage theory fails to describe the intricacy and complexity of children's thinking and might lead adults to focus on what children are supposedly not able to do, thus falsely lowering expectations. We need to keep these cautions in mind if we look to Piagetian theory for guidance in selecting books for children and planning literature experiences.

Piaget's main contribution to our understanding of cognitive development was his recognition of the child as a meaning maker. Piaget's work and the work of cognitive psychologists since the mid-1900s have helped us view children as individuals. We can expect them to think about their experiences differently as they develop, and we can expect that thinking to change as they move toward adulthood. Thus, it is still useful for us to look at some of the characteristics of children's thinking described by Piaget and to compare them with those of the children with whom we work. Then we can consider how children's thinking patterns are related to the books they like and to their responses to literature.

During the preschool and kindergarten years, children learn to represent the world symbolically through language, play, and drawing. Their thinking seems to be based on direct experience and perception of the present moment. Many of the particular features ascribed to this stage of thought seem to be reflected in young children's response to literature. During these years, children have a hard time holding an image in mind as it changes form or shape. They enjoy predictable stories like "The Gingerbread Boy" or *It's Quacking Time!* by Martin Waddell. The built-in repetition in these stories carries the sequence of the action along from page to page. Older children who are able to follow the more complex logic of stories can remember the events without aid and often say that the repetitious language is boring.

Most children of elementary-school age would be described as being in the concrete operational stage according to Piaget's theory. Classifying and arranging objects in series are important abilities within children's command during this period, making

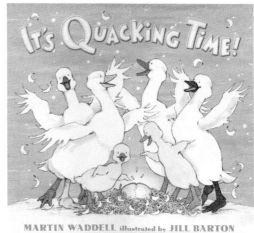

Author Martin Waddell is a master at telling engaging, predictable stories for toddlers, such as *It's Quacking Time!*

It's Quacking Time! Written by Martin Waddell. Illustrations copyright © 2005 by Jill Barton. Reproduced by permission of the publisher, Candlewick Press, Inc., Somerville, MA, on behalf of Walker Books Ltd., London

them more systematic and orderly thinkers. Their thought also becomes flexible and reversible, allowing them to unravel and rearrange a sequence of events. It is no surprise, then, that elementary-age children begin to like mysteries and to understand stories with more complex plot features such as flashbacks or a story within a story. Older elementary-age children also seem to identify more spontaneously with different points of view. Books like *The Wolf's Story* by Toby Forward or *Red Ridin' in the Hood* by Patricia Santos Marcantonio suit this developmental level well because readers understand what the author has done with the structure of a familiar tale and can also begin to see the events through the eyes of a new narrator or a new culture.

As students begin the transitional period that corresponds roughly to the middle-school years, they begin to develop abstract theoretical thought; they are no longer dependent on concrete evidence but can reason from hypotheses to logical conclusions. This allows them to think of possibilities for their lives that are contrary to their prior experience and enables them to see the future in new ways. Complex novels and science fiction in particular begin to have appeal for students at this level. Also, students gain understanding of the use of symbols, such as letters for numbers in algebra or symbolic meanings in literature. While they have understood the use of obvious symbols like the fish in L. S. Matthews's *Fish,* they can now deal with the layers of meaning found in some poetry and complex stories like Lois Lowry's *The Giver.*

However we look at cognitive development, we need to remember that it is only one part of a much larger picture of growth patterns that influence interests and responses.

Language Development

The pattern of language learning moves from an infant babbling and cooing to the use of single words, to simple sentences and transformations such as questions and negatives. Language development proceeds at a phenomenal pace during the preschool years. By the end of that time, children will have learned to express their thoughts in longer sentences that combine ideas or embed one idea within another. In short, they will have gained access to the basic structure of grammar—all this by about age 4, whatever their native language.[12]

Children improvise and explore words as they learn, chanting and playing with language as they gain confidence. Rhythmic rhymes and nonsense verses are natural choices for preschoolers because they fit this pattern so well. However, children's fun in playing with language as various forms are mastered is not limited to the very young. Middle-grade children, with their wider range of language competence, are fascinated by the variety of jokes, riddles, tongue twisters, and folklore miscellany offered by Alvin Schwartz in collections like *Whoppers: Tall Tales and Other Lies*. They are also intrigued by ingenious uses of language in a story context, as in Pamela Edwards's *Some Smug Slug*, Norton Juster's *The Phantom Tollbooth*, or Christopher Paul Curtis's *Mr. Chickee's Funny Money*.

We know that children's language growth continues through the elementary grades and beyond, although the rate is never again as dramatic as during the preschool years. The average length and complexity of their statements, both oral and written, increase as children progress through school.[13] We also know, however, that children's capacity to produce language consistently lags behind their ability to understand it. This suggests that we owe students of all ages the opportunity to read and hear good writing that is beyond the level of their own conversation. Seven-year-olds, for instance, cannot speak with the eloquence and humor that characterize William Steig's picturebooks, such as *Zeke Pippin* or *Doctor De Soto*. Still, they can understand the language in its story context, and hearing it will add to their knowledge of how language sounds and works. Books by Virginia Hamilton or E. L. Konigsburg might serve the same function for older students. Unlike novels that do little more than mirror contemporary speech, the work of these and other fine writers can give children a chance to consider the power of language used with precision and imagination.

Moral Development

Piaget's extensive studies of children included special attention to their developing ideas about fairness and justice. According to Piaget, the difference between younger and older children's concepts is so pronounced that there are really "two moralities" in childhood.[14] Other researchers such as Lawrence Kohlberg[15] and Carol Gilligan have contributed to our understanding of moral development in children.

According to both Piaget's and Kohlberg's descriptions of the general direction of elementary children's development, as children grow in intellect and experience, they move away from ideas of morality based on authority and adult constraint and toward morality based on the influence of group cooperation and independent thinking. To the later stages of this development Gilligan adds a dimension based on gender.[16] She suggests that as girls mature, their sense of their identity is influenced by interconnections with others to a greater degree than for boys. Consequently, their moral judgment develops along lines of an enhanced sense of responsibility and caring for others. Girls might seem less decisive than boys in discussing moral dilemmas because they are trying to take into account a whole network of people who could be affected by a choice. This concern for others is present in boys' thinking as well, but seldom takes precedence over their ideas about what is "fair."

Some of the contrasts between the moral judgment of younger and older children are as follows:

- Young children judge the goodness or badness of an act according to its likelihood of bringing punishment or reward from adults; in other words, they are constrained by the rules that adults have made. Older elementary-age children usually understand that there are group standards for judging what is good or bad and by then are very conscious of situations where they can make their own rules.

- In a young child's eyes, behavior is totally right or totally wrong, with no allowance for an alternate point of view. More-mature children are willing to consider the possibility that circumstances and situations make for legitimate differences of opinion.

- Young children tend to judge an act by its consequences, regardless of the actor's intent. By third or fourth grade, most children have switched to considering motivation rather than consequences alone in deciding what degree of guilt is appropriate.

- Young children believe that bad behavior and punishment go together; the more serious the deed, the more severe the punishment they would prescribe. Its form would not necessarily be related to the offense, but it would automatically erase the offender's guilt. Older children are not so quick to suggest all-purpose pain. They are more interested in finding a "fair" punishment, one that somehow fits the crime and will help bring the wrongdoer back within the rules of the group.

These developmental differences are apparent in the responses of two groups of children to Taro Yashima's *Crow Boy*. When asked what the teacher in the story should do about shy Chibi, who hid under the schoolhouse on the first day, many first graders said "Spank him!" Nine- and 10-year-olds, however, suggested explaining to him that there was nothing to be afraid of or introducing him to classmates so he wouldn't be shy. Many stories for children present different levels of moral complexity that have the potential for stimulating rich discussions among children. In *The Teddy Bear,* David McPhail provides younger children with a chance to consider the impulse to help others over their own wants and desires. *On My Honor* by Marion Dane Bauer and *Millions* by Frank Cottrell Boyce provide older readers with a chance to discuss the complexities of a tragic personal experience.

Working through dilemmas, the experts suggest, allows us to move from one level of moral judgment toward another. Literature provides a means by which children can rehearse and negotiate situations of conflict without risk, trying out alternative stances to problems as they step into the lives and thoughts of different characters.

Personality Development

Every aspect of a child's growth is intertwined with every other. All learning is a meshing of cognitive dimensions, affective or emotional responses, social relationships, and value orientation. This is the matrix in which personality develops. The process of "becoming" is a highly complex one indeed. For children to become "fully functioning" persons, their basic needs must be met. They need to feel they are loved and understood; they must feel they are members of a group significant to them; they must feel they are achieving and growing toward independence. Psychologist Abraham Maslow's research suggests that a person develops through a "hierarchy of needs," from basic animal-survival necessities to the "higher" needs that are more uniquely human and spiritual.[17] Self-actualization might take a lifetime, or it might never be achieved. But the concept that the individual is continually "becoming" is a more positive view than the notion that little change can take place in personality.

Literature can provide opportunities for people of all ages to satisfy higher-level needs, but it is important to remember that books alone cannot meet children's basic needs.

Psychologist Erik Erikson sees human emotional and social development as a passage through a series of stages.[18] Each stage centers around the individual's meeting a particular goal or concern associated with that stage. Erikson theorized that accomplishments at later stages depend on how well the individual was able to meet the goals of preceding stages. According to this theory, a sense of trust must be gained during the first year; a sense of autonomy should be realized by age 3; between 3 and 6 years the sense of initiative is developed; and a sense of duty and accomplishment or industry occupies the period of childhood from 6 to 12 years. In adolescence a sense of identity is built. A sense of intimacy, a parental sense of productivity, and a sense of integrity are among the tasks of adulthood.

The audience for children's books can be grouped according to their orientations toward achieving initiative, accomplishment, and identity. Preschool and early primary children can be described as preoccupied with first ventures outside the circle of familiar authority. Most elementary children are caught up in the period of industry, or "task orientation," proud of their ability to use skills and tools, to plan projects, and to work toward finished products. Middle-school students are more concerned with defining values and personal roles. Writers of

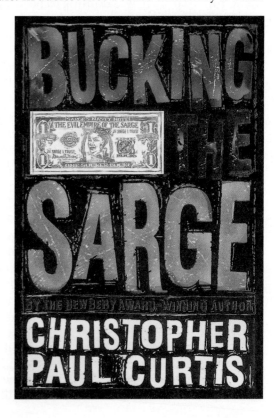

children's books sometimes suggest a natural audience for their work by bringing one of these orientations into the foreground. In Beatrix Potter's *The Tale of Peter Rabbit,* Peter's adventures demonstrate a developing sense of initiative like that of the preschoolers listening to the story. The fearsome aspects of taking those first steps away from Mother are reflected in Phyllis Root's *Oliver Finds His Way. Bucking the Sarge* by Christopher Paul Curtis speaks to the adolescent's struggle for identity and independence.

Guides for Ages and Stages

Adults who are responsible for children's reading need to be aware of child development and learning theory and of children's interests. They must keep in mind characteristics and needs of children at different ages and stages of development. At the same time, it is important to remember that each child has a unique pattern of growth. **Teaching Feature 2.1: Books for Ages and Stages** summarizes some characteristic growth patterns, suggests implications for selection and use of books, and provides examples of suitable books for a particular stage of development. Remember that the age levels indicated are only approximates. Also, books suggested as appropriate for one category might fit several other categories as well.

teaching feature 2.1

Books for Ages and Stages

Characteristics	Implications	Examples
Preschool and Kindergarten: Ages 3, 4, and 5		
Rapid development of language.	Interested in words. Enjoys rhymes, nonsense, and repetition and cumulative tales. Enjoys retelling simple folktale and "reading" stories from books without words.	*Where Is the Green Sheep?* (Fox) *Bears* (Krauss) *The Three Bears* (Rockwell) *Dinnertime!* (Williams)
Very active, short attention span.	Requires books that can be completed in one sitting. Enjoys participation such as naming, pointing, singing, and identifying hidden pictures. Should have a chance to hear stories several times each day.	*The Noisy Way to Bed* (Whybrow) *The Wheels on the Race Car* (Zane) *Each Peach Pear Plum* (Ahlberg) *The Very Hungry Caterpillar* (Carle)
Child is center of own world. Interest, behavior, and thinking are egocentric.	Likes characters that are easy to identify with. Normally sees only one point of view.	*Best Best Friends* (Chodos-Irvine) *Leonardo, the Terrible Monster* (Willems) *No, David!* (Shannon) *Bunny Cakes* (Wells)

(continued)

teaching feature 2.1

Characteristics	Implications	Examples
Curious about own world.	Enjoys stories about everyday experiences, pets, playthings, home, and people in the immediate environment.	*When You Were Born* (Aston) *The Family Book* (Parr) *My Cat, the Silliest Cat in the World* (Bachelet) *The Wildest Brother* (Funke)
Beginning interest in how things work and the wider world.	Books feed curiosity and introduce new topics.	*One Little Lamb* (Greenstein) *A Truck Goes Rattley-Bumpa* (London) *My Mom's Having a Baby!* (Butler) *Sea Horse: The Shyest Horse in the Sea* (Butterworth)
Building concepts through many firsthand experiences.	Books extend and reinforce child's developing concepts.	*This Is Me and Where I Am* (Fitzgerald) *My Pet Hamster* (Rockwell) *My Car* (Barton) *Eating the Alphabet* (Ehlert)
Has little sense of time. Time is "before now," "now," and "not yet."	Books can help children begin to understand the sequence of time.	*Cluck O'Clock* (Gray) *Hickory Dickory Dock* (Baker) *Clocks and More Clocks* (P. Hutchins) *A Second Is a Hiccup* (H. Hutchins)
Learns through imaginative play; make-believe world of talking animals and magic seems very real.	Enjoys stories that involve imaginative play. Likes personification of toys and animals.	*Below* (Crews) *When an Elephant Comes to School* (Ormerod) *Corduroy* (Freeman) *We're Going on a Bear Hunt* (Rosen)
Seeks warmth and security in relationships with family and others.	Likes to hear stories that provide reassurance. Bedtime stories and other read-aloud rituals provide positive literature experiences.	*Shhhhh! Everybody's Sleeping* (Markes) *I Will Hold You 'til You Sleep* (Zuckerman) *Edward, Unready for School* (Wells) *Little Bear* (Minarik)
Beginning to assert independence. Takes delight in own accomplishments.	Books can reflect emotions. Enjoys stories where small characters show initiative.	*Myrtle* (Pearson) *Alfie Gets in First* (Hughes) *Molly's Family* (Garden) *Will I Have a Friend?* (M. Cohen)

Characteristics	Implications	Examples
Makes absolute judgments about right and wrong.	Expects bad behavior to be punished and good behavior to be rewarded. Requires poetic justice and happy endings.	*Superdog: The Heart of a Hero* (Buehner) *The Little Red Hen* (Barton) *The Gingerbread Man* (Aylesworth) *The Tale of Peter Rabbit* (Potter)

Early Primary: Ages 6 and 7

Characteristics	Implications	Examples
Continued development and expansion of language.	Frequent story times during the day provide opportunity to hear the rich and varied language of literature. Wordless books and simple tales encourage storytelling.	*Rainstorm* (Lehman) *Sylvester and the Magic Pebble* (Steig) *The Boy Who Loved Words* (Schotter) *The Adventures of the Dish and the Spoon* (Grey)
Attention span increasing.	Prefers short stories; may enjoy a continued story provided each chapter is a complete episode.	*Tales from the Waterhole* (Graham) *Zelda and Ivy: The Runaways* (Kvasnosky) *Library Lion* (Knudson) *Aggie and Ben: Three Stories* (Ries)
Striving to accomplish skills expected by adults.	Proud of accomplishments in reading and writing. Needs reassurance that everyone progresses at own rate. First reading experiences should be enjoyable, using familiar or predictable stories.	*Duck, Duck, Goose!* (Beaumont) *A Splendid Friend, Indeed* (Bloom) *The Day of Ahmed's Secret* (Heide) *You Read to Me, I'll Read to You* (Hoberman)
Learning still based on immediate perception and direct experiences.	Uses information books to verify as well as extend experience. Much value in watching guinea pigs or tadpoles before using a book.	*Actual Size* (Jenkins) *On the Way to the Beach* (H. Cole) *My Puppy Is Born* (J. Cole) *Chameleon, Chameleon* (Cowley)
Continued interest in own world; more curious about a wider range of things. Still sees world from an egocentric point of view.	Needs a wide variety of books. TV has expanded interests beyond home and neighborhood.	*Bee-Bim Bop!* (Park) *Bebé Goes Shopping* (Elya) *I Live in Tokyo* (Takabayashi) *And Tango Makes Three* (Richardson)

(continued)

teaching feature 2.1

Characteristics	Implications	Examples
Vague concepts of time.	Needs to learn basics of telling time and the calendar. Simple biographies and historical fiction may give a feeling for the past, but accurate understanding of chronology is beyond this age group.	*Mimmy and Sophie, All Around the Town* (Cohen) *The House on Maple Street* (Pryor) *Ox-Cart Man* (D. Hall) *When I Was Young in the Mountains* (Rylant)
More able to separate fantasy from reality; more aware of own imagination.	Enjoys fantasy. Likes to dramatize simple stories or use feltboard, puppets, etc.	*Ker-splash!* (O'Connor) *Traction Man Is Here!* (Grey) *Where the Wild Things Are* (Sendak) *I Know an Old Lady* (Taback)
Beginning to develop empathy for others.	Adults can ask such questions as "What would you have done?" "How would you have felt?"	*Rickie and Henri* (Goodall) *Crow Boy* (Yashima) *The Teddy Bear* (McPhail) *Fly Away Home* (Bunting)
Has a growing sense of justice. Demands application of rules, regardless of circumstances.	Expects poetic justice in books.	*Guji Guji* (Chen) *Flossie and the Fox* (McKissack) *Too Many Tamales* (Soto) *The Tale of Tricky Fox* (Aylesworth)
Humor is developing.	Needs to hear many books read aloud for pure fun. Enjoys books and poems that have surprise endings, plays on words, incongruous situations, and slapstick comedy. Likes to be in on the joke.	*Once Upon a Banana* (Armstrong) *Meet Wild Boars* (Rosoff) *My Little Sister Hugged an Ape* (Grossman) *Broom Mates* (Palatini)
Shows curiosity about gender differences and reproduction.	Teachers need to accept and be ready to answer children's questions about sex.	*It's Not the Stork: A Book About Girls, Boys, Babies, Bodies, Families and Friends* (Harris) *How I Was Born* (Wabbes) *Making Animal Babies* (Collard) *How You Were Born* (J. Cole)

Characteristics	Implications	Examples
Physical contour of the body is changing; permanent teeth appear; learning to whistle and developing other fine motor skills.	Books can help the child accept physical changes in self and differences in others.	*I Lost My Tooth in Africa* (Diakité) *Whistling* (Partridge) *You'll Soon Grow into Them, Titch* (P. Hutchins) *Hue Boy* (Phillips)
Continues to seek independence from adults and to develop initiative.	Needs opportunities to select own books and activities. Enjoys stories of responsibility and successful ventures.	*Elena's Serenade* (Campbell) *My Rows and Piles of Coins* (Mollel) *Adèle & Simon* (McClintock) *Ira Sleeps Over* (Waber)
Continues to need warmth and security in family relationships.	Books may emphasize universal human characteristics in a variety of lifestyles.	*For You Are a Kenyan Child* (Cunnane) *The Biggest Soap* (Schaefer) *A Bear for Miguel* (Alphin) *Henry's First Moon Birthday* (Look)

Middle Elementary: Ages 8 and 9

Characteristics	Implications	Examples
Attaining independence in reading skill. May read with complete absorption; or may still be having difficulty learning to read. Wide variation in ability and interest.	Discovers reading as an enjoyable activity. Prefers an uninterrupted block of time for independent reading. During this period, many children become avid readers.	*Ruby Lu, Empress of Everything* (Look) *Judy Moody Declares Independence* (McDonald) *Shredderman: Attack of the Tagger* (Van Draanen) *Martin Bridge: Sound the Alarm!* (Kerrin)
Reading level may still be below appreciation level.	Essential to read aloud to children each day in order to extend interests, develop appreciation, and provide balance.	*The Fish in Room 11* (Dyer) *The Pepins and Their Problems* (Horvath) *The Penderwicks* (Birdsall) *If Dogs Were Dinosaurs* (Schwartz)
Peer-group acceptance becomes increasingly important.	Children need opportunities to recommend and discuss books. Sharing favorites builds a sense that reading is fun and has group approval. Popular books may provide status and be much in demand.	*Owen Foote, Super Spy* (Greene) *Lucy Rose: Big on Plans* (Kelly) *Mercy Watson: Princess in Disguise* (DiCamillo) *Clementine's Letter* (Pennypacker)

(continued)

teaching feature 2.1

Characteristics	Implications	Examples
Developing standards of right and wrong. Begins to see viewpoints of others.	Books provide opportunities to relate to several points of view.	*Honeysuckle House* (Cheng) *Alec's Primer* (Walter) *Freedom on the Menu* (Weatherford) *Through My Eyes* (Bridges)
Less egocentric; developing empathy for others. Questioning death.	Accepts some books with a less-than-happy ending. Discussion helps children explore their feelings for others.	*Each Little Bird That Sings* (Wiles) *Michael Rosen's Sad Book* (M. Rosen) *The Cat with the Yellow Star* (Rubin) *Stone Fox* (Gardiner)
Time concepts and spatial relationships developing. This age level is characterized by thought that is flexible and reversible.	Interested in biographies, life in the past, in other lands, and the future. Prefers fast-moving, exciting stories.	*Maritcha: A Nineteenth Century American Girl* (Bolden) *Sequoyah* (Rumford) *Being Teddy Roosevelt* (Mills) *The Green Book* (Walsh)
Enjoys tall tales and slapstick humor in everyday situations. Appreciates imaginary adventure.	Teachers need to recognize the importance of literature for laughter, releasing tension, and providing enjoyment.	*The Golden Goose* (King-Smith) *Oh No! Where Are My Pants?* (Hopkins) *Grandy Thaxter's Helper* (Rees) *Wake the Dead* (M. Harris)
Cognitive growth and language development increase capacity for problem solving and word play.	Likes the challenge of solving puzzles and mysteries. High interest in twists of plot, secret codes, riddles, and other language play.	*Can You See What I See?* (Wick) *Math Potatoes* (Tang) *Cam Jansen and the New Girl Mystery* (Adler)
Improved coordination makes proficiency in sports and games possible and encourages interest in crafts and hobbies.	Interested in sports books; wants specific knowledge about sports. Enjoys how-to-do-it books.	*The Jumbo Book of Needlecrafts* (Sadler) *National Geographic Photography Guide for Kids* (Johnson) *The Visual Dictionary of Baseball* (Buckley Jr.) *Africa for Kids* (Croze)
Sees categories and classifications with new clarity; interest in collecting is high.	Likes to collect and trade paperback books. Begins to look for books of one author or series books.	*Dragon of the Red Dawn* (Osborne) *The Extreme Team: Wild Ride* (Christopher) *Horrible Harry Cracks the Code* (Kline) *Meet Addy* (Porter)

Characteristics	Implications	Examples
Seeks specific information to answer questions; may go to books beyond own reading ability to search out answers.	Enjoys books that collect facts, nonfiction, and identification books. Requires guidance in locating information within a book and in using the library.	*Insectology* (Blobaum) *Where Did the Butterfly Get Its Name?* (Berger) *New Beginnings: Jamestown and the Virginia Colony* (D. Rosen) *The Tomb of the Boy King* (Frank)

Later Elementary: Ages 10 and 11

Rate of physical development varies widely. Rapid growth precedes beginning of puberty. Girls are about two years ahead of boys in development. Both increasingly curious about all aspects of sex.	Guide understanding of the growth process and help children address personal problems. Continued differentiation in reading preferences of boys and girls.	*Are You There, God? It's Me, Margaret* (Blume) *Llama in the Library* (Hurwitz) *What's the Big Secret? Talking About Sex with Girls and Boys* (L. Brown and M. Brown) *The Period Book* (K. Gravelle and J. Gravelle)
Understanding of sex role is developing; boys and girls form ideas about their own and each other's identity.	Books may provide identification with gender roles and impetus for discussion of stereotypes.	*Stanford Wong Flunks Big-Time* (Yee) *Project Mulberry* (Park) *Under the Watsons' Porch* (Shreve) *Guys Write for Guys Who Read* (Scieszka)
Increased emphasis on peer group and sense of belonging.	Book choices often influenced by peer group. Books can highlight problems with peer pressure.	*Moon Runner* (Marsden) *Some Friend* (Bradby) *No Talking* (Clements) *Wringer* (Spinelli)
Deliberate exclusion of others; some expressions of prejudice.	Books can emphasize unique contributions of all. Discussion can be used to clarify values.	*Days of Tears* (Lester) *Yankee Girl* (Rodman) *Roll of Thunder, Hear My Cry* (Taylor) *Lizzie Bright and the Buckminster Boy* (Schmidt)
Family patterns changing; may challenge parents' authority. Highly critical of siblings.	Books may provide some insight into these changing relationships.	*Eggs* (Spinelli) *Millions* (Boyce) *Al Capone Does My Shirts* (Choldenko) *Rules* (Lord)

(continued)

teaching feature 2.1

Characteristics	Implications	Examples
Begins to have models other than parents drawn from TV, movies, sports figures, books. Beginning interest in future vocation.	Biographies may provide models. Career books broaden interests and provide useful information.	*Nelson Mandela* (Kramer) *When Marian Sang* (Ryan) *What to Do About Alice?* (Kerley) *Freedom Walkers* (Freedman)
Sustained, intense interest in specific activities.	Seeks book about hobbies and other interests.	*Out Standing in My Field* (Jennings) *Galileo for Kids* (Panchyk) *Bodies from the Ash* (Deem) *Berry Smudges and Leaf Prints* (Senisi)
A peak time for voluntary reading.	Avid readers welcome challenges and repeated contact with authors, genres.	*Harry Potter and the Half-Blood Prince* (Rowling) *The Search for Belle Prater* (White) *Permanent Rose* (McKay) *The Book without Words* (Avi)
Seeks to test own skills and abilities; looks ahead to a time of complete independence.	Enjoys stories of survival and "going it alone."	*Fish* (Matthews) *Gnat Stokes and the Foggy Bottom Swamp Queen* (Keehn) *Hatchet* (Paulsen) *The Higher Power of Lucky* (Patron)
Increased cognitive skill can be used to serve the imagination.	Tackles complex and puzzling plots in mysteries, science fiction, fantasy. Can appreciate more subtlety in humor.	*The Calder Game* (Balliett) *A Thief in the House of Memory* (Wynne-Jones) *Framed* (Boyce) *The Clue of the Linoleum Lederhosen* (Anderson)
Increased understanding of the chronology of past events; developing sense of own place in time. Begins to see many dimensions of a problem.	Literature provides opportunities to examine issues from different viewpoints. Guidance needed for recognizing biased presentations.	*A Dream of Freedom* (McWhorter) *Adam Canfield of the Slash* (Winerip) *The Friends* (Yumoto) *Emil and Karl* (Glatshteyn)

Characteristics	Implications	Examples
Highly developed sense of justice and concern for others.	Willing to discuss many aspects of right and wrong; likes "sad stories"; shows empathy for victims of suffering and injustice.	*Gentle's Holler* (Madden) *Billy Creekmore* (Porter) *The Killer's Tears* (Bondoux) *Bud, Not Buddy* (Curtis)
Searching for values; interested in problems of the world. Can deal with abstract relationships; becoming more analytical.	Valuable discussions may grow out of teacher's reading aloud prose and poetry to this age group. Questions may help students gain insight into both the content and the literary structure of a book.	*The Other Side of Truth* (Naidoo) *Under the Persimmon Tree* (Staples) *Shadows of Ghadames* (Stolz) *The View from Saturday* (Konigsburg)

Middle School—Ages 12, 13, and 14

Characteristics	Implications	Examples
Wide variation in physical development; both boys and girls reach puberty by age 14. Developing sex drive; intense interest in sexuality and world of older teens.	Books provide insight into feelings, concerns. Guidance needed to balance students' desire for frank content with lack of life experience.	*It's Perfectly Normal* (Harris) *What My Mother Doesn't Know* (Sones) *Am I Blue?* (Bauer) *The Big Game of Everything* (Lynch)
Self-concept continues to grow. Developing a sense of identity is important.	Books help students explore roles, rehearse journey to identity. Many stories based on myth of the hero.	*A Wizard of Earthsea* (LeGuin) *The Hero and the Crown* (McKinley) *Shadows on the Stars* (Barron) *Absolute Brightness* (Lecesne)
Peer group becomes increasingly influential; relationships with family are changing.	Concerns about friends and families reflected in books. School should provide chance to share books and responses with peer group.	*How to Build a House* (Reinhardt) *Breaking Through* (Jiménez) *A Step from Heaven* (Na) *Criss Cross* (Perkins)
New aspects of egocentrism lead to imagining self as center of others' attention and feeling one's own problems are unique.	Students begin to enjoy introspection; may identify with characters who are intense or self-absorbed.	*The Absolutely True Diary of a Part-Time Indian* (Alexie) *Jazmin's Notebook* (Grimes) *Jacob Have I Loved* (Paterson) *White Darkness* (McCaughrean)

(continued)

teaching feature 2.1

Characteristics	Implications	Examples
Cognitive abilities are increasingly abstract and flexible, but not consistently so. New capacity to reason from imaginary premises, manipulate symbolic language, and make hypothetical judgments.	Students read more complex stories, mysteries, and high fantasy that call for complex logic; enjoy science fiction and high adventure. Metaphor, symbols, and imagery are understood at a different level.	*The Land of the Silver Apples* (Farmer) *The Fire-Eaters* (Almond) *Darkwing* (Oppel) *The Star of Kazan* (Ibbotson)
Able to apply ideas of relativity to questions of values; girls might see moral issues differently than boys do.	Students need discussion time to negotiate meanings in stories that pose moral dilemmas.	*Shabanu* (Staples) *The Giver* (Lowry) *Keeping Corner* (Sheth) *The Diary of Pelly D* (Adlington)
Sensitive to great complexity in human feelings and relationships.	Students seek richer and more complex stories.	*Tamar* (Peet) *Like Sisters on the Home Front* (Williams-Garcia) *Copper Sun* (Draper) *Sunrise Over Fallujah* (Myers)
Cumulative effects of development and life experience produce wide variation among individuals in abilities and interests.	Reading ability and interests in one class may range from early elementary to adult.	*The Hobbit* (Tolkien) *Honeybee* (Nye) *Ghost Circles* (J. Smith) *The Secret Under My Skin* (McNaughton)

Response in the Classroom

Understanding children's responses to literature would be much easier if it were possible to peer inside children's heads. Instead, teachers must be satisfied with secondary evidence. Children's perceptions and understandings are revealed in many different ways—as the children choose and talk about books, and as they write, paint, play, or take part in other classroom activities.

Classroom responses can be obvious and direct (primary children have been known to kiss a favorite book) or hidden within a situation that appears to have little to do with literature (such as block corner play). Many responses are verbal, many come without words. Some are spontaneous, bubbling up out of children too delighted to be still, or shyly offered in confidence. Other responses would not be expressed at all without the direct invitation of teachers who plan extension activities or discussions (see Chapter 10) to generate thoughtful reaction to literature. To understand any of these observed responses, it is helpful to be acquainted with a few basic theoretical perspectives.

Theories of Response

What really goes on between a reader and a story or poem is a complex question with many answers. Theories about reader response draw from many disciplines, including psychology, linguistics, aesthetics, and, of course, literature and education.

Some theories focus on what is read; others focus on the reader. For instance, some researchers have examined in careful detail the structure of stories, noting the precise arrangement of words and sequence of ideas. These patterns are called "story grammars," and studies indicate that they can affect the way readers understand and recall a story.[19] Other theorists are more concerned with individual readers and how their personalities can influence their ideas about what they read.[20] Still other researchers emphasize the cultural or social aspects of response. According to Richard Beach, "While all these theoretical perspectives rest on different assumptions about meaning, they ultimately intersect and overlap. The local—the focus on readers' textual knowledge and experience—is embedded within the global, larger social and cultural contexts." All categories of reader response research focus on the reader's textual knowledge and experience, but they are embedded within larger social and cultural contexts.[21]

One important point on which scholars agree is that the process of reading and responding is active rather than passive. The words and ideas in the book are not transferred automatically from the page to the reader. Rather, as Louise Rosenblatt has argued:

> The literary work exists in the live circuit set up between reader and text: the reader infuses intellectual and emotional meanings into the pattern of verbal symbols, and those symbols channel his thoughts and feelings.[22]

Response is dynamic and open to continuous change as readers anticipate, infer, remember, reflect, interpret, and connect. The "meaning" and significance of stories like David Almond's *Skellig* or Lois Lowry's *The Giver* will vary from reader to reader, depending on age and personal experience as well as experience with literature. However, each reader's response will also change, given time for reflection, discussion, or repeated readings.

Reader response theory also points out that readers approach works of literature in special ways. James Britton proposes that in all our uses of language we can be either *participants* or *spectators*.[23] In the participant role, we read in order to accomplish something in the real world, as in following a recipe. In the spectator role, we focus on what the language says as an end in itself, attending to its forms and patterns, as we do in enjoying poetry.

Rosenblatt suggests that reading usually involves two roles, or stances, and that we shift our emphasis from one to the other according to the material and our purposes for reading it.[24] In the *efferent* stance, we are most concerned with what information can be learned from the reading. In the *aesthetic* stance, our concern is for the experience of the reading itself, the feelings and images that come and go with the flow of the words. Most readers, of course, find themselves switching back and forth from one of these stances to the other as they read. One thing teachers can do to help children share the world the author has created is to help them find an appropriate stance as they begin to read.

Types of Response

Teachers who are familiar with reader response theories and who study children's responses to literature will discover that they provide a basis for deepening children's satisfaction with books and for supporting children's growth in interpretation.

The most common expressions of response to literature are statements, oral or written. In their most polished form, such responses are known as literary criticism, and for many years research in literature involved measuring young people's statements against a standard of mature critical ability.

Where children are concerned, it is important to remember that direct comment is only one of many ways of revealing what goes on between the book and its audience. Language used in other ways—to tell or write stories based on other stories, for instance—often provides good clues about a child's feelings and understandings about the original. Parents and teachers of young children also recognize nonverbal behaviors as signs of response. For instance, young listeners almost always show their involvement, or lack of it, in body postures and facial expressions. Children's artwork, informal drama, and other book extension activities (see Chapter 10) also provide windows on response.

Interpreting Children's Responses

Previous research in response to literature provides teachers and librarians with a framework for interpreting their students' reactions to books. This classroom-based research can give us a deeper understanding of children's responses.

Recognizing Patterns of Change Teachers and researchers alike have observed that when children at different grade levels read and respond in ways that are comfortable for them, their responses will be alike in some ways and different in others. What might teachers expect to see in a fourth-grade classroom? What are typical first-grade responses? No one can answer these questions with exactness, for every child is a unique reader and every classroom represents a different composite of experiences with literature and with the world. Even so, it is helpful to know what researchers and teachers have discovered about the responses of their students at various grade levels. This section outlines some of these findings to provide information on the patterns of change in responses that usually take place as children have experiences with literature in the elementary school.[25] Although these findings are presented in an age-level sequence, keep in mind that any of these characteristics can be seen at other ages, depending on the child, the situation, and the challenge presented by the material. Like the Teaching Feature 2.1: Books for Ages and Stages chart, this guide is more useful for making predictions about a class than for making predictions about an individual child.

Younger Children (Preschool to Primary) Younger children are motor oriented. As listeners, they respond with their whole selves, chiming in on refrains or talking back to the story. They lean closer to the book, point at pictures, clap their hands. They use body movements to try out some of the story's action, "hammering" along with *John Henry* by Julius Lester or making wild faces to match the illustrations in Maurice Sendak's *Where the Wild Things Are*. Actions to demonstrate meaning ("Like this") might be given as answers to a teacher's questions. These easily observable responses go undercover as children mature; older children reveal feelings through subtle changes of expression and posture.

At this age, children spontaneously act out stories or bits of stories using actions, roles, and conventions of literature in their dramatic play. Witches, kings, "wild things," and other well-defined character types appear naturally, showing how well children have assimilated elements of favorite tales. Examples of story language ("We lived happily ever after") are sometimes incorporated. Spontaneous dramatic play disappears from the classroom early in the primary years (although it persists out of school with some children) and is replaced by more structured drama of various kinds. Older children are usually much more conscious of their own references to literature.

These children respond to stories piecemeal. Their responses deal with parts rather than wholes. A detail of text or illustration might prompt more comment than the story itself, as children make quick associations with their own experience: "I saw a bird like that once," or "My sister has bunk beds just like those." This part-by-part organization can also be seen in very young children's art, where the pictures show individual story items without any indication of relationship ("This is the baby bear's chair, and this is Goldilocks, and this is the house the bears lived in, and here is the bed."). This is the same sort of itemization or cataloging of characters, objects, and events that children sometimes use when asked to tell something about a story. Young children are more likely to respond to the story as a whole if they have heard it many times or if an adult provides that focus by asking good questions.

Children at this age use embedded language in answering direct questions about stories. Because young children see the world in literal, concrete terms, their answers are likely to be couched in terms of the characters, events, and objects found in the story. One first grader made a good attempt to generalize the lesson of "The Little Red Hen," but couldn't manage without some reference to the tale: "When someone already baked the cake and you haven't helped, they're probably just gonna say 'No'!" A teacher or other adult who shares the child's context—who knows the story, has heard or read it with the child, and knows what other comments have been made—will understand the intent of such a statement more readily than a casual observer will.

Children in Transition (Primary to Middle Grades) Children in transition from the primary to the middle grades develop from being listeners to becoming readers. They go through a period of focus on the accomplishment of independent reading. They make many comments about quantity—number of pages read, the length of a book, or the number of books read. Conventions of print and of bookmaking might draw their attention. One third grader refused to read any of the poems from Shel Silverstein's *Where the Sidewalk Ends* without locating them in the index first; a classmate was fascinated with the book's variety of word and line arrangements for poetry. Another child studied the front matter of a picturebook and pronounced it "a dedicated book." So-called independent reading may be more sociable than it sounds because many children like to have a listener or reading partner and begin to rely on peers as sounding boards for their response.

At this age, children become more adept at summarizing in place of straight re-telling when asked to talk about stories. This is a skill that facilitates discussion and becomes more useful as it is developed. Summarizing is one of the techniques that undergirds critical commentary, but adults use it more deliberately and precisely than children do.

These children classify or categorize stories in some of the same ways that adults do. Middle graders who are asked to sort out a random pile of books use categories like "mysteries," "humorous books," "make-believe," and "fantasy." If you ask kinder-gartners to do the same, they are more likely to classify the books by their physical properties ("fat books," "books with pretty covers," "red books") than by content. Children at this age *attribute personal reactions to the story* itself. A book that bores an 8-year-old will be thought of as a "boring book," as if "boring" were as much a property of the story as its number of pages or its first-person point of view. Children judge a story on the basis of their response to it, regardless of its qualities as literature or its appeal to anyone else. This is a very persistent element in response; it affects the judgment of students of children's literature and of professional book review-ers as well as children in elementary school. Personal response can never be totally eliminated from critical evaluation; but with experience, readers can develop more objectivity in separating a book's literary characteristics from its personal appeal.

These children also use borrowed characters, events, themes, and patterns from literature in their writing, just as younger children do in dramatic play. In the earli-est stages, much of this is unconscious and spontaneous. One example is a 7-year-old who was convinced that her story about a fish with paint-splashed insides was "made up out of my own head," even when reminded that the class had just heard Robert McCloskey's *Burt Dow, Deep Water Man*. A 9-year-old spontaneously combined a favorite character with a field-trip experience in his story "Paddington Bear Goes to Franklin Park Conservatory," but he was aware of his idea sources. Other children produce their own examples of patterns, forms, or genres. The direction of growth is toward more conscious realization of the uses of literature in writing.

Older Children (Middle Grades to Middle School) Older children express stronger pref-erences, especially for personal reading. Younger children seem to enjoy almost ev-erything that is reasonably appropriate, but older ones do not hesitate to reject books they do not like. Some children show particular devotion to certain authors or genres or series at this time. Some children also become more intense and protective about some of their reactions, and they should not be pressed to share those feelings that demand privacy.

At this age, children are more skillful with language and more able to deal with abstractions. They can deduce ideas from a story and put them in more generalized terms, as in stating a universal moral for a particular fable.

These children also begin to see (but not consistently) that their feelings about a book are related to identifiable aspects of the writing. Responses like "I love this book because it's great" develop into "I love this book because the characters say such funny things" or "*Strider* [by Cleary] is my favorite because Leigh is a lot like me."

Older children go beyond categorizing stories toward a more analytical percep-tion of why characters behave as they do, how the story is put together, or what the author is trying to say. They begin to test fiction against real life and understand it better through the comparison. They use some critical terminology, although their understanding of terms may be incomplete. In talk and writing, children who are encouraged to express ideas freely begin to stand back from their own involvement and take an evaluative look at literature. One sixth grader had this to say about *A Taste of Blackberries* by Doris Buchanan Smith:

> I thought the author could have put more into it. I really didn't know much about the kid who died. I mean, it really happened fast in the book. It started out pretty soon and told about how sad he was and what they used to do. All the fun things they used to do together. I wished at the beginning they would have had all the things that he talked about and then have him thinking about what a good friend he is and then all of a sudden he dies—a little closer to the end. Because when he died, you didn't much care 'cause you didn't really know him. But I guess the author wanted to talk about how it would be, or how people feel, or maybe what happened to her—how it felt when one of her friends died like that.[26]

In general, children's responses move toward this sort of conscious comment. Young children sometimes make stunningly perceptive observations about stories, but they are not usually able to step back and see the importance of what they have said. Older children begin to have a deeper understanding of their observations and can then take command of it. This allows them to layer mature appreciation on top of the beginner's natural delight.

However, older children's increasing capacity for abstraction, generalization, and analysis should *not* be interpreted as a need for programs of formal literary analysis or highly structured study procedures. Opportunities to read, hear, and talk about well-chosen books under the guidance of an interested and informed teacher will allow elementary school children to develop their responses to their full potential.

Children, no matter what their age, will respond to a story on their own terms of understanding. It does little good (and can be destructive to the enjoyment of literature) if younger children are pushed to try to formulate the abstractions achieved by more mature children. However, James Britton maintains that teachers may refine and develop the responses that children are already making by gradually exposing them to stories with increasingly complex patterns of events.[27]

Collecting Children's Responses

Finding out how children understand literature and which books they like is such essential information for elementary teachers and librarians that it should not be left to chance. Techniques for discovering responses that are simple and fit naturally into the ongoing business of classrooms and library media centers are discussed in the context of planning the school literature program in Chapter 10.

As elementary teachers become aware of the way they can tune in to children's responses to literature, they will see the value of examining the nature of children's thinking about it. We all believe that literature is important for children, but we do not truly know what difference it makes in a child's life, if any. An in-depth study of children's responses to books is just as important as, if not more important than, the studies of children's interests in books. We should explore the developmental nature of response and conduct longitudinal studies of a child's responses over the years. As teachers and librarians, we need to listen to what the children are telling us about their involvement with books and what it means to them.

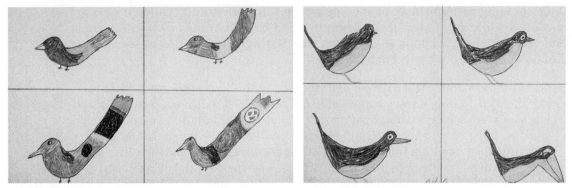

When asked to replicate Leo Lionni's story of *The Biggest House in the World* using a new main character, two children demonstrated different levels in their understanding of the theme. The 8-year-old (left picture) showed a bird growing more elaborate; the 10-year-old (right picture) portrayed a change leading to the bird's self-destruction. Tremont Elementary School, Upper Arlington Public Schools, Upper Arlington, Ohio. Jill Boyd, teacher.

Notes

1. *2008 Kids and Family Reading Report* <www.scholastic.com/aboutscholastic/news/readingreport.htm>.

2. See, for example, Christina Clark and Amelia Foster, *Children's and Young People's Reading Habits and Preferences: The Who, What, Why, Where and When,* National Literacy Trust (December 2005); Mary-Jo Fresch, "Self-Selection Strategies of Early Literacy Learners," *Reading Teacher 49* (November 1995): 220–27; Alan Purves and Richard Beach, *Literature and the Reader: Research in Response to Literature, Reading Interests, and the Teaching of Literature* (Urbana, Ill.: National Council of Teachers of English, 1972), pp. 69–71.

3. Amanda Ferguson, "Reading Is Cool," *Publishers Weekly* 245 (12 October 1998): 28–31.

4. Glenda Childress, "Gender Gap in the Library: Different Choices for Boys and Girls," *Top of the News* 42 (fall, 1985): 69–73; Helen Huus, "Interpreting Research in Children's Literature," in *Children, Books and Reading* (Newark, Del.: International Reading Association, 1964), p. 125.

5. Christine Hall and Martin Coles, *Children's Reading Choices* (London: Routledge, 1999), p. 136.

6. Christina Clark and Amelia Foster, *Children's and Young People's Reading Habits and Preferences: The Who, What, Why, Where and When* (London: National Literacy Trust, 2005).

7. Jo Worthy, Megan Moorman, and Margo Turner, "What Johnny Likes to Read Is Hard to Find in School," *Reading Research Quarterly* 34.1 (1999): 20.

8. Susan I. Hepler and Janet Hickman, "'The Book Was Okay. I Love You'—Social Aspects of Response to Literature," *Theory into Practice* 21 (autumn, 1982): 279.

9. See Andre Favat, *Child and Tale: The Origins of Interest* (Urbana, Ill.: National Council of Teachers of English, 1977), and Norma Marian Schlager, "Developmental Factors Influencing Children's Responses to Literature" (Ph.D. dissertation, Claremont Graduate School, 1974).

10. Barbel Inhelder and Jean Piaget, *The Growth of Logical Thinking* (New York: Basic Books, 1962); Barry J. Wadsworth, *Piaget's Theory of Cognitive and Affective Development* (Reading, Mass.: Addison-Wesley, 1996).

11. Margaret Donaldson, *Children's Minds* (New York: Norton, 1979), chap. 2.

12. Dan I. Sobin, "Children and Language: They Learn the Same Way All around the World," in *Contemporary Readings in Child Psychology,* 2nd ed., eds. E. Mavis Hetherington and Ross D. Parke (New York: McGraw-Hill, 1981), pp. 122–26.

13. Walter Loban, *Language Development: Kindergarten through Grade Twelve* (Urbana, Ill.: National Council of Teachers of English, 1976).

14. Jean Piaget, *The Moral Judgment of the Child,* trans. M. Gabain (New York: Free Press, 1965).

15. Lawrence Kohlberg, *The Meaning and Measurement of Moral Development* (Worcester, Mass.: Clark University Heinz Wemer Institute, 1981).

16. Carol Gilligan, *In a Different Voice: Psychological Theory and Women's Development* (Cambridge, Mass.: Harvard University Press, 1982).

17. Abraham H. Maslow, *Motivation and Personality,* rev. ed. (Reading, Mass.: Addison-Wesley, 1987).

18. Erik H. Erikson, *Childhood and Society,* rev. ed. (New York: Norton, 1993).

19. Dorothy S. Strickland and Joan Feeley, "Development in the Elementary School Years," *Handbook of Research on Teaching the English Language Arts,* eds. James Flood, Julie Jensen, Diane Lapp, and James Squire (New York: Macmillan, 1991), pp. 386–402.

20. Norman H. Holland, *Five Readers Reading* (New Haven, Conn.: Yale University Press, 1975).

21. Richard Beach, *A Teacher's Introduction to Reader-Response Theories* (Urbana, Ill.: National Council of Teachers of English, 1993), p. 9.

22. Louise M. Rosenblatt, *Literature as Exploration,* 5th ed. (New York: Modern Language Association, 1996), p. 25.

23. James Britton, et al., *The Development of Writing Abilities (11–18),* Schools Council Research Studies (London: Macmillan Education Limited, 1975).

24. Louise M. Rosenblatt, *The Reader, the Text, the Poem: The Transactional Theory of the Literary Work* (Carbondale: Southern Illinois University Press, 1994).

25. This section is based on observations with reference to the work of Arthur Applebee, *The Child's Concept of Story* (Chicago, Ill.: University of Chicago Press, 1978), pp. 123–25; Janet Hickman, "A New Perspective on Response to Literature," *Research in the Teaching of English* 15 (1981): 343–54; and others.

26. Recorded in the classroom of Lois Monaghan, teacher, Barrington School, Upper Arlington, Ohio.

27. James Britton, in *Response to Literature,* ed. James R. Squire (Champaign, Ill.: National Council of Teachers of English, 1968), p. 4.

Children's Literature

Go to **www.mhhe.com/kiefer1e** to access the *Children's Literature Database,* which includes information on thousands of children's books. Following are some of the titles you will find in the database.

Titles in blue = multicultural titles

Adler, David A. *Young Cam Jansen and the New Girl Mystery.* Viking, 2004.

Adlington, L. J. *The Diary of Pelly D.* Greenwillow, 2005.

Ahlberg, Janet, and Allan Ahlberg. *Each Peach Pear Plum.* Viking, 1978.

Alexie, Sherman. *The Absolutely True Diary of a Part-Time Indian.* Little, 2007.

Almond, David. *The Fire-Eaters.* Delacorte, 2004.

———. *Skellig.* Delacorte, 1999.

Alphin, Elaine Marie. *A Bear for Miguel.* Illustrated by Joan Sanders. HarperCollins, 1996.

Anderson, M. T. *The Clue of the Linoleum Lederhosen.* Harcourt, 2006.

Armstrong, Jennifer. *Once Upon a Banana.* Illustrated by David Small. Simon, 2006.

Aston, Dianna Hutts. *When You Were Born.* Illustrated by E. B. Lewis. Candlewick, 2004.

Avi. *The Book without Words: A Fable of Medieval Magic.* Hyperion, 2005.

Aylesworth, Jim. *The Gingerbread Man.* Illustrated by Barbara McClintock. Scholastic, 1998.

———. *The Tale of Tricky Fox: A New England Trickster Tale.* Illustrated by Barbara McClintock. Scholastic, 2001.

Bachelet, Gilles. *My Cat, the Silliest Cat in the World.* Abrams, 2006.

Baker, Keith. *Hickory Dickory Dock.* Harcourt, 2007.

Balliett, Blue. *The Calder Game.* Scholastic, 2008.

Barron, T. A. *The Great Tree of Avalon: Shadows on the Stars.* Philomel, 2005.

Barton, Byron. *The Little Red Hen.* HarperCollins, 1993.

———. *My Car.* HarperCollins, 2001.

Bauer, Marion Dane. *Am I Blue? Coming Out from the Silence.* HarperCollins, 1994.

———. *On My Honor.* Clarion, 1986.

Beaumont, Karen. *Duck, Duck, Goose!* Illustrated by Jose Aruego and Ariane Dewey. HarperCollins, 2004.

Berger, Melvin, and Gilda Berger. *Where Did the Butterfly Get Its Name? Questions and Answers about Butterflies and Moths.* Scholastic, 2003.

Birdsall, Jeanne. *The Penderwicks: A Summer Tale of Four Sisters, Two Rabbits, and a Very Interesting Boy.* Knopf, 2005.

Blobaum, Cindy. *Insectology: 40 Hands-On Activities to Explore the Insect World.* Chicago Review, 2005.

Bloom, Suzanne. *A Splendid Friend, Indeed.* Boyds Mills, 2005.

Blume, Judy. *Are You There, God? It's Me, Margaret.* Bradbury, 1970.

Bolden, Tonya. *Maritcha: A Nineteenth Century American Girl.* Abrams, 2005.

Bond, Michael. *A Bear Called Paddington.* Illustrated by Peggy Fortnum. Houghton, 1998.

Bondoux, Anne-Laure. *The Killer's Tears.* Translated from the French by Y. Maudet. Delacorte, 2006.

Boyce, Frank Cottrell. *Framed.* HarperCollins, 2006.

———. *Millions.* HarperCollins, 2004.

Bradby, Marie. *Some Friend.* Atheneum, 2004.

Bridges, Ruby. *Through My Eyes.* Scholastic, 1999.

Brimner, Larry Dane. *The Littlest Wolf.* Illustrated by Jose Aruego and Ariane Dewey. HarperCollins, 2002.

Brown, Laurene Krasny, and Marc Brown. *What's the Big Secret? Talking About Sex with Girls and Boys.* Little, 1997.

Bryant, Sarah Cone. *The Burning Rice Fields.* Illustrated by M. Funai. Holt, 1963.

Buckley Jr., James. *The Visual Dictionary of Baseball.* DK, 2001.

Buehner, Caralyn. *Superdog: The Heart of a Hero.* Illustrated by Mark Buehner. HarperCollins, 2004.

Bunting, Eve. *Fly Away Home.* Illustrated by Ron Himler. Clarion, 1991.

Butler, Dori Hillestad. *My Mom's Having a Baby!* Illustrated by Carol Thompson. Whitman, 2005.

Butterworth, Christopher. *Sea Horse: The Shyest Horse in the Sea.* Illustrated by John Lawrence. Candlewick, 2006.

Campbell, Geeslin. *Elena's Serenade.* Illustrated by Ana Juan. Atheneum, 2004.

Carle, Eric. *The Very Hungry Caterpillar.* Philomel, 1969.

Chen, Chih-Yuan. *Guji Guji.* Kane/Miller, 2004.

Cheng, Andrea. *Honeysuckle House.* Front St., 2004.

Chodos-Irvine, Margaret. *Best Best Friends.* Harcourt, 2006.

Choldenko, Gennifer. *Al Capone Does My Shirts.* Putnam, 2004.

———. *Notes from a Liar and Her Dog.* Putnam, 2001.

Christopher, Matt. *The Extreme Team: Wild Ride.* Illustrated by Michael Koelsch. Little, 2005.

Cleary, Beverly. *Strider.* Illustrated by Paul O. Zelinsky. HarperCollins, 2001.

Clements, Andrew. *No Talking.* Simon. 2007.

Cohen, Miriam. *Mimmy and Sophie, All Around the Town.* Illustrated by Thomas F. Yezerski. Farrar, 2004.

———. *Will I Have a Friend?* Illustrated by Lillian Hoban. Macmillan, 1971.

Cole, Henry. *On the Way to the Beach.* Greenwillow, 2003.

Cole, Joanna. *How You Were Born.* Morrow, 1984.

———. *My Puppy Is Born.* Photographs by Margaret Miller. Morrow, 1990.

Collard III, Sneed B. *Making Animal Babies.* Illustrated by Steve Jenkins. Houghton, 2000.

Cowley, Joy. *Chameleon, Chameleon.* Photographs by Nic Bishop. Scholastic, 2005.

Crews, Nina. *Below.* Holt, 2006.

Croze, Henry. *Africa for Kids.* Chicago Review, 2006.

Cunnane, Kelly. *For You Are a Kenyan Child.* Illustrated by Ana Juan. Atheneum, 2006.

Curtis, Christopher Paul. *Bucking the Sarge.* Lamb/Random, 2004.

———. *Bud, Not Buddy.* Delacorte, 1999.

———. *Mr. Chickee's Funny Money.* Lamb/Random, 2005.

Dahl, Roald. *The BFG.* Illustrated by Quentin Blake. Farrar, 1982.

Dane, Larry. *The Littlest Wolf.* Illustrated by Jose Aruego and Ariane Dewey. HarperCollins, 2000.

Deem, James. *Bodies from the Ash: Life and Death in Ancient Pompeii.* Houghton, 2005.

Diakité, Penda. *I Lost My Tooth in Africa.* Illustrated by Baba Wagué Diakité. Scholastic, 2006.

DiCamillo, Kate. *Mercy Watson: Princess in Disguise.* Candlewick, 2007.

Draper, Sharon. *Copper Sun.* Atheneum, 2006.

Dyer, Heather. *The Fish in Room 11.* Scholastic, 2004.

Edwards, Pamela Duncan. *Some Smug Slug.* Illustrated by Henry Cole. HarperCollins, 1996.

Ehlert, Lois. *Eating the Alphabet.* Harper, 1989.

Elya, Susan Middleton. *Bebé Goes Shopping.* Illustrated by Steven Salerno. Harcourt, 2006.

Farmer, Nancy. *The Land of the Silver Apples.* Atheneum, 2007.

Fitzgerald, Joanna. *This Is Me and Where I Am.* Fitzhenry and Whiteside, 2004.

Forward, Toby. *The Wolf's Story: What Really Happened to Little Red Riding Hood.* Illustrated by Izhar Cohen. Candlewick, 2005.

Fox, Mem. *Where Is the Green Sheep?* Illustrated by Judy Horacek. Harcourt, 2004.

Frank, John. *The Tomb of the Boy King.* Illustrated by Tom Pohrt. Farrar, 2001.

Freedman, Russell. *Freedom Walkers: The Story of the Montgomery Bus Boycott.* Holiday, 2006.

———. *The Voice That Challenged a Nation: Marian Anderson and the Struggle for Civil Rights.* Clarion, 2004.

Freeman, Don. *Corduroy.* Viking, 1968.

Funke, Cornelia. *The Wildest Brother.* Illustrated by Oliver Latsch. Scholastic, 2006.

Garden, Nancy. *Molly's Family.* Illustrated by Sharon Wooding. Farrar, 2004.

Gardiner, John Reynolds. *Stone Fox.* Illustrated by Greg Hargreaves. HarperCollins, 1992.

Glatshteyn, Yankev. *Emil and Karl.* Translated by Jeffrey Shandler. Roaring Brook, 2006.

Goodall, Jane. *Rickie and Henri.* Illustrated by Alan Marks. Putnam, 2004.

Graham, Bob. *Tales from the Waterhole.* Candlewick, 2004.

Gravelle, Karen, and Jennifer Gravelle. *The Period Book: Everything You Don't Want to Ask (But Need to Know).* Walker, 2006.

Gray, Kes. *Cluck O'Clock.* Illustrated by Mary McQuillan. Holiday, 2004.

Greene, Stephanie. *Owen Foote, Super Spy.* Clarion, 2005.

Greenstein, Elaine. *One Little Lamb*. Viking, 2004.

Grey, Mini. *The Adventures of the Dish and the Spoon*. Knopf, 2006.

———. *Traction Man Is Here!* Knopf, 2005.

Grimes, Nikki. *Jazmin's Notebook*. Dial, 1998.

Grossman, Bill. *My Little Sister Hugged an Ape*. Illustrated by Kevin Hawkes. Knopf, 2004.

Hall, Donald. *Ox-Cart Man*. Illustrated by Barbara Cooney. Viking, 1979.

Harris, Monica A. *Wake the Dead*. Illustrated by Susan Estelle Kwas. Walker, 2004.

Harris, Robie H. *It's Not the Stork: A Book About Girls, Boys, Babies, Bodies, Families and Friends*. Illustrated by Michael Emberly. Candlewick, 2006.

———. *It's Perfectly Normal: A Book About Changing Bodies, Growing Up, Sex, and Sexual Health*. Illustrated by Michael Emberley. Candlewick, 1994.

Heide, Florence Parry, and Judith Heide Gilliland. *The Day of Ahmed's Secret*. Illustrated by Ted Lewin. Lothrop, 1990.

Hoberman, Mary Ann. *You Read to Me, I'll Read to You: Very Short Stories to Read Together*. Illustrated by Michael Emberley. Little, 2001.

Hodges, Margaret. *The Wave*. Illustrated by Blair Lent. Houghton, 1964.

Hopkins, Lee Bennett. *Oh, No! Where Are My Pants? and Other Disasters: Poems*. Illustrated by Wolf Erlbruch. HarperCollins, 2005.

Horvath, Polly. *The Pepins and Their Problems*. Farrar, 2004.

Hughes, Shirley. *Alfie Gets in First*. Lothrop, 1981.

Hurwitz, Joanna. *Llama in the Library*. Morrow, 1999.

Hutchins, Hazel. *A Second Is a Hiccup*. Scholastic, 2007.

Hutchins, Pat. *Clocks and More Clocks*. Macmillan, 1994 [1970].

———. *You'll Soon Grow into Them, Titch*. Greenwillow, 1983.

Ibbotson, Eva. *The Star of Kazan*. Illustrated by Kevin Hawkes. Dutton, 2004.

Jenkins, Steve. *Actual Size*. Houghton, 2004.

Jennings, Patrick. *Out Standing in My Field*. Scholastic, 2005.

Jiménez, Francisco. *Breaking Through*. Houghton, 2001.

Johnson, Neil. *National Geographic Photography Guide for Kids*. National Geographic, 2001.

Juster, Norton. *The Phantom Tollbooth*. Random, 1961.

Keehn, Sally. *Gnat Stokes and the Foggy Bottom Swamp Queen*. Philomel, 2005.

Kelly, Katy. *Lucy Rose: Big on Plans*. Illustrated by Adam Rex. Delacorte, 2005.

Kerley, Barbara. *What to Do About Alice? How Alice Roosevelt Broke the Rules, Charmed the World, and Drove Her Father Teddy Crazy*. Illustrated by Edwin Fotheringham. Scholastic, 2008.

Kerrin, Jessica Scott. *Martin Bridge: Sound the Alarm!* Illustrated by Joseph Kelly. Kids Can, 2007.

King-Smith, Dick. *The Golden Goose*. Illustrated by Ann Kronheimer. Knopf, 2005.

Kline, Suzy. *Horrible Harry Cracks the Code*. Illustrated by Frank Remkiewicz. Viking, 2007.

Knudsen, Michelle. *Library Lion*. Illustrated by Kevin Hawkes. Candlewick, 2006.

Konigsburg, E. L. *The View from Saturday*. Atheneum, 1996.

Kramer, Ann. *Nelson Mandela: The Tribal Prince Who Grew Up to Be President*. National Geographic, 2005.

Krauss, Ruth. *Bears*. Illustrated by Maurice Sendak. HarperCollins, 2005.

Kvasnosky, Laura McGee. *Zelda and Ivy: The Runaways*. Candlewick, 2006.

Lecesne, James. *Absolute Brightness*. Harper, 2008.

Le Guin, Ursula K. *A Wizard of Earthsea*. Illustrated by Ruth Robbins. Parnassus, 1968.

Lehman, Barbara. *Rainstorm*. Houghton, 2007.

Lester, Julius. *Days of Tears: A Novel in Dialogue*. Hyperion, 2005.

———. *John Henry*. Illustrated by Brian Pinkney. Dial, 1994.

Lionni, Leo. *The Biggest House in the World*. Dragonfly, 1973.

London, Jonathan. *A Truck Goes Rattley-Bumpa*. Illustrated by Denis Roche. Holt, 2005.

Look, Lenore. *Henry's First Moon Birthday*. Illustrated by Yumi Heo. Atheneum, 2001.

———. *Ruby Lu, Brave and True*. Illustrated by Anne Wilsdorf. Simon, 2004.

———. *Ruby Lu, Empress of Everything*. Illustrated by Anne Wilsdorf. Simon, 2006.

Lord, Cynthia. *Rules*. Scholastic, 2006.

Lowry, Lois. *The Giver*. Houghton, 1993.

Lynch, Chris. *The Big Game of Everything*. HarperCollins, 2008.

Madden, Kerry. *Gentle's Holler*. Viking, 2005.

Marcantonio, Patricia Santos. *Red Ridin' in the Hood and Other Cuentos*. Illustrated by Ranato Alarcão. Farrar, 2005.

Markes, Julie. *Shhhhh! Everybody's Sleeping*. Illustrated by David Parkins. HarperCollins, 2005.

Marsden, Carolyn. *Moon Runner*. Candlewick, 2005.

Martin, Ann. *A Dog's Life: The Autobiography of a Stray*. Scholastic, 2005.

Matthews, L. S. *Fish*. Delacorte, 2004.

McCaughrean, Geraldine. *White Darkness*. HarperCollins, 2007.

McClintock, Barbara. *Adèle & Simon*. Farrar, 2006.

McCloskey, Robert. *Burt Dow, Deep Water Man*. Viking, 1963.

——. *Make Way for Ducklings*. Viking, 1941.

McCully, Emily. *Four Hungry Kittens*. Dial, 2001.

McDonald, Megan. *Judy Moody Declares Independence*. Candlewick, 2005.

McKay, Hilary. *Permanent Rose*. Simon, 2005.

McKinley, Robin. *The Hero and the Crown*. Greenwillow, 1984.

McKissack, Patricia C. *Flossie and the Fox*. Illustrated by Rachel Isadora. Dial, 1986.

McNaughton, Janet. *The Secret under My Skin*. HarperCollins, 2005.

McPhail, David. *The Teddy Bear*. Holt, 2002.

McWhorter, Diane. *A Dream of Freedom: The Civil Rights Movement from 1954–1968*. Scholastic, 2004.

Mills, Claudia. *Being Teddy Roosevelt*. Illustrated by R. W. Alley. Farrar, 2007.

Minarik, Else Holmelund. *Little Bear*. Illustrated by Maurice Sendak. Harper, 1957.

Mollel, Tolowa. *My Rows and Piles of Coins*. Illustrated by E. B. Lewis. Clarion, 1999.

Myers, Walter Dean. *Sunrise Over Fallujah*. Scholastic, 2008.

Na, An. *A Step from Heaven*. Front St., 2001.

Naidoo, Beverley. *The Other Side of Truth*. HarperCollins, 2001.

Nye, Naomi Shihab. *Honeybee*. Greenwillow, 2008.

O'Connor, George. *Ker-splash!* Simon, 2005.

Oppel, Kenneth. *Darkwing*. Eos, 2007.

Ormerod, Jan. *When an Elephant Comes to School*. Orchard, 2005.

Osborne, Mary Pope. *Dragon of the Red Dawn*. Illustrated by Sal Murdocca. Random, 2007.

Palatini, Margie. *Broom Mates*. Illustrated by Howard Fine. Hyperion, 2003.

Panchyk, Richard. *Galileo for Kids: His Life, Ideas and 25 Activities*. Chicago Review, 2005.

Parish, Peggy. *Amelia Bedelia*. Illustrated by Fritz Siebel. Harper, 1963.

Park, Linda Sue. *Bee-Bim Bop!* Illustrated by Ho Baek Lee. Clarion, 2005.

——. *Project Mulberry*. Clarion, 2005.

Parr, Todd. *The Family Book*. Little, 2003.

Partridge, Elizabeth. *Whistling*. Illustrated by Anna Grossnickle Hines. Greenwillow, 2003.

Paterson, Katherine. *Jacob Have I Loved*. Crowell, 1980.

Patron, Susan. *The Higher Power of Lucky*. Atheneum, 2006.

Paulsen, Gary. *Hatchet*. Bradbury, 1987.

Pearson, Tracy Campbell. *Myrtle*. Farrar, 2004.

Peet, Mal. *Tamar*. Candlewick, 2007.

Pennypacker, Sara. *Clementine's Letter*. Illustrated by Marla Frazee. Hyperion, 2008.

Pericoli, Matteo. *The True Story of Stellina*. Knopf, 2006.

Perkins, Lynne Rae. *Criss Cross*. Greenwillow, 2005.

Phillips, Rita Mitchell. *Hue Boy*. Illustrated by Caroline Binch. Dial, 1993.

Pitzer, Susanna. *Not Afraid of Dogs*. Illustrated by Larry Day. Walker, 2006.

Porter, Connie. *Meet Addy* (the American Girl collection). Illustrated by Nancy Niles. Pleasant, 1990.

Porter, Tracey. *Billy Creekmore*. HarperCollins, 2007.

Potter, Beatrix. *The Tale of Peter Rabbit*. Warne, 1902.

Pryor, Bonnie. *The House on Maple Street*. Illustrated by Beth Peck. Morrow, 1987.

Rees, Douglas. *Grandy Thaxter's Helper*. Illustrated by S. D. Schindler. Atheneum, 2004.

Reinhardt, Dana. *How to Build a House*. Random, 2008.

Reiser, Lynn. *Little Clam*. Greenwillow, 1998.

Richardson, Justin, and Peter Parnell. *And Tango Makes Three*. Illustrated by Henry Cole. Simon, 2005.

Ries, Lori. *Aggie and Ben: Three Stories*. Illustrated by Frank W. Dormer. Charlesbridge, 2006.

Rockwell, Anne. *My Pet Hamster*. Illustrated by Bernice Lum. HarperCollins, 2002.

——. *The Three Bears and Fifteen Other Stories*. Crowell, 1975.

Rodman, Mary Ann. *Yankee Girl*. Farrar, 2004.

Root, Phyllis. *Oliver Finds His Way*. Illustrated by Christopher Denise. Candlewick, 2002.

——. *What Baby Wants*. Illustrated by Jill Barton. Candlewick, 1998.

Rosen, Daniel. *New Beginnings: Jamestown and the Virginia Colony, 1607–1699*. National Geographic, 2005.

Rosen, Michael. *Michael Rosen's Sad Book*. Candlewick, 2005.

——. *We're Going on a Bear Hunt*. Illustrated by Helen Oxenbury. McElderry, 1989.

Rosoff, Meg. *Meet Wild Boars*. Illustrated by Sophie Blackall. Holt, 2005.

Rowling, J. K. *Harry Potter and the Half-Blood Prince*. Scholastic, 2005.

Rubin, Susan Goldman. *The Cat with the Yellow Star: Coming of Age in Terezin*. Holiday House, 2006.

Rumford, James. *Sequoyah. The Cherokee Man Who Gave His People Writing*. Translated by Anna Sixkiller Huckaby. Houghton, 2004.

Ryan, Pam Muñoz. *When Marian Sang*. Illustrated by Brian Selznick. Scholastic, 2002.

Rylant, Cynthia. *When I Was Young in the Mountains*. Illustrated by Diane Goode. Dutton, 1982.

Sachar, Louis. *Holes*. Farrar, 1998.

Sadler, Judy Ann. *The Jumbo Book of Needlecrafts*. Kids Can, 2005.

Schaefer, Carole Lexa. *The Biggest Soap*. Illustrated by Stacy Dressen-McQueen. Farrar, 2004.

Schmidt, Gary D. *Lizzie Bright and the Buckminster Boy*. Clarion, 2004.

Schotter, Roni. *The Boy Who Loved Words*. Illustrated by Giselle Potter. Random, 2006.

Schwartz, Alvin. *Whoppers: Tall Tales and Other Lies*. Illustrated by Glen Rounds. HarperCollins, 1975.

Schwartz, David. *If Dogs Were Dinosaurs*. Illustrated by James Warhola. Scholastic, 2005.

Scieszka, Jon, ed. *Guys Write for Guys Who Read: Boys' Favorite Authors Write About Being Boys*. Viking, 2005.

Sciurba, Katie. *Oye, Celia! A Song for Celia Cruz*. Illustrated by Edel Rodriguez. Holt, 2007.

Sendak, Maurice. *Where the Wild Things Are*. Harper, 1963.

Senisi, Ellen B. *Berry Smudges and Leaf Prints: Finding and Making Colors from Nature*. Dutton, 2001.

Shannon, David. *No David!* Scholastic, 1998.

Sheth, Kashmira. *Keeping Corner*. Hyperion, 2009.

Shreve, Susan. *Under the Watsons' Porch*. Knopf, 2004.

Silverstein, Shel. *Runny Babbit: A Billy Sook*. HarperCollins, 2005.

———. *Where the Sidewalk Ends*. Harper, 1963.

Smith, Doris Buchanan. *A Taste of Blackberries*. Illustrated by Charles Robinson. Crowell, 1973.

Smith, Jeff. *Bone: Ghost Circles*. Scholastic, 2008.

Sones, Sonya. *What My Mother Doesn't Know*. Simon, 2001.

Soto, Gary. *Too Many Tamales*. Illustrated by Ed Martinez. Putnam, 1993.

Spinelli, Jerry. *Eggs*. Little, 2007.

———. *Maniac Magee*. Little, 1990.

———. *Wringer*. HarperCollins, 1997.

Staples, Suzanne Fisher. *Shabanu: Daughter of the Wind*. Knopf, 1989.

———. *Under the Persimmon Tree*. Farrar, 2005.

Steig, William. *Doctor De Soto*. Farrar, 1982.

———. *Sylvester and the Magic Pebble*. Simon, 1969.

———. *Zeke Pippin*. HarperCollins, 1994.

Stolz, Joëlle. *The Shadows of Ghadames*. Delacorte, 2004.

Taback, Sims. *I Know an Old Lady*. Dial, 1997.

Takabayashi, Mari. *I Live in Tokyo*. Houghton, 2001.

Tang, Greg. *Math Potatoes*. Illustrated by Harry Briggs. Scholastic, 2005.

Taylor, Mildred. *Roll of Thunder, Hear My Cry*. Dial, 1976.

Tolkien, J. R. R. *The Hobbit*. Illustrated by Michael Hague. Houghton, 1989 [1938].

Van Draanen, Wendelin. *Shredderman: Attack of the Tagger*. Knopf, 2004.

Wabbes, Marie. *How I Was Born*. Tambourine, 1991.

Waber, Bernard. *Ira Sleeps Over*. Houghton, 1973.

Waddell, Martin. *It's Quacking Time!* Illustrated by Jill Barton. Candlewick, 2005.

Walsh, Jill Paton. *The Green Book*. Illustrated by Lloyd Bloom. Farrar, 1982.

Walter, Mildred Pitts. *Alec's Primer*. Illustrated by Larry Johnson. Vermont Folklife Center, 2004.

Weatherford, Carole Boston. *Freedom on the Menu: The Greensboro Sit-Ins*. Illustrated by Jerome Lagarrigue. Dial, 2005.

Wells, Rosemary. *Bunny Cakes*. Dial, 1998.

———. *Edward, Unready for School*. Dial, 1995.

White, Ruth. *Belle Prater's Boy*. Farrar, 1996.

———. *The Search for Belle Prater*. Farrar, 2005.

Whybrow, Ian. *The Noisy Way to Bed*. Illustrated by Tiphanie Beeke. Scholastic, 2004.

Wick, Walter. *Can You See What I See? Picture Puzzles to Search and Solve*. Scholastic, 2002.

Wiles, Deborah. *Each Little Bird That Sings*. Harcourt, 2005.

Willems, Mo. *Leonardo, the Terrible Monster*. Hyperion, 2004.

Williams, Sue. *Dinnertime!* Illustrated by Kerry Argent. Harcourt, 2002.

Williams-Garcia, Rita. *Like Sisters on the Home Front*. Dutton, 1995.

Winerip, Michael. *Adam Canfield of the Slash*. Candlewick, 2005.

Wynne-Jones, Tim. *A Thief in the House of Memory*. Farrar, 2005.

Yashima, Taro. *Crow Boy*. Viking, 1955.

Yee, Lisa. *Stanford Wong Flunks Big-Time*. Scholastic, 2005.

Yumoto, Kazumi. *The Friends*. Illustrated by Cathy Hirano. Farrar, 1996.

Zane, Alexander. *The Wheels on the Race Car*. Illustrated by James Warhola. Orchard, 2005.

Zuckerman, Linda. *I Will Hold You 'til You Sleep*. Illustrated by Jon J. Muth. Scholastic, 2006.

Part Two

Exploring Genres in Children's Books

Chapter Three

Picturebooks

Chapter Outline

It's Friday afternoon and the first-grade children are taking turns going to the "library" in the corner of the classroom to "check out" books for the weekend. Soon the teacher hears the elevation of voices that she has come to recognize as the precursor to a visit to the "negotiation table" to talk it out. She looks over to the corner and sees a tug of war going on, each child holding on to the book cover. Rachel clutches the front; Lorinda has the back. "Let go!" Rachel screamed!

"Nooooooooo, you let go!" Lorinda screamed back. They were so intent on the tugging that neither one of them realized the teacher was standing over them. When they did, the pulling stopped and the book fell to the floor with a plop. The classroom copy of *Where the Wild Things Are* lay on the floor, each child looking from the book to the teacher's face and back to the book again.

"What is the problem here?" asks the teacher.

Rachel quickly explains, "I want to take that book home." Lorinda replies, "No, I want to." The teacher asks each of them why this particular book was so important. Lorinda says, "I like how the wild things stomped around and looked so funny." Rachel, with tears welling up in her eyes says, "I think it's pretty and it has the medal on it."

We have heard the adage: A picture is worth a thousand words. Well, in this case the picture was worth a good tug of war! The 1964 Caldecott Medal winner *Where the Wild Things Are* still evokes a powerful aesthetic response with these twenty-first-century first graders. This powerful response to the art in books is often at the root of what motivates many young readers to engage with a book.

The Picturebook Defined

Picturebooks are those books in which images and ideas join to form a unique whole. In the best picturebooks, the illustrations are as much a part of our experience with the book as the written text (if there is one). A picturebook provides the reader with an aesthetic experience that is more than the sum of the book's parts. (See **Teaching Feature 3.1: A Brief History of the Picturebook** on page 60.)

Any book with a picturebook format can be included under the umbrella term *picturebook*. A picturebook might be a wordless book, an alphabet book, a counting book, a concept book, or a picture storybook. The illustrations for a concept book or an alphabet book can depict a different object or an animal on each page, providing for much variety in the pictures. In a nonfiction book (discussed in Chapter 9) the illustrations can help support important concepts and clarify ideas. They can also emphasize themes and understandings that the author is trying to convey.

In a picture storybook, the message is conveyed equally through two media—picture and word. In a well-designed book in which the total format reflects the meaning of the story, both the illustrations and the text must bear the burden of narration. The pictures help tell the story, showing the action and expressions of the characters, the changing settings, and the development of the plot.

Maurice Sendak's *Where the Wild Things Are* shows how pictures and words work together to create the kind of passionate responses to books we saw in Rachel and Lorinda. The cover shows an intriguing and gigantic creature, asleep beside an empty boat. The child reader is immediately invited to co-construct this story by asking such questions as "Who is in the boat?" "Is this monster scary?" The bold black letters of the title and author's name seem to offer stability and a reassuring answer. In addition, the monster is captured within the lines of type and by the white space of the borders. This monster is not likely to enter the child's world, just the imagination. The shape of the book is horizontal rather than vertical and implies movement over a broad landscape. The end papers, full of lush leaves seen through a screen of cross-hatching lines, burst with energy and invite entry into the book. These forms are not

A Brief History of the Picturebook

The picturebooks we know today have roots that we might trace back to cave paintings of the prehistoric era. An African (Egyptian) papyrus that dates from approximately 1295 B.C. depicts a humorous tale that includes an antelope and a lion seated on chairs engaged in a board game. Books as we know them today—folded leaves bound between hard covers—date from the first century C.E., and many of these included images as well as words. Such books would blossom into incredibly beautiful works of art by the fourteenth century.

With the invention of a printing press with movable type in the 1450s, the images in books began to take a back seat to the convenience of mass production. Full-color, hand-painted, and hand-written books were replaced with black-and-white wood engravings or black prints. However, images in books were still highly popular with the reading audience. That audience might have included children, but until the 1600s books were not usually created for an audience of children. As society began to place more emphasis on a culture of childhood and the need to educate children in religious as well as secular matters, picturebooks were created to meet these needs. Many of these educational books were emblem books that followed a pictorial format in which a verse or couplet was illustrated with a small picture. Johann Amos Comenius's *Orbis Pictus* (The World in Pictures) was translated into English in 1659 and published with many woodcuts illustrating everyday objects. It is often referred to as the first picturebook for children.

In 1744, John Newbery published *A Little Pretty Pocket-Book,* which was meant to entertain as well as educate children, and modern children's book publishing was born. Many of the books written for children in the eighteenth and nineteenth centuries included illustrations, but they were still most often printed in black and white. In the late 1800s, a printer named Edmund Evans perfected a method of color printing that ushered in the golden age of children's picturebooks. Evans's extraordinary talent as an engraver and his important improvements in color printing techniques were responsible for dramatic changes in picturebooks for children. Evans recruited artists who would become the best-known illustrators of the nineteenth century—Walter Crane, Randolph Caldecott, and Kate Greenaway. The success of their many books opened the door to other illustrators of the twentieth century such as Beatrix Potter, Ernest Shepard, and Arthur Rackham.

Printing techniques continued to be refined over the rest of the twentieth century until computer scanning and laser reproduction removed some of the tedious technical tasks from the artist and allowed almost any artistic medium to be reproduced. At the same time the audience for picturebooks expanded beyond the very young to children of all ages. In our current era, the picturebook is melding into a variety of multimodal forms and will likely continue to change in format and in the audience it attracts.

the vegetation of the everyday world; however, they convey an unfamiliar world and imply that something magical may be at work. Sendak's use of soft, muted watercolor washes over delicate line drawings evokes a sense of unreality or mystery throughout the book. Sendak also creates cross-hatched lines that set up emotional tensions that ebb and flow across the pages. He uses curving shapes to create movement within each picture and to move our eyes across each page. The layout of each double-page spread creates a rhythm as we proceed through the book. The small size of the early illustrations reflects the disciplinary reins placed on Max by his mother. As he sets off on his imaginary journey, those pictures break out of their rectangular white borders and grow out to the edges of the single page. They then begin to grow across the double-page spread until Max arrives upon his island. When the "wild rumpus" starts, there is no longer a need for white space or words at all. The three double-page spreads create a visual equivalent of three booming drumbeats, and the pictures fill the space just as sounds of the wild rumpus must fill the air. We know the book has reached a climax of excitement here because on the next double-page spread the picture begins to shrink and white space and words reappear. Max returns home to his room on the last page, but he is not the same child. Sendak removes the white border and sharp edge that began Max's adventure and leaves him on the right-hand page in a full bleed (i.e., the picture extends to the edge of the page.) *Where the Wild Things Are* represents the type of real marriage between pictures and text that we hope to find in good picturebooks.

Creating Meaning in Picturebooks

A picturebook, then, must be a seamless whole conveying meaning through both the art and the text. Moreover, in a picturebook that tells a story, the illustration does not merely reflect the idea or action on a single page but shares in moving a story forward and in engaging the reader with the narrative on both an intellectual and an emotional level. Throughout the narration the pictures should convey, enhance, and extend the meaning behind the story.

The Elements of Design

Crucial to the visual meaning in a picturebook are the choices artists make about certain elements of design, particularly the use of line, shape, color, and space, as they decide what to illustrate in the story and how best to do it. Just as words can convey meaning on several levels, the elements of art have the capacity to convey meaning and evoke emotion.

Line and Shape Line is so inherently a part of every illustration that we forget that this element, too, can convey meaning. A horizontal line suggests repose and peace, a vertical line gives stability, and a diagonal line suggests action and movement. In *Stevie*, John Steptoe uses a heavy black outline for his figures to emphasize Robert's resentment of Stevie, the little boy his mother takes care of during the day. The tiny, sketchy lines in Marcia Brown's version of Perrault's *Cinderella* suggest the somewhat fussy elegance of the story's sixteenth-century French setting. Chris Raschka uses the element of line to great effect in books like *The Hello, Goodbye Window* by Norton Juster. Raschka's bold, scribbled lines predominate the page, defining the characters, creating energy, and moving the plot forward.

A line that encloses space creates shape, and this element is equally evocative of meaning. Shapes with sharp edges and corners can portray tension and movement, as they do in Christopher Meyers's *Black Cat*. On the other hand, when shapes have nongeometric curving forms found in nature, they can breathe a sense of life into illustrations, as we see in Suzanne Bloom's simple, rounded shapes in the pages of *A Splendid Friend, Indeed.*

What are you doing?
Are you reading?

Suzanne Bloom's use of naturalistic shapes reflects the characters' feelings and leads the eye across the page in the delightful *A Splendid Friend, Indeed. A Splendid Friend, Indeed,* copyright © 2005 by Suzanne Bloom. Published by Boyd's Mills Press, Inc. Reprinted by permission.

Sophie is a volcano,
ready to explode.

And when Sophie
gets angry—
really, really angry...

In Molly Bang's *When Sophie Gets Angry—Really, Really Angry....* a young child finds space for a tantrum and room to calm down again. From *When Sophie Gets Angry—Really, Really Angry....* by Molly Bang. Copyright © 1999 by Molly Bang. Reprinted by permission of Blue Sky Press, an imprint of Scholastic Inc.

Color Colors can evoke strong emotional connections in readers. Many classic picturebooks did not use color in the illustrations, such as the sepia pictures of Robert McCloskey's *Make Way for Ducklings* and the well-loved black-and-white illustrations for *Millions of Cats* by Wanda Gág. Modern publishing techniques make it much easier and less expensive to publish full-color books, but many illustrators are still using black-and-white graphics to create exciting picturebooks.

The choice of colors should depend on the theme of the book. Molly Bang's *When Sophie Gets Angry—Really, Really Angry . . .* is a fine example of judicious use of color. Sophie, a rambunctious preschooler, is infuriated by an older sister who grabs her favorite toy. Sophie gets so angry, "she kicks, she screams, she wants to smash the world to smithereens." Bang's intense reds and oranges represent Sophie's rage perfectly. As she runs outside into the wider world and her anger diminishes, the colors turn to cool greens and blues, which follow her back home to the embrace of her now peaceful family. The final page is a pleasing family scene done in a full-color palette that provides a reassuring message that harmony and balance have returned.

Value The element of value can be defined as the amount of light and dark in a picture. Illustrator Chris Van Allsburg uses the element of value to create a dramatic three-dimensional effect for all his books. His masterful depiction of light and dark in books like *The Polar Express* and *Probuduti* suggests that the figures and objects might leap off the page at any moment. On the other hand, the values in Jon Muth's illustrations for Karen Hesse's *Come On, Rain!* are uniform and muted. The paintings thus convey the still, hot air of a summer's day just before a welcoming rainstorm.

Space The illustrations in a picturebook exist on a two-dimensional plane. However, artists can choose to use elements such as color, value, or line to create a feeling of realism and depth, as in E. B. Lewis's illustrations for Richard Michelson's *Across the Alley*. The creative use of space can also enhance the underlying themes in a picturebook. In *Come Along, Daisy!*—Jane Simmons's story about a wayward duck who becomes separated from her mother—we see a tiny Daisy almost invisible in the expanse of a huge blue-green world. Simmons's use of space effectively emphasizes Daisy's fright at being separated from her mother. In *The Three Pigs*, David Wiesner violates the traditional use of space in picturebooks. When the three pigs step out of their familiar story, Wiesner emphasizes the pure white space of the page instead of filling up the double-page spread with images. This reinforces the feeling that we are entering a new world, one beyond our expectations.

David Wiesner's *The Three Pigs* breaks picturebook traditions when the pigs break out of their traditional story to write a new ending. Illustration from *The Three Pigs* by David Wiesner. Copyright © 2001 by David Wiesner. Reprinted by permission of Clarion Books, an imprint of Houghton Mifflin Harcourt Publishing Company. All rights reserved.

The batter slams a power hit soaring past the shortstop's mitt.

Bill Thomson uses unusual points of view for dramatic effect in *Baseball Hour* by Carol Nevius. Illustration reprinted from *Baseball Hour* by Carol Nevius, illustrated by Bill Thomson, with permission of Marshall Cavendish.

Perspective or Point of View Just as an author decides what would be the best voice in which to tell a story, so too does an artist think about point of view. One way to obtain action in what might otherwise be a static series of pictures is to change the focus, just as a movie camera changes perspective or shows close-ups and then moves back to pan the whole scene. Part of the perfection of Carole Boston Weatherford's poetic *Moses* is that illustrator Kadir Nelson uses shifting perspectives to portray the shifting fortunes of Harriet Tubman's struggles. The perspective in Chris Van Allsburg's surrealistic pictures for *Jumanji* changes from a worm's-eye point of view to a bird's-eye view, adding to the constant shifts between reality and fantasy in that story. Bill Thomson gives us highly dramatic points of view in Carol Nevius's *Baseball Hour* and *Karate Hour*. Not all artists work with changing perspectives, but when they do, it is interesting to ask why and look to see how this adds to the meaning of the story.

Composition In good picturebooks, no single element of art exists apart from the others. Rather, the illustrator uses principles of composition to unify elements on each page and on each succeeding page. By arranging the elements on each page, including the printed type, the artist tries to obtain an effective balance between unity and variety, and creates certain visual patterns that may be carried from page to page. Illustrators try to ensure that the eye moves from one part of each double-page spread to another through elements within the picture that tie the picture to the printed text. This in turn sets up a subtle rhythm that can be carried throughout the book. All of these choices contribute to a whole that is greater than the sum of its parts. We have discussed how effective Sendak's choices in composition are in *Where the Wild Things Are*. Adam Rex's comical *Pssst!* tells of a child's visit to the zoo. As she makes her way around the exhibits, each animal catches her attention with "Pssst!" and asks for one unlikely object after another. The increasingly perplexed child does her best to accommodate the animals. The page layouts vary rhythmically. One double-page spread shows a drawing of the zoo landscape. On the next page, we see small rectangular vignettes of animal and child on the left-hand page, followed by a full-color picture of the child on an otherwise blank space on the right-

Adam Rex creates interesting compositions on each double-page spread and throughout the pages of his amusing *Pssst!* Illustrations from *Pssst!*, copyright © 2007 by Adam Rex, reproduced by permission of Houghton Mifflin Harcourt Publishing Company.

hand page. This pattern continues throughout the book until the climatic double-page spread shows a full-color picture of what it was the animals wanted all those objects for.

The Artist's Choice of Media

Children accept and enjoy a variety of media in the illustrations of their picturebooks. The illustrator's choice of original media can be as important to the meaning of the book as the choice of the elements of design. Many artists today are using the picturebook as a vehicle for experimentation with new and interesting media and formats. For example, Christopher Meyers's *Black Cat* is created using a combination of photographs, ink, and opaque paint. This mixed media heightens the emotional depth of this poetic story of a lonely cat wandering the streets of a city. The layers created in Meyers's paintings also suggest underlying metaphors for human survival in urban environments.

In today's creative experimentation with picturebooks, the medium the artist uses is not nearly as important as the appropriateness of the medium choice for a particular book and how effectively the artist uses it. Nevertheless, teachers and children are fascinated with the various aspects of illustrating and always ask what medium is used. This is becoming increasingly difficult to answer, as artists these days use a combination of media and printing techniques to achieve a particular effect. Some publishing houses provide information on the art techniques of some of their outstanding books. This might be found in a foreword, on the copyright page, or on a jacket flap. It is a service that teachers and librarians hope more companies will provide. **Teaching Feature 3.2** on page 66 gives a brief overview of some of the media choices open to the artist.

The Artist's Media Choices

Medium	Description	Examples*
Printmaking	The process of cutting into metal or wood, applying ink to the surface, and pressing on paper.	Mary Azarian: *Snowflake Bentley* (Jacqueline Briggs Martin) Holly Meade: *On the Farm* (David Elliot)
Collage and Construction	Pictures are created by building up a variety of materials and textures onto a surface.	Cathryn Falwell: *Scoot!* David Diaz: *Smoky Night* (Eve Bunting) Ed Young: *Twenty Heartbeats* (Dennis Haseley)
Stitchery and Cloth	Pieces of cloth and sewn threads or yarns are used to created pictures.	Anna Grossnickle Hines: *1, 2, Buckle My Shoe* María Hernández de la Cruz: *The Journey of Tunuri and the Blue Deer* (James Endredy)
Paints, Pen, and Ink	Applying pigments mixed with a binder and medium such as water or oil to a surface.	Meilo So: *The Cat's Tale* (Doris Orgel) Christopher Myers: *Jazz* (Walter Dean Myers) Duane Smith: *Seven Miles to Freedom* (Janet Halfman)
Drawing Materials	Process of making marks on a surface; includes materials such as crayon, charcoal, pastel chalks, and scratchboard.	Ed Young: *My Mei Mei* Beth Krommes: *The House in the Night* (Susan Marie Swanson) Kurt Cyrus: *Mammoths on the Move* (Lisa Wheeler)
Computer-Generated Art	Use of computer applications to create pictures.	Craig Frazier: *Stanley Goes Fishing* Stian Hole: *Garmann's Summer*
Mixed Media	Combinations of paint, drawing, collage, and other media.	Simms Taback: *Joseph Had a Little Overcoat* Nicoletta Ceccoli: *The Girl in the Castle Inside the Museum* (Kate Bernheimer)

*Book's author is in parentheses, if other than illustrator.

Mary Azarian's Caldecott Medal–winning woodcuts for Jacqueline Briggs Martin's *Snowflake Bentley* evoke the time and place of nineteenth-century Vermont.

Illustration from *Snowflake Bentley* by Jacqueline Briggs Martin, illustrated by Mary Azarian. Illustrations copyright © 1998 by Mary Azarian. Reprinted by permission of Houghton Mifflin Harcourt Publishing Company. All rights reserved.

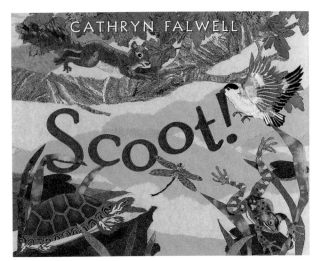

Cathryn Falwell's use of collage in *Scoot!* reflects the natural textures of her setting. *Scoot* by Cathryn Falwell. Used by permission of HarperCollins Publishers.

Each page of Anna Grossnickle Hines's *1, 2, Buckle My Shoe* is part of a larger handmade quilt. Illustration from *1, 2, Buckle My Shoe*, copyright © 2008 by Anna Grossnickle Hines, reproduced by permission of Houghton Mifflin Harcourt Publishing Company.

Beth Krommes's scratchboard drawings bring a gentle glow to Susan Marie Swanson's lovely bedtime story, *The House in the Night*. Illustration from *The House In The Night* by Susan Marie Swanson, pictures by Beth Krommes. Illustrations copyright © 2008 by Beth Krommes. Reprinted by permission of Houghton Mifflin Harcourt Publishing Company. All rights reserved.

Meilo So's transparent watercolors convey the delicate story of grandmother, granddaughter, and cat in Doris Orgel's *The Cat's Tale*. From *The Cat's Tale* by Doris Orgel. Used by permission of Roaring Brook Press, a division of Henry Holt and Company, LLC.

Simms Taback's Caldecott Medal–winning *Joseph Had a Little Overcoat* is a fine example of the use of mixed media— ink, watercolor, colored pencil, and collage. From *Joseph Had a Little Overcoat* by Simms Taback, copyright © 1999 by Simms Taback, illustrations. Used by permission of Penguin Group (USA) Inc.

Nicoletta Ceccoli has combined digital media with paint, clay models, and photography for the magical *The Girl in the Castle Inside the Museum* by Kate Bernheimer. "Illustrations" by Nicoletta Ceccoli, copyright © 2008 by Nicoletta Ceccoli, from *The Girl in the Castle Inside the Museum* by Kate Bernheimer, Illustrated by Nicoletta Ceccoli. Used by permission of Schwartz and Wade Books, an imprint of Random House Children's Books, a division of Random House, Inc.

Choosing Artistic Conventions

Artists may choose to borrow conventions or ways of depicting that we have come to associate with certain historical or cultural periods—such as Renaissance art or Impressionism—or art associated with a people—such as art of Tibetans or of the Northern Plains Indian tribes. Such choices often add authenticity to a story set "once upon a time" or one that originated in a particular society or culture.

A wonderful example of an homage to Impressionism can be found in the Monet-like paintings by Maurice Sendak for *Mr. Rabbit and the Lovely Present,* written by Charlotte Zolotow. In luscious shades of blues and greens, Sendak has created a dreamlike world where a very sophisticated rabbit and a little girl wander about the countryside looking for presents of red, yellow, green, and blue (her mother's favorite colors) for the little girl's mother. The dappled endpapers for this book are examples of Impressionistic techniques in themselves.

Many artists illustrating stories, folktales, or legends make use of the conventions found in art forms of their respective countries or cultures. David Diaz uses elements of Mexican folk art to tell contemporary stories set within Mexican and Mexican/American cultures. In Eve Bunting's *Going Home,* the story of a farm family returning to Mexico for Christmas, Diaz creates endpapers that feature close-up photographs of brilliant "artesanias Mexicanas," decorative objects,

David Diaz's Mexican folk art motifs mirror Oaxacan ceramic figures and provide a culturally rich visual setting for Eve Bunting's *Going Home.* Illustration from *Going Home* by Eve Bunting, illustrations by David Diaz. Illustrations copyright © 1996 by David Diaz. Photographs by Cecelia Zeiba-Diaz. Joanna Cotler Books. Used by permission of HarperCollins Publishers, Inc.

figures, and other popular arts found in the marketplaces of Mexico. This "arté popular" then forms the background on which the paintings and type are placed. Folk art silhouettes outline these panels; they are also found on the title page and the final page, set against a brilliant presidential blue background. **Teaching Feature 3.3: Historical and Cultural Conventions in Picturebooks** summarizes other historical and cultural conventions and suggests art and picturebooks for further study.

Paul O. Zelinsky's *Rapunzel* pays homage to Renaissance artists, in this case to Raphael's painting, "Madonna of the Meadow." From *Rapunzel* by Paul O. Zelinsky, copyright © 1997 by Paul O. Zelinsky. Used by permission of Dutton Children's Books, a division of Penguin Putnam Inc.

teaching feature 3.3

Historical and Cultural Conventions in Picturebooks

 Go to **www.mhhe.com/kieferbrief1e** for the latest Web links to the "Examples in Painting."

Historical Style and Description	Example in Painting	Example in Picturebooks
Historical Conventions		
Early Christian Art/Near Eastern Art: A clear uniform message was desired. Dramatic form was subdued for repetition of motifs and conventional symbols. This style can be found in Middle Eastern and Russian art today.	Sultan Mohammed, *Shahnama*	Demi: *The Hungry Coat*
Gothic: A style that began with architecture and sculpture; showed a movement toward more natural although still decorative depiction of religious subjects.	Giotto, *The Death of St. Francis*	Tomie dePaola: *The Clown of God*
Late Gothic: A movement away from stylized, two-dimensional depictions toward a renewed interest in realism. Symbolism survives but in increasingly realistic form.	Jan van Eyck, *The Marriage of Giovanni Arnolfini*	Nancy Eckholm Burkert: *Snow White and the Seven Dwarfs* (Grimm)
Renaissance: A move toward realism; an emphasis on forms, proportioning of space, and dramatic lighting.	Raphael, *Madonna of the Meadow*	Paul Zelinsky: *Rapunzel*
Rococo Art: Centered in France with a move to genre scenes or mythology set in idealized park settings. Characterized by highly decorated, almost fussy use of curving lines, flowing forms, and lightened colors.	Jean-Honore Fragonard, *The Swing*	Barbara McClintock: *Cinderella* (Perrault)
Romanticism: Late 18th to mid-19th century movement influenced by romantic literature of Goethe and Byron. Nostalgic identification with nature and the past. Often focused on melancholy, emotional subjects.	Caspar David Friedrich, *Moonrise over the Sea*	Chris Van Allsburg: *The Polar Express, The Wreck of the Zephyr*
Impressionism: Concerned with a momentary and spontaneous view of a scene; characterized by broken color, softened contours.	Claude Monet, *Woman Seated under the Willows*	Maurice Sendak: *Mr. Rabbit and the Lovely Present* (Zolotow)
Expressionism: Emotionally rooted, intense themes, characterized by brilliant, shocking colors, rough rapid brush work.	Georges Rouault, *The Old King*	John Steptoe: *Stevie* Susan Guevera: *Chato's Kitchen* (Soto)
Surrealism: Acknowledged the irrational and the power of imagination. Mixed a realistic style with bizarre, dislocated imagery.	René Magritte, *Time Transfixed*	Anthony Browne: *Changes*

Historical Style and Description Cultural Conventions	Example in Painting	Example in Picturebooks*
African Art: A broad and diverse category that is often characterized by simplified forms and/or bright colors, with an emphasis on form and decoration rather than realism.	Angola, Chokwe peoples, *Chibinda Ilunga Figure*	G. Haley: *A Story, a Story*
Folk Art: A term applied to crafts (more often than to painting) that use traditional designs. Often produced in rural communities these are typified by Tibetan, Indian, and Central and South American embroideries.	Oaxacan ceramic figures Gansevoort Limner, *Susanna Truax*	David Diaz: *Going Home* (Bunting) Barbara Cooney: *The Ox-Cart Man* (Hall)
Asian Art: A method of painting using silk, fine papers, and inks that promoted exploration of linear and spatial effects. The style is rooted in calligraphy and involves controlled handling of the brush.	Guo Xi, *Early Spring*	Ed Young: *The Sons of the Dragon King* Demi: *Chingis Khan*
Japanese Prints: Woodblock prints of the seventeenth through nineteenth centuries were characterized by flattened forms, large areas of color, and decorative tensions created by use of line and shape.	Hokusai, *Tokaido* Yoshida	Leo and Diane Dillon: *The Tale of the Mandarin Ducks* (Paterson)

*Book's author is in parentheses, if other than illustrator.

An Artist's Personal Style

Few picturebook artists use only one style of art; they adapt their work to meet the requirements of a particular story. At the same time, many of them do develop a recognizable personal style that can be identified by their preference for a particular pictorial style of art, use of medium, or even choice of content. For example, we have come to associate the use of collage with Leo Lionni, Ezra Jack Keats, and Eric Carle, even though they differ in how they use it. The amusing animals in the stories by Pat Hutchins are frequently stylized with patterned fur and feathers. Her birds and animals in *We're Going on a Picnic, What Game Shall We Play?* and that self-assured hen in *Rosie's Walk* are vintage Hutchins.

Style, then, is an elusive quality of the artist, which changes and varies over the years and with the particular demands of the work. Today there is more freedom to experiment in illustrating children's picturebooks. Many artists are taking advantage of this new freedom and producing fresh and original art. Exposure to a variety of art styles through fine picturebooks can help children develop visual maturity and appreciation. Certainly there is no one style that is appropriate for children or preferred by children. The major consideration in evaluating style is how well it conveys and enhances meaning.

The Format of the Book

A picturebook is not made up of single illustrated pictures but conveys its message through a series of images. The impact of the total format of the book is what creates the art object known as the picturebook. Book size and shape are often decisions made jointly by the illustrator and the art director of the publishing house. They might search for a size that will enhance the theme of the story. The size of *The Bear* by Raymond Briggs is almost fifteen inches tall—big enough, it seems, to contain the huge bear within. Oliver Dunrea's Gossie books, about a tiny gosling and her circle of friends, are small in size, just right for its preschool audience. The shape of some books suggests their content. The shape of *Fish Eyes* by Lois Ehlert is long and narrow like a fish or small aquarium. *A Tree Is Nice* by Janice Udry, illustrated by Marc Simont, is tall and vertical in shape, much like the tree described in the book.

Both the cover and dust jacket of a book should receive careful attention. The primary purpose of the jacket is to call attention to the book. The cover of Doreen Rappaport's *Martin's Big Words* needs no words. Bryan Collier's elegant, almost life-size, close-up of Martin Luther King, Jr.'s face is instantly recognizable. Publishers are increasingly duplicating the image from the dust jacket on the book's cover rather than preparing a separate cloth cover that few people ever see. However, a peek beneath a dust jacket can still reveal pleasant surprises. David Wiesner's books such as *Flotsam* and *The Three Pigs* have lovely embossed designs on their cloth covers.

Jerry Pinkney's exquisitely painted endpapers for Hans Christian Andersen's *The Ugly Duckling* reflect thoughtful care in book design. Illustration from *The Ugly Duckling* by Hans Christian Andersen, illustrations by Jerry Pinkney. Illustrations copyright © 1999 by Jerry Pinkney. Used by permission of HarperCollins Publishers.

The endpapers of a hardcover picturebook can also add to its attractiveness. These are the first and last pages of the book; one half of each is glued to the inside of the cover, while the other is not pasted down. Endpapers are usually of stronger paper than printed pages. In picturebooks, endpapers are often of a color that harmonizes with the cover or other pictures in the book, and frequently they are illustrated. Decorated endpapers can reflect the setting, the theme, or the content of the book and serve as a special invitation into the book. Jerry Pinkney's exquisitely painted endpapers for Hans Christian Andersen's *The Ugly Duckling* are as much a part of the storytelling as the other pages in the book. The opening endpapers show a parade of ducks swimming and diving in a pristine stream with an odd-looking bird struggling to bring up the rear. At the book's end a glorious, full-grown white swan is depicted in the same locale.

Even the title page of a picturebook can be beautiful, informative, and symbolic. The title page of *Just Plain Fancy* by Patricia Polacco provides the clue to the origin of the fancy peacock egg that Naomi and Ruth found in the tall grass by the drive. In Bob Graham's *"Let's Get a Pup!" Said Kate,* the story actually begins before the title page. On the book's very first page, usually reserved for the title, Kate lies in bed missing her dead cat, Tiger, who died the previous winter. But Kate suddenly has a brilliant idea and is out of bed in a snap. "Let's get a pup!" she calls to her still sleeping parents, and the story proceeds.

All aspects of a book's design can reinforce or extend the meaning of the story. The layout of pictures and text on each double-page spread and on succeeding pages can have an important impact on the meaning and movement of a story. Full-size pictures might be interspersed with smaller ones, or a page might show a sequence of pictures. This visual pattern can set up a rhythm akin to a musical refrain. The spacing of the text on the page, the choice of margins, and the white space within a book contribute to the making of a quality picturebook. In Virginia Lee Burton's *The Little House,* the arrangement of the text on the page suggests the curve of the road in the opposite picture.

Appropriate type design is also a matter for consideration. Type is the name given to all printed letters, and typeface refers to the thousands of letter styles available today. Before the advent of computer-created fonts, printers chose from some six thousand different styles then available. Now the computer allows artists much more freedom. David Diaz designed the fonts for Eve Bunting's *Going Home* to resemble the linear forms of the Mexican folk art that fills the book. Whether they are traditional or computer-created, typefaces, or fonts, vary in legibility and the feeling they create. Some seem bold, others delicate and graceful, some crisp and businesslike. The type should enhance or extend the overall design of the book.

In sum, no single element creates an outstanding picturebook. All elements work together to create a cohesive whole that pleases the eye and delights the imagination.

The Language of Picturebooks

The words of picturebooks are as important as the illustrations; they can help children develop an early sensitivity to the imaginative use of language and add to their overall experience with a picturebook. Since many of these books are read to children rather than by them, there is no reason to oversimplify or write down to today's knowledgeable and sophisticated child. Beatrix Potter knew that, given the context of *The Tale of Peter Rabbit* and the picture of Peter caught in the gooseberry net, most children would comprehend the words "his sobs were overheard by some friendly sparrows, who flew to him in great excitement, and implored him to exert himself" (p. 45). This is the way children increase their vocabularies—by hearing or reading words they do not know but in a context that provides a general sense of the meaning.

Evaluating Picturebooks

Guidelines

 Go to **www.mhhe.com/kieferbrief1e** *to access an expanded version of this evaluation form.*

The following questions are meant to help determine the strengths of the book. Not every question is appropriate for every book.

Content

- How appropriate is the content of the book for its intended age level?
- Is this a book that will appeal to children, or is it really written for adults?
- When and where does it take place? How has the artist portrayed this?
- Are the characters well delineated and developed?
- Are stereotypes regarding race, gender, and others avoided?
- What is the quality of the language of the text?
- How is the theme developed through text and illustrations?

Illustrations

- In what ways do the illustrations help create the meaning of the text?
- How are pictures made an integral part of the text?
- Do the illustrations extend the text in any way? Do they provide clues to the action of the story?
- Are the pictures accurate and consistent with the text?
- Where the setting calls for it, are the illustrations authentic in detail?

Medium and Style of Illustrations

- What medium has the illustrator chosen to use? Is it appropriate for the mood of the story?
- How has the illustrator used line, shape, and color to extend the meaning of the story?

- How would you describe the style of the illustrations? Is the style appropriate for the story?
- How has the illustrator varied the style and technique? What techniques seem to create rhythm and movement?
- How has the illustrator created balance in composition?

Format

- Does the size of the book seem appropriate to the content?
- Does the jacket design express the theme of the book?
- Do the cover design and endpapers convey the spirit of the book?
- In what way does the title page anticipate the story to come?
- Is the type design well chosen for the theme and purpose of the book?
- What is the quality of the paper?
- How durable is the binding?

Overall Evaluation

- How is this work similar to or different from other works by this author and/or illustrator?
- How is this story similar to or different from other books with the same subject or theme?
- What comments have reviewers made about this book? Do you agree or disagree with them?
- What has the artist said about her or his work?
- Will this book make a contribution to the growing body of children's literature? How lasting do you think it will be?

In evaluating picture storybooks, it is important to remember that a story should be told quickly because the action must be contained within a 32- to 64-page book. Even with this limitation, the criteria developed in Chapter 1 for all fiction apply equally well to picturebooks that tell stories. Both text and illustrations should be evaluated. The artistry of the words should be equal to the beauty of the illustrations. See **Guidelines: Evaluating Picturebooks** for some questions that can help you evaluate picturebooks.

The Content of Picturebooks

The content of picturebooks is as rich and varied as today's world. Picturebooks are not just for younger children; they are increasingly addressed to children in the middle grades and older. This seems appropriate for today's visually minded child. However, as the age range for picturebooks increases, it becomes imperative to evaluate the appropriateness of the content for the age level of its intended audience. You do not want to share *Hiroshima No Pika* (The Flash of Hiroshima) by Toshi Maruki with young children any more than you would read *Goodnight Moon* by Margaret Wise Brown to older children.

Other considerations regarding the content of picturebooks need to be examined. For example, does the book avoid race, gender, and age stereotyping? Gender stereotyping begins early. Examples can be found in pictures as well as in text. In the imaginative story *Can I Keep Him?* by Steven Kellogg, Albert asks his mother if he can keep one pet after another, ranging from real to imaginary to human. His distraught mother is always pictured attending to such household chores as scrubbing, ironing, and cleaning the toilet bowl. She explains in very literal terms why Albert cannot keep his pets; for example, a snake's scales could clog the vacuum. While the contrast between Albert's highly original ideas and his mother's mundane preoccupation with household duties is funny, it is also a stereotyped image of the traditional housewife.

Books that counteract gender stereotyping are not as hard to find as they were when *William's Doll,* by Charlotte Zolotow, was published in 1972. William is a little boy who desperately wants a doll but is misunderstood by family and teased by friends. Only his grandmother understands how he feels, and so she brings him a baby doll "to hug . . . so that when he's a father . . . he'll know how to care for his baby." More and more books portray characters who are willing to step outside of traditional roles to have fulfilling lives. In *Max* by Rachel Isadora, a young baseball player decides to take ballet lessons. He finds that it is a super way to warm up for baseball.

We have picturebooks that portray the experiences of more diverse cultures than ever before, although the total number of multicultural books is still small compared with the proportion of ethnic and racial groups in the population. Many people from parallel cultures are now represented in stories about contemporary children as well as in folktales. *This House Is Made of Mud,* by Ken Buchanan, celebrates the joy of living in a Navajo hogan. The desert is its yard, the mountains its fence, and all the animals and birds are welcome visitors. Lovely clear watercolors by Libba Tracy add to the beauty of this simple story.

The past few years have seen an increase in books about Latino and Asian cultures, in bilingual books, and in translated books. Alexis O'Neill's *Estela's Swap* is a story

The Chinese setting of Catherine Gower's *Long-Long's New Year* is visualized through He Zhihong's adaptation of traditional painting styles. From *Long-Long's New Year* by Catherine Gower and He Zhihong. Published by Frances Lincoln Ltd., copyright © 2005. Reproduced by permission of Frances Lincoln Ltd.

about a young Hispanic girl who brings her music box to the swap meet her father attends each week. She wants to earn money for folk-dance lessons and hopes to sell the box. She leaves it behind in a sudden windstorm to go help an older flower seller. When she returns, the box has been damaged, and Estela thinks she's lost the chance to earn her money. But the flower seller gives her a beautiful "falda," a special skirt for dancing in the Ballet Folklórico. The old woman, grateful for Estela's help in cleaning up her flower stall, tells her, "Since we are at a swap meet, it is only fair that we swap." Illustrator Enrique O. Sanchez created richly textured, bright paintings to convey this warmhearted story. In modern-day China, Long-Long also hopes to make money when he accompanies his grandfather to market in *Long-Long's New Year* by Catherine Gower. Long-Long's hopes to buy presents for his family seem thwarted at first until, like Estela, Long-Long's kindness to others saves the day and he returns home with many presents. He Zhihong's watercolor illustrations resemble traditional Chinese screen paintings and lend cultural authenticity to the setting.

Though there are now more books about older people than ever before, we can find stereotypes among these, too. One young-appearing grandfather went to a bookstore recently and said he wanted "a book about a grandfather in which the main character doesn't die." Many grandparents today in their sixties and seventies are vigorous and healthy; we might well ask if they are being portrayed this way. Author Janet Lord and illustrator Julie Paschkis celebrate the vitality of the older generation in *Here Comes Grandma!* showing a determined grandmother riding a bike, strapping on skis, and catching a hot air balloon just to visit her grandchildren.

Picturebooks frequently give children their first impressions of various ethnic and racial groups. Only when our books portray characters of both sexes, all ages, and all ethnic and racial groups in a wide range of occupations and from a great variety of socioeconomic backgrounds and settings will we have moved away from stereotyping to a more honest portrayal of the world for children. **Teaching Feature 3.4: A Sampling of Picturebooks** provides an introduction to the many topics found in today's picturebooks.

A Sampling of Picturebooks

Author, Illustrator	Title	Target Grade Level	Description
ABC and Counting Books			
Linda Ashman and Nancy Carpenter	*M Is for Mischief*	1 and up	Twenty-six highly offensive children cavort through the pages of this book.
Eric Carle	*10 Little Rubber Ducks*	PreK–1	Rubber ducks fall off a container ship and head in different directions.
Lois Ehlert	*Eating the Alphabet*	PreK–1	Fruits and vegetables are shown for every letter of the alphabet.
Catheryn Falwell	*Feast for Ten*	PreK–2	Beginning with one grocery cart, these textured collages show an African American family preparing a family feast.
Anita Lobel	*Animal Antics A–Z*	PreK–2	Animals play with the letters from A to Z, while acrobats form them with their bodies.
David McLimans	*Gone Wild: An Endangered Animal Alphabet*	K and up	McLimans's vivid artistic style draws attention to endangered species.
Margaret Musgrove and Leo and Diane Dillon	*Ashanti to Zulu: African Traditions*	2–5	Illustrations feature the people, their homes, and an artifact from twenty-six African tribes.
Wordless Books			
Suzy Lee	*Wave*	PreK–3	A little girl explores the rhythms of the ocean in this lovely two-color book.
Barbara Lehman	*Rainstorm*	PreK–3	A rainy day inspires an imaginative adventure.
Mark Newgarden and Megan Montague Cash	*Bow-Wow Bugs a Bug*	PreK–2	A dog is bugged by a bug and bugs back.

(continued)

teaching feature 3.4

Author, Illustrator	Title	Target Grade Level	Description
Gregory Rogers	*Midsummer Knight*	PreK–8	Shakespeare inspires a medieval bear to attempt the life of a soldier.
Shaun Tan	*The Arrival*	4–8	A man must flee his family and country and adjust to a totally new place and culture.
Brinton Turkle	*Deep in the Forest*	PreK–2	This is a wonderful reversal of the traditional Goldilock's story.
David Wiesner	*Flotsam*	PreK–8	A boy finds an unusual camera while at the beach.

Family Stories

Author, Illustrator	Title	Target Grade Level	Description
Nancy Garden and Sharon Wooding	*Molly's Family*	PreK–1	Molly shares her picture of her family but is distraught when her fellow kindergarteners tell her no one has two mothers.
Maurie J. Manning	*Kitchen Dance*	PreK–1	Children wake to find their Mama and Papa dancing in the kitchen.
Linda Sue Park and Ho Baek Lee	*Bee-Bim Bop!*	PreK–2	A Korean American girl looks forward to eating "mix, mix rice" with her family.
Elizabeth Winthrop and Pat Cummings	*Squashed in the Middle*	1–4	A girl who feels lost between older and younger siblings makes herself known.
Belle Yang	*Hannah Is My Name*	1–4	A Chinese American girl describes her family's emigration from Taiwan.

Relatives

Author, Illustrator	Title	Target Grade Level	Description
Andrea Cheng and Ange Zhang	*Grandfather Counts*	K–3	Helen and her Chinese grandfather learn to speak each other's language.
Stian Hole	*Garmann's Summer*	K–2	Garmann's three great aunts come for a visit and help him with his fears about starting school.

Author, Illustrator	Title	Target Grade Level	Description
Elizabeth Fitzgerald Howard and James Ransome	*Aunt Flossie's Hats (and Crab Cakes Later)*	1–4	Two sisters listen to the stories of their great-great aunt's many hats.
René Colato Laínez	*Playing Lotería /El juego de la lotería*	K–3	A young boy learns to speak Spanish while visiting his grandmother.
Leonore Look and Yumi Heo	*Uncle Peter's Amazing Chinese Wedding*	K–3	Jenny feels left out on the day of her uncle's wedding.
Sonia Manzano and Jon Muth	*No Dogs Allowed*	K–3	Members of an extended Latino family trek off to the beach with the pet dog only to find that no dogs are allowed.

Family History

Sandra Belton and Cozbi A. Cabrera	*Beauty, Her Basket*	K–3	Grandmother shares the history of the Sea Islands baskets with her granddaughter.
Karen English and Sean Qualls	*The Baby on the Way*	K–3	Grandmother tells her grandson about her own childhood.
Janice N. Harrington and Jerome Lagarrigue	*Going North*	2–6	An African American family makes the long trip north for a better life.
Margaree King Mitchell	*Uncle Jed's Barbershop*	2–5	Uncle Jed puts off his dreams to help others during the Depression.
Uri Shulevitz	*How I Learned Geography*	2–6	Shulevitz looks back on his childhood as a refugee in a far-off land.
Jacqueline Woodson and E. B. Lewis	*Coming on Home Soon*	2–5	A young girl and her grandmother are separated from Mama when she moves north to work during WWII.

Familiar Experiences

Tomie dePaola	*Stage Struck*	K–3	Young Tommy tries to take over the class play when he doesn't get the lead role.

(continued)

teaching feature 3.4

Author, Illustrator	Title	Target Grade Level	Description
Marla Frazee	*A Couple of Boys Have the Best Week Ever*	PreK–2	Two best friends spend a happy week at the beach.
Robie H. Harris and Michael Emberley	*Mail Harry to the Moon!*	PreK–2	An older brother knows just what to do to get rid of a new sibling.
Antonio Hernández Madrigal and Gerrardo Suzán	*Blanca's Feather*	K–3	A little girl loses her pet hen at the blessing of the animals on St. Francis of Assisi Day.
Leslea Newman and Ron Himler	*The Best Cat in the World*	K–3	A young boy struggles to deal with the death of his cat and a new kitten who is very different in nature.
Mary Ann Rodman and E. B. Lewis	*My Best Friend*	2–6	A young girl tries hard to make friends with an older girl at the swimming pool.
Vera B. Williams	*Music, Music for Everyone*	K–3	Rosa uses her birthday accordion to earn money to help pay the bills.

Children Around the World

Author, Illustrator	Title	Target Grade Level	Description
Florence Parry Heide, Judith Heide Gilliland and Ted Lewin	*Sami and the Time of the Troubles*	2–6	A young boy must struggle to maintain a normal life during the war in Lebanon.
Tololwa Mollel and E. B. Lewis	*My Rows and Piles of Coins*	K–3	A young Tanzanian boy is trying to save enough money to buy a bicycle so he can help his mother deliver her goods to market.
Naomi Shihab Nye and Nancy Carpenter	*Sitti's Secret*	2–5	A Palestinian American girl goes to visit her grandmother in Palestine.
Karen Lynn Williams and Catherine Stock	*Galimoto*	K–3	A young Malawian boy succeeds in making his own toy car.
Karen Lynn Williams and Khadra Mohammed	*Four Feet, Two Sandals*	3–6	Two girls in a Pakistani refugee camp agree to share the pair of sandals they find.

Author, Illustrator	Title	Target Grade Level	Description
Social and Environmental Concerns			
Jeannie Baker	*Home*	1–4	A wordless picturebook shows a neighborhood changing over time.
Eve Bunting	*Fly Away Home*	1–4	A young boy and his father must live in an airport concourse.
Eleanor Coerr and Ed Young	*Sadako*	3–5	A young Japanese girl develops leukemia as a result of the atomic bomb.
Katie Smith Milway and Eugenie Fernandes	*One Hen*	2–5	An Ashanti boy receives a micro loan and buys a hen to begin a thriving business.
Tim Tingle and Jeanne Rorex Bridges	*Crossing Bok Chito*	3–5	Native Americans aid runaway slaves in prebellum Mississippi.
Ruth Vander Zee and Robert Innocenti	*Erika's Story*	3–5	A Jewish couple makes a terrible choice in order to save their baby.
Animals as People			
Bonny Becker and Kady MacDonald Denton	*A Visitor for Bear*	PreK–1	An insistent mouse finally convinces reclusive Bear that friends are nice to have.
Chih-Yaun Chen	*Guji Guji*	K–3	An alligator hatched with ducklings shows nurture can triumph over nature.
Doreen Cronin and Harry Bliss	*Diary of a Spider* *Diary of a Worm*	1–4	The world as seen through the eyes (and words) of a young spider and a worm.
Robert Kraus and José Aruego	*Leo the Late Bloomer*	PreK–2	Leo, a baby tiger, can't do anything right until he's ready to.
Edel Rodriguez	*Sergio Makes a Splash!*	PreK–1	Sergio the Penguin can do just about anything—except swim!

(continued)

teaching feature 3.4

Author, Illustrator	Title	Target Grade Level	Description
Modern Folktale Style			
Colin and Jacqui Hawkins	*Fairytale News*	K–4	Mother Hubbard's son Jack delivers papers to fairy tale characters to earn money to fill their cupboards.
Patricia McKissack, Onawumi Jean Moss, and Kyrsten Brooker	*Precious and the Boo Hag*	2–4	A little girl manages to trick a trickster when she is left at home alone.
Pat Mora and Raúl Colón	*Doña Flor: A Tall Tale About a Woman with a Big Heart*	2–4	A kind and helpful woman rescues her village from a giant puma.
Jerdine Nolen and Kadir Nelson	*Hewitt Anderson's Great Big Life*	K–4	This is an African American twist on Tom Thumb.
Diane Stanley	*The Giant and the Beanstalk*	2–4	"Jack and the Beanstalk" is told from the giant's point of view.
Humorous Picturebooks			
Jon Agee	*Terrific*	2–6	Eugene Crumb, the world's most pessimistic man, meets a parrot who improves his outlook.
Emily Gravett	*Little Mouse's Big Book of Fears*	4 and up	A mouse's phobias are brought to visual life in a highly inventive way.
Kathleen Krull, Paul Brewer, and Boris Kulikov	*Fartiste*	K–3	A Frenchman makes his mark as master of his sphincter—based on a true story.
James Marshall	*George and Martha*	K–3	Brief stories about the adventures of two hippo friends are both poignant and hysterical.
Susan Meddaugh	*Perfectly Martha*	1–4	Martha the Talking Dog copes with a crooked dog training scam.

Author, Illustrator	Title	Target Grade Level	Description
Meg Rosoff and Sophie Blackall	*Meet Wild Boars* *Wild Boars Cook*	K–3	A quartet of wild boars stands in for the most ill-behaved children ever.
Fantasy			
Corneila Funke and Kerstin Meyer	*The Princess Knight*	1–4	The king's daughter is determined to be a knight very much against her father's wishes.
Mimi Grey	*Traction Man Is Here!* *Traction Man Meets Turbo Dog*	K–3	An action figure comes to life in these delightful fantasies.
Barbara Jean Hicks and Alexis Deacon	*Jitterbug Jam: A Monster Tale*	K–3	A young monster is scared of the boy hiding under his bed.
Kevin O'Malley and Patrick O'Brien	*Captain Raptor and the Moon Mystery*	1–6	Captain Raptor of the planet Jurassica saves human visitors from a dangerous monster.
Zachary Pullen	*Friday My Radio Flyer Flew*	PreK–2	A boy discovers his father's radio flyer wagon and eventually takes off!
Sean Taylor and Bruce Ingman	*Boing!*	1–4	This is a giddy tale of a trampoline champion turned superhero.

Bow-Wow Bugs a Bug by Mark Newgarden and Megan Montague Cash exemplifies visual storytelling in this delightful wordless book. Illustrations from *Bow-Wow Bugs a Bug,* copyright © 2007 by Mark Newgarden and Megan Montague Cash, reproduced by permission of Houghton Mifflin Harcourt Publishing Company.

Maurie J. Manning's *Kitchen Dance* is a warm family story and a perfect goodnight book.
Illustration from *Kitchen Dance* by Maurie J. Manning. Copyright © 2008 by Maurie J. Manning. Reprinted by permission of Houghton Mifflin Harcourt Publishing Company. All rights reserved.

Four Feet, Two Sandals, illustrated by Doug Chayka and written by Karen Williams and Khadra Mohammed, provides an intimate chld's point of view to news items that may seem very distant to children. *Four Feet, Two Sandals* by Karen Lynn Williams and Khadra Muhammed and illustrated by Doug Chayka © 2007 Wm. B. Eerdmans Publishing Company, Grand Rapids, MI. Reprinted by permission of the publisher. All rights reserved.

Katie Smith Milway's *One Hen*, illustrated by Eugenie Fernandes, shows how the gift of an animal can change the lives of poor people in dramatic ways. Material from *One Hen: How One Small Loan Made a Big Difference*, written by Katie Smith Milway, illustrated by Eugenie Fernandes and is used by permission of Kids Can Press Ltd., Toronto. Illustration © 2008 Eugenie Fernandes.

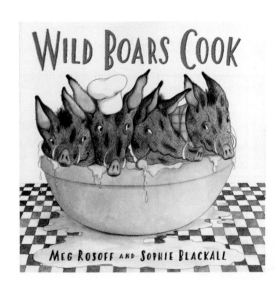

Sophie Blackall creates wonderfully funny illustrations for Meg Rosoff's *Wild Boars Cook.* Cover of *Wild Boars Cook* by Meg Rosoff, illustrated by Sophie Blackall. Text copyright © 2008 by Meg Rosoff. Illustrations copyright © by Sophie Blackall. Reprinted by permission of Henry Holt and Company, LLC.

Challenging Perspectives on Picturebooks

We have explored some qualities of picturebooks that affect children's emotional and intellectual responses to books, which we hope will lead to a lifelong appreciation of literature and art. The illustrations in picturebooks can help teach any number of prereading and independent reading skills that fall under the rubric of higher-level critical thinking (such as formulating questions about the material you are reading—especially questions that analyze, hypothesize, or evaluate). Understanding the concept of "book" is an important milestone on the road to literacy. Children with prior book experience may already know some concepts about print, such as turning pages, recognizing the differences between print and pictures, and so on. It is at the next skill level—looking at pictures (illustrations) in books—that children are reaching benchmarks related to inference (a conclusion drawn from evidence or reasoning) and making meaning in literacy learning.

When young children look at pictures in texts, how are their inferences culturally bound? How can a teacher's understanding of the cultural context of aesthetic responses support or get in the way of how he or she introduces, discusses, and assesses picturebooks with children?

At the beginning of this chapter, an exchange between two students initially presented what can be a daily scenario in any classroom, one book with two children vying for it. As the story played out, the reason was not one of selfishness. It was what can be labeled an aesthetic response. The one child thought the book was "pretty" enough to fight for it, suggesting that the artistic style of the picturebook, *Where the Wild Things Are,* engaged this student in ways that would move her to want to read the book again and again. This level of response, while rooted in a small conflict, begs for a closer look into the underlying reasons to the responses to the illustrations in picturebooks, which may be culturally connected.

Earlier in this chapter we also discussed how color, as one of the elements of design, can elicit strong emotions that affect a viewer's response to a book. Colors, for example, can be full of symbolism. Cultural referents can be linked to geography, parental preferences, and any other number of things related to the culture in which one was raised. For example, brides in the eastern hemisphere wear red, while often brides in the western hemisphere wear white. **Table 3.1** on page 86 lists other color connections to consider.

Market researchers work hard to determine what consumers will like or dislike. The use of color in marketing, for example, is not random. They use many markers of difference (race, gender, social class, geography) and trends are used to determine what the logos and marketing layouts for their products will be. Given the attention to color and style, the illustrators of children's books realize that the colors and mediums they choose are more than tangential to the creation of a picturebook. They are aware that very young children tend to prefer brighter colors, and thus use modern publishing techniques to create exciting, full-color picturebooks.

Again the choice of colors should depend on the theme of the book. However, as teachers encourage aesthetic responses, it should be put in the cultural context of children's lived experiences. Using the example of Molly Bang's *When Sophie Gets Angry—Really, Really Angry,* we find Bang's intense reds and oranges represent Sophie's rage. As she runs outside into the wider world and her anger diminishes, the

table 3.1	Color Around the World

Color	Country/Ethnicity/Culture	Meaning
Red	Eastern hemisphere	Worn by brides
	Western hemisphere	Excitement, danger, love, passion, stop, Christmas (with green)
	China	Good luck, celebration, summoning
	India	Purity
	Russia	Communism
	South Africa	Color of mourning
	Cherokee	Success, triumph
Orange	Western hemisphere	Halloween (with black), creativity, autumn
	Ireland	Religious (Protestants)
Yellow	Western hemisphere	Hope, hazards, coward
	China	Nourishing
	Egypt	Color of mourning
	India	Merchants
	Japan	Courage
Green	Western hemisphere	Spring, new birth, go, St. Patrick's Day, Christmas (with red)
	China	Green hats indicate a man's wife is cheating on him; exorcism
	India	Islam
	Ireland	Symbol of the entire country
Blue	Western hemisphere	Depression, sadness, conservative, corporate, "something blue" bridal tradition
	Iran	Heaven, spirituality
	Cherokee	Defeat, trouble
Purple	Western hemisphere	Royalty
	Thailand	Color of mourning (widows)
White	Eastern hemisphere	Funerals
	Western hemisphere	Brides, angels, "good guys," hospitals, doctors, peace (white dove)
	Japan	White carnation symbolizes death
Black	Western hemisphere	Funerals, death, Halloween (with orange), "bad guys," rebellion
	China	Color for young boys

colors turn to cool greens and blues that follow her back home to the embrace of her now peaceful family. Teachers using this book might ask if red denotes anger and intensity in every culture. Can the use of red have a cultural referent that would cause a student to think something else is going on with the protagonist? For example, in some South African communities, red is used as symbol of mourning.

The response to literature that includes the aesthetic response is a critical part of the enjoyment of reading. However, we know that in the art world, artistic works can be labeled controversial and political. Few lists of criteria for the selection of a picturebook to read with children includes evaluation for the social-political construction of what is art and how that may affect children's aesthetic responses. Alternatively, what are the controversies in the art world that may have some impact on what shows up in illustrator's choices of artistic form in children's books? Children can participate in topics of conversations that include controversy. They can be taught the evaluative language of art, the explanations of artistic elements, and the principles of design to help them express their ideas and aesthetic responses.

We can help children have deeper understandings of how the use of various artistic elements represents different things to different people. For example, an important aspect of literacy instruction is reading comprehension. When reading a picturebook with a child, we often facilitate the development of comprehension with a series of questions. These questions ask students to go beyond immediately available information in the text. Through careful questioning and discussion, students realize the illustration contains hints that imply a whole network of information: clues to deeper understanding of the story. To push beyond what is written in the text, ask children to find clues within the illustrations, examine them, and discuss what inferences (meanings) are justified. This enhances reading comprehension through inference.

The question then becomes, *"How can we increase their understandings of cultural perspectives?"* For example, Sharon Dennis Wyeth's, *Something Beautiful* with illustrations by Chris Soentpiet, can best demonstrate these concepts. The book begins with a little girl leaving her home for school. As she is closing the door, she sees the word "die" scrawled in red graffiti on her front door. After reading the first page of this story, the classroom teachers can pause and begin engaging children in a conversation about

Sharon Wyeth's *Something Beautiful*, illustrated by Chris K. Soentpiet, is an example of the type of picturebook that can open up critical understandings for children. "Illustrations" by Chris K. Soentpiet, copyright © 1998 by Chris K. Soentpiet, from *Something Beautiful* by Sharon Wyeth, illustrated by Chris K. Soentpiet. Used by permission of Random House Children's Books, a division of Random House, Inc.

figure 3.1

The Ten-Point Model for Teaching Controversial Issues Picturebooks

Step	Task	To Consider
1. Prompt with the initial question.	Prompt children's response with: • "Why did the illustrator _____?" • "What does it mean in your family or community?" • "What does it mean in different cultures?"	Ground rules are needed to moderate the nature of contributions to the discussion. The purpose of such rules is to enable the free flow of ideas in a safe, nonthreatening environment with the goal of having students think about and question their assumptions, and listen to others' ideas about the artist's use of line, shape, form, space, texture, value, and color.
2. Create a list of "Things to find out more about."	As children brainstorm concepts or ideas that are not directly tied to the elements of art, record them for later discussions.	Be explicit about learning more about the visual arts (drawing, painting, sculpture, architecture, photography, film, or printmaking) and the use of color in different cultural communities and around the world.
3. Assign information-gathering homework.	Encourage children to gather information about art, artistic styles, and controversies from multiple sources, television, newspapers, and artists. Have students find out everything they can about the initial question.	Find out about your students' cultural backgrounds as much as possible. Remind students that parents, caregivers, other family members, and friends in their community would be their best sources of information.
4. Share again responses to the initial question in a brainstorming session.	Require students to cite the quality of the evidence of which claims are made, whether from an outside source, from their experiences, from media, or family.	Provide as much support as you have available. Invite local artists, museum curators, and illustrators to your classroom.
5. Continue the process of gathering information.	Have the students share information. Identify things to find out more about for as long as the topic seems interesting. Encourage students to listen to and learn from each other.	Brainstorming can encourage students to work as a group to see all possible aspects of a controversial issue and can be used for a range of purposes. The teacher's role is an active one—facilitating, clarifying, and questioning—but the teacher does not impose information.
6. If a concept emerges that sparks interest, confusion, or conflict, pose it as a new question.	If the topic begins with use of color in cultural contexts but evolves into a discussion of use of media, you may have two lines of inquiry going on simultaneously, or change the topic.	Mediating negative comments and strong emotions is an important aspect of ensuring a "smooth" approach to controversial issues. Ask for evidence, analyze underlying assumptions, and ask for other viewpoints.
7. Periodically give the children assignments in class to summarize their thoughts.	The assignment can be individual or shared writing. Prompts could be worded as: • "What you know about the use of color" • "Things you don't understand about illustrators' color choices" • "In my family, using the color _____ means _____." Share the compositions in a public space.	Find ways to help crystallize your students' individual thinking about the art of picturebooks.

figure 3.1 *(continued)*

Step	Task	To Consider
8. As individual or group projects emerge, follow up on them.	The class may decide to write letters to illustrators of their favorite books or books that are part of past or contemporary controversies. One or two children may decide to pursue a challenging research topic to report on to the group or other interested communities.	Be flexible.
9. Let others know what you are doing.	Many picturebook illustrators do school and bookstore visits. Invite them to your classroom or take children to where they may be speaking. Local artists usually welcome the opportunity to visit schools and discuss their choices for composition.	Encourage dialogue with parents, colleagues, and the community.
10. End your project with something either public or permanent.	If possible, create a space for a class presentation. This may be to the rest of the school about what they have learned, or an article for the school paper or the local newspaper or art community.	It's critical to make the experience relevant to the lives of the children. Looking for opportunities for authentic learning experiences will help children create real-world connections.

Source: Adapted from Kreidler, W. *Elementary Perspectives: Teaching Concepts of Peace and Conflict.* Copyright © 1990, Educators for Social Responsibility, Cambridge, MA. www.esrnational.org. Used by permission.

the cultural referents of color before continuing the story. *What color is the word? Why do you think the illustrator used red? What does it mean when you see the color red? Does it mean anything in your family if people wear red? Do you know if it means something in other cultures? Is there a right or a wrong way to use the color red?*

As students participate in a discussion of this type, they will share their cultural referents to color, those that are positive and negative to their lived experiences. Helping students understand the variety of viewpoints related to the use of color can open a space for understanding the multiple perspectives that people have around the globe in the arts and other areas. A critical analysis of the text and the illustrations helps them to engage in conversations and more reflective responses to what they read or what is read to them.

Picturebooks are for all ages, and they can be about all subjects. They can enrich children's lives, stretch their imaginations, and increase their sensitivities. The growth of beautiful picturebooks for children of all ages is an outstanding accomplishment of the past fifty years of publishing. Children do not always recognize the beauty of these books, but early impressions do influence the development of children's permanent tastes as they grow up. The challenge for teachers will be to change the lens through which the art of the picturebook is seen for one that offers critique and inclusion of cultural referents.

Figure 3.1 gives examples on how to use the Ten-Point Model to address perceptions and controversial issues related to picturebooks.

Using Picturebooks to Address Standards

Through the use of enchanting stories and visual creativity, picturebooks spark ideas in the imagination of students, help them see themselves reflected in the characters, and introduce readers to times, events, and places that give them insight into their past and hope for their future. The variety of styles and stories that encompass the genre of picturebooks offer a starting point for implementing curriculum standards in the classroom. For example, students can explore the ways texts are constructed in David Wiesner's *The Three Pigs*, or learn about the diversity of people and places other than their own in René Colato Laínez's *Playing Lotería*, Linda Sue Park's *Bee-Bim Bop!*, or Tololwa Mollel's *My Rows and Piles of Coins*. Curricular connections can be made to math concepts through books like Cathryn Falwell's *Feast for Ten* or Marge Palatini's *Three French Hens*. Discussions about science concepts such as animal habitats can be sparked by reading about the animal characters in Suzanne Bloom's *A Splendid Friend, Indeed*. Simple machines and aerodynamics come to life in Pablo Bernasconi's *Captain Arsenio: Inventions and (Mis) Adventures in Flight*. Picturebooks also provide a chance for students to make textual connections as they read or are read to. Examples of books that may inspire such associations include Karen Hesse's *Come On, Rain!*, Kam Mak's *My Chinatown*, and Robert McCloskey's *One Morning in Maine*.

Standards in Action: The English Language Arts

For example, let's examine the following text in regard to the NCTE/IRA Standards for the English Language Arts:

Cronin, D. (2006) *Diary of a Spider* New York: HarperCollins.

Diary of a Spider uses multiple genres to showcase the day-to-day adventures in the life of a spider. There are family photos, a postcard, a diagram, a newspaper article, lists of directions, and flash cards that provide perspective into the ups and downs of the spider's life. Each genre is cleverly used to highlight the social relationships within the spider's world that parallel the reader's own use of texts.

English Language Arts Standard 6

Students apply knowledge of language structure, language conventions (e.g., spelling and punctuation), media techniques, figurative language, and genre to create, critique, and discuss print and nonprint texts.

- Students can create multigenre books about their daily life that include the same texts found in the spider's life: photos, to-do lists, postcards, charts, newspaper articles, calendars, etc.
- Students can describe and contrast the different language conventions used by different types of texts within the book and within their own projects.
- Students can draw diagrams of a special place they like to visit or would like to visit. They should label all parts of their diagram and write a caption for their text.

English Language Arts Standard 7

Students conduct research on issues and interests by generating ideas and questions, and by posing problems. They gather, evaluate, and synthesize data from a variety of sources (e.g., print and nonprint texts, artifacts, people) to communicate their discoveries in ways that suit their purpose and audience.

- Students can engage in inquiry projects about the lives of other animals. Students can each take a different animal or work in groups. The projects can include factual research reports, fictionalized accounts of personified animals, and dramatic presentations of how their animals would interact with others.

Source: Standards are from the NCTE/IRA Standards for the English Language Arts.

Children's Literature

OLC *Go to www.mhhe.com/kiefer1e to access the Children's Literature Database, which includes information on thousands of children's books. Following are some of the titles you will find in the database.*

Titles in blue = multicultural titles

Agee, Jon. *Terrific.* Hyperion, 2005.

Andersen, Hans. *The Ugly Duckling.* Illustrated by Jerry Pinkney. Morrow, 1999.

Ashman, Linda. *M Is for Mischief: An A to Z of Naughty Children.* Illustrated by Nancy Carpenter. Dutton, 2008.

Baker, Jeannie. *Home.* Greenwillow, 2004.

Bang, Molly. *When Sophie Gets Angry—Really, Really Angry.* Scholastic, 1999.

Becker, Bonny. *A Visitor for Bear.* Illustrated by Kady MacDonald Denton. Candlewick, 2008.

Belton, Sandra. *Beauty, Her Basket.* Illustrated by Cozbi A. Cabrera. Amistad, 2004.

Bernasconi, Pablo. *Captain Arsenio: Inventions and (Mis) Adventures in Flight.* Houghton, 2006.

Bernheimer, Kate. *The Girl in the Castle inside the Museum.* Illustrated by Nicoletta Ceccoli. Random, 2008.

Bloom, Suzanne. *A Splendid Friend, Indeed.* Boyds Mills, 2005.

Briggs, Raymond. *The Bear.* Random, 1994.

Brown, Margaret Wise. *Goodnight Moon.* Illustrated by Clement Hurd. Harper, 1975 [1947].

Browne, Anthony. *Changes.* Knopf, 1986.

Buchanan, Ken. *This House Is Made of Mud/Esta casa esta hecha de lodo.* Illustrated by Libba Tracy. Rising Moon, 1991.

Bunting, Eve. *Fly Away Home.* Illustrated by Ronald Himler. Clarion, 1991.

———. *Going Home.* Illustrated by David Diaz. HarperCollins, 1996.

———. *Smoky Night.* Illustrated by David Diaz. Sandpiper, 1999.

Burton, Virginia Lee. *The Little House.* Houghton, 1942.

Carle, Eric. *10 Little Rubber Ducks.* HarperCollins, 2005.

Chen, Chih-Yuan. *Guji Guji.* Kane/Miller, 2004.

Cheng, Andrea. *Grandfather Counts.* Illustrated by Ange Zhang. Lee, 2003.

Coerr, Eleanor. *Sadako.* Illustrated by Ed Young. Putnam, 1993.

Cronin, Doreen. *Diary of a Spider.* Illustrated by Harry Bliss. HarperCollins, 2006.

———. *Diary of a Worm.* Illustrated by Harry Bliss. HarperCollins, 2005.

Demi. *Chingis Khan.* Holt, 1991.

———. *The Hungry Coat.* Simon, 2004.

dePaola, Tomie. *The Clown of God.* Harcourt, 1978.

———. *Stage Struck.* Putnam, 2005.

Dunrea, Olivier. *Gossie.* Houghton, 2002.

Ehlert, Lois. *Eating the Alphabet.* Harcourt, 1989.

———. *Fish Eyes: A Book You Can Count On.* Harcourt, 1990.

Elliot, David. *On the Farm.* Illustrated by Holly Meade. Candlewick, 2008.

Endredy, James. *The Journey of Tunuri and the Blue Deer: A Huichol Indian Story.* Illustrated by María Hernández de la Cruz and Casimiro de la Cruz López. Bear Cub Books, 2003.

English, Karen. *The Baby on the Way.* Illustrated by Sean Qualls. Farrar, 2005.

Falwell, Cathryn. *Feast for Ten.* Clarion, 1993.

———. *Scoot!* HarperCollins, 2008.

Frazee, Marla. *A Couple of Boys Have the Best Week Ever.* Harcourt, 2008.

Frazier, Craig. *Stanley Goes Fishing.* Chronicle, 2006.

Funke, Cornelia. *The Princess Knight.* Translated by Anthea Bell. Illustrated by Kerstin Meyer. Scholastic, 2004.

Gág, Wanda. *Millions of Cats.* Coward-McCann, 1928.

Garden, Nancy. *Molly's Family.* Illustrated by Sharon Wooding. Farrar, 2004.

Geisert, Arthur. *Oops.* Houghton, 2006.

Gower, Catherine, and He Zhihong. *Long-Long's New Year.* Tuttle, 2005.

Graham, Bob. *"Let's Get a Pup!" Said Kate.* Candlewick, 2001.

———. *Oscar's Half Birthday.* Candlewick, 2005.

Gravett, Emily. *Little Mouse's Big Book of Fears.* Macmillan, 2007.

Grey, Mini. *Traction Man Is Here!* Knopf, 2005.

———. *Traction Man Meets Turbo Dog.* Knopf, 2008.

Grimm brothers. *Snow White and the Seven Dwarfs.* Translated by Randall Jarrell. Illustrated by Nancy Ekholm Burkert. Farrar, 1972.

Haley, Gail. *A Story, a Story.* Atheneum, 1970.

Halfman, Janet. *Seven Miles to Freedom: The Robert Smalls Story.* Illustrated by Duane Smith. Lee, 2008.

Hall, Donald. *The Ox-Cart Man.* Illustrated by Barbara Cooney. Viking, 1979.

Harrington, Janice. *Going North.* Illustrated by Jerome Lagarrigue. Farrar, 2004.

Harris, Robie H. *Mail Harry to the Moon!* Illustrated by Michael Emberley. Little, 2008.

Haseley, Dennis. *Twenty Heartbeats.* Illustrated by Ed Young. Roaring Brook, 2008.

Hawkins, Colin, and Jacqui Hawkins. *Fairytale News.* Candlewick, 2004.

Heide, Florence Parry, and Judith Heide Gilliland. *Sami and the Time of the Troubles*. Illustrated by Ted Lewin. Clarion, 1992.

Hesse, Karen. *Come On, Rain!* Illustrated by Jon J. Muth. Scholastic, 1999.

Hicks, Barbara Jean. *Jitterbug Jam: A Monster Tale*. Illustrated by Alexis Deacon. Farrar, 2005.

Hines, Anna Grossnickle. *1, 2, Buckle My Shoe*. Harcourt, 2008.

Hole, Stian. *Garmann's Summer*. Translated by Don Bartlett. Eerdmans, 2008.

Howard, Elizabeth Fitzgerald. *Aunt Flossie's Hats (and Crab Cakes Later)*. Illustrated by James Ransome. Houghton, 1991.

Hutchins, Pat. *We're Going on a Picnic!* Greenwillow, 2002.

——. *What Game Shall We Play?* Greenwillow, 1990.

——. *Rosie's Walk*. Macmillan, 1968.

Isadora, Rachel. *Max*. Aladdin, 1984.

Juster, Norton. *The Hello, Goodbye Window*. Illustrated by Chris Raschka. Hyperion, 2005.

Kellogg, Steven. *Can I Keep Him?* Dial, 1971.

Kraus, Robert. *Leo the Late Bloomer*. Illustrated by José Aruego. Crowell, 1971.

Krull, Kathleen, and Paul Brewer. *Fartiste*. Illustrated by Boris Kulikov. Simon, 2008.

Laínez, René Colato. *Playing Lotería /El juego de la lotería*. Illustrated by Jill Arena. Luna Rising, 2005.

Lee, Suzy. *Wave*. Chronicle, 2008.

Lehman, Barbara. *Rainstorm*. Houghton, 2007.

Lobel, Anita. *Animal Antics A–Z*. Greenwillow, 2005.

Look, Leonore, and Yumi Heo. *Uncle Peter's Amazing Chinese Wedding*. Atheneum, 2006.

Lord, Janet. *Here Comes Grandma!* Illustrated by Julie Paschkis. Holt, 2005.

Madrigal, Antonio Hernández. *Blanca's Feather*. Illustrated by Gerrardo Suzán. Rising Moon/Northland, 2000.

Mak, Kam. *My Chinatown: One Year in Poems*. HarperCollins, 2001.

Manning, Maurie J. *Kitchen Dance*. Houghton, 2008.

Manzano, Sonia. *No Dogs Allowed*. Illustrated by Jon J. Muth. Simon, 2005.

Marshall, James. *George and Martha: The Complete Stories of Two Best Friends*. Houghton, 1997.

Martin, Jacqueline Briggs. *Snowflake Bentley*. Illustrated by Mary Azarian. Houghton, 1998.

Maruki, Toshi. *Hiroshima No Pika (The Flash of Hiroshima)*. Lothrop, 1980.

McCloskey, Robert. *Make Way for Ducklings*. Viking, 1941.

——. *One Morning in Maine*. Viking, 1952.

McCully, Emily. *Picnic*. HarperCollins, 1984.

McKissack, Patricia, and Onawumi Jean Moss. *Precious and the Boo Hag*. Illustrated by Kyrsten Brooker. Atheneum, 2005.

McLimans, David. *Gone Wild: An Endangered Animal Alphabet*. Walker, 2006.

Meddaugh, Susan. *Perfectly Martha*. Houghton, 2004.

Meyers, Christopher. *Black Cat*. Scholastic, 1999.

Michelson Richard. *Across the Alley*. Illustrated E. B. Lewis. Putnam, 2006.

Milway, Katie Smith. *One Hen*. Illustrated by Eugenie Fernandes. Kids Can, 2008.

Mitchell, Margaree King. *Uncle Jed's Barbershop*. Illustrated by James Ransome. Simon, 1993.

Mollel, Tololwa. *My Rows and Piles of Coins*. Illustrated by E. B. Lewis. Clarion, 1999.

Mora, Pat. *Doña Flor: A Tall Tale About a Woman with a Big Heart*. Illustrated by Raúl Colón. Knopf, 2005.

Musgrove, Margaret. *Ashanti to Zulu: African Traditions*. Illustrated by Leo and Diane Dillon. Dial, 1976.

Myers, Walter Dean. *Jazz*. Illustrated by Christopher Myers. Holiday, 2006.

Nevius, Carol. *Baseball Hour*. Illustrated by Bill Thomson. Marshall Cavendish, 2008.

——. *Karate Hour*. Illustrated by Bill Thomson. Marshall Cavendish, 2004.

Newgarden, Mark, and Megan Montague Cash. *Bow-Wow Bugs a Bug*. Harcourt, 2007.

Newman, Leslea. *The Best Cat in the World*. Illustrated by Ron Himler. Eerdmans, 2004.

Nolen, Jerdine. *Hewitt Anderson's Great Big Life*. Illustrated by Kadir Nelson. Simon, 2005.

Nye, Naomi Shihab. *Sitti's Secret*. Illustrated by Nancy Carpenter. Four Winds, 1994.

O'Malley, Kevin. *Captain Raptor and the Moon Mystery*. Illustrated by Patrick O'Brien. Walker, 2005.

O'Neill, Alexis. *Estela's Swap*. Illustrated by Enrique O. Sanchez. Lee, 2002.

Orgel, Doris. *The Cat's Tale: Why the Years Are Named for Animals*. Illustrated by Meilo So. Roaring Brook, 2008.

Palatini, Marge. *Three French Hens*. Illustrated by Richard Egielski. Hyperion, 2005.

Park, Linda Sue. *Bee-Bim Bop!* Illustrated by Ho Baek Lee. Clarion, 2005.

Paterson, Katherine. *The Tale of the Mandarin Ducks*. Illustrated by Leo and Diane Dillon. Dutton, 1990.

Perrault, Charles. *Cinderella*. Illustrated by Marcia Brown. Macmillan, 1954.

——. *Cinderella*. Illustrated by Barbara McClintock. Scholastic, 2005.

Polacco, Patricia. *Just Plain Fancy*. Doubleday, 1990.

Potter, Beatrix. *The Tale of Peter Rabbit*. Warne, 1902.

Pullen, Zachary. *Friday My Radio Flyer Flew*. Simon, 2008.

Rappaport, Doreen. *Martin's Big Words*. Illustrated by Bryan Collier. Hyperion, 2001.

Rex, Adam. *Pssst!* Harcourt, 2007.

Rodman, Mary Ann. *My Best Friend*. Illustrated by E. B. Lewis. Viking, 2005.

Rodriguez, Edel. *Sergio Makes a Splash!* Little, 2008.

Rogers, Gregory. *Midsummer Knight*. Roaring Brook, 2007.

Rosoff, Meg. *Meet Wild Boars*. Illustrated by Sophie Blackall. Holt, 2005.

———. *Wild Boars Cook*. Illustrated by Sophie Blackall. Holt, 2008.

Schaefer, Carole Lexa. *Kids Like Us*. Illustrated by Pierr Morgan. Viking, 2008.

Sendak, Maurice. *Where the Wild Things Are*. Harper, 1963.

Shulevitz, Uri. *How I Learned Geography*. Farrar, 2008.

Simmons, Jane. *Come Along, Daisy!* Little, 1998.

Soto, Gary, and Susan Guevara. *Chato's Kitchen*. Putnam, 1997.

Stanley, Diane. *The Giant and the Beanstalk*. HarperCollins, 2004.

Steptoe, Javaka. *The Jones Family Express*. Lee, 2003.

Steptoe, John. *Stevie*. Harper, 1969.

Swanson, Susan Marie. *The House in the Night*. Illustrated by Beth Krommes. Houghton, 2008.

Taback, Simms. *Joseph Had a Little Overcoat*. Viking, 1999.

Tan, Shaun. *The Arrival*. Scholastic, 2007.

Taylor, Sean. *Boing!* Illustrated by Bruce Ingman. Candlewick, 2005.

Tingle, Tim. *Crossing Bok Chitto*. Illustrated by Jeanne Rorex Bridges. Cinco Puntos, 2006.

Turkle, Brinton. *Deep in the Forest*. Dutton, 1976.

Udry, Janice May. *A Tree Is Nice*. Illustrated by Marc Simont. Harper, 1956.

Van Allsburg, Chris. *Jumanji*. Houghton, 1981.

———. *The Polar Express*. Houghton, 1985.

———. *The Wreck of the Zephyr*. Houghton, 1983.

Vander Zee, Ruth. *Erika's Story*. Illustrated by Roberto Innocenti. Creative Editions, 2003.

Weatherford, Carole Boston. *Moses: When Harriet Tubman Led Her People to Freedom*. Illustrated by Kadir Nelson. Hyperion, 2006.

Wheeler, Lisa. *Mammoths on the Move*. Illustrated by Kurt Cyrus. Harcourt, 2006.

Wiesner, David. *Flotsam*. Clarion, 2006.

———. *The Three Pigs*. Clarion, 2001.

Willems, Mo. *Leonardo the Terrible Monster*. Hyperion, 2005.

Williams, Karen Lynn. *Galimoto*. Illustrated by Catherine Stock. Lothrop, 1990.

Williams, Karen Lynn, and Khadra Mohammed. *Four Feet, Two Sandals*. Illustrated by Doug Chayka. Eerdmans, 2007.

Williams, Vera B. *Music, Music for Everyone*. Greenwillow, 1984.

Winthrop, Elizabeth. *Squashed in the Middle*. Illustrated by Pat Cummings. Holt, 2005.

Woodson, Jacqueline. *Coming on Home Soon*. Illustrated by E. B. Lewis. Putnam, 2004.

Wyeth, Sharon Dennis. *Something Beautiful*. Illustrated by Chris K. Soentpiet. Doubleday, 1998.

Yang, Belle. *Hannah Is My Name*. Candlewick, 2004.

Young, Ed. *My Mei Mei*. Philomel, 2006.

———. *The Sons of the Dragon King*. Atheneum, 2004.

Zelinsky, Paul. *Rapunzel*. Dutton, 1997.

Zolotow, Charlotte. *Mr. Rabbit and the Lovely Present*. Illustrated by Maurice Sendak. Harper, 1962.

———. *William's Doll*. Illustrated by William Pène Du Bois. HarperCollins, 1972.

Chapter Four

Traditional Literature

Chapter Outline

Mrs. Ramirez's fifth-grade social studies class has been involved in a year-long study of North Carolina, the United States, Europe, and South America by considering, comparing, and connecting those studies to the study of Africa, Asia, and Australia. As the students examined the social, economic, and political institutions, they analyzed similarities and differences among societies. Mrs. Ramirez wanted to culminate this year's study with a special focus on the primary discipline of geography, especially cultural geography. She developed a unit using Cinderella tales from around the world.

As a class they constructed a comparison chart to show differences and similarities they found in tales from China, Indonesia, the Caribbean, Korea, and other countries. Mrs. Ramirez has brought in a new book, Paul Fleischman's *Glass Slipper, Gold Sandal: A Worldwide Cinderella* and is sharing the book during read-aloud time. The

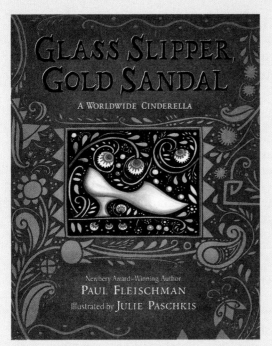

In *Glass Slipper, Gold Sandal,* Paul Fleischman and illustrator Julie Paschkis weave together motifs from the many "Cinderella" tales found in cultures throughout the world. Cover from *Glass Slipper, Gold Sandal* by Paul Fleischman, illustrated by Julie Paschkis. Illustration copyright © 2007 by Julie Paschkis. Reprinted by permission of Henry Holt and Company, LLC.

students are particularly taken by the book and almost immediately notice that Fleischman, through his words, and Julie Paschkis, through her illustrations, had woven motifs from many of the stories they have studied. "It's like all these people heard somebody tell this same story," one student remarked.

Mrs. Ramirez explained it appears that way because humans share many common experiences as they try to explain themselves and their world. What made the sun and the moon and the stars? Why are the animals made the way they are? What caused night and day, the seasons, the cycle of life itself? Why are some people greedy and some unselfish, some ugly and some handsome, some dull and some clever? As people pondered these questions and many more, they created stories that helped explain the world. And so people created their myths and their folktales, their legends and epics. Then as they were written down, we can learn about their particular cultural beliefs.

The students created elaborate Wiki pages (a Wiki being a type of Web site, or a collection of Web pages, that allows multiple users to create and add to the content) of the geographic and cultural elements of each story. Mrs. Ramirez helped provide additional historical, economic, and religious issues (local, regional, national, and global) related to the background of the cultures represented so that the students' pages would contain the rich heritage of stories that have come down to us from generations and generations around the world.

A Perspective on Traditional Literature

Traditional literature refers to all of the stories born of the oral tradition, the stories most often labeled "folklore," "folk literature," or "mythology." Generally we say that myths are about gods and the creation of things; legends are about heroes and their mighty deeds before the time of recorded history; and folktales, fairy tales, and fables are simple stories about talking beasts, woodcutters, and princesses who reveal human behavior and beliefs while playing out their roles in a world of wonder and magic.

In Western literature, two writers today strongly associated with folk literature are the Grimm brothers. However, when brothers Jacob and Wilhelm Grimm published the first volume of their *Household Stories* in 1812, they did not intend it for children. These early philologists were studying the language and grammar of such traditional tales. Today anthropologists study folklore in order to understand the inherent values and beliefs of a culture. Psychologists look at folktales and myths to learn about human motivation and feelings. Folklorists collect and categorize various stories, types, and motifs from around the world. These are all adult scholars of folk literature, which itself was first created by adults and usually told to an adult community. How, then, did folk literature become associated with children's literature, and what value does this kind of literature have for children?

Originally folklore was the literature of the people; stories were told to young and old alike. Families or tribes of the king's court would gather to hear a famous storyteller in much the same way that an entire family today will watch their favorite television program together. With the age of scientific enlightenment, these stories were relegated to the nursery, often kept alive by resourceful nursemaids or grandmothers, much to the delight of children.

Children today still enjoy these tales because they are good stories. Born of the oral tradition, these stories usually are short and have fast-moving plots. They frequently are humorous and almost always end happily. Poetic justice prevails; the good and the just are eventually rewarded; the evil are punished. This appeals to children's sense of justice and their moral judgment. Wishes come true, but usually not without the fulfillment of a task or trial. The littlest child, the youngest child, or the smallest animal succeeds; the oldest or the largest is frequently defeated. Youngsters, who are the little people of their world, thrive on such turns of events.

Beyond the function of pure entertainment, folktales can kindle the child's imagination. Behind every great author, poet, architect, mathematician, or diplomat are that person's dreams of what she or he hopes to achieve. These dreams or ideals have been created by the power of imagination. If we always give children stories of "what is"—stories that only mirror the living of today—then we have not helped them to imagine "what might have been" or "what might be."

Our speech and vocabulary reflect many contributions from traditional literature. Think of the figures of speech that come from Aesop's fables: "sour grapes," "dog in the manger," "boy who cried wolf." Our language is also replete with words and phrases from the myths—*narcissistic, cereal, labyrinth, siren,* and many more.

Traditional literature is a rightful part of a child's literary heritage and lays the groundwork for understanding all literature. Poetry and modern stories allude to traditional literature, particularly the Greek myths, Aesop's fables, and Bible stories. As you meet recurring patterns or symbols in mythlike floods, savior heroes, cruel stepmothers, the seasonal cycle of the year, and the cycle of a human life, you begin to build a framework for literature. Poetry, prose, and drama become more emotionally significant as you respond to these recurring archetypes.

This chapter discusses children's literature that comes from the oral tradition. It also includes a description of folktales, fables, myths, epics, and stories from the Bible, which are all a part of traditional literature. Modern parodies of traditional tales are discussed in Chapter 3 and modern literary fairy tales written by known authors are discussed in Chapter 5.

Folktales

Folktales have been defined as "forms of narrative written or oral which have been handed down over the years."[1] We think of these narratives as relatively brief stories with simple plots, sometimes simplistic characters, and generally happy endings.

Questions often arise about which of the available print versions of a tale is the "correct" or authentic text. From a folklorist's point of view, a tale is recreated every time it is told, and therefore *every* telling is correct in its own way. A great deal of variation is also acceptable in print versions, where literary style carries the same uniqueness as the teller's voice. Authors and illustrators may also add original twists, customize their stories for a chosen audience, or adapt a familiar tale to an unfamiliar setting, as oral storytellers do. There might be a problem, however, when a print version suggests by its title, or lack of an author's note, that it represents a tale derived directly from a previously printed source. Readers of a story identified as recorded and published by the Grimm brothers, for instance, have a right to find that this tale has been subsequently published without major additions, omissions, or distortions.

Types of Folktales

The folktales that have found their way into the hands and hearts of children come from many cultures. There will be features of these stories that are unique to each culture, but children will also find particular aspects of plot or characterization that occur across cultures. Recognizable literary patterns can be found in cumulative tales, pourquoi tales, beast tales, wonder tales, and realistic tales.

Cumulative Tales Very young children are fascinated by such cumulative stories as "The Old Woman and Her Pig" with its "Rat! rat! gnaw rope; rope won't hang butcher; butcher won't kill ox; ox won't drink water; water won't quench fire; fire won't burn stick; stick won't beat dog; dog won't bite pig; piggy won't get over the stile; and I shan't get home tonight." (See

The Old Woman and Her Pig: An Appalachian Folktale by Margaret Read MacDonald is a cumulative tale, one that repeats each previous episode as the story progresses. From *The Old Woman and Her Pig: An Appalachian Folktale* by Margaret Read MacDonald and illustrated by John Kanzler, copyright © 2007. Used by permission of HarperCollins Publishers.

versions by Margaret Read MacDonald and Eric Kimmel.) In cumulative tales, the story itself is not as important as the increasing repetition of the details building up to a quick climax.

The story of the gingerbread boy who ran away from the old woman, defiantly crying "Catch me if you can!" as in Paul Galdone's *The Gingerbread Boy,* has been told in many different versions, including Jim Aylesworth's *The Gingerbread Man* and Jan Brett's *Gingerbread Baby.* Richard Egielski has created an entirely modern setting for this traditional tale in his *The Gingerbread Boy.* Construction workers, street musicians, and other urban mainstays chase the mischievous cookie through the streets of New York City instead of the countryside.

In another familiar cumulative tale, one day an acorn falls on Henny Penny (see Steven Kellogg's *Chicken Little*). Thinking the sky is falling down, she persuades Cocky-Locky, Ducky-Daddles, Goosey-Poosey, and Turkey-Lurkey to go along with her to tell the king. Children delight in the sound of the rhyming double names, which are repeated over and over. Young children, especially, enjoy extending and personalizing these cumulative tales through dramatic play. You will find repetitive stories in practically all folklore.

Pourquoi Tales Some folktales are "why," or *pourquoi,* stories that explain certain animal traits or characteristics or human customs. In "How the Animals Got Their Tails" in *Beat the Story-Drum, Pum-Pum,* Ashley Bryan tells an African tale of a time when all animals were vegetarians. Then the god Raluvhimba created a mistake: flies who were flesh eaters and bloodsuckers. "I can't take back what I've done. After all, that's life," the god said. But he did give the rest of the animals tails with which to swish away the flies.

Many Native American stories are "why" stories that explain animal features, the origin of certain natural features, or how humans and their customs came to be. Paul Goble's retelling of a Cheyenne myth in *Her Seven Brothers* explains the origins of the Big Dipper. The Cherokee *Story of the Milky Way* has been retold by Joseph Bruchac and Gayle Ross.

Beast Tales Probably the favorite folktales of young children are beast tales in which animals act and talk like human beings. The best known of these frequently appear in newly illustrated versions. In his version of *The Three Little Pigs,* Paul Galdone portrays the wolf as a ferocious doggy creature. James Marshall's red-capped wolf looks like a thug in his red-striped polo shirt. Barry Moser's version has a particularly detestable wolf and an ultra-hip third little pig. Other beast tales found in several versions include Asbjørnsen and Moe's *The Three Billy Goats Gruff* (versions illustrated by Marcia Brown and Glen Rounds), *The Little Red Hen* (Jerry Pinkney, Paul Galdone, Margot Zemach), and *Puss in Boots* (Perrault).

Many African stories are "wise beast/foolish beast" tales of how one animal, such as a spider or rabbit, outwits a lion, hyena, leopard, or other foe. In Verna Aardema's *Rabbit Makes a Monkey of Lion,* Rabbit and Turtle steal Lion's honey and continually trick him into letting them go. So Lion hides in Rabbit's house in hopes of eating him for supper. But Rabbit notices the beast's footprints and calls out, "How-de-do, Little House." When the house doesn't reply, Rabbit pretends to be puzzled. "Little House, you always tell me *how-de-do.* Is something wrong today?" Of course, the confused Lion answers for the house, reveals his presence, and is tricked once again.

Many beast tales that traveled to the United States with enslaved Africans were collected by Joel Chandler Harris in the late 1800s. These have been retold by Julius Lester in a series that begins with *The Tales of Uncle Remus: The Adventures of Brer Rabbit.*

Talking animals appear in folktales of all cultures. Fish are often in English, Scandinavian, German, and South Seas stories. Tales of bears, wolves, and the fire-bird are found in Russian folklore. Spiders, rabbits, tortoises, crocodiles, monkeys, and lions are very much a part of African tales; rabbits, badgers, monkeys, and even bees are represented in Japanese stories. A study of just the animals in folklore would be fascinating.

Wonder Tales Children call wonder tales about magic and the supernatural "fairy tales." Very few tales have fairies or even a fairy godmother in them, but the name persists. Wicked witches, Baba Yaga in Russian folklore, demons such as the *oni* of Japanese tales, or monsters and dragons abound in these stories. Traditionally we have thought of the fairy tale as involving romance and adventure. "Cinderella," "Snow White and the Seven Dwarfs," and "Beauty and the Beast" all have elements of both. The long quest tales—such as the Norwegian tale told in George Dasent's *East o'the Sun and West o'the Moon*—are complex wonder tales in which the hero, or heroine, triumphs against all odds to win the beautiful princess, or handsome prince, and makes a fortune. Children know that these tales will end with ". . . and they lived happily ever after." In fact, part of the appeal of the fairy tale is the secure knowledge that no matter what happens, love, kindness, and truth will prevail—and hate, wickedness, and evil will be punished. Wonder tales have always represented the glorious fulfillment of human desires.

Realistic Tales Surprisingly, there are a few realistic tales included in folklore. The story in Marcia Brown's *Dick Whittington and His Cat* could have happened; in fact, there is evidence that a Richard Whittington did indeed live and was mayor of London. Like the American story in Reeve Lindbergh's *Johnny Appleseed,* the tale began with a real person but has become so embroidered through various tellings that it takes its place in the folklore of its culture.

Dianne Snyder's *The Boy of the Three-Year Nap* is a humorous realistic folktale involving trickery. A poor widow, tired of supporting her son Taro, who is "lazy as a rich man's cat," pesters him to go to work for a rich rice merchant. Declining to work, the boy tricks the merchant into betrothing him to his daughter. Taro's mother works her own ruse, however, and in the end Taro is caught in his own tricks.

Teaching Feature 4.1: A Cross-Cultural Study of Folktale Types on page 100 is the first of two boxes in this chapter that group folktales from various countries in specific ways to help teachers more easily plan curricula. This box groups together titles that tell similar tales.

Evaluating Folktales

Because folktales have been told and retold from generation to generation within a particular culture, we may ask how they reflect the country of their origin and its oral tradition. An authentic tale from Africa will include references to the flora and fauna of Africa and to the tribespeople's food, huts, customs, foibles, and beliefs. It will sound like it is being *told*. Although folktales have many elements in common, it would be difficult to confuse a folktale from Japan with a folktale from the fjords of

A Cross-Cultural Study of Folktale Types

Tale (Author)	Culture or Country/Place of Origin
Cumulative Tales: An increasing repetition of the details builds up to a quick climax.	
Chicken Little (Kellogg)	England
The Little, Little House (Souhami)	Eastern European, Jewish
One Fine Day (Hogrogian)	Armenia
Only One Cowry (Gershator)	Dahomey, Africa
The Rooster Who Went to His Uncle's Wedding (Ada)	Cuba
What about Me? (Young)	Sufi (Middle East)
Pourquoi Tales: Folktales that explain why (French "pourquoi") certain animal traits or characteristics or human customs have developed.	
The Cat's Purr (Bryan)	West Indian
The Golden Flower (Jaffee)	Puerto Rico
How Chipmunk Got His Stripes (Bruchac and Bruchac)	Native American
Tuko and the Birds (Climo)	Philippines
Why the Sun and the Moon Live in the Sky (Dayrell)	Africa
Beast Tales: Tales in which animals act and talk like human beings.	
Beat the Story-Drum, Pum-Pum (Bryan)	Africa
The Bremen-Town Musicians (Grimm brothers, Orgel)	Germany
King Pom and the Fox (Souhami)	Japan
Mabela the Clever (MacDonald)	Africa
The Rabbit's Tail (Han)	Korea
Wonder Tales: Longer and more complicated tales about magic and the supernatural, often called *fairy tales*.	
The Bearskinner (Schlitz)	Germany
The Castle of Cats (Kimmel)	Ukraine
The Great Smelly, Slobbery, Small-Tooth Dog (MacDonald)	Great Britain
The Tale of the Firebird (Spirin)	Russia
Realistic Tales: Stories from the oral tradition that involve no magic.	
The Boy of the Three-Year Nap (Snyder)	Japan
Dick Whittington and His Cat (Brown, Hodges)	England
The Empty Pot (Demi)	China
Fire on the Mountain (Kurtz)	Ethiopia
Something from Nothing (Gilman)	Jewish

Norway. What are some of the things to look for when reading folktales? What are the characteristics common to all folktales? The box **Guidelines: Evaluating Traditional Literature** summarizes the criteria that need to be considered when evaluating this genre for children.

Characteristics of Folktales

Plot Structures Of the folktales best known in children's literature, even the longer stories are usually simple and direct. A series of episodes maintains a quick flow of action. If it is a "wise beast/foolish beast" story, the characters are quickly delineated, the action shows the inevitable conflict and resolution, and the ending is usually brief. If the tale is a romance, the hero or heroine sets forth on a journey, often helps the poor on the way, frequently receives magical power, overcomes obstacles, and returns to safety. The plot that involves a weak or innocent child going forth to meet the monsters of the world is another form of the "journey-novel." In the Grimm brothers' *Hansel and Gretel,* the children go out into a dark world and meet the witch, but goodness and purity triumph. Almost all folktale plots are success stories of one kind or another (unlike many myths, in which characters meet a sad end through their own human failings).

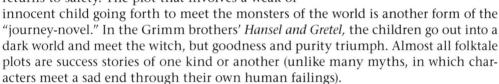

Guidelines

Evaluating Traditional Literature

Go to **www.mhhe.com/kieferbrief1e** *to access an expanded version of this evaluation form.*

Consider the following when evaluating folktales for children:

- Is there some mention or citation of the original source for folktales?
- Is the plot simple and direct?
- Is the language lively and engaging and in keeping with the oral tradition?

- Does a theme emerge from the telling of the tale? If so, what is the story's message or moral?
- Do illustrations add to and extend the story? Are illustrations and details true to the culture represented?
- Does the story represent cultural norms, or is it rewritten to conform to Western mores?

Repetition is a basic element in many folktale plots, and "three" is often the magic number. There are three little pigs whose three houses face the puffing of the wolf. The wolf gives three challenges to the pig in the brick house—to get turnips, to get apples, and to go to the fair. In the longer tales, each of the three tasks becomes increasingly more difficult, and the intensity of the wonders becomes progressively more marvelous. This repetition satisfies listeners or readers with its orderliness.

Time and place are established quickly in the folktale. Virginia Hamilton opens *The Girl Who Spun Gold* with "There be this tale told about a tiny fellow who could hide in a foot of shade amid old trees." Time is always past and frequently described by such conventions as "Once upon a time" or "In olden times when wishing still helped." The setting of the folktale is not specific, but in some faraway land, in a cottage in the woods, or in a beautiful palace.

The conclusion of the story follows the climax very quickly and includes few details. In Laura Amy Schlitz's *The Bearskinner,* a poor solider makes a pact with the devil. He must wear a bearskin for seven years in return for all the money he wants. A gambler's middle daughter promises to wait for the loathsome Bearskinner in return for settling her father's debts. When the soldier returns, rid of his bearskin and looking young and handsome, the middle daughter recognizes him by his kind eyes. The story ends as follows:

> So the middle daughter married the Bearskinner. The love between them lasted a lifetime and so did the soldier's fortune. He always had more than enough and always shared with people who had nothing.
> And never again did he bargain with the devil. (unpaged)[2]

Even this is a long ending compared with "And so they were married and lived happily ever after."

The structure of the folktale, with its quick introduction, economy of incident, and logical and brief conclusion, maintains interest through suspense and repetition. Because the storyteller has to keep the attention of the audience, each episode must contribute to the theme of the story. Written versions, then, should follow the oral tradition, adding little description and avoiding lengthy asides or admonitions.

Characterization Characters in folktales are shown in flat dimensions, symbolic of the completely good or entirely evil. Character development is seldom depicted. The beautiful girl is usually virtuous, humble, patient, and loving. Stepmothers are ugly, cross, and mean. The hero, usually fair-haired or curly-haired, is strong, virile, brave, kind, and sympathetic. The poor are often kind, generous, and long-suffering; the rich are imperious, hard-hearted, and often conniving, if not actually dishonest. Physical characteristics may be described briefly, but readers form their own pictures as they read.

Qualities of character or special strengths or weaknesses of the characters are revealed quickly because this factor will be the cause of conflict or lead to resolution of the plot. The heroine in *Clever Beatrice* by Margaret Willey is established in a few phrases:

> "Sure, she was little but Beatrice loved riddles and tricks and she could think fast on her feet. Sharp as a tack," said her mother.[3]

Seeing folktale characters as symbols of good, evil, power, trickery, wisdom, and other traits, children begin to understand the basis of literature that distills the essences of human experience.

Style Folktales offer children many opportunities to hear rich qualitative language and a wide variety of language patterns. Story introductions may range from the familiar "Once upon a time" to the Persian "There was a time and there wasn't a time"; and then there is the African tale that starts: "We do not mean, we do not really mean that what we are going to say is true."

The introductions and language of the folktale should maintain the "flavor" of the country but still be understood by its present audience. Some folktales include proverbs of the country. For example, in Diane Wolkstein's *The Magic Orange Tree*, a king says to his followers after hearing the story of a man whose second wife murdered his son: "Choose whom you want to marry, but if you choose a tree that has fruit, you must care for the fruit as much as for the tree."

Frequently storytellers imitate the sounds of the story. In Verna Aardema's retelling of a West African tale in *Why Mosquitoes Buzz in People's Ears,* a python slithers into a rabbit's hole *wasawusu, wasawusu, wasawusu,* and the terrified rabbit scurries away *krik, krik, krik.* These onomatopoeic words help listeners hear the story and are wonderful additions for those who tell and read stories to children.

When the tales are written as though the storyteller is speaking directly to the reader, the oral tradition is more clearly communicated. Joyce Arkhurst uses this style effectively in *The Adventures of Spider:*

> I have already told you, and you have already seen for yourselves, that Spider was very full of mischief. He was often naughty and always greedy. But sometimes, in his little heart, he wanted very much to be good. . . . He tried hard, but his appetite almost always got in the way. In fact, that is why Spider has a bald head to this day. Would you like to hear how it got that way? (p. 21)

Dialect enhances a story, but it is difficult for children to read. The teacher will need to practice reading or telling a story with dialect, but it is worth the effort if it is done well. Julius Lester, in his retellings of the Uncle Remus stories collected by Joel Chandler Harris, tried to do what Harris had done: namely, to write tales "so that the reader (listener) would feel as if he or she were being called into a relationship of warmth and intimacy with another human body."[4] His contemporary storyteller communicates through asides, imagery, and allusions. For instance, in "Brer Rabbit Gets Even," in Julius Lester's *Uncle Remus: The Complete Tales,* Brer Rabbit decides to visit with Miz Meadows and the girls:

> Don't come asking me who Miz Meadows and her girls were. I don't know, but then again, ain't no reason I got to know. Miz Meadows and the girls were in the tale when it was handed to me, and they gon' be in it when I hand it to you. And that's the way the rain falls on that one. . . . (p. 16)

The major criteria for style in the written folktale, then, are that it maintain the atmosphere of the country and culture from which it originated and that it sound like a tale *told* by a storyteller.

Themes The basic purpose of the folktale is to tell an entertaining story, yet these stories do present important themes. Some tales might be merely humorous accounts of foolish people who are so ridiculous that the listeners see their own foolish ways exaggerated in them. Many of the stories once provided an outlet for feelings against the kings and nobles who oppressed the poor. Values of the culture are expressed in

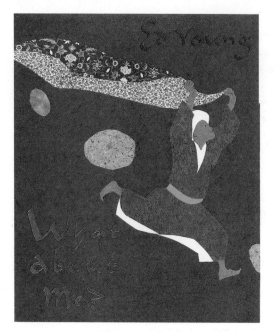

folklore. Humility, kindness, patience, sympathy, hard work, and courage are invariably rewarded. These rewards reflect the goals of people—long life, a good spouse, beautiful homes, fine clothing, plenty of food, and freedom from fear of the ogre or giant. Sometimes these themes are stated explicitly at the end of the book as in Ed Young's *What About Me?* In this story a young boy approaches the Grand Master to ask for knowledge. He is sent out to get a small carpet for the Master's work. This, of course, is not as simple a task as it sounds. After many arduous trials the boy finds that the knowledge he sought was already his. The Grand Master cautions, "Some of the most precious gifts that we receive are those we receive when we are giving," and "Often, knowledge comes to us when we least expect it." (p. 32)

Many folktales feature the small and powerless achieving good ends by perseverance and patience. In Gail Haley's African tale *A Story, a Story,* Anansi the spider man wins stories for his people by outsmarting a leopard, the hornets, and a fairy and presenting them all to the Sky God. Characters such as Blanche in Robert D. San Souci's *The Talking Eggs* and Manyana in John Steptoe's *Mufaro's Beautiful Daughters* have good luck when they are kind to objects and animals.

Feminists have expressed concern that folktale themes most often favor courageous, independent boy adventurers and leave girl characters languishing at home. Though it is true that it is easier to find tales that feature plucky boys, there are folktales that portray resourceful, courageous, clever, and independent girls. In the Grimm brothers' *Princess Furball,* the heroine doesn't need a fairy godmother; she wins a prince because of her own cleverness. In Katrin Tchana's *Sense Pass King,* the heroine receives that name because she is smarter than the ruler. Because of her sense and great courage, she outsmarts the king. She becomes the ruler in his stead and gains a new name, Queen Ma'antah.

Parents, teachers, and some psychologists have expressed concern about themes of cruelty and horror in folktales. "Little Red Riding Hood," for example, has been rewritten so that the wolf eats neither the grandmother nor the heroine. Goals are not accomplished easily in folktales; they frequently require sacrifice. But usually harsh acts occur very quickly with no sense of pain and no details. In the Grimm brothers' *Snow White and the Seven Dwarfs,* illustrated by Nancy Ekholm Burkert, Snow White's stepmother dances to death in her iron shoes but we do not see this action, only the empty shoes at the top of a staircase. Children accept these stories as they are—symbolic interpretations of life in an imaginary land of another time.

Motifs and Variants Folklorists analyze folktales according to motifs or patterns, numbering each tale and labeling its episodes. *Motif* has been defined as the smallest part of a tale that can exist independently.[5] Motifs can be seen in the recurring parade of characters in folktales—the younger brother, the wicked stepmother, the abused child, the clever trickster—or in supernatural beings like the fairy godmother, the evil witch, and the terrifying giant. The use of magical objects (such as a slipper, a doll, a ring, a tablecloth) is another pattern found in many folktales. Stories of enchantment, long sleeps, or marvelous transformations are typical motifs. Some motifs have been repeated so frequently that they have been identified as a type of folk story. Thus we have beast tales about talking animals and wonder tales about supernatural beings.

Even the story plots have recurring patterns—three tasks to be performed, three wishes that are granted, three trials to be endured. A simple tale will have several motifs; a complex one will have many. Recognizing some of the most common motifs in folklore will help a teacher to suggest points of comparison and contrast in a cross-cultural approach to folk literature.

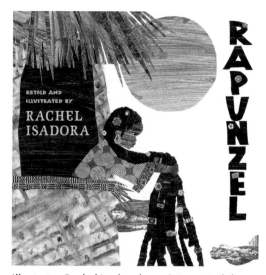

Illustrator Rachel Isadora has reinterpreted the traditional Grimm brothers' story of *Rapunzel* with an African setting. From *Rapunzel* by Rachel Isadora and illustrated by Rachel Isadora, copyright © 2008. Used by permission of Penguin Group (USA) Inc., 345 Hudson Street, New York, NY 10014. All rights reserved.

When a folktale is from a single source but interpreted differently by an illustrator, we refer to it as a *version* of a folktale. Rachel Isadora and Niki Daly have interpreted several tales from the Brothers Grimm, including *The Fisherman and His Wife, Rapunzel,* and *Pretty Salma: A Red Riding Hood Story from Africa* (Daly). Both provide lively African settings for their tales. Although Isadora has been faithful to the Grimm version in her stories, Eric Kimmel and illustrator Martha Aviles have set the Grimm brothers' story of "The Fisherman and His Wife" in the Aztec culture in *The Fisherman and the Turtle.*

In contrast to folktale versions, folktale *variants* do not derive from the same original source but share many characters, similarities, or motifs in common. For example, in Robert D. San Souci's retelling of an African American story in *The Talking Eggs,* a poor girl is kind to an old woman and in return is given some plain eggs that become riches when tossed behind her. Later her greedy stepsister is critical and unhelpful to the old woman. She chooses to take fancy eggs instead of plain ones, but when these are tossed, out come stinging insects. In John Steptoe's *Mufaro's Beautiful Daughters,* the sister who takes time to stop and help people is the one who wins the prince's love. The theme of rewards for a generous and willing person and punishment for a greedy and disobedient one seems to be universal.

As we saw in the opening vignette, a comparison of the variants of what we would call a "Cinderella" story illustrates differences in theme and motif that can be found in cultures from around the world. Scholars have found versions of this story in ancient Egypt, in ninth-century China, and in tenth-century Iceland. Cinderella receives her magical gifts in many different ways. In the French and most familiar version (see Charles Perrault's *Cinderella* illustrated by Marcia Brown), a fairy godmother gives them to her; in the Grimms' version, a dove appears on the tree that grew from the tears she had shed on her mother's grave; in Ai-Ling Louie's Chinese version titled *Yeh-Shen,* magical fish bones bestow gifts on her. She attends three balls in some stories, and her treatment of the stepsisters varies from blinding them to inviting them to live at the palace.

Knowledge of the variants of a tale, common motifs, and common types of folktales enable teachers to help children see similar elements in folktales across cultures. Knowledge of the folklore of a particular country or cultural group aids in identifying the uniqueness and individuality of that group. Both approaches to a study of folklore seem essential.

Every culture has produced folklore. In-depth studies of the folktales of Asia, Africa, the Middle East, or indigenous America can provide insights into the beliefs of these peoples, their values, their jokes, their lifestyles, and their histories. At the same time, a cross-cultural study of folk literature by types, motifs, and variants can help children discover the universal qualities of humankind. **Teaching Feature 4.2: A Cross-Cultural Study of Folktale Motifs and Variants** can help you organize tales by variants for classroom presentation.

teaching feature 4.2

A Cross-Cultural Study of Folktale Motifs and Variants

Theme (Author)	Culture or Country/Place of Origin
Cinderella	
Adelita (dePaola)	Mexico
Cendrillon (R. San Souci)	Caribbean
Cinderella (Perrault)	France
The Egyptian Cinderella (Climo)	Egypt
Fair, Brown, and Trembling (Daly)	Ireland
The Gift of the Crocodile (Sierra)	Indonesia
The Golden Sandal (Hickox)	Middle East
Kongi and Potgi (Han)	Korea
The Korean Cinderella (Climo)	Korea
The Little Gold Star (R. San Souci)	Spanish American
Moss Gown (Hooks)	United States
Princess Furball (Grimm brothers)	Germany

teaching feature 4.2

Theme (Author)	Culture or Country/Place of Origin
The Rough-Face Girl (Martin)	Native American
Yeh-Shen (Louie)	China
Magical Objects or Gifts	
The Bachelor and the Bean (Fowles)	Moroccan Jewish
"The Lad Who Went to the North Wind," in *East o' the Sun and West o' the Moon* (Asbjørnsen and Moe)	Norway
The Magic Gourd (Diakité)	Mali
The Magic Porridge Pot (Galdone)	Germany
The Table, the Donkey, and the Stick (Grimm brothers)	Germany
Tunjur! Tunjur! Tunjur! (MacDonald)	Palestine
Willa and the Wind (Del Negro)	Scandinavia
Generous Person/Greedy Person	
The Impudent Rooster (Rascol)	Romania
Mufaro's Beautiful Daughters (Steptoe)	Africa (Zimbabwe)
Me-An and the Magic Serpent (Diakité)	Mali
The Talking Eggs (R. San Souci)	African American
Toads and Diamonds (Huck)	France
The Well at the End of the World (R. San Souci)	England
Helpful Companions	
Anansi the Spider (McDermott)	West Africa
The Fool of the World and the Flying Ship (Ransome)	Russia
Iron John (Kimmel)	Germany
The Seven Chinese Brothers (Mahy)	China
The Shark God (Martin)	Hawaii
The Silver Charm (R. San Souci)	Japan
Naming	
Ananse and the Lizard (Cummings)	West Africa
Duffy and the Devil (H. Zemach)	England
The Girl Who Spun Gold (Hamilton)	West Indies
Rumpelstiltskin (Grimm brothers)	Germany

Fables

Fables are usually associated with Aesop, a Greek slave who is supposed to have been born in Asia Minor about 600 B.C. Some scholars doubt his actual existence and believe that his works were the product of several storytellers. We know that some of the fables appeared in Greek literature two centuries before Aesop's birth and in India and Egypt before that. The first written fables were in Greek, translated into Latin and again into English by William Caxton, and printed in 1484.

Other sources for fables are the Jataka tales—animal stories that told of the previous births of the Buddha—and the *Panchatantra,* which was written for the purpose of instructing the young princes of India. These stories, longer than Aesop's fables, have moralistic verses interspersed throughout. When these are removed, the tales are closer to folktales.

A third common source for fables is the work of Jean De La Fontaine, a French poet, who wrote his fables in verse form. However, he drew largely on the collections of Aesop's fables that were available in the seventeenth century.

Characteristics of Fables

Fables are brief, didactic tales in which animals, or occasionally the elements, speak as human beings. Examples of these might be the well-known race between the hare and the tortoise or the contest between the sun and the north wind. Humans do appear in a few fables, such as *The Boy Who Cried Wolf* (Hennessy). The characters are impersonal, with no name other than "fox," rabbit," or "cow." They do not have the lively personalities of Anansi the spider or Raven the trickster of folktale fame. The animals merely represent aspects of human nature—the lion stands for kingliness, the fox for cunning, the sheep for innocence and simplicity, and so on. Fables seldom have more than three characters, and the plots are usually based on a single incident. Fables were primarily meant to instruct. Therefore, all of them contain either an implicit or an explicit moral.

Because of their brevity, fables appear to be simple. However, they convey an abstract idea in relatively few words, and for that very reason they are highly complex. Younger children might appreciate some fables, but they are not usually able to extract a moral spontaneously until about second or third grade. There are many fine collections of fables to share with children.

Editions

Jerry Pinkney applies his characteristic style to *Aesop's Fables* with grand results. His exquisite watercolor illustrations for sixty of Aesop's best tales make this an essential collection for classrooms and libraries. The book is meticulously designed, and Pinkney's multicultural interpretation of human and animal characters is highly original. Veronica Uribe expands her sights beyond Aesop to include fables from around the world in *Little Book of Fables.* Constanza Bravo's stylish illustrations complement Uribe's delightful and lively retellings. John Bierhorst, a distinguished collector and editor of Native American literature, discovered that Aesop's fables had been recorded by the Aztecs in the sixteenth century. His *Doctor Coyote* is a collection of these stories, translated from the Aztec manuscript, in which the main character of each fable became Coyote, a Native American trickster. Bierhorst's cohesive collection of twenty fables weaves one story into the next and shows Coyote getting a little wiser with each "lesson."

Other illustrators have chosen single tales for interpretation. Startling close-ups heighten the drama of "little and big" in Ed Young's black-and-white illustrations for *The Lion and the Mouse*. By contrast, Young's vividly colored collages for the Indian fable *Seven Blind Mice* highlight the patchwork nature of understanding that these mice bring to their definition of an elephant.

Older children might enjoy comparing treatments of several of these fables. In this way they would become familiar with the spare language, the conventional characters, and the explicit or implied morals of fables. They will appreciate Amy Lowry Poole's Chinese setting for a retelling of "The Grasshopper and the Ant," and they will enjoy reading modern writers of fables, such as William Steig, whose *Amos and Boris* mirrors "The Lion and the Mouse." After such comparisons, discussions, and readings, they would then be well prepared to write their own fables and variations.

Myths

Mythology evolved as primitive peoples searched their imaginations and related events to forces as they sought explanations of the earth, sky, and human behavior. These explanations moved slowly through the stages of a concept of one power or force in human form, who controlled the phenomena of nature; to a complex system in which the god or goddess represented such virtues as wisdom, purity, or love; to a worshipping of the gods in organized fashion. Gods took the forms of men and women, but they were immortal and possessed supernatural powers.

Myths deal with human relationships with the gods, with the relationships of the gods among themselves, with the way people accept or fulfill their destiny, and with people's struggles with good and evil forces both within themselves and outside themselves. The myths are good stories, too, for they contain action, suspense, and basic conflicts. Usually each story is short and can be enjoyed by itself, without deep knowledge of the general mythology.

Many myths can be characterized by the type of explanation they offer about the beginnings of the world or about some natural phenomenon. Other myths might focus on difficult tasks or obstacles to be overcome by the hero or heroine.

Creation Myths

Every culture has a story about how the world began, how people were made, and how the sun and the moon got into the sky. These are called creation myths, or origin myths; they give an explanation for the beginnings of things. Virginia Hamilton chose creation stories from around the world for her collection *In the Beginning*.

> These myths from around the world were created by people who sensed the wonder and glory of the universe. Lonely as they were, by themselves, early people looked inside themselves and expressed a longing to discover, to explain who they were, why they were, and from what and where they came. (p. xi)

Barry Moser's watercolor portraits and representations are mysterious and dramatic accompaniments to these tales. An Eskimo story tells how Raven the Creator made a pea pod from which humans sprang. A Chinese story explains how Phan Ku burst from a cosmic egg to create the world. A California Indian legend, "Turtle Dives to the Bottom of the Sea," begins with a sea turtle that dives underwater to bring up enough earth to make dry land.

Nature Myths

The nature myths include stories that explain seasonal changes, animal characteristics, earth formations, constellations, and the movements of the sun and earth. Many Native American nature myths are easier for young children to comprehend than are the creation myths. Some of these myths have been previously discussed in the section "Pourquoi Tales."

The Greek story of Demeter and Persephone explains the change of seasons. Hades, god of the underworld, carried Persephone off to the underworld to be his bride, and Demeter, her mother, who made plants grow, mourned so for her daughter that she asked Zeus to intercede. It was granted that the girl might return if she had eaten nothing in Hades. Because she had eaten four seeds of a pomegranate, she was compelled to return to Hades for four months each year, during which time the earth suffered and winter came. Warwick Hutton has illustrated a picturebook edition of *Persephone*.

Hero Myths

The hero myths, found in many cultures, do not attempt to explain anything at all. These myths have some of the same qualities as wonder stories—the hero is given certain tasks or, in the case of Heracles, labors, to accomplish. Frequently the gods help (or hinder) a particular favorite (or disliked) mortal. Monsters, such as gorgons, hydras, and chimeras, are plentiful in the Greek stories, but these provide the hero with a challenge. Characteristic of the hero or heroine is that he or she accepts all dangerous assignments and accomplishes the quest or dies in one last glorious adventure. Robert Byrd has created a fine introduction to the Greek hero Theseus in *The Hero and the Minotaur*.

Editions

Greek mythology is composed of many stories of gods and goddesses, heroes, and monsters. The Greeks were the first to see their gods in their own image. As their culture became more sophisticated and complex, so too did their stories of the gods. These personified gods could do anything that humans could do, but on a much mightier scale. The gods, although immortal, freely entered into the lives of mortals, helping or hindering them, depending on their particular moods. Their strength was mighty and so was their wrath. Many of the myths are concerned with the gods' conflicts and loves. Their jealousy and their struggles for power often caused trouble for humans. (Some of the stories concerning the loves and quarrels of the immortals are inappropriate for children.)

Children who have a good background in folktales will find that many of the same elements are present in the Greek myths. In *D'Aulaires' Book of Greek Myths* the story of King Midas is economically told in two pages with a bold stone lithograph illustration. The D'Aulaires' collection presents a well-woven selection of tales ranging from the birth of Cronus's children to the stories of the mortal descendants of Zeus. Geraldine McCaughrean's *Greek Gods and Goddesses* provides an introduction to the pantheon.

Norse myths appeal to the child's imagination, with their tales of giants and dwarfs, eight-legged horses and vicious wolves, magic hammers, and rings. Primarily they are bold, powerful stories of the relationships among the gods and their battles against the evil frost giants. Odin is the serious protector of the humans he created, willingly sacrificing one of his eyes to obtain wisdom that would allow him to see deep into their hearts. The largest and the strongest of the gods is Thor, owner of a magic hammer that will hit its mark and then return to his hands. And Balder, the tragic god of light, is the most loved by all the other gods. Ingri D'Aulaire and Edgar Parin D'Aulaire's *Book of Norse Myths,* out of print for some years, has been recently reissued and is a good introduction to the body of Norse myths and heroes for children of all ages.

Epic and Legendary Heroes

An epic is a long narrative or a cycle of stories clustering around the actions of a single hero. Epics grew out of myths or along with them, since the gods still intervene in earlier epics like the *Iliad* and the *Odyssey.* Gradually, the center of action shifted from the gods to human heroes, so that in tales like "Robin Hood" the focus is completely on the daring adventures of the man himself.

The epic hero is a cultural or national hero embodying all the ideal characteristics of greatness in his time. The Epic of Gilgamesh, composed more than four thousand years ago in Mesopotamia, is one of the oldest hero stories. It is a tale about the power and importance of human compassion. The epic poem, first discovered written on clay tablets in the library of Assur-Bani-Pal, an Assyrian king who ruled from 668 to 626 B.C., is probably the compilation of many earlier myths. The Greek hero Odysseus and Penelope, his wife, represented the Greek ideals of intelligence, persistence, and resourcefulness. Odysseus survived by his wit rather than his great strength. The hero Beowulf battles three terrible foes, including Grendel to save the Danish Kingdom of Heorot. King Arthur and Robin Hood appealed to the English's love of justice and freedom: King Arthur and his knights represented the code of chivalry; Robin Hood was the champion of the commoner—the prototype of the "good outlaw." The epics, then, express the highest moral values of a society. A knowledge of the epics gives children an understanding of a particular culture; but more importantly, it provides them with models of greatness through the ages.

Editions

Canadian author Ludmila Zeman has retold and illustrated three episodes of the Gilgamesh epic in a highly readable trio of picture books. In *Gilgamesh the King* we are introduced to the god-king who plays the central role in the three books. He is a bitter and cruel king because he has not experienced the power of human companionship. When his desire to build a great wall threatens his people's survival, the sun god sends Enkidu, another man as strong as Gilgamesh, to earth, where he lives in the forest and cares for the animals. When he threatens one of Gilgamesh's hunters, Gilgamesh sends the lovely singer Shamat to tempt Enkidu out of the forest. In spite of his beastly appearance, she teaches him about human love and they leave the forest to confront Gilgamesh. The two men engage in a terrible struggle on Gilgamesh's famous wall, but because their powers are equal they seem to be at an impasse. Then Gilgamesh stumbles on a stone and would fall to his death except that Enkidu reaches out a hand to help him. Gilgamesh's experience with human kindness is transforming, and the two become like brothers. In the second book, *The Revenge of Ishtar,* the two meet the goddess Ishtar, who offers to marry Gilgamesh and give him a chariot of gold. When he spurns her, he makes a great enemy who will plague him all his life and cause the deaths of Shamat and Enkidu. In *The Last Quest of Gilgamesh,* the great king is so heartbroken by the death of his friends that he sets out to find the secret of immortality. When he learns that Utnapishtim is the only human who knows that secret, Gilgamesh endures a terrible journey across the waters of death to Utnapishtim's island. Utnapishtim explains that he arrived on the island on a great ark after he had been warned of a terrible flood that would destroy the earth. Gilgamesh cannot accomplish the task that Utnapishtim sets him to become immortal, and after one more battle with Ishtar he returns home heartbroken at his failure. Enkidu is sent by the gods to show him that the immortality he craves is there in the great civilization he has created. Zeman's majestic illustrations, done in mixed media and incorporating motifs from Mesopotamian art, have a wonderful sense of timelessness. Geraldine McCaughrean has provided a superb retelling of the epic for older readers in *Gilgamesh the Hero.*

Homer's *The Odyssey* is the story of the hazardous ten-year journey of Odysseus (called Ulysses by the Romans) from Troy to his home in Ithaca, following the end of the war. Odysseus has one terrifying experience after another, which he manages to survive by his cunning. For example, he defeats the horrible one-eyed Cyclops by blinding him and then strapping his men to the undersides of sheep, which were allowed to leave the cave. His ship safely passes between the whirlpool of Charybdis and the monster Scylla, but later is shipwrecked and delayed for seven years. A loyal servant and his son aid the returned hero in assuming his rightful throne and saving his wife, Penelope, who has had a difficult time discouraging the many suitors who wished to become king. While children or teachers might be acquainted with episodes from the story, it is the total force of all of Odysseus's trials that presents the full dimensions of this hero. The wanderings of Odysseus have also come to provide the template for many contemporary journey stories. A good introduction to the epic is the Tales from the Odyssey series by Mary Pope Osborne. In books such as *The One-Eyed Giant* and *Mermaids and Monsters,* illustrated by Troy Howell, Osborne retells one of the episodes from Odysseus's journey. Geraldine McCaughrean and Rosemary Sutcliff have both written versions of the *Odyssey* for middle-grade readers. Sutcliff's *Black Ships before Troy: The Story of the Iliad* is a fine companion book. Padraic Colum's *The Children's Homer* keeps the essence of the traditional poem, and Willy Pogany's illustrations distinguish this book from others. An edition suitable for older readers is Colum's *The Trojan War and the Adventures of Odysseus,* illustrated by Barry Moser.

The epic of Beowulf has been interpreted in two fine editions for children. Nicky Raven's *Beowulf: A Tale of Blood, Heat, and Ashes* is illustrated by reknown fantasy artist John Howe and at seventy-two pages is suitable for older readers. Raven includes a foreword describing the tale's origins and an appendix containing character biographies. James Rumford's *Beowulf: A Hero's Tale Retold* is shorter than Raven's and suitable for middle graders and older. Extraordinarily, Rumford has told the story using only words that can be traced back to Old English. In addition, he includes Old English words and pronunciation guides. An afterword is included with information about the origin of the story and the language in which it was originally told.

It took Beowulf half a day to reach the bottom. There Grendel's mother was watching.

In a whoosh she was on him, sticking her sharp claws into his iron-woven shirt.

When she could not break through to his flesh, she let her dragons tear at him with their tusks and teeth and claws.

Beowulf withstood them all, and, one by one, they swam away.

The mouth of the hag's lair—made so that no water seeped inside—beckoned.

He went in.

A fire blazed inside. In its glow stood Grendel's mother, in all her might.

James Rumford has retold the epic *Beowulf: A Hero's Tale Retold* in English words that can be traced back to the original Old English. Illustration from *Beowulf: A Hero's Tale Retold* by James Rumford. Copyright © 2008 by James Rumford. Reprinted by permission of Houghton Mifflin Harcourt Publishing Company. All rights reserved.

The *Ramayana* is the great epic tale of India that tells how the noble Rama, his devoted brother, and his beautiful, virtuous wife, Sita, manage to defeat the evil demon Ravana. Heir to the throne, Rama is banished from his home through the trickery of his stepmother. Prince Rama, his brother Lakshmana, and the devoted Sita spend fourteen years in wandering and adventure. One day Sita vanishes, kidnapped by Ravana. Rama searches for her unsuccessfully and then turns to a tribe of monkeys for help. Finally Sita is found, and with the help of an entire army of monkeys, Rama rescues her. To be cleansed from her association with the demon, Sita must withstand a trial by fire. Her faithfulness proved, she is united with her beloved Rama. Peace and plenty prevail during Rama's reign.

Composed in India by the sage Vlamiki during the fourth century B.C., the *Ramayana* represented some 24,000 couplets that were memorized and repeated. It constitutes part of the gospel of Hindu scripture, for Rama and his wife are held as the ideal man and woman. Rama is believed to be an incarnation of the god Vishnu come to earth in human form.

Surely Western children should know something of this epic hero who is so important to a large part of the world. Jessica Souhami's *Rama and the Demon King* is a picturebook version that focuses on Rama's exile and his battle with Ravana. Souhami's cut-paper illustrations recall Indian folk art forms and provide the story with a dramatic touch. David Weitzman pays visual homage to Indonesian stick puppets in his illustrations for *Rama and Sita: A Tale from Ancient Java*. A longer version of Rama and Sita's story can be found in *The Story of Divaali*, retold by Jatinder Verma.

The Bible as Literature

All children deserve to know the spiritual and religious beliefs that have shaped the world in which they live. This religious heritage is often conveyed in the form of stories. As we have seen in this chapter, many peoples around the world have their creation stories, and there are numerous recountings of a great flood. In particular, many Native American stories reflect the religious beliefs of their tellers. The Jataka and Panchatantra stories come from Buddhist traditions and the *Ramayana* from Hindu scriptures. The Bible has an important and rightful place in any comprehensive discussion of traditional literature because it is a written record of people's continuing search to understand themselves and their relationships with others and their creator. It makes little sense to tell children the story of Jack the Giant Killer and then deny them the stories about David and Goliath or Samson. They read of the wanderings of Odysseus, but not those of Moses. They learn in Gilgamesh that Utnapishtim built an ark and survived a flood, but do not know the story of Noah. Our fear should not be that children will know the Bible; rather, it should be that they will not know it. Whatever our religious persuasion or nonpersuasion, children should not be denied their right to knowledge of the traditional literature of the Bible. Children cannot fully understand other literature unless they are familiar with the outstanding characters, incidents, poems, proverbs, and parables of this literature of the Western world of thought.

We must clarify the difference between the practice of religious customs, indoctrination in one viewpoint, and study of the Bible as a great work of literature. In 1963 the Supreme Court asserted that "religious exercises" in public schools violated the First Amendment, but also encouraged study of the Bible as literature.

Collections of Bible Stories

When a school staff agrees that children should have an opportunity to hear or read some of the great stories from the Bible, it will find many highly regarded versions available. In *Does God Have a Big Toe?* Marc Gellman, a rabbi, follows a long-held Jewish tradition of telling midrashim, stories about stories in the Bible. These involve readers with their often humorous, contemporary tellings. For instance, Noah doesn't have the heart to tell his friends what God has told him, so he hints: "You know, Jabal, this might be a very good time for you to take those swimming lessons you have been talking about for so long" (p. 31). Jane Breskin Zalben has retold a midrash title *Light* originally written by Rabbi Isaac Luri, the founder of Kabbalah.

Many individual picturebooks based on individual stories from the Bible are especially useful to introduce children to this literature. The story of the first humans is retold by Jane Ray in *Adam and Eve and the Garden of Eden*. Ray's patterned, folk art paintings evoke the original purity of Adam and Eve and provide for their future as mortal beings. Jerry Pinkney brings his accomplished watercolor and pencil illustrations to tell the story of *Noah's Ark* and creates a detailed and majestic visual interpretation of the story. Brian Wildsmith has created several retellings of Bible stories, including *Joseph, Jesus,* and *Exodus.* The books sparkle and glow with Wildsmith's wonderfully rich colors and patterns and are printed using gold as a fifth color.

The Bible, myths and legends, fables, and folktales represent literature of people through the ages. Folk literature has deep roots in basic human feelings. Through this

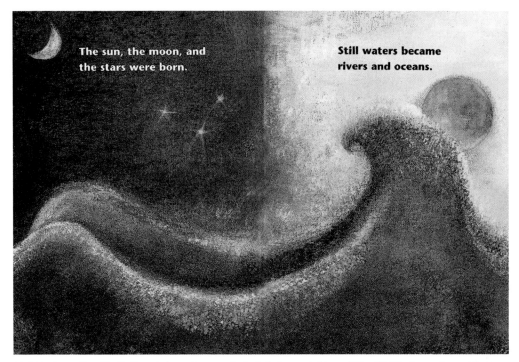

The sun, the moon, and the stars were born.

Still waters became rivers and oceans.

Light by Jane Breskin Zalben is based on a scholarly interpretation of the Old Testament creation story. From *Light* by Jane Breskin Zalben, copyright © 2007 by Jane Breskin Zalben. Used by permission of Dutton, a Division of Penguin Young Readers Group, a Member of Penguin Group (USA) Inc., 345 Hudson Street, New York, NY 10014. All rights reserved.

literature, children can form a link with the common bonds of humanity from the beginnings of recorded time, as well as form a foundation for much of their future reading.

Challenging Perspectives on Traditional Literature

An important point to consider when teaching traditional literature is that not all children will view fairy tales in predictable ways. Some children will opt not to participate in classroom activities that center on reading fairy tales, fables, or myths. Simply put, this would not be their genre of choice. Their perceptions about traditional literature present particular challenges for the classroom teacher. This can be especially challenging if fairy tales, well liked by the teacher, are used to teach across the curriculum. In that context, a student's lack of engagement and lack of response can eventually create a barrier to academic achievement.

Some educators assert that there are universals across all children's experiences and these universals are the places in discussions that reading and responding to traditional literature are best facilitated. This is not always the case. Teachers' childhood experiences and those of their students, particularly those from diverse backgrounds, may find themselves at disparate crossroads. Therefore the mediation of responses rooted in lived experiences may be especially challenging. There are some lived experiences that fuel responses to literature that are germane to a particular set of everyday life understandings.[6,7] For example, a study conducted by Tyson with African American male fifth-grade students reported the children were not engaged in the classroom when the story of Little Red Riding Hood was part of a unit to teach several literacy skills. This led her to explore the teaching and learning implications connected to the selection and use of traditional children's literature. In this study, she opened the door to extended responses to the literature and coupled it with the use of contemporary realistic fiction. She stated,

> As they responded to the texts, the boys began to discover and supplement the fictional information with factual information. They began to scrutinize and interrupt the information through cause and effect, hypothesizing ideas and predictions, inferring or deciphering character traits or identifying the author's purpose, as well as bringing personal insight and their own experience to their literary interpretations . . . they did look for connections to their lives including, but not limited to, school, family, and community experiences.[8]

Tyson later concluded that their responses were often related to their own lives. The boys in the study began to respond to the issues raised in the texts in ways that increased their engagement and enhanced their success with literacy tasks.

> . . . He added to his response a discussion of the things that Little Red Riding Hood could have done to protect herself, what her grandmother could have done differently, and what the neighborhood could do to get rid of the wolf.

So the questions arise: When looking at reader response and reading engagement, how do we recognize that culture, geography, language, and other influences impact reader response? How can a teacher meet the challenge of using traditional literature with children that may not connect and engage with the genre?

First, teachers and librarians can look outside the realm of what is the traditional. Throughout this chapter we have highlighted many texts that are considered the "classics" in traditional children's literature. Today's teachers should remember that children, even the youngest learners in our classrooms, are no longer only exposed to what is on the shelves of their neighborhood, classroom, and home libraries. They are no longer even confined to the "traditional" printed page.

Children today may have more options. They can download books and podcasts from the Internet to their iPods, view multilingual simulcasts, and much more. Given the wealth of cross-over technological experiences that children can have in a multimodal literary world, the first responses to the traditional genre of literature may not be "traditional" at all. Smith[9] conducted a study where she explored body punctuation as a part of children's response to literature, adding depth of meaning to spoken responses that were absent to written ones. In her article, "Body Punctuation: Reader-Response in Motion," Smith focused on particular body language used by students as part of their response process, which she called "body punctuation." Smith defined the gestures and the exaggerated body movements as ways that students extended their understandings and responses to literature, suggesting procedures and clues for processes that might be used by all teachers.

Second, teachers can expand their understanding of what it means to respond to traditional literature.[10] If the only legitimate way to respond is to discuss the literature within in its genre—plot structures, style, themes, motif and variants, and other measures used to capture students' responses to literature—then we may lose the opportunity to use traditional literature to open up a whole world of imagination, cross-cultural understanding, and pure enjoyment. Children will come to the classroom with many varied lived experiences that will be the foundation of engagement and response to literature. What happens when a teacher wants to use a traditional folktale to teach all the objectives found in a reading standard and some of the children's responses indicate they are not engaged with the text? The teacher may decide to continue with the unit and hope those students will change their attitude or the teacher may want to develop teaching strategies that will facilitate creating classroom spaces for multiple ways of responding to literature. The Ten-Point Model below (**Figure 4.1**) provides suggestions for using traditional literature to respond to the perspectives some children bring to a reading of this genre. This model provides additions to a repertoire of many successful strategies for differentiated instruction.

figure 4.1   **The Ten-Point Model for Teaching Controversial Issues**
Teaching Traditional Literature

Step	Task	To Consider
1. Raise the initial question and have the children brainstorm all their initial responses.	Ask students to critically analyze traditional literature (such as folktales, myths, or legends).	For example, ask what a different perspective of the story would be. What would Red Riding Hood think or do differently if her grandmother's house was in your neighborhood?
2. Create a list of "Things to find out more about."	As children read variations of traditional literature they can compare and contrast different versions of the story, asking which is the "correct one" and why. What is the author's viewpoint? Can you detect propaganda techniques in the writing of traditional literature?	Many cultures approach "strangers" in different ways. Ask if Little Red Riding Hood grew up in your house, what would have been expected of her when she met the wolf that was a stranger? Do you think other children are taught to respond differently?
3. Assign information-gathering homework.	Children can illustrate ways to compare various tales or to note similarities and differences in the main character, setting, conflict, advice, animals, and resolution of conflict. Students should gather, evaluate, and synthesize information in a variety of ways, perhaps using multimodal approaches to information gathering and display.	Traditional literature is a powerful tool for teaching critical reading. It offers children the opportunity to actively engage with the texts while simultaneously considering ideas, values, and ethical questions. For example, ask what would Little Red Riding Hood have done to solve the conflict with the wolf if she lived a big city? Small town? Rural town?

(continued)

figure 4.1 *(continued)*

Step	Task	To Consider
4. Share again responses to the initial question in a brainstorming session.	Have students share their "discoveries" with each other.	Continue to discuss and expand the topic: If you were going to retell the story of Little Red Riding Hood to a group of children that have never heard the story, how would you tell the story? Would it matter where the children lived? If so, why and what would be different?
5. Continue the process of gathering information.	Students should explore what a variety of children think is the good definition of a folktale, and a good reason for restating the oral folktale into the written or contemporary forms.	Using modern variants of traditional texts is an effective technique to share with students, offering perspectives on both traditional and contemporary literature.
6. If a concept emerges that sparks interest, confusion, or conflict, pose it as a new question.	A new way to reframe this issue could be: • How can you compare the culturally specific details of stories with international variations of the tale? • How can the similarities and differences among cultures and, ultimately, the stereotypes of characters compare with those of real life?	What happens when a group of students do not find the traditional tales interesting and others do? Using open-ended questions students can be asked to critique the literature, developing a list of criteria that they feel would be reflective of how their peers would respond to the text. They then could use that list to develop a "marketing campaign." Ask them to develop ways to make the text more appealing to young readers.
7. Periodically give the children assignments in class to summarize their thoughts.	A prompt could be worded as follows: What stories are read/told in your family? Your friend's family? Told to your parents? Grandparents? Did the stories change over time? How? Are they better? What criteria did you use to determine this?	The assignment can be individual or shared writing.
8. As individual or group projects emerge, follow up on them.	The class may decide to examine the diversity and the large scope of legends and fables that extend from local stories and how they travel around the world. Students can investigate which stories were popular among children in one part of the world and spread to other parts of the world and why.	This issue is well demonstrated by stories like Little Red Riding Hood and Cinderella. There are several variants nationally and internationally that students could read for comparing and contrasting multiple perspectives on a traditional story line.
9. Let others know what you are doing.	Invite students' parents, grandparents, caregivers, and other community members to come in and tell variations of stories from their childhood.	Collect some of the contemporary variants of the traditional tales and compare and contrast for content, context, themes, and conflict.
10. End your project with something either public or permanent.	Children could write their own versions of traditional tales, using more contemporary elements.	"Self-publish" the revised stories and make them available in the school library.

Source: Adapted from Kreidler, W. *Elementary Perspectives: Teaching Concepts of Peace and Conflict.* Copyright © 1990, Educators for Social Responsibility, Cambridge, MA. www.esrnational.org. Used by permission.

Using Traditional Literature to Address Standards

Traditional literature can provide windows into many people, places, and experiences. It brings to life the values and material surroundings of groups all over the world, demonstrating both our differences and our similarities. The variety of styles and stories that encompass the genre of traditional literature offer an opportunity for implementing curriculum standards in the classroom. For example, students can hone their critical thinking skills by comparing multiple versions of similar stories across cultures and perspectives, such as Young's *Lon Po Po*, Forward's *The Wolf's Story: What Really Happened to Little Red Riding Hood*, and Grimm and Hyman's *Little Red Riding Hood*. Curriculum connections can be made to social studies concepts such as geography and environments through stories including Del Negro's *Willa and the Wind*, Kimmel's *Rimonah of the Flashing Sword*, or Grifalconi's *The Village of Round and Square Houses*, all of which take place in distinctive locations. Different types of money and market places can be seen in books like Daikité's *The Hat Seller and the Monkeys* or Demi's *The Donkey and the Rock*.

The example below utilizes science standards as a context for the use of traditional literature to make curriculum connections.

Standards in Action: Science

> *East o'the Sun and West o'the Moon*
> Lewis, Naomi, trans. (2005). *East o'the Sun and West o'the Moon*. Cambridge, Mass.: Candlewick.

East o'the Sun and West o'the Moon is a Scandinavian fairy tale that is full of adventure, deception, and magic. It begins with the quest of a prince who has been cursed to take the form of a white bear by day. White Bear strikes a deal with a poor farmer to trade the life of his youngest, prettiest daughter for instant riches. She convinces the White Bear to take her to see her family by agreeing to a special condition, which she breaks and causes bad luck to befall both of them. After realizing the consequences of her actions, she sets off on a quest to find her prince charming and break his spell. She encounters obstacles along the way, but eventually is reunited with her true love.

Apply to Science Content Standard B – Physical Science
Properties of objects and materials; position and motion of objects, light, heat, electricity, and magnetism, motions and forces.

- Students can create pourquoi ("why") tales about events in nature. Afterward students can research the science behind those events. Then, students can compare the stories they wrote with the scientific information.
- Since the main character in the story is carried to the castle by the four winds, students can experiment to see how much force it would take to move small objects such as a scrap of paper or a paper clip through the air.
- Students can experiment with different solvents to discover which materials remove wax from cloth most effectively in order to guess what the main character used to win her challenge.

Apply to Science Content Standard C – Life Science
The characteristics of organisms; life cycles of organisms; organisms and environments; populations and ecosystems; diversity and adaptations of organisms.

- Students can illustrate and/or act out adaptations and transformations that occur in nature (i.e., seed to flower; day to night; pupa to butterfly; brown hare to snowshoe hare; child to adult). Students can brainstorm the reasons that these transformations may be helpful for these organisms and compare such transformations with those of physical materials (i.e., water to ice; day to night; hot to cold).

(continued)

curriculum connections

(continued)

- Students can chart the characteristics of all the characters from the story and compare those characteristics with those of people and animals in real life.

Apply to Science Content Standard E – Science and Technology

Abilities of technological design; understanding about science and technology; abilities to distinguish between natural objects and objects made by humans including the ability to evaluate a product or design.

- Students can invent a device that would have helped one of the characters in the story. Ask students to explain their device to the class with text, illustrations, and figures. Students can evaluate the designs of each others' devices and make models of ones they find most helpful.

Source: Tyson, C. (1999) Shut My Mouth Wide Open: Realistic Fiction and Social Action. *Theory into Practice, 38*(3), pp. 155–159. Copyright 1999 by the College of Education and Human Ecology, The Ohio State University. All rights reserved.

Notes

1. Northrop Frye, *The Educated Imagination* (Bloomington, Ind.: Indiana University Press, 1964), p. 48.
2. Laura Amy Schlitz, *The Bearskinner: A Tale of the Brothers Grimm,* illustrated by Max Grafe (Candlewick, 2007).
3. Margaret Willey, *Clever Beatrice,* illustrated by Heather Solomon (Atheneum, 2001).
4. Julius Lester, "The Storyteller's Voice: Reflections on the Rewriting of Uncle Remus," *New Advocate* 1.3 (summer, 1988): 144.
5. Stith Thompson, *Motif Index of Folk Literature,* 6 vols. (Bloomington, Ind.: Indiana University Press, 1955–1958).
6. R. Sims Bishop, "Mirrors, Windows, and Sliding Glass Doors," *Perspectives* 6 (1990): ix–xi.
7. V. Harris, *Teaching Multicultural Literature in Grades K–8* (Norwood, Mass.: Christopher-Gordon Publishers, 1992).
8. C. Tyson, "'Shut My Mouth Wide Open': Realistic Fiction and Social Action," *Theory into Practice* 38.3 (1999): 155–59.
9. E. B. Smith, "Body Punctuation: Reader-Response in Motion," in *Reader Response in Elementary Classrooms: Quest and Discovery,* ed. Nicholas J. Karolides (Mahwah, N.J.: Lawrence Erlbaum Associates, 1997).
10. L. Eckert, *How Does It Mean? Engaging Reluctant Readers through Literary Theory* (Portsmouth, N.H.: Heinemann, 2006).

Children's Literature

OLC Go to **www.mhhe.com/kiefer1e** *to access the Children's Literature Database, which includes information on thousands of children's books. Following are some of the titles you will find in the database.*

Titles in blue = multicultural titles

Except where obvious from the title, the country or culture of origin follows each entry in parentheses. Dates in square brackets are original publication dates.

Folktales

Aardema, Verna. *Rabbit Makes a Monkey of Lion.* Illustrated by Jerry Pinkney. Dial, 1989. (Africa, Tanzania)

———. *Who's in Rabbit's House?* Illustrated by Leo Dillon and Diane Dillon. Dial, 1977. (West Africa)

———. *Why Mosquitoes Buzz in People's Ears.* Illustrated by Leo Dillon and Diane Dillon. Dial, 1975.

Ada, Alma Flor. *The Rooster Who Went to His Uncle's Wedding.* Illustrated by Kathleen Kuchera. Putnam, 1993. (Cuba)

Arkhurst, Joyce Cooper. *The Adventures of Spider: West African Folk Tales.* Illustrated by Jerry Pinkney. Scholastic, 1969.

Asbjørnsen, Peter Christian, and Jorgen E. Moe. *East o'the Sun and West o'the Moon.* Translated by George Webbe Dasent. Dover, 1970 [1842–1843]. (Norway)

———. *The Three Billy Goats Gruff.* Illustrated by Marcia Brown. Harcourt, 1957. (Norway)

Aylesworth, Jim. *The Gingerbread Man.* Illustrated by Barbara McClintock. Scholastic, 1998. (English)

Brett, Jan. *Gingerbread Baby.* Putnam, 1999.

Brown, Marcia. *Dick Whittington and His Cat.* Scribner's, 1950. (England)

Bruchac, Joseph, and James Bruchac. *How Chipmunk Got His Stripes: A Tale of Bragging and Teasing.* Illustrated by Jose Aruego and Ariane Dewey. Dial, 2001. (Native American)

Bruchac, Joseph, and Gayle Ross. *The Story of the Milky Way.* Illustrated by Virginia Stroud. Dial, 1995. (Cherokee)

Bryan, Ashley. *Beat the Story-Drum, Pum-Pum.* Atheneum, 1980. (Africa)

———. *The Cat's Purr.* Macmillan, 1993.

Climo, Shirley. *The Egyptian Cinderella.* Illustrated by Ruth Heller. Crowell/Harper, 1989.

———. *The Korean Cinderella.* Illustrated by Ruth Heller. HarperCollins, 1993.

———. *Tuko and the Birds: A Tale from the Philippines.* Illustrated by Francisco X. Mora. Holt, 2008.

Cooper, Susan. *Tam Lin.* Illustrated by Warwick Hutton. McElderry, 1991. (Scotland)

Cummings, Pat. *Ananse and the Lizard. A West African Tale.* Holt, 2002.

Daly, Jude. *Fair, Brown and Trembling: An Irish Cinderella Story.* Farrar, 2001.

Daly, Niki. *Pretty Salma: A Red Riding Hood Story from Africa.* Clarion, 2007.

Dasent, George. *East o'the Sun and West o'the Moon.* Illustrated by Gillian Barlow. Philomel, 1988. (Norway)

Dayrell, Elphinstone. *Why the Sun and the Moon Live in the Sky.* Illustrated by Blair Lent. Houghton, 1968. (Africa)

Del Negro, Janice. *Willa and the Wind.* Illustrated by Heather Solomon. Cavendish, 2005. (Scandinavia)

Demi. *The Empty Pot.* Holt, 1990. (China)

dePaola, Tomie. *Adelita: A Mexican Cinderella Story.* Putnam, 2002.

———. *Strega Nona.* Prentice-Hall, 1975. (Italy)

Diakité, Baba Wagué. *The Magic Gourd.* Scholastic, 2003. (Mali)

———. *Me-An and the Magic Serpent: A Folktale from Mali.* Groundwood, 2007.

Egielski, Richard. *The Gingerbread Boy.* HarperCollins, 1997. (English)

Fleischman, Paul. *Glass Slipper, Gold Sandal: A Worldwide Cinderella.* Illustrated by Julie Paschkis. Holt, 2007.

Fowles, Shelley. *The Bachelor and the Bean.* Farrar, 2004. (Moroccan Jewish)

French, Fiona. *Lord of the Animals: A Miwok Indian Creation Myth.* Millbrook, 1997.

Galdone, Paul. *The Gingerbread Boy.* Clarion, 1984 [1968]. (England)

———. *The Little Red Hen.* Clarion, 1979 [1974]. (England)

———. *The Magic Porridge Pot.* Clarion, 1979 [1976]. (Germany)

———. *The Three Little Pigs.* Clarion, 1981 [1973]. (Norway)

Gershator, Phillis. *Only One Cowry: A Dahomean Tale.* Illustrated by David Soman. Orchard, 2000.

Gilman, Phoebe. *Something from Nothing.* Scholastic, 1992. (Jewish)

Goble, Paul. *Her Seven Brothers.* Bradbury, 1988. (Native American)

Grimm brothers. *The Bremen-Town Musicians.* Retold and illustrated by Ilse Plume. Doubleday, 1980. (Germany)

———. *The Fisherman and His Wife.* Illustrated by Rachel Isadora. Putnam Penguin, 2008. (Germany)

———. *The Frog Prince or Iron Henry.* Translated by Naomi Lewis. Illustrated by Binette Schroeder. North-South, 1998. (Germany)

———. *Princess Furball.* Retold by Charlotte Huck. Illustrated by Anita Lobel. Greenwillow, 1989. (Germany)

———. *Rumpelstiltskin.* Retold and illustrated by Paul O. Zelinksy. Dutton, 1986. (Germany)

———. *Snow White and the Seven Dwarfs.* Translated by Randall Jarrell. Illustrated by Nancy Ekholm Burkert. Farrar, 1972. (Germany)

———. *The Table, the Donkey, and the Stick.* Illustrated by Paul Galdone. McGraw-Hill, 1976.

Haley, Gail E. *A Story, a Story.* Atheneum, 1970. (Africa)

Hamilton, Virginia. *The Girl Who Spun Gold.* Illustrated by Leo Dillon and Diane Dillon. Scholastic, 2000. (West Indies)

———. *The Magical Adventures of Pretty Pearl.* Harper, 1983.

Han, Suzanne Crowder. *The Rabbit's Tail: A Tale from Korea.* Illustrated by Richard Wehrman. Holt, 1999.

Hickox, Rebecca. *The Golden Sandal: A Middle Eastern Cinderella.* Illustrated by Will Hillenbrand. Holiday, 1998.

Hodges, Margaret. *Dick Whittington and His Cat.* Illustrated by Mélisande Potter. Harcourt, 2006.

Hogrogian, Nonny. *One Fine Day.* Macmillan, 1971. (Armenia)

Hong, Lily Toy. *Two of Everything.* Whitman, 1993. (China)

Hooks, William. *Moss Gown.* Illustrated by Donald Carrick. Clarion, 1987. (United States)

Huck, Charlotte S. *Toads and Diamonds.* Illustrated by Anita Lobel. Greenwillow, 1996.

Huth, Holly. *The Son of the Sun and the Daughter of the Moon: A Sammi Folktale*. Illustrated by Anna Votech. Atheneum, 2000. (Scandinavia)

Isadora, Rachel. *Rapunzel*. Putnam, 2008.

——. *The Fisherman and His Wife*. Putnam, 2008.

Jaffe, Nina. *The Golden Flower: A Taino Myth from Puerto Rico*. Illustrated by Eric O. Saná. Piñata, 2005.

Kellogg, Steven. *Chicken Little*. Morrow, 1988. (United States)

Kimmel, Eric A. *Baba Yaga: A Russian Folktale*. Illustrated by Megan Lloyd. Holiday, 1991.

——. *The Castle of Cats*. Illustrated by Katya Krenina. Holiday, 2004. (Ukraine)

——. *The Fisherman and the Turtle*. Illustrated by Martha Aviles. Cavendish, 2008. (Germany)

——. *Iron John*. Illustrated by Trina Schart Hyman. Holiday, 1994. (German)

——. *The Old Woman and Her Pig*. Illustrated by Giora Carmi. Holiday, 1993. (English)

Kurtz, Jane. *Fire on the Mountain*. Illustrated by E. B. Lewis. Simon, 1994. (Ethiopia)

Lester, Julius. *Uncle Remus: The Complete Tales*. Illustrated by Jerry Pinkney. Dial, 1999. (African American)

Lindbergh, Reeve. *Johnny Appleseed*. Illustrated by Kathy Jakobsen. Little, 1990. (United States)

Louie, Ai-Ling. *Yeh-Shen: A Cinderella Story from China*. Illustrated by Ed Young. Philomel, 1982.

MacDonald, Margaret Read. *The Great Smelly, Slobbery, Small-Tooth Dog: A Folktale from Great Britain*. Julie Paschkis. August, 2007.

——. *Mabela the Clever*. Illustrated by Tim Coffey. Whitman, 2001. (Limba/Africa)

——. *The Old Woman and Her Pig: An Appalachian Folktale*. Illustrated by John Kanzler. HarperCollins, 2007.

——. *Tunjur! Tunjur! Tunjur! A Palestinian Folktale*. Illustrated by Alik Arzoumanian. Cavendish, 2006.

Mahy, Margaret. *The Seven Chinese Brothers*. Illustrated by Jean Tseng and Mou-Sien Tseng. Scholastic, 1990.

Martin, Rafe. *Foolish Rabbit's Big Mistake*. Illustrated by Ed Young. Putnam, 1985. (India)

——. *The Rough-Face Girl*. Illustrated by David Shannon. Putnam, 1992. (Native American)

——. *The Shark God*. Illustrated by David Shannon. Levine, Scholastic, 2001. (Hawaii)

McDermott, Gerald. *Anansi the Spider*. Holt, 1972. (Africa)

Orgel, Doris. *The Bremen Town Musicians: And Other Animal Tales from Grimm*. Illustrated by Bert Kitchen. Roaring Brook, 2004. (Germany)

Perrault, Charles. *Cinderella*. Illustrated by Marcia Brown. Scribner's, 1954. (France)

——. *Puss in Boots*. Translated by Malcolm Arthur. Illustrated by Fred Marcellino. Farrar, 1993 [1990]. (France)

Pinkney, Jerry. *The Little Red Hen*. Dial, 2006. (England)

Ransome, Arthur. *The Fool of the World and the Flying Ship*. Illustrated by Uri Shulevitz. Farrar, 1968. (Russia)

Rascol, Sabin I. *The Impudent Rooster*. Illustrated by Holly Berry. Orchard, 2004. (Romania)

Rodanas, Kristina. *Follow the Stars: A Native American Woodlands Tale*. Cavendish, 1998.

Sanfield, Steve. *The Adventures of High John the Conqueror*. Illustrated by John Ward. Orchard, 1989. (African American)

San Souci, Robert D. *Cendrillon, a Caribbean Cinderella*. Illustrated by Brian Pinkney. Simon, 1998.

——. *The Little Gold Star. A Spanish American Cinderella Story*. Illustrated by Sergio Martinez. HarperCollins, 2000.

——. *The Silver Charm: A Folktale from Japan*. Illustrated by Yoriko Ito. Doubleday, 2002.

——. *The Talking Eggs*. Illustrated by Jerry Pinkney. Dial, 1989. (African American)

——. *The Well at the End of the World*. Illustrated by Rebecca Walsh. Chronicle, 2004. (England)

Schlitz, Laura Amy. *The Bearskinner: A Tale of the Brothers Grimm*. Illustrated by Max Grafe. Candlewick, 2007. (Germany)

Sierra, Judy. *The Gift of the Crocodile: A Cinderella Story*. Illustrated by Reynold Ruffins. Simon, 2000. (Indonesia)

Singer, Isaac Bashevis. *Mazel and Shlimazel, or the Milk of a Lioness*. Illustrated by Margot Zemach. Farrar, 1967. (Jewish)

——. *Zlateh the Goat, and Other Stories*. Translated by the author and Elizabeth Shub. Illustrated by Maurice Sendak. Harper, 1966. (Jewish)

Snyder, Dianne. *The Boy of the Three-Year Nap*. Illustrated by Allen Say. Houghton, 1988. (Japan)

Souhami, Jessica. *King Pom and the Fox*. Frances Lincoln, 2007. (Japan)

——. *The Little, Little House*. Frances Lincoln, 2006. (Jewish)

Spirin, Gennady. *The Tale of the Firebird*. Translated by Tatiana Popova. Philomel, 2002. (Russia)

Steptoe, John. *Mufaro's Beautiful Daughters: An African Tale*. Lothrop, 1987. (Zimbabwe)

Tchana, Katrin. *Sense Pass King: A Story from Cameroon*. Illustrated by Trina Schart Hyman. Holiday, 2002.

Uchida, Yoshiko. *The Magic Purse.* Illustrated by Keiko Narahasi. McElderry, 1993. (Japan)

White, Carolyn. *Whuppity Stoorie.* Illustrated by S. D. Schindler. Putnam, 1997. (Scotland)

Willey, Margaret. *Clever Beatrice.* Illustrated by Heather Solomon. Atheneum, 2001. (Canada)

Winthrop, Elizabeth. *The Little Humpbacked Horse.* Illustrated by Alexander Koshkin. Clarion, 1997. (Russia)

——. *Vasilissa the Beautiful.* Illustrated by Alexander Koshkin. HarperCollins, 1991. (Russia)

Wolkstein, Diane. *The Day Ocean Came to Visit.* Illustrated by Steve Johnson and Lou Fancher. Harcourt/Gulliver, 2001. (Nigeria)

——. *The Magic Orange Tree and Other Haitian Folktales.* Illustrated by Elsa Henriquez. Knopf, 1978.

Young, Ed. *What about Me?* Philomel, 2002. (Sufi)

Zemach, Harve. *Duffy and the Devil.* Illustrated by Margot Zemach. Farrar, 1973. (England)

Zemach, Margot. *The Little Red Hen: An Old Story.* Farrar, 1993.

Fables

Bierhorst, John. *Doctor Coyote: A Native American Aesop's Fables.* Illustrated by Wendy Watson. Aladdin, 1996.

Hennessy, B. G. *The Boy Who Cried Wolf.* Illustrated by Boris Kulikov. Simon, 2006.

Pinkney, Jerry. *Aesop's Fables.* North-South, 2000.

Poole, Amy Lowry. *The Ant and the Grasshopper.* Holiday, 2000.

Steig, William. *Amos and Boris.* Farrar, 1971.

Uribe, Veronica. *Little Book of Fables.* Translated by Susan Ouriou. Illustrated by Constanza Bravo. Groundwood, 2004.

Young, Ed. *Seven Blind Mice.* Philomel, 1992.

Myths and Legends

Byrd, Robert. *The Hero and the Minotaur: The Fantastic Adventures of Theseus.* Dutton, 2005.

Climo, Shirley. *Stolen Thunder.* Illustrated by Alexander Koshkin. Clarion, 1994.

Colum, Padraic. *The Children's Homer: The Adventures of Odysseus and the Tale of Troy.* Illustrated by Willy Pogany. Macmillan, 1962.

——. *The Trojan War and the Adventures of Odysseus.* Illustrated by Barry Moser. Morrow, 1997.

D'Aulaire, Ingri, and Edgar Parin D'Aulaire. *D'Aulaires' Book of Greek Myths.* Doubleday, 1962.

——. *D'Aulaires' Book of Norse Myths.* New York Review of Books, 2005 [1967].

Hamilton, Virginia. *In the Beginning: Creation Stories from around the World.* Illustrated by Barry Moser. Harcourt, 1988.

Hutton, Warwick. *Persephone.* McElderry, 1994.

McCaughrean, Geraldine. *Gilgamesh the Hero.* Illustrated by David Parkins. Eerdmans, 2004.

——. *Greek Gods and Goddesses.* Illustrated by Emma Chichester Clark. McElderry, 1998.

——. *The Odyssey.* Illustrated by Victor Ambrus. Oxford UP, 1997.

Osborne, Mary Pope. *Mermaids and Monsters.* Illustrated by Troy Howell. Hyperion, 2003.

——. *The One-Eyed Giant.* Illustrated by Troy Howell. Hyperion, 2003.

Raven, Nicky. *Beowulf: A Tale of Blood, Heat, and Ashes.* Illustrated by John Howe. Candlewick, 2007.

Rumford, James. *Beowulf: A Hero's Tale Retold.* Houghton, 2007.

Souhami, Jessica. *Rama and the Demon King: An Ancient Tale from India.* DK, 1997.

Sutcliff, Rosemary. *Black Ships before Troy: The Story of the Iliad.* Illustrated by Alan Lee. Delacorte, 1993.

——. *The Wanderings of Odysseus: The Story of the Odyssey.* Illustrated by Alan Lee. Delacorte, 1996.

Verma, Jatinder. *The Story of Divaali.* Illustrated by Nilesh Mistry. Barefoot, 2002.

Weitzman, David. *Rama and Sita: A Tale from Ancient Java.* Godine, 2003.

Zeman, Ludmila. *Gilgamesh the King.* Tundra, 1995.

——. *The Last Quest of Gilgamesh.* Tundra, 1995.

——. *The Revenge of Ishtar.* Tundra, 1995.

The Bible

Gellman, Marc. *Does God Have a Big Toe? Stories about Stories in the Bible.* Illustrated by Oscar de Mejo. Harper, 1989.

Goldin, Barbara Diamond. *Journeys with Elijah: Eight Tales of the Prophet.* Illustrated by Jerry Pinkney. Gulliver/Harcourt, 1999.

Ray, Jane. *Adam and Eve and the Garden of Eden.* Eerdmans, 2005.

Wildsmith, Brian. *Exodus.* Eerdmans, 1998.

——. *Jesus.* Eerdmans, 2000.

——. *Joseph.* Eerdmans, 1997.

Zalben, Jane Breskin. *Light.* Dutton, 2007.

Chapter Five

Modern Fantasy

Chapter Outline

Bree, a fifth grader, read Philip Pullman's *The Golden Compass* and found it "stupendous." She passed it on to her best friend Madeline who also responded to it with passionate enthusiasm. Soon the two were in a continuing dialogue about Pullman's daemons, pronunciations, and auroras. By the following September, they both had the same idea—to dress up as *Golden Compass* characters for Halloween. Bree ended up being Lyra, and Madeline went as a girl Lyra would meet on the other side of the Aurora. (The sequels, *The Subtle Knife* and *The Amber Spyglass*, weren't out yet.) They were both "lured" by hopes of seeing the aurora borealis. Bree looked for it at camp in Quebec, and Madeline on a trip to Norway. They loved assigning daemons to each other. Then, during sleepovers, they began assigning each person they knew their *true* type of daemon. *The Golden Compass* became their measuring stick for other fantasy. They asked each other, "But is it as good as *The*

Golden Compass? Are the characters as realistic? Is the setting as vivid? Is the plot as compelling?" For these friends, fantasy became a way of examining their own worlds and evaluating the world of literature.

Fantasy for Today's Child

Some educators and parents question the value of fantasy for today's child. They argue that children want contemporary stories that are relevant and speak to the problems of daily living—"now" books about the real world, not fantasies about unreal worlds. Others object to any fantasy at all for children, afraid that reading about goblins, trolls, and witches will lead children to practices of satanism or belief in the occult. But good fantasy might be critical to children's understanding of themselves and of the struggles they will face as human beings. Lloyd Alexander, master of the craft of writing fantasy, argues that fantasy is of the utmost value for children.

> We call our individual fantasies dreams, but when we dream as a society, or as a human race, it becomes the sum total of all our hopes. Fantasy touches our deepest feelings and in so doing, it speaks to the best and most hopeful parts of ourselves. It can help us learn the most fundamental skill of all—how to be human.[1]

The great fantasies frequently reveal new insights into the world of reality. Both E. B. White's *Charlotte's Web* and Kenneth Grahame's *The Wind in the Willows* detail the responsibilities and loyalties required of true friendship. The fundamental truth underlying Ursula Le Guin's story *A Wizard of Earthsea* is that each of us is responsible for the wrong that we do and that we are free of it only when we face it directly. In a book of realism, such a theme might appear to be a thinly disguised religious lesson; in fantasy it becomes an exciting quest for identity and self-knowledge. Fantasy consistently asks the universal questions concerning the struggle of good versus evil, the humanity of humankind, and the meaning of life and death.

A modern realistic fiction novel can be out of date in five years, but well-written fantasy endures. Hans Christian Andersen's *The Nightingale* speaks directly to this century's adoration of mechanical gadgetry to the neglect of what is simple and real.

Artist Jerry Pinkney visualizes Hans Christian Andersen's *The Nightingale* in a fabled kingdom in Morocco. From *The Nightingale* by Hans Christian Andersen, adapted and translated by Jerry Pinkney, copyright © 2002 by Jerry Pinkney. Used by permission of Phyllis Fogelman Books, a Division of Penguin Young Readers Group, a Member of Penguin Group (USA) Inc., 345 Hudson Street, New York, NY 10014. All rights reserved.

Lois Lowry's *The Giver* asks how the freedom of an individual can be weighed against the needs of the group. Natalie Babbitt's *Tuck Everlasting* questions whether anything or anyone would wish to live forever.

More important, however, fantasy helps the child develop imagination. To be able to imagine, to conceive of alternative ways of life, to entertain new ideas, to create strange new worlds, to dream dreams—these are all skills vital to human survival.

These arguments aside, children themselves have shown that they continue to want books that satisfy this hunger. J. K. Rowling's Harry Potter books are undoubtedly the most popular children's books to be published in the past fifty years. E. B. White's *Charlotte's Web*, Brian Jacques's Redwall series, C. S. Lewis's Narnia series, and Madeleine L'Engle's *A Wrinkle in Time* are all fantasies that rank among children's favorite books. And many of the classics, books that have endured through generations—such as Lewis Carroll's *Alice in Wonderland*, A. A. Milne's *Winnie the Pooh*, Kenneth Grahame's *The Wind in the Willows*, and J. M. Barrie's *Peter Pan*—are also fantasies.

The modern literature of fantasy is diverse. We have contemporary fairy tales; stories of magic, talking toys, and other wonders; quests for truth in lands that never were; and narratives that speculate on the future. Though these types of stories might seem very different, they do have something in common: they have roots in earlier sources—in folktales, legends, myths, and the oldest dreams of humankind.

All literature borrows from itself, but the fantastic genre is particularly dependent. The motifs, plots, characters, settings, and themes of new fantasy books often seem familiar. And well they should, for we have met them before, in other, older stories.

Many authors borrow directly from the characters and motifs of folklore. The African American folk heroes John de Conquer and John Henry Roustabout enliven the unusual fantasy *The Magical Adventures of Pretty Pearl* by Virginia Hamilton. Ian Beck's Tom Trueheart series, Sarah Beth Durst's *Into the Wild,* and Lyn Gardner's *Into the Woods* are peopled by characters from German and English folktales. Nancy Farmer (*The Islands of the Blessed*), Mollie Hunter (*A Stranger Came Ashore*), and Kate Thompson (*The Last of the High Kings*) all rely on places, motifs, and creatures from Celtic and Norse mythology to tell their thrilling stories. Greek mythology forms the basis for Gail Carson Levine's *Ever* and for Rick Riordan's popular Percy Jackson series including *The Battle of the Labyrinth*.

The ultimate taproot of all fantasy is the human psyche. Like the ancient taletellers and the medieval bards, modern fantasy writers speak to our deepest needs, our darkest fears, and our highest hopes. In fantasy for children, adults might find many of the collective images or shared symbols called archetypes by the great psychologist Carl Jung. Children will simply recognize that such a fantasy is "true." All our best fantasies, from the briefest modern fairy tale to the most complex novel of high adventure, share this quality of truth.

Types of Fantasy

Literary Fairy Tales

The traditional folklore or fairy tale had no identifiable author but was passed on by retellings by one generation to the next. Even though the names Grimm and Jacobs have become associated with some of these tales, they did not write the stories; they compiled and edited the folktales of Germany and England. The modern literary fairy tale utilizes the form of the old but has an identifiable author.

Hans Christian Andersen is generally credited with being the first author of modern fairy tales, although some of his stories, such as *The Wild Swans*, are definite adaptations of the old folktales. Many of Andersen's stories bear his unmistakable stamp of gentleness, melancholy, and faith in God. Often even his retellings of old tales are embellished with deeper meanings, making them very much his creations.

Other well-known authors have been captivated by the possibilities of the literary fairy tale. Kenneth Grahame's *The Reluctant Dragon* is the droll tale of a peace-loving dragon who is forced to fight Saint George. James Thurber's *Many Moons* is the story of a petulant princess who desires the moon. Contemporary authors such as Diane Stanley's *The Giant and the Beanstalk* or Colin and Jacqui Hawkins's *Fairytale News* have brought a sense of playfulness to such fractured tales. (See Modern Folktale Style in Chapter 3.)

Animal Fantasy

Children might first be introduced to fantasy through tales of talking animals, toys, and dolls. The young child frequently ascribes powers of thought and speech to pets or toys and might already be acquainted with some of the Beatrix Potter stories or the more sophisticated tales of William Steig.

One of the most beloved animal fantasies of our time is E. B. White's delightful tale *Charlotte's Web*. While much of our fantasy is of English origin, *Charlotte's Web* is as American as the Fourth of July and just as much a part of our children's heritage. Eight-year-old Fern can understand all of the animals in the barnyard—the geese who always speak in triplicate ("certainly-ertainlyyertainly"); the wise old sheep; and Templeton, the crafty rat—yet she cannot communicate with them. The true heroine of the story is Charlotte A. Cavatica—a beautiful large gray spider who befriends Wilbur, a humble little pig. When the kindly old sheep inadvertently drops the news that as soon as Wilbur is nice and fat he will be butchered, Charlotte promises to save the hysterical pig. By miraculously spinning words into her web that describe the pig as "radiant," "terrific," and "humble," she makes Wilbur famous. The pig is saved, but Charlotte dies alone at the fairgrounds. Wilbur manages to bring Charlotte's egg sac back to the farm so that the continuity of life in the barnyard is maintained. Wilbur never forgets his friend Charlotte, though he loves her children and grandchildren dearly. This story has humor, pathos, wisdom, and beauty. Its major themes speak of the web of true friendship and the cycle of life and death. All ages find meaning in this most popular fantasy.

The well-loved *The Wind in the Willows* by Kenneth Grahame endures even though it is slow-paced, idyllic, and more sentimental than a more modern animal fantasy. It is the story of four friends: kindly and gruff old Badger; practical and good-natured Ratty; gullible Mole; and boisterous, expansive, and easily misled Toad. Toad gets into one scrape after another, and the other three loyally rescue their errant friend and finally save his elegant mansion from a band of wicked weasels and stoats. The themes of friendship, the importance of a home place, and love of nature pervade this pastoral fantasy.

The villainous animals threatening Toad Hall in *The Wind in the Willows* are the same sorts who threaten Redwall Abbey in Brian Jacques's Redwall books. But this series is swiftly told, complexly plotted, and action-packed by comparison. Redwall tells

Elise Broach's *Masterpiece* is a story of a human boy and a highly intelligent beetle who can draw like a Renaissance master. Both are called upon to save a masterpiece from thieves. Cover of *Masterpiece* by Elise Broach, illustrated by Kelly Murphy. Illustrations copyright © 2005 by Kelly Murphy. Reprinted by permission of Henry Holt and Company, LLC.

of Matthias, a clumsy, young, and peace-loving mouse, who galvanizes himself to defeat the evil rat, Cluny the Scourge. Aided by Cornflower the Fieldmouse, Constance the Badger, and Brother Methuselah, Matthias's efforts to fortify the Abbey alternate with chapters of the terrible Cluny subduing woodland creatures to his will. The sinister names of Cluny's band (Fangborn, Cheesethief, Ragear, Mangefur) alert young readers to the evil characters. In fact, one of the major appeals of the Redwall stories is that one never doubts that good will triumph.

Elise Broach's *Masterpiece* is an animal fantasy that takes place in our own world with a human and an insect as co-protagonists. In this case, a beetle represents the animal character and a human boy is his partner in solving a theft of a precious drawing by Renaissance artist Albrecht Dürer. The human boy is astonished to find a beetle who can communicate to him in gestures and in drawing. This device makes the story more believable for the older, more skeptical child reader.

The World of Toys and Dolls

As authors have endowed animals with human characteristics, so, too, have they personified toys and dolls. Young children enjoy stories that bring inanimate objects such as a tugboat or a steam shovel to life. Seven-, 8-, and 9-year-olds still like to imagine that their favorite playthings have a life of their own.

Probably no one has made toys seem quite so much like people as has A. A. Milne in his well-loved Pooh stories. Each chapter contains a separate adventure about the favorite stuffed toys of Milne's son, Christopher Robin. The good companions introduced in *Winnie the Pooh* include Winnie-the-Pooh, "a bear of little brain"; Eeyore, the doleful donkey; Piglet, the happy follower and devoted friend of Pooh; and Rabbit, Owl, Kanga, and little Roo. A bouncy new friend, Tigger, joins the group in Milne's second book, *The House at Pooh Corner*. They all live in the "100 Aker Wood" and spend most of their time getting into—and out of—exciting and amusing situations. The humor in these stories is not hilarious but quiet, whimsical, and subtle. If teachers and children know only the Disney version of these stories, they are in for a treat when they read the original Milne.

Kate DiCamillo has created a memorable rabbit doll in *The Miraculous Journey of Edward Tulane*. Edward is a very handsome, very narcissistic doll made almost entirely of china—with real rabbit-hair ears and tail and a wardrobe of elegant costumes. He is passionately loved by his mistress, Abilene, but he is coldly immune to her affections. It is only when he falls overboard on an ocean voyage that his travail and his humanization begin. Passed over the years from one human to another, Edward gradually comes to open his heart to his need for love. Although the book is sure to remind readers of Margery Williams's *The Velveteen Rabbit*, DiCamillo has created a fresh and moving examination of the relationship between children and their beloved toys.

Elizabeth Winthrop's *The Castle in the Attic* also examines responsibility for one's own actions. Although an accomplished gymnast, 10-year-old William lacks confidence in himself. When he hears that Mrs. Phillips, his lifelong friend and live-in baby-sitter, is returning to her native England, he is crushed but determined to find a way to make her stay. Inside her parting gift to him, a huge model of a castle that has been in her family for generations, William discovers a tiny lead knight that comes to life at his touch. The knight shows William a charm that can be used to miniaturize objects or people, and William uses it to reduce his baby-sitter to toy size and keep her in the castle. Regretting this hasty act, he submits himself to the charm, travels back in time with the knight, and recovers the amulet that will reverse the spell. On this quest William discovers unexpected strengths in himself. He returns victorious, prepared to wish Mrs. Phillips farewell.

Eccentric Characters and Preposterous Situations

Many fantasies for children are based on eccentric characters or preposterous situations. Cars or people might fly, eggs might hatch into dinosaurs or dragons, ancient magical beings might come up against modern technology. Often these characters and situations occur in otherwise very normal settings—which allows readers to believe more readily.

Pippi Longstocking, a notoriously funny character created by Astrid Lindgren, has delighted children for more than fifty years. Pippi is an orphan who lives alone with her monkey and her horse in a child's utopian world where she tells herself when to go to bed and when to get up! Although she is only 9 years old, Pippi can hold her own with anyone, for she is so strong that she can pick up a horse or a man and throw him into the air. Children love this amazing character who always has the integrity to say what she thinks, even if she shocks adults. Seven-, 8-, and 9-year-olds enjoy her madcap adventures in *Pippi Longstocking* and in the sequels, *Pippi Goes on Board*, *Pippi in the South Seas*, and *Pippi on the Run*.

Mr. Popper's Penguins by Richard Atwater and Florence Atwater has long been the favorite funny story of many primary-grade children. Mr. Popper is a mild little house painter whose major interest in life is the study of the Antarctic. When an explorer presents Mr. Popper with a penguin, he promptly names him Captain Cook, and he obtains Greta from the zoo to keep Captain Cook company. After the arrival of ten baby penguins, Mr. Popper puts a freezing plant in the basement of his house and moves his furnace upstairs to the living room. The Atwaters' serious account of a highly implausible situation adds to the humor of this truly funny story.

Roald Dahl's many books are populated with highly eccentric characters involved in highly preposterous adventures. One of the most popular fantasies for children is Dahl's tongue-in-cheek morality tale *Charlie and the Chocolate Factory*. Mr. Willie

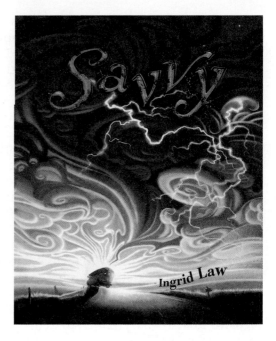

Wonka suddenly announces that the five children who find the gold seal hidden in their chocolate bar wrappers will be allowed to visit his fabulous factory. One by one the children disobey Willie and meet with horrible accidents in the chocolate factory, except of course for the virtuous and humble Charlie, who by the story's conclusion has brought his poor family to live in the chocolate factory and is learning the business from his benefactor.

Sally Keehn and Ingrid Law turn to American folklore and tall tales in creating their larger than life heroines. Keehn's Gnat in *Gnat Stokes and the Foggy Bottom Swamp Queen* is a motherless child who is an outcast in her Appalachian community. When she sets out to battle the evil Swamp Queen to rescue a young man who has gone missing, she finds danger, adventure, and her own identity, not to mention a wonderful cat named Eat-More-Beans. Based on the "Tam Lin" folktale, Keehn's version is both funny and suspenseful. Gnat's colloquial, first-person narrative makes this a natural story to read aloud. Keehn has followed up with an equally eccentric and outlandish distant cousin of Gnat's in *Magpie Gabbard and the Quest for the Buried Moon*. In Law's *Savvy*, each of the members of the Beaumont family find a special gift ("savvy") revealed on their thirteenth birthday. Brother Rocket puts out electrical charges, young Fish causes storms and hurricanes when he gets upset. Two days before her own thirteenth birthday, young Mibs eagerly awaits the revelation of her own savvy. The funny events that take place as she sets off on her journey to identity lighten the tone, but don't hide the worthy theme that we all have our individual savvy, magical or not.

Extraordinary Worlds

When Alice followed the White Rabbit down his rabbit hole and entered a world that grew "curiouser and curiouser," she established a pattern for many modern books of fantasy. Often starting in the world of reality, they move quickly into a world where the everyday becomes extraordinary, yet still believable. The plausible impossibilities of Lewis Carroll's *Alice's Adventures in Wonderland* include potions and edibles that make poor Alice grow up and down like an elevator. Always the proper Victorian young lady, however, Alice maintains her own personality despite her bizarre surroundings, and her acceptance of this nonsense makes it all seem believable. She is the one link with reality in this amazingly fantastic world.

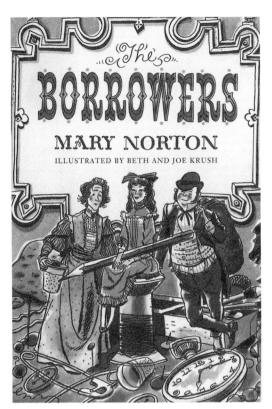

The British landscape where Alice's adventures began has formed the setting for many other fine works of fantasy. *Harry Potter and the Sorcerer's Stone*, the first book in J. K. Rowling's phenomenally popular series, begins in what seems to be a run-of-the-mill middle-class neighborhood as Mr. Dursley picks up his briefcase, bids his wife and son goodbye, and heads off to work. As he drives off, however, he fails to notice a cat sitting on the street reading a map. Mr. Dursley might be clueless, but readers know immediately that this is no ordinary work of realism. They are soon immersed in the magical world of Harry Potter, his awful Dursley relatives, and a host of magical and muggical characters. Rowling has adapted the familiar characters of school stories—a well-meaning and earnest hero and his likable friends, a school bully, an acerbic teacher, and a kind-hearted one, and finally a wise if uneducated janitor to whom the kids go for advice and comfort. Her plots are fast moving and straightforward. The hero is confronted with serious problems that, in spite of many obstacles, are eventually solved. What makes these books so enjoyable are the good humor and obvious zest with which Rowling writes and the wonderful details of Harry's extraordinary world.

Miniature worlds have always fascinated children, and Mary Norton's Borrowers series tells a fascinating story about tiny people who try to coexist with normal-size humans. The Borrowers derive their names from their occupation, which is "borrowing" from human "beans," those "great slaves put there for them to use." "Borrowing" is a dangerous trade, for if one is seen by human beings, disastrous things may happen. Therefore, in *The Borrowers*, Pod and Homily Clock are understandably alarmed when they learn of their daughter Arrietty's desire to explore the world upstairs. In the end, the Borrowers are "discovered" and flee for their lives. This surprise ending leads directly to the sequel, *The Borrowers Afield*. Strong characterizations and apt descriptions of setting make the small-scale world of the Borrowers come alive. Other titles continue the series.

Once children have discovered the delights of series fantasy, they will want to be introduced to others. See **Teaching Feature 5.1: Chronicles, Sagas, and Trilogies: Recent Fantasy Series for Children** on page 132 for descriptions of more popular series fantasies.

Chronicles, Sagas, and Trilogies: Recent Fantasy Series for Children

Author	Series Title	Description	Grade Level
T. A. Barron	The Great Tree of Avalon	These stories of the battle between good and evil take place in the legendary land of Avalon.	5 and up
——	The Lost Years of Merlin	These tales relate the childhood of Merlin and his rise to power.	5 and up
Ian Beck	Tom Trueheart	Tom, youngest of seven brothers all named Jack, enters the land of stories to seek happy endings.	3–6
Patrick Carman	Atherton	Edgar lives on an artificial world that has three levels strictly divided by class.	4–7
Tony DiTerlizzi and Holly Black	The Spiderwick Chronicles	Three children move into an old estate and experience new adventures with fairies and other magical creatures.	3–6
Jeanne DuPrau	The City of Ember	Lina and Doon struggle to escape their existence in a devastated future world.	4–7
Nancy Farmer	Islands of the Blessed	Jack, a young Saxon boy, enters into adventures with heroes from Celtic and Norse mythology.	5 and up
Jean Ferris	Marigold series	An amusing take on traditional fairy tales in which young Marigold is pitted against a wicked Queen.	4–7
Cornelia Funke	Inkheart	Meggie and her father can live in two worlds, their own and the world of the book.	4–7
Debi Gliori	Pure Dead	An over-the-top comedy series featuring the Strega-Borgia clan.	4–7
Erin Hunter	Warriors	The cats of the Thunder Clan face trials and tribulations.	4 and up
Brian Jacques	Redwall	A large cast of animal characters fight for right in the mythical medieval kingdom of Redwall.	4 and up
Catherine Jinks	Genius Squad	Thaddeus Roth is a young genius who is recruited into the Axis Institute for World Domination.	5 and up
William Nicholson	The Wind on Fire Trilogy	Twins Bowman and Kestral lead their people on a journey to their ancestral home.	5 and up
Jenny Nimmo	Magician Trilogy	Gwyn, a young Welsh boy, learns that he is descended from wizards and with the help of magical gifts battles villains from Wales' past.	4–7
Kenneth Oppel	Silverwing	A young bat ventures out into the wide world to save his colony and find his identity.	3–6

Author	Series Title	Description	Grade Level
Christopher Paolini	Inheritance	A boy bonds with a dragon to fight evil in his kingdom.	4–7
Tamora Pierce	Circle of Magic, The Circle Opens, The Circle Reforged	These three series follow the adventures of four mages from their training to the major roles they play in their society.	4–7
Philip Reeve	The Hungry City Chronicles	In a future world, mechanized cities travel around the globe trying to destroy each other.	5 and up
——	Larklight and Starcross	Mad adventure and wacky episodes follow Art and his sister Myrtle through a Victorian world set in outer space.	5 and up
Rick Riordan	Percy Jackson and the Olympians	A boy with attention-deficit hyperactivity disorder finds out he is the half-human son of a Greek god. His quest is to restore order in the supernatural realm and discover his true identity.	5–9
Jan Scieszka	The Time Warp Trio	A magic book provides adventures in time to three zany boys.	2 and up
Gloria Skurzynski	The Virtual War Chronologs	Teens of a future world battle with evil in cyberspace.	5 and up
Trenton Lee Stewart	The Benedict Society	Four uniquely talented youngsters are recruited to fight evil.	4–6
Jonathan Stroud	The Bartimaeus Trilogy	Bartimaeus, the djinni, an ambitious young magician, and a young resistance fighter struggle for power in an alternate Victorian universe.	5 and up
Kate Thompson	T'ír na n'Og	A family of Irish musicians travel back and forth between the present and the land of Faerie.	7 and up
Anne Ursu	Cronus Chronicles	Charlotte and Zee are drawn into a plot that involves Greek gods, Shadow Children, and the Lord of the Dead.	4–7
Carol Wilkinson	Dragon Keeper	Ping, a Chinese slave girl, becomes guardian to the last of the Imperial Dragons.	4–7
Patricia Wrede	Enchanted Forest Chronicles	The unconventional Princess Cimorene befriends dragons, battles wizards, and rescues princesses in this lighthearted series.	4–7
Laurence Yep	The Tiger's Apprentice	A young Chinese boy is trained in magic by a shape-changing tiger.	4–7

Magical Powers

The children in books of fantasy often possess a magical object, know a magical saying, or have magical powers themselves. In *Half Magic* by Edward Eager, the nickel that Jane finds turns out to be a magical charm, or at least half of a magical charm, for it provides half of all the children's wishes, so that half of them will come true.

Jane Langton has written a story of mystery and magical powers surrounding the Halls, who live in a strange old turreted house in Concord, Massachusetts. *The Fledgling*, centers upon 8-year-old Georgie Halls's desire, and eventual ability, to fly. She is befriended by the Goose Prince, who takes her on his back and teaches her to glide in the air by herself. Although Georgie outgrows her gift and the goose falls prey to a gun, he leaves her with a magical present—a ball that projects an image of the whole world and the admonition "Take good care of it." Langton's descriptions give the story a warm and comfortable tone; her evocation of flying might make earth-bound readers' spirits soar.

Authors Sarah Prineas and Sid Fleischman set their fantasies in a much lighter vein. Prineas's protagonist in *The Magic Thief* is Conn, a wily, young pickpocket. When he picks the pocket of the wizard Nevery Elinglas, Conn has met his match, and he finds himself apprenticed to a mage whose difficult task is to discover why magic is seeping out of the city of Wellmet. A lively battle of wits between Nevery and the villainous Underlord ensues with Conn playing the role of a bumbling if ingenious helper. Sid Fleischman's *The Midnight Horse* takes place near the fictionalized New England town of Cricklewood, New Hampshire: "Population 217: 216 Fine Folks & 1 Infernal

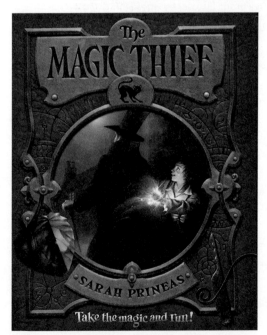

Young Conn is a pickpocket who picks the wrong pocket in *The Magic Thief* by Sarah Prineas. From *The Magic Thief* by Sarah Prineas. Used by permission of HarperCollins Publishers.

Grouch." When Touch, a young orphan, comes to claim his inheritance from the infernal grouch Judge Wigglesforth, the judge tries to force him to sign for his inheritance, thirty-seven cents. No fool, Touch refuses to sign and escapes to a ramshackle inn. In fast-paced, humorous, short chapters, Touch discovers his real inheritance, saves the inn, and unmasks both the thief and the judge. Fleischman's ear for comic dialogue, his inspired similes, and his ability to strip a tale to its essentials put this a lively fantasy in the same vein as his story *The Whipping Boy*.

Older readers with a tolerance for invented worlds and the ability to follow a large cast of characters will enjoy the many books by Diana Wynne Jones. *Howl's Moving Castle* features Sophie Hatter, an adolescent who is turned into an old woman by the Wicked Witch of the Waste. In *Charmed Life* the magician Chrestomanci must help young Eric Chant (called "Cat" for short) to discover his own powers while he preserves his household against the evil that assails it from outside the castle walls. *The Lives of Christopher Chant*, a prequel, is about the boyhood of Chrestomanci, who is able to dream himself into strange worlds and bring back from these places what others cannot. Like Eric, he is naive about adult motives, an unwitting accomplice to his uncle's wicked plans, and an unwilling heir to the previous Chrestomanci's power. Chrestomanci returns in other books including Jones's *House of Many Ways*. These imaginatively plotted stories reveal the author's wry humor, her love of language, and her ability to balance aspects of time and space in impossible but believable ways.

Suspense and the Supernatural

Interest in the occult and the supernatural, usually an adult preoccupation, also captures the imagination of children. They enjoy spooky, scary stories, just as they like being frightened by TV or theater horror stories. This may in part explain the popularity of authors like John Bellairs, whose mysteries, such as *The House with a Clock in Its Walls*, are full of spooky old houses, scary characters, fast-moving plots, and plenty of dialogue. Increasingly, publishers are issuing finely crafted suspense fantasies that are often superior to the usual ghost story or mystery tale. These well-written tales of suspense and the supernatural deserve attention.

Several recent books don't pull any stops when it comes to horror. All involve resourceful heroines who are forced to act in the face of their terror when their parents disappear. Neil Gaiman's *Coraline* is an only child, out of sorts with the world and left to fend for herself by her preoccupied parents. Coraline explores the house they have just moved into, and discovers a door that leads to a dark hallway—and to a terrifying alternative universe. This other world is a nightmare reflection of her own, and Coraline has let loose events that she cannot control. Gaiman masterfully builds the tension as the true horror of this other world is revealed. Coraline realizes that she must somehow undo the wrong she has committed and restore normalcy. *Coraline* is horror writing at its best, with intriguing characters, a well-constructed and eerie setting, and a thrilling and suspenseful plot. Gaiman and illustrator Craig Russell have collaborated in a graphic novel version of *Coraline*.

Joseph Bruchac's *The Dark Pond*, *Whisper in the Dark*, and *Skeleton Man*, although set in the present, are based on traditional Native American tales. In *Skeleton Man*, the heroine, Molly, relates this traditional Abenaki tale at the beginning of her own narrative story. As her story proceeds, Molly becomes involved with a mysterious great-uncle who turns up when her parents disappear. Locked in her room each night, Molly suspects that the uncle may be Skeleton Man, a legendary creature who devoured himself and then, still hungry, ate everyone around him. Molly realizes that, like the young girls in the original tale, she is the only one who can defeat him. These novels are flat-out terrifying through their final pages.

Mary Downing Hahn's ghost stories are not for the fainthearted. In *Wait Till Helen Comes*, a ghost child named Helen has perished in a fire and now waits by a pond to drag children to their deaths as play companions. When Molly and Michael's mother remarries, their new father's child joins the family, but Heather is a brat who forever whines about imagined injustices. Nobody believes Heather's stories of the ghostly Helen until Molly begins to develop some sympathy for her stepsister's point of view. In a chilling ending, Molly pieces together the mystery, saves Heather from a sure death, and forges a hopeful beginning of a loving family. In Hahn's *All the Lovely Bad Ones*, two mischievous children think it would be great fun to awaken the ghosts reputed to haunt their grandmother's inn. They soon find that fun is nowhere in the

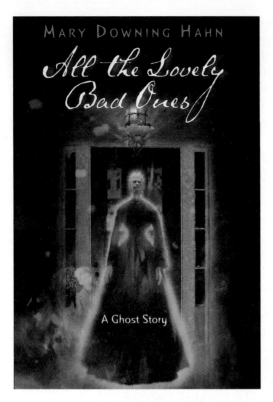

MARY DOWNING HAHN

All the Lovely Bad Ones

A Ghost Story

mix as they struggle to put the ghosts back to rest. Hahn's fast-paced stories consistently win young-readers' awards presented by various states, showing how much children appreciate a good, scary ghost story.

Sweet Whispers, Brother Rush by Virginia Hamilton is a haunting story of the supernatural in which fourteen-year-old Tree must take care of her older brother Dab while her mother, Viola, works in another city as a practical nurse. Tree painfully accepts her mother's absences and devotes her time to schoolwork and caring for her brother. As Dab's occasional bouts of sickness suddenly become more frequent, a spectral character named Brother Rush appears to Tree and enables her to understand what is happening. Making use of African American cadences and inflections, Hamilton has created complex characters whose steady or fumbling reachings for each other may linger with middle-school readers long past the end of this story.

Time-Shift Fantasy

Probably everyone at one time or another has wondered what it would be like to visit the past. Recognizing this, authors of books for children have written many fantasies that are based on characters who appear to shift easily from their particular moment in the present to a long-lost point in someone else's past. Usually these time leaps are linked to a tangible object or place that is common to both periods. In *Tom's Midnight Garden* by Philippa Pearce, for example, the old grandfather clock that strikes thirteen hours serves as the fixed point of entry for the fantasy.

No one is more skillful in fusing the past with the present than L. M. Boston in her stories of Green Knowe, the mysterious old English house in which the author lived. Each story of Green Knowe blends a child of the present with characters and situations from previous centuries while creating for the reader a marvelous sense of place.

While the characters in most time fantasies slip in and out of the past, the problem in *Tuck Everlasting* is that the Tuck family is trapped forever in the present. Natalie Babbitt's elegant prose leads the reader to expect a quiet Victorian fantasy, but the book holds many surprises—including a kidnapping, a murder, and a jailbreak. The simplicity of the Tucks and their story belies the depth of the theme of *Tuck Everlasting*. With its prologue and epilogue, the story is reminiscent of a play, a kind of *Our Town* for children.

In some books where characters are shifted from modern times into specific periods of history, the concern with social and political issues of the past is very strong. David Wiseman's *Jeremy Visick* explores the conditions of child laborers in England's nineteenth-century copper mines when the hero's school assignment leads him into a mine disaster of a previous century. Jane Yolen's devastating story of the Holocaust, *The Devil's Arithmetic*, begins in the present when Hannah, bored with all the remembering of the Passover Seder, opens the door to welcome symbolically the prophet Elijah and finds herself in the unfamiliar world of a Polish village in the 1940s.

Susan Cooper has created a richly detailed time-travel story in *King of Shadows*. Nat Field is a passionate actor and a member of a group of boys who have been chosen to perform William Shakespeare's *A Midsummer Night's Dream* at the recently opened replica of the Globe Theatre in London. Nat keeps himself busy with rehearsals and throws himself into his role as Puck, partly out of love for acting and partly to block out thoughts about his father's suicide. Soon after his arrival in London, Nat becomes ill and wakes from his fever to find himself in sixteenth-century London. There he is still called Nat Field and he is still an actor. But now he finds he is to play the part of Puck alongside Will Shakespeare on the boards of the original Globe. Readers captivated by the world of the Elizabethan theater in *King of Shadows* will also enjoy Jane Louise Curry's *The Black Canary*. In this time-shift fantasy, 13-year-old James, a biracial child, has rejected the musical world of his career-oriented parents. When he accompanies them to London, he finds a mysterious door in the cellar of their borrowed flat. Stepping through, James is plunged into Elizabethan times, where he is forced to join the Queen's performers. In addition to dealing with issues of race, Curry tells a gripping coming-of-age story in *The Black Canary*. Both *The Black Canary* and *King of Shadows* introduce themes of interest to early adolescents. In addition, they present readers with the historical background of a vivid age.

Imaginary Realms

Many authors of fantasy create believability by setting their stories in an imaginary society where kings and queens rule feudal societies that resemble the Middle Ages. Often lighter in tone than high fantasy, these stories might nonetheless feature some of its attributes—such as a human character's search for identity, a quest, or the struggle against evil—and are good introductions to the more complex and more serious works of high fantasy. Children are often drawn to this kind of fantasy, as it seems so closely related in many ways to folktales and traditional literature.

Authors have long enjoyed playing with the characters and elements of traditional tales. Gail Carson Levine, Diane Stanley, and Patricia Wrede are three writers who have relied on familiar fairy tales to create humorous, highly readable fantasies. In *Ella Enchanted*, Levine has taken the Cinderella story and provided a reasonable interpretation for Cinderella's subservience to her stepmother and stepsisters. A well-meaning fairy has given her the gift of obedience, but the gift turns into a curse when her stepfamily starts ordering her around. This wily heroine eventually breaks the wish through willing self-sacrifice and wins the Prince through her own devices. In *Bella at Midnight*, Diane Stanley serves up a delightful twist on the Cinderella story, with a bit of the Joan of Arc legend thrown in. Patricia Wrede's Enchanted Forest Chronicles feature the unconventional Princess Cimorene. In *Dealing with Dragons*, Cimorene runs off to be librarian and cook for the dragon Kazul rather than stay in the palace, sew, and wait for a suitor. This same audience will appreciate the many series of books by

The protagonist of *Princess Ben*, by Catherine Gilbert Murdock, is a younger member of a royal family who suddenly finds herself groomed as a future queen. Cover from *Princess Ben* by Catherine Gilbert Murdock. Front cover photo-illustration © Larry Rostant. Reprinted by permission of Houghton Mifflin Harcourt Publishing Company. All rights reserved.

Tamora Pierce, which feature characters who will not stay put in the roles their societies have dictated for them. Catherine Gilbert Murdock's *Princess Ben* is another character who won't stick to traditional gender roles. When her mother and her Uncle the King are killed and her father disappears, Ben suddenly becomes heir to the kingdom. Her aunt Sophia, the former queen, is determined to train her in the ways of royalty and to marry her off to a neighboring prince (not in her estimation anything like Charming). In a story that borrows from Sleeping Beauty, Ben finally wakes up to her own individual powers, saves her kingdom, and finds her prince.

Gerald Morris, Nancy Springer, and Kevin Crossley-Holland have placed their stories squarely within the tradition of Arthurian legend. We have chosen to discuss these books in the fantasy chapter because of some instances of magic and their focus on legendary characters such as Arthur and Morgan le Fay. However, these books are so well researched in the history of the Middle Ages that they could qualify as historical fiction. Morris's stories are clearly set in mythical Arthur's time period. *The Squire's Tale* and *The Squire, His Knight and His Lady* are the somewhat lighthearted stories of 14-year-old Terence's apprenticeship to Sir Gawain and his adventures at King Arthur's court. Springer's *I Am Mordred* and *I Am Morgan le Fay* are more somber but ultimately uplifting stories of the traditional villains in King Arthur's tale. Crossley-Holland's series, which includes *The Seeing Stone*, *At the Crossing Place*, and *King of the Middle March*, takes place in the latter part of the twelfth century in England. This England is not a mythical place but a carefully researched historical setting. It is a time when the English face great danger as the villainous King John assumes the throne after King Richard's death. *Crossing to Paradise* follows Arthur's childhood friend Gatti, a young field girl, who is asked to accompany Lady Gwyneth as a maidservant on a pilgrimage to the Holy Land. In return for her services on this dangerous journey, Gatti will be taught to read and write and to be trained in how to use her marvelous singing voice. The geographical journey is mirrored by Gatti's journey to self-understanding and self-confidence.

High Fantasy

Many readers who learn to enjoy popular stories of magic, ghosts, time travel, and the like go on to become fans of a more serious and demanding type of story called high fantasy. These complex narratives, which often extend into sequels, are characterized by certain recurring themes and motifs. For instance, the stories frequently take place in created worlds or imaginary realms. Characters might call on ancient and fundamental powers, for good or ill. The conflict between these opposing forces becomes the focus of many stories. Frequently the protagonists of high fantasy have a quest to fulfill. Finally, although there may be touches of humor, the overall tone of high fantasy is serious, because its purpose is serious. High fantasy concerns itself with cosmic questions and ultimate values: goodness, truth, courage, wisdom.

The age-old conflicts between good and evil, light and darkness, life and death are recurring themes in modern fantasy as well as in traditional literature. The setting for the struggle might be the world as we know it, or an invented land like Narnia, which some children know as well as their own backyards or city blocks. C. S. Lewis, a well-known English scholar and theologian, created seven fantasies about the country of Narnia. The best of the series is the first one published, *The Lion, the Witch, and the Wardrobe*, although it was the second in the sequence according to the history of Narnia.

Susan Cooper has written a series of five books about the cosmic struggle between good and evil. The second book in the series, *The Dark Is Rising*, features Will Stanton who discovers that he is the last of the Old Ones, immortals dedicated throughout the ages to keeping the world safe from the forces of evil, the Dark. Will must find the six Signs of Life in order to complete his power and defeat, even temporarily, the rising of the Dark. While rich in symbolism and allegory, the story is grounded in reality so that both Will's "real" life and his quest in suspended time are distinct, yet interwoven. In the fourth book of the series, *The Grey King*, Will once again must prepare for the coming battle between the Dark and the Light. *Silver on the Tree* draws together characters from the previous four novels for a final assault on the Dark. Much that was hidden in the other tales is made explicit here, and knowledge of the major threads of the first four books is necessary to understand this exciting and fulfilling climax to the saga.

T. A. Barron has also drawn on myths surrounding King Arthur in his five-book The Lost Years of Merlin series. This saga begins with a young boy who finds himself lying on a rocky shore robbed of his memory and his identity. Over the course of the series this child will uncover his past and his magical gifts. More important, however, as he faces increasingly difficult trials, he will learn to control his marvelous talents and to accept the responsibilities that come with power. Barron's Great Tree of Avalon series continues his exploration of Celtic lore and the myth of Merlin.

Philip Pullman, whose skillful writing has given us such fine books as the suspenseful *The Ruby in the Smoke*, the supernatural *Clockwork*, and the farcical *The Firework-Maker's Daughter* and *I Was a Rat*, has created high fantasy of matchless proportion in

In his Great Tree of Avalon series, T. A. Barron has created complex works of high fantasy based in ancient legends and myths. *The Great Tree of Avalon: The Eternal Flame*, Book III by T. A. Barron, copyright © 2002 by T.A. Barron. Used by permission of Philomel Books, a division of Penguin Young Readers Group, a Member of Penguin Group (USA) Inc., 345 Hudson Street, New York, NY 10014. All rights reserved.

His Dark Materials series. The trilogy, which includes *The Golden Compass*, *The Subtle Knife*, and *The Amber Spyglass*, is a richly complex work of the imagination. Inspired by a phrase from Milton's *Paradise Lost*, Pullman wrestles with profound issues of innocence, individuality, and spirituality. These compelling books, with their connections to Judeo-Christian traditions, their underpinnings in literary classics, and their references to theories of quantum physics, demand much of readers, but those willing to accept the challenging puzzles will be rewarded with an exceptionally satisfying experience.

High fantasy is almost always the story of a search—for treasure, justice, identity, understanding—and of a hero figure who learns important lessons in the adventuring. Welsh legends and mythology are the inspiration for the intriguing chronicles of the imaginary land of Prydain as told by Lloyd Alexander. In *The Book of Three*, the reader is introduced to Taran, an assistant pigkeeper who dreams of becoming a hero. With a strange assortment of companions, he pursues Hen Wen, the oracular pig, and struggles to save Prydain from the forces of evil. The chronicles are continued in the most exciting of all the books, *The Black Cauldron*. Over the course of the chronicles Taran gradually learns what it means to become a man among men. He experiences treachery, tragedy, and triumph; yet a thread of humor runs throughout to lighten the tension. Good does prevail, and Taran has matured and is ready for his next adventure. *The High King*, the masterful conclusion to this cycle of stories about the kingdom of Prydain, received the Newbery Medal.

A superior tale against which other novels of high fantasy may be judged is *A Wizard of Earthsea* by Ursula K. Le Guin. Studying at the School for Wizards, Sparrow-hawk is taunted by a jealous classmate to use his powers before he is ready. Pride and arrogance drive him to call up a dreadful malignant shadow that threatens his life and all of Earthsea. Thus begins a chase and the hunt between the young wizard and the shadowbeast across the mountains and the waters of this world. Sparrow-hawk, or Ged, his true name known only by his most trusted friends, is a well-developed character who transforms from an intelligent, impatient adolescent into a wise and grateful mage, or wizard. A major theme of the story is the responsibility that each choice carries with it. The power of knowing the true name of someone or something, a common motif in traditional literature, is of central importance to this story. So, too, is the value of self-knowledge:

> Ged's "ultimate quest . . . had made him whole: a man who knowing his whole true self, cannot be used or possessed by another power other than by himself, and whose life therefore is lived for life's sake and never in the service of ruin, or pain, or hatred, or the dark." (p. 203)

The metaphors in all Le Guin's books speak clearly and profoundly to today's world.

Science Fiction

The line between fantasy and science fiction has always been difficult to draw, particularly in children's literature. Children are likely to use the label *science fiction* for any book that includes the paraphernalia of science, although critics make finer distinctions. It has been suggested that fantasy (even "science fantasy") presents a world that never was and never could be, whereas science fiction speculates on a world that, given what we now know of science, might just one day be possible.

Science fiction is relevant for today's rapidly changing world. Writers must speculate about future technology and how new discoveries will affect our daily lives and thoughts. To do this, they must construct a world in which scientific frontiers of genetic engineering, artificial intelligence, space exploration, or robotics have advanced beyond our present knowledge. As in modern fantasy, detailed descriptions of these "scientific principles" and the characters' acceptance of them make the story believable. In addition, authors who speak to today's reader about the future must consider the ethical or social implications inherent in the scientific issues they raise.

Science fiction of the highest level presents the reader with complex hypotheses about the future of humankind. Many novels raise questions about the organization of society or the nature of the world following a massive ecological disaster. Writers such as Madeleine L'Engle imagine other life forms and their interactions with our world. In L'Engle's *A Swiftly Tilting Planet*, the past is altered to change the present and future. Throughout these novels of speculation runs the question of which human qualities and responsibilities will become—or remain—essential in time to come. *A Wrinkle in Time* suggests that love and individuality will continue to be important for the future. If there is a classic in the field of science fiction for children, it might be this Newbery Medal winner by Madeleine L'Engle. See **Teaching Feature 5.2: Exploring Possible Futures** for an overview of recent science fiction about future worlds.

One of the values of science fiction is its ability to develop children's imagination and intuition as well as exercise their speculative and improvisational abilities. Most literature offers a view of society as it is; science fiction assumes a vastly different society. Much science fiction that considers cosmic questions falls within the realm of young-adult novels. For instance, in *The Diary of Pelly D*, and the sequel *Cherry Heaven*, L. J. Adlington imagines a seemingly utopian world where growing prejudice about genetic ancestry leads society to a futuristic holocaust. In *Eva*, Peter Dickinson considers the consequences when the mind of a human girl is transferred from her ruined body to that of a healthy chimpanzee. *The Adoration of Jenna Fox* by Mary E. Pearson and Nancy Farmer's *The House of the Scorpion* deal with ethical issues and cloning. M. T. Anderson's *Feed* contemplates a frightening future where at birth almost everyone is wired to the Internet through brain implants. These books demand maturity in their readers but raise important questions about the world these young adults will inherit.

Lois Lowry's *The Giver* imagines a future that at first seems benign and idyllic. Pollution is gone, family life is tranquil, and communities are orderly and peaceful. In this world, young Jonas approaches the Ceremony of Twelve with anticipation, for this is when he will be assigned to his life's work. He is stunned when his name is passed over during the

In her Newbery Medal–winning book *The Giver*, Lois Lowry raises fundamental questions about human nature and human society. Cover from *The Giver* by Lois Lowry. Copyright © 1993 by Lois Lowry. Reprinted by permission of Houghton Mifflin Harcourt Publishing Company. All rights reserved.

Exploring Possible Futures: Science Fiction for Today's Youth

Author	Title	Description	Grade Level
L. J. Adlington	*The Diary of Pelly D.*; *Cherry Heaven*	Settlers of a distant planet find they have repeated all the mistakes that led them to abandon earth.	7 and up
Julie Bertagna	*Exodus*; *Zenith*	Greenhouse gases have finally destroyed most of the planet and refugees from the last island try to find sanctuary.	7 and up
Clare B. Dunkle	*The Sky Inside*	This view of the pros and cons of creating a utopian future is reminiscent of Lois Lowry's *The Giver*.	4–8
Brian Falkner	*The Tomorrow Code*	A binary code from the future is sent back to two children in the present and they discover a threat to the entire human race.	4–8
Helen Fox	*Eager*	Eager is a robot in a future world where rich and poor are vastly separated.	4–8
Michael Grant	*Gone*	Everyone over the age of 14 has disappeared and the survivors are not too skilled at taking care of themselves.	6–9
Margaret Haddix	*Among the Hidden*	Third children are illegal in a future world and thus exist in great peril.	4–7
Peter Hautman	*Rash*	In a future, highly constrained society, young Bo is sent to a prison/pizza factory and forced to join the football team.	7 and up
Will Hobbs	*Go Big or Go Home*	When a meteorite crashes into earth, Brady picks up a piece of it and starts to develop unusual powers and worrisome physical symptoms.	4–6
Susan Beth Pfeffer	*Life as We Knew It*	An asteroid hits earth and causes havoc for human society.	7 and up

ceremony, but then the Chief Elder announces that Jonas has been selected to be the next Receiver of Memory. This is the one person in the community who holds memories, not just of events, but of feelings. As he is instructed by the old Receiver, now the Giver, he comes to understand the fullness of human experience in all its color, joy, and pain. He also begins to see beneath the orderly surface of his existence and to understand the terrible price his people have paid for their serenity. Determined to change the course of the future, Jonas and the Giver plan for his escape. But at the last moment a terrible threat to Gabriel, a foster child about whom Jonas cares deeply, forces a change of plan, and Jonas sets out on a journey that might lead to his end or might bring him full circle to his humanity. *The Giver* is a richly rewarding fantasy, full of subtle clues, connections, and ideas. Lowry has given each reader the wonderful gift that Jonas's community lacked, the gift of choice. This is a book to be read, enjoyed, and understood on an intensely personal level.

The ability to change lives is the power of such good writing. Fantasy for children needs no defense. Whether a modern fairy tale like *Many Moons* or *The Little Prince*, modern fantasy like *Charlotte's Web* or *The Dark Is Rising*, or the science fiction of *A Wrinkle in Time* or *The Giver*, these lasting books can speak for our time and the times to come. They stretch children's imaginations, present our own world in a new perspective, and ask readers to consider how present actions might affect earth's ecological, political, and social future.

Evaluating Modern Fantasy

Well-written fantasy, like other fiction, has a well-constructed plot, convincing characterization, a worthwhile theme, and an appropriate style. However, additional considerations must guide the evaluation of fantasy. The primary concern is the way the author makes the fantasy believable. A variety of techniques can be used to create belief in the unbelievable. Many authors firmly ground a story in reality before gradually moving into fantasy. Not until chapter 3 in *Charlotte's Web* does author E. B. White suggest that Fern can understand the farm animals as they talk. And even then, Fern never talks to the animals; she only listens to them. By the end of the story Fern is growing up and really is more interested in listening to Henry Fussy than to the animals. White's description of the sounds and smells of the barnyard allows readers to experience the setting as well.

Creating belief by careful attention to the detail of the setting is a technique also used by Mary Norton in *The Borrowers*. Norton's graphic description of the Borrowers' home beneath the clock enables the reader to visualize this domestic background and to feel what it would be like to be as small as the Borrowers. J. K. Rowling has created such wonderfully detailed settings for her Harry Potter series that children have no trouble accepting the magical creatures and the fantastic events that occur at Hogwarts School of Witchcraft and Wizardry.

Having one of the characters mirror the disbelief of the reader is another device for creating convincing fantasy. In *Jeremy Visick*, David Wiseman has portrayed his protagonist, Matthew, as a boy who thinks history is rubbish. Therefore, when even he is persuaded that the past lives again, the reader shares Matthew's terror as he descends to sure disaster within the depths of the Wheal Maid mine.

The use of appropriate language adds a kind of authenticity to fantasy. In *The Fox Busters*, a clever story full of wordplay and puns, Dick King-Smith creates languages for a farm community in which chickens speak Hennish while the foxes speak Volpine. When one of the hens curses, using "fowl language," she tells a fox, "Go fricassee yourself," and calls a human a "stupid scrambled boy." The hens are named after famous farm-implement companies like Massey-Harris or Allis-Chalmers, which adds further authenticity to this delightful fantasy.

The proof of real objects gives an added dimension of truth in books. How can we explain the origin of Greta's kitten or her father's penknife if not from Blue Cove in Julia Sauer's story *Fog Magic*? In *Tom's Midnight Garden* by Philippa Pearce, it is the discovery of a pair of ice skates that confirms the reader's belief in Tom's adventures.

Another point to be considered when evaluating fantasy is the consistency of the story. Each fantasy should have a logical framework and an internal consistency in the world set forth by the author. For instance, characters should not become invisible whenever they face difficulty unless invisibility is a well-established part of their natures. The laws of fantasy may be strange indeed, but they must be obeyed.

Lloyd Alexander explains the importance of internal consistency within the well-written fantasy:

> Once committed to his imaginary kingdom, the writer is not a monarch but a subject. Characters must appear plausible in their own setting, and the writer must go along with the inner logic. Happenings should have logical implications. Details should be tested for consistency. Shall animals speak? If so, do *all* animals speak? If not, then which—and how? Above all, why? Is it essential to the story, or lamely cute? Are there enchantments? How powerful? If an enchanter can perform such-and-such, can he not also do so-and-so?[2]

Finally, while all plots should be original, the plots of fantasy must be ingenious and creative. A contrived or trite plot seems more obvious in a fanciful tale than in a realistic story.

Modern fantasy makes special demands on authors. The box **Guidelines: Evaluating Modern Fantasy** summarizes the criteria that need to be considered when evaluating this genre for children.

Challenging Perspectives on Modern Fantasy

Children have always loved fantasy. Whether it is Beatrix Potter's *Tales of Peter Rabbit*, Maurice Sendak's *Where the Wild Things Are*, or the lovable adventures of Don Freeman's *Corduroy*, children young and old have read and reread and come back for more. In fantasies, people and animals live in a make-believe world. Some fantasies begin realistically or contain bits of reality so that they seem believable to the reader.

As children enter the world of make-believe through imagination and play, reading provides a conduit for expanding the terrain of what is. It is often with fantasy through nursery rhymes, fairy tales, and folk tales that younger children engage in

Guidelines

Evaluating Modern Fantasy

Go to **www.mhhe.com/kieferbrief1e** *to access an expanded version of this evaluation form.*

Consider the following when evaluating modern fantasy:

- What are the fantasy elements of the story?
- How has the author made the story believable?
- Is the story logical and consistent within the framework established by the author?

- Is the plot original and ingenious?
- Is there a universal truth underlying the metaphor of the fantasy?
- How does the story compare with other books of the same kind or by the same author?

dramatic play. Pretending that inanimate objects can come to life has always been popular for readers of all ages.

Some parents, caregivers, and teachers have become concerned when reading materials, either selected for or given to their children, include tales of fantasy that in their minds is an affront to religious and spiritual family values. However, the question of appropriateness is not a new one. In the early work of Piaget (a developmental psychologist known for his work studying children and his theory of cognitive development), he determined that children move through several stages of development (see Chapter 2). It is in and through each of these stages that children progress developmentally from abstract to more concrete understandings of events. While approximate ages have been assigned to the stages (sensory-motor: from birth to age 2—children experience the world through movement and senses and learn object permanence; preoperational: from ages 2 to 7—acquisition of motor skills; concrete operational: from ages 7 to 11—children begin to think logically about concrete events; formal operational stage: after age 11—development of abstract reasoning), there are no absolute ages for each of these stages. Some teachers and parents often cite this work to support claims that children are not developmentally ready to traverse between the worlds of imagination and reality. However, researchers continue to find that children who are encouraged to engage in these imaginative ways make significant gains in readiness skills.[3,4]

Children are not born with imagination. The development and later use of imagination, however, is crucial to their intellectual and social development. The ability to suspend belief to expand their worlds through fantasy can develop not only school readiness for younger children but also fosters creativity.

The major challenge, however, is to respond to criticisms that fantasy is dangerous literature for children. Parents and guardians of children have the expressed right to determine what their children read. It is not the teacher's role to determine if parents or caregivers should include or exclude fantasy from their child's "personal-at-home" library.

What does fall under the purview of teachers is to engage in language arts instruction that is not limited to grammar and vocabulary, or even to the development of language skills. They must encourage creative language and understand that the role of imagination in reading good children's literature can be facilitated with the genre of fantasy in ways that for some children can jump-start their imagination and increase the development of general skills and specific strategies of the reading process.

An unofficial standard of meeting the needs of the families and community in which you may teach is real. Pressure from the outside into the classrooms of teachers related to reading material can have you before a principal, or school board, depending on the media coverage. The challenge that remains, however, is how a teacher can deal with a parent's objection to a particular book. Should teachers, as professionals, be free to exercise their judgment in the selection of children's literature to be read in the classroom? The professional autonomy of teachers can be an important source of strength in an education system, and as such, should be valued by the broader society as well as by colleagues of the profession. Using children's literature is just one area where teachers are experiencing many limitations and challenges to their professional autonomy. These challenges can be met in many cases when teachers work in partnership with parents, guardians, and school administrators to

Step	Task	To Consider
1. Raise the initial question and have the children brainstorm all their initial responses.	Prompt children's response with: • "Is censorship in schools a good idea?" • "Is it necessary to ban books?" • "Why are certain books the target of individuals or groups who want them banned or censored?"	Ground rules are needed to moderate the nature of contributions to the discussion. The purpose of such rules is to enable the free flow of ideas in a safe, nonthreatening environment with the goal of having students think about and question their assumptions and listen to others' ideas.
2. Create a list of "Things to find out more about."	As children brainstorm their ideas about banned or censored books, ask them to create a list of what they know about the topic and about what they need to find out more.	Be explicit about the First Amendment to the Constitution and the right to one's own opinion, censorship, hate speech, obscenity and defamation laws, the most challenged books, the American Library Association's stand, etc.
3. Assign information-gathering homework.	Encourage children to gather examples of banned or censored books and to learn about the history of banning books in America and abroad.	Local librarians and constitutional law lawyers in the community may be your best sources.
4. Share again responses to the initial question in a brainstorming session.	Require students to cite the quality of the evidence from which claims are made—whether from an outside source, from their experiences, from the media, or from family members.	Provide as much support as you have available, including information from court cases. Invite local librarians and legal experts to participate.
5. Continue the process of gathering information.	Share information and identify things to find out more about. Encourage students to listen to and learn from each other.	Students can find out how to stop a book from becoming banned by contacting the American Library Association's Freedom to Read campaign or the National Coalition Against Censorship.

negotiate the best way to approach these controversial topics as they arise with challenged texts.

Some school districts have established policies on the rights of teachers to teach good literature, thereby supporting the selection of fantasy, science fiction, and other genres of children's literature. If a policy does not exist, it may be appropriate to first talk with an administrator in the building to discuss if the book has been used before or how challenges to the use of controversial texts has been dealt with in the past. It might also require a note home to parents letting them know before a book is used in the classroom, and that an alternative reading assignment may be given to their child if they so choose. It could also be helpful to check with other teachers in the building as well as district or local professional teacher organizations for advice. There are no predetermined rules to follow since every community context is different. It is best to gather as much information as you can and make your best professional decision. Sur-

figure 5.1 *(continued)*

Step	Task	To Consider
6. If a concept emerges that sparks interest, confusion, or conflict, pose it as a new question.	Some children may agree that books should be banned. Allow each side of the debate to express their views.	Mediating negative comments and strong emotions is an important aspect of ensuring a "smooth" approach to controversial issues. Ask for evidence, analyze underlying assumptions, and ask for other viewpoints.
7. Periodically give the children assignments in class to summarize their thoughts.	An assignment to educate the public about books that are banned or censored locally can include writing a letter to the editor of the local newspaper or helping local librarians with Banned Books Week.	Find ways to help crystallize your students' individual thinking about banned or censored books.
8. As individual or group projects emerge, follow up on them.	One or two children may decide to pursue a challenging research topic to report on to the group or other interested communities.	Often when teaching controversial issues, it can become very emotional. Keep up with the progress on either side of the issue and remind students that everyone is entitled to an opinion.
9. Let others know what you are doing.	Students can contact organizations such as the American Booksellers Foundation for Free Expression or the Thomas Jefferson Center for the Protection of Free Expression for speakers to present issues to the community.	Encourage dialogue with parents, colleagues, and the community. Find out what books have been challenged in the past and what happened. Inform parents of books that may be challenged, giving them options for alternative reading material for their child.
10. End your project with something either public or permanent.	If possible, facilitate a school and/or community dialogue about understanding and defending the First Amendment, and supporting local librarians who may be facing attempts to restrict library materials and services.	It is critical to make the experience relevant to the lives of the children. Looking for opportunities for authentic learning experiences will help children create real-world connections.

Source: Adapted from Kreidler, W. *Elementary Perspectives: Teaching Concepts of Peace and Conflict.* Copyright © 1990, Educators for Social Responsibility, Cambridge, MA, www.esrnational.org. Used by permission.

prisingly, the types of controversies that may arise, such as with J. K. Rowling's Harry Potter books, often actually generate even greater reader interest and enthusiasm in the books!

If the challenge to a book prohibits using it in the classroom, this could lead to what is called a "teachable moment." Language arts teacher Shiela Siegfried wrote, "teachers must be ready at the drop of a hat to leap into curriculum development. The teachable moment is also the curriculum-design moment. The children are letting us know what sparks their interest all the time." She further stated, "Spur-of-the-moment curriculum development should be occurring regularly in our classrooms. Opportunities arise daily that lend themselves to further exploration" (p. 285).[5] For example, a teacher could use an opportunity to have discussions with her students about books that are banned or censored (challenged) using the Ten-Point Model for discussing controversial issues. (See **Figure 5.1**.)

In his book, *Critical Incidents in Teaching: Developing Professional Judgment*, David Tripp states, ". . . we have to develop professional judgment, when we have to move beyond our everyday 'working' way of looking at things." He argues that teachers need a "professional consciousness" to meet the everyday challenges to teaching.[6] It is this professional consciousness that should permeate teachers' decisions in the selection and use of any genre of children's literature. The consciousness will help teachers respond to the pressure of contemporary concerns while simultaneously showing high degrees of skill and competence in their instruction of fantasy literature.

curriculum connections

Using Modern Fantasy to Address Standards

As a genre, fantasy opens up possibilities to explore alternative societies that emulate and expose the hopes, despairs, and possibilities of our own society. In fantasy, the characters are not only people like us, but also trolls, kings, fairies, and sorcerers who form coalitions to fight against darkness and evil. Fantasy provides a space for characters and readers alike to wrestle with the inadequacies of our human limits and imagine ways our world might be otherwise. The genre has strong connections to the language arts because of many titles' dependence on epic structures and more traditional extended narratives. Titles that rely on these textual patterns include Philip Pullman's Golden Compass trilogy, or T. A. Barron's Great Tree of Avalon series. Topics in science such as the physics of flight can be studied after reading books in the Harry Potter series by J. K. Rowling, while Kenneth Opel's Silverwing series is a wonderful introduction to a study of bats. Finally, Jon Scieszka's historical romps in the Time Warp Trio series are excellent entries into a variety of topics in history, math, and science.

Standards in Action: Social Studies

I, Coriander
> Gardner, S. (2005). *I, Coriander*. New York: Dial Books.

This book blends historical fiction and fantasy in the story of a young girl who is the daughter of a wealthy London merchant and his fairy-princess wife. Her life is profoundly shaped by her mother's early death and the arrival of her cruel stepmother as well as the larger social context of Puritan England. Coriander travels back and forth between both worlds, experiencing adventures full of danger. In the end she must decide to which world she ultimately belongs.

Apply to Social Studies Standard 4: Individual Development and Identity
Personal identity is shaped by one's culture, by groups, and by institutional influences. Students should consider such questions as: How do people learn? Why do people behave as they do? What influences how people learn, perceive, and grow? How do people meet their basic needs in a variety of contexts? How do individuals develop from youth to adulthood?

- Students can illustrate the different communities that they feel they are a part of. Who are the key people in these different communities? Where are the communities physically located? What are possible differences or conflicts between these different communities? What connects them to these communities?

Apply to Social Studies Standard 6: Power, Authority, and Governance

Understanding the historical development of structures of power, authority, and governance and their evolving functions in contemporary U.S. society and other parts of the world is essential for developing civic competence. In exploring this theme, students confront questions such as: What is power? What forms does it take? Who holds it? How is it gained, used, and justified? What is legitimate authority? How are governments created, structured, maintained, and changed? How can individual rights be protected within the context of majority rule?

- Students can compare and contrast the way that power and governance operated in both of Coriander's worlds. They can consider questions such as: Who is in charge? How did they get to be in charge? What could people do to change who was in charge? Who had the least power? Who had the most?

Apply to Social Studies Standard 7: Production, Distribution, and Consumption

Because people have wants that often exceed the resources available to them, a variety of ways have evolved to answer such questions as: What is to be produced? How is production to be organized? How are goods and services to be distributed? What is the most effective allocation of the factors of production (land, labor, capital, and management)?

- Students can create a class map of London as Coriander describes the city. They should consider the range of businesses that are mentioned and businesses that we might expect that were not mentioned. After creating some of the products mentioned in the story, students can hold a fair or market where they trade (or "sell") their goods with one another.
- Students can explore the role of ships and waterways in business and trade during the 1600s. Students can use maps to chart the routes Coriander's father's ships would have sailed and think about why the geography of England made them so dependent on water travel.

Source: Standards are from the National Council for the Social Studies and can be found online at www.socialstudies.org/standards.

Notes

1. Lloyd Alexander, "Fantasy and the Human Condition," *New Advocate* 1.2 (spring, 1983): 83.
2. Lloyd Alexander, "The Flat-Heeled Muse," in *Children and Literature*, ed. Virginia Haviland, p. 243. Reprinted from the March/April 1965 issue of *The Horn Book Magazine* by permission of The Horn Book, Inc.
3. D. G. Singer and J. L. Singer, eds., *Handbook of Children and the Media* (Thousand Oaks, Cal.: Sage Publications, 2001).
4. D. G. Singer and J. L. Singer, *The House of Make-Believe* (Cambridge, Mass.: Harvard University Press, 1992).
5. S. Siegfried, "Carpe diem," *Language Arts* 69 (1992): 284–85.
6. D. Tripp, *Critical Incidents in Teaching: Developing Professional Judgment* (New York: Routledge, 1993).

Children's Literature

Go to www.mhhe.com/kiefer1e to access the Children's Literature Database, which includes information on thousands of children's books. Following are some of the titles you will find in the database.

Titles in blue = multicultural titles

Adlington, L. J. *The Diary of Pelly D.* Greenwillow, 2005.
——. *Cherry Heaven.* Greenwillow, 2008.
Alexander, Lloyd. *The Black Cauldron.* Holt, 1965.
——. *The Book of Three.* Holt, 1964.
——. *The Castle of Llyr.* Holt, 1966.
——. *The High King.* Holt, 1968.
——. *Taran Wanderer.* Holt, 1967.
Andersen, Hans Christian. *The Nightingale.* Illustrated by Jerry Pinkney. Fogelman/Putnam, 2002.
——. *The Wild Swans.* Retold by Amy Ehrlich. Illustrated by Susan Jeffers. Dial, 1981.
Atwater, Richard, and Florence Atwater. *Mr. Popper's Penguins.* Illustrated by Robert Lawson. Little, 1938.
Avi. *Poppy.* Illustrated by Brian Floca. Orchard, 1995.
Babbitt, Natalie. *Tuck Everlasting.* Farrar, 1975.
Barron, T. A. *The Fires of Merlin.* Philomel, 1998.
——. *The Great Tree of Avalon: Child of the Dark Prophecy.* Philomel, 2004.
——. *The Great Tree of Avalon: The Eternal Flame.* Philomel, 2006.
——. *The Great Tree of Avalon: Shadows on the Stars.* Philomel, 2005.
——. *The Lost Years of Merlin.* Philomel, 1996.
Beck, Ian. *The Secret History of Tom Trueheart.* HarperCollins, 2007.
——. *Tom Trueheart and the Land of the Dark Stories.* HarperCollins, 2008.
Bellairs, John. *The House with a Clock in Its Walls.* Dial, 1973.
Bernstein, Nina. *Magic by the Book.* Farrar, 2005.
Bertagna, Julie. *Exodus.* Walker, 2008.
——. *Zenith.* Walker, 2009.
Boston, L. M. *The Children of Green Knowe.* Illustrated by Peter Boston. Harcourt, 1955.
——. *An Enemy at Green Knowe.* Illustrated by Peter Boston. Harcourt, 1964.
——. *The River at Green Knowe.* Illustrated by Peter Boston. Harcourt, 1959.
——. *The Treasure of Green Knowe.* Illustrated by Peter Boston. Harcourt, 1958.
Broach Elise. *The Masterpiece.* Holt, 2008.
Bruchac, Joseph. *The Dark Pond.* HarperCollins, 2004.

——. *Skeleton Man.* HarperCollins, 2001.
——. *Whisper in the Dark.* HarperCollins, 2005.
Carman, Patrick. *Into the Mist.* Land of Elyon. Scholastic, 2007.
——. *Rivers of Fire.* Atherton. Little, 2008.
Carroll, Lewis [Charles L. Dodgson]. *Alice's Adventures in Wonderland and Through the Looking Glass.* Illustrated by John Tenniel. Macmillan, 1963 [1865, 1872].
Cooper, Susan. *The Dark Is Rising.* Illustrated by Alan E. Cober. Atheneum, 1973.
——. *The Grey King.* Atheneum, 1975.
——. *King of Shadows.* McElderry, 1999.
——. *Over Sea, Under Stone.* Illustrated by Marjorie Gill. Harcourt, 1966.
——. *Silver on the Tree.* Atheneum, 1977.
Crossley-Holland, Kevin. *At the Crossing Place.* Scholastic, 2002.
——. *Crossing to Paradise.* Scholastic, 2008.
——. *King of the Middle March.* Scholastic, 2004.
——. *The Seeing Stone.* Scholastic/Levine, 2001.
Curry, Jane Louise. *The Black Canary.* Simon, 2005.
Dahl, Roald. *Charlie and the Chocolate Factory.* Illustrated by Joseph Schindelman. Knopf, 1972.
DiCamillo, Kate. *The Miraculous Journey of Edward Tulane.* Illustrated by Bagram Ibatoulline. Candlewick, 2006.
DiTerlizzi, Tony, and Holly Black. *The Field Guide: The Spiderwick Chronicles.* Simon, 2003.
——. *The Nixie's Song.* Beyond the Spiderwick Chronicles. Simon, 2007.
Dunkle, Clare B. *The Sky Inside.* Atheneum, 2008.
DuPrau, Jeanne. *The City of Ember.* Random, 2003.
Durst, Sarah Beth. *Into the Wild.* Razorbill, 2007.
Eager, Edward. *Half Magic.* Illustrated by N. M. Bodecker. Harcourt, 1954.
Falkner, Brian. *The Tomorrow Code.* Random, 2008.
Farmer, Nancy. *The Islands of the Blessed.* Atheneum, 2009.
——. *The Land of the Silver Apples.* Atheneum, 2007.
Ferris, Jean. *Once upon a Marigold.* Harcourt, 2002.
——. *Twice upon a Marigold.* Harcourt, 2008.
Fleischman, Sid. *The Midnight Horse.* Illustrated by Peter Sis. Greenwillow, 1990.
——. *The Whipping Boy.* Illustrated by Peter Sis. Greenwillow, 1986.
Fox, Helen. *Eager.* Random, 2004.
——. *Eager's Nephew.* Random, 2006.
Funke, Cornelia. *Inkdeath.* Scholastic, 2008.
——. *Inkheart.* Scholastic, 2003.

——. *Inkspell*. Scholastic, 2005.

Gaiman, Neil. *Coraline*. Illustrated by Dave McKean. HarperCollins, 2002.

Gardener, Sally. *I, Coriander*. Dial, 2005.

Gliori, Debi. *Pure Dead Magic*. Knopf, 2001.

Grahame, Kenneth. *The Reluctant Dragon*. Illustrated by Ernest H. Shepard. Holiday, 1938.

——. *The Wind in the Willows*. Illustrated by E. H. Shepard. Scribner's, 1940 [1908].

Grant, Michael. *Gone*. HarperTeen, 2008.

Haddix, Margaret. *Among the Hidden*. Simon, 1999.

Hahn, Mary Downing. *All the Lovely Bad Ones*. Clarion, 2008.

——. *Wait Till Helen Comes: A Ghost Story*. Houghton, 1986.

Hamilton, Virginia. *The Magical Adventures of Pretty Pearl*. Harper, 1983.

——. *Sweet Whispers, Brother Rush*. Philomel, 1982.

Hautman, Peter. *Rash*. Simon, 2006.

Hawkins, Colin, and Jacqui Hawkins. *Fairytale News*. Candlewick, 2004.

Hobbs, Will. *Go Big or Go Home*. HarperCollins, 2008.

Jacques, Brian. *Redwall*. Illustrated by Gary Chalk. Philomel, 1987.

Jones, Diana Wynne. *Charmed Life*. Greenwillow, 1989.

——. *House of Many Ways*. Greenwillow, 2008.

——. *Howl's Moving Castle*. Harper, 2001.

——. *The Lives of Christopher Chant*. Greenwillow, 1988.

Keehn, Sally M. *Magpie Gabbard and the Quest for the Buried Moon*. Philomel, 2007.

King-Smith, Dick. *The Fox Busters*. Illustrated by Jon Miller. Delacorte, 1988.

Langrish, Katherine. *Troll Blood*. HarperCollins, 2008.

——. *Troll Fell*. Harper, 2004.

——. *Troll Mill*. HarperCollins, 2006.

Langton, Jane. *The Fledgling*. Harper, 1980.

Law, Ingrid. *Savvy*. Dial, 2008.

Le Guin, Ursula K. *The Farthest Shore*. Illustrated by Gail Garraty. Atheneum, 1972.

——. *The Tombs of Atuan*. Illustrated by Gail Garraty. Atheneum, 1971.

——. *A Wizard of Earthsea*. Illustrated by Ruth Robbins. Parnassus, 1968.

L'Engle, Madeleine. *A Swiftly Tilting Planet*. The Time Trilogy. Farrar, 1978.

——. *A Wind in the Door*. The Time Trilogy. Farrar, 1973.

——. *A Wrinkle in Time*. The Time Trilogy. Farrar, 1962.

Levine, Gail Carson. *Ella Enchanted*. HarperCollins, 1997.

Lewis, C. S. *The Horse and His Boy*. Illustrated by Pauline Baynes Macmillan, 1962.

——. *The Last Battle*. Illustrated by Pauline Baynes. Macmillan, 1964.

——. *The Lion, the Witch, and the Wardrobe*. Illustrated by Pauline Baynes. Macmillan, 1961.

——. *The Magician's Nephew*. Illustrated by Pauline Baynes. Macmillan, 1964.

——. *Prince Caspian: The Return to Narnia*. Illustrated by Pauline Baynes. Macmillan, 1964.

——. *The Silver Chair*. Illustrated by Pauline Baynes. Macmillan, 1962.

——. *The Voyage of the "Dawn Treader."* Illustrated by Pauline Baynes. Macmillan, 1962.

Lindgren, Astrid. *Pippi Goes on Board*. Translated by Florence Lamborn. Illustrated by Louis S. Glanzman. Viking, 1957.

——. *Pippi in the South Seas*. Translated by Florence Lamborn. Illustrated by Louis S. Glanzman. Viking, 1959.

——. *Pippi Longstocking*. Illustrated by Louis S. Glanzman. Viking, 1950.

——. *Pippi on the Run*. Viking, 1976.

Lowry, Lois. *The Giver*. Houghton, 1993.

Mayne, William. *Earthfasts*. Dutton, 1967.

Milne, A. A. *Winnie the Pooh*. Illustrated by Ernest H. Shepard. Dutton, 1926.

Morris, Gerald. *The Squire, His Knight and His Lady*. Houghton, 1999.

——. *The Squire's Tale*. Houghton, 1998.

Murdock, Catherine Gilbert. *Princess Ben: Being a Wholly Truthful Account of Her Various Discoveries and Misadventures, Recounted to the Best of Her Recollections, in Four Parts*. Houghton, 2008.

Nicholson, William. *The Wind Singer*. The Wind on Fire Trilogy. Hyperion, 2000.

Nimmo, Jenny. *The Chestnut Soldier*. Scholastic, 2007.

——. *The Emlyn's Moon*. Scholastic, 2007.

——. *The Snow Spider*. Scholastic, 2006.

Norton, Mary. *The Borrowers*. Illustrated by Beth and Joe Krush. Harcourt, 1953.

——. *The Borrowers Afield*. Illustrated by Beth and Joe Krush. Harcourt, 1955.

Oppel, Kenneth. *Silverwing*. Simon, 1997.

Paolini, Christopher. *Eragon*. Knopf, 2003.

Pearce, Philippa. *Tom's Midnight Garden*. Illustrated by Susan Einzig. Lippincott, 1959.

Pfeffer, Susan Beth. *The Dead and the Gone*. Harcourt, 2008.

Pierce, Tamora. *Magic Steps*. The Circle Opens. Scholastic, 2000.

——. *Sandry's Book*. Circle of Magic, Book 1. Scholastic, 1997.

———. *The Will of the Empress*. The Circle Reforged. Scholastic, 2005.

Prineas, Sarah. *The Magic Thief*. HarperCollins, 2008.

Pullman, Philip. *The Amber Spyglass*. His Dark Materials. Knopf, 2000.

———. *Clockwork: Or All Wound Up*. Scholastic, 1998.

———. *The Firework-Maker's Daughter*. Illustrated by S. Saelig Gallagher. Levine, 1999.

———. *The Golden Compass*. His Dark Materials. Knopf, 1996.

———. *I Was a Rat*. Knopf, 2000.

———. *The Ruby in the Smoke*. Knopf, 1994.

———. *The Subtle Knife*. His Dark Materials. Knopf, 1997.

Reeve, Philip. *Larklight*. Illustrated by David Wyatt. Bloomsbury, 2006.

———. *Mortal Engines*. The Hungry City Chronicles. HarperCollins, 2003.

———. *Predator's Gold*. The Hungry City Chronicles. HarperCollins, 2003.

———. *Starcross*. Bloomsbury, 2007.

Riordan, Rick. *The Lightning Thief*. Percy Jackson and the Olympians, Book 1. Hyperion, 2005.

Rowling, J. K. *Harry Potter and the Sorcerer's Stone*. Scholastic, 1998.

Saint-Exupéry, Antoine de. *The Little Prince*. Translated by Katherine Woods. Harcourt, 1943.

Sauer, Julia. *Fog Magic*. Illustrated by Lynd Ward. Viking, 1943.

Scieszka, Jon. *Da Wild, Da Crazy, Da Vinci*. Viking, 2004.

———. *The Frog Prince, Continued*. Illustrated by Steve Johnson. Puffin, 1994.

Skurzynski, Gloria. *The Clones: Virtual War Chronologs*. Simon/Atheneum, 2002.

Springer, Nancy. *I Am Mordred: A Tale from Camelot*. Philomel, 1998.

———. *I Am Morgan le Fay*. Philomel, 2002.

Stanley, Diane. *Bella at Midnight: The Thimble, the Ring, and the Slippers of Glass*. Illustrated by Bagram Ibatoulline. Harper, 2006.

——. *The Giant and the Beanstalk*. HarperCollins, 2004.

Stewart, Trenton Lee. *The Mysterious Benedict Society*. Illustrated by Carson Ellis. Little, 2007.

——. *The Mysterious Benedict Society and the Perilous Journey*. Illustrated by Carson Ellis. Little, 2008.

Stroud, Jonathan. *The Amulet of Samarkand*. The Bartimaeus Trilogy, Book 1. Hyperion, 2003.

Thompson, Kate. *The Last of the High Kings*. Greenwillow, 2008.

——. *The New Policeman*. Greenwillow, 2007.

Thurber, James. *Many Moons*. Illustrated by Marc Simont. Harcourt, 1990.

Tolkien, J. R. R. *The Fellowship of the Ring. The Two Towers. The Return of the King*. The Lord of the Rings trilogy. Houghton, 1965.

——. *The Hobbit*. Houghton, 1938.

Ursu, Anne. *Shadow Thieves*. Cronus Chronicles. Simon, 2006.

——. *Siren Song*. Cronus Chronicles. Simon, 2007.

Walsh, Jill Paton. *A Chance Child*. Farrar, 1978.

White, E. B. *Charlotte's Web*. Illustrated by Garth Williams. Harper, 1952.

Wilkinson, Carole. *Dragon Keeper*. Hyperion, 2005.

——. *Dragon Moon*. Hyperion, 2008.

——. *Garden of the Purple Dragon*. Hyperion, 2007.

Williams, Margery. *The Velveteen Rabbit*. Illustrated by William Nicholson. Doubleday, 1969 [1922].

Winthrop, Elizabeth. *The Castle in the Attic*. Holiday, 1985.

Wiseman, David. *Jeremy Visick*. Houghton, 1981.

Wrede, Patricia C. *Dealing with Dragons*. Harcourt, 1990.

Yep, Laurence. *Tiger's Apprentice*. HarperCollins, 2004.

Yolen, Jane. *The Devil's Arithmetic*. Viking Penguin, 1990.

Chapter Six

Poetry

Chapter Outline

A little boy and his mother board a crowded city bus and find two seats together toward the front. As the bus leaves the stop, the child begins to sing softly to himself; his legs dangling a few inches from the floor keeping pace with his song:

> Going for a bus ride
> Going for a bus ride
> Going for a BUS ride
> Bus Bus Bus Bus Bus
> Going for a BUS ride

Oblivious to the passing world, he continues these refrains through several more stops, altering the variations in pitch and beat to suit his happy mood. Like most young children, he has a ready affinity for the elements of poetry—the delightful musicality he finds in his language. And he has no hesitation in creating his own poems to accompany the rhythms of his life.

Poetry for Children

There is an elusiveness about poetry that makes it defy precise definition. It is not so much what it is that is important, as how it makes us feel. In her *Poems for Children*, Eleanor Farjeon tells us that poetry is "not a rose, but the scent of the rose. . . . Not the sea, but the sound of the sea."[1] Fine poetry is this distillation of experience that captures the essence of an object, a feeling, or a thought. Such intensification requires a more highly structured patterning of words than prose does. Each word must be chosen with care for both sound and meaning, because poetry is language in its most connotative and concentrated form. Laurence Perrine defines poetry as "a kind of language that says more and says it more intensely than ordinary language."[2]

Poetry for children differs little from poetry for adults, except that it comments on life in dimensions that are meaningful for children. Its language should be poetic and its content should appeal directly to children. For example, in "Firefly July," poet J. Patrick Lewis captures the magic of a summer night from a child's point of view.

Firefly July
When I was ten, one summer night,
The baby stars that leapt
Among the trees like dimes of light,
I cupped, and capped, and kept.

—**J. PATRICK LEWIS.** © 2008 by J. Patrick Lewis. Used by permission.

The emotional appeal of children's poetry should reflect the real emotions of childhood. Poetry that is cute, coy, nostalgic, or sarcastic might be *about* children, but it is not *for* them. Whittier's "The Barefoot Boy," for example, looks back on childhood in a nostalgic fashion characteristic of adults, not children.

Sentimentality is another adult emotion that is seldom felt by children. Joan W. Anglund's poetry is as cute and sentimental as her pictures of "sweet little boys and girls." The poem "Which Loved Best," frequently quoted before Mother's Day, drips with sentiment and morality. Poems that are about childhood or aim to instruct are usually disliked by children.

Yet children do feel deep emotions; they can be hurt, fearful, bewildered, sad, happy, expectant, and satisfied. The best poetry for children succeeds in capturing the real feelings of children, and the best poets have found many ways of speaking to the needs and interests of children.

Where Poetry Begins

For many children, finger plays, nursery rhymes, and songs are their first introduction to the world of literature. These folk rhymes are passed down from generation to generation and are found across many cultures. What is the attraction of nursery rhymes that makes them so appealing to these young children? What accounts for their survival through these many years? Much of the language in these rhymes is obscure; for example, modern-day children have no idea what "curds" and "whey" are, yet they delight in "Little Miss Muffet." Nothing in current literature has replaced the venerable traditional finger plays and rhymes for the nursery-school age.

Nursery Rhymes and Games Finger rhymes are a traditional way to provide for young children's participation as they play "Five Little Pigs" or sing "Where Is Thumbkin?" and the ever popular "Eensy, Weensy Spider." Finger plays date back to the time of Friedrich Froebel, the so-called father of the kindergarten movement, who collected the finger plays and games that the peasant mothers in the German countryside were using with their children. Jane Yolen and Adam Stemple have collected many favorites in *This Little Piggy: And Other Rhymes to Sing and Play*, illustrated by Will Hillenbrand. As teachers recognize, this folklore of childhood continues beyond the preschool set and onto the grade-school playground. *Over in the Pink House* by Rebecca Kai Dotlich, *Miss Mary Mack and Other Children's Street Rhymes* by Joanna Cole, and *Schoolyard Rhymes: Kids' Own Rhymes of Rope-Skipping, Hand Clapping, Ball Bouncing, and Just Plain Fun* by Judy Sierra are wonderful collections to keep in the classroom library.

Mother Goose The terms *nursery rhymes* and *Mother Goose rhymes* are interchangeable. The character of Mother Goose has come to represent the type of speech play we have discussed but the reason for the association of these traditional rhymes with a character called Mother Goose is unclear. The oldest surviving nursery rhyme book was published by Mary Cooper in 1744 in two or perhaps three little volumes under the title *Tommy Thumb's Pretty Song Book*; a single copy of volume 2 is a treasured possession of the British Museum.

Today's children are fortunate in being able to choose among many beautifully illustrated Mother Goose editions. There is no *one* best Mother Goose book, for this is a matter for individual preference. The children in every family deserve at least one of the better editions, however. Preschool and primary teachers will also want to have one that can be shared with small groups of children who might not have been fortunate enough ever to have seen a really beautiful Mother Goose. Some of the most delightful collections are *Tomie dePaola's Mother Goose*, Iona Opie and Rosemary Wells's *My Very First Mother Goose* and *Here Comes Mother Goose*, and Leo and Diane Dillon's *Mother Goose: Numbers on the Loose*.

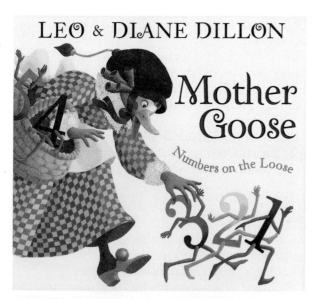

Leo and Diane Dillon provide an imaginative counting journey in *Mother Goose: Numbers on the Loose*. Book cover from *Mother Goose: Numbers on the Loose*, compilation and illustrations copyright © 2007 by Leo Dillon and Diane Dillon, reproduced by permission of Houghton Mifflin Harcourt Publishing Company.

The Elements of Poetry

As children become more sophisticated through their exposure to films and television, the dividing line between what is poetry for adults and what is poetry for children becomes fainter. It is, however, possible to identify those poems that contain the elements of fine poetry that still speak to children.

Rhythm The young child is naturally rhythmical. She beats on the tray of her high chair, kicks her foot against the table, and chants her vocabulary of one or two words in a singsong fashion. She delights in the sound of "Pat-a-cake, pat-a-cake, baker's man" or "Ride a cock-horse to Banbury Cross" before she understands the meaning of the words. This response to a measured beat is as old as humans themselves. Primitive people had chants, hunting and working songs, dances, and crude musical instruments. Rhythm is a part of the daily beat of our lives—the steady pulse rate, regular breathing, and pattern of growth.

Poetry satisfies the child's natural response to rhythm. In poetry, it is the stresses and pauses in language that set up the rhythm. The term *meter* refers to this pattern of stresses that fall in each line. The rhythm helps create a kind of music of its own, and the child responds to it. The very young child enjoys the rocking rhythm of Mother Goose and expects it in all other poems. In the following poem from *The Llama Who Had No Pajama*, Mary Ann Hoberman explores various rhythms in the child's life as she links weather and seasonal patterns to the rhythm of a child's swinging

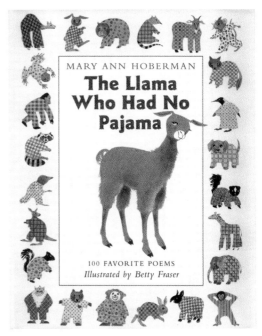

Collections such as Mary Ann Hoberman's *The Llama Who Had No Pajama* introduce children to the delights of poetry. Book cover from *The Llama Who Had No Pajama: 100 Favorite Poems* by Mary Ann Hoberman, illustrations copyright © 1998 by Betty Fraser, reproduced by permission of Houghton Mifflin Harcourt Publishing Company.

Hello and Good-bye

Hello and good-bye
When I'm in a swing
Swinging low and then high,
Good-bye to the ground
Hello to the sky.
Hello to the rain
Good-bye to the sun,
Then hello again sun
When the rain is all done.
In blows the winter,
Away the birds fly.
Good-bye and hello
Hello and good-bye.

—**MARY ANN HOBERMAN.** "Hello and Good-bye," from *The Llama Who Had No Pajama: 100 Favorite Poems*. Copyright © 1959 and renewed 1987 by Mary Ann Hoberman. Reprinted with permission of Houghton Mifflin Harcourt Publishing Company.

In some poems, both the rhythm and the pattern of the lines are suggestive of the movement or mood of the poem. The arrangement of these poems forces the reader to emphasize a particular rhythm. For example, in Eleanor Farjeon's "Mrs. Peck-Pigeon," "Mrs. Peck-Pigeon is picking for bread, Bob-bob-bob goes her little round head"—the repetition of the hard sounds of *b* and *p* help create the bobbing rhythm of the pigeon herself.

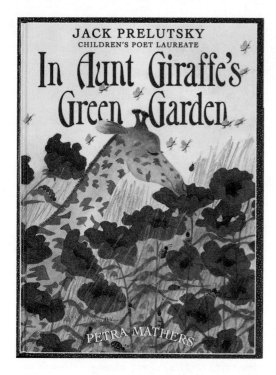

JACK PRELUTSKY
CHILDREN'S POET LAUREATE
In Aunt Giraffe's
Green Garden

PICTURES BY
PETRA MATHERS

Jack Prelutsky's *In Aunt Giraffe's Green Garden*, illustrated by Petra Mathers, is a collection of lighthearted poetry for younger children. From *In Aunt Giraffe's Green Garden* by Jack Prelutsky and illustrated by Petra Mathers. Used by permission of HarperCollins Publishers, HarperCollins Children's Books.

Rhyme and Sound In addition to the rhythm of a poem, children respond to its rhyme—for rhyme helps to create the musical qualities of a poem, and children enjoy the "singingness of words." The Russian poet Kornei Chukovsky maintains that in the beginning of childhood we are all "versifiers," and that it is only later in life that we begin to speak in prose.[3] Chukovsky is referring to the young child's tendency to double all syllables, so that *mother* is first "mama" and *water* is "wa-wa." This, plus the regular patterning of such words as *daddy, mommy, granny,* and so on, makes for a natural production of rhyme. The young child's enjoyment of Mother Goose is due almost entirely to the rhyme and rhythm of these verses.

Rhyme is only one aspect of sound; *alliteration*, or the repetition of initial consonant sounds, is another; *assonance*, or the repetition of particular vowel sounds, is still another. Jack Prelutsky frequently uses alliteration to create the humor in his poetry collections such as *In Aunt Giraffe's Green Garden* and *My Dog May Be a Genius*. The quiet *s* sound and the repetition of the double *o* in *moon* and *shoon* suggest the mysterious beauty of the moon in Walter de la Mare's poem "Silver" (in Helen Ferris's *Favorite Poems Old and New*). The term *onomatopoeia* refers to the use of words that make a sound like the action represented by the word, such as *crack, hiss,* and *sputter.* Occasionally a poet will create an entire poem that resembles a particular sound. Tony Mitten has successfully imitated the sound of a railroad train in "Rickety Train Ride."

Rickety Train Ride
I'm Taking the Train to Ricketywick
Clickety clickety clack.
I'm sat in my seat
With a sandwich to eat
As I travel the trickety track.

It's ever so rickety trickety train,
And I honestly thickety think.
That before it arrive
At the end of the line
I will tip up my drippety drink.

—**Tony Mitten.** "Rickety Train Ride," in *Here's a Little Poem,* ed. Jane Yolen and Andrew Fusek Peters. Originally published in *Pip,* Scholastic Inc., NY.

Repetition is another way the poet creates particular sound effects in a poem. Robert Frost frequently used repetition of particular lines or phrases to emphasize meaning in his poems. The repetition of the last line "miles to go before I sleep" in his famous "Stopping by Woods on a Snowy Evening" (in de Regniers et al., *Sing a Song of Popcorn*) adds to the mysterious element in that poem.

Children are intrigued with the sound of language and enjoy unusual and ridiculous combinations of words. The gay nonsense of Laura Richards's "Eletelephony" is as much in the sound of the ridiculous words as in the plight of the poor elephant who tried to use the "telephant." Children love to trip off the name "James James Morrison Morrison Weatherby George Dupree" in A. A. Milne's "Disobedience." Poets use rhyme, rhythm, and the various devices of alliteration, assonance, repetition, and coined words to create the melody and sound of poetry loved by children.

Imagery Poetry draws on many kinds of language magic. The imagery of a poem involves direct sensory images of sight, sound, touch, smell, or taste. This aspect of poetry has particular appeal for children, as it reflects one of the major ways they explore their world. The very young child grasps an object and immediately puts it in her mouth. Children love to squeeze warm, soft puppies, and they squeal with delight as a pet mouse scampers up their arms. Taste and smell are also highly developed in the young child.

Poetry can never be a substitute for actual sensory experience. A child can't develop a concept of texture by hearing a poem or seeing pictures of the rough bark of a tree; he must first touch the bark and compare the feel of a deeply furrowed oak with the smooth-surfaced trunk of a beech tree. Then the poet can call up these experiences and extend them or make the child see them in a new way.

Because children are visually minded, they respond readily to the picture-making quality of poetry. In Tennyson's "The Eagle," the description of the eagle is rich in the use of visual imagery. In the first verse the reader can see the eagle perched on the crest of a steep mountain, posed and ready for his swift descent whenever he sights his quarry. But in the second verse the poet "enters into" the eagle's world and describes it from the bird's point of view. Looking down from his lofty height, the might of the waves is reduced to wrinkles and the sea seems to crawl:

> He clasps the crag with crooked hands;
> Close to the sun in lonely lands,
> Ringed with the azure world, he stands.
>
> The wrinkled sea beneath him crawls;
> He watches from his mountain wall,
> And like a thunderbolt he falls.

—**ALFRED, LORD TENNYSON.** "The Eagle," in *Piping Down the Valleys Wild*, ed. Nancy Larrick.

The lonely, peaceful scene is shattered by the natural metaphor of the final line: "And like a thunderbolt he falls." In your mind's eye you can see, almost feel, the wind on your wings as you plunge down the face of the cliff.

Most poetry depends on visual and auditory imagery to evoke a mood or response, but imagery of touch, taste, and smell is also used. Psychologists tell us that some of children's earliest memories are sensory, recalling particularly the way things smell and taste. Most children have a delicate sense of taste that responds to the texture and smell of a particular food. Rose Rauter captures both the feel of a fresh-picked peach and its delicious taste in "Peach":

> Touch it to your cheek and it's soft
> as a velvet newborn mouse
> who has to strive to be alive.
> Bite in. Runny
> honey blooms on your tongue—
> as if you've bitten open
> a whole hive.

> —**ROSE RAUTER.** "Peach," from *Knock at a Star: A Child's Introduction to Poetry* by Dorothy M. Kennedy. Copyright © 1988 by X. J. Kennedy and Dorothy M. Kennedy (text). Copyright © 1999 by Karen Lee Baker (illustrations). By permission of Little, Brown & Company.

Figurative Language: Comparison and Contrast Because the language of poetry is so compressed, every word must be made to convey the meaning of the poem. Poets do this by comparing two objects or ideas with each other in such a way that the connotation of one word gives added meaning to another. In "Peach," Rose Rauter compared the soft fuzzy feel of a peach to a velvety newborn mouse; its sweet taste made her think of a whole hive of honey. In "Geode," John Frank compares the inside of a stone to an everyday breakfast dish.

Geode
I cracked a stone egg
dark as smoke,
and found, inside,
a crystal yolk
as purple as
a sheet of sky
pulled over twilight's
closing eye.

> —**JOHN FRANK.** "Geode," from *Keepers* by John Frank. Reprinted by permission of Henry Hold and Co. LLC.

When writers compare one thing with another, using such connecting words as *like* or *as*, they are using a *simile*. In a

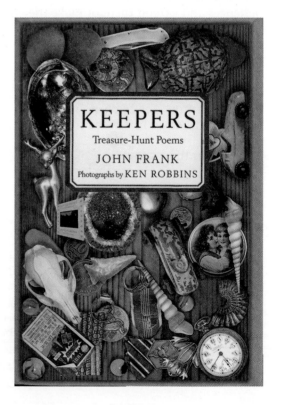

John Frank's *Keepers: Treasure-Hunt Poems* finds beauty in the small things that children find and collect. From *Keepers: Treasure-Hunt Poems* by John Frank and photographs by Ken Robbins. Used by permission of Roaring Brook Press, a division of Henry Holt and Company, LLC.

metaphor the poet speaks of an object or idea as if it *were* another object. In recent years we have paid little attention to the difference between these two techniques, referring to both as examples of metaphorical or figurative language.

It is not important that children know the difference between a simile and a metaphor. It is important that they know what is being compared and that the comparison is fresh and new and helps them view the idea or object in a different and unusual way. Two well-known poems containing metaphors that help children see their world afresh are Carl Sandburg's "Fog" and Vachel Lindsay's "The Moon's the North Wind's Cookie" (both in Jack Prelutsky's *The Random House Book of Poetry for Children*). Perhaps the reason these poems have endured is that they also reveal a true understanding of a child's point of view.

Personification is a way of speaking about inanimate objects and animals as though they were persons. Human beings have always personified inanimate objects. Young children personify their toys; adolescents and adults name their computers, their cars, and boats. Poetry simply extends this process to a wider range of objects. In *Dirty Laundry Pile: Poems in Different Voices*, Paul Janeczko has collected twenty-seven poems written in the voices of animals such as mosquitoes, cats, and turtles and objects like washing machines, scarecrows, and kites. Diane Siebert personifies the river in her book *Mississippi*, the desert in *Mojave*, and the Sierra Nevada Mountains in *Sierra*.

Shape The first thing children notice about reading a poem is that it looks different from prose. And usually it does. Most poems begin with capital letters for each line and have one or more stanzas. Increasingly, however, poets are using the shape of their poems to reinforce the image of the idea. In "The Grasshopper" (in his *One at a Time*), David McCord describes the plight of a grasshopper that fell down a deep well. As luck would have it, he discovers a rope and up he climbs one word at a time! The reader must read up the page to follow the grasshopper's ascent. Abram Bunn Ross writes about siblings sharing the same sleeping space in "Two in Bed." The words form the shape of an arrowhead—or the sharp pain of a brother's knee poking into one's back.

Two in Bed

When my brother Tommy
Sleeps in bed with me
He doubles up
And makes
himself
exactly
like
a
V
And 'cause the bed is not so wide
A part of him is on my side.

—**ABRAM BUNN ROSS.** "Two in Bed," in *Days Like This*, ed. Simon James. Copyright © 2000.

Children enjoy mounting their own poems on a piece of paper shaped in the image of their poem, such as a verse about a jack-o'-lantern on a pumpkin shape or a poem about a plane mounted on the silhouette of a plane. Later, the words themselves may form the shape of the content, as in concrete poetry.

The Overall Impact of Poetry

We have seen how sound, language, and the shape of a poem can all work together to create the total impact of the poem. Considered individually, the rhyme scheme, imagery, figurative language, and appearance of the poem are of little importance unless all of these interrelate to create an emotional response in the reader. The craft of the poem is not the poem.

In the following poem, a modern poet writes of the way two children feel when caught in the vortex of their parents' quarrel:

Listening to grownups quarreling,
standing in the hall against the
wall with my little brother, blown
like leaves against the wall by their
voices, my head like a pingpong ball
between the paddles of their anger:
I knew what it meant
to tremble like a leaf.
Cold with their wrath, I heard
the claws of the rain
pounce. Floods
poured through the city,
skies clapped over me,
and I was shaken, shaken
like a mouse between their jaws.

—**RUTH WHITMAN.** "Listening to Grownups Quarreling," from *The Marriage Wig and Other Poems.* Compilation copyright © 1968 and renewed 1996 by Ruth Whitman. Reprinted by permission of Houghton Mifflin Harcourt Publishing Co.

All elements of this poem work together to create the feeling of being overpowered by a quarrel between those you love most. A teacher could destroy the total impact of this poem for children by having them count the number of metaphors in it, looking at their increasing force and power. Children should have a chance to hear it, comment on it if they wish, or compare it with other similar poems.

Good poetry has the power to make readers moan in despair, catch their breath in fear, gasp in awe, smile with delight, or sit back in wonder. Poetry heightens emotions and increases one's sensitivity to an idea or mood.

Evaluating Poetry

A child responds to the total impact of a poem and should not be required to analyze it. However, teachers need to understand the language of poetry if they are to select the best to share with children. How, for example, can you differentiate between real poetry and mere verse? Mother Goose, jump-rope rhymes, tongue twisters, and the lyrics of some songs are not poetry; but they *can* serve as a springboard for diving into real poetry. Elizabeth Coatsworth, who has written much fine poetry and verse for children, refers to rhyme as "poetry in petticoats."[4] Such rhymes might have the sound of poetry, but they do not contain the quality of imagination or the depth of emotion that characterizes real poetry.

In looking for real poetry for children, teachers should examine the content and form of the poetry. However, it is important to note that modern poets are breaking traditional molds in both content and form. Frequently the words are spattered across pages in a random fashion, or they become poem-pictures, as in concrete poetry. Many authors are revisiting story in one of its earliest forms, the epic narrative poem. Writers for older children and young adults are using poetry to redefine the form of the novel. Juan Felipe Herrera has written *Downtown Boy*, a novel in verse about a young Mexican migrant worker who tries to hold his life together when his family moves to San Francisco. Marilyn Nelson chose the traditional fourteenth-century Petrarchan form called a heroic crown of sonnet to reflect upon life and death in *A Wreath for Emmett Till*.

Teachers need to be able to identify the characteristics of good poetry and be aware of new trends in contemporary poetry in order to make wise selections to share with children. They need to know the various kinds of poetry and the range of content of poetry for children. Then they can select poetry that will gradually develop children's appreciation of it and its form. The questions listed in the feature **Guidelines: Evaluating Poetry for Children** would not be appropriate to use for every poem. However, they can serve as a beginning way to look at poetry for children.

Guidelines

Evaluating Poetry for Children

 Go to **www.mhhe.com/kieferbrief1e** *to access an expanded version of this evaluation form.*

Consider the following when evaluating poetry:

- How does the rhythm of the poem reinforce and create the meaning of the poem?
- If the poem rhymes, does it sound natural or contrived?
- How does the sound of the poem add to its meaning?
- Does the poem use alliteration? Onomatopoeia? Repetition?
- Does the poem create sensory images of sight, touch, smell, or taste?
- Are these images related to children's delight in their particular senses?
- What is the quality of imagination in the poem? Does the poem make the child see something in a fresh, new way, or does it rely on tired clichés?

- Is the figurative language appropriate to children's lives? Are the similes and metaphors ones that a child would appreciate and understand?
- What is the tone of the poem? Does it patronize childhood by talking down to it? Is it didactic and preachy? Does it see childhood in a sentimental or nostalgic way?
- Is the poem appropriate for children? Will it appeal to them, and will they like it?
- How has the poet created the emotional intensity of the poem? Does every word work to heighten the feelings conveyed?
- Does the shape of the poem—the placement of the words—contribute to the poem's meaning?
- What is the purpose of the poem? To amuse? To describe in a fresh way? To comment on humanity? To draw parallels to our lives? How well has the poet achieved this purpose?

Once Upon a Poem, **collected by Kevin Crossley-Holland, contains storytelling poems that are consistent favorites of children.** From *Once Upon a Poem* by Kevin Crossley-Holland. Scholastic Inc., The Chicken House. Cover illustration copyright © 2004 by Scholastic Inc. Reprinted by permission.

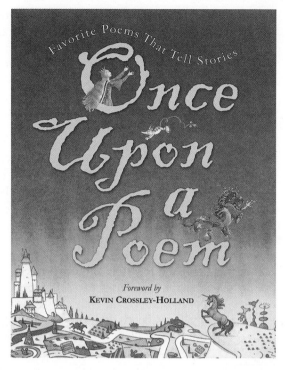

Forms of Poetry for Children

Children are more interested in the "idea" of a poem than in knowing about the various forms of poetry. However, teachers will want to expose children to various forms of poetry and note their reactions. Do these children like only narrative poems? Do they think all poetry must rhyme, or will they listen to some free verse? Are they ready for the seemingly simple, yet highly complex, form of haiku? Understanding of and appreciation for a wide variety of poetry grow gradually as children are exposed to different forms and types of poems. Paul Janeczko's *A Kick in the Head: An Everyday Guide to Poetic Forms* is a lively introduction to forms of poetry that will appeal to children. Each form is accompanied by poems of example and a brief explanation of structure. Janeczko's choice of poems and Chris Raschka's illustrations liven up what might otherwise be just a tedious list of definitions. Although we do not have the space in this chapter to cover the many forms found in *A Kick in the Head,* we have singled out a few that are worth sharing with children in **Teaching Feature 6.1: Forms of Poetry for Children.**

teaching feature 6.1

Forms of Poetry for Children

Forms	Title/ Author	Age
Narrative The narrative poem relates a particular event or episode or tells a long tale. It may be a lyric, a sonnet, or free verse; its one requirement is that it must tell a story. – Ballad	"The Night Before Christmas" (or "A Visit from St. Nicholas") (Moore)	6–10
	"The Tale of Custard the Dragon" (Nash)	4–8
	Once Upon a Poem: Favorite Poems That Tell Stories (Crossley-Holland)	6–10

teaching feature 6.1

Forms	Title/ Author	Age
Lyrical The term *lyrical* derives from the word *lyric* and means poetry that sings its way into the minds and memories of its listeners. It is usually personal or descriptive poetry, with no prescribed length or structure other than its melody.	"The Swing" and "The Wind," both in *A Child's Garden of Verses* (Stevenson) "The Lone Dog" (McLeod in Ferris) "Sea Fever" (Maesfield in Ferris)	4–8 8–12 8–12
Limerick This is a five-line verse in which the first and second lines rhyme, the third and fourth rhyme, and the fifth line rhymes with lines 1 and 2 and usually is a surprise or humorous statement. Freak spellings, oddities, and humorous twists characterize this form of poetry.	"Limericks" in *Knock at a Star* (Kennedy and Kennedy) *Boo! Halloween Poems and Limericks* (Hubbell) *Grimericks* (Pearson)	6–10 6–10 6–10
Free Verse Free verse does not have to rhyme but depends on rhythm or cadence for its poetic form. It may use some rhyme, alliteration, and pattern. Though it frequently looks different on the printed page, it sounds very much like other poetry when read aloud.	"How to Eat a Poem" (Merriam in Cullinan) "April Rain Song" (Hughes) *This Is Just to Say* (Sidman) *All the Small Poems and Fourteen More* (Worth)	7–12 6–10 7–12 7–12
Haiku Haiku is an ancient Japanese verse form that can be traced back to the thirteenth century. There are only seventeen syllables in the haiku; the first and third lines contain five syllables, the second line seven. Almost every haiku can be divided into two parts: first, a simple picture-making description that usually includes some reference, direct or indirect, to the season; and second, a statement of mood or feeling. A relationship between these two parts is implied—either a similarity or a telling difference.	*The Stars Are Whispering* and *Today and Today* (Issa Kobayashi) *If Not for the Cat* (Prelutsky) *Stone Bench in an Empty Park* (Janeczko) *Birds on a Wire* (Lewis and Janeczko) *Yum! ¡Mmmm! ¡Qué Rico: America's Sproutings* (Mora) *Dogku* (Clements)	6–10 6–10 8–12 8–12 6–8 6–8
Sijo See Joe A Korean form consisting of three lines of 14–16 syllables, each totaling 44–46 syllables. The first two lines set forth a situation or event and the third line concludes the poem with a humorous twist.	*Tap Dancing on the Roof: Sijo Poems* (Park)	8–10
Concrete Concrete poems are picture poems that make the reader see what they are saying. The message of the poem is presented not only in the words (sometimes just letters or punctuation marks) but in the arrangement of the words. Meaning is reinforced, or even carried, by the shape of the poem.	*A Poke in the I* (Janeczko) *Flicker Flash* (Graham) *Doodle Dandies* (Lewis) *Blue Lipstick: Concrete Poems* (Grandits) *Meow Ruff* (Sidman)	8–12 6–10 6–10 12 and up 5–8

Art and words combine to create poems about light in Joan Graham's book of concrete poetry, *Flicker Flash*, with illustrations by Nancy Davis.

Birthday Candles

Like shooting stars that blaze the dark, you flame — then disappear. But when I look, I see your light in faces, circled near.

Selecting Poetry for Children

Before they enter school, children seem to have a natural enthusiasm for the sounds and rhythms of language. School-teachers and librarians will want to select poems and poets that will build upon these inclinations and that appeal to children's interests. They will also want to find ways to extend and deepen children's initial preferences into a life-long love of poetry.

Children's Poetry Preferences

Starting in the early 1920s, children's interest in poetry has been the subject of many research studies. The interesting fact about all these studies is the similarity of the findings and the stability of children's poetry preferences over the years. According to Ann Terry, these studies suggest the following:

1. Children are the best judges of their preferences.
2. Reading texts and courses of study often do not include the children's favorite poems.
3. Children's poetry choices are influenced by (1) the poetry form, (2) certain poetic elements, and (3) the content, with humor and familiar experience being particularly popular.
4. A poem enjoyed at one grade level may be enjoyed across several grade levels.
5. Children do not enjoy poems they do not understand.
6. Thoughtful, meditative poems are disliked by children.
7. Some poems appeal to one sex more than the other; girls enjoy poetry more than boys do.
8. New poems are preferred over older, more traditional ones.
9. Literary merit is not necessarily an indication that a poem will be liked.[5]

Terry also reported that in her study of children in grades 4 through 6, narrative poems, such as John Ciardi's "Mummy Slept Late and Daddy Fixed Breakfast" (in *A Jar of Tiny Stars*, ed. Bernice E. Cullinan), and limericks, including both modern and traditional, were the children's favorite forms of poetry. Haiku was consistently disliked by all grade levels. Elements of rhyme, rhythm, and sound increased children's enjoyment of the poems, as evidenced by their preference for David McCord's "The Pickety Fence" (in *A Jar of Tiny Stars*, ed. Bernice E. Cullinan) and "Lone Dog" (in *Favorite Poems Old and New*, ed. Helen Ferris). Poems that contained much figurative language or imagery were disliked. Children's favorite poems at all three grade levels contained humor or were about familiar experiences or animals. All children preferred contemporary poems containing modern content and today's language to the older, more traditional poems. Research by Carol Fisher and Margaret Natarella[6] found similar preferences among first, second, and third graders, as did Karen Kutiper[7] among seventh, eighth, and ninth graders.

How then can we most effectively select poetry for children? Certainly a teacher will want to consider children's needs and interests, their previous experience with poetry, and the types of poetry that appeal to them. A sound principle to follow is to begin where the children are. Teachers can share poems that have elements of rhyme, rhythm, and sound, such as Tony Mitten's "Rickety Train Ride" in Jane Yolen and Andrew Fusek Peters's *Here's a Little Poem* or David McCord's "The Pickety Fence" in *A Jar of Tiny Stars,* ed. Bernice E. Cullinan. They can read many narrative verses and limericks and look for humorous poems and poems about familiar experiences and animals. They should share only those poems that they really like themselves; enthusiasm for poetry is contagious. However, teachers will not want to limit their sharing only to poems that they know children will like, for taste needs to be developed, too. Children should go beyond their delight in humorous and narrative poetry to develop an appreciation for variety in both form and content. We want children to respond to more poetry and to find more to respond to in poetry.

Poetry Books for Children

Today poetry anthologies do not stay in print as long as they used to, because time limits are usually placed on permissions to use certain poems. This has meant the publication of fewer large anthologies and the proliferation of many specialized collections containing fewer than twenty poems. Teachers will want to have a good classroom library of anthologies and specialized collections. These can be enhanced by selecting volumes from the school library for special studies that link poetry to all the many areas of the curriculum.

Poetry Anthologies Every family with children will want to own at least one excellent anthology of poetry for children. Teachers will want to have several, including some for their personal use and some for the children's use.

Many parents and teachers will be attracted to the large *Random House Book of Poetry for Children*, with its 572 poems selected by Jack Prelutsky and profusely illustrated with Arnold Lobel's lively pictures. Though much of the book is dominated by humorous verse (including some 38 poems by Prelutsky himself), fine poems by Robert Frost, Eve Merriam, Eleanor Farjeon, Emily Dickinson, Myra Cohn Livingston, Dylan Thomas, and others are interspersed with them. Arnold Lobel's humorous full-color illustrations also draw children to this anthology.

Knock at a Star: A Child's Introduction to Poetry, compiled by the well-known adult poet and anthologist X. J. Kennedy and his wife, Dorothy, is a memorable collection of poetry for children 8 years old and up. The poets represented range widely, from adult poets like James Stephens, Emily Dickinson, Robert Frost, and William Stafford to children's poets Aileen Fisher, David McCord, and Lillian Morrison. Many

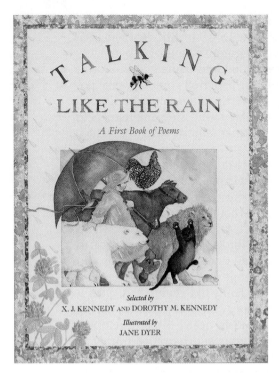

X. J. Kennedy and Dorothy M. Kennedy's poetry and Jane Dyer's illustrations provide in inviting introduction to poetry for young children in *Talking Like the Rain*. From the cover of *Talking Like the Rain: A First Book of Poems* by X. J. Kennedy and Dorothy M. Kennedy, illustrated by Jane Dyer. Illustrations copyright © 1992 by Jane Dyer. By permission of Little, Brown, and Company, Inc.

familiar poems are here, but most are new and fresh to children's collections. The three section headings in this book also are addressed to children and provide an understanding of how poetry does what it does: (1) "What Do Poems Do?" (make you laugh, tell stories, send messages, share feelings, start you wondering); (2) "What's Inside a Poem?" (images, word music, beats that repeat, likenesses); and (3) "Special Kinds of Poems." Teachers, librarians, and parents as well as children can learn from this wise book, which teaches at the same time as it develops enthusiasm for poetry.

X. J. Kennedy and Dorothy M. Kennedy's *Talking Like the Rain*, illustrated by Jane Dyer, contains a mixture of old and new poems that have the kind of sound and wordplay that is particularly appealing to younger children. *Talking Like the Rain* contains 123 poems, ranging from Robert Louis Stevenson's "The Swing" to Myra Cohn Livingston's "Working with Mother." Donald Hall's *The Oxford Illustrated Book of American Children's Poems* is a wonderful collection that includes poems from contemporary poets and classic favorites. Those in Michael Rosen's *Poems for the Very Young* have been chosen with special consideration for "the physical side of language," those sound elements that intrigue the youngest child. Polly Dunbar provides exuberant illustrations to accompany Jane Yolen and Andrew Fusek Peters's collection for younger children titled *Here's a Little Poem: A Very First Book of Poetry*.

Paul Janeczko's *Seeing the Blue Between* and *The Place My Words Are Looking For* are two superb collections that provide insight into how some poets work and how they feel about their poems. In *Seeing the Blue Between*, thirty-two poets share advice for aspiring writers of poetry and then several of their poems that illustrate their advice. In *The Place My Words Are Looking For*, Jack Prelutsky, X. J. Kennedy, Myra Cohn Livingston, and others talk about how they create their poetry by providing personal comments and examples of their poems. Pictures of the poets accompany each section so that children can see what their favorite poet looks like.

One of the most enduring current anthologies is *Reflections on a Gift of Watermelon Pickle and Other Modern Verses*, edited by Stephen Dunning and others. Illustrated with superb black-and-white photographs surrounded by much space, this anthology appeals to the eye as well as the ear of older students in middle school. They will take delight in "Sonic Boom" by John Updike, "Ancient History" by Arthur Guiterman, "Dreams" by Langston Hughes, and "How to Eat a Poem" by Eve Merriam. They will appreciate the honesty and realistic viewpoint of "Husbands and Wives,"

in which Miriam Hershenson tells of couples who ride the train from station to station without ever speaking to each other.

Several volumes of multicultural poetry for older children deserve to be considered among the "must-haves" in any home or classroom. Catherine Clinton has edited a fine anthology of poetry called *I, Too, Sing America: Three Centuries of African American Poetry*. Illustrated in muted tones by Stephen Alcorn, the book provides a chronological history of African American poetry by including poets from the 1700s to today. Poet and anthologist Naomi Shihab Nye has edited beautiful books that bring together poems from all over the world: *The Space Between Our Footsteps: Poems and Paintings from the Middle East* and *This Same Sky: A Collection of Poems from Around the World* are international collections with universal connections.

Specialized Collections As mentioned earlier, as poetry permissions have become more expensive and more difficult to obtain for long lengths of time, anthologists have turned to making small, specialized collections. Most of these are organized for a particular age level or around certain subjects, such as dogs or seasons. Some are related to the ethnic origin of the poems, such as poetry of Native Americans or poems that celebrate the experiences of African Americans. An increasing number of specialized collections contain stunning illustrations. Some of the best of these are listed in **Teaching Feature 6.2: Specialized Collections of Poetry** on page 170. Children will find imaginative connections to themes such as time or animals and to subjects as varied as American history, music, and science through many of these books.

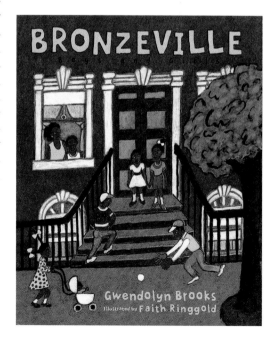

Specialized Collections of Poetry

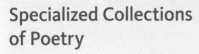 teaching feature 6.2

Compiler	Title	Age Level	Description
Children's Everyday Experiences			
Ralph Fletcher	*A Writing Kind of Day: Poems for Young Poets*	8–12	A fictional narrator composes poems about writing poetry.
Kristine O'Connell Georgew	*Swimming Upstream*	11–14	George turns her talents to poems about being in middle school.
Nikki Grimes	*It's Raining Laughter*	6–8	Bright photographs illustrate this sunny collection of poetry about everyday experiences.
Sara Holbrook	*By Definition: Poems of Feelings*	4-8	Holbrook captures the young adolescents' emotions in poems ranging from giddiness to guilt.
Lee Bennett Hopkins	*Oh, No! Where Are My Pants? and Other Disasters*	7–12	This collection focuses on events that often spell disaster for a child—some funny, some poignant.
Pat Mora	*Love to Mama: A Tribute to Mothers*	9–12	Poems honor mothers, grandmothers, and caregiving women.
Naomi Shihab Nye	*A Maze Me*	12 and up	Nye's poems reflect the inner life and concerns of adolescent girls.
Joyce Sidman	*This Is Just to Say*	7 and up	Sidman imagines a class of sixth graders writing poems of apology and their addressees writing back poems of forgiveness.
Gary Soto	*Fearless Fernie* and *Worlds Apart*	9–12	These two volumes contain sensitive, funny, and beautifully written poems about childhood friends.
Dorothy S. Strickland and Michael R. Strickland	*Families: Poems Celebrating the African American Experience*	5–8	Poems celebrating African American family life make up this volume.
Poetry of Nature and Seasons			
Douglas Florian	*Autumnblings, Handsprings, Summersaults,* and *Winter Eyes*	5–10	Lovely watercolors illustrate these four volumes of poetry about the seasons.
Kristine O'Connell George	*Toasting Marshmallows: Camping Poems*	5–10	Simple and short, these poems capture the joys of camping outdoors.

Compiler	Title	Age Level	Description
Paul Paolilli and Dan Brewer	*Silver Seeds*	5–8	These acrostic poems describe familiar sights and objects in the young child's world.
Joanne Ryder	*Toad by the Road*	5–8	Keenly observed poems about the life cycle of toads.
Steven Schnur	*Winter: An Alphabet Acrostic*	6–10	This book completes Schnur's acrostic poems about the four seasons.
Joyce Sidman	*Song of the Water Boatman*	7–12	Poems in the voices of pond dwellers are accompanied by exquisite woodcut illustrations and convey factual information about pond ecology.
Marilyn Singer	*Central Heating* and *Footprints on the Roof*	7–12	These volumes center on the elements of earth and fire.
Jane Yolen	*Color Me a Rhyme*, *Shape Me a Rhyme*, and *Wild Wings*	6–10	Yolen and her photographer son, Jason Stemple, collaborate on several volumes about the natural world.
Animal Poems			
Francisco X. Alarcón	*Animal Poems of the Iguazú/ Animalario del Iguazú*	5–8	Animals speak of their lives in the South American rainforest.
David Greenberg	*Bugs!*	5–8	This delicious menu of funny poems about insects comes from the subversive author of *Slugs*.
Lee Bennett Hopkins	*Dinosaurs*	8 and up	These eighteen poems, including "The Last Dinosaur" and "How the End Might Have Been," are useful for discussion and dinosaur units.
Marjorie Maddox	*A Crossing of Zebras: Animal Packs in Poetry*	5–8	Maddox uses collective nouns such as schools of fish as an inspiration for poetry.
Jack Prelutsky, ed.	*The Beauty of the Beast*	7–12	Meilo So's exquisite watercolor paintings make these beasts truly beautiful. More than two hundred poems celebrate the animal world.
Jack Prelutsky	*If Not for the Cat*	7–12	Different animals are the subject of these haiku poems.

(continued)

teaching feature 6.2

Compiler	Title	Age Level	Description
Judy Sierra	*Antarctic Antics*	4–8	Lively verses celebrate the emperor penguin (from the penguin's point of view).
Amy E. Sklansky	*From the Doghouse: Poems to Chew On*	4–8	Sklansky gives children a lighthearted and lively look at dogs.
Valerie Worth	*Animal Poems*	4–8	This collection of poems has been beautifully illustrated with collages by Steve Jenkins.
Wade Zahares	*Big, Bad, and a Little Bit Scary: Poems That Bite Back!*	6–11	Zahares provides wonderful artistic interpretations of poems about scary animals.

Humorous Poetry

Compiler	Title	Age Level	Description
David Greenberg	*Don't Forget Your Etiquette! The Essential Guide to Misbehavior*	6–8	A child's humorous antidote to rules of good behavior.
Lee Bennett Hopkins	*Oh, No! Where Are My Pants? and Other Disasters*	7–12	Poems about embarrassing events in the lives of children.
J. Patrick Lewis	*Once Upon a Tomb: Gravely Humorous Verses*	7–10	These silly and slightly gruesome epitaphs will leave children giggling.
Susan Pearson	*Grimericks*	5–10	A funny collection of limericks about grisly creatures.
Jack Prelutsky	*My Dog May Be a Genius*	5–10	Lively colored illustrations by James Stevenson add to the humor in Prelutsky's latest collection of funny poems.
Adam Rex	*Frankenstein Makes a Sandwich*	5–8	Well-known monsters deal with the humdrum of everyday life.
Shel Silverstein	*Where the Sidewalk Ends*	7 and up	Every child's favorite collection of poems.

Multicultural Poetry Collections

Compiler	Title	Age Level	Description
Arnold Adoff	*I Am the Darker Brother: An Anthology of Modern Poems by Black Americans*	10 and up	This collection contains some of the best-known poetry of Langston Hughes, Gwendolyn Brooks, and Countee Cullen, as well as some modern poets.
Francisco X. Alarcón	*Angels Ride Bikes*, *From the Bellybutton Moon*, *Iguanas in the Snow*, and *Laughing Tomatoes*	5–8	Four bilingual volumes celebrate the singular joys of each season.

Compiler	Title	Age Level	Description
Jorge Argueta	*A Movie in My Pillow/Una película en mi almohada*	10–14	Bilingual poems describe growing up in El Salvador and San Francisco.
Gwendolyn Brooks	*Bronzeville Boys and Girls*	6–8	Faith Ringgold has illustrated a new edition of Brooks's classic collection.
Lori Marie Carlson	*Cool Salsa* and *Red Hot Salsa*	12 and up	Two collections of bilingual poems describe growing up Latino.
Eloise Greenfield	*In the Land of Words*	5–8	New poems and old favorites make up this collection from noted poet Greenfield.
Nikki Grimes	*A Pocketful of Poems*	7–10	The narrator takes readers through the seasons on pairs of free verse/haiku poems.
Langston Hughes	*The Dream Keeper*	7 and up	This is a must-have collection of poems from a great American poet.
Naomi Shihab Nye	*19 Varieties of Gazelle: Poems of the Middle East*	10 and up	Nye holds up a magnifying glass to capture the smallest nuances of Middle Eastern culture.
Joyce Carol Thomas	*The Blacker the Berry*	7–10	These collections celebrate African American identities.
Janet Wong	*Twist: Yoga Poems*	6–8	Each poem focuses on a different yoga position.

Creating a Climate for Enjoyment

There have always been teachers who love poetry and who share their enthusiasm for poetry with students. There are teachers who make poetry a natural part of the daily program of living and learning. They realize that poetry should not be presented under the pressure of a tight time schedule, but should be enjoyed every day. Children should be able to relax and relish the humor and beauty that the sharing of poetry affords.

Finding Time for Poetry

Teachers who would develop children's delight in poetry will find time to share poetry with them sometime each day and find ways to connect poetry to the experiences in children's lives. They know that anytime is a good time to read a poem to children, but they will especially want to capitalize on exciting experiences like the first snow, a birthday party, or the arrival of a classmate's new baby brother. Perhaps there has been a fight on the playground and someone is still grumbling and complaining—that might be a good time to share poetry about feelings. The teacher could read Karla Kuskin's "When I Woke Up This Morning" (in *Moon, Have You Met My Mother?*), and then everyone could laugh the bad feelings away. Poetry can also be thought of as a delicious snack to nibble on during transition times between going out to recess or the last few minutes of the day. Anytime is a good time for a poetry snack!

One way to be sure to share poetry every day is to relate children's favorite prose stories to poetry. One teacher who keeps a card file of poems always slips one or two cards into the book that is to be read aloud that day. For example, after sharing *Whistle for Willie* by Ezra Jack Keats, Jack Prelutsky's "Whistling" (in *Read-Aloud Rhymes for the Very Young*) could be read. A fifth-grade teacher paired Gail Carson Levine's *Ella Enchanted* with Laura Whipple's *If the Shoe Fits: Voices from Cinderella*. Students then went on to read other novelizations of fairy tales and to write poems in the voices of the characters. Librarians and teachers will want to make their own poetry/prose connections.

Teachers have also found that a good way to integrate poetry into the entire day is to link poems to content areas. A science unit could be built around Douglas Florian's four seasons books or Joyce Sidman's three books about ecosystems, *Welcome to the Night*, *Butterfly Eyes*, and *Song of the Water Boatman*. (See the **Curriculum Connections** feature on page 181.) A math lesson might be introduced with one of the poems from Lee Bennett Hopkins's collection *Marvelous Math*. Many poems can enhance social studies. Geography need not be neglected with appealing collections such as Hopkins's *My America: A Poetry Atlas of the United States* and *Got Geography!* as well as Lewis's *A World of Wonders: Geographic Travels in Verse and Rhyme*. American history is also well represented by collections such as Hopkins's *Lives: Poems about Famous Americans* and Susan Katz's *A Revolutionary Field Trip*. *Remember the Bridge: Poems of a People*, a collection of poems by Carole Boston Weatherford, is a fine introduction to Black History for adolescents. Bobbi Katz's *We the People* begins with "The First Americans" and takes us to the edge of the twenty-first century in "Imagine." In each poem Katz speaks through the voice of a person, real or imagined, who experienced important events in American history. In *Heroes and Sheroes*, J. Patrick Lewis pays tribute to men and women from around the world, some who are well known and others who may have gone unnamed.

Several volumes pair poetry and art in unique ways. Jan Greenberg, with Sandra Jordan, has written many books about twentieth-century art, inviting poets to choose a work of twentieth-century art and write a poem about it. The results, *Heart to Heart* and *Side to Side,* are a delight and a revelation. In *Talking to the Sun*, by Kenneth Koch and Kate Farrell, the editors have matched paintings with poems.

Children will also be delighted with excellent poetry books on sports, such as Jack Prelutsky's *Good Sports*, Robert Burleigh's *Goal* and *Hoops*, and Lee Bennett Hopkins's *Extra Innings*. There are poems on every subject, from dinosaurs to quasars and black holes.

Reading Poetry to Children

Poetry should be read in a natural voice with a tone that fits the meaning of the poem. Generally, the appropriate pace for reading poetry is slower than for reading prose. It is usually recommended that a poem be read aloud a second time, perhaps to refresh

Poems from books such as *Song of the Water Boatman* by Joyce Sidman can serve as models for writing or springboards for curriculum studies. Illustration from *Song of the Water Boatman and Other Pond Poems* by Joyce Sidman, illustrated by Beckie Prange. Illustrations copyright © 2005 by Beckie Prange. Reprinted by permission of Houghton Mifflin Harcourt Publishing Company. All rights reserved.

children's memories, to clarify a point, or to savor a particular image. Most poetry, especially good poetry, is so concentrated and compact that few people can grasp its meaning in one exposure. Following the reading of a poem, discussion should be allowed to flow. In certain instances, discussion is unnecessary or superfluous. Spontaneous chuckles might follow the reading of Kaye Starbird's "Eat-It-All Elaine" (in *The Random House Book of Poetry for Children*, ed. Jack Prelutsky), while a thoughtful silence might be the response to Robert P. Tristram Coffin's "Forgive My Guilt" (in *Reflections on a Gift of Watermelon Pickle*, ed. Stephen Dunning et al.). It is not necessary to discuss or do something with each poem read, other than enjoy it. The most important thing you as a teacher or librarian can do when you are reading poetry is share your enthusiasm for the poem.

A former United States poet laureate provides four simple but useful tips for reading poetry aloud. These tips are elaborated on the Library of Congress Poetry 180 project Web site. They are in brief:

1. Read the poem slowly. A good way for a reader to set an easy pace is to pause for a few seconds between the title and the poem's first line.

2. Read in a normal, relaxed tone of voice. Let the words of the poem do the work.
3. Poems come in lines but pausing at the end of every line will create a choppy effect and interrupt the flow of meaning. Readers should pause only where there is punctuation, just as you would when reading prose.
4. Use a dictionary to look up unfamiliar words. In some cases a reader might want to write a poem phonetically as a reminder of how it should sound.[8]

Choral Reading

The reading and sharing of poetry through choral speaking is another way to foster interest in poetry. Choral speaking or reading is the interpretation of poetry by several voices speaking as one. At first, young children *speak* it as they join in the refrains. Middle-grade children might prefer to *read* their poems. They are not always read in unison; in fact, this is one of the most difficult ways to present a poem.

Several types of choral speaking are particularly suited for use in the elementary school. In the "refrain" type, one person (teacher or child) reads the narrative and the rest of the class joins in on the refrain. The teacher might use the well-known folk poem that begins "In a dark, dark wood there was a dark, dark path" and let children join in on the "dark darks." Eve Merriam's "Windshield Wiper" (in *Knock at a Star*, ed. X. J. Kennedy and D. M. Kennedy) and Sara Holbrook's "Copycat" (in *Wham! It's a Poetry Jam*) are good echo poems to try.

Another way to do a group reading, called antiphonal, is to divide the class into two groups and let the groups take turns reading each verse. An effective approach with young children is the "line-a-child" arrangement, where different children say, or read, individual lines, with the class joining in unison at the beginning or end of the poem. "One, Two, Buckle My Shoe" is a good rhyme to introduce this type of choral reading.

Several books come ready-made for multiple-voice readings. Younger children can get started on this technique with Mary Ann Hoberman's series of books beginning with *You Read to Me, I'll Read to You: Very Short Stories to Read Together* or David Harrison's *Farmer's Dog Goes to the Forest: Rhymes for Two Voices*. Older children particularly enjoy practicing reading Paul Fleischman's poems for multiple voices found in his Newbery Medal book *Joyful Noise* and in his *I Am*

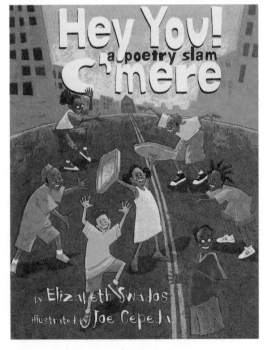

Joe Cepeda's intense paintings for Elizabeth Swados's *Hey You! C'Mere: A Poetry Slam* seem to dance right off the page. Cover illustration copyright © 2002 by Joe Cepeda from *Hey You! C'mere: A Poetry Slam* by Elizabeth Swados. Arthur A. Levine Books/Scholastic Inc./Scholastic Press. Reprinted with permission.

Phoenix. In *Big Talk*, Fleischman challenges older readers by presenting poems for four voices.

If children are to develop appreciation for the deep satisfactions that poetry brings, they should have many opportunities to share poetry in interesting and meaningful situations. Appreciation for poetry develops slowly. It is the result of long and loving experience with poetry over a period of years. Children who are fortunate enough to have developed a love of poetry will always be the richer for it.

Challenging Perspectives on Poetry

During playground duty, Ms. Berlyn walked toward two little girls playing what looked like a game of very sophisticated patty-cake. The rhythm and rhyme of the game was almost hypnotic. The girls were singing and reciting the words of a popular rhyme, "Apple on the stick, you make me sick, you make my heart go 246, not because you dirty, not because you clean, not because you kiss the boy behind the magazine! Come on girls let's have some fun, here comes Jenny with the short skirt on." The rhyme went on and then Ms. Berlyn realized that the rhyme went "down hill" as the girls' language became profane and inappropriate.

"Let's find another game to play," Ms. Berlyn interrupted.

Startled, one little girl asked why. Ms. Berlyn responded, "The language is not school language and you should not be talking about some of those things—you are too young."

"It's just like poetry," Crystal protested. "It rhymes and everything!"

Ms. Berlyn did not know what to say. "Well, that's not poetry, find something else to do." The girls walked away discussing in hushed tones their feelings about Ms. Berlyn's request.

Poetry can be extremely engaging and fun word play for children, but today certain uses present challenges for teachers. Its value begins in the early grades, when poetry can be used to jump-start language development and as a support for a wide range of literacy skills, including phonemic awareness, repetition, and predictability, and to enhance reading fluency and emergent writing, especially for children with limited vocabulary.

While many children know what poetry is, a group of first-graders described poetry as the following:

"It's *Def Poetry Jam,* on HBO, you know what that is, right?"
"It's like a poetry slam and people read or just say from memory while music is playing in the background. And the people listen; if they like it they get real excited."

Poetry today is not "your mother's poetry." For many young people, the most popular form of poetry is called *spoken word*. Spoken word is a performance in which the formal elements of poetry (allegory, alliteration, assonance, denotation/connotation, diction, imagery, irony, metaphor, meter, rhyme, simile, symbol, tone, and word order) are dramatic events and recitation. Often song lyrics are part of the recitation, again spoken rather than sung. As the first-grader above stated, spoken word is often accompanied by a musical background, but emphasis is on the words and the speaker.

Spoken word is often performed competitively. Poetry slams—a competitive event in which poets perform their work and are judged based on content and performance by members of the audience—are organized locally, nationally, and internationally. These events, open to anyone who signs up, invite poets to participate in either the individual or group categories for awards, prize money, and possibly network or cable television exposure. In *performance poetry* the poet either reads previously published poems, or reads poems specifically written to be performed aloud. Another kind of spoken word poetry gaining popularity recently is political and social commentary, which is more artistic than a typical speech.

In 2002, nine gifted poets and performers, a talented DJ to add music to their words, one of Hollywood's most prolific directors of television and films, and a master visionary who has long-shaped the evolution of pop and urban culture created *Russell Simmons Def Poetry Jam on Broadway*, a presentation of performance poetry inspired by today's world. Previously an award-winning HBO television series, the Broadway show received a Tony Award for Special Theatrical Event.

Def Poetry Jam on Broadway was performed to sell-out crowds throughout the world. One reviewer stated, "The show gave poetry a new level of respect in the culture . . . to some, this may seem like a lot of energy and effort and fuss for what is, in the end, just poetry. Yeah, just poetry. Just ear-ringing, heart-charging, truth-telling, life-affirming, life-*changing* poetry."[9]

A look at the publicity for the performance leads us to one of the challenges that teachers meet as poetry has gained new popularity in this context. The advertisement for the performance included a warning that read: "May be inappropriate for 11 and under. (Strong Language)." Clearly, even though the performance became massively popular and promoted poetry, the use of this and other examples of performance poetry is not a given for all classrooms.

Outside of the classical poetry taught in schools, the poetry of today, in slams for example, are full of social and political commentary and are often mixed with great energy, enthusiasm, and strong language. From radio personalities to the music industry, debates regarding language include one's First Amendment rights to free speech to controversy over misogyny (primarily sexist or degrading comments to or about women) and racism. This context provides an exciting segue for teachers to discuss the wonderful world of poetry with their students in the classroom. The challenge is, however, how to use contemporary forms of expression in poetry and negotiate use of controversial language and content.

This can be a slippery slope. Some language is deeply political and loaded with the historical baggage of oppression. From Huck Finn to hip-hop, some would argue the use of the "N-word" needs to be in school as a symbol of intellectual freedom. After all, isn't the liberty taken by an artist or a writer in deviating from conventional forms—unconventional language or facts to achieve a desired effect—poetic license? The challenge is deeply rooted in the historical considerations of language and dialect. When language dialects are heard as deficits—markers of class and discrimination—then issues of identity and validation are part of the teaching and learning process. If we want children to adopt the language of schooling, teachers should not view language variation as deficits. Lisa Delpit, in her book *The Skin That We Speak*, provides a variety of positive ways to view the language variations that students bring to school. "Since language is one of the most intimate expressions of identity, indeed, 'the skin that we speak,' then to reject a person's language can only feel as if we are rejecting him" (p. 47).[10]

This is not suggesting that the use of oppressive or what is now deemed "strong language" is appropriate for school. When students use language in poetry or other forms of creative writing there is a way to simultaneously affirm a student's home language and provide a segue to teaching and learning standard, edited English. Most often the discussion of affirming a student's home language is in part helping English Language Learners (ELL) to speak, read, write, and communicate in English. However, this perspective, affirming what a student brings to the classroom in language, can help a teacher work with all students, learning from their use of language and providing ideas to develop further as they learn more about their students' lives. For example, in *Rethinking Schools*, author Linda Christensen uses the poem "Raised by Women" by Kelly Norman Ellis. This poem connects home and heritage in a celebration of the women in the poet's life. Christensen stated she uses poetry to "build community and teach poetic traits . . . to build relationships with students and between students." She further says, "I love Ellis' celebration of the women in her life, her use of home language, and the wit and wisdom of her rhythmic lines."[11] Christensen uses poetry to help honor the use of students' home language rather than standard English, and, like the poet, encouraged students to experiment with language in their poems. The students felt validated while they learned about metaphor, meter, rhyme, simile, and tone.

Using this approach, we start by affirming a student's home language and cultural practices. We begin not with what is lacking, but with the skills the student already possesses. By changing our vantage point and becoming learners of our students, we are better able to recognize and appreciate all that is involved in being a "family translator." In this way, we come to understand, affirm, and draw upon students' vigorous linguistic and cultural practices for their own learning and development.

Using the many new and familiar voices found in poetry written for children, teachers can engage students in reading, writing, and performing poetry in ways that can serve as a bridge to reading and understanding other forms of classical work. Teachers can engage students in conversations of the debates around language and literary works in contemporary times by the Ten-Point Model for Teaching Controversial Issues (see **Figure 6.1** on p. 180). The ultimate goal is to get students to read, and write, and then read and write again and again—increasing student engagement and participation with all genres.

figure 6.1

The Ten-Point Model for Teaching Controversial Issues
Language Choices in Poetry

Step	Task	To Consider
1. Raise the initial question and have the children brainstorm all their initial responses.	Prompt children's response with: • "What is poetic license?" • "Does this freedom give poets the authority to use language that some deem offensive?"	Ground rules are needed to moderate the nature of contributions to the discussion. The purpose of such rules is to enable the free flow of ideas in a safe, nonthreatening environment with the goal of having students think about and question their assumptions and listen to others' ideas.
2. Create a list of "Things to find out more about."	Create a list of "Things About Contemporary Language" and use debates to find out more.	For example: When is it okay to use a racial slur?
3. Assign information-gathering homework.	Students should gather, evaluate, and synthesize data from a variety of sources (e.g., print and nonprint texts, artifacts, people, etc.) and communicate their discoveries in ways that suit their purpose and audience.	How is the information similar/different from each of these resources?
4. Share again responses to the initial question in a brainstorming session.	Having students share their responses with the class "puts everything on the table" for further exploration and discussion.	Provide as much support as you have available.
5. Continue the process of gathering information.	Students should be encouraged to comb the Internet for blogs, electronic magazines, and other news sources to gather information about the most current debates in broadcast and print media.	The teacher's role is an active one—facilitating, clarifying, monitoring, and questioning. But the teacher does not impose information.
6. If a concept emerges that sparks interest, confusion, or conflict, pose it as a new question.	New ways to reframe this issue could be: • "Is there a double standard?" • "Can some groups of people use some language that others are not allowed to use?" • "What about the First Amendment?" • "What responsibility comes with freedom of expression?"	Mediating negative comments and strong emotions is an important aspect of ensuring a "smooth" approach to controversial issues. Ask for evidence, analyze underlying assumptions, and ask for other viewpoints.
7. Periodically give the children assignments in class to summarize their thoughts.	The assignment could be individual or shared writing. Potential prompts include: • "What is the rule in your family or community?" • "Are there words and phrases that you could or could not use in your writing to a wider audience?" • "Who should be considered in the creative writing process before publishing poetry?"	What other ways can you find to help crystallize your students' individual thinking about the use of language in poetry?
8. As individual or group projects emerge, follow on them.	The class may decide to attend poetry readings or a poetry "slam." This can be an opportunity for students' follow-up on initial considerations of language use.	For example, students could interview poets by asking, "If poetry relies on language for imagery, is it the user or the audience that should decide what is appropriate usage?"

figure 6.1 *(continued)*

Step	Task	To Consider
9. Let others know what you are doing.	Find spoken-word artists/poets in your local area and invite them to your classroom to discuss how they deal with the issues of free speech and censorship. This can be as simple as a one-day visit to read poems and lead a workshop, or as ambitious as a long-term residency over a week, a term, or even longer.	Encourage dialogue with parents, colleagues, and the community.
10. End your project with something either public or permanent.	Hold an open forum with a group of students on the topic of language use in creative work. Invite those who are on both sides on the issue.	Teachers will need to facilitate carefully the expressive nature of the interactive communications with limitations on various words or phrases that may be sensitive.

Source: Adapted from Kreidler, W. *Elementary Perspectives: Teaching Concepts of Peace and Conflict.* Copyright © 1990 Educators for Social Responsibility, Cambridge, MA, www.esrnational.org. Used by permission.

curriculum connections

Using Poetry to Address Standards

The topic of poetry often gets groans from students and teachers alike who relate the genre more to ancient verse than to the new, imaginative, and engaging titles for children that have come out more recently. With recent publications, poetry can be a tool to explore language, emotion, and the world around you while also implementing curriculum standards. For example, students can explore the application of math concepts to everyday life in *Marvelous Math* with poems selected by Lee Bennett Hopkins. Language Arts standards that address rhyme, rhythm, and figurative language come to life in books such as *Blues Journey* by Walter Dean Myers, *Jazz A-B-Z: An A to Z Collection of Jazz Portraits* by Wynton Marsalis, and *Peacock and Other Poems* by Valerie Worth. Poetic forms of all types are beautifully illustrated in Paul Janeczko's *A Kick in the Head: An Everyday Guide to Poetic Forms.* Some poetry books bring social studies to life in an alternative form with creative language and illustrations. For example, Marilyn Nelson's *A Wreath for Emmett Till* highlights the tragedy of his murder in the segregated South by using iambic pentameter and sonnets. *Mural on Second Avenue and Other City Poems*, by Lillian Moore, uses words to describe the social and material environments of children in the city. Some books such as *Meow Ruff: A Story in Concrete Poetry* by Joyce Sidman and Joan Graham's *Flicker Flash* combine their poetry with art and design elements that add a graphic dimension to the text.

Standards in Action: Science

> *Handsprings*
> Florian, D. (2006). *Handsprings*. New York: Greenwillow.

Handsprings is the fourth title in Florian's series of poetry about the seasons. It contains a collection of

(continued)

(continued)

short poems that use rhyme, figurative language, and shape to explore various aspects of spring. Students may enjoy reading poems that describe springtime environment, weather, and activities. Poems are accompanied by whimsical watercolor illustrations.

Apply to Science Content Standard C – Life Science
The characteristics of organisms; life cycles of organisms; organisms and environments; populations and ecosystems; diversity and adaptations of organisms.

- Following the poem "Growing," students can keep observation notebooks of plant and animal life that they see growing during this season.

- Following the poem "Spring Is When," students can explore different migrating animal populations that live in their community. Students can document sightings of these animals and can use maps to trace the migration patterns.

Apply to Science Content Standard D – Earth and Space Science
Properties of earth materials; objects in the sky; changes in earth and sky. Properties and changes of properties in matter; motions and forces; transfer of energy.

- Following the poems, "Good-bye, Winter," "Winter and Spring," and "The First Day of Spring," stu-

dents could create a Venn diagram with words or images describing the characteristics of weather and life in winter and spring.

- Following the poem "In Winter," observe and record weather during the change from winter to spring. Look up weather information from previous years. Compare and contrast both sets of data and make a hypothesis about what next year's temperatures might be.

- Following the poem "March Wind," students can make weather vanes to indicate the direction of the wind. Students can place the weather vanes at different points around the school building and can compare the directions on different days and in the different locations.

- Following the poem "Rain Song," students can go out in the rain and observe using all of their senses. This sense data can be compiled and the students can write sensory poems to reflect their experiences.

Source: Standards are from the National Science Content Standards by the National Committee on Science Education Standards and Assessment, the National Research Council, and the Center for Science, Mathematics, and Engineering Education (1996).

Notes

1. *Poetry* originally appeared in *Sing for Your Supper.* Copyright © 1938 by Eleanor Farjeon; renewed 1966 by Gervase Farjeon. Used by permission of Harper-Collins Publishers, New York, NY.
2. Laurence Perrine, *Sound and Sense: An Introduction to Poetry*, 10th ed. (New York: Harcourt Brace Jovanovich, 2000), p. 3.
3. Kornei Chukovsky, *From Two to Five*, trans. and ed. Miriam Morton (Berkeley: University of California Press, 1963), p. 64.
4. Elizabeth Coatsworth, *The Sparrow Bush*, ill. Stefan Martin (New York: Norton, 1966), p. 8.
5. Ann Terry, "Children's Poetry Preferences: A National Survey of the Upper Elementary Grades," *NCTE Research Report* 16 (Urbana, Ill.: National Council of Teachers of English, 1974), p. 10.
6. Carol J. Fisher and Margaret A. Natarella, "Young Children's Preferences in Poetry: A National Survey of First, Second and Third Graders," *Research in the Teaching of English* 16 (December 1982): 339–53.

7. Karen Sue Kutiper, *A Survey of the Adolescent Poetry Preferences of Seventh, Eighth and Ninth Graders* (Ed.D. dissertation, University of Houston, 1985).

8. Poetry 180, October 2008 <www.loc.gov.poetry/180/p180-howtoread.html>. Used by permission of Billy Collins.

9. Robert Faires, "After Conquering Broadway, Def Jam Goes National and Pro Arts Snags Them," *Austin Chronicle* (13 Feb. 2004) 2008 <www.austinchronicle.com/gyrobase/Issue/story?oid=oid%A196859>.

10. L. Delpit and J. Dowdy, eds. *The Skin That We Speak: Thoughts on Language and Culture in the Classroom* (New York: New Press, 2002).

11. L. Christensen, "Raised by Women: Building Relationships Through Poetry," *Rethinking Schools* 21.3. (2007). Also online at <www.rethinkingschools.org/archive/21_03/21_03.shtml>.

Children's Literature

OLC Go to **www.mhhe.com/kiefer1e** *to access the Children's Literature Database, which includes information on thousands of children's books. Following are some of the titles you will find in the database.*

Titles in blue = multicultural titles

Adoff, Arnold, ed. *I Am the Darker Brother: An Anthology of Modern Poems by Black Americans.* Macmillan, 1970.

Alarcón, Francisco X. *Angels Ride Bikes: And Other Fall Poems/Los Angeles Andan En Cicicleta: Y Otros Poemas de Otoño.* Children's, 2005.

———. *Animal Poems of the Iguazú/Animalario del Iguazú.* Illustrated by Maya Christina Gonzalez. Children's Book Press, 2008.

———. *From the Bellybutton of the Moon and Other Summer Poems.* Illustrated by Maya Christina Gonzalez. Children's, 1998.

———. *Iguanas in the Snow and Other Winter Poems.* Illustrated by Maya Christina Gonzalez. Children's, 2001.

———. *Laughing Tomatoes: And Other Spring Poems/Jitomates Risueños: Y Otros Poemas de Primavera.* Children's, 2005.

Argueta, Jorge. *A Movie in My Pillow/Una película en mi almohada.* Illustrated by Elizabeth Gómez. Children's, 2001.

Brooks, Gwendolyn. *Bronzeville Boys and Girls.* Illustrated by Faith Ringgold. HarperCollins, 2007.

Burleigh, Robert. *Goal.* Illustrated by Stephen T. Johnson. Silver Whistle, 2001.

———. *Hoops.* Illustrated by Stephen T. Johnson. Silver Whistle, 1997.

Carlson, Lori M., ed. *Cool Salsa: Bilingual Poems on Growing Up Latino in the United States.* Holt, 1994.

———. *Red Hot Salsa: Bilingual Poems on Being Young and Latino in the United States.* Holt, 2005.

Clements, Andrew. *Dogku.* Illustrated by Tim Bowers. Simon, 2007.

Clinton, Catherine. *I, Too, Sing America: Three Centuries of African American Poetry.* Illustrated by Stephen Alcorn. Houghton, 1998.

Cole, Joanna, and Stephanie Calmenson. *Miss Mary Mack and Other Children's Street Rhymes.* Illustrated by Alan Tiegreen. Harper, 1990.

Crossley-Holland, Kevin. *Once upon a Poem: Favorite Poems That Tell Stories.* Chicken House/Scholastic, 2004.

Cullinan, Bernice E., ed. *A Jar of Tiny Stars: Poems by NCTE Award-Winning Poets.* Boyds Mills, 1996.

dePaola, Tomie. *Tomie dePaola's Mother Goose.* Putnam, 1988.

Dillon, Leo and Diane. *Mother Goose: Numbers on the Loose.* Harcourt, 2007.

Dotlich, Rebecca Kai. *Over in the Pink House.* Illustrated by Melanie W. Hall. Boyds, 2004.

Dunning, Stephen, Edward Lueders, and Hugh Smith. *Reflections on a Gift of Watermelon Pickle and Other Modern Verse.* Lothrop, 1966.

Ferris, Helen, ed. *Favorite Poems Old and New.* Illustrated by Leonard Weisgard. Doubleday, 1957.

Fleischman, Paul. *Big Talk: Poems for Four Voices.* Illustrated by Beppe Giacobbe. Candlewick, 2000.

———. *I Am Phoenix: Poems for Two Voices.* Illustrated by Ken Nutt. Harper, 1985.

———. *Joyful Noise: Poems for Two Voices.* Illustrated by Eric Beddows. Harper, 1988.

Fletcher, Ralph. *A Writing Kind of Day: Poems for Young Poets.* Boyds Mills, 2005.

Florian, Douglas. *Autumnblings.* Greenwillow, 2003.

———. *Comets, Stars, the Moon, and Mars: Space Poems and Paintings.* Harcourt, 2007.

———. *Handsprings.* Greenwillow, 2006.

———. *Summersaults.* Greenwillow, 2002.

———. *Winter Eyes.* Greenwillow, 1999.

———. *zoo's who.* Harcourt, 2005.

Frank, John. *Keepers: Treasure-Hunt Poems.* Photographs by Ken Robbins. Roaring Brook, 2008.

Frost, Robert. *Stopping by Woods on a Snowy Evening.* Illustrated by Susan Jeffers. Dutton, 1978.

George, Kristine O'Connell. *Swimming Upstream: Middle School Poems.* Illustrated by Debbie Tilley. Clarion, 2002.

———. *Toasting Marshmallows: Camping Poems.* Illustrated by Kate Kiesler. Clarion, 2001.

Graham, Joan Bransfield. *Splish, Splash.* Illustrated by Steve Scott. Ticknor & Fields, 1994.

Grandits, John. *Blue Lipstick: Concrete Poems.* Clarion, 2007.

Greenberg, David T. *Bugs!* Illustrated by Lynn Munsinger. Little, 1997.

———. *Don't Forget Your Etiquette! The Essential Guide to Misbehavior.* Illustrated by Nadine Bernard Westcott. Farrar, 2006.

Greenberg, Jan, ed. *Side by Side: New Poems Inspired by Art from around the World.* Abrams, 2008.

Greenfield, Eloise. *In the Land of Words: New and Selected Poems.* Illustrated by Jan Spivey Gilchrist. Amistad, 2004.

Grimes, Nikki. *It's Raining Laughter.* Photographs by Myles C. Pinkney. Dial, 1997.

———. *A Pocketful of Poems.* Illustrated by Javaka Steptoe. Clarion, 2001.

Harrison, David L. *Farmer's Dog Goes to the Forest: Rhymes for Two Voices.* Boyds, 2005.

Herrera, Juan Felipe. *Downtown Boy.* Scholastic, 2005.

Hoberman, Mary Ann. *The Llama Who Had No Pajama.* Illustrated by Betty Fraser. Harcourt, 1998.

———. *You Read to Me, I'll Read to You: Very Short Stories to Read Together.* Illustrated by Michael Emberley. Little, 2001.

Holbrook, Sara. *By Definition: Poems of Feeling.* Illustrated by Scott Mattern. Boyds, 2003.

Hopkins, Lee Bennett, selector. *America at War: Poems Selected by Lee Bennett Hopkins.* Illustrated by Stephen Alcorn. Simon, 2008.

———, selector. *Dinosaurs.* Illustrated by Murray Tinkelman. Harcourt, 1987.

———, ed. *Extra Innings: Baseball Poems.* Illustrated by Scott Medlock. Harcourt, 1993.

———, selector. *Got Geography!* Illustrated by Phillip Stanton. Greenwillow, 2006.

———. *Incredible Inventions.* Illustrated by Julia Sarcone-Roach. Greenwillow, 2009.

———, selector. *Marvelous Math.* Illustrated by Karen Barbour. Simon, 1997.

———, selector. *My America: A Poetry Atlas of the United States.* Illustrated by Stephen Alcorn. HarperCollins, 2000.

———, selector. *Oh, No! Where Are My Pants? and Other Disasters: Poems.* Illustrated by Wolf Erlbruch. Harper, 2005.

Hubbell, Patricia. *Boo! Halloween Poems and Limericks.* Illustrated by Jeff Spackman. Cavendish, 1998.

Hudson, Wade, ed. *Pass It On: African American Poetry for Children.* Illustrated by Floyd Cooper. Scholastic, 1993.

Issa. *See* Kobayashi, Issa.

James, Simon, selector. *Days Like This: A Collection of Small Poems.* Candlewick, 2000.

Janeczko, Paul B., selector. *Dirty Laundry Pile: Poems in Different Voices.* Illustrated by Melissa Sweet. HarperCollins, 2001.

———, comp. *A Kick in the Head: An Everyday Guide to Poetic Forms.* Illustrated by Chris Raschka. Candlewick, 2005.

———, ed. *The Place My Words Are Looking For.* Bradbury, 1990.

———, selector. *A Poke in the I: A Collection of Concrete Poems.* Illustrated by Chris Raschka. Candlewick, 2001.

———. selector. *Seeing the Blue Between: Advice and Inspiration for Young Poets.* Candlewick, 2001.

Katz, Susan. *A Revolutionary Field Trip: Poems of Colonial America.* Illustrated by R. W. Alley. Simon, 2004.

Keats, Ezra Jack. *Whistle for Willie.* Viking, 1964.

Kennedy, X. J., and Dorothy M. Kennedy, comp. *Knock at a Star: A Child's Introduction to Poetry.* Illustrated by Karen Ann Weinhaus. Little, 1999 [1982].

———. *Talking Like the Rain.* Illustrated by Jane Dyer. Little, 1992.

Kobayashi, Issa. *The Stars Are Whispering: A Haiku Journey with Poems.* Illustrated by G. Brian Karas. Scholastic, 2005.

———. *Today and Today.* Illustrated by G. Brian Karas. Scholastic, 2007.

Kuskin, Karla. *Moon, Have You Met My Mother?* Illustrated by Sergio Ruzzier. Harper, 2003.

Larrick, Nancy, ed. *Piping Down the Valleys Wild.* Illustrated by Ellen Raskin. Delacorte, 1985 [1968].

Lear, Edward. *The Complete Nonsense Book.* Dodd, 1946.

Levine, Gail Carson. *Ella Enchanted.* HarperCollins, 1997.

Lewis, J. Patrick. *Doodle Dandies.* Illustrated by Lisa Desimini. Atheneum, 1998.

———. *Heroes and She-roes: Poems of Amazing and Everyday Heroes.* Illustrated by Jim Cooke. Dial, 2005.

———. *Once upon a Tomb: Gravely Humorous Verses.* Illustrated by Simon Bartram. Candlewick, 2006.

———. *A World of Wonders: Geographic Travels in Verse and Rhyme.* Illustrated by Alison Jay. Dial, 2002.

Maddox, Marjorie. *A Crossing of Zebras: Animal Packs in Poetry.* Illustrated by Philip Huber. Boyds, 2008.

McCord, David. *One at a Time.* Illustrated by Henry B. Kane. Little, 1977.

Moore, Clement. *The Night Before Christmas.* Illustrated by Jan Brett. Putnam, 1998.

Mora, Pat. *Love to Mama: A Tribute to Mothers.* Illustrated by Paula S. Barragán. Lee, 2001.

Nash, Ogden. *The Tale of Custard the Dragon.* Illustrated by Lynn Munsinger. Little, 1995.

Nelson, Marilyn. *A Wreath for Emmett Till.* Illustrated by Philippe Lardy. Houghton, 2005.

Nye, Naomi Shihab. *19 Varieties of Gazelle: Poems of the Middle East.* Greenwillow, 2002.

———. *A Maze Me: Poems for Girls.* Greenwillow, 2005.

———. *The Space Between Our Footsteps: Poems and Paintings from the Middle East.* Simon, 1998.

———. *This Same Sky: A Collection of Poems from Around the World.* Four Winds, 1992.

Opie, Iona, ed. *Here Comes Mother Goose.* Illustrated by Rosemary Wells. Candlewick, 1999.

———, ed. *My Very First Mother Goose.* Illustrated by Rosemary Wells. Candlewick, 1996.

Paolini, Paul, and Dan Brewer. *Silver Seeds: A Book of Nature Poems.* Illustrated by Steve Johnson and Lou Fancher. Viking, 2001.

Park, Linda Sue. *Tap Dancing on the Roof: Sijo Poems.* Illustrated by Istvan Banyai. Clarion, 2007.

Pearson, Susan. *Grimericks.* Illustrated by Gris Grimley Cavendish, 2005.

Prelutsky, Jack. *The Beauty of the Beast: Poems from the Animal Kingdom.* Illustrated by Meilo So. Knopf, 1997.

———. *Good Sports: Rhymes About Running, Jumping, Throwing and More.* Illustrated by Chris Raschka. Knopf, 2007.

———. *If Not for the Cat.* Illustrated by Ted Rand. Greenwillow, 2004.

———. *In Aunt Giraffe's Green Garden.* Illustrated by Petra Mathers. Greenwillow, 2007.

———. *My Dog May Be a Genius.* Illustrated by James Stevenson. Greenwillow, 2008.

———. ed. *The Random House Book of Poetry for Children.* Illustrated by Arnold Lobel. Random, 1983.

———. *Read-Aloud Rhymes for the Very Young.* Illustrated by Marc Brown. Knopf, 1986.

Rex, Adam. *Frankenstein Makes a Sandwich.* Harcourt, 2006.

Schnur, Steven. *Winter: An Alphabet Acrostic.* Clarion, 2002.

Sidman, Joyce. *Butterfly Eyes and Other Secrets from the Meadow.* Beth Krommes. Houghton, 2006.

———. *Meow Ruff: A Story in Concrete Poetry.* Illustrated by Michelle Berg. Houghton, 2007.

———. *Song of the Water Boatman and Other Pond Poems.* Illustrated by Beckie Prange. Houghton, 2005.

———. *This Is Just to Say.* Illustrated by Pamela Zagarenski. Houghton, 2007.

———. *Welcome to the Night: Mysteries of the Night Woods.* Illustrated by Rick Allen. Houghton, 2010.

Siebert, Diane. *Mojave.* Illustrated by Wendell Minor. Crowell, 1988.

———. *Sierra.* Illustrated by Wendell Minor. Crowell, 1991.

Sierra, Judy. *Antarctic Antics: A Book of Penguin Poems.* Illustrated by Jose Aruego and Ariane Dewey. Gulliver, 1998.

———. *Schoolyard Rhymes: Kids' Own Rhymes for Rope-Skipping, Hand Clapping, Ball Bouncing, and Just Plain Fun.* Illustrated by Melissa Sweet. Knopf, 2005.

Silverstein, Shel. *Where the Sidewalk Ends: Poems and Drawings.* Harper, 1974.

Singer, Marilyn. *Central Heating: Poems About Fire and Warmth.* Illustrated by Meilo So. Knopf, 2005.

———. *Footprints on the Roof: Poems About the Earth.* Illustrated by Meilo So. Knopf, 2002.

Sklansky, Amy E. *From the Doghouse: Poems to Chew On.* Illustrated by Karla Firehammer, Karen Dismukes, Sandy Koeser, and Cathy McQuitty. Holt, 2002.

Soto, Gary. *Fearless Fernie: Hanging Out with Fernie and Me.* Illustrated by Regan Dunnick. Putnam, 2002.

———. *Worlds Apart: Traveling with Fernie and Me.* Putnam, 2005.

Stevenson, Robert Louis. *A Child's Garden of Verses.* Illustrated by Diane Goode. Morrow, 1998.

Strickland, Dorothy S., and Michael R. Strickland. *Families: Poems Celebrating the African American Experience.* Illustrated by John Ward. Boyds Mills/Wordsong, 1994.

Thomas, Joyce Carol. *The Blacker the Berry.* Illustrated by Floyd Cooper. HarperCollins, 2005.

Whipple, Laura. *If the Shoe Fits: Voices from Cinderella.* Illustrated by Laura Beingessner. McElderry, 2002.

Worth, Valerie. *All the Small Poems and Fourteen More.* Illustrated by Natalie Babbitt. Farrar, 1994.

———. *Animal Poems.* Illustrated by Steve Jenkins. Farrar, 2007.

Yolen, Jane. *Color Me a Rhyme: Nature Poems for Young People.* Photographs by Jason Stemple. Wordsong, 2000.

Yolen, Jane, and Andrew Fusek Peters. *Here's a Little Poem: A Very First Book of Poetry.* Illustrated by Polly Dunbar. Candlewick, 2007.

Zahares, Wade. *Big, Bad, and a Little Bit Scary: Poems That Bite Back!* Viking, 2001.

Chapter Seven

Contemporary Realistic Fiction

It was Thursday—library day at Garfield Elementary school. Madison loved library day. She was always excited to get a new book to read. As she stood in line waiting for her class to walk down the hall, she asked Carolyn if she was excited about library day. "No," she replied. "Why not?" Madison asked. "Library day is fun and . . ." Before Madison could finish her sentence, Carolyn interrupted, "All the library books are dumb and I hate to read!" Overhearing the conversation, Mr. Douglas asked, "Carolyn, why do you hate to read?" With her head down, she quietly shrugged her shoulders. "Tell me," he continued, "what do you like to watch on television?" "I like real stories and the Discovery Channel." Mr. Douglas quickly realized that contemporary realistic fiction just might be of interest to Carolyn. "How about this, Carolyn. If I make a suggestion for a book, will you at least try it out?" "Okay," she answered. Mr. Douglas went to the shelves of the school library and quickly found a book for Carolyn. Later that day, when the children were given free time before recess, Mr. Douglas noticed that Carolyn was reading the book. Mr. Douglas smiled to himself thinking "Yes! Got her!" But quickly he began to ask himself, "Now how can I keep her reading?"

Realism in Contemporary Children's Literature

Realistic fiction may be defined as imaginative writing that accurately reflects life as it was lived in the past or could be lived today. Everything in such a story can conceivably happen to real people living in our natural physical world, in contrast to fantasy, where impossible happenings are made to appear quite plausible even though they are not possible. Historical fiction (see Chapter 8) portrays life as it may have been lived in the past; contemporary realism focuses on the problems and issues of living today. In this chapter we arbitrarily chose the 1950s as the dividing line between contemporary and historical fiction.

Though other genres in children's literature, such as fantasy, are popular, children consistently are found to prefer realistic fiction. The books discussed in this chapter can be categorized as contemporary realistic fiction for children. Many are stories about growing up today and finding a place in the family, among peers, and in modern society. In addition, aspects of coping with the problems of the human condition may be found in contemporary literature for children. Books that are humorous or reflect special interests—such as animal or sports stories and mysteries—are also classified as realistic literature and so are included in this chapter.

Realistic fiction serves children who are in the process of understanding and coming to terms with themselves. Books that honestly portray the realities of life help children gain a fuller understanding of human problems and human relationships and, thus, a fuller understanding of themselves and their own potential.

This is not a function unique to contemporary realism. Other types of books can show children a slice of the world. Some fantasy is nearer to truth than realism; biography and autobiography frequently provide readers with models of human beings who offer "hope and courage for the journey." The ability to maintain one's humanity and courage in the midst of deprivation is highlighted in *Number the Stars*, Lois Lowry's historical fiction about Danish efforts to save Jewish citizens in World War II. Personal bravery and responsible behavior under dire circumstances is also one of the themes of the high fantasy *A Wizard of Earthsea* by Ursula Le Guin. However, most children appear to identify more readily with characters in books of contemporary realism than with those of historical fiction or fantasy.

Realistic fiction helps children enlarge their frames of reference while seeing the world from another perspective. For example, human rights abuses in Haiti are memorably portrayed in Frances Temple's *Taste of Salt*. No one reading about the plight of these characters could think of them as "other." Instead, Temple places the reader directly in her characters' shoes. Children who have had little contact with the problems of the elderly might come to understand the older adults as real people through

THE BIRTHDAY ROOM KEVIN HENKES

In *The Birthday Room*, twelve-year-old Ben learns that the long-standing relationship between his mother and his uncle has an important effect on his own self-awareness. From *The Birthday Room* by Kevin Henkes and illustrated by Jim Burke. Cover art copyright © 2001 by Jim Burke. Used by permission of HarperCollins Publishers.

M. J. Auch's *Wing Nut* or Kazumi Yumoto's *The Friends*. Stories like these help young people develop compassion for and an understanding of human experiences.

Realistic fiction also reassures young people that they are not the first in the world to have faced problems. In Hilary McKay's *Permanent Rose*, Kimberly Willis Holt's *When Zachary Beaver Came to Town*, and Marion Dane Bauer's *A Question of Trust*, they read of other children whose parents have separated or divorced. In Kevin Henkes's *The Birthday Room*, Lynne Rae Perkins's *Criss Cross*, and Joan Bauer's *Stand Tall*, they read about characters who are beginning to be concerned about relationships with the opposite sex. They gain some solace from recognizing the problems a low-income background poses for Jamal in Walter Dean Myers's *Scorpions*, Livy Two in Kerry Madden's *Gentle's Holler*, or Jazmin in Nikki Grimes's *Jazmin's Notebook*. This knowledge that they are not alone brings a kind of comfort to child readers.

Realistic fiction can also illuminate experiences that children have not had. A child with loving parents whose only chore consists of making a bed may have a deeper need to read Katherine Paterson's *The Same Stuff as Stars* than a child of poverty whose life is more nearly reflected in the story. A child who takes school for granted might gain much from Ann Cameron's poignant *The Most Beautiful Place in the World*, about a Guatemalan who desperately wants an education. Realistic fiction can be a way of experiencing a world we do not know.

Some books also serve as a kind of preparation for living. Far better to have read Katherine Paterson's *Bridge to Terabithia* or Kimberly Willis Holt's *Keeper of the Night* than to experience firsthand at age 10 or 12 the death of your best friend or the suicide of your mother. For many years, death was a taboo subject in children's literature. Yet, as children face the honest realities of life in books, they are developing a kind of courage for facing problems in their own lives. Madeleine L'Engle, whose *Meet the Austins* was among the first works of modern children's literature to treat the subject of death, maintained that "to pretend there is no darkness is another way of extinguishing light."[1]

Realistic fiction for children does provide many possible models, both good and bad, for coping with problems of the human condition. As children experience these stories, they may begin to filter out some meaning for their own lives. This allows children to organize and shape their own thinking about life as they follow, through stories, the lives of others.

More controversy surrounds the writing of contemporary realistic fiction for children than perhaps any other kind of literature. Everyone is a critic of realism, for everyone feels he or she is an expert on what is real in today's world. But realities clash, and the fact that "what is real for one might not be real for another" is a true and lively issue. Some of the questions that seem uniquely related to contemporary realism in writing for children need to be examined.

What Is Real?

The question of what is "real" or "true to life" is a significant one. C. S. Lewis, the British author of the well-known Narnia stories, described three types of realistic content:

> But when we say, "The sort of thing that happens," do we mean the sort of thing that usually or often happens, the sort of thing that is typical of the human lot? Or do we mean "The sort of thing that might conceivably happen or that, by a thousandth chance, may have happened once?"[2]

Middle graders reading the Narnia series know that these stories are fantasy and couldn't happen in reality. However, middle graders might read stories like Gary Paulsen's *Hatchet*, or N. D. Wilson's *Leepike Ridge* and believe that children can survive any hardship or crisis if only they possess determination. These well-written books cast believable characters in realistic settings facing real problems. Teachers might ask readers to compare these books to Graham Salisbury's *Night of the Howling Dogs*, which is based on Salisbury's cousin's experience surviving a tsunami. Book discussions can help readers ask whether this sort of thing "by a thousandth chance, may have happened once."

Adding to the question of what is real is the recent trend toward magic realism in literature for children. In other cultures the belief that the spirit world is as real as the one we can see and touch is common. Increasingly, authors from the United States, Great Britain, Canada, and Australia feel no compunction in blending these worlds. We have dealt with some of these books in "Modern Fantasy" (Chapter 5). In this chapter we include others when we feel the thrust of the book speaks to contemporary real-life concerns. We suspect that as the twenty-first century moves forward, the lines between traditional genres will become more and more blurred.

Night of the Howling Dogs is a thrilling survival story based on real events that were experienced by author Graham Salisbury's cousin. Jacket cover from *Night of the Howling Dogs* by Graham Salisbury. Used by permission of Wendy Lamb Books, an imprint of Random House Children's Books, a division of Random House, Inc.

How Real May a Children's Book Be?

Much controversy centers on how much graphic detail may be included in a book for children. How much violence is too much? How explicit may an author be in describing bodily functions or sexual relations? These are questions that no one would have asked thirty-five years ago. But there are new freedoms today. Childhood is not the innocent time we like to think it is (and it probably never was). In addition, authors of young adult literature (defined in the American Library Association's Printz Award as ages 12–18) have been more willing to tackle issues for adolescents as frankly as they would in a book for adults. In this book, we focus on children ages 6 to 14. It is therefore often difficult to make decisions about what literature is appropriate for those adolescents in middle school. Basically, we have worked under the assumption that although these youth might not need protection, they do still need the perspective that good literature can give. A well-written book makes the reader aware of the human suffering resulting from inhumane acts by others.

Media coverage of local killings or the body count in the latest "peacekeeping" effort seldom show the pain and anguish that each death causes. The rebuilding of human lives is too slow and tedious to portray in a five-minute newscast. Even many video games are based on violence. The winner of the game is the one who can eliminate or destroy the "enemy." Reasons or motivations are never given, and the aftereffects of violence are not a part of the game.

By way of contrast to the media world, a well-written story provides perspective on the pain and suffering of humankind. In a literary story the author has time to develop the characters into fully rounded human beings. The reader knows the motives and pressures of each individual and can understand and empathize with the characters. If the author's tone is one of compassion for the characters, if others in the story show concern or horror for a brutal act, the reader gains perspective.

A story that makes violence understandable without condoning it is Suzanne Fisher Staples's *Shabanu: Daughter of the Wind*. In the Pakistani desert culture in which 12-year-old Shabanu lives, obedience to rules has enabled many tribes to live in peace in an environment that offers little material comfort. When Shabanu runs away to avoid an arranged marriage to a middle-aged man, she discovers her favorite camel has broken its leg. In choosing to remain with the camel, Shabanu tacitly agrees to the rules of her clan. Her father catches up with her and beats her severely. But she is soaked with his tears as he does what he must, and the reader realizes both are trapped in roles their society has defined for them.

James Giblin, a former children's book editor, suggests that a book can be realistic without being overly graphic:

> For instance, if the young detective in a mystery story was attacked by a gang of bullies, I wouldn't encourage an author to have them burn his arms with a cigarette to get him to talk (although that might conceivably happen in an adult mystery). However, I would accept a scene in which the gang *threatened* to do so: that would convey the reality and danger of the situation without indulging in all the gory details.[3]

Giblin maintains that very few subjects are inappropriate in themselves; it is all in how the author treats them. The facts of a situation, ugly as they might be, can be presented with feeling and depth of emotion, which carry the reader beyond the particular subject.

The same criteria are appropriate for evaluating explicitness about sex and bodily functions in books for children. Betty Miles raises this issue in *Maudie and Me and the Dirty Book*. When seventh grader Kate Harris teams up with a classmate to read aloud to first graders, one of her choices—a story about a puppy being born— triggers a discussion among the 6-year-olds about human birth and conception. Although Kate handles the discussion with poise, a parent complaint eventually brings about a town meeting concerning what is appropriate in the elementary classroom curriculum. Miles treats the topics of conception, birth, and censorship in an open and forthright way. Chris Crutcher presents a similar situation regarding issues in *The Sledding Hill*. Here, a controversy is sparked by the reading of a young adult novel that includes a gay character. Crutcher's work is more heavy-handed in its message about censorship than is Miles's, but it will certainly prompt interesting discussions. Furthermore, the essence of the book is about friendship and healing rather than sexual orientation.

Bias and Stereotyping

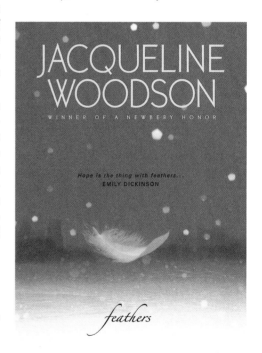

Children's books have always reflected the general social and human values of a society, so it is not surprising that they are also scrutinized for implied attitudes or biases of that society. Contemporary realistic fiction is examined for racism, cultural inaccuracies, sexism, ageism, and treatment of people with physical or mental impairments. Because consciousness generally has been raised in the world of children's book publishing, there are now more books that present diverse populations positively and fairly.

The political and social activism of the 1960s contributed to an awareness of racism in children's books. Since the beginning of the twenty-first century, children have been able to find fully realized characters from diverse cultures in books such as Virginia Hamilton's *Cousins*, Linda Sue Park's *Project Mulberry*, Pam Muñoz Ryan's *Becoming Naomi Leon*, and Jacqueline Woodson's *Feathers*. Still, adults need to be alert to reissues of books from an earlier era—such as the 1945 Newbery Honor Book *The Silver Pencil*,[4] which contains many racist descriptions of people in Trinidad. Books like this help us recognize the gains of recent decades.

Because scholars have made us more aware of the subtle ways in which literature has perpetuated stereotypes, contemporary realistic fiction now does a much better job of portraying the complexity of gender expectations and roles. Girls can find caring female role models outside of the family; intelligent, independent, and strong girls and women; and romance as a consequence of strong friendship are all found in realistic fiction of the present decade. They can also find

Jacqueline Woodson's *Feathers* is a beautifully written story about a child's hopes and fears, with an African American character whose story will appeal to children of all cultures. *Feathers* by Jacqueline Woodson, copyright © 2007 by Jacqueline Woodson. Used by permission of Putnam, a Division of Penguin Young Readers Group, a Member of Penguin Group (USA) Inc., 345 Hudson Street, New York, NY 10014. All rights reserved.

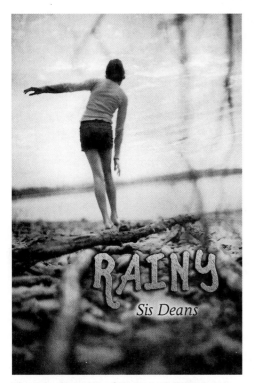

The title character of Sis Deans's *Rainy* is a 10-year-old girl who struggles to control her ADHD while away from her supportive family at summer camp. Cover of *Rainy* by Sis Deans. Cover copyright © 2005 by Henry Holt and Company. Reprinted by permission of Henry Holt and Company, LLC.

characters like Frankie in *The Disreputable History of Frankie Landau-Banks* by E. Lockhart, who are willing to challenge traditional role models and expectations.

Boys, too, can get beyond such beliefs as "men don't cry." Modern realistic fiction shows that everyone may cry as they grieve, as do a boy and his father following the drowning of a friend in *On My Honor* by Marion Dane Bauer. The issue of presenting multiple role models in books for boys has led to a campaign by popular author Jon Scieszka. Scieszka's Web site, called Guys Read <www.guysread.com>, has suggestions for books and activities that will appeal to boys. Scieszka has also selected various male authors to contribute to *Guys Write for Guys Read*, a collection of short stories for boys.

People with mental or physical impairments have in the past been depicted as "handicapped" or "disabled." Books such as Tracie Vaughn Zimmer's *Reaching for the Sun* or Sis Deans's *Rainy* provide more enlightened views that suggest that the person is more important than the impairment; one can be differently abled without necessarily being disabled. Older people (and other adults) in children's literature have often been dismissed as irrelevant in a young person's life, as ineffectual in contrast to the vibrancy of young spirits, or as unable to do certain things because of their age. High-quality contemporary realistic fiction stories depict adults and older people in many ways—as mentors to young people, for instance, and as having their own romances, problems, and triumphs.

Children's books have made great gains in the depiction of our changing society. However, today's books need to continue to reflect the wide ranges of occupations, education, speech patterns, lifestyles, and futures that are possible for all, regardless of race, gender, age, ability, or belief.

The Author's Background

The subject of an author's racial background has become another source of controversy in children's contemporary realistic fiction. Must an author be black to write about African Americans, or Native American to write about Native Americans? As Virginia Hamilton states:

> It happens that I know Black people better than any other people because I am one of them and I grew up knowing what it is we are about. . . . The writer uses the most comfortable milieu in which to tell a story, which is why my characters are Black. Often being Black is significant to the story; other times, it is not. The writer will always attempt to tell stories no one else can tell.[5]

It has been generally accepted that an author should write about what he or she knows. But Ann Cameron, an Anglo-American author who has lived in Guatemala for many years, is the author of many books about children from diverse places and cultures, including *The Stories Julian Tells, Gloria Rising, The Most Beautiful Place in the World*, and *Colibrí*. Cameron maintains a different point of view:

> It seems to me that the people who advise "write about what you know" drastically underestimate the human capacity for imagining what lies beyond our immediate knowledge and for understanding what is new to us. Equally, they overestimate the extent to which we know ourselves. A culture, like a person, has blind spots. . . . Often the writer who is an outsider—an African writing about the United States, an American writing about China—sees in a way that enriches him as an observer, the culture he observes, and the culture he comes from.[6]

Moreover, although it may be true that Cameron and other writers who have spent years living and working in other countries (Elizabeth Laird, Jane Kurtz, and Nancy Farmer, for example) may not be able to give a culturally authentic picture of the characters they write about, they do Western children a great service by pointing out issues of social justice and human rights. As world cultures become more and more interdependent in the twenty-first century, offering such service is surely a worthwhile goal.

Evaluating Contemporary Fiction

The hallmark of fine writing is the quality of imagining it calls forth from us. Imagination is not the exclusive trait of any race or gender but is a universal quality of all fine writers. No authors or artists want to be limited to writing about or portraying only the experiences of persons of a single race or cultural background, nor should they be. We need to focus on two aspects of every book: (1) What is its literary merit? and (2) Will children enjoy it? For additional criteria to keep in mind, see **Guidelines: Evaluating Contemporary Realistic Fiction.**

Guidelines

Evaluating Contemporary Realistic Fiction

 Go to **www.mhhe.com/kieferbrief1e** *to access an expanded version of this evaluation form.*

Consider the following when evaluating realistic fiction:

- Does the book honestly portray the realities of life for today's children?
- Does the book illuminate problems and issues of growing up in today's world?
- Does the story transcend the contemporary setting and have universal implications?
- Are the characters convincing and credible to today's child?

- Are controversial topics such as sexuality dealt with in an open and forthright way?
- If violence or other negative behavior is part of the story, does the author provide motivations and show aftereffects?
- Does the author avoid stereotyping?
- Does the book truly represent the experience of the culture depicted?
- Does the book help children enlarge their personal points of view and develop appreciation for our ever-changing pluralistic society?

Categorizing Literature

Reviewers, educators, and curriculum makers often categorize books according to their content. Categorizing serves textbook authors by allowing them to talk about several books as a group. It serves educators who hope to group books around a particular theme for classroom study. While one person might place Katherine Paterson's *Bridge to Terabithia* in a group of books about "making friends," it could just as easily be placed in other groups, such as books about "growing up" or "learning to accept death," or "well-written books." It is a disservice to both book and reader if, in labeling a book, we imply that this is all the book is about. Readers with their own purposes and backgrounds will see many different aspects and strengths in a piece of literature. It is helpful to remember that our experiences with art occur at many different, unique, and personal levels. Even though teachers might wish to lead children to talk about a particular aspect of a book, they will not want to suggest that this is the only aspect worth pursuing. Author Jean Little argues that teachers need to trust children to find their own messages in books:

> Individual readers come to each story at a slightly different point in their life's journey. If nobody comes between them and the book, they may discover within it some insight they require, a rest they long for, a point of view that challenges their own, a friend they may cherish for life. If we, in the guise of mentor, have all the good messages listed or discussed in small groups . . . the individual and vitally important meeting of child and story may never happen.[7]

A second issue in the categorizing of literature is age-appropriateness. Realistic fiction is often categorized as being for upper elementary or middle-grade and junior high or young-adult readers. Yet anyone who has spent time with 9- to 14-year-old readers has surely noticed the wide ranges of reading interests, abilities, and perceptions present. Betsy Byars's *The Pinballs* and Judy Blume's *Are You There, God? It's Me, Margaret* have challenged and entertained readers from fourth grade through high school. To suggest that these titles are only "for 10- to 12-year-old readers" would ignore the ages of half the readership of these popular authors.

The story of every man and every woman is the story of growing up, of becoming a person, of struggling to become one's own person. The kind of person you become has its roots in your childhood experiences—how much you were loved, how little you were loved; the people who were significant to you, the ones who were not; the places you've been, and those you did not go to; the things you had, and the things you did not get. Yet a person is always more than the totality of these experiences; the way a person organizes, understands, and relates to those experiences makes for individuality. Childhood is not a waiting room for adulthood but the place where adulthood is shaped by one's family, peers, society, and, most important, the person one is becoming. The passage from childhood to adulthood is a significant journey for each person. It is no wonder that children's literature is filled with stories about growing up in our society today.

In **Teaching Feature 7.1: A Sampling of Contemporary Realism for Children**, books are arranged according to categories based on theme and content merely for convenience of presentation. They could have been arranged in many other ways. The ages of main characters are noted, as a clue to potential readership.

A Sampling of Contemporary Realism for Children

teaching feature 7.1

Author	Title	Grade Level	Description
Families			
Beverly Cleary	*Ramona's World*	2–4	As with previous titles about this family, Ramona continues to be her irrepressible, dramatic self.
Patricia MacLachlan	*Journey*	4–6	Eleven-year-old Journey is devastated and angered when his mother leaves him with his grandparents.
Katherine Paterson	*Jacob Have I Loved*	6–8	The complicated relationship between two sisters echoes themes of the biblical Jacob and Esau.
Cynthia Voigt	*Homecoming*	4–6	This story of motherless children finding a family recalls epic journeys such as that in *The Odyssey*.
Jacqueline Woodson	*Feathers*	6–8	A young African American girl tries to deal with unspoken fears about her family.
Friends			
Kimberly Willis Holt	*When Zachary Beaver Came to Town*	4–6	Events in a small Texas town are set in motion by the arrival of side-show subject Zachary Beaver, but center around the ups and downs of long-time friends and the forging of new friendships.
E. L. Konigsburg	*The View from Saturday*	6–8	Four sixth-graders form strong bonds as they compete in a middle-school academic bowl.
Katherine Paterson	*Bridge to Terabithia*	4–6	This powerful story of a friendship between two misfits has become a modern-day classic.
Lynne Rae Perkins	*Criss Cross*	6–8	This story explores adolescents caught on the brink of discovering their identities largely through the intertwining relations of old friends.
Jerry Spinelli	*Wringer*	4–6	Spinelli examines the serious consequences of peer pressure as 9-year-old Palmer is pushed to be "one of the boys" by enduring physically painful rituals.
Growing Toward Maturity			
Marion Dane Bauer	*On My Honor*	4–6	The story explores themes about facing the tragic consequences of your own actions with the help of a loving family.

(continued)

teaching feature 7.1

Author	Title	Grade Level	Description
Terence Blacker	*Boy2Girl*	7 and up	Questions about gender identity are explored through short, first-person narratives by the boys, girls, parents, and teachers in a British middle school.
Walter Dean Myers	*Scorpions*	6–8	Two friends struggle to come of age in an inner-city environment that calls for life-altering choices.
Susan Patron	*The Higher Power of Lucky* and *Lucky Breaks*	4–6	An 11-year-old girl trying to discover her identity is a keen observer of her world.
Gary D. Schmidt	*Trouble*	5–8	A boy from a privileged background must confront his own prejudices on the road to self-understanding.
Jacqueline Woodson	*I Hadn't Meant to Tell You This*	6–8	Woodson raises critical questions about class, race, abuse, and loyalty in the context of this beautifully realized friendship.

Survival

Author	Title	Grade Level	Description
Nancy Farmer	*A Girl Named Disaster*	5–8	A young African girl runs away from her village and travels by river from Mozambique to Zimbabwe to find her father.
Jean Craighead George	*Julie of the Wolves*	5–8	A Native Alaskan girl finds herself alone on the Alaskan tundra and must depend on a pack of wolves to survive.
L. S. Matthews	*Fish*	3–6	A young boy whose own survival is at risk is determined to keep a rescued fish alive as he and his parents flee a war-torn African country.
Gary Paulsen	*Hatchet*	4 and up	On his way to meet his father, the pilot of the aircraft suffers a heart attack and Brian manages to land the plane in a lake in the Canadian wilderness.
Graham Salisbury	*Night of the Howling Dogs*	4 and up	Based on a true story, this is a thrilling account of a group of Hawaiian scouts who are stranded by a tsunami while on a camping trip.

Problems of the Human Condition

Author	Title	Grade Level	Description
Sis Deans	*Rainy*	4–6	A young girl with attention deficit hyperactivity disorder must learn to live with her behavior.
Jack Gantos	*Joey Pigza Swallowed the Key*	4–6	This is the first in a series of books about a boy with ADHD.

Author	Title	Grade Level	Description
Kimberly Willis Holt	*My Louisiana Sky*	4–6	Tiger Ann Parker must cope with the developmental disabilities of her own parents.
Ann Martin	*A Corner of the Universe*	4–6	Twelve-year-old Hattie's worldview is dramatically changed when her previously unknown Uncle Adam is discharged from his mental hospital and returns home.
Kazumi Yumoto	*The Friends*	4–6	Three Japanese boys begin to spy on a reclusive old neighbor, hoping to watch him die.
Tracie Vaughn Zimmer	*Reaching for the Sun*	6–8	A girl with cerebral palsy tells of her seventh-grade year.

Living in a Diverse Community

Author	Title	Grade Level	Description
Joseph Bruchac	*Eagle Song*	4–6	Danny Bigtree, a young Mohawk, moves to Brooklyn with his family so that his ironworker father can find work.
Sundee T. Frazier	*Brendan Buckley's Universe, and Everything in It*	4–6	A biracial boy collects rocks, practices Tae Kwon Do, and learns he has a grandfather he has never met.
Nikki Grimes	*Jazmin's Notebook*	6–8	Jazmin, an adolescent girl living in Harlem, keeps a notebook to record her observations of life and to write her poetry.
Virginia Hamilton	*M. C. Higgins, the Great*	6–8	M. C. daydreams of moving his family away from the slow-moving slag heap that threatens to engulf their southern Ohio home.
Lensey Namioka	*Yang the Youngest and His Terrible Ear*	4–6	This is the first in a series of stories about irrepressible members of a Chinese American family.
Pam Muñoz Ryan	*Becoming Naomi Leon*	4–6	A girl discovers her dual Mexican American heritage.

Understanding World Cultures

Author	Title	Grade Level	Description
Daniella Carmi	*Samir and Yonatan*	4–6	Samir, a Palestinian boy, must spend several months in an Israeli hospital on a ward with Jewish children who have also been damaged by the Israeli/Palestinian conflict.
Berlie Doherty	*The Girl Who Saw Lions*	7 and up	Two girls with Tanzanian roots grow up in widely different circumstances.
Deborah Ellis	*Parvana's Journey*	4–6	A young girl must masquerade as a boy as she tries to find her family in post-Taliban Afghanistan.

(continued)

teaching feature 7.1

Author	Title	Grade Level	Description
Henning Mankell	*Secrets in the Fire*	7 and up	This story of a girl caught in the civil war in Mozambique is based on the experiences of a real person.
Beverley Naidoo	*Journey to Jo'burg*	4–8	Naledi is forced to face the terrible realities of South African apartheid when she journeys from her sheltered village to Johannesburg.
Frances Temple	*Taste of Salt*	7 and up	Parallel narratives follow the trials of two young people under brutal dictatorship.

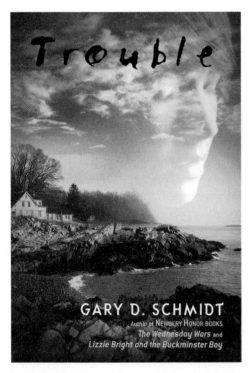

Gary Schmidt's *Trouble* is a powerful coming-of-age story that follows a boy through the process of grief and self-acceptance. Cover from *Trouble* by Gary Schmidt. Jacket illustration copyright © 2008 by Ericka O'Rourke. Reprinted by permission of Clarion Books, an imprint of Houghton Mifflin Harcourt Publishing Company. All rights reserved.

In Sundee T. Frazier's *Brendan Buckley's Universe*, Brendan collects rocks and is a participant in Tae Kwon Do when he meets a grandfather about whom he has never known. Jacket cover from *Brendan Buckley's Universe and Everything in It* by Sundee T. Frazier. Copyright © 2007. Used by permission of Delacort Press, an imprint of Random House Children's Books, a division of Random House, Inc.

Joseph Bruchac's warm and realistic *Eagle Song* is one of the few books for children that feature a Native American character in a contemporary setting.

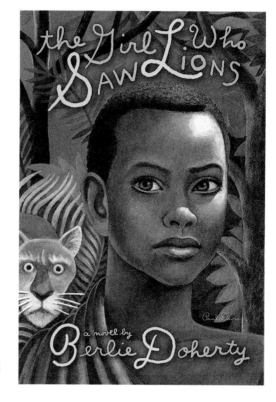

Two girls of African heritage grow up in two very different worlds in Berlie Doherty's moving *The Girl Who Saw Lions*.

Popular Types of Realistic Fiction

Certain categories of realistic fiction are so popular that children ask for them by name. They want a good animal story, usually about a dog or horse; a sports book; a "funny" book; or a good mystery. Each decade seems to have a popular series, as well, that lingers on the bookshelves. From Gertrude Chandler Warner's Boxcar Children to Ann Martin's Baby-Sitters Club series, from Nancy Drew and the Hardy Boys to Patricia Reilly Giff's Kids of Polk Street School series, children read one volume of a series and demand the next. Although many of these books are not high-quality literature, they do serve the useful function of getting children hooked on books so that they will move on to better literature.[8] Children also develop fluency and reading speed as they quickly read through popular books or a series.

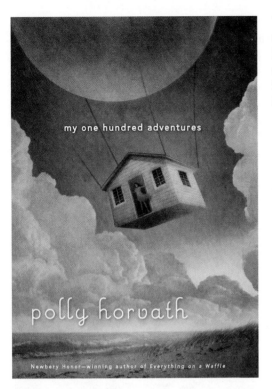

Told in Polly Horvath's singular comedic style, *My One Hundred Adventures* is the story of a sheltered 12-year-old who longs for adventures. Jacket cover from *My One Hundred Adventures* by Polly Horvath. Copyright © 2008. Used by permission of Schwartz and Wade Books, an imprint of Random House Children's Books, a division of Random House, Inc.

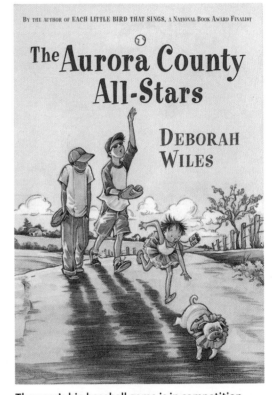

The year's big baseball game is in competition with the big county pageant in Deborah Wiles's funny *The Aurora County All-Stars*, and it looks like star pitcher House Jackson is in for trouble. Book cover from *The Aurora County All-Stars*, copyright © 2007 by Deborah Wiles, reproduced by permission of Houghton Mifflin Harcourt Publishing Company.

A troubling disappearance at a famous London landmark is the setting for Siobhan Dowd's *The London Eye Mystery*. Jacket cover from *The London Eye Mystery* by Siobhan Dowd. Copyright © 2008 by Siobhan Dowd. Used by permission of David Fickling Books, an imprint of Random House Children's Books, a division of Random House, Inc.

A highly intelligent pit bull is the main character in *Dog Lost*, Ingrid Lee's heartwarming story about a boy and his dog. From *Dog Lost* by Ingrid Lee. Scholastic Inc., The Chicken House. Cover illustration copyright © 2008 by Scholastic Inc. Reprinted by permission.

"A breathless page-turner . . . brutally honest . . . wonderfully heart-rousing."—Ann M. Martin

Dog Lost

INGRID LEE

Happily, the categories of popular fiction include many well-written, award-winning books, and children who love the easier series books have found their way to excellent titles such as Louis Sachar's *Holes*, Ellen Raskin's *The Westing Game*, and Phyllis Reynolds Naylor's *Shiloh*. Each of these books fits under the categories of "popular" literature but have transcended clichés of genre to win the John Newbery Medal. Newer, well-written works that middle-grade and middle-school readers will enjoy include Polly Horvath's *My One Hundred Adventures*, Deborah Wiles's *The Aurora County All-Stars*, and Siobhan Dowd's *The London Eye Mystery*. Knowing and honoring the books children like increases an adult adviser's credibility, while also allowing him or her to recommend other titles that can broaden children's reading choices. In **Teaching Feature 7.2: Popular Fiction for Today's Readers**, we have selected some of the best fiction in categories that are especially appealing to children.

teaching feature 7.2

Popular Fiction for Today's Readers

Author	Title	Grade Level	Description
Humorous Stories			
Jeanne Birdsall	*The Penderwicks on Gardam Street*	4–6	A lively group of sisters are intent on keeping their widowed father from dating.
Judy Blume	*Tales of a Fourth Grade Nothing*	2–5	In the first of a series about Peter Hatcher and his younger brother Fudge, 2-year-old Fudge, whose real name is Farley Drexel Hatcher, eats Peter's pet turtle but the long-suffering Peter earns a pet dog.
Jeff Kinney	*Diary of a Wimpy Kid*	4–6	Greg Heffley suffers the indignities and pains of adolescence in this funny graphic novel.

(continued)

teaching feature 7.2

Author	Title	Grade Level	Description
Barbara Park	*Skinnybones*	2–5	Alex (also known as "Skinnybones") is telling his story about trying to enter a cat food commercial contest. In addition, Alex, the self-acclaimed funniest person in the sixth grade, has been a size "small" in Little League for six years and is the butt of the class bully's jokes.
Thomas Rockwell	*How to Eat Fried Worms*	2–5	To win a fifty-dollar bet, Billy plans to eat fifteen worms in fifteen days. Each ingestion becomes more bizarre the closer Billy comes to winning his bet.

Animal Stories

Author	Title	Grade Level	Description
Sheila Burnford	*The Incredible Journey*	4–6	The story recounts the odyssey of three runaway pets, a young Labrador retriever, an old bull terrier, and a Siamese cat, whwo try to reach their home more than 250 miles away.
Ingrid Lee	*Dog Lost*	2–5	A young boy bonds with a pit-bull puppy until his father gets rid of it. The puppy survives on its wits while the community is set on banning pitbulls.
Allison Lester	*The Quicksand Pony*	4–6	Ten-year-old Biddy is finally allowed to go on the family muster that rounds up the cattle that have been grazing wild in the Australian back country.
Phyllis Reynolds Naylor	*Shiloh*	4–6	Marty decides to hide an abused dog in the woods of his West Virginia mountain hollow. He deceives his family until a crisis forces him to fight for his principles and confront the owner of the dog.
Pam Muñoz Ryan	*Paint the Wind*	4–6	Maya has grown up sheltered and overprotected by her grandmother until she finds herself at the Wyoming ranch of her other grandmother.

Sports Stories

Author	Title	Grade Level	Description
Chris Lynch	*Gold Dust*	5–8	Set in Boston in 1975, the story focuses on the friendship and baseball dreams of two seventh graders, one from a white working-class family and the other the son of a professor of Caribbean literature, newly arrived from the Dominican Republic.

Author	Title	Grade Level	Description
Carolyn Marsden	*Moon Runner*	4–6	A reserved fourth-grade girl finds success, friendship, and her identity on a track team.
Linda Sue Park	*Keeping Score*	4–6	Ten-year-old Maggie is a passionate Brooklyn Dodger fan who spends her baseball season with her firefighter father's chums at the firehouse, listening to baseball and learning to keep score.
Robert B. Parker	*Edenville Owls*	5–8	In 1945, an eighth grader organizes his friends into a basketball team and amateur detective society.
Deborah Wiles	*The Aurora County All-Stars*	4–6	Twelve-year-old star pitcher House Jackson has been out of commission due to a broken elbow. When he can finally pitch for the all-star game, he finds it is scheduled at the same time as the Aurora County Pageant.

School Stories

Beverly Cleary	*Ramona Quimby, Age 8*	2–4	Ramona arrives in third grade, where she enjoys her teacher's "Dear" (Drop Everything and Read) time, and stages a hilarious parody of a cat food commercial for her book report.
Andrew Clements	*No Talking*	4–6	Fifth-grade boys are pitted against girls in a contest to see who can go without talking the longest.
Walter Dean Myers	*Darnell Rock Reporting*	5–7	Darnell is a typical underachieving middle-school student until he joins the school newspaper, and becomes a champion for a homeless man he has interviewed.
Gary Schmidt	*The Wednesday Wars*	5–7	A sixth grader has to spend Wednesday afternoons with his English teacher who lures him into reading (and liking) Shakespeare and discovering himself.
Michael Winerip	*Adam Canfield: Watch Your Back!*	5–7	Sixth-grade Adam is overscheduled and overworked as he tries to juggle his school newspaper editorship.

Mysteries

Blue Balliett	*The Calder Game*	5–7	Three friends investigate their third art-related mystery with a set of pentominoes and a trip to England.

(continued)

teaching feature 7.2

Author	Title	Grade Level	Description
Elise Broach	*Shakespeare's Secret*	5–7	A shy sixth-grade girl, an elderly woman, and a popular eighth-grade boy set out to solve the mystery of a missing diamond that may once have belonged to Anne Boleyn.
Siobhan Dowd	*The London Eye Mystery*	5–7	Two British children watch their visiting cousin board the London Eye. When he doesn't get out at the end of the ride, they are intent on solving the mystery of his disappearance.
Carl Hiaasen	*Hoot*	4–6	Twelve-year-old hero Roy Eberhardt fights the corporate executives of Mother Paula's All-American Pancake House, who want to destroy the habitat of burrowing owls in order to put up their latest restaurant.
Ellen Raskin	*The Westing Game*	4–6	At the reading of a millionaire's will, sixteen characters are presented with a directive to discover the identity of his murderer and other clues cleverly hidden within the will.

Challenging Perspectives on Realistic Fiction

The genre of contemporary realistic fiction includes books that are fictionalized narratives with plots, characters, and settings that might be found in real life. These stories reflect contemporary life, take place in familiar settings, and present situations with which the reader can identify. These stories are also often based on socially significant events. The classification of realistic fiction is given to stories that are convincingly true to life and that help children see their own lives, empathize with other people, and see the complexity of human interaction. For example, Elinor Batezat Sisulu's picturebook *The Day Gogo Went to Vote* is a fictionalized account of a South African grandmother who votes in the first democratic election in South Africa that permitted Black South Africans to participate. Another is Eve Bunting's 1995 Caldecott Medal–winner *Smoky Night*, a fictional account of the Los Angeles riots, which occurred after three police officers were acquitted of criminal charges for the beating of Rodney King.

The question of whether to use contemporary realistic fiction in the classroom and how to use it continues to create challenges for teachers today. Some people have questioned the relevance of the topics in this type of fiction to the lives of children. Should we offer to children realistic depictions of social issues in literature? Claudia Mills, in *The Ethics of Representation: Realism and Idealism in Children's Fiction*, states:

> . . . in defense of realism, is the argument for the value of truth, for "telling it like it is," for an honest witness to the world as we actually find it. Children, this argument goes, have a right to be told the truth, as best as we can tell it. Besides, if we don't tell them the truth, they'll find it out anyway, eventually, and then distrust us for having withheld it from them.[9]

In recent times, what some deem inappropriate topics are featured in some contemporary realistic fiction. These topics have been identified as unsuitable for certain age groups, and they include offensive language, acts of racism, implied sexual content, glorified violence, and nudity, to name a few. The appropriate or inappropriateness of these topics poses a challenge for the classroom teacher when using a genre of literature that features them. Teachers should always give attention to developmentally appropriate content and practices for children. Suggested guidelines for appropriate content were first introduced in 1987 by the National Association for the Education of Young Children[10] in order to enhance the quality of educational experiences for early childhood programs serving children from birth through age 8. Although the guidelines reflected a consensus definition of developmentally appropriate practices involving the input from thousands of early childhood professionals, a number of controversies, confusions, and myths surrounded their arrival in the field.

The appropriateness of content continues to be fodder for many lively debates in education circles, and as a result the titles of many contemporary realistic children's literature books are relegated to the shelves of teachers' personal collections and are rarely a part of the curriculum development for teaching in content areas. This debate cannot be resolved in the few paragraphs of this chapter. However, we know that many children from all walks of life experience the difficulties of our world that are described in these books. This is not to suggest children living with violence, homelessness, poverty, or other injustices should only read or be read stories about protagonists dealing with the tough issues of life. It does suggest that children "need to have the book as a mirror—to mirror their physical self, their lives, and family experiences . . . they also need the window—the book that takes them into other worlds, that expands their horizons."[11] Using the genre of contemporary realistic fiction, we can help children to begin what we hold as a life-long learning goal: to develop and respect the multiple ways of "seeing," "knowing," and "creating meaning in the world." The teacher is one who can guide, observe, facilitate, pose problems, extend discussions and activities, and, in Lev Vygotsky's (1978) words, "create a natural moment" in the child's environment.[12]

Finally, when using children's literature that has a focus on contemporary issues and problems, a teacher's choices should always reflect both the age and individual needs of the child and the goal of creating learning experiences that are meaningful for the child. This should not discourage the use of literature, but rather should encourage its use to increase a child's ability to critique and ultimately participate in solving many of the problems in their world—the same problems we will depend on future generations to solve. (See **Figure 7.1** to address contemporary realistic fiction with the Ten-Point Model for Teaching Controversial Issues.)

figure 7.1 · The Ten-Point Model for Teaching Controversial Issues Using Contemporary Realistic Fiction

Step	Task	To Consider
1. Raise the initial question and have the children brainstorm all their initial responses.	The essential question is: What is meant by "realistic"? How does censorship relate to controversial literature?	Certain topics may be deemed objectionable in children's literature, such as violence, nudity, sexual orientation, offensive language, religion, the occult, and drug and alcohol abuse. For example, discuss why the picturebook *And Tango Makes Three*—based on actual events about a couple of male penguins in the Central Park Zoo raising a hatchling—has topped the American Library Association's list of the Most Challenged Books of 2006.
2. Create a list of "Things to find out more about."	What is questioned in one culture may not be in another. By whose standard should we decide if a book is too realistic?	Students can research locally what books have been challenged in their state and neighboring states. As they gather the information, they can see who is involved in the committees that make the decisions. Then discuss who is included and who is not and why.
3. Assign information-gathering homework.	Students should gather, evaluate, and synthesize data from a variety of sources (e.g,. print and nonprint texts, artifacts, and people) to communicate their discoveries in ways that suit their purpose and audience.	Assign individual students or small groups to gather information on the First Amendment of the Bill of Rights to the U.S. Constitution, the U.S. Supreme Court notable First Amendment court cases, and freedom of speech and press. Then using that information, debate the issues of censorship and book banning.
4. Share again responses to the initial question in a brainstorming session.	Having students share their responses with the class will allow a space to put everything "on the table" for further exploration and discussion.	Have students share the information they have gathered about their schools and community and any books that have been on banned or challenged book lists.
5. Continue the process of gathering information.	Students should explore information from educational and psychological communities to determine what the "experts" say about children and books that may contain objectionable content but are important and worthwhile because they explore themes that address real-life scenarios.	As they gather information, students should be encouraged to search the Internet for blogs, electronic magazines, and other news sources to gather information about the most current debates in broadcast and print media.
6. If a concept emerges that sparks interest, confusion, or conflict, pose it as a new question.	Explore the histories of two authors and their books that are routinely kept out of school libraries such as J. K. Rowling and the Harry Potter books (accused of implicitly endorsing witchcraft and satanism) and Judy Blume (adult themes and profanity).	Children's books with gay themes often stir this kind of controversy. What is particularly troubling about these incidents is the widespread effect they appear to have, curtailing the availability and publication of more of these kinds of books.

figure 7.1 *(continued)*

Step	Task	To Consider
		New questions could be posed: What are the similarities and differences of this controversial issue and others? What were the circumstances and underlying assumptions for the variety of viewpoints? Who should decide? Teachers? Librarians? Parents?
7. Periodically give the children assignments in class to summarize their thoughts.	Prompts could be: • What is the rule in your family and community? • Are there words and phrases that you could or could not use in your writing to a wider audience? • Who should be considered in the creative writing process before publishing?	The assignment can be individual or shared writing.
8. As individual or group projects emerge, follow up on them.	Children may identify compelling issues found in the literature and identify projects that can advocate for change within their communities.	Research resources, including organizations, databases, and publications focused on activism projects. Some projects may require that children partner with adults to be really effective. The American Library Association's Web site ‹www.ala.org› has many resources to help teachers and librarians offer support for dealing with or reporting challenges to library materials. There is a sample checklist with ideas for working with community leaders that could be adapted for student use.
9. Let others know what you are doing.	Invite authors, illustrators, teachers, librarians, school administrators, publishers, parents/caregivers, and children to discuss their own perspectives and experiences with difficult issues: censorship, violence, raw images in picturebooks, depictions of minorities, gender issues, political correctness, ethical heroes, and more.	Encourage dialogue with parents, colleagues, and the community. This could be a space to support dialogue about issues in the community and nationally. For example, students could contact the Freedom to Read Foundation (Chicago, Ill.) for quarterly news, articles, and timely reports on censorship trends, current court cases, and more.
10. End your project with something either public or permanent.	Children could use a survey format to gather student opinions on the use of contemporary realistic fiction in classrooms and libraries.	Students could collect the information school or district-wide and share the responses with teachers and other interested constituent groups.

Source: Adapted from Kreidler, W. *Elementary Perspectives: Teaching Concepts of Peace and Conflict.* Copyright © 1990. Educators for Social Responsibility, Cambridge, MA, www.esrnational.org. Used by permission.

Using Realistic Fiction to Address Standards

Realistic fiction provides opportunities for students to engage in discussions about contemporary topics and see people their age who struggle with familiar issues but prevail in the end. With the diversity of settings, characters, and conflicts, these books provide many opportunities for integration across the curriculum. For example, *Hoot* by Carl Hiaasen, makes environmental activism and ecological knowledge central to the plot. Paul Fleischman's *Seedfolks* features neighbors growing a variety of crops in an urban community garden. Even the physical changes of growing up are addressed in texts such as *The Secret Blog of Raisin Rodriguez* by Judy Goldschmidt and *Then Again, Maybe I Won't* by Judy Blume. Immigration, a key component of many social studies curricula, can be explored by reading titles such as *Step from Heaven* by An Na and *Swimming to America* by Alice Mead. These, of course, are in addition to books set in international locations. Getting along in a diverse society is the theme of both *The Misfits* by James Howe and *My Louisiana Sky* by Kimberly Willis Holt.

Standards in Action: Language Arts

Project Mulberry
Park, L. (2005). *Project Mulberry*. New York: Clarion Books.

Project Mulberry follows Julia Song and her friend Patrick as they work on a project for the state fair. At the suggestion of Julia's mother, the two decide to grow silkworms and make their own thread just as Julia's mother had done as a girl in Korea. Julia repeatedly wishes they could do a more "American" project, but the two persevere and learn about issues of identity, prejudice, and sustainable farming in addition to raising their silkworms. The book breaks from traditional form by interspersing dialogue between Julia and the author between chapters.

Apply to English Language Arts Standard 4

Students adjust their use of spoken, written and visual language (e.g., conventions, style, vocabulary) to communi-cate effectively with a variety of audiences and for different purposes.

- Students can create a chart to compare Julia's dialogue with different characters such as her little brother, Kenny, and her neighbor, Mr. Dixon. Students should analyze the differences in tone and word choice and discuss how they change their own language when communicating with different audiences.
- Students can engage in word studies of English words derived from Greek and Latin roots just as Patrick does with the words *phobia* and *entomologist*. Students can keep a running list of the words they learn that are also used in the book.

Apply to English Language Arts Standard 7

Students conduct research on issues and interests by generating ideas and questions, and by posing problems. They gather, evaluate, and synthesize data from a variety of sources (e.g., print and nonprint texts, artifacts, people) to communicate their discoveries in ways that suit their purpose and audience.

- Students can research the lifecycle of a particular animal and can create a multigenre project to synthesize their learning from the variety of sources consulted. Julia and Patrick's combination of photos, video, journaling, and embroidery can be an example.

Apply to English Language Arts Standard 11

Students participate as knowledgeable, reflective, creative, and critical members of a variety of literacy communities.

- Students can write a letter to the author of one of their favorite books, taking the perspective of the main character just as Julia writes to Ms. Park. Students can critique the author's choices and offer different perspectives on the text that the main character may have.

Source: Standards are from the NCTE/IRA Standards for the English Language Arts.

Notes

1. Madeleine L'Engle, in a speech before the Florida Library Association, May 1965, Miami.
2. C. S. Lewis, *An Experiment in Criticism* (Cambridge: Cambridge University Press, 1961), p. 57.
3. James Cross Giblin, *Writing Books for Young People* (Boston: Writer, 1990), p. 73.
4. Alice Dalgliesh, *The Silver Pencil* (New York: Puffin, 1991 [1944]).
5. Virginia Hamilton, "Writing the Source: In Other Words," *Horn Book Magazine* (December 1978): 618.
6. Ann Cameron, "Write What You Care About," *School Library Journal* 35.10 (June 1989): 50.
7. Jean Little, "A Writer's Social Responsibility," *New Advocate* 3 (spring, 1990): 83.
8. See Margaret Mackey's "Filling the Gaps: 'The Baby-Sitters Club,' the Series Book, and the Learning Reader," *Language Arts* 67.5 (September 1990): 484–89; and "Bad Books, Good Reading," special issue of *Bookbird* 33.3/4 (fall/winter, 1995–1996).
9. Claudia Mills, "The Ethics of Representation: Realism and Idealism in Children's Fiction," report from the Institute for Philosophy and Public Policy, vol. 19, no. 1 (winter, 1999): 13–18.
10. S. Bredekamp and C. Copple, eds., *Developmentally Appropriate Practice in Early Childhood Programs*, rev. ed. (Washington, DC: NAEYC, 1997).
11. R. Sims Bishop, "Mirrors, Windows, and Sliding Glass Doors," *Perspectives* 6 (1990): ix–xi.
12. L. S. Vygotsky, "Interaction Between Learning and Development," in *Minds in Society*, ed. M. Cole, V. John-Steiner, S. Scribner, and E. Souberman (Cambridge, Mass.: Harvard University Press, 1978).

Children's Literature

Go to **www.mhhe.com/kiefer1e** *to access the Children's Literature Database, which includes information on thousands of children's books. Following are some of the titles you will find in the database.*

Titles in blue = multicultural titles

An, Na. *A Step from Heaven*. Front St., 2001.

Applegate, Katherine. *Home of the Brave*. Feiwel, 2007.

Auch, M. J. *Wing Nut*. Holt, 2005.

Balliett, Blue. *The Calder Game*. Illustrated by Brett Helquist. Scholastic, 2008.

Bauer, Joan. *Stand Tall*. Putnam, 2002.

Bauer, Marion Dane. *A Question of Trust*. Houghton, 1994.

——. *On My Honor*. Houghton, 1986.

Birdsall, Jeanne. *The Penderwicks on Gardam Street*. Knopf, 2008.

Blacker, Terence. *Boy2Girl*. Farrar, 2005.

Blume, Judy. *Are You There God? It's Me, Margaret*. Bradbury, 1970.

——. *Tales of a Fourth Grade Nothing*. Illustrated by Roy Doty. Dutton, 1972.

Broach, Elise. *Shakespeare's Secret*. Holt, 2005.

Bruchac, Joseph. *Eagle Song*. Dial, 1997.

Bunting, Eve. *Smoky Night*. Illustrated by David Diaz. Harcourt, 1994.

Burnford, Sheila. *The Incredible Journey*. Illustrated by Carl Burger. Little, 1961.

Byars, Betsy. *The Pinballs*. Harper, 1977.

Cameron, Ann. *Colibrí*. Farrar, 2003.

——. *Gloria Rising*. Illustrated by Lis Toth. Farrar, 2002.

——. *The Most Beautiful Place in the World*. Illustrated by Thomas B. Allen. Knopf, 1988.

——. *The Stories Huey Tells*. Illustrated by Roberta Smith. Knopf, 1995.

——. *The Stories Julian Tells*. Illustrated by Ann Strugnell. Knopf, 1981.

Carmi, Daniella. *Samir and Yonatan*. Levine/Scholastic, 2000.

Choldenko, Gennifer. *Notes from a Liar and Her Dog*. Putnam, 2001.

Cleary, Beverly. *Ramona Quimby, Age 8*. Illustrated by Alan Tiegreen. Morrow, 1981.

——. *Ramona's World*. Illustrated by Alan Tiegreen. Morrow, 1999.

Cleaver, Vera, and Bill Cleaver. *Where the Lilies Bloom*. Illustrated by James Spanfeller. Lippincott, 1969.

Clements, Andrew. *No Talking*. Simon, 2007.

Crutcher, Chris. *The Sledding Hill*. Greenwillow, 2005.

Deans, Sis. *Rainy*. Holt, 2005.

Doherty, Berlie. *The Girl Who Saw Lions*. Roaring Brook, 2008.

Dowd, Siobhan. *The London Eye Mystery*. Random, 2008.

Ellis, Deborah. *Parvana's Journey*. Groundwood, 2002.

Farmer, Nancy. *A Girl Named Disaster*. Orchard, 1996.

Frazier, Sundee T. *Brendan Buckley's Universe, and Everything in It*. Delacorte, 2007.

Gantos, Jack. *Joey Pigza Swallowed the Key*. Farrar, 1998.

George, Jean Craighead. *Julie of the Wolves*. Illustrated by John Schoenherr. Harper, 1972.

Gipson, Fred. *Old Yeller*. Illustrated by Carl Burger. Harper, 1956.

Grimes, Nikki. *Jazmin's Notebook*. Dial, 1998.

Hamilton, Virginia. *M. C. Higgins, the Great*. Macmillan, 1974.

Henkes, Kevin. *The Birthday Room*. Greenwillow, 1999.

Hiaasen, Carl. *Hoot*. Knopf, 2002.

Holt, Kimberly Willis. *Keeper of the Night*. Holt, 2003.

———. *My Louisiana Sky*. Holt, 1998.

———. *When Zachary Beaver Came to Town*. Holt, 1999.

Horvath, Polly. *My One Hundred Adventures*. Random, 2008.

Jiménez, Francisco. *The Circuit: Stories from the Life of a Migrant Child*. Houghton, 2001.

Johnson, Angela. *Heaven*. Simon, 1998.

Kinney, Jeff. *Diary of a Wimpy Kid*. Abrams, 2007.

Konigsburg, E. L. *The View from Saturday*. Atheneum, 1996.

Kurtz, Jane. *Jakarta Missing*. HarperCollins, 2001.

Lee, Ingrid. *Dog Lost*. Scholastic, 2008.

L'Engle, Madeleine. *Meet the Austins*. Dell, 1981 [1960].

Le Guin, Ursula K. *A Wizard of Earthsea*. Illustrated by Ruth Robbins. Houghton, 1968.

Lester, Alison. *The Quicksand Pony*. Houghton, 1998.

Lockhart, E. *The Disreputable History of Frankie Landau-Banks*. Hyperion, 2008.

Lowry, Lois. *Number the Stars*. Houghton, 1989.

Lynch, Chris. *Gold Dust*. HarperCollins, 2000.

MacLachlan, Patricia. *Journey*. Delacorte, 1991.

Madden, Kerry. *Gentle's Holler*. Viking, 2005.

Mankell, Henning. *Secrets in the Fire*. Annick, 2003.

Marsden, Carolyn. *Moon Runner*. Candlewick, 2005.

Martin, Ann M. *A Corner of the Universe*. Scholastic, 2002.

Matthews, L. S. *Fish*. Delacorte, 2004.

McKay, Hilary. *Forever Rose*. Simon, 2008.

Miles, Betty. *Maudie and Me and the Dirty Book*. Knopf, 1980.

Myers, Walter Dean. *Darnell Rock Reporting*. Delacorte, 1994.

———. *Scorpions*. Harper, 1988.

Naidoo, Beverley. *Journey to Jo'burg*. Illustrated by Eric Velasquez. Lippincott, 1986.

Namioka, Lensey. *Yang the Youngest and His Terrible Ear*. Illustrated by Kees de Kiefte. Little, 1992.

Naylor, Phyllis Reynolds. *Shiloh*. Atheneum, 1991.

Park, Barbara. *Skinnybones*. Knopf, 1982.

Park, Linda Sue. *Keeping Score*. Clarion, 2008.

———. *Project Mulberry*. Clarion, 2005.

Parker, Robert B. *Edenville Owls*. Philomel, 2007.

Paterson, Katherine. *Bridge to Terabithia*. Illustrated by Donna Diamond. Crowell, 1977.

———. *Jacob Have I Loved*. Harper, 1980.

———. *The Great Gilly Hopkins*. Crowell, 1978.

———. *The Same Stuff as Stars*. Clarion, 2002.

Patron, Susan. *The Higher Power of Lucky*. Illustrated by Matt Phelan. Atheneum, 2006.

———. *Lucky Breaks*. Atheneum, 2009.

Paulsen, Gary. *Hatchet*. Bradbury, 1987.

Perkins, Lynne Rae. *Criss Cross*. Greenwillow, 2005.

Raskin, Ellen. *The Westing Game*. Dutton, 1978.

Rawlings, Marjorie Kinnan. *The Yearling*. Illustrated by Edward Shenton. Scribner's, 1938.

Rockwell, Thomas. *How to Eat Fried Worms*. Watts, 1973.

Ryan, Pam Muñoz. *Becoming Naomi Leon*. Scholastic, 2004.

———. *Paint the Wind*. Scholastic, 2007.

Salisbury, Graham. *Night of the Howling Dogs*. Random, 2007.

Schmidt, Gary D. *Trouble*. Clarion, 2008.

———. *The Wednesday Wars*. Clarion, 2007.

Scieszka, Jon. *Guys Write for Guys Read: Boys' Favorite Authors Write About Being Boys*. Viking, 2005.

Sisulu, Elinor Batezat. *The Day Gogo Went to Vote*. Illustrated by Sharon Wilson. Little, 1996.

Spinelli, Jerry. *Wringer*. HarperCollins, 1997.

Staples, Suzanne Fisher. *Shabanu: Daughter of the Wind*. Knopf, 1989.

Temple, Frances. *Taste of Salt*. Orchard, 1992.

Voigt, Cynthia. *Homecoming*. Atheneum, 1981.

Wiles, Deborah. *The Aurora County All-Stars*. Harcourt, 2007.

Winerip, Michael. *Adam Canfield: Watch Your Back!* Candlewick, 2007.7

Woodson, Jacqueline. *Feathers*. Putnam, 2007.

———. *I Hadn't Meant to Tell You This*. Delacorte, 1994.

Yumoto, Kazumi. *The Friends*. Translated by Cathy Hirano. Farrar, 1996.

Wilson, N. D. *Leepike Ridge*. Random, 2007.

Zimmer, Tracie Vaughn. *Reaching for the Sun*. Bloomsbury, 2007.

Chapter Eight

Historical Fiction

Chapter Outline

This is Amanda's first year as an elementary school teacher. She has been assigned fifth grade and is very excited about the opportunity. When she met with her other fifth-grade colleagues to plan for the upcoming year, the annual discussion about social studies being the students' least favorite subject came up. Again they were faced with how to cover the soon-to-be-tested information and increase the students' engagement. This was surprising to Amanda. She had majored in history and always loved many parts of the integrated social studies (geography, economics, anthropology, political science). She asked her colleagues if they ever included historical fiction when teaching social studies. They replied that they had in the past, but not recently. Together they then planned several thematic units integrating historical fiction titles with the social studies curriculum. Much to their surprise, the authenticity of setting, the language that reflected the period, the characters who behaved according to the standards of the times, and worthwhile themes had tremendous appeal. The students were getting excited about social studies!

Historical Fiction for Today's Child

Historical fiction must draw on two sources, fact and imagination—the author's information about the past and her or his power to speculate about how it was to live in that time. By personalizing the past and making it live in the mind of the reader, such books can help children understand both the public events that we usually label "history" and the private struggles that have characterized the human condition across the centuries.

Historical fiction is not as popular with readers today as it was a generation or two ago. Today's children generally select realistic fiction, the so-called "I" stories with modern-day characters and settings. Even so, children have more historical fiction available now than in the 1980s. Publishers have capitalized on children's interest in series books by developing collectible sets of historical fiction titles. The American Girl books, published by the Pleasant Company, offer seven different series, each chronicling the adventures of a girl in a particular time. These books, along with the expensive dolls and period costumes that go with them, have been phenomenally successful. Other publishers have also targeted the 7-to-11 age range. In 1996, Scholastic introduced the Dear America series of fictional journals by young girls, which provide "eyewitness" accounts of events in American history. All the books are written by well-known authors, though with mixed results. Joyce Hansen's *I Thought My Soul Would Rise and Fly* received a Coretta Scott King Honor Book Award in 1998; other titles have been severely criticized.[1] Perhaps most disturbing is the series' attempt to look like authentic diaries rather than like fiction. No author's name is given on the cover or spine. Following the diary entries is an epilogue describing what happened to the character following the accounts in the diary. An historical note and archival photographs follow. Buried at the back of the book is a brief "About the Author" section, and the dedication, acknowledgments, and CIP information are given on the final page. It is no wonder that many children and teachers believe these stories are real accounts. The popularity of the series has spawned three others that use a similar format. The My America series is for a younger audience and has a continuing series of books narrated by the same fictional character. The My Name Is America series features fictional boys' reports of significant happenings in American history, and the Royal Diaries series provides fictional chronicles of famous young women such as Elizabeth I and Cleopatra. Teachers who want to share these books with children will want to select titles carefully and ensure that children read them with a critical eye.[2]

Historical fiction continues to provide ideas to authors and illustrators of picture storybooks that portray the life of a particular period. For example, children can experience the terror of slaves traveling on the Underground Railroad in Deborah Hopkinson's *Under the Quilt of Night* with James Ransome's vivid oil paintings to illuminate

Kadir Nelson's illustrations for *Henry's Freedom Box* by Ellen Levine represent the dramatic true story of a slave's escape from Virginia to Philadelphia. Cover illustration copyright © 2007 by Kadir Nelson from *Henry's Freedom Box* by Ellen Levine. Scholastic Inc./Scholastic Press. Reprinted by permission.

the fearful journey. They can cheer for the extraordinary bravery of Henry Brown as he escapes from slavery by shipping himself from Richmond to Philadelphia in *Henry's Freedom Box* by Ellen Levine and Kadir Nelson. In Eve Bunting's *Dandelions* readers can travel across the prairie, or they can greet the arrival of Lewis and Clark from a Native American perspective in Virginia Driving Hawk Sneve's *Bad River Boys*. They can experience the detention of a young Chinese immigrant newly arrived in San Francisco in Katrina Saltonstall Currier's *Kai's Journey to Gold Mountain*. They can walk among the tenements of an immigrant community in New York City in Elisa Bartone's *Peppe the Lamplighter* or experience the horrors of World War II and the Holocaust in books such as *The Cats in Krasinski Square* by Karen Hesse, *Rose Blanche* by Roberto Innocenti and Christophe Gallaz, or *Hiroshima No Pika* by Toshi Maruki. "Easy-to-read" books about historical events are also readily available, including Louise Borden's *Sleds on Boston Common* and Patricia Lee Gauch's *Aaron and the Green Mountain Boys*, both about the American Revolution.

The Value of Historical Fiction

Historical novels for children help a child to experience the past—to enter into the conflicts, the suffering, the joys, and the despair of those who lived before us. There is no way children can feel the jolt of a covered wagon, the tediousness of the daily trek in the broiling sun, or the constant threat of danger unless they take an imaginative journey in books like Jean Van Leeuwen's *Bound for Oregon* or *A Heart for Any Fate* by Linda Crew. Well-written historical fiction offers young people the vicarious experience of participating in the life of the past.

Historical fiction encourages children to think as well as feel. Every book set in the past invites a comparison with the present. In addition, opportunities for critical thinking and judgment are built into the many novels that provide conflicting views on an issue and force characters to make hard choices. Readers of *My Brother Sam Is Dead* by James L. Collier and Christopher Collier can weigh Sam's Patriot fervor against his father's Tory practicality as young Tim tries to decide which one is right. Readers will question Will Page's dislike of his uncle because he refused to fight the Yankees in Carolyn Reeder's *Shades of Gray*, and have an opportunity to consider the battles faced by conscientious objectors to every war in which this nation has participated.

An historical perspective also helps children see and judge the mistakes of the past more clearly. They can read such books as *Day of Tears* by Julius Lester, *Nory Ryan's Song* by Patricia Reilly Giff, or *Under the Blood-Red Sun* by Graham Salisbury and realize the cruelty people are capable of inflicting on each other, whether by slavery, persecution, or the internment of Japanese-Americans in "relocation centers." Such books will quicken children's sensibilities and bring them to a fuller understanding

Louise Erdrich's *The Porcupine Year* continues the story of Omakays and her Ojibwa community in the mid-nineteenth century. Cover from *The Porcupine Year* by Louise Erdrich. Used by permission of HarperCollins Children's Books, HarperCollins Publisher.

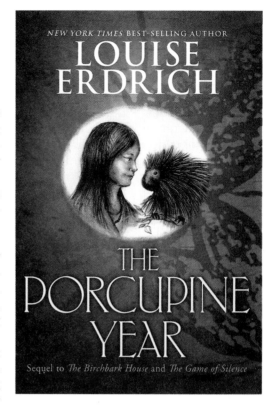

of human problems and human relationships. We hope that our children will learn not to repeat the injustices of the past. Many years ago George Santayana cautioned: "Those who cannot remember the past are condemned to repeat it."

Stories of the past help children see that times change, nations rise and fall, but universal human needs have remained relatively unchanged. All people need and want respect, belonging, love, freedom, and security, regardless of whether they lived during the period of the Vikings or the pioneers or are alive today. The pain of moving from home to home and place to place is present in many books such as Louise Erdrich's *The Birchbark House*, *The Game of Silence,* and *The Porcupine Year*. But the solace drawn from loving families is what gives all the characters hope. Children today living in tenements, trailers, or suburban homes seek the same feeling of warmth and family solidarity that Erdrich portrays so effectively in her books.

Historical fiction also enables children to see human interdependence. We are all interconnected and interrelated. We need others as much as Christopher needed Asha-po in Kathleen Karr's *Worlds Apart* or Ellen Rosen needed Annemarie Johansen's family in order to escape the Nazis in Lois Lowry's award-winning book *Number the Stars*. Such books also dramatize the courage and integrity of the thousands of "common folk" who willingly take a stand for what they believe. History does not record their names, but their stories are frequently the source of inspiration for books of historical fiction.

Children's perceptions of chronology are inexact and develop slowly. Even so, stories about the past can develop a feeling for the continuity of life and help children to see themselves and their present place in time as part of a larger picture. Books such as Bonnie Pryor's *The House on Maple Street* provide this sense for younger elementary students. In Pryor's book, lost objects from early times are unearthed in a contemporary child's yard. Paintings by Beth Peck link past and present, showing changes that came to that specific setting over the intervening centuries. Reading historical fiction is one way children can develop this sense of history and begin to understand their place in the sweep of human destiny.

Types of Historical Fiction

The term *historical fiction* can be used to designate all realistic stories that are set in the past. Even though children tend to see these in one undifferentiated category (because all the action happened "in the olden days" before they were born), students of literature will want to keep in mind that various distinctions can be made on the basis of the author's purpose and the nature of the research and writing tasks required. Teachers and librarians should help children differentiate between the fictionalized aspects and the factual aspects in all types of historical fiction.

In the most obvious type of historical fiction, an author weaves a fictional story around actual events and people of the past. *Johnny Tremain* by Esther Forbes, the story of a fictional apprentice to Paul Revere, is a novel of this sort. The author had previously written a definitive adult biography of Revere and had collected painstakingly accurate details about life in Boston just before the Revolutionary War: the duties of apprentices, the activities of the Committee for Public Safety, and much, much more. Johnny Tremain's personal story, his development from an embittered boy into a courageous and idealistic young man, is inextricably connected with the political history and way of life of his place and time. It is not uncommon in recent books of historical fiction to find that the author has added an author's note and bibliography of sources at the end of the book.

In other stories of the past, fictional lives are lived with little or no reference to recorded historical events or real persons. However, the facts of social history dictate the background for how the characters live and make their living; what they wear, eat, study, or play; and what conflicts they must resolve. Australian writer Sonya Hartnett's *Thursday's Child* is of this type. Written about a family struggling to cope with their circumstances during the Great Depression in the Australian outback, this superb book is a moving examination of a family torn apart by circumstances beyond their control. The rural Midwest and western America provide the setting for several books whose main thrust is humor rather than historical detail. Richard Peck's books *The Teacher's Funeral*, *A Year Down Yonder*, and *A Long Way from Chicago* are set in rural Illinois in the nineteenth and mid-twentieth centuries. Their main focus is on wonderfully eccentric characters and amusing plot lines. These same qualities make David Ives's *Scrib*, about a 16-year-old boy who makes a precarious living writing letters for "ill-literates" in the "wild" West of the 1860s, so appealing.

More often in this type of historical fiction the historical setting simply provides the background for ripping good adventure stories that rely on the structures of Robert Louis Stevenson's *Treasure Island* or Johann David Wyss's *The Swiss Family Robinson*. Stories that fall into this category would include Eva Ibbotson's *The Star of Kazan*, about a young girl involved in mystery and intrigue in early-twentieth-century Vienna. *Operation Red Jericho* and *Operation Typhoon Shore* by Joshua Mowll are 1920s adventures that blend aspects of Jules Verne and Indiana Jones. The books, whose shape and cover mimic old journals, are purportedly told by the very person who has inherited and researched the archives of a secret society. Mowll includes maps, diagrams, and photographs found in the archives as well as excerpts from teenage heroine Becca's diary and her brother Doug's sketchbook.

Some historical fiction turns traditional female roles upside down. In Avi's *The True Confessions of Charlotte Doyle* and Louis A. Meyer's stories about Mary "Jacky" Faber, such as *Bloody Jack* and *My Bonny Light Horseman*, the heroines assume the roles of able sailor lads and prove their grit when trouble strikes their ships. Nancy Springer and Julia Golding have chosen an historical London setting for their likable mystery series. Springer's heroine Enola Holmes is the very rebellious younger sister to Mycroft and Sherlock Holmes and determined to solve her own mysteries in books such as *The Case of the Bizarre Bouquets* and *The Case of the Peculiar Pink Fan*. Julia Golding's *The Diamond*

Julia Golding's *Cat Among the Pigeons* features heroine Cat Royal and is the second of a series of adventures set in London during the 1790s. Cover from *Cat Among the Pigeons* by Julia Golding. Used by permission of Roaring Brook Press, NY, a division of Henry Holt and Company, LLC.

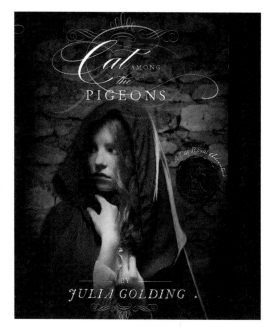

of Drury Lane and *Cat Among the Pigeons* are set in the theater world of 1790s London and feature a feisty orphan named Cat Royal. In *Den of Thieves*, Golding's heroine Cat travels to the French Revolution. Often such historical adventure stories rely on circumstances that border on the fantastic, although the settings are built on historical sources.

In a third type of historical fiction, authors recreate, largely from memory, their own personal experiences of a time that is "history" to their child audience. The Little House books, for example, are all based on actual childhood experiences in the life of their author, Laura Ingalls Wilder, or her husband. Such books require searching one's memory for details and then sorting and imaginatively retelling significant events, but extensive research is seldom done and books written in the past often reflect the prejudices of the past. This is one reason to make sure to offer children many books about a time period. Louise Erdrich's *The Birchbark House, The Game of Silence*, and *The Porcupine Year* take place during the same time period as Wilder's Little House books but present historical events from the point of view of a Native American community.

In other instances, a purely contemporary story about a significant event might endure until it acquires historical significance. *Snow Treasure* by Marie McSwigan is the exciting story of Norwegian children who heroically strapped gold bullion under their sleds and slid downhill to the port past the watchful Nazi commandant. Written as realism in 1942, this book is read by children today as historical fiction. We must also realize that Katherine Paterson's *Park's Quest* and other books about the Vietnam War might be read as historical fiction by today's child, despite the fact that for many of us these events were lived firsthand.

Some historical stories defy commonly accepted classifications. Walter Mosley's graphically moving *47* vividly portrays the experiences of slavery in 1832 Georgia. The story's narrator is named only Number Forty-Seven, following the practice of dehumanization that was common to slave owners in the South. However, Forty-Seven is looking back on his life from the ripe old age of 180. Furthermore, the other major character in the story is a runaway slave named Tall John, whom many on the plantation suspect of being the legendary African hero High John the Conqueror. Instead of being this mythical African, however, Tall John is actually an alien from another planet. Clearly, Mosley has broken the format of traditional historical fiction for children. But the book presents such an accurate and brutal picture of slavery that it will provide important historical insights to mature readers.

A few authors tell stories of the past in the guise of another genre to draw the hesitant reader in more quickly. Jane Yolen's devastating story of the Holocaust, *The Devil's*

Arithmetic, begins in the present when Hannah, bored with all the remembering of the Passover Seder, opens the door to welcome symbolically the prophet Elijah and finds herself in the unfamiliar world of a Polish village in the 1940s. In Lois Ruby's *Steal Away Home* and its companion book *Soon Be Free*, 12-year-old Dana Shannon finds a skeleton in a closet after her family moves into an old house in Kansas. A small black diary found with the skeleton helps Dana discover that the skeleton is that of Lizbeth Charles, who had died 130 years earlier. Alternate chapters take the reader back to the 1850s, when the house was owned by a Quaker family and was part of the Underground Railroad. In *Tennyson*, Lesley M. M. Blume's heroine Tennyson Fontaine lives in a decrepit Louisiana mansion, and at night she dreams of her home during its heyday before the Civil War and while under attack by the Yankees during the war.

Historical fiction has also been shaped in the form of theatrical scripts. *Bull Run* by Paul Fleischman, *Day of Tears* by Julius Lester, *Good Masters! Sweet Ladies!* by Laura Amy Schlitz, and *Colonial Voices* by Kay Winters all contain multiple voices witnessing historical events and provide children with wonderful opportunities for dramatic presentation. Categorizing books like these is far less important than bringing them to the attention of children, for they all tell good stories and make their subjects memorable.

No type of historical story is intrinsically better than another. However, the type of story might influence a teacher's selection process when choosing books for specific classroom purposes. And in applying the criteria for evaluating historical fiction, which are described in the following section, standards of authenticity must be applied most rigorously to stories that give a prominent place to real people and real events.

Evaluating Historical Fiction

Books of historical fiction must first of all tell a story that is interesting in its own right. The second, and unique, requirement is balancing fact with fiction. Margery Fisher maintains that a good story should not be overwhelmed by facts:

> For the more fact he [the author] has to deal with, the more imagination he will need to carry it off. It is not enough to be a scholar, essential though this is. Without imagination and enthusiasm, the most learned and well-documented story will leave the young reader cold, where it should set him on fire.[3]

Historical fiction *does* have to be accurate and authentic. However, the research should be thoroughly digested, making details appear as an essential part of the story, not tacked on for effect. Mollie Hunter, a well-known Scottish writer of fine historical fiction for children, maintains that an author should be so steeped in the historical period of the book that "you could walk undetected in the past. You'd wake up in the morning and know the kind of bed you'd be sleeping in, . . . even the change you'd have in your pocket!"[4] The purpose of research, she said, is

> to be able to think and feel in terms of a period so that the people within it are real and three-dimensional, close enough to hear the sound of their voices, to feel their body-warmth, to see the expression in their eyes.[5]

This obligation applies not only to details of person, place, and time but also to the values and norms of the culture or cultures depicted. To provide a faithful representation of a culture, an author needs to grasp the language, emotions, thoughts, concerns, and experiences of her character rather than shape that character to fit a mainstream point of view. In Ann Rinaldi's *My Heart Is on the Ground: The Diary of Nannie Little Rose, a Sioux Girl*, in addition to many factually inaccurate details, there are cultural miscues as well. For example, Lakota (Sioux) children are taught to be deferential and respectful to their elders and would be unlikely to criticize their mothers. Yet Nannie's disdain for her mother is a thread that runs throughout the book. Her continuing disapproval of her brother's actions also conflicts with the special bond that existed between Lakota brother and sister, one that even exceeded the bond between husband and wife.[6] Comparing these relationships with those of the Ojibwa family in Louise Erdrich's *The Porcupine Year*, *The Birchbark House*, and *The Game of Silence* can reveal the importance of accurate depiction of culture in historical fiction for children. To fail in this regard is, at the very least, insensitive to children who are members of that culture. Such a failure also does a disservice to children from outside that culture whose worldview and understanding could be enriched by exposure to the attitudes, values, and goals of another group.

Although fictional characters and invented turns of plot are accepted in historical novels, nothing should be included that contradicts the actual record of history. If President Lincoln was busy reviewing Union troops in Virginia on a given day in 1863, an author must not "borrow" him for a scene played in New York City, no matter how great the potential dramatic impact. It breaks the unwritten contract between author and child reader to offer misinformation in any form.

Stories must accurately reflect the spirit and values of the time, as well as the events. Historical fiction can't be made to conform to today's more enlightened point of view concerning medical knowledge, women's rights, or civil rights. George Washington can't be saved with a shot of penicillin. Although in Carol Ryrie Brink's *Caddie Woodlawn*, Caddie's father allows her to be a tomboy while she is growing up in the Wisconsin backwoods, it is highly unlikely that girls raised in the Victorian era could refuse to assume the persona of a "proper lady" in adulthood. Many African-Americans may have suffered the indignity of racism in silence as the family in William Armstrong's *Sounder* did. But there were also people of many cultures in our history who fought against the roles that society dictated for them. Authors of historical fiction can inspire us with their stories in books based on real characters such as Kirkpatrick Hill's *Dancing at the Odinochka*, Sheila P. Moses's *The Legend of Buddy Bush* and *The Return of Buddy Bush*, and Christopher Paul Curtis's *Elijah of Buxton*.

The historian Christopher Collier, who has collaborated with his brother James Lincoln Collier on several novels set during the era of the American Revolution, maintains that authors should pay careful attention to historiography, "that is, the way that professional historians have approached and interpreted the central episode of the story."[7] Collier believes that authors should weigh opposing views on the causes or meaning of a conflict and decide which should be predominant in the story, but also find a way to include the other significant interpretations. One way is to have different characters espouse different points of view. In *Bull Run*, Paul Fleischman deals with this reality by telling the story of this early battle of the Civil War through the voices of sixteen different characters—northerner and southerner, male and female, civilian and military, slave and free.

However, fiction that draws the reader into the thoughts and feelings of a central character cannot be truly impartial. In the middle of a massacre scene, a bleeding settler

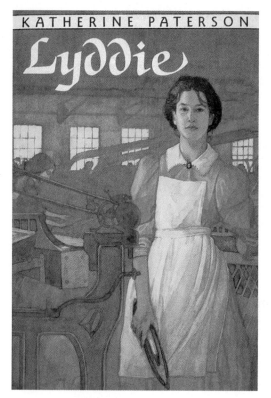

KATHERINE PATERSON

Lyddie

who cries "But the Indians are only fighting for what is theirs!" will sacrifice the story's credibility. Many fine books, like K. M. Grant's *Blood Red Horse*, Carolyn Reeder's *Shades of Gray*, and Avi's *The Fighting Ground*, do let the reader feel more than one side of an issue. But for a more inclusive viewpoint, teachers and librarians will want to provide a variety of books, each with its own point of view and approach to the topic.

The authenticity of language in historical fiction should be given careful attention. We have no recordings of the speech of people from much earlier times, but the spoken word in a book with an historical background should give the flavor of the period. However, too many *prithee*s and *thou*s will seem artificial and might discourage children's further reading. Some archaic words can be used if they are explained in the content. For example, the book *The Cabin Faced West* notes that George Washington "bated" at the Hamiltons. The author, Jean Fritz, makes it very clear by the action in the story that "bated" means "stopped by for dinner."

Some words commonly used in earlier times are offensive by today's standards. Authors must consider whether it would be misleading to omit such terms entirely and how necessary such language is for establishing a character. In Graham Salisbury's *Under the Blood-Red Sun*, "haoles," or white Hawaiians, refer to the Japanese as "Japs." The word "nigger" is used by African American authors Julius Lester in *Day of Tears*, Sheila P. Moses in *The Legend of Buddy Bush*, and Walter Mosley in *47*. It would have defeated the purpose and softened the brutality of the times of these stories to have these characters use more acceptable language. Walter Mosley explains 47's use of the phrase "a nigger like me" in a footnote: "That was before I met Tall John and he taught me about the word 'nigger' and how wrong it was for me to use such a term" (p. 7). Authors' notes about the reasons for choices they have made regarding language are useful to both students and teachers. Explaining the dilemma she faced in *Crooked River*, a story about the clash of Anglo and Native Americans in Ohio in 1812, Shelley Pearsall remarks:

> Sadly, the language of the past also reflected the prejudices and hatreds of the past. Some of the characters in *Crooked River* use words such as *savages*, *half-breeds*, and *beasts* to describe the Native American people. It was with a heavy heart that I put those

words into the story. They were used on the frontier and found in the historical documents I read. Appallingly, even the governor of Ohio used this language in an 1812 address to the Ohio Legislature where he called the Indians "hordes of barbarians." As a historical writer I could not ignore the language of the past, but I hope that it causes readers to reflect upon the destructive power that words of hate can wield. (p. 239)

Pearsall also counteracts the sting of such language by her sensitive shaping of the character of John Mic, an Ojibwa Indian who is accused of the murder of a white man. In the chapters narrated by John, Pearsall chose to use story poems, which she felt best expressed "the powerful, descriptive language" of the Ojibwa.

Teachers should try to be aware of the reasoning behind authors' decisions and should be prepared to discuss controversial issues that arise in books like these with students and their parents.

Well-written historical fiction also makes use of figurative language that is appropriate for the times and characters in the story. For example, in Katherine Paterson's powerful story *Lyddie*, about a farm girl who goes to work in the fabric mills of Lowell, Massachusetts, in the 1840s, all allusions and metaphors are those of an uneducated rural girl. In the very beginning of the story, a bear gets into their farm cabin and Lyddie stares him down while the other children climb the ladder to the loft. Finally she herself backs up to the ladder, climbs it, and pulls it up behind her. Throughout the book Lyddie alludes to "staring down the bears." She thinks of the huge machines as "roaring clattering beasts . . . great clumsy bears" (p. 97). And when she throws a water bucket at the overseer to get him to let go of a young girl, she laughs as she imagines she hears the sound of an angry bear crashing the oatmeal bucket in the cabin. Everything about this book works together to capture Lyddie's view of the world. At the same time, the long thirteen hours a day of factory work, life in the dormitories, the frequency of tuberculosis, and the treatment of women all reflect the spirit and the values of the times. More important than the authenticity of the writing is the fast-paced story and Lyddie's grit, determination, and personal growth.

A book of historical fiction should do even more than relate a good story of the past authentically and imaginatively. It should illuminate today's problems by examining those of other times. The themes of many historical books are basic ones about the meaning of freedom, loyalty and treachery, love and hate, acceptance of new ways, closed minds versus questioning

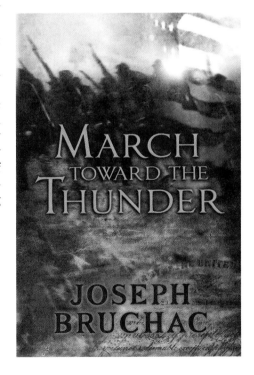

Joseph Bruchac's *March Toward the Thunder* is based on the story of Bruchac's Abenaki great-grandfather's service in the Irish Brigade in 1864. Cover from *March Toward the Thunder* by Joseph Bruchac, copyright © 2008. Used by permission of Dial Books for Young Readers, a Division of Penguin Young Readers Group, a Member of Penguin Group (USA) Inc., 345 Hudson Street, New York, NY 10014. All rights reserved.

Evaluating Historical Fiction

 Go to **www.mhhe.com/kieferbrief1e** *to access an expanded version of this evaluation form.*

Consider the following when evaluating historical fiction for children:

- Does the book tell a good story? Is fact blended with fiction in such a way that the background is subordinate to the story?
- Is the story as accurate and authentic as possible?
- Does the author provide background information in an afterword or author's note that will help readers distinguish between what is fact and what has been fictionalized?
- Does the story accurately reflect the values and norms of the culture depicted?
- Does the author avoid any contradiction or distortion of the known events of history?

- Are background details authentic, in keeping with accurate information about the period?
- Does the story accurately reflect the values and spirit of the time?
- Are different points of view on the issues of the time presented or acknowledged?
- Does the dialogue convey a feeling of the period without seeming artificial? Does it reflect character as well as setting?
- Is the language of the narrative appropriate to the time, drawing figures of speech from the setting?
- Does the theme provide insight and understanding for today's problems as well as those of the past?

ones, and, always, the age-old struggle between good and evil. Many tales of the past echo recent experience. Books like *Catherine, Called Birdy* by Karen Cushman, *Lyddie* by Katherine Paterson, *Prairie Songs* by Pam Conrad, and *The Hope Chest* by Karen Schwabach could well be used in a discussion of the history of women's roles. All these books can shed light and understanding on today's problems.

To summarize, historical fiction must first meet the requirements of good writing, but it demands special criteria beyond that. In evaluating historical fiction the reader will want to consider whether the story meets these specialized needs. Historical fiction can dramatize and humanize facts of history that can seem sterile in so many textbooks. It can give children a sense of participation in the past and an appreciation for their historical heritage. It should enable the child to see that today's way of life is a result of what people did in the past and that the present will influence the way people live in the future. For some of the most important criteria to keep in mind, see **Guidelines: Evaluating Historical Fiction**.

Classroom Approaches to Historical Fiction

One way to approach historical fiction is to look at common topics or themes as they are presented in different settings across the centuries and to group titles by such themes. Such a thematic approach helps emphasize the universality of human experi-

teaching feature 8.1

A Thematic Approach to Historical Fiction

The Clash of Cultures

The Arrow Over the Door (Bruchac)	American Revolution, 1777
Crooked River (Pearsall)	Ohio, 1812
The Lantern Bearers (Sutcliff)	Fifth-century England
The Man from the Other Side (Orlev)	Poland, World War II
Walk Across the Sea (Fletcher)	California, 1886
Witness (Hesse)	Vermont, 1924
Worlds Apart (Karr)	South Carolina, 1600s
Year of Impossible Goodbyes (Choi)	North Korea, 1940s

The Human Cost of War

Lord of the Nutcracker Men (I. Lawrence)	Britain, World War II
My Brother Sam Is Dead (Collier and Collier)	American Revolution
Private Peaceful (Morpurgo)	World War I
March Toward the Thunder (Bruchac)	U.S. Civil War
Sunrise Over Fallujah (Meyers)	Iraq, 2003

In Quest of Freedom

Black Storm Comin' (Wilson)	Pre–Civil War Nevada and California
The Clay Marble (Ho)	Cambodia, 1980s
Copper Sun (Draper)	American South, 1730s
Elijah of Buxton (Curtis)	Ontario, Canada, 1849
The Hope Chest (Schwabach)	Tennessee, 1920
Jump Ship to Freedom (Collier and Collier)	United States, 1780s

Dealing with Disabilities

T4 (LeZotte)	Nazi Germany
Apple Is My Sign (Riskind)	United States, early 1900s
The Door in the Wall (de Angeli)	Medieval England
The King's Shadow (Alder)	Medieval England
A Way of His Own (Dyer)	Prehistoric America
Wintering Well (Wait)	Maine, 1820s

ences over time and place. (See **Teaching Feature 8.1: A Thematic Approach to Historical Fiction**.)

Another approach is to plan to read books chronologically, according to the periods and settings they represent. This approach follows the more traditional social studies curriculum. (See **Teaching Feature 8.2.: A Chronological Approach to Historical Fiction**.)

A Chronological Approach to Historical Fiction for Children

Author	Title	Time/Place
Ancient Times		
Caroline Lawrence	The Roman Mysteries series: including *The Prophet from Ephesus*, *The Thieves of Ostia*, *The Secrets of Vesuvius*, *The Fugitive from Corinth*, *The Gladiators from Capua*, *The Pirates of Pompeii*, and *The Beggar of Volubilis*	Roman Empire, first century C.E.
Julius Lester	*Pharaoh's Daughter*	Egypt in the time of Moses
Eloise McGraw	*Mara, Daughter of the Nile* *The Golden Goblet*	Egypt in the time of Queen Hatshepsut Ancient Egypt
Jill Rubalcaba	*A Place in the Sun*	Egypt, thirteenth century B.C.
Rosemary Sutcliff	*The Eagle of the Ninth*	Roman Britain
The Middle Ages		
Elizabeth Alder	*The King's Shadow*	England, 1053
Avi	*Crispin: The Cross of Lead*	England, fourteenth century
Kevin Crossley-Holland	*Crossing to Paradise*	1200, England to Jerusalem
Karen Cushman	*Catherine, Called Birdy* *The Midwife's Apprentice*	England, 1290 England
Marguerite de Angeli	*The Door in the Wall*	England, fourteenth century
K. M. Grant	*Blood Red Horse* *Green Jaspar* *Blaze of Silver*	The Crusades
Elizabeth Janet Gray	*Adam of the Road*	England, thirteenth century
Geraldine McCaughrean	*The Kite Rider*	China, thirteenth century in the time of Genghis Kahn
Linda Sue Park	*A Single Shard*	Korea, twelfth century
Laura Amy Schlitz	*Good Masters! Sweet Ladies! Voices from a Medieval Village*	English village, 1255

Author	Title	Time/Place
The Renaissance		
Gary Blackwood	*The Shakespeare Stealer* *Shakespeare's Scribe*	England c. sixteenth century in the time of Shakespeare
J. B. Cheaney	*The Playmaker* *The True Prince*	England c. sixteenth century in the time of Shakespeare
Mary Hoffman	*The Falconer's Knot*	Italy, fourteenth century
E. L. Konigsburg	*The Second Mrs. Giaconda*	Italy, early sixteenth century in the time of Leonardo daVinci
Pilar Molina Llorente	*The Apprentice*	Renaissance, Florence
Lensey Namioka	*Den of the White Fox* *The Coming of the Bear* *Island of Ogres*	Feudal Japan
Katherine Paterson	*The Sign of the Chrysanthemum* *Of Nightingales That Weep* *The Master Puppeteer*	Feudal Japan
Exploration by Sea		
Alan Armstrong	*Raleigh's Page*	Initial exploration of Roanoke Island and the Chesapeake Bay 1585
Henry Garfield	*The Lost Voyage of John Cabot*	Voyage of John Cabot
Karen Hesse	*Stowaway*	Voyage of James Cook
Michelle Torrey	*To the Edge of the World*	Voyage of Magellan
Stories of the Western Hemisphere: Native Americans		
Joseph Bruchac	*The Winter People*	Abenaki village in Canada c. 1759
Louise Erdrich	*The Birchbark House* *The Game of Silence* *The Porcupine Year*	c. 1847, Lake Superior Ojibwa tribe
Kirkpatrick Hill	*Dancing at the Odinochka*	Native Americans in Russian Alaska, late 1800s
Theodora Kroeber	*Ishi, Last of His Tribe*	Yahi Indians of California, early 1900s

(continued)

teaching feature 8.2

Author	Title	Time/Place
Peter Lerangis	*Smiler's Bones*	Native Greenlanders return to the U.S. with Robert Peary, late 1800s

Colonial America

Elisa Carbonne	*Blood on the River*	First settlement at Jamestown, 1607–1610
Jean Fritz	*The Cabin Faced West*	Pre-Revolution, western counties in Pennsylvania
Kathleen Karr	*Worlds Apart*	South Carolina, 1670
Katherine Kirkpatrick	*Escape Across the Wide Sea*	French Huguenots flee to America, 1686
Elizabeth George Speare	*The Witch of Blackbird Pond*	Puritan Connecticut, 1687

The Revolutionary Era

Laurie Halse Anderson	*Chains*	African American sisters in Revolutionary War, New York City
Avi	*The Fighting Ground*	Battle near Trenton, N.J., 1787
James Lincoln Collier and Christopher Collier	*My Brother Sam Is Dead*	Two brothers on opposing sides during the Revolution
	Jump Ship to Freedom *War Comes to Willy Freeman* *Who Is Carrie?*	African Americans' experiences during the Revolution
Esther Forbes	*Johnny Tremain*	Prior to and during the Revolutionary War
Jean Fritz	*Early Thunder*	Loyalist in Massachusetts, 1775
Scott O'Dell	*Sarah Bishop*	British loyalist during Revolutionary period
Kay Winters	*Colonial Voices*	Multiple voices describing events leading to the Revolution

An Expanding Nation

Pam Conrad	*Prairie Songs*	Nebraska, 1880s
Karen Cushman	*The Ballad of Lucy Whipple*	California gold rush, 1880s
Kirby Larson	*Hattie Big Sky*	Montana homesteader, early 1900s
Diane Lee Wilson	*Black Storm Comin'*	Pony Express route, c. 1860

Resistance to Slavery

James Berry	*Ajeemah and His Son*	Father and son are slaves in early 1800s Jamaica
Christopher Paul Curtis	*Elijah of Buxton*	Free settlement of former slaves, Canada early 1860s

Author	Title	Time/Place
Sharon Draper	*Copper Sun*	Parallel stories of an African girl and a white indentured servant who find themselves subject to a brutal slave owner
Julius Lester	*Day of Tears*	Slave auction, 1859 Georgia
Mary E. Lyons	*Letters from a Slave Girl*	Based on the life of Harriet Jacobs
	Letters from a Slave Boy	Based on the life of Joseph Jacobs
Gary Paulsen	*Nightjohn*	Slaves on a Southern plantation, c. 1850

The Civil War

Joseph Bruchac	*March Toward the Thunder*	Abenaki Indian youth in Irish Brigade, 1864
James Lincoln Collier and Christopher Collier	*With Every Drop of Blood*	Southern boy and African American Union soldier
Patricia Lee Gauch	*Thunder at Gettysburg*	Girl caught in the middle of Battle of Gettysburg
Margaret McMullan	*How I Found the Strong*	Southern boy leaves to care for his family
Carolyn Reeder	*Shades of Gray*	Son of a confederate soldier and his pacifist uncle
Rosemary Wells	*Red Moon at Sharpsburg*	Virginia, beginning in 1862

The Age of Economic Revolution

M. J. Auch	*Ashes of Roses*	1911, Triangle Shirt Factory
Katherine Paterson	*Lyddie*	1843, Massachusetts mills
	Bread and Roses	c. 1912, Massachusetts mill strike
Richard Peck	*Fair Weather*	1893, Chicago World's Fair
Tracey Porter	*Billy Creekmore*	1900, coal mines
Elizabeth Winthrop	*Counting on Grace*	1910, Vermont mill town

Immigrants

Patricia Reilly Giff	*Nory Ryan's Song*	Ireland, 1845–1852
	A House of Tailors	Germany to United States, 1870s
	Water Street	Ireland to United States, 1870s
Karen Hesse	*Brooklyn Bridge*	Russian immigrants, 1903
Donna Jo Napoli	*The King of Mulberry Street*	Italy to New York City, late 1800s
Pam Muñoz Ryan	*Esperanza Rising*	Mexico to United States, Great Depression

(continued)

teaching feature 8.2

Author	Title	Time/Place
Laurence Yep	*Dragon's Gate*	China to U.S., 1867
	Dragonwings	China to U.S., 1906
	The Dragon's Child	China to U.S., 1922

The Struggle for Civil Rights

Christopher Paul Curtis	*Bud, Not Buddy*	1930s, Michigan
David L. Dudley	*The Bicycle Man*	1920s, Georgia
Karen English	*Francie*	1940s, Alabama
Shiela Moses	*The Legend of Buddy Bush*	1947, North Carolina
Gary D. Schmidt	*Lizzie Bright and the Buckminster Boy*	1910, Maine
Karen Schwabach	*The Hope Chest*	Women's rights movement
Kashmira Sheth	*Keeping Corner*	India, 1918 during the time of Narmad, peace activist and poet
Mildred Taylor	*Roll of Thunder, Hear My Cry*	1930, Mississippi
Padma Venkatraman	*Climbing the Stairs*	WWII India during the time of Ghandi

The Great Depression

Lesley M. M. Blume	*Tennyson*	Mississippi, 1932
Cynthia DeFelice	*Nowhere to Call Home*	Hoboing on a train west to California
Marian Hale	*The Truth About Sparrows*	Texas
Karen Hesse	*Out of the Dust*	Oklahoma

The World at War

Joseph Bruchac	*Code Talker*	WWII, Navajo soldiers
Iain Lawrence	*Lord of the Nutcracker Men*	WWI
Michael Morpurgo	*Private Peaceful*	WWI
Walter Dean Myers	*Sunrise Over Fallujah*	Iraq, 2003
Margaret I. Rostkowski	*After the Dancing Days*	WWI, aftermath

Escape and Resistance WWII

Susan Campbell Bartoletti	*The Boy Who Dared*	WWII Germany
Sook Nyul Choi	*Year of Impossible Goodbyes*	WWII and aftermath, Korea

Author	Title	Time/Place
David Chotjewitz	*Daniel Half Human and the Good Nazi*	WWII Germany
Yankev Glatshteyn	*Emil and Karl*	Pre-WWII Vienna
Esther Hautzig	*The Endless Steppe*	WWII Siberia
Lois Lowry	*Number the Stars*	WWII Denmark
Linda Sue Park	*When My Name Was Keoko*	Japanese-occupied Korea
Sandi Toksvig	*Hitler's Canary*	WWII Denmark

Linda Sue Park won the Newbery Medal for *A Single Shard*, the story of a young orphan, Tree-Ear, who becomes a master potter of Korea's fabled celadonware. Cover from *A Single Shard* by Linda Sue Park. Jacket and case cover copyright © 2001 by Jean and Mou-sien Tseng. Reprinted by permission of Clarion Books, an imprint of Houghton Mifflin Harcourt Publishing Company. All rights reserved.

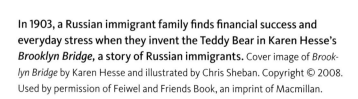

In 1903, a Russian immigrant family finds financial success and everyday stress when they invent the Teddy Bear in Karen Hesse's *Brooklyn Bridge,* a story of Russian immigrants. Cover image of *Brooklyn Bridge* by Karen Hesse and illustrated by Chris Sheban. Copyright © 2008. Used by permission of Feiwel and Friends Book, an imprint of Macmillan.

Challenging Perspectives on Historical Fiction

When children are asked to name their least favorite school subject, the answer is often social studies. Anything to do with history, ancient or modern, seems to turn off young readers. The question for educators then becomes, "How can I pique the interest of my students in historical events? And especially those events that link the past experiences of people near and far to the lived experiences of contemporary times?"

Researchers and observant teachers have concluded that students' interest in social studies (geography, economics, anthropology, political science, etc.) and their ability to learn, retain, and think critically about information increases considerably when their instruction included literature.[8,9]

One efficient way to accomplish this is by integrating social studies education into the language arts curriculum using historical fiction. In almost every classroom—under the umbrella of literacy—students write formal essays, creative stories, poetry, songs, and dialogues. Students can apply the social studies skills, as they read primary sources, secondary sources, historical fiction, and historical nonfiction. One would be hard pressed to find anything that a language arts teacher does that would not integrate smoothly the teaching of social studies curriculum. For example, students can be helped to understand that their social studies book is one source for information, but there are many primary sources, such as documents, photographs, and other artifacts that were created at the time of an event. These primary resources also help to reveal more information about the event in history, often from the narratives from those who lived during that historical time period.

A book that lends itself to this integration is Sharon Draper's *Copper Sun*, a Coretta Scott King Award winner. One review noted: "The historian, if honest, gives us a photograph of the past: the storyteller gives us a painting."[10]

The use of historical fiction raises a challenge for some who believe there is a "truth," and factual evidence of an event should not be distorted by fictional accounts. For example, some teachers did not want to use Faith Ringgold's book, *Aunt Harriet's Underground Railroad in the Sky*. In the book, Cassie returns to the skies, flying way up, so far up that the mountains look like rock candy and the oceans like tiny cups of tea. Cassie and her brother, BeBe, encounter a fantastic train—the Underground Railroad train—and a tiny woman in a conductor's uniform. The woman is Harriet Tubman, who takes Cassie and BeBe on an imaginary journey to the terrifying world of a slave plantation and on a desperate, but ultimately triumphant, escape to freedom.

Drawing on historical accounts of the Underground Railroad, the facts of Harriet Tubman's life, and on the rich resources of her own imagination, Ringgold created a book that both recounts the chilling realities of slavery and joyfully celebrates freedom. How can this award-winning book be a problem? One teacher reported, "After spending so much time on the Underground Railroad—teaching the children it was not a REAL railroad but a metaphor for the escape route of enslaved Africans—the last thing I needed was a book that said it was in the sky!" The dilemma for this teacher was the facts of history put side by side with a fictional account, which confused her young readers. While the accuracy of historical events have a place in the curriculum, when using a work of historical fiction, the focus should be placed on expanding the reader's perspective of a given time and sparking an interest for further investigation and the development of their historical thinking.

Yet another concern is how history is fraught with controversy. When discussing historical fiction and controversial issues, the most common objection raised is, "Why should we impose contemporary values and ideals upon the past?" As mentioned in earlier chapters, discussing controversial issues with children helps to foster their critical thinking and problem-solving ability. Using historical fiction creates an open forum for debating the historical issues juxtaposed with contemporary concerns. As children recognize a selection as a reflection of its social, cultural, and historical context (trying to decipher the past as it was then), they read considering the issues raised in light of situations, conflicts, and themes common to the human experience of the time. Contemporary values may only juxtapose for the purpose of critique or debate and cannot be easily imposed upon the past.

One example is the picturebook *Carl the Complainer* by Michelle Knudsen. Set in Colonial America, the protagonist Carl learns how to turn complaints into petitions and use personal involvement, action, and voice to become a more effective citizen. This story shows that one person can make a difference through determination and perseverance. The petition for redress of grievance to government or existing authority was the method used to establish legal and moral credibility by our nation's founders. It is an individual political right acknowledged and guaranteed to every citizen of a state of the Union in the First Amendment to the Constitution of the United States. Reading Carl's story, students will examine how Carl went from complainer to nonviolent activist. Students can then research Article I of the Constitution and debate how in history and in contemporary times Congress has made laws respecting an establishment of religion, or prohibiting the free exercise thereof, or has abridged the freedom of speech or the press, or the right of the people to peaceably assemble and to petition the government for a redress of grievances.

With careful selection, one can find examples of historical fiction through which two or more strands of the social studies can be taught, and engaging discussions of historical and contemporary controversial issues will promote increased literacy skills. This can happen while the children suspend belief and are enthralled with the story. The Ten-Point Model for Teaching Controversial Issues (**Figure 8.1**, p. 232) can facilitate classroom discussion and support projects for deeper, more focused treatment of historical fiction. Given that historical fiction centers around people and events, it is also the hope that reading, analyzing, and interpreting this genre can facilitate the development of an increased understanding of human dignity, basic rights, and responsibilities of citizens in a democracy—and open-minded respect for individual and cultural differences.

figure 8.1

The Ten-Point Model for Teaching Controversial Issues Using Historical Fiction

Step	Task	To Consider
1. Raise the initial question and have the children brainstorm all their initial responses.	Tackle current controversial issues in history. Ask, "Which episodes in the past still upset people today?"	This is when the sensitive questions about history and memory can be asked: the extermination of Jews in Europe, enslavement of Africans, immigration, etc. These issues are often at the root of controversy in society and school curricula.
2. Create a list of "Things to find out more about."	Students should research historical events and chronology, seeking to find contradictory information and discourse.	They should examine how historians have formulated and organized their arguments, learning to position their ideas and to shape their own historical arguments.
3. Assign information-gathering homework.	Students should gather, evaluate, and synthesize data from a variety of sources (e.g., newspapers, directories, maps, and cookbooks, oral histories from parents and grandparents, diaries, letters, photographs, and/or paintings), to uncover details of historical events.	This will provide opportunities for students to make their own personal, but reasoned, opinion, backed up by research. These opinions can be presented in a classroom-debate format.
4. Share again responses to the initial question in a brainstorming session.	Having students "check in" to share their responses with the class will "put everything on the table" for further exploration and discussion, allowing them to share their perspectives, while respecting the opinions of others.	As students continue to share their perspectives, over time this will facilitate multiple opportunities for students to negotiate and debate opinions that may differ from theirs.
5. Continue the process of gathering information.	Students should research information from historical communities to explore what the "experts" say about the controversies related to history.	As the process of gathering information continues, students should be encouraged to research historical and current debates, using primary documents, and analyze them for reliability. Develop questions regarding the strengths and weaknesses of various sources and identify possible biases and inaccuracies.
6. If a concept emerges that sparks interest, confusion, or conflict, pose it as a new question.	A new way to reframe this issue could be: • What sources should be seen as "the truth"—primary documents (written by the actual person); secondary accounts (written by a historian interpreting events); historical fiction (written by an author dramatizing the historian's interpretation)? • What are the similarities and differences?	Many students have not been encouraged to think critically in their prior learning experiences. They are ready to accept what is in print as "the truth." Here students will be asked to think critically and interpretatively as they make decisions about the validity of all sources.
7. Periodically give the children assignments in class to summarize their thoughts.	A lesson that uses graphic organizers can help students analyze assumptions, scrutinize facts, and discern patterns.	Lists, diagrams, wheels, and charts help students assimilate information from diverse resources and encourage critical thinking.
8. As individual or group projects emerge, follow up on them.	In groups, students could brainstorm a list of questions the protagonist in historical fiction might be asked if he or she were interviewed for a pop magazine or television talk show. Or, have students work in pairs, posing as an interviewer and interviewee.	The interviews could be video or audiotaped and peer-critiqued for authentic voice and historical detail.

figure 8.1 *(continued)*

Step	Task	To Consider
9. Let others know what you are doing.	Encourage dialogue. Invite an author of historical fiction for a visit to discuss his or her process in researching and writing historical fiction.	A local historian that has published on a particular event and an oral historian can come in to compare and contrast "fact" and "fiction."
10. End your project with something either public or permanent.	Students can work with the local historical society and/or museum curators to make special collections of documents, diaries, letters, photos, and so on that correlate with historical fiction available in the school and public libraries.	It's critical to make the experience relevant to the lives of the children. Looking for opportunities for authentic learning experiences will help children create real-world connections.

Source: Adapted from Kreidler, W. *Elementary Perspectives: Teaching Concepts of Peace and Conflict.* Copyright © 1990, Educators for Social Responsibility, Cambridge, MA, www.esrnational.org. Used by permission.

curriculum connections

Using Historical Fiction to Address Standards

Historical fiction provides children with a lens to the past. By reading and engaging in discussions about fictionalized historical events, students have the opportunity to experience a range of emotions and gain knowledge about what life was like during different time periods. Themes such as clashes among cultures (*Crooked River* by Pearsall); war (*When My Name Was Keoko* by Linda Sue Park); freedom (*Jump Ship to Freedom* by Christopher and James Collier); and conflicts in premodern times (*Crispin* by Avi) can be explored by reading historical fiction books. However, connections to other content areas are also possible. For example, Karen Hesse's *Out of the Dust* provides an opportunity to examine the craft of writing in verse, while *Witness* is written in prose from the perspectives of multiple characters. While math concepts are not central to this genre, *The Birchbark House* by Louise Erdrich highlights money and trade, and *Code Talker* by Joesph Bruchac deals with language patterns.

Books such as *Molly Bannaky* by Alice McGill and *A Single Shard* by Linda Sue Park illustrate the science involved in farming and creating pottery.

Standards in Action: Social Studies

> *Henry's Freedom Box: A True Story from the Underground Railroad.*
> > Levine, E. (2007). *Henry's Freedom Box: A True Story from the Underground Railroad.* New York: Scholastic.

Ellen Levine brings to life the courageous tale of Henry Brown in *Henry's Freedom Box: A True Story from the Underground Railroad.* This engaging and well-written picturebook captures the horrific conditions of slavery and the dangerous journey that one man was willing to undertake for freedom. The beautifully detailed illustrations capture the desperation and triumph of Henry's life and his quest for freedom.

(continued)

curriculum connections

(continued)

Apply to Social Studies Standard 2:
Time, Continuity, and Change

Human beings seek to understand their historical roots and to locate themselves in time. Knowing how to read and reconstruct the past allows one to develop a historical perspective and to answer questions such as: Who am I? What happened in the past? How am I connected to those in the past? How has the world changed, and how might it change in the future? Why does our personal sense of relatedness to the past change? This theme typically appears in courses in history and others that draw upon historical knowledge and habits.

- Students can create a cultural autobiography to explore their history and connections to historic events or movements.
- Students can research a significant event from the past that occurred in the town in which they live and can trace the effects of that event to current-day interactions. They can also use the information they gain to predict how this event will shape the future.

Apply to Social Studies Standard 6:
Power, Authority, and Governance

Understanding the historical development of structures of power, authority, and governance and their evolving functions in contemporary U.S. society and other parts of the world is essential for developing civic competence. In exploring this theme, students confront questions such as: What is power? What forms does it take? Who holds it? How is it gained, used, and justified? What is legitimate authority? How are governments created, structured, maintained, and changed? How can individual rights be protected within the context of majority rule? In schools, this theme typically appears in units and courses dealing with government, politics, political science, history, law, and other social sciences.

- Students can create a plan of study that defines power from the perspectives of local government, slaveholders, abolitionists, and slaves. By drawing upon examples in the book, they can provide examples of how each group of people gained and justified their use of power during slavery.
- Students can research how disenfranchised groups responded to unequal forms of power in the U.S. and societies around the world. This information can be shared through drama, music, dance, or song.
- Students can create a government ABC book that explains how different governments protect the rights of their citizens around the world. The book can include different forms of government, political maps, comparisons of the U.S. branches of government to other countries, world leaders, human rights organizations, and list of laws that were changed or created in response to citizen protest.

Source: Standards are from the National Council for the Social Studies and can be found online at <www.socialstudies.org/standards>.

Notes

1. See Marlene Atleo, et al., "A Critical Review of Ann Rinaldi's *My Heart Is on the Ground*," and Beverly Slapin's "A Critical Review of Ann Turner's *The Girl Who Chased Away Sorrow*," available on the World Wide Web at <www.oyate.org>.
2. See Daniel Hade, "Storyselling: Are Publishers Changing the Way Children Read?" *Horn Book Magazine* 78.5 (2002): 509.
3. Margery Fisher, *Intent Upon Reading: A Critical Appraisal of Modern Fiction for Children* (New York: Watts, 1962), p. 225.
4. Mollie Hunter in a lecture at Ohio State University, Columbus, Ohio, November 1968.
5. Mollie Hunter, "Shoulder the Sky," in *Talent Is Not Enough* (New York: Harper, 1976), pp. 43–44.

6. Atleo, et al., "A Critical Review of Ann Rinaldi's *My Heart Is on the Ground*," 1 Aug. 2008 <http://www.oyate.org/bookstoavoid/myHeart.html>.
7. Christopher Collier, "Criteria for Historical Fiction," *School Library Journal* 28 (August 1982): 32.
8. M. Cai, "Variables and Values in Historical Fiction for Children," *The New Advocate* 5.4 (1992): 279–91.
9. E. Freeman and L. Levstick, "Recreating the Past: Historical Fiction in the Social Studies Curriculum," *Elementary School Journal* 88.4 (1988): 329–37.
10. Leon Garfield, "Historical Fiction for Our Global Times," *Horn Book Magazine* 64.6 (1988): 736–39.

Children's Literature

OLC Go to **www.mhhe.com/kiefer1e** to access the *Children's Literature Database, which includes information on thousands of children's books. Following are some of the titles you will find in the database.*

Titles in blue = multicultural titles

Alder, Elizabeth. *The King's Shadow*. Farrar, 1995.

Anderson, Laurie Halse. *Chains*. Simon, 2008.

Armstrong, Alan. *Raleigh's Page*. Random, 2007.

Armstrong, William H. *Sounder*. Illustrated by James Barkley. Harper, 1969.

Auch, M. J. *Ashes of Roses*. Holt, 2002.

Avi [Avi Wortis]. *Crispin: The Cross of Lead*. Hyperion, 2002.

——. *The Fighting Ground*. Lippincott, 1984.

——. *The True Confessions of Charlotte Doyle*. Orchard, 1990.

Bartoletti, Susan Campbell. *The Boy Who Dared*. Scholastic, 2008.

Bartone, Elisa. *Peppe the Lamplighter*. Illustrated by Ted Lewin. Lothrop, 1993.

Berry, James. *Ajeemah and His Son*. HarperCollins, 1992.

Blackwood, Gary. *Shakespeare's Scribe*. Dutton, 2000.

——. *The Shakespeare Stealer*. Dutton, 1998.

Blume, Lesley M. M. *Tennyson*. Knopf, 2008.

Borden, Louise. *Sleds on Boston Common: A Story from the American Revolution*. Illustrated by Robert Andrew Parker. McElderry, 2000.

Brink, Carol Ryrie. *Caddie Woodlawn*. Illustrated by Trina Schart Hyman. Macmillan, 1973.

Bruchac, Joseph. *The Arrow Over the Door*. Dial, 1998.

——. *Code Talker*. Scholastic, 2005.

——. *March Toward the Thunder*. Dial, 2008.

——. *The Winter People*. Dial, 2002.

Bunting, Eve. *Dandelions*. Illustrated by Greg Shed. Harcourt, 1995.

Cheaney, J. B. *The Playmaker*. Knopf, 2002.

——. *The True Prince*. Knopf, 2002.

Choi, Sook Nyul. *Year of Impossible Goodbyes*. Houghton, 1991.

Chotjewitz, David. *Daniel Half Human and the Good Nazi*. Translated by Doris Orgel. Atheneum, 2004.

Clapp, Patricia. *Constance: A Story of Early Plymouth*. Lothrop, 1968.

Collier, James Lincoln, and Christopher Collier. *Jump Ship to Freedom*. Delacorte, 1981.

——. *My Brother Sam Is Dead*. Four Winds, 1974.

——. *War Comes to Willy Freeman*. Delacorte, 1983.

——. *Who Is Carrie?* Delacorte, 1984.

——. *With Every Drop of Blood*. Delacorte, 1994.

Conrad, Pam. *Prairie Songs*. Illustrated by Darryl Zudeck. Harper, 1985.

Crew, Linda. *A Heart for Any Fate: Westward to Oregon, 1845*. Oregon Historical Society, 2005.

Curtis, Christopher Paul. *Bud, Not Buddy*. Delacorte, 1999.

——. *Elijah of Buxton*. Scholastic, 2007.

——. *The Watsons Go to Birmingham—1963*. Delacorte, 1995.

Cushman, Karen. *The Ballad of Lucy Whipple*. Clarion, 1996.

——. *Catherine, Called Birdy*. Clarion, 1994.

——. *The Midwife's Apprentice*. Clarion, 1995.

de Angeli, Marguerite. *The Door in the Wall*. Doubleday, 1949.

DeFelice, Cynthia C. *Nowhere to Call Home*. Farrar, 1999.

Draper, Sharon. *Copper Sun*. Atheneum, 2006.

Dudley, David L. *The Bicycle Man*. Clarion, 2005.

Dyer, T. A. *A Way of His Own*. Houghton, 1981.

English, Karen. *Francie*. Farrar, 1999.

Erdrich, Louise. *The Birchbark House*. Hyperion, 1999.

——. *The Game of Silence*. HarperCollins, 2005.

——. *The Porcupine Year*. HarperCollins, 2008.

Ernst, Kathleen. *Betrayal at Cross Creek*. American Girl, 2004.

Fleischman, Paul. *Bull Run*. HarperCollins, 1993.

Fletcher, Susan. *Walk Across the Sea*. Atheneum, 2001.

Forbes, Esther. *Johnny Tremain*. Illustrated by Lynd Ward. Houghton, 1946.

Fritz, Jean. *The Cabin Faced West*. Illustrated by Feodor Rojankovsky. Coward-McCann, 1958.

——. *Early Thunder*. Illustrated by Lynd Ward. Coward-McCann, 1967.

Frost, Helen. *The Braid*. Farrar, 2006.

Garfield, Henry. *The Lost Voyage of John Cabot*. Atheneum, 2004.

Gauch, Patricia Lee. *Aaron and the Green Mountain Boys*. Boyds Mills, 2005.

——. *Thunder at Gettysburg*. Illustrated by Stephen Gammell. Putnam, 1990 [1975].

Giff, Patricia Reilly. *All the Way Home*. Delacorte, 2001.

——. *A House of Tailors*. Random, 2004.

——. *Lily's Crossing*. Delacorte, 1997.

——. *Maggie's Door*. Random, 2003.

——. *Nory Ryan's Song*. Delacorte, 2000.

Glatshteyn, Yankev. *Emil and Karl*. Translated by Jeffrey Shandler. Roaring Brook, 2006.

Grant, K. M. *Blaze of Silver*. de Granville Trilogy. Walker, 2006.

——. *Blood Red Horse*. de Granville Trilogy. Walker, 2005.

——. *Green Jasper*. de Granville Trilogy. Walker, 2006.

Gray, Elizabeth Janet. *Adam of the Road*. Illustrated by Robert Lawson. Viking, 1942.

Hahn, Mary Downing. *Stepping on the Cracks*. Clarion, 1991.

Hale, Marian. *The Truth About Sparrows*. Holt, 2004.

Hansen, Joyce. *The Captive*. Scholastic, 1994.

——. *I Thought My Soul Would Rise and Fly: The Diary of Patsy a Freed Girl*. Scholastic, 1997.

Hartnett, Sonya. *Thursday's Child*. Candlewick, 2002.

Hautzig, Esther. *The Endless Steppe: Growing Up in Siberia*. Crowell, 1968.

Hesse, Karen. *Brooklyn Bridge*. Illustrated by Chris Sheban. Feiwel, 2008.

——. *The Cats in Krasinski Square*. Illustrated by Wendy Watson. Scholastic, 2004.

——. *Out of the Dust*. Scholastic, 1997.

——. *Stowaway*. McElderry, 2000.

——. *Witness*. Scholastic, 2001.

Hill, Kirkpatrick. *Dancing at the Odinochka*. McElderry, 2005.

Ho, Minfong. *The Clay Marble*. Farrar, 1991.

Hoffman, Mary. *The Falconer's Knot: A Story of Friars, Flirtation and Foul Play*. Bloomsbury, 2007.

Holm, Anne. *North to Freedom*. Translated by L. W. Kingsland. Harcourt, 1965.

Hoobler, Dorothy, and Thomas Hoobler. *The Demon in the Tea-house*. Philomel, 2001.

——. *In Darkness, Death*. Philomel, 2005.

——. *The Ghost in the Tokaido Inn*. Philomel, 1999.

Hopkinson, Deborah. *Under the Quilt of Night*. Illustrated by James E. Ransome. Simon, 2001.

Ibbotson, Eva. *The Star of Kazan*. Illustrated by Kevin Hawkes. Dutton, 2004.

Innocenti, Roberto, and Christophe Gallaz. *Rose Blanche*. Illustrated by Roberto Innocenti. Creative Education, 1985.

Ives, David. *Scrib*. HarperCollins, 2005.

Jones, Elizabeth McDavid. *Mystery on Skull Island*. Pleasant, 2002.

Karr, Kathleen. *Worlds Apart*. Cavendish, 2005.

Kirkpatrick, Katherine. *Escape Across the Wide Sea*. Holiday, 2004.

Konigsburg, E. L. *A Proud Taste for Scarlet and Miniver*. Atheneum, 1973.

——. *The Second Mrs. Giaconda*. Macmillan, 1978.

Kroeber, Theodora. *Ishi, Last of His Tribe*. Illustrated by Ruth Robbins. Parnassus, 1964.

Larson, Kirby. *Hattie Big Sky*. Delacorte, 2006.

Lawrence, Caroline. *The Beggar of Volubilis*. Orion, 2008.

——. *The Fugitive from Corinth*. Roaring Brook, 2006.

——. *The Gladiators from Capua*. Roaring Brook, 2005.

——. *The Pirates of Pompeii*. Roaring Brook, 2003.

——. *The Prophet from Ephesus*. Orion, 2009.

——. *The Scribes from Alexandria*. Orion, 2008.

——. *The Secrets of Vesuvius*. Roaring Brook, 2002.

——. *The Thieves of Ostia*. Roaring Brook, 2002.

Lawrence, Iain. *Lord of the Nutcracker Men*. Delacorte, 2001.

——. *The Smugglers*. Delacorte, 2000.

Lerangis, Peter. *Smiler's Bones*. Scholastic, 2005.

Lester, Julius. *Day of Tears: A Novel in Dialogue*. Hyperion, 2005.

——. *Pharaoh's Daughter: A Novel of Ancient Egypt*. Harcourt, 2000.

LeZotte, Ann Clare. *T4*. Houghton, 2008.

Llorente, Pilar Molina. *The Apprentice*. Translated by Robin Longshaw. Illustrated by Juan Ramón Alonso. Farrar, 1993.

Lowry, Lois. *Number the Stars*. Houghton, 1989.

Lunn, Janet. *The Root Cellar*. Macmillan, 1983.

Lyons, Mary E. *Letters from a Slave Boy: The Story of Joseph Jacobs*. Atheneum, 2007.

——. *Letters from a Slave Girl: The Story of Harriet Jacobs*. Scribner's, 1992.

MacLachlan, Patricia. *Sarah, Plain and Tall*. Harper, 1985.

Maruki, Toshi. *Hiroshima No Pika* (The Flash of Hiroshima). Lothrop, 1980.

McCaughrean, Geraldine. *The Kite Rider*. HarperCollins, 2002.

McGraw, Eloise Jarvis. *The Golden Goblet*. Viking Penguin, 1986 [1961].

——. *Mara, Daughter of the Nile*. Viking Penguin, 1985 [1953].

McMullan, Margaret. *How I Found the Strong*. Houghton, 2005.

McSwigan, Marie. *Snow Treasure*. Illustrated by Alexander Pertzoff. HarperCollins, 1991.

Meyer, Louis A. *Bloody Jack: Being an Account of the Curious Adventures of Mary "Jacky" Faber, Ship's Boy*. Bloody Jack Adventures. Harcourt, 2004.

——. *Curse of the Blue Tattoo: Being an Account of the Misadventures of Jack Faber, Midshipman and Fine Lady*. Bloody Jack Adventures. Harcourt, 2005.

———. *My Bonny Light Horseman: Being an Account of the Further Nautical Adventures of Jacky Faber in Love and War.* Harcourt, 2008.

———. *Under the Jolly Roger: Being an Account of the Further Nautical Adventures of Jacky Faber.* Bloody Jack Adventures. Harcourt, 2005.

Morpurgo, Michael. *Private Peaceful.* Scholastic, 2004.

Morrow, Honoré. *On to Oregon!* Beech Tree, 1991 [1946].

Moses, Sheila. *The Legend of Buddy Bush.* McElderry, 2004.

———. *The Return of Buddy Bush.* McElderry, 2005.

Mosley, Walter. *47.* Little, 2005.

Mowll, Joshua. *Operation Red Jericho.* Candlewick, 2005.

———. *Operation Typhoon Shore.* Candlewick, 2006.

Myers, Walter Dean. *Sunrise Over Fallujah.* Scholastic, 2008.

Namioka, Lensey. *The Coming of the Bear.* HarperCollins, 1992.

———. *Den of the White Fox.* Harcourt, 1997.

———. *Island of Ogres.* Harper, 1989.

Napoli, Donna Jo. *Daughter of Venice.* Random, 2002.

———. *The King of Mulberry Street.* Random, 2005.

O'Dell, Scott. *Sarah Bishop.* Houghton, 1980.

Orlev, Uri. *The Man from the Other Side.* Translated by Hillel Halkin. Houghton, 1991.

Park, Linda Sue. *A Single Shard.* Clarion, 2001.

———. *When My Name Was Keoko.* Clarion, 2002.

Paterson, Katherine. *Bread and Roses, Too.* Clarion, 2006.

———. *Lyddie.* Lodestar, 1988.

———. *The Master Puppeteer.* Harper, 1975.

———. *Of Nightingales That Weep.* Harper, 1974.

———. *The Sign of the Chrysanthemum.* Harper, 1973.

Paulsen, Gary. *Nightjohn.* Delacorte, 1993.

Pearsall, Shelley. *Crooked River.* Knopf, 2005.

Peck, Richard. *Fair Weather.* Dial, 2001.

———. *A Long Way from Chicago.* Dial, 1999.

———. *The Teacher's Funeral: A Comedy in Three Parts.* Dial, 2004.

———. *A Year Down Yonder.* Dial, 2000.

Perez, N. A. *The Slopes of War.* Houghton, 1984.

Porter, Tracey. *Billy Creekmore: A Novel.* HarperCollins, 2007.

Pryor, Bonnie. *The House on Maple Street.* Illustrated by Beth Peck. Morrow, 1987.

Reeder, Carolyn. *Shades of Gray.* Macmillan, 1989.

Rinaldi, Ann. *My Heart Is on the Ground: The Diary of Nannie Little Rose, a Sioux Girl (Dear America).* Scholastic, 1999.

Riskind, Mary. *Apple Is My Sign.* Houghton, 1981.

Rostkowski, Margaret I. *After the Dancing Days.* Harper, 1986.

Rubalcaba, Jill. *A Place in the Sun.* Clarion, 1997.

Ruby, Lois. *Soon Be Free.* Simon, 2000.

———. *Steal Away Home.* Macmillan, 1994.

Ryan, Pam Muñoz. *Esperanza Rising.* Scholastic, 2000.

Salisbury, Graham. *Under the Blood-Red Sun.* Delacorte, 1994.

Schlitz, Laura Amy. *Good Masters! Sweet Ladies! Voices from a Medieval Village.* Illustrated by Robert Byrd. Candlewick, 2008.

Schmidt, Gary D. *Lizzie Bright and the Buckminster Boy.* Clarion, 2004.

Schwabach, Karen. *The Hope Chest.* Random, 2008.

Sheth, Kashmira. *Keeping Corner.* Hyperion, 2007.

Sneve, Virginia Driving Hawk. *Bad River Boys: A Meeting of the Lakota Sioux with Lewis and Clark.* Illustrated by Bill Farnsworth. Holiday, 2005.

Snyder, Zilpha Keatley. *Cat Running.* Delacorte, 1994.

Speare, Elizabeth George. *The Sign of the Beaver.* Houghton, 1983.

———. *The Witch of Blackbird Pond.* Houghton, 1958.

Steele, William O. *The Buffalo Knife.* Illustrated by Paul Galdone. Harcourt, 1952.

———. *Winter Danger.* Illustrated by Paul Galdone. Harcourt, 1954.

Sutcliff, Rosemary. *The Eagle of the Ninth.* Illustrated by C. W. Hodges. Walck, 1954.

Taylor, Mildred. *Roll of Thunder, Hear My Cry.* Illustrated by Jerry Pinkney. Dial, 1976.

Temple, Frances. *The Ramsey Scallop.* Orchard, 1994.

Toksvig, Sandi. *Hitler's Canary.* Roaring Brook, 2007.

Torrey, Michelle. *To the Edge of the World.* Knopf, 2003.

Van Leeuwen, Jean. *Bound for Oregon.* Illustrated by James Watling. Dial, 1994.

Venkatraman, Padma. *Climbing the Stairs.* Putnam, 2008.

Vos, Ida. *Hide and Seek.* Translated by Terese Edelstein and Inez Smidt. Houghton, 1991.

Wait, Lea. *Wintering Well.* McElderry, 2004.

Wells, Rosemary. *Red Moon at Sharpsburg.* Viking, 2007.

Wilder, Laura Ingalls. *Little House on the Prairie.* Illustrated by Garth Williams. Harper, 1953 [1935].

———. *Little Town on the Prairie.* Illustrated by Garth Williams. Harper, 1953 [1932].

Wilson, Diane Lee. *Black Storm Comin'.* McElderry, 2005.

Winthrop, Elizabeth. *Counting on Grace.* Random, 2006.

Wiseman, David. *Jeremy Visick.* Houghton, 1981.

Wood, Frances M. *Daughter of Madrugada.* Delacorte, 2002.

Wyss, Johann David. *The Swiss Family Robinson.* Sharon, 1981 [1814].

Yep, Laurence, with Kathleen S. Yep. *The Dragon's Child: A Story of Angel Island.* Harper, 2008.

———. *Dragon's Gate.* HarperCollins, 1993.

———. *Dragonwings.* Harper, 1977.

Yolen, Jane. *The Devil's Arithmetic.* Viking Penguin, 1990.

Chapter Nine

Nonfiction

Chapter Outline

Celia is a lively 6-year-old who loves to go to the school library because there she can choose any book she wants. At story time she listens eagerly to picture storybooks and other fiction, but the books she chooses to check out, to keep for a time and to pore over at home, are nonfiction. Her favorites are about animals, insects, and the natural world. She often chooses books far above her level of understanding. Part of her fun is looking at the illustrations over and over again, but she also wants an adult to "read" these difficult books to her. In this case, she means reading the picture captions and talking through main ideas or intriguing details in response to her many questions. She joins in the reading by looking for words she knows or can figure out in the boldface headings or diagram labels.

Nonfiction for Today's Child

The audience for nonfiction books is broad, including young children as well as older students, girls as well as boys. Adult ideas about what is appropriate for a given age level are often less important than a child's desire to know about a particular topic. A reader's approach to a nonfiction book might not always be to read pages in order from first to last, as fiction demands. In this type of reading, visual materials play a vital part by focusing interest and clarifying or extending information. Most of all, our example of Celia shows how nonfiction literature can provide a powerful motivation to read and to enjoy experiences with books. Children are curious about the world and how it works, and they develop passionate attachments to the right books at the right time. They deserve teachers and librarians who can help them discover this particular kind of satisfaction in reading.

What Is Nonfiction?

For many years, children's literature scholars have used the term *informational* books rather than *nonfiction* books to designate literature for children that is based in the actual rather than the imagined. One recent trend in children's literature is the movement to the term *nonfiction* rather than *informational*. Author Penny Colman argues that the term *informational* tends to make people think of encyclopedias and textbooks.

> The term does not readily trigger associations with the variety of nonfiction books— biographies, history, true adventures, science, sports, photographic essays, memoirs, etc.—that are available and accessible for children and young adults and that can be just as compelling, engaging and beautifully written as good fiction.[1]

In this chapter we will most often use the term *nonfiction* rather than *informational* to refer to this body of literature, as is common with adult literature.

New worlds and new interests lay waiting for children between the covers of nonfiction books. The secrets of a water droplet, the fascinating world of entomologists, or the search for the legendary pink dolphin have all been revealed in attractive and inviting formats. For proof, have a look at Walter Wick's *A Drop of Water*, Donna M. Jackson's *The Bug Scientists*, or Sy Montgomery's *Encantado: Pink Dolphin of the Amazon*. Nonfiction books also offer children new perspectives on familiar topics, as can be found in Patricia Lauber's *What You Never Knew About Tubs, Toilets, and Showers* or Alexandra Siy and Dennis Kunkel's *Mosquito Bite*. Some nonfiction books, like Darlyne A. Murawski's *Face to Face with Caterpillars* or Stephen Kramer's *Hidden Worlds: Looking Through a Scientist's Microscope*, have tremendous eye appeal and invite browsing. Others are designed to reward sustained attention, like Susan Campbell Bartoletti's *Black Potatoes: The Story of the Great Irish Famine, 1845–1850* or Scott Reynolds Nelson and Marc Aronson's *Ain't Nothing But a Man: My Quest to Find the Real John Henry*. Nonfiction books for children are more numerous, more various, and more appealing than ever.

Awards for Nonfiction

For many years, nonfiction books were overlooked in awards given to children's literature. In 1981, author Betty Bacon pointed out that nonfiction books had won the Newbery Medal only six times in fifty-eight years, and those winners were from history or biography, in which the chronological narrative form is very much like

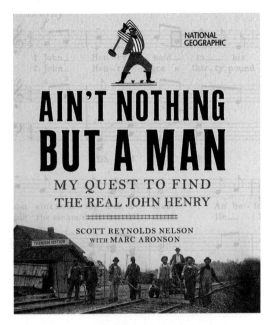

fiction.[2] This is quite a contrast to literature for adults, where authors like John McPhee and Tracy Kidder regularly win critical acclaim for their work, and nonfiction frequently dominates the best-sellers lists. As a result of this imbalance, in 1990 the National Council of Teachers of English established the Orbis Pictus Award for Outstanding Nonfiction for Children. Its name commemorates what is thought to be the first book of facts produced for children, dating back to the seventeenth century. Winners include Tonya Bolden's *M.L.K.: Journey of a King*, Russell Freedman's *Franklin Delano Roosevelt*, Sy Montgomery and Nic Bishop's *Quest for the Tree Kangaroo: An Expedition to the Cloud Forest of New Guinea*, and Jim Murphy's *An American Plague*.

In 2000, the Association of Library Services to Children established the Robert F. Sibert Informational Book Award. This award is meant to honor an author whose work of nonfiction has made a significant contribution to the field of children's literature in a given year. Peter Sis's *The Wall: Growing Up Behind the Iron Curtain*, Susan Campbell Bartoletti's *Black Potatoes: The Story of the Great Irish Famine, 1845–1850*, and James Cross Giblin's *Secrets of the Sphinx* are among those titles named as Sibert Award winners or honor books. The Boston Globe–Horn Book Awards have included a nonfiction category for many years. Some of the books recognized in this category have been Loree Griffin Burns's *Tracking Trash: Flotsam, Jetsam, and the Science of Ocean Motion*, Robie H. Harris's *It's Perfectly Normal: A Book About Changing Bodies, Growing Up, Sex, and Sexual Health*, Nicholas Debon's *The Strongest Man in the World: Louis Cyr*, and Phillip Hoose's *The Race to Save the*

M.L.K.

Tonya Bolden

Lord God Bird. With the Boston Globe–Horn Book recognition and other prestigious awards, there are now many more opportunities for all kinds of nonfiction books to receive the acclaim they deserve.

Evaluating Nonfiction Books

Critic Jo Carr has suggested that teachers and librarians who want to choose the very best books available should be guided by her view that a nonfiction writer is first a teacher, then an artist, and should be concerned with feeling as well as thinking and passion as well as clarity.[3] Specific criteria can be used to help identify this level of achievement. Being familiar with these criteria and with the types of books in which information is presented will make it easier to choose the best books at the right time. The individual reviewer must judge the relative value of the various criteria in terms of particular books. Sometimes a book's strengths in one or two categories may far outweigh its weakness in others. See **Guidelines: Evaluating Nonfiction Books** on page 242 for an overview of these criteria.

Accuracy and Authenticity

Accuracy is of primary importance in nonfiction books for children. No one wants inaccurate information, no matter how well it is presented, especially because many children believe that anything printed in a book is true. The author's qualifications, the way in which the author presents facts and generalizations, the correctness of the illustrations, and many other factors need to be considered in evaluating a book's accuracy and authenticity.

The Author's Qualifications Nonfiction books are written by people who are authorities in their fields, such as astronaut Sally Ride, or they are written by writers who study a subject, interview specialists, and compile the data. A few, like naturalist Jean Craighead George, are both specialists and writers. It is always a good idea to check the book's jacket copy, title page, introduction, or "About the Author" page at the back for information about the author's special qualifications, often expressed in terms of professional title or affiliation. Expertise in one field does not necessarily indicate competency in another, however, so we expect a high degree of authenticity only if the author has limited the book to what appears to be his or her specialty.

If a book is written by a "writer," not by an expert in the field, facts can be checked by authorities and the authorities cited. For example, Donna M. Jackson is an insect enthusiast but is not a trained scientist. In *The Bug Scientists*, however, she acknowledges and names a long list of experts she interviewed and consulted, and photo credits show that the illustrations were furnished by individuals and universities with an established expertise. The record of sources and research provided here gives assurance that the book is accurate. A number of authors have earned the reputation of writing dependably good nonfiction books. When in doubt, teachers and librarians are likely to turn first to writers who have proven their integrity with facts— Penny Colman, Patricia Lauber, James Cross Giblin, Russell Freedman, Milton Meltzer, Laurence Pringle, Seymour Simon, and Helen Roney Sattler, among others. But authorship, while it may be a valuable rule of thumb, is a dangerous final criterion. Each book must be evaluated on its own merits.

Evaluating Nonfiction Books

 Go to www.mhhe.com/kieferbrief1e *to access an expanded version of this evaluation form.*

Consider the following when evaluating nonfiction books for children:

Accuracy and Authenticity

- Is the author qualified to write about this topic?
- Has the manuscript been checked by authorities in the field?
- Are the facts accurate according to other sources?
- Is the information up-to-date?
- Are all the significant facts included?
- Do text and illustrations reveal diversity and avoid stereotypes?
- Are generalizations supported by facts?
- Is there a clear distinction between fact and theory?
- Are the text and illustrations free of anthropomorphism and teleological explanations?

Content and Perspective

- For what purpose was the book designed?
- Is the book within the comprehension and interest range of its intended audience?
- Is the subject adequately covered?
- Are different viewpoints presented?
- Does the book lead to an understanding of the scientific method?
- Does it foster the spirit of inquiry?

- Does the book show interrelationships?
- If it is a science book, does it indicate related social issues? *at least 2 or 3*

Style

- Is information presented clearly and directly?
- Is the text appropriate for the intended audience?
- Does the style create the feeling of reader involvement?
- Is the language vivid and interesting?

Organization

- Is the information structured clearly, with appropriate subheadings?
- Does the book have reference aids that are clear and easy to use, such as a table of contents, index, bibliography, glossary, and appendix?

Illustrations and Format

- Do illustrations clarify and extend the text or speak plainly for themselves?
- Are size relationships made clear?
- Are media suitable to the purposes for which they are used?
- Are illustrations explained by captions or labels where needed?
- Does the total format contribute to the clarity and attractiveness of the book?

Factual Accuracy Fortunately, many of the errors of fact in children's nonfiction books are minor. Children who have access to a variety of books on one topic should be encouraged to notice discrepancies and pursue the correct answer, a valuable exercise in critical reading.

Errors that teachers and children recognize are less distressing than those that pass for fact because the topic is unfamiliar or highly specialized; then the reader must depend on a competent reviewer to identify inaccuracies. Ideally, a book with technical information should be reviewed by someone with expertise in that field. *Appraisal: Science Books for Young People* is a periodical that offers paired reviews, one by a science professional and one by a teacher or librarian. *Science Books and Films* includes reviews by specialists in the field. *Horn Book Magazine* singles out science books for special reviewing efforts, although other nonfiction is included. The *School Library Journal* often provides helpful criticism. *Social Education* and *Science and Chil-*

dren magazines also give some attention to appropriate books, and both publish a list of outstanding books in their respective fields each year. Both of these lists can be accessed through the Children's Book Council Web site at <www.cbcbooks.org>. Generally speaking, science books are more likely to be challenged by experts than are those about history or other topics in the humanities.

Up-to-Dateness Some books that are free of errors at the time of writing become inaccurate with the passage of time, as new discoveries are made in the sciences or as changes occur in world politics. Books that focus on the past are less likely to be rapidly outdated, although new discoveries in archaeology or new theories in history and anthropology call for a reevaluation of these materials also. Kathleen Weidner Zoehfeld's *Dinosaur Parents, Dinosaur Young* details the mistakes that, for many years, led scientists to believe that dinosaur parents did not care for their young. She then describes how scientists Michael Novacek and Mark Norell were able to deduce that the oviraptor actually sat on its nest and incubated its eggs. This type of information helps children to understand how what we know about an extinct species changes as scientists continue to ask questions. Books that focus on subjects in which vigorous research and experimentation are being done, such as viruses and disease or space technology, are even more quickly outdated. It is worth noting, however, that the latest trade books are almost always more up-to-date than the latest textbooks or print encyclopedias.

It is also difficult, but important, to provide children with current information about other countries where national governments are emerging or where future political developments are uncertain. Current events that generate an interest in books about a particular country also call attention to the fact that those books might be out-of-date. Internet sites would be an excellent way to keep track of current events, although these too require critical evaluation. The American Library Association lists more than seven hundred great sites for children. (Go to <www.ala.org> and search "Great Web Sites for Kids.") Teachers will want to make note of other sites vetted by professional organizations, such as the Web site for the National Council for the Social Studies <www.ncss.org> and the Web site for the National Science Teachers Association <www.nsta.org>. Books about minority cultures also need to include material on contemporary experience, as well as heritage. Books like *Celebrating Ramadan* by Diane Hoyt-Goldsmith, show families who take pride in continuing their traditions but who also are clearly people of today's world. Being up-to-date is one of the ways that books of this kind can combat stereotypes.

Inclusion of All the Significant Facts Although the material presented in a book might be current and technically correct, the book cannot be totally accurate if it omits significant facts. Forty years ago science books that dealt with animal reproduction frequently glossed over the specifics of mating or birth. In Robert McClung's *Possum*, the process was explained like this: "All night long the two of them wandered through the woods together. But at dawn each went his own way again. Possum's babies were born just twelve days later."[4] Fortunately, the changing social mores that struck down taboos in children's fiction have also encouraged a new frankness in nonfiction books. For instance, close-up photographs and forthright text in *How You Were Born* by Joanna Cole mark this as a straightforward book about human reproduction and birth. Gail Saltz's *Amazing You!* is a frank and engaging look at male and female sexual organs.

Human reproduction and sexuality have so often been distorted by omissions that books with accurate terminology and explicit information are particularly welcome. Robie H. Harris's *It's Not the Stork! A Book About Girls, Boys, Babies, Bodies, Families, and Friends* is aimed at children in grades kindergarten to third. Older children and adolescents will find that Harris's *It's So Amazing: A Book About Eggs, Sperm, Birth, Babies, and Families* or *It's Perfectly Normal: A Book About Changing Bodies, Growing Up, Sex, and Sexual Health* are thorough and frank guides to adolescent and adult sexuality. In each of these books Michael Emberley's detailed illustrations add a wonderful touch of humor to what is often a touchy subject for this age group.

The honest presentation of all information necessary for understanding a topic is just as important in historical or cultural accounts as in the sciences. This may be difficult to achieve because social issues are complex, and writing for a young audience requires that the author be brief. Judging whether a book includes all the significant facts can also be difficult, for deciding what really counts is a matter of interpretation, often dependent on the book's intended audience. For many years,

Careful research by Catherine O'Neill Grace and Margaret M. Bruchac for *1621: A New Look at Thanksgiving* helps undo many of the stereotypes about the first "Thanksgiving" feast. Photograph from *1621: A New Look at Thanksgiving* by Catherine O'Neill Grace and Margaret M. Bruchac with Plimouth Plantation. Published by the National Geographic Society. Photography copyright © 2001 by Sisse Brimberg and Cotton Coulson.

myths surrounding the first Thanksgiving went unchallenged. In *1621: A New Look at Thanksgiving* Catherine O'Neill Grace and Margaret M. Bruchac, in cooperation with the staff of Plimoth Plantation, show how those myths evolved and present new information. They state:

> In 1947, the founders of Plimoth Plantation created a museum to honor the 17th-century English colonists who would come to be known to the world as the Pilgrims. In doing so, the founders left out the perspective of the Wampanoag people who had lived on the land for thousands of years. At Plimoth Plantation today, we ask questions about what really happened in the past. We draw from the new research of scholars who study documents, artifacts, home sites, culture, and formerly untapped sources such as the Wampanoag people themselves. (p. 7)

This fascinating account includes photographs taken at the museum site and shows children what the harvest festival was probably like. The book also provides an important lesson about historical research and the need to include many sources and many points of view when interpreting historical events.

Avoidance of Stereotypes A book that omits significant facts tells only part of the truth; a book that presents stereotypes pretends, wrongly, to have told the truth. One very common sort of stereotyping is by omission. If we never see women or minorities in science books, for instance, we are left with the incorrect impression that all scientists must be white males. In recent years, fortunately, more authors, illustrators, and publishers have made conscious efforts to represent the great variety of roles that women and minorities play in science and the world of work. Susan Kuklin's *Families*, which includes photographs and voices of children describing their families, surveys the many groupings of loving adults and children who make up today's families. This no-fanfare approach helps combat stereotypes because it encourages children to understand the contributions of people as a matter of course.

Another way authors try to avoid stereotyping is by relating the story of one individual within a community. Diane Hoyt-Goldsmith's books about Native Americans focus on one tribe and then on a particular child's family, school, and community experiences. Readers associate the facts in these books with specific persons and places. Consequently, they should be less likely to assume that this description of Native American life represents the way *all* people of Native American heritage live.

Use of Facts to Support Generalizations To be distinguished from stereotype or simple opinion, a proper generalization needs facts for support. Phillip Hoose provides such support throughout *The Race to Save the Lord God Bird*. Hoose is careful to make sure his readers understand that scientists are not sure if the ivory-billed woodpecker (nicknamed the Lord God Bird for its magnificent plumage) is extinct or not. Instead, Hoose takes readers through the tantalizing mystery of the bird's existence with facts about the sightings and search for the elusive bird. He also provides extensive notes of his sources in an afterword. Laurence Pringle builds a convincing case that global warming is indeed under way in *Global Warming: The Threat of Earth's Changing Climate* through fourteen short chapters that begin with the facts about global warming and end with a call to action to address the challenges of the future. Critical readers need to be aware of generalizations and judge for themselves whether adequate facts are provided to support them.

Distinction Between Fact and Theory In their introduction to *The World Made New: Why the Age of Exploration Happened & How It Changed the World*, Marc Aronson and John W. Glenn state:

> In this book you will often notice us saying "we are not sure" . . . That is not because we were lazy and forgot to check. Rather it is that, recently, historians have been re-examining evidence on these issue and making exciting new discoveries. (p. 5)

Careful writers like these make distinctions between fact and theory; but even so, children need guidance in learning to recognize the difference. Often the distinction depends on key words or phrases—such as *scientists believe, so far as we know*, or *perhaps*. Consider the importance of the simple phrase *may have* in this description of a prehistoric reptile: "Pterodactyls lived near the shores of prehistoric seas and may have slept hanging from trees." Books about the disappearance of the dinosaurs make

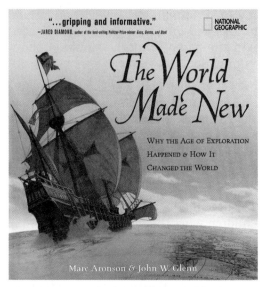

"...gripping and informative."
—JARED DIAMOND, author of the best-selling Pulitzer-Prize winner Guns, Germs, and Steel

NATIONAL GEOGRAPHIC

The World Made New

WHY THE AGE OF EXPLORATION HAPPENED & HOW IT CHANGED THE WORLD

Marc Aronson & John W. Glenn

Marc Aronson and John W. Glenn explain that what we know about history is constantly being updated by new research in *The World Made New: Why the Age of Exploration Happened & How It Changed the World*. From *The World Made New: Why the Age of Exploration Happened & How It Changed the World* by Marc Aronson and John W. Glenn. Published by the National Geographic Society.

good material for helping children sort out the difference between fact and theory, because the problem is dramatic and the evidence provides for legitimate disagreement among scientists. Franklyn Branley's *What Happened to the Dinosaurs?* does a particularly good job of helping primary-age children understand what a theory is.

Although it is important to distinguish between fact and theory in all of the sciences, including the social sciences, the matter receives most attention in books dealing with evolution and human origins. In some communities this is a very sensitive topic, but it would seem that children everywhere have a right to information about scientists' discoveries and theories regarding our origins. Steve Jenkins and Christopher Sloan have provided scientifically valid explanations. Jenkins's *Life on Earth: The Story of Evolution* is an excellent and visually appealing introduction for younger readers. Christopher Sloan's *The Human Story: Our Evolution from Prehistoric Ancestors to Today* is aimed at older children and adolescents and concentrates on the scientific process that built our present-day understanding. It is reassuring to note that balanced coverage of this important topic is available in nonfiction books at a time when many school districts are reluctant to include the topic in their curricula.

Avoidance of Anthropomorphism In poetry and fiction, the assignment of human feelings and behavior to animals, plants, or inanimate objects is called *personification*—an accepted literary device that can be used with great effect. In science, however, this device is unacceptable and is known as *anthropomorphism*. Science writer

Millicent Selsam addressed the problem of interpreting what animals do in one of her early books on animal behavior:

> It is hard to keep remembering that animals live in a different kind of world from our own. They see, hear, smell, and taste things differently. And they do not have human intelligence or emotions, so we must avoid interpreting their behavior in terms of our own feelings and thoughts. For example, it looks to us as though parent birds are devoted to their young in the same way that human parents are devoted to theirs. But only experimental work can show whether this interpretation is true.[5]

Many books with these anthropomorphic touches are still being published. Lorrie Mack's *Animal Families*, aimed at a preschool to primary-grade audience, looks at first glance as if it has all the qualities we ask for in nonfiction. There is a table of contents, a simple glossary and an index, appealing photographs and attractive layout. The style of writing seems typically expository: "There are all kinds of animal families with different ways of life" (p. 8). Look more closely, however, and you will see that in addition to captions and labels on photographs there are speech bubbles where the animal "talks" to the audience. "'My brothers and sisters and I are all VERY hungry,' states a grizzly bear cub" (p. 13). Then in one double-page spread in addition to the speech bubble, a baby duck actually narrates the entire text. In *Antarctica*, an otherwise lovely book about the animal life on this great continent, Helen Cowcher tries to convey the negative impact of human intrusion on the animal life. She states, "Out at sea anxious songs ring out from the depths. Weddell seals call to their friends under the ice."[6] The words *anxious* and *friends* attribute human emotions and human relationships to the seals and may lead children to the types of interpretation that Selsam cautions against. Sandra Markle's *A Mother's Journey* is also an emotionally gripping book about the Antarctic and its emperor penguins, but Markle and illustrator Alan Marks achieve that response through good writing and fine illustration.

Content and Perspective

Consideration of the purpose of a book, its intended audience, and the objectivity of its author can help readers evaluate a nonfiction book's content and perspective. A good nonfiction book should also foster reflective inquiry in children and enable them to see relationships across disciplines.

Purpose It is futile to try to pass judgment on the content of a nonfiction book without first determining the purpose for which the book was designed. Identifying the scope of the book lets us know what we can reasonably expect. A quick look at James Buckley, Jr.'s *The Visual Dictionary of Baseball* reveals a fascinating collection of facts for browsing, whereas both the title and the appearance of Martin Redfern's *The Kingfisher Young People's Book of Space* indicate a comprehensive treatment of the topic. Titles can be misleading, particularly those that promise to tell "all about" a subject but offer limited coverage instead. At best, titles indicate the scope of the book's content and pique the reader's curiosity, as do titles such as *Secrets from the Rocks: Dinosaur Hunting with Roy Chapman Andrews* by Albert Marrin and *Hidden Worlds: Looking Through a Scientist's Microscope* by Stephen Kramer. More about the scope and purpose of nonfiction books can be found in **Teaching Feature 9.1: Types of Nonfiction**.

Types of Nonfiction

Type	Description	Example Title	Author	Grade level
Biography	Well-documented accounts of a person or persons' lives	*My Name Is Celia/ Me llamo Celia*	Monica Brown	1–3
		She Touched the World: Laura Bridgeman, Deaf-Blind Pioneer	Sally Hobart Alexander	4 and up
		Maritcha: A Remarkable Nineteenth-Century American Girl	Tonya Bolden	1–3
		Young Thomas Edison	Michael Dooling	1–3
		Rachel Carson	Ellen Levine	5 and up
Concept Books	Explore the characteristics of a class of objects or of an abstract idea	*A Second Is a Hiccup: A Child's Book of Time*	Hazel Hutchins	PreK–2
		In Your Face	Donna M. Jackson	PreK–2
		Sisters and Brothers	Steve Jenkins and Robin Page	PreK–2
		Black? White! Day? Night!	Laura Seeger	PreK–2
Craft and How-To Books	Give directions for making and doing	*The Big Book for Little Hands*	Marie-Pascale Cocagne	PreK–2
		Ecology Crafts for Kids: 50 Great Ways to Make Friends with Planet Earth	Bobbe Needham	2–5
Documents and Journals	Based on sketchbooks, journals, and original documents	*Antarctic Journal*	Jennifer Owings Dewey	2–5
		Top to Bottom, Down Under	Ted Lewin and Betsy Lewin	2–5
		A Dream of Freedom	Diane McWhorter	4 and up
Experiment and Activity Books	Present activities or experiments to clarify concepts	*Exploring the Solar System*	Mary Kay Carson	2–6
		More Science Experiments You Can Eat	Vicki Cobb	2–5
		African Crafts: Fun Things to Make and Do from West Africa	Lynne Garner	3–6
		Cool Chemistry Concoctions: 50 Formulas That Fizz Foam, Splatter and Ooze	Joe Rhatigan and Veronica Gunter	3–6

Type	Description	Example Title	Author	Grade level
Identification Books	Generally naming books, usually with simple drawings or photographs with appropriate labels	*Tool Book* *Stars and Planets* *Rocks and Minerals*	Gail Gibbons John O'Byrne Edward Ricciuti	PreK–2 3–6 3–6
Life-Cycle Books	Cover all or some part of the cycle of life of animals or plants	*Owls* *Wings of Light: The Migration of the Yellow Butterfly*	Gail Gibbons Stephen Swinburne	K–3 3–6
Nonfiction Picturebooks	Convey information in well-designed picture book format	*An Egg Is Quiet* *Leonardo's Horse* *Pale Male* *Did Dinosaurs Have Feathers?*	Dianna Aston Jean Fritz Janet Schulman Kathleen Weidner Zoehfeld	PreK–3 3 and up 1–4 K–3
Photographic Essays	Photographs are used to particularize general information, to document emotion, to assure the reader of truth in an essentially journalistic fashion	*Capoeira: Game! Dance! Martial Art!* *Face to Face with Wolves* *Owen & Mzee: The True Story of a Remarkable Friendship*	George Ancona Jim Brandenburg Isabella Hatkoff, Craig Hatkoff, and Paula Kahumbu	2–6 2–5 K–3
Specialized Books	Designed to give specific information about a relatively limited topic	*The Story of Salt* *An American Plague* *Quest for the Tree Kangaroo: An Expedition to the Cloud Forest of New Guinea*	Mark Kurlansky Jim Murphy Sy Montgomery	3–6 4 and up 4 and up
Survey Books	Give an overall view of a substantial topic and furnish a representative sampling of facts, principles, or issues	*Steve Caney's Ultimate Building Book* *Those Amazing Musical Instruments!* *Dinosaurs* *Venom* *Chew on This: Everything You Don't Want to Know About Fast Food*	Steve Caney Genevieve Helsby Nigel Marven Marilyn Singer Eric Schlosser and Charles Wilson	4 and up 4 and up 4 and up 4 and up 6–9

Eye-catching photographs and an appealing title will invite children to pick up *Hidden Worlds: Looking Through a Scientist's Microscope* by Stephen Kramer. From *Hidden Worlds: Looking Through a Scientist's Microscope* by Stephen Kramer, photographs by Dennis Kunkel. Jacket photographs copyright © 2001 by Dennis Kunkel. Reprinted by permission of Houghton Mifflin Harcourt Publishing Company. All rights reserved.

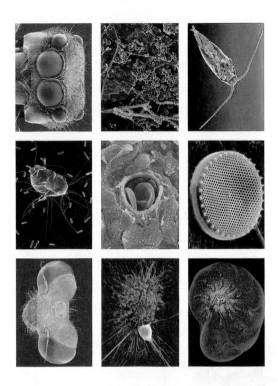

Rafael Lopez's illustrations for *My Name is Celia/Me llamo Celia*, Monica Brown's bilingual picturebook biography of Celia Cruz, sizzles with all the vibrancy of the music of this noted Cuban singer. *My Name is Celia/Me llamo Celia (Bilingual): The Life of Celia Cruz/La vida de Celia Cruz* by Monica Brown and illustrated by Rafael Lopez. Copyright © 2004. Luna Rising Books, a division of Cooper Square Publishing, National Book Network.

Intended Audience Before evaluating content, we have to know not just for what the book was intended, but for whom. Book jackets and book reviews often indicate an age range according to reading level or interest. It is difficult to know whether one or both of these factors are reflected in the age recommendation. Generally, a book's reading level is not as important as its content in relation to the reader's actual interest in a subject. Older students and adults might turn to children's nonfiction books for introductory material on an unfamiliar topic. In using nonfiction books, children will read "beyond their abilities" when reading for particular facts. Children will frequently turn to difficult books if they contain many pictures or useful diagrams. At the same time, vocabulary, sentence length, size of type, and the book's organization are factors to be considered. Children might reject a book that contains useful information if they see crowded pages, relatively small type, and few pictures.

The choice of topic, then, is an important factor in determining whether a book will be suitable for its intended audience. Books for young children most often reflect their basic egocentric concerns and their curiosity about themselves and other living things; it is a mistake to assume that they will not be interested in other subjects, however. Many early primary children enjoy browsing through the widely diverse titles of the Eyewitness series, such as Brian Cosgrove's *Weather* or Lawrence Mound's *Insect*, even though these books are designed for an older audience. On the other hand, books that look like picturebooks are frequently aimed at upper-grade children. Some of these may require readers to keep track of some complex concepts while they follow the ins and outs of the visual and verbal narrative.

Adequacy of Coverage Recognizing the purpose of a book and its intended level, the reader has a basis for deciding if the author has said too much about the topic or too little. Jim Murphy's many fine books, such as *The Great Fire* and *An American Plague*, are close to two hundred pages. The focus of the topic is limited, but the treatment is detailed. Broader topics, like the history or culture of a nation, might require many pages in order to give even brief attention to all the significant material. History textbooks have earned particularly harsh criticism for faulty coverage,[7] and good trade books help fill in perspectives that the textbooks omit. A generation ago, Gerald Johnson expressed the need for careful writing in the introduction to his book *America Is Born*:

> Part of the story is very fine, and other parts are very bad, but they all belong to it, and if you leave out the bad parts you never understand it all. (pp. viii–ix)[8]

Authors who fail to acknowledge more than one viewpoint or theory fail to help children learn to examine issues. Even young children should know that authorities do not always agree, though the context might be simple. It is far more common, though, and certainly more necessary, for books about complex issues to deal with varying points of view.

Demonstration of Scientific Inquiry Because we are concerned about *how* as well as *what* children learn, it is important to note what kind of thinking a book encourages, as well as the body of facts it presents. Nonfiction books should illustrate the process of scientific inquiry, the excitement of discovery. James Cross Giblin's *The Mystery of the Mammoth Bones: And How It Was Solved* and Pamela S. Turner's *Life on Earth—and Beyond; An Astrobiologist's Quest* give readers a good idea of the problems scientists try to solve and the kind of day-to-day work that is involved.

While these are fine accounts of the scientific method at work, the reader's involvement is still vicarious. Some books are designed to give children more direct experience with the skills of inquiry. Millicent Selsam's *How to Be a Nature Detective* encourages children to ask "What happened, who was here, and where did he go?" in order to learn how to read animal tracks. At each step of the process, Marlene Donnelly's illustrations help children follow this sequence as if they were actually outdoors tracking various animals. Many of Jim Arnosky's books, such as *Wild Tracks! A Guide to Nature's Footprints* and *The Brook Book: Exploring the Smallest Streams*, direct attention to important features in the outdoor environment and give background information that helps children interpret what they see.

Methods of scientific inquiry apply to the social sciences, too. In *Ain't Nothing But a Man: My Quest to Find the Real John Henry*, Scott Reynolds Nelson reveals the story of his own historical research as he attempts to find the story behind the legend of John Henry. The search leads him into many dead ends but he eventually lays out a case for what he believes is the truth. The book is a fascinating tale of a real person who might have been behind the legend, and Nelson includes details about the building of a railroad in the story. *Ain't Nothing But a Man* is also a guide to conducting historical research with an afterword by Marc Aronson that encourages students to do their own research. Penny Colman's *Thanksgiving: The True Story* is also told in the first person and begins with the results of an informal survey she sent out asking adults and teens several questions about their understanding of the Thanksgiving story. One hundred percent of the teens and a majority of adults surveyed had learned that the first Thanksgiving was celebrated by Pilgrims and Indians in Plymouth, Massachusetts, in 1621. Colman went on to conduct further research and found at least twelve competing claims for holding the holiday first, from Texas in 1541 to Boston in 1631. In subsequent chapters Colman elucidates on the competing claims, some of the oldest traditions of the holiday, Sarah Josepha Hale's campaign to have a national day of Thanksgiving, and the "Pilgrim and Indian" Story. The book's second section surveys the types of gatherings, the food, and the activities that usually take place on Thanksgiving. The methodology and the organization of the book could easily be replicated by students who want to conduct their own research.

Interrelationships and Implications A list of facts is fine for an almanac, but nonfiction books should be expected to put facts into some sort of perspective. After all, linking facts in one way or another transforms information into knowledge. Thomas Locker's *Sky Tree* shows how the same tree changes through the seasons and how it interacts with the animals, the earth, and the sky around it throughout the year. In *The Tree* by Karen Gray Ruelle and *Building Manhattan* by Laura Vila, time lines put growth in the natural world with perspectives on the growth of human communities.

Interrelationships of a different sort are pointed out in Barbara Brenner's *If You Were There in 1492*. This book helps readers see the cultural context in which a major event, Columbus's first voyage, took place. The author describes the world as it would have been known to ordinary people in Spain in terms of food, clothing, education, books, the arts, crime, ships, and many other aspects. The vivid presentations of the 1492 expulsion of Jews from Spain and the everyday life of the Lucayan people on the island where Columbus landed are especially good for prompting discussion about the relationship of one culture to another.

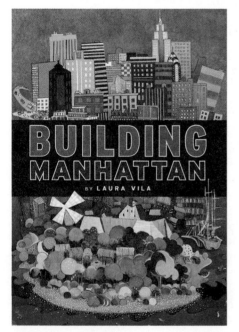

Intertwining science and technology with modern culture has become crucial, and many recent nonfiction books have taken this issue as a focus. *A Home by the Sea: Protecting Coastal Wildlife* by Kenneth Mallory discusses effects of commercial and residential development on coastal wildlife in New Zealand and the efforts being made to protect wildlife species. Even books not specifically designed to call attention to the related social problems of science and technology ought to acknowledge that such problems exist. Where the uses of science have serious implications for society, the relationships should be made clear.

Laura Vila's *Building Manhattan* demonstrates the interrelationships between people and places over time. Cover from *Building Manhattan* by Laura Vila. Copyright © 2008 by Laura Vila. Used by permission of Viking Children's Books, a Division of Penguin Young Readers Group, a Member of Penguin Group (USA) Inc., 345 Hudson Street, New York, NY 10014. All rights reserved.

Style

The style of a nonfiction book can be crucial in attracting children to the book and in helping them understand the concepts presented there. The clarity of presentation and the appropriateness of the language for its intended audience are important matters to consider in evaluating a book's style. In addition, the writing should involve readers in the topic and provide them with an absorbing and vivid learning experience. Author Penny Colman suggests that in evaluating nonfiction writing we should ask how authors effect transitions, craft the ending, "establish a point of view, create a sense of time, use adjectives, adverbs, metaphors, or varied sentence lengths."[9] These qualities of style are just as important in nonfiction as they are in fiction.

Clarity and Directness It is difficult to list all of the criteria that influence clarity. The use of precise language and specific detail is one important factor. Nothing is vague in Miriam Schlein's description of a vampire bat's dinner in *Billions of Bats*. She names the animals that are likely prey ("a horse, a cow, a donkey, or even a chicken"), describes the approach and the bite ("only about a tenth of an inch long"), and goes on to explain how the bat curves its tongue into a funnel shape and sucks in blood ("for about a half hour"). The language is simple and direct, giving the reader a clear picture of the process.

Many writers and publishers of nonfiction for children seem to believe that information needs to be presented in the guise of fiction. Some of the most popular nonfiction picturebooks of recent years are the Magic School Bus stories by Joanna Cole and Bruce Degen. *The Magic School Bus inside the Earth* was followed by other titles. Although the story element in books like this might help children understand facts, they could also confuse children who are still sorting out real and make believe. In addition when a picturebook is only loosely based in fact, as in Emily Arnold McCully's *The Bobbin Girl* or Pam Conrad's *Call Me Ahnighito*, we cannot call it nonfiction (perhaps *informational fiction* or *faction*[10] would be good terms)—and we need to make sure children understand the difference. Across grade levels teachers will need to help children develop their own criteria for evaluating nonfiction that includes ever finer distinctions between what is made up and what is not made up.

Level of Difficulty Although the vocabulary does have to be within the child's range, books for primary-grade children need not be restricted to a narrow list of words. New terms can be explained in context. In *Follow the Water from Brook to Ocean*, Arthur Dorros provides a two-paragraph description of the effects of moving water before introducing the word *erosion*. He also gives helpful context through examples and illustrations for the words *meanders* and *reservoir*. Context does not serve to explain everything, however; a writer aware of the background of the intended audience takes pains to make new words clear. Words that look unpronounceable are another stumbling block for most children. A glossary is helpful, but youngsters who are intent on a book's content might not take time to look in the back. In some cases, authors provide pronunciation guides in parentheses for daunting words. Such is the case in Caroline Arnold's *Pterosaurs* and Cathy Camper's *Bugs Before Time: Prehistoric Insects and Their Relatives*.

Reader Involvement Authors use many different techniques to engage their readers' attention and help them stay involved with a book's subject matter. Alexandra Siy begins *Mosquito Bite* with black-and-white photographs of a girl and a boy playing a backyard game of hide-and-seek. As the boy peeks from behind a tree, the tantalizing text reads like the introduction to a horror film:

> He listens. He hears the girl's footsteps near the garden, or the driveway, now by the flowers along the walk. She's getting closer. Suddenly there's another sound. A droning buzz. The boy's hand flutters across his face and brushes the back of this neck. Something else is looking for the boy. (p. 5)

Siy and photographer Dennis Kunkel then go on to describe the life cycle of the *Culex pipiens* mosquito using stunning colorized electron micrographs.

Nonfiction authors also use direct address—sentences that speak to the reader as "you." Sometimes an author asks direct questions to claim a bond of communication with the reader. Paul Showers hooks the primary-grade audience for *How Many Teeth?* with a variety of rhymes interspersed throughout the text to ask "How many teeth have you?"

One technique that lends itself to nonfiction for children is called "creative nonfiction." Such writers of adult nonfiction as Annie Dillard and Frank Conroy have long used this approach to invigorate their topics.[11] Author Penny Colman explains that in writing creative nonfiction, "I adhere to the basic tenets of nonfiction writing as well as use stylistic and narrative strategies traditionally found in fiction."[12] Colman begins *Corpses, Coffins, and Crypts: A History of Burial* with her own reflection about spending the day with her uncle's dead body, and in subsequent chapters she relays the real-life experiences of many others to cover subjects such as autopsies, embalming and cremation, and burial customs. These real-life experiences and personal reflections add zest to her explanations, yet her meticulous research and attention to detail are evident not only in her writing but also in her extensive use of archival material and site visits. The results are highly engaging books like *Corpses, Coffins, and Crypts* and *Rosie the Riveter: Women Working on the Home Front in World War II.*

Vividness of Language The writer of nonfiction books uses the same techniques as the writer of fiction to bring a book to life, although the words must be accurate as well as attractive. Imagery is used to appeal to the senses, as in Barbara Bash's *Ancient Ones: The World of the Old-Growth Douglas Fir*:

> Walking into an old-growth forest, you enter a strangely silent world. The Earth feels moist and springy underfoot, and the air is thick with the fragrance of decomposing needles. (p. 7)

This quiet beginning in Jim Murphy's *Gone A-Whaling* provides a sense of anticipation:

> The water in the bay was calm. Mewing gulls soared and dipped feverishly, searching for fish, before gliding off toward the rocky shore. For a few seconds, all was quiet. (p. 9)

When a forty-ton whale erupts out of the sea, the reader's emotional leap is all the more exciting. Children probably will not be able to describe an author's style, but they certainly will respond to it. They know that a well-written nonfiction book somehow does not sound the same as an encyclopedia essay, and they enjoy the difference.

Organization

Even if a book is vividly written, accurate, and in command of its topic, children will not find it very useful unless it also furnishes a clear arrangement of information.

The way a book's content is structured and the reference aids it includes should help readers find and understand key concepts and facts.

Structure Every author must choose a structure, or organizing principle, as a basis for presenting facts. Sometimes an author uses a very obvious principle, such as organizing a collection of facts alphabetically. This format allows Jonathan Chester to introduce readers to interesting details about mountain climbing in *The Young Adventurer's Guide to Everest: From Avalanche to Zopkio*. In this book, as in others, the alphabet device makes a good format for browsing and is easily understood by children, although it pays less attention to the relationship among facts.

The question-and-answer approach has become more widely used in recent years. For very young children, questions and pictured answers can change a concept book into an engaging guessing game. Several of Margaret Miller's books, such as *Guess Who?* repeat a question and suggest four silly answers; turn the page and discover a word or phrase and the photographs of the correct answer. Melvin Berger and Gilda Berger's Question and Answer series includes hard-to-resist titles such as *How Do Frogs Swallow with Their Eyes? Where Did the Butterfly Get Its Name?* and *Why Do Volcanoes Blow Their Tops?* These books, meant for middle graders, begin with a brief, one-page overview followed by such questions as "How hot is it inside the earth?" "Does all rock melt?" and "What makes a volcano erupt?"

A common and sensible arrangement for many books, especially about history or biological processes, is based on chronology. Kate Waters's *Samuel Eaton's Day* and *Sarah Morton's Day* allow modern-day children to compare their own morning-to-nighttime activities to those of children who lived almost four hundred years ago. *Cactus Hotel* by Brenda Guiberson reveals both history and science in its account of the two-hundred-year growth of a giant saguaro cactus.

Regardless of its topic, a general-survey type of book should have a system of headings that helps the reader get an overview of the content, unless the book is very brief and has pictures that serve as graphic guides for skimming. The longer the book and the more complex its topic, the greater the need for manageable division. Subheadings are helpful as indicators of structure, especially for less-practiced readers.

Reference Aids With the exception of certain simple and special types, factual books should offer help at both front and back for the reader who needs to locate information quickly. It is important for children to develop reference skills early, so a table of contents and an index should be included in any book whose structure warrants it. Ann Morris's concept books for younger children, including *Shoes, Shoes, Shoes*, provide visual indexes with additional information about each of the countries that she has visited in photographs in the books. A map identifies each of the countries shown in the pictures. This is a good way to introduce younger readers to indexes and other reference aids. For older children, an index will be truly useful only if it is complete and has necessary cross-references. It is difficult to think of all the possible words children might use to look up a topic or to answer a question, yet writers should consider as many possibilities as seem reasonable.

Other helpful additions to a book are glossaries, bibliographies, suggestions for further reading, and nonfiction appendixes. Picture glossaries are on the increase with the growing number of nonfiction picturebooks. Nancy Winslow Parker and Joan Richards Wright include an illustrated glossary that summarizes growth patterns and adds detail about anatomy in their joint production *Bugs*. This book would be good for demonstrating to children the use of reference aids, because it has touches of humor that add appeal as well as a full range of devices for locating and extending information.

If children are to understand methods of inquiry, they need to learn that a writer uses many sources of information. Penny Colman's *Corpses, Coffins and Crypts* has five pages of references. In an author's note Colman provides information about the people whose experiences she related, and she lists the sources that were particularly helpful to her. Photo credits that include many of her own photographs show how thorough and wide-ranging her research was.

Appendixes are used to extend information in lists, charts, or tabulations of data that would seem cumbersome in the text itself. *Commodore Perry in the Land of the Shogun*, Rhoda Blumberg's award-winning account of the opening of Japanese harbors to American ships, seems all the more credible because of the documents and lists presented in the appendixes. Having read that lavish gifts were exchanged during the negotiations, children can discover in an appendix that the emperor was offered more than thirty items, including two telegraph sets, a copper lifeboat, champagne, tea, muskets, swords, and two mail-bags with padlocks.

Illustrations and Format

In our visually oriented culture, readers of all ages demand that a book's illustrations make it more interesting and attractive. In a nonfiction book, the illustrations and design must do that, and much more. Researchers who have traditionally focused on the grammar or structures of written text have turned to the construction of visual text and have demonstrated how important these visual elements are to understanding of meaning and concepts, especially in nonfiction. Even young children readily learn to "read" the information in pictures and format.

Clarification and Extension of Text One of the basic functions of the visual material in nonfiction books is to clarify and extend the text. The visual material consists of illustrations and photographs but also can include such devices as labels, cutaways, cross-sections, diagrams, and graphs. Books by Gail Gibbons such as *Corn* and *Monarch Butterfly* provide younger readers with a first look at these visual devices.

The more abstract the topic, the more important it is that pictures help children "see" explanations. Latitude, longitude, and other mapping concepts, for instance, are often hard for children to grasp, so it is especially important that they be illustrated clearly, as Harriet Barton has done for Jack Knowlton's introductory book *Maps and Globes*. These big, bright pictures use color to focus attention on the equator, contour lines, and other specific aspects of simplified maps.

Illustrations are especially important in clarifying size relationships. Paul Facklam's illustrations for Margery Facklam's *The Big Bug Book* show the actual size of really big bugs and then place them with familiar objects to help children visualize just how large they really are. Illustrator Steve Jenkins has delighted younger children with his *Actual Size* and *Prehistoric Actual Size*, both of which make use of an extra-large trim size, double-page spreads, and foldouts to give children a sense of their own size in relation to different animals. For example, only the teeth of the great white shark are shown on a twelve-inch by twenty-inch double-page spread. Not many topics lend themselves to life-size portrayals, of course, and that makes it important for artists to find other ways to be clear. Photographs and drawings often show magnified parts or wholes, and often some information about actual size is needed.

In many books the visual materials add detail and extend the information of the text; in others the illustrations themselves provide the bulk of the information, or become the subject of the text. In Walter Wick's *A Drop of Water*, the amazing photographs invite the reader to ask questions about such things as how a straight pin can indent the surface of water in a glass or how a huge bubble can rest on a metal frame. The text functions here to clarify and extend the pictures rather than the other way around. When illustrations are this important to a book, they need to have substantive content, high-quality reproduction, and a logical presentation or layout. For other good examples of effective presentation, look at Seymour Simon's books about the planets or Patricia Lauber's *Volcano: The Eruption and Healing of Mt. St. Helen's*.

In nonfiction books such as *Corn* by Gail Gibbons, children learn to recognize visual materials such as cross-sections, labels, and diagrams. Illustration from *Corn* by Gail Gibbons, used by permission of Holiday House.

Suitability of Media Both illustrations and photographs can be clear and accurate, but one medium might be more suitable than another for a given purpose. We have talked with some young children who believe that a book is nonfiction because it has photographs and fiction because it has illustrations. It is important for teachers to help students think about why a particular medium has been chosen for a particular subject.

Paul Carrick and Bruce Shillinglaw's paintings in *Dinosaur Parents, Dinosaur Young: Uncovering the Mystery of Dinosaur Families* by Kathleen Weidner Zoehfeld are important in allowing the reader to visualize the circumstances that may have led to the creation of the oviraptor fossils. Illustrators can also create cutaways, diagrams, and other visuals that would not be possible with photographs. On the other hand, paintings would not create the sense of wonder that photographs do in *Hidden Worlds: Looking through a Scientist's Microscope* by Stephen Kramer. It is important for teachers to help children consider the reasons for the choices of media for nonfiction books. Diagrams and drawings have an impact of their own and also have many uses especially appropriate to science books. Diagrams can reduce technological processes to their essentials or show astronomical relationships that represent distances too great to be photographed.

Sometimes the perception of a graphic artist is vital to the purpose of a book. David Macaulay's *The Way Things Work* and *The Way We Work* explain how mechanical devices and human bodies work, and though both books have an engaging, almost lighthearted approach, they both represent years of research from this talented author. His *Cathedral*, *City*, *Castle*, *Pyramid*, and *Mosque* lead us step-by-step through the building of these amazing constructions and also demonstrate the ways in which humans have been involved in their conception and their use. Macaulay certainly set the standard for excellence, attention to detail, and touches of humor in his illustrated nonfiction.

In spite of the range of media available for nonfiction books, the medium of choice is now photography. Photographs help establish credibility for real-life stories like Diane Hoyt-Goldsmith's *Las Posadas: An Hispanic Christmas Celebration* and add to the fascination of such topics as bog people in James M. Deem's *Bodies from the Ash*. Photographs reveal the natural world in its astonishing variety, recording minute detail in an instant. The photos by Nic Bishop for Joy Cowley's *Chameleon, Chameleon* and *Red-Eyed Tree Frog* reveal marvels of skin textures, colors, and patterns that would be difficult to reproduce with complete accuracy in a painting.

Photographs in nonfiction books furnish more than technical accuracy, however. Photographers can be artists as well as recorders of information. Sometimes artistry results not from a single photographer's work but from the careful choice of pictures to accompany a nonfiction text. The photographs that illustrate Seymour Simon's many books come from a variety of sources, but their effect is breathtaking in such books as *Guts, Horses, Galaxies,* and *Crocodiles and Alligators*.

Captions Children need to be able to look at an illustration and know what they are seeing, and that requires a wise use of captions and labels. Many writers use the text itself, if it is brief, to explain the pictures, eliminating the need for additional captions. The short paragraphs in much of Kathryn Lasky's *Interrupted Journey: Saving Endangered Sea Turtles* are clearly situated next to Christopher G. Knight's photographs. The arrangement of the text on the page and clear references to details in each picture help readers get maximum information about the rescue efforts of Kemp's ridley turtles by the staff of the New England Aquarium.

Sometimes it is helpful to have labels or other text printed within the illustration itself. In *Maps: Getting from Here to There* by Harvey Weiss, many drawings and diagrams include labels and arrows to show specifically where items like "a south latitude" or "an east longitude" are represented on the globe. Explanation within the pictures also helps identify contour lines and the features of a marine chart. Only occasionally does Weiss use a conventional caption to refer to an entire illustration. However an author chooses to use captions, they should be clear.

Format The total look of a book is its *format*, involving type size, leading (space between the lines), margins, placement of text and pictures, and arrangement of front and back matter—these include title and copyright pages in the front and indexes, bibliographies, and other aids at the back. *Mummies Made in Egypt* by Aliki incorporates hieroglyphic writing on the dedication and half-title pages, and many of the illustrations are arranged like the friezes that decorated the tombs of antiquity. This author frequently arranges sequences of pictures on the page in a comic strip or storyboard variation.

There are no absolute rules for format; the look of a book should be responsive to its purpose and its content. The broad coverage of topic intended in the Eyewitness series published by DK makes the busy layout of its pages seem rich rather than crowded. On the other hand Steve Jenkins nonfiction books for younger children including *Actual Size* and *Prehistoric Actual Size* feature a less complicated page layout with bright full-color collage illustrations. Even a book that is sparingly illustrated can be notable for its overall design. Spacious margins and tastefully ornamented headings can make a long text seem less forbidding. The format of a nonfiction book is an asset if it contributes to clarity or if it makes the book more appealing to its audience.

Challenging Perspectives on Nonfiction

Children are naturally curious about the world around them. For some children, however, reading nonfiction may be difficult as it requires a different repertoire of skills, or a mastery of a different set of reading strategies, than those needed to read fiction. As teachers help students learn to read in the content areas (such as math, science, and social studies), the understanding of the structure and specialized vocabulary of nonfiction produce particular challenges for both teaching and learning.

When reading fiction, we start at the beginning of the book, we read all the words, on all the pages, until we get to the end of the text. This strategy is fine for reading fiction, but it cannot be transferred to reading other texts. For example, when reading *Green Eggs and Ham Cookbook*, students would not read it from beginning to end if they want to find out how to cook green eggs. They would go to the page with that recipe on it and follow those directions. Similarly, students reading *National Geographic Our World: A Child's First Picture Atlas* would not read all the pages of an atlas if they want to know where Johannesburg, South Africa, is.

Gathering of information and learning about new things may require more time when reading nonfiction books. For example, it may take more time to study the illustrations, diagrams, charts, and graphs, and less time reading the text. To increase comprehension, readers will have to stop and think about what they are reading and make sure they understand what they are reading before proceeding in the book. It may require students to look in other books for more information and to learn unfamiliar vocabulary.

For elementary classroom teachers, the controversies with this genre are usually reduced to how much "reality" children can handle. For example, the National Council of Teachers of English (NCTE) 2007 Orbis Pictus Award winner for outstanding nonfiction for children, *Quest for the Tree Kangaroo: An Expedition to the Cloud Forest of New Guinea* by Sy Montgomery, might be used by many teachers in science to study animals or as a study of Papua, New Guinea. However, some teachers may find another notable book, the 2008 Orbis Pictus Honorable Mention *Freedom Walkers: The Story of the Montgomery Bus Boycott*, a story by Russell Freedman about how racism was confronted during the civil rights era, is not developmentally appropriate for young readers.

As with contemporary realistic fiction, some parents and community members feel that some nonfiction materials are excessively violent or too scary for children. Concerns about material range from texts with mature themes (such as human sexuality or graphic language) to disturbing illustrations some feel are unsuitable for children. Examples of children's books that have received both school and public library request for removal include:

- *Dr. Ruth Talks to Kids: Where You Came from, How Your Body Changes and What Sex Is All About* by Dr. Ruth Westheimer. Concerns were expressed about an overly permissive stance on sexuality.
- *Life Doesn't Frighten Me* by Maya Angelou. Concerns were expressed that biographical material included in the book was not appropriate for children.
- *Mommy Laid an Egg* by Babette Cole. Concerns were expressed that content was inappropriate for children.

There is no recipe or formula that a teacher can use to know which book will be appropriate or not. Teachers must know their children in order to make selections that are appropriate to the development of their students. The nonfiction collections found in classrooms and school libraries are intended to serve a wide variety of interests and a very diversified student population. When an issue of current interest seems controversial or unresolved, the classroom teacher should gather from the genre, nonfiction in this case, materials showing a variety of viewpoints and differing opinions on that issue. Today's children have an immense capacity to analyze, critique, and challenge the realities of their daily lives. Using nonfiction can be just one tool to help facilitate increasing the knowledge base as children continue to make sense of the world.

There are a number of important reasons that support using nonfiction with children:[13]

- **Nonfiction provides the key to success in later schooling.** As readers advance in grade, they more frequently face content-area textbooks as well as informational passages on tests. Including more nonfiction texts in early schooling puts them in a better position to handle reading and writing demands in later grades.

- **Nonfiction prepares students to handle real-life reading.** Studies show that adults read a great deal of nonfiction both at home and on the job.[14,15] Also, there is a growing reliance upon Web-based material and the need for information competency, including how to interpret and evaluate information. Thus, students must be able to read and write informational text.

- **Nonfiction appeals to readers' preferences.** As Ron Jobe and Mary Dayton-Sakari describe in *Info-kids: How to Use Nonfiction to Turn Reluctant Readers into Enthusiastic Learners*, some students simply prefer information text. Using these resources in your classroom may improve attitudes toward reading and even serve as a catalyst for overall literacy development.[16]

- **Nonfiction addresses students' questions and interests.** Many studies have illustrated that regardless of readers' text preferences, when the text *topic* interests them, their reading is likely to improve. Not surprisingly then, approaches emphasizing reading for the purpose of addressing students' real questions tend to lead to higher achievement and motivation.[17]

- **Nonfiction builds knowledge of the natural and social world.** Students who are reading and listening to nonfiction will develop a greater knowledge of the world,[18,19] acquiring background knowledge that will help them comprehend subsequent texts.[20] Overall, the more background knowledge readers have, the stronger their comprehension skills are likely to be.

- **Nonfiction boosts vocabulary and other kinds of literacy knowledge.** According to researchers, parents and teachers focus more on vocabulary and literacy concepts when reading nonfiction texts aloud versus when they read narrative text.[21,22] This extra attention from parents and teachers may make nonfiction well suited for building a student's word knowledge.[23,24] Learning to read diagrams, tables, and other graphical devices that are often part of informational text may develop visual literacy.

See **Figure 9.1** for ways to use the Ten-Point Model to incorporate nonfiction into the classroom.

figure 9.1 The Ten-Point Model for Teaching Controversial Issues Using Nonfiction

Step	Task	To Consider
1. Raise the initial question and have the children brainstorm all their initial responses.	An open-ended question could begin the discussion of age and developmentally appropriate use of nonfiction. • Who should decide when a work of children's literature is "objectionable"? • Does the same criteria apply to nonfiction? • Who decides what is appropriate or not?	Children have a natural sense of fairness and could participate in discussions and make compelling arguments for "who" gets to decide what is appropriate or not. While they may not have the final decisions, engaging them in the conversation will help them develop higher thinking skills of analysis, synthesis, and evaluation.
2. Create a list of "Things to find out more about."	Students should research their school district's policies that govern the selection and use of children's literature in general and nonfiction texts in particular.	Children should have exposure very early to research and reference skills. Helping them learn how to use the many technological references, books, and resources will lay a foundation for later academic success.
3. Assign information-gathering homework.	Students should gather, evaluate, and synthesize data from a variety of sources (e.g., parents, grandparents, community members, book store owners, religious leaders, librarians, P.T.A. members, school board members, city government officials, state department of education representatives, and so on).	This will provide opportunities for students to make their own personal but reasoned opinion, backed up by research.
4. Share again responses to the initial question in a brainstorming session.	Students could create a Web-based threaded discussion, permitting others in the classroom to check in and share their information and responses with each other.	This creates a "cyber" safe-space to put everything "on the table" for further exploration and discussion, sharing their perspectives while respecting the opinions of others.
5. Continue the process of gathering information.	Students should explore information from teachers to determine how decisions are guided when choosing nonfiction for classroom library collections, student assignments, and as supplemental resources.	Teachers could also be surveyed for their opinions related to using nonfiction children's literature so students will know the "truth." What sources should be seen as "the truth"?
6. If a concept emerges that sparks interest, confusion, or conflict, pose it as a new question.	A new way to reframe this issue could be: • Should authors/illustrators and librarians be proactive, pushing teachers to provide children with accuracy? • When should parents' feelings or opinions be considered?	In this age of testing, we are living in an academic world of the "right" answer. While creative imagination has its place, inaccurate information may lead to children making other flawed assumptions.
7. Periodically give the children assignments in class to summarize their thoughts.	A lesson that introduces students to the skill set necessary to compare and contrast texts will help them first determine why a nonfiction text could be controversial. After developing a set of criteria to determine if it is "fact" or "fiction," students can use their ability to engage in describing, explaining, instructing, persuading, and retelling to compile the information gathered.	Once a determination is made, the students could discuss if the book should or should not be used with students at their grade level.

(continued)

figure 9.1 *(continued)*

Step	Task	To Consider
8. As individual or group projects emerge, follow up on them.	Students will no doubt "take sides" as the information about the text are gathered and critiqued. Put them into groups to continue with similar perspectives.	Later they can debate the issue in either writing or discussion.
9. Let others know what you are doing.	A letter home to parents will alert them of the use of books that may seem controversial. If you are not certain, discuss this with your school administrator and librarian.	A permission form sent to parents with possible "controversial" titles may create unnecessary alarm, but will allow parents to decide if something is objectionable material for either religious or cultural traditions.
10. End your project with something either public or permanent.	Students can work with other students in their school and school district to continue the discussion of what is appropriate and who gets to decide.	It's critical to make the experience relevant to the lives of the children. Looking for opportunities for authentic learning experiences will help children create real-world connections.

Source: Adapted from Kreidler, W. *Elementary Perspectives: Teaching Concepts of Peace and Conflict.* Copyright © 1990, Educators for Social Responsibility, Cambridge, MA, www.esrnational.org. Used by permission.

curriculum connections

Using Nonfiction to Address Standards

Nonfiction books have been written on many topics, but even books on a single topic can be used to support content standards from a range of subjects. For example, books about the weather could teach about social studies, language arts, and even math concepts in addition to science. Weather-related events and their effects on people, whether from the distant past like the Ice Age or from a more recent event like Hurricane Katrina, can come to life for students through books. Jim Murphy's *Blizzard! The Storm That Changed America* (2000) recounts an 1888 winter storm through riveting text and historic illustrations and photographs. Michael Cooper's *Dust to Eat* (2004) describes the Dust Bowl of the West and the resulting migration of people to California. *Dust to Eat* contains poems and song lyrics popular at the time, which could be a way to introduce language arts skills in addition to social studies information. The Dr. Seuss series The Cat in the Hat's Learning Library contains *Oh Say Can You Say What's the Weather Today?* (Rabe, 2004) that teaches about weather entirely in rhyme. Language arts standards can also be met in books that deal with weather more scientifically, such as *Earth's Wild Winds* by Sandra Friend (2002) and *Wild Weather* by Warren Faidley and Caroline Harris (2005),

(continued)

through the study of various types of texts and text features, including charts, tables, diagrams, and descriptive passages. Lynda DeWitt's *What Will the Weather Be?* (1991) even introduces a variety of tools for weather measurement, which could be integrated with math lessons.

Standards in Action: Science

Weather

Simon, Seymour. (2006). *Weather*. New York: HarperCollins.

This revised edition of Simon's 1993 *Weather* explores multiple aspects of weather-related phenomena. It includes high-quality photographs of weather events to help illustrate Simon's discussion of the causes of weather patterns. Students who are interested in taking the knowledge of weather-related events to a higher level will find the information and layout of this book engaging and informative.

Apply to Science Content Standard B—Physical Science

Properties of objects and materials; position and motion of objects; light, heat, electricity, and magnetism; motions and forces.

- Students will participate in a variety of demonstrations such as rubbing balloons together, or rubbing a small plastic comb with wool and holding it near a metal doorknob to gain deeper understanding about the relationship between static electricity and lightning.

- Students will conduct research on electricity, light, and heat and use the information they learn to create fact books.
- Students will explore the effects that wind speed has on objects by using leaves, feathers, paper, and tissue to determine which object is carried farthest by the wind. This experience will allow them to investigate and explore the motion and forces of wind.

Apply to Science Content Standard D—Earth and Space Science

Properties of earth materials; objects in the sky; changes in earth and sky; properties and changes of properties in matter; motions and forces; transfer of energy.

- Students will collect data about local weather patterns to analyze changes that occur over time. They will use spreadsheets and charts to collect, display, and discuss their findings.
- Students will also observe and record clouds daily as they research different cloud types. Students will use this information to create a cloud mural, using photographs, illustrations, or 3-D representations of the four basic cloud types. This information will be used to assist students to create forecasts for their area.

Source: Standards are from the National Science Content Standards by the National Committee on Science Education Standards and Assessment, the National Research Council, and the Center for Science, Mathematics, and Engineering Education (1996).

Notes

1. Penny Colman, "Nonfiction Is Literature Too," *New Advocate* 12.3 (summer, 1999): 217.
2. Betty Bacon, "The Art of Nonfiction," *Children's Literature in Education* 12 (spring, 1981): 3.
3. Jo Carr, "Writing the Literature of Fact," in *Beyond Fact: Nonfiction for Children and Young People* (Chicago: American Library Association, 1982), pp. 3–12.
4. Robert McClung, *Possum* (New York: Morrow, 1963), p. 41.
5. Millicent Selsam, *Animals as Parents*, illustrated by John Kaufmann (New York: 1965), p. 16.
6. Helen Cowcher, *Antarctica* (New York: Farrar, Strauss & Giroux, 1990), unpaged.

7. See Frances FitzGerald, *America Revised* (Boston: Atlantic/Little, Brown, 1979).

8. Gerald White Johnson, *America Is Born*, illustrated by Leonard Everett Fisher (New York: William Morrow, 1959).

9. Colman, "Nonfiction Is Literature Too," p. 220.

10. See Carol Avery, "Nonfiction Books: Naturals for the Primary Level," in *Making Facts Come Alive: Choosing Quality Nonfiction for Children*, ed. Rosemary Banford and Janice Kristo (Norwood, Mass.: Christopher Gordon, 1998).

11. Lee Gutkind, "From the Editor: The 5R's of Creative Nonfiction," *Creative Nonfiction* 6 (1996): 1–16.

12. Colman, "Nonfiction Is Literature Too," p. 219.

13. N. K. Duke, V. S. Bennett-Armistead, and E. M. Roberts, "Bridging the Gap Between Learning to Read and Reading to Learn," in *Literacy and Young Children: Research-Based Practice*, ed. D. M. Barone and L. M. Morrow (New York: Guilford Press, 2003), pp. 226–42.

14. R. L. Venezky, "The Origins of the Present-Day Chasm Between Adult Literacy Needs and School Literacy Instruction," *Visible Language* 16, (1982): 112–27.

15. M. C. Smith, "The Real-World Reading Practices of Adults," *Journal of Literacy Research* 32 (2000): 25–32.

16. L. J. Caswel and N. K. Duke, "Non-Narratives as a Catalyst for Literacy Development," *Language Arts* 75 (1998): 108–117.

17. J. T. Guthrie, P. Van Meter, A. D. McCann, A. Wigfield, L. Bennett, et al. Growth in Literacy Engagement: Changes in Motivations and Strategies During Concept-Oriented Reading Instruction," *Reading Research Quarterly* 31 (1996): 306–32.

18. E. Anderson and J. T. Guthrie, *Motivating Children to Gain Conceptual Knowledge from Text: The Combination of Science Observation and Interesting Texts*, paper presented to the annual meeting of the American Educational Research Association, Montreal, Canada, April 1999.

19. N. K. Duke and J. Kays, "Can I Say Once Upon a Time? Kindergarten Children Developing Knowledge of Information Book Language," *Early Childhood Research Quarterly* 13 (1998): 295–318.

20. P. T. Wilson and R. C. Anderson, "What They Don't Know Will Hurt Them: The Role of Prior Knowledge in Comprehension," in *Reading Comprehension from Research to Practice*, ed. J. Oransano (Hillside, N.J.: Erlbaum, 1986).

21. J. M. Mason, C. L. Peterman, B. M. Powell, and B. M. Kerr, "Reading and Writing Attempts by Kindergarteners After Book Reading by Teachers, in *Reading and Writing Connections*, ed. J. M. Mason (Boston: Allyn & Bacon, 1989), pp. 105–120.

22. A. D. Pelligrini, J. C., Perlmutter, L. Galda, and G. H. Brody, "Joint Reading Between Head Start Children and Their Mothers," *Child Development* 61 (1990): 443–53.

23. M. J. Dreher, "Fostering Reading for Learning," in *Engaging Young Readers: Promoting Achievement and Motivation*, ed. L. Baker, M. J. Dreher, and J. Guthrie (New York: Guilford, 2000), pp. 94–118.

24. N. K. Duke, V. S. Bennett-Armistead, and E. M. Roberts, "Incorporating Information Text in the Primary Grades," in *Comprehensive Reading Instruction Across Grade Levels*, ed. C. Roller (Newark, Del.: International Reading Association, 2002).

Children's Literature

Go to **www.mhhe.com/kiefer1e** *to access the Children's Literature Database, which includes information on thousands of children's books. Following are some of the titles you will find in the database.*

Titles in blue = multicultural titles

Nonfiction

Alexander, Sally Hobart, and Robert Alexander. *She Touched the World: Laura Bridgeman, Deaf-Blind Pioneer*. Clarion, 2008.

Aliki [Aliki Brandenberg]. *Mummies Made in Egypt*. Crowell, 1979.

Ancona, George. *Capoeira: Game! Dance! Martial Art!* Lee, 2007.

Anderson, Maxine. *Amazing Leonardo da Vinci: Inventions You Can Build Yourself*. Nomad Press, 2006.

Armstrong, Jennifer. *Shipwreck at the Bottom of the World: The Extraordinary True Story of Shackleton and the Endurance*. Crown, 1988.

Arnold, Caroline. *Pterosaurs: Rulers of the Skies in the Dinosaur Age*. Illustrated by Laurie Caple. Clarion, 2004.

Arnosky, Jim. *The Brook Book: Exploring the Smallest Streams*. Dutton, 2008.

———. *Wild Tracks! A Guide to Nature's Footprints*. Sterling, 2008.

Aronson, Marc, and John W. Glenn. *The World Made New: Why the Age of Exploration Happened & How It Changed the World*. Illustrated by Gil Davies. National Geographic, 2007.

Aston, Dianna. *An Egg Is Quiet*. Illustrated by Sylvia Long. Chronicle, 2006.

Bartoletti, Susan Campbell. *Black Potatoes: The Story of the Great Irish Famine, 1845–1850*. Houghton, 2001.

———. *Growing Up in Coal Country*. Houghton, 1996.

———. *Hitler Youth: Growing Up in Hitler's Shadow*. Scholastic, 2005.

Bash, Barbara. *Ancient Ones: The World of the Old-Growth Douglas Fir*. Sierra Club, 1994.

Berger, Melvin, and Gilda Berger. *How Do Frogs Swallow with Their Eyes?* Illustrated by Karen Carr. Scholastic, 2003.

———. *Where Did the Butterfly Get Its Name? Questions and Answers About Butterflies and Moths*. Scholastic, 2005.

———. *Why Do Volcanoes Blow Their Tops?* Illustrated by Higgins Boyd. Scholastic, 2002.

Blumberg, Rhoda. *Commodore Perry in the Land of the Shogun*. Lothrop, 1985.

Bolden, Tonya. *Maritcha: A Remarkable Nineteenth-Century American Girl*. Abrams, 2005.

———. *M.L.K.: Journey of a King*. Abrams, 2007.

Branley, Franklyn M. *What Happened to the Dinosaurs?* Illustrated by Marc Simont. Crowell, 1989.

Brenner, Barbara. *If You Were There in 1492*. Bradbury, 1991.

Brown, Monica. *My Name Is Celia/Me llamo Celia: The Life of Celia Cruz/La vida de Celia Cruz*. Illustrated by Rafael Lopez. Luna Rising, 2004.

Buckley, James, Jr. *The Visual Dictionary of Baseball*. DK, 2001.

Burns, Marilyn. *Good for Me! All About Food in 32 Bites*. Little, 1978.

Camper, Cathy. *Bugs Before Time: Prehistoric Insects and Their Relatives*. Illustrated by Steve Kirk. Simon, 2002.

Caney, Steve. *Steve Caney's Ultimate Building Book*. Illustrated by Lauren House. Running Press, 2006.

Carson, Mary Kay. *Exploring the Solar System: A History with 22 Activities*. Chicago Review Press, 2006.

Chester, Jonathan. *The Young Adventurer's Guide to Everest: From Avalanche to Zopkio*. Tricycle, 2002.

Cobb, Vicki. *More Science Experiments You Can Eat*. Illustrated by Peter Lippman. Lippincott, 1972.

Cocagne, Marie-Pascale. *The Big Book for Little Hands*. Illustrated by Bridget Strevens-Marzo. Tate, 2007.

Cole, Joanna. *How You Were Born*. Photographs by Margaret Miller. HarperCollins, 1994.

———. *The Magic School Bus and the Science Fair Expedition*. Illustrated by Bruce Degen. Scholastic, 2006.

Colman, Penny. *Corpses, Coffins and Crypts: A History of Burial*. Holt, 1997.

———. *Rosie the Riveter: Women Working on the Home Front in World War II*. Crown, 1994.

———. *Thanksgiving: The True Story*. Holt, 2008.

Conrad, Pam. *Call Me Ahnighito*. Illustrated by Richard Egielski. HarperCollins, 1995.

Cooper, Michael. *Dust to Eat: Drought and Depression in the 1930s*. Clarion, 2004.

Cosgrove, Brian. *Weather*. DK, 2007.

Cowcher, Helen. *Antarctica*. Farrar, 1990.

Cowley, Joy. *Chameleon, Chameleon*. Photographs by Nic Bishop. Scholastic, 2005.

———. *Red-Eyed Tree Frog*. Photographs by Nic Bishop. Scholastic, 1999.

Davies, Nicola. *Ice Bear: In the Steps of the Polar Bear*. Illustrated by Gary Blythe. Candlewick, 2005.

Debon, Nicolas. *The Strongest Man in the World: Louis Cyr*. Groundwood, 2007.

Dewey, Jennifer Owings. *Antarctic Journal: Four Months at the Bottom of the World*. HarperCollins, 2001.

———. *Mud Matters*. Photographs by Stephen Trimble. Cavendish, 1998.

DeWitt, Lynda. *What Will the Weather Be?* Illustrated by Caroline Croll. HarperCollins, 1991.

Dooling, Michael. *Young Thomas Edison*. Holiday House, 2005.

Dorros, Arthur. *Follow the Water from Brook to Ocean*. HarperCollins, 1991.

Facklam, Margery. *The Big Bug Book*. Illustrated by Paul Facklam. Little, 1994.

Faidley, Warren, and Caroline Harris. *Wild Weather*. Kingfisher, 2005.

Freedman, Russell. *Franklin Delano Roosevelt*. Clarion, 1990.

Friend, Sandra. *Earth's Wild Winds*. 21st Century, 2002.

Fritz, Jean. *Leonardo's Horse*. Illustrated by Hudson Talbot. Putnam, 2001.

Garner, Lynne. *African Crafts: Fun Things to Make and Do from West Africa*. Chicago Review Press, 2008.

Gibbons, Gail. *Corn*. Holiday, 2008.

———. *Monarch Butterfly*. Holiday, 1989.

———. *Owls*. Holiday, 2005.

———. *Tool Book*. Holiday, 1982.

Giblin, James Cross. *The Mystery of the Mammoth Bones: And How It Was Solved*. HarperCollins, 1999.

———. *Secrets of the Sphinx*. Illustrated by Bagram Ibatoulline. Clarion, 2005.

Grace, Catherine O'Neill, and Margaret M. Bruchac. *1621: A New Look at Thanksgiving*. Photographs By Sisse Brimberg and Cotton Coulson. National Geographic, 2001.

Harris, Robie H. *It's Not the Stork! A Book About Girls, Boys, Babies, Bodies, Families, and Friends*. Illustrated by Michael Emberley. Candlewick, 2006.

———. *It's Perfectly Normal: A Book About Changing Bodies, Growing Up, Sex, and Sexual Health.* Illustrated by Michael Emberley. Candlewick, 1994.

———. *It's So Amazing: A Book About Eggs, Sperm, Birth, Babies, and Families.* Illustrated by Michael Emberley. Candlewick, 1999.

Hatkoff, Isabella, Craig Hatkoff, and Paula Kahumbu. *Owen & Mzee: The True Story of a Remarkable Friendship.* Photos by Peter Greste. Scholastic, 2006.

Helsby, Genevieve. *Those Amazing Musical Instruments!* Sourcebooks, 2007.

Hoose, Phillip. *The Race to Save the Lord God Bird.* Farrar, 2004.

Hoyt-Goldsmith, Diane. *Celebrating Ramadan.* Photographs by Lawrence Migdale. Holiday, 2001.

———. *Potlatch: A Tsimshian Celebration.* Photographs by Lawrence Migdale. Holiday, 1997.

Hutchins, Hazel. *A Second Is a Hiccup: A Child's Book of Time.* Illustrated by Kady MacDonald Denton. Scholastic, 2007.

Jackson, Donna M. *The Bug Scientists.* Houghton, 2002.

———. *In Your Face: The Facts About Your Face.* Viking, 2004.

Jenkins, Steve. *Actual Size.* Houghton, 2004.

———. *Life on Earth: The Story of Evolution.* Houghton, 2002.

———. *Prehistoric Actual Size.* Houghton, 2005.

Jenkins, Steve, and Robin Page. *Sisters and Brothers: Sibling Relationships in the Animal World.* Houghton, 2008.

Kramer, Stephen. *Hidden Worlds: Looking Through a Scientist's Microscope.* Photographs by Dennis Kunkel. Houghton, 2001.

Kuklin, Susan. *Families.* Hyperion, 2006.

Kurlansky, Mark. *The Story of Salt.* Illustrated by S. D. Schindler. Putnam, 2006.

Lasky, Kathryn. *Interrupted Journey: Saving Endangered Sea Turtles.* Photographs by Christopher G. Knight. Candlewick, 2001.

Levine, Ellen. *Rachel Carson.* Viking, 2007.

Lewin, Ted, and Betsy Lewin. *Top to Bottom, Down Under.* HarperCollins, 2005.

Locker, Thomas, with Candace Christiansen. *Sky Tree.* HarperCollins, 1995.

Macaulay, David. *Castle.* Houghton, 1977.

———. *Cathedral: The Story of Its Construction.* Houghton, 1973.

———. *City: The Story of Roman Planning and Construction.* Houghton, 1974.

———. *Mosque.* Houghton, 2003.

———. *Pyramid.* Houghton, 1975.

———. *The Way Things Work.* Houghton, 1988.

———. *The Way We Work.* Houghton, 2008.

Mack, Lorrie. *Animal Families.* DK, 2008.

Mallory, Kenneth. *A Home by the Sea: Protecting Coastal Wildlife.* Gulliver, 1998.

Markle, Sandra. *A Mother's Journey.* Illustrated by Alan Marks. Charlesbridge, 2005.

Marrin, Albert. *Secrets from the Rocks: Dinosaur Hunting with Roy Chapman Andrews.* Dutton, 2002.

Marven, Nigel. *Dinosaurs.* Kingfisher, 2007.

McCully, Emily Arnold. *The Bobbin Girl.* Dial, 1996.

McWhorter, Diane. *A Dream of Freedom: The Civil Rights Movement from 1954–1968.* Scholastic, 2004.

Montgomery, Sy. *Encantado: Pink Dolphin of the Amazon.* Photographs by Diane Taylor Snow. Illustrated by Liddy Hubbell. Houghton, 2002.

———. *Quest for the Tree Kangaroo: An Expedition to the Cloud Forest of New Guinea.* Photographs by Nic Bishop. Houghton, 2006.

Morris, Ann. *Shoes, Shoes, Shoes.* Lothrop, 1995.

———. *Weddings.* Lothrop, 1995.

Murawski, Darlyne A. *Face to Face with Caterpillars.* National Geographic, 2007.

Murphy, Jim. *An American Plague: The True and Terrifying Story of the Yellow Fever Epidemic of 1793.* Houghton, 2003.

———. *Blizzard! The Storm That Changed America*. Scholastic, 2000.

———. *Gone A-Whaling: The Lure of the Sea and the Hunt for the Great Whale*. Clarion, 1998.

———. *The Great Fire*. Scholastic, 1995.

Nelson, Kadir. *We Are the Ship: The Story of Negro League Baseball*. Hyperion, 2008.

Nelson, Scott Reynolds, with Marc Aronson. *Ain't Nothing But a Man: My Quest to Find the Real John Henry*. National Geographic, 2008.

O'Byrne, John. *My First Pocket Guide: Stars and Planets*. National Geographic, 2002.

Parker, Nancy Winslow, and Joan Richards Wright. *Bugs*. Illustrated by Nancy Winslow Parker. Greenwillow, 1987.

Patent, Dorothy Hinshaw. *Shaping the Earth*. Photographs by William Muñoz. Clarion, 2000.

Pelta, Kathy. *Discovering Christopher Columbus: How History Is Invented*. Lerner, 1991.

Perl, Lila. *The Great Ancestor Hunt: The Fun of Finding Out Who You Are*. Clarion, 1989.

Pringle, Laurence. *Global Warming: The Threat of Earth's Changing Climate*. SeaStar, 2001.

Rabe, Tish, and Aristides Ruiz. *Oh Say Can You Say What's the Weather Today?* Dr. Seuss series The Cat in the Hat's Learning Library. Random, 2004.

Redfern, Martin. *The Kingfisher Young People's Book of Space*. Kingfisher, 1998.

Reinhard, Johann. *Discovering the Inca Ice Maiden: My Adventure on Ampato*. National Geographic, 1998.

Rhatigan, Joe, and Veronika Gunter. *Cool Chemistry Concoctions: 50 Formulas That Fizz, Foam, Splatter and Ooze*. Illustrated by Tom La Baff. Lark, 2007.

Ricciuti, Edward. *Rocks and Minerals*. Scholastic, 1998.

Schlosser, Eric, and Charles Wilson. *Chew on This: Everything You Don't Want to Know About Fast Food*. Houghton, 2006.

Seeger, Laura. *Black? White! Day? Night!* Roaring Brook, 2006.

Showers, Paul. *How Many Teeth?* Illustrated by True Kelley. HarperCollins, 1991.

Simon, Seymour. *Animal Fact/Animal Fable*. Illustrated by Diane de Groat. Crown, 1987.

———. *Crocodiles and Alligators*. HarperCollins, 1999.

———. *Galaxies*. Morrow, 1988.

———. *Guts*. HarperCollins, 2005.

———. *Horses*. HarperCollins, 2006.

———. *Weather*. HarperCollins, 2006.

Singer, Marilyn. *Venom*. Darby Creek, 2007.

Sis, Peter. *The Wall: Growing Up Behind the Iron Curtain*. Farrar, 2007.

Siy, Alexandra, and Dennis Kunkel. *Mosquito Bite*. Charlesbridge, 2005.

Sloan, Christopher. *The Human Story: Our Evolution from Prehistoric Ancestors to Today*. National Geographic, 2004.

Swinburne, Stephen R. *Wings of Light: The Migration of the Yellow Butterfly*. Illustrated by Bruce Hiscock. Boyds Mills, 2006.

Thimmesh, Catherine. *Team Moon: How 400,000 People Landed Apollo 11 on the Moon*. Houghton, 2006.

Watts, Claire. *Disaster*. DK, 2006.

Webb, Sophie. *My Season with Penguins: An Antarctic Journal*. Houghton, 2000.

Weiss, Harvey. *Maps: Getting from Here to There*. Houghton, 1991.

Weitzman, David. *My Backyard History Book*. Illustrated by James Robertson. Little, 1975.

Wick, Walter. *A Drop of Water*. Scholastic, 1997.

Zoehfeld, Kathleen Weidner. *Did Dinosaurs Have Feathers?* Illustrated by Lucia Washburn. HarperCollins, 2004.

———. *Dinosaur Parents, Dinosaur Young: Uncovering the Mystery of Dinosaur Families*. Illustrated by Paul Carrick and Bruce Shillinglaw. Clarion, 2001.

Part Three

The Literature Program Across the Curriculum

Chapter Ten

Planning the
Literature Program

Chapter Outline

Students in a combined fifth- and sixth-grade class unanimously agreed that *The Pinballs* by Betsy Byars was their favorite book. Their teacher then asked them to discuss the book, telling what it was that made them like it so much. Part of their discussion follows:

> Lenny says, "This is the best book I've ever read. I'd like to know Harvey because I'd like to cheer him up." He decides that "he shows real courage because he has two broken legs." Barb adds, "All the kids do because they have to go to a foster home." "So does Thomas J. because the twins are going to die and he has to go to the hospital to see them," says Will. Jack talks about Carlie, saying, "She's really funny because she's so rude." The teacher suggests that a book that is "basically serious can have funny elements." Tom says, "You know that Carlie is really tough." Then Tom goes on to explain the title by saying, "Carlie thinks they're pinballs because they are always being thrown around like pinballs."

By April of that year, eighteen of the class had read *The Pinballs*. They also were reading other Betsy Byars books; thirteen had read *The Summer of the Swans*, eight *Goodbye, Chicken Little*.[1] Individual children had read many books (from 24 to 122 over the year), yet they singled out *The Pinballs* as their favorite. Though it was still difficult for them to articulate why they liked the story, they had moved beyond the usual circular kind of statement, "I liked it because it was good." They were beginning to recognize the importance of character development and readily identify with Carlie and Harvey. Lenny, who was not a particularly good reader and had read few books, empathized with Harvey to the point of wanting to comfort him. These students had extended their horizons to imagine the courage it would require to live in a foster home away from their family and to have to visit people who are dying in the hospital. Tom attempted a rough statement of the meaning of the title without any prompting.

In this class, book discussions occurred every day during the last fifteen minutes of an hour-long period for sustained silent reading. The children readily supported each other in their selection of books and in their evaluations; they exemplify a "community of readers." It is obvious from their discussion that they were gaining a greater sense of form and were beginning to see more in books than just story.

It takes time for reading and literature to grow in a classroom. The children in this class had, for the most part, been exposed to good literature throughout their school attendance. The teacher had been working on a literature-based curriculum over a period of several years to develop children who loved reading. From this base she added a growing appreciation for and understanding of good literature.

Purposes of the Literature-Based Curriculum

Each school's staff will want to develop its own curriculum in terms of the background and abilities of the children it serves. Teachers and librarians need to know both their children and the potential of their material and have an understanding of the structure of literature; then they will be free to make the right match between child and book. This chapter can suggest guidelines and give examples, but it cannot prescribe the literature-based curriculum that will work with all children.

One of the major purposes of any literature-based curriculum is to provide children with the opportunity to experience literature, to enter into and become involved in a book. The goal of all such programs should be not only to teach children to learn but also to help them learn to love reading, to discover joy in reading. Their every activity, every assignment, should pass this test: "Will this increase children's desire to read? Will it make them want to continue reading?" A literature-based curriculum must get children excited about reading, turned on to books, tuned in to literature.

A second goal of a literature-based curriculum is to build critical knowledge and understanding (currently represented by content-area standards) through integrated experiences with genres and disciplines. This type of integration builds on current theories of how individual children develop and learn.[2] It gives children opportunities for critical inquiry in areas that have relevance to their lives and futures. A literature-based curriculum also allows teachers to provide opportunities for learning for children of widely differing abilities and interests.[3] **Teaching Feature 10.1: Fact and Fiction: Books to Use Together** provides examples of how to link various genres of books with themes of study at different grade levels.

A school literature program should also help children develop literary awareness and appreciation. We want children to develop an understanding of literary genres and to recognize the unique qualities and criteria of many types of literature. We want to introduce children to literary classics and to the authors and illustrators who create the books that they love. We expect that over time children will become familiar with the many components of fiction and nonfiction literature. However, their knowledge

A story map of "The Story of the Three Little Pigs" helped first-grade children to retell the story. Columbus Public Schools, Columbus, Ohio. Connie Compton, teacher.

about literature should be secondary to their wide experiencing of literature. Too frequently, we have substituted the study of literary criticism for the experience of literature itself. Attention to content should precede consideration of form.

teaching feature 10.1

Fact and Fiction: Books to Use Together

Eggs (Grades K–1)

An Egg Is Quiet (Aston)	Nonfiction
Egg (Burton)	Nonfiction
The Perfect Nest (Friend)	Nonfiction
Nana's Big Surprise / Nana, ¡que sorprésa! (Peréz)	Picturebook
An Extraordinary Egg (Lionni)	Picturebook
A Nestful of Eggs (P. Jenkins)	Nonfiction
Just Plain Fancy (Polacco)	Picturebook
Guess What Is Growing Inside This Egg? (Posada)	Nonfiction
Where Do Chicks Come From? (Sklansky)	Nonfiction
When Chickens Grow Teeth (de Maupassant)	Picturebook
From Chick to Chicken (Powell)	Nonfiction
The Odd Egg (Gravett)	Picturebook
Cook-a-Doodle-Doo! (Stevens and Stevens)	Picturebook
The Talking Eggs (San Souci)	Traditional
Big Fat Hen (Baker)	Counting Book
Chicken Man (Edwards)	Picturebook
Daniel's Mystery Egg (Ada)	Easy Picturebook
Hilda Hen's Search (Wormell)	Picturebook

Bugs (Grades 2–3)

Bugs (Parker and Wright)	Nonfiction
Bugs: Poems about Creeping Things (Harrison)	Poetry
It's a Butterfly's Life (Kelly)	Nonfiction
Monarch Butterfly (Gibbons)	Nonfiction
Ladybug (Bernhard)	Nonfiction
The Big Bug Book (Facklam)	Nonfiction
The Tarantula Scientist (Montgomery)	Nonfiction
Face to Face with Caterpillars (Murawski)	Nonfiction
Flit, Flutter, Fly (Hopkins)	Poetry
Big Bugs (Simon)	Nonfiction
Joyful Noise (Fleischman)	Poetry
Honey in a Hive (Rockwell)	Nonfiction
The Little Buggers (Lewis)	Poetry
What's That Bug? (Froman)	Nonfiction

(continued)

teaching feature 10.1

Bugs (Grades 2–3) (continued)

Bugs! (Greenberg)	Poetry
Bugs Are Insects (Rockwell)	Nonfiction
James and the Giant Peach (Dahl)	Fantasy
Bugs: Poems About Creeping Things (Harrison)	Poetry
Creepy Crawlies (Wallace)	Nonfiction
Spiders (Bishop)	Nonfiction
Diary of a Spider (Cronin)	Picturebook
Diary of a Fly (Cronin)	Picturebook

Wet Weather (Grades 1–3)

Weather (Cosgrove)	Nonfiction
Wild Science Projects About Earth's Weather (Gardner)	Nonfiction
Terrible Storm (Hurst)	Picturebook
Down Comes the Rain (Branley)	Nonfiction
Come a Tide (Lyon)	Picturebook
A Rainy Day (Markle)	Nonfiction
Peter Spier's Rain (Spier)	Picturebook
Flash, Crash, Rumble and Roll (Branley)	Nonfiction
Hurricane! (London)	Picturebook
The First Tortilla: A Bilingual Story (Anaya)	Picturebook
Rainstorm (Lehman)	Picturebook
Thunderstorms (Sipiera and Sipiera)	Nonfiction
Twister (Beard)	Picturebook
Storms (Simon)	Nonfiction
In the Rain with Baby Duck (Hest)	Picturebook
Weather! Watch How Weather Works (Rupp)	Nonfiction
Where Does the Butterfly Go When It Rains? (Garelick)	Picturebook
The Tree That Rains (Bernhard and Bernhard)	Traditional
Rain Talk (Serfozo)	Picturebook
The Magic Bean Tree (Van Laan)	Traditional

Native Americans on the Plains (Grades 3–5)

Lana's Lakota Moons (Sneve)	Fiction
The Porcupine Year (Erdrich)	Historical Fiction
An Indian Winter (Freedman)	Nonfiction
Shingebiss: An Ojibwe Legend (Van Laan)	Traditional
Indian Chiefs (Freedman)	Nonfiction
Sootface: An Ojibwa Cinderella (San Souci)	Traditional
Children of the Wild West (Freedman)	Nonfiction
Dancing with the Indians (Medearis)	Picturebook

Native Americans on the Plains (Grades 3–5) (*continued*)

. . . If You Lived with the Sioux Indians (McGovern)	Nonfiction
Bad River Boys (Sneve)	Picturebook Nonfiction
What Is the Most Beautiful Thing You Know About Horses? (Van Camp)	Picturebook
Buffalo Hunt (Freedman)	Nonfiction
The First Americans: The Story of Where They Came from and Who They Became (Aveni)	Nonfiction
Geronimo (Bruchac)	Historical Fiction
The Game of Silence (Erdrich)	Historical Fiction
Follow the Stars (Rodanas)	Traditional
The Birchbark House (Erdrich)	Historical Fiction
The Lost Children (Goble)	Traditional

Once Upon the Prairie (Grades 3–6)

Prairie (Mayer)	Nonfiction
Sod Houses on the Great Plains (Rounds)	Nonfiction
The Prairie Builders (Collard)	Nonfiction
Children of the Wild West (Freedman)	Nonfiction
On the Trail of Sacagawea (Lourie)	Nonfiction
Prairies (Patent)	Nonfiction
Prairie Willow (Trottier)	Picturebook
Pioneer Girl: Growing Up on the Prairie (Warren)	Nonfiction
Sarah, Plain and Tall (MacLachlan)	Historical Fiction Biography
Prairie Songs (Conrad)	Historical Fiction
Dandelions (Bunting)	Picturebook
My Daniel (Conrad)	Historical Fiction
Dakota Dugout (Turner)	Picturebook
Calling Me Home (Hermes)	Historical Fiction
Three Names (MacLachlan)	Picturebook
Worth (LaFaye)	Fiction
My Prairie Christmas (Harvey)	Picturebook

Slavery and Freedom (Grades 4–6)

Slavery and Resistance (Jordan)	Nonfiction
Escape from Slavery (Rappaport)	Nonfiction
Night Running (Carbone)	Nonfiction
Steal Away Home (Ruby)	Historical Fiction
To Be a Slave (Lester)	Nonfiction
Letters from a Slave Girl (Lyons)	Historical Fiction

(continued)

teaching feature 10.1

Slavery and Freedom (Grades 4–6) *(continued)*

Letters from a Slave Boy (Lyons)	Historical Fiction
Christmas in the Big House, Christmas in the Quarters (McKissack and McKissack)	Nonfiction
Jip: His Story (Paterson)	Historical Fiction
I Thought My Soul Would Rise and Fly (Hansen)	Historical Fiction
Amistad Rising: The Story of Freedom (Chambers)	Nonfiction
Sarny (Paulsen)	Historical Fiction
From Slave Ship to Freedom Road (Lester)	Nonfiction
Stealing Freedom (Carbone)	Historical Fiction
The Underground Railroad for Kids (Carson)	Nonfiction
Nightjohn (Paulsen)	Historical Fiction
Days of Jubilee (McKissack and McKissack)	Nonfiction
Silent Thunder (Pinkney)	Historical Fiction
Lincoln: A Photobiography (Freedman)	Biography
Jayhawker (Beatty)	Historical Fiction
Harriet Beecher Stowe and the Beecher Preachers (Fritz)	Biography
With Every Drop of Blood (Collier and Collier)	Historical Fiction
Anthony Burns: The Defeat and Triumph of a Fugitive Slave (Hamilton)	Biography
Forty Acres and Maybe a Mule (Robinett)	Historical Fiction
Nettie's Trip South (Turner)	Picturebook
North by Night: A Story of the Underground Railroad (Ayres)	Historical Fiction
The Middle Passage (Feelings)	Picturebook
Ajeemah and His Son (Berry)	Historical Fiction
Sky Sash So Blue (Hathorn)	Picturebook
Alec's Primer (Walter)	Historical Fiction
In the Time of the Drums (Siegelson)	Picturebook
The House of Dies Drear (Hamilton)	Fiction
Pink and Say (Polacco)	Picturebook
Days of Tears (Lester)	Historical Fiction
The Captive (Hansen)	Historical Fiction
47 (Mosley)	Fantasy
Honey Bea (Siegelson)	Fantasy
I, Too, Sing America: Three Centuries of African American Poetry (Clinton)	Poetry

Difficult Journeys (Grades 5–8)
World War II

In Defiance of Hitler (McClafferty)	Nonfiction
The Secret of the Priest's Grotto (Taylor and Nicola)	Nonfiction
One Thousand Tracings (Judge)	Nonfiction

Difficult Journeys (Grades 5–8) (*continued*)
World War II (continued)

Hitler's Canary (Toksvig)	Historical Fiction
T4 (LeZotte)	Historical Fiction
Emil and Karl (Glatshteyn)	Historical Fiction
At the Firefly Gate (Newbery)	Historical Fiction
Rose Blanche (Gallaz and Innocenti)	Picturebook
I Am an American (Stanley)	Nonfiction
The Lily Cupboard (Oppenheim)	Picturebook
Baseball Saved Us (Mochizuki)	Picturebook
Milkweed (Spinelli)	Historical Fiction
The Bracelet (Uchida)	Picturebook
Number the Stars (Lowry)	Historical Fiction
Journey to Topaz (Uchida)	Historical Fiction
The Man from the Other Side (Orlev)	Historical Fiction
Under the Blood-Red Sun (Salisbury)	Historical Fiction
Greater Than Angels (Matas)	Historical Fiction
My Friend the Enemy (Cheaney)	Historical Fiction
My Freedom Trip (Park and Park)	Historical Fiction
Eyes of the Emperor (Salisbury)	Historical Fiction
The Endless Steppe (Hautzig)	Historical Fiction
Hitler Youth: Growing Up in Hitler's Shadow (Bartoletti)	Nonfiction
Remember World War II: Kids Who Survived Tell Their Stories (Nicholson)	Nonfiction
Year of Impossible Goodbyes (Choi)	Historical Fiction
So Far from the Bamboo Grove (Watkins)	Historical Fiction
The Hidden Children (Greenfeld)	Nonfiction
War and the Pity of War (Philip)	Poetry
Rescue (Meltzer)	Nonfiction
When My Name Was Keoko (Park)	Fiction
One More Border: The True Story of One Family's Escape from War-Torn Europe (Kaplan)	Nonfiction
Shadow Life: A Portrait of Anne Frank and Her Family (Deneberg)	Nonfiction
Daniel Half Human and the Good Nazi (Chotjewitz)	Historical Fiction
Surviving Hitler: A Boy in the Nazi Camps (Warren)	Nonfiction
No Pretty Pictures: A Child of War (Lobel)	Memoir
Anne Frank (Poole)	Picturebook; Biography
The Cats in Krasinski Square (Hesse)	Picturebook
Always Remember Me: How One Family Survived World War II (Russo)	Picturebook
Hidden Child (Millman)	Picturebook

(continued)

Difficult Journeys (Grades 5–8) *(continued)*
Modern-Day Refugees

Escape from Saigon (Warren)	Nonfiction
A Haitian Family (Greenberg)	Nonfiction
A Nicaraguan Family (Malone)	Nonfiction
The Lost Boys of Natinga: A School for Sudan's Young Refugees (Walgren)	Nonfiction
The Journey That Saved Curious George (Borden)	Nonfiction
Memories of Survival (Krinitz)	Biography
On the Wings of Eagles: An Ethiopian Boy's Story (Schrier)	Picturebook
How Many Days to America? (Bunting)	Picturebook
My Name Is María Isabel (Ada)	Fiction
Kiss the Dust (Laird)	Fiction
Tonight, by Sea (Temple)	Fiction
Grab Hands and Run (Temple)	Fiction
Goodbye Vietnam (Whelan)	Fiction
Secrets in the Fire (Mankell)	Fiction
Under the Persimmon Tree (Staples)	Fiction
The Frozen Waterfall (Hiçyilmaz)	Fiction
Colibrí (Cameron)	Fiction
Behind the Mountains (Danticat)	Fiction
The Garbage King (Laird)	Fiction
Flight to Freedom (Veciana-Suarez)	Fiction
The Trouble Begins (Himelblau)	Fiction
The Girl Who Saw Lions (Doherty)	Fiction
La Linea (Jaramillo)	Fiction

Components of a Literature Program

The day-to-day routines in classrooms centered around children's literature may vary greatly according to the age of the students, the needs of the community, and the dictates of local and state curricula. But children in all literature-based classrooms need to be surrounded by enthusiastic, book-loving adults and many, many good books.

The most important aspect of the classroom environment is the teacher. She or he creates the climate of the classroom and arranges the learning environment. If the teacher loves books, shares them with children, and provides time for children to read and a place for them to read, children will become enthusiastic readers. The teacher who reads to the children every day, talks about books and characters in books as if they were good friends, and knows poems and stories to tell is serving the class as an adult model of a person who enjoys books.

One teacher regularly used to read a new children's book while her class was reading. She would keep the book in an old beat-up briefcase that she delighted in carrying. A kind of game she played with her 7- and 8-year-old students was to keep the book hidden from them. Their delight was to find out what book she was reading, so they could read the same one. Of course they always found out, which was what she had in mind in the first place. Enthusiasm for books is contagious; if the teacher has it, so will the children.

If we want children to become readers, we will want to surround them with books of all kinds. We know that wide reading is directly related to accessibility; the more books available and the more time for reading, the more children will read and the better readers they will become.

Books should be a natural part of the classroom environment. There should be no argument about whether to have a classroom collection of books or a library media center; both are necessary. Children should have immediate access to books whenever they need them. The books in the classroom collection will vary from those in the library media center. Many classrooms have an extensive paperback collection (400 to 500 titles). Frequently, there are five or six copies of the same title, so several children can read the same book and have an in-depth discussion of it.

The classroom teacher will also want to provide for a changing collection of books depending on the themes or units the children are studying. The librarian might provide a rolling cart of materials that will enhance children's study of insects or folktales or the Civil War or explorers. It is important that teachers be thoroughly acquainted with the content of these books so they can help their students use them. If the library media center does not have particular books that the children or the teacher needs, they might be obtained from local public libraries or from a bookmobile. Some state libraries will send boxes of books to teachers in communities that are not serviced by public libraries. An increasing number of teachers are demanding and receiving their share of monies allocated for instructional materials. Teachers using real books as the heart of their curriculum should receive the same amount of money as those using basal readers, workbooks, social studies, science, and other textbooks. We admire the number of teachers who spend their own money to buy trade books for their classrooms, but at the same time we question the practice. Real books are essential to the making of a fluent reader and should be an unquestioned item of every school budget.

Sharing Literature with Children

Because literature serves many educational purposes in addition to entertainment and enjoyment, teachers should place a high priority on sharing literature with children. Boys and girls of all ages should have the opportunity to hear good literature every day.

One of the best ways to interest children in books is to read to them frequently from the time they are first able to listen. Preschoolers and kindergartners should have an opportunity to listen to stories three or four times a day. Parent or grandparent volunteers, high school students, college participants, community members—all can be encouraged to read to small groups of children throughout the day. Children should have a chance to hear their favorite stories repeated over and over again at a listening/multimedia center. A child from a book-loving family might have heard over a thousand bedtime stories before she ever comes to kindergarten; some children might never have heard one.

Teachers accept the idea of reading at least twice a day to the primary-grade child. The daily read-aloud time is advocated by almost all authorities in reading. The research reported in Chapter 1 emphasizes the importance of reading aloud to all children, not only for enjoyment but also for their growth in reading skills. Reading to children improves children's reading. Rereading favorite books is as important as the initial reading.

Unfortunately, daily story times are not as common in the upper elementary and middle-school grades as in the primary grades, yet we know that they are just as essential for those age groups. Older children, like many adults, like to be read to, as evidenced by the many books available on CD-ROM and other downloadable formats. Reading comprehension is improved as students listen to and discuss events, characters, and motivation. They learn to predict what will happen in exciting tales like Mollie Hunter's *A Stranger Came Ashore* or Louis Sachar's *Holes*. Their vocabulary increases as they hear fine texts such as Sy Montgomery's *Quest for the Tree Kangaroo* or Jack Prelutsky's *The Wizard*. Older students can discuss homelessness and prejudice as they hear Paula Fox's *Monkey Island* or Leon Tillage's *Leon's Story*. They can add to their knowledge of Abraham Lincoln's presidency by reading Russell Freedman's remarkable photobiography *Lincoln*. Teachers can take advantage of this time to introduce various genres, such as fantasy, biography, or poetry, that students might not be reading on their own.

Primarily, however, the read-aloud time will cause children to want to read. For older children it models the cadence and fluency of good oral reading. Once children have heard a good book read aloud, they can hardly wait to savor it again. Reading aloud thus generates further interest in books, language, and literary events. Good oral reading should develop a taste for fine literature.

Selecting Books to Read Aloud

Teachers and librarians will want to select read-aloud books in terms of the children's interests and background in literature and the quality of writing. Usually teachers will not select books that children in the group are reading avidly on their own or books that may appear to be controversial. This is the time to stretch their imaginations, to extend interests, and to develop appreciation of fine writing and alternative perspectives. If children have not had much experience in listening to stories, begin where they are. Appreciation for literature appears to be developmental and sequential. Six- and 7-year-olds who have had little exposure to literature still need to hear many traditional fairy tales, including "Hansel and Gretel," "Sleeping Beauty," and *Ananse and the Lizard* by Pat Cummings. They delight in such favorite picture storybooks as Jan Ormerod's *When an Elephant Comes to School*, Patricia C. McKissack's *Flossie and the Fox*, and Karma Wilson's *Bear Wants More*.

Other young children who have had much exposure to literature might demand longer chapter books like *Ramona Forever* by Beverly Cleary, *James and the Giant Peach* by Roald Dahl, or *The Pepins and Their Problems* by Polly Horvath. Older children with a strong foundation and wide exposure to literature might enjoy series chapter books by authors such as Ann Brashares, Mildred Taylor, J. K. Rowling, and Sharon Draper.

Picturebooks are no longer just for "little kids." There is a real place for sharing beautiful picturebooks with older children as well as younger ones. *Dawn* by Uri Shulevitz creates the same feeling visually as one of Emily Dickinson's clear, rarefied poems. It is a literary experience for all ages, but particularly for anyone who has felt a deep connection with the world before the sunrise. Older students particularly enjoy Jon Scieszka's *Seen Art?* and Kevin O'Malley's rip-roaring *Captain Raptor and the Moon Mystery*.

The teacher should strive for balance in what is read aloud to children. Like children, teachers tend to enjoy what they know best. Expanding the repertoire of what is read aloud may require researching multiple book lists for reviews, asking for recommendations from other teachers, and looking up professional organizations whose focus is children's literature.

Many teachers have thought of read-aloud time as a time to read fiction to children. However, there is a wealth of excellent nonfiction that is every bit as compelling as a good fictional story. For example, the book *Freedom Walkers: The Story of the Montgomery Bus Boycott* gives the historical account of the events that led to the civil rights movement, but its prose style also captivates readers as a narrative, using the actual recorded words of the people whose experiences tell the story.

Poetry is another genre that can be read aloud, even in the brief minutes of transition between subjects or before lunch or recess breaks. Word play and spoken word can engage the reluctant reader as well as the better reader. Reading poems for two or more voices can help children enhance fluency in reading aloud. They will find it irresistible fun to work together dramatically reading aloud poetry.

Primary-grade teachers should read many books to their children. Middle-grade teachers might present parts of many books to their students during book talks or as teasers to interest children in reading the books. But how many entire books will a teacher read in the course of one school year? An educated guess might be that starting with 8-year-olds—when teachers begin to read longer, continuous stories to boys and girls—an average of some six to ten books are read aloud during the year. This means that for the next four years, when children are reaching the peak of their interest in reading, they might hear no more than forty or so books read by their teachers!

Today when there are thousands of children's books in print, read-aloud choices must be selected with care in terms of their relevance for students and the quality of their writing. Only a teacher who knows the children, their interests, and their background of experience can truly select appropriate books for a particular class. The teacher will want to consider children's backgrounds in literature, or lack of background, as he or she selects appropriate books to capture their attention. A read-aloud program should be planned. What books are too good to miss? These should be included in the overall plan.

Teachers should keep a record of the books that they have shared with the children they teach and a brief notation of the class's reaction to each title. This enables teachers to see what kind of balance is being achieved and what the particular favorites of the class are. Such a record provides the children's future teachers with information on the likes and dislikes of the class and their exposure to literature. It also might prevent the situation that was discovered by a survey of one school in which every teacher in the school, with the exception of the kindergarten and the second-grade teachers, had read E. B. White's *Charlotte's Web* aloud to the class! *Charlotte's Web* is a great book, but not for every class several years in a row. Perhaps teachers in a school need to agree on what is the most appropriate time for reading particular favorites. Teachers and librarians should be encouraged to try reading new books to children, instead of always reading the same ones. But some self-indulgence should be allowed every teacher who truly loves a particular book because that enthusiasm can't help but rub off on children.

Effective oral reading is an important factor in capturing children's interest. Some teachers can make almost any story sound exciting; others plod dully through. The storyteller's voice, timing, and intonation patterns should communicate the meanings and mood of the story. To read effectively, the teacher should be familiar with the story and communicate his or her enthusiasm for the book. **Teaching Feature 10.2: Effective Practices for Reading Aloud** might prove useful. Check the list before selecting and reading a story to a whole class.

teaching feature 10.2

Effective Practices for Reading Aloud

1. Select a book appropriate to the developmental age of the children and their previous exposure to literature.
2. Determine whether you will share the book with the whole class, a small group, or an individual child.
3. Select books that will stretch children's imaginations, extend their interests, and expose them to fine art and writing.
4. Read a variety of types of books to capture the interests of all.
5. Remember that favorite books should be reread at the primary level.
6. Plan to read aloud several times a day.
7. Select a story that you like so that you can communicate your enthusiasm.
8. Choose a book or section that can be read in one session.
9. Read the book first so that you are familiar with the content.
10. Seat the children close to you so that all can see the pictures.
11. Hold the book so that children can see the pictures at their eye level.
12. Communicate the mood and meaning of the story and characters with your voice.
13. Introduce books in various ways:
    - Through a display
    - Through a brief discussion about the author or illustrator
    - By asking children to predict what the story will be about through looking at the cover and interpreting the title
    - By linking the theme, author, or illustrator to other books children know
14. Encourage older children to discuss the progress of the story or predict the outcome at the end of the chapter.
15. Help children to link the story with their own experiences or other literature.
16. Keep a list of the books read aloud to the whole class that can be passed on to their next teachers.

For more on effective practices for reading aloud, see Caroline Feller Bauer's *New Handbook for Storytellers* (Chicago: American Library Association, 1995).

Storytelling

A 5-year-old said to his teacher: "Tell the story from your face." His preference for the story told by the teacher or librarian instead of the story read directly from the book is echoed by boys and girls everywhere. The art of storytelling is frequently neglected in the elementary school today. There are so many beautiful books to share with children, we rationalize, and our harried life allows little time for learning stories. Yet children should not be denied the opportunity to hear well-told stories. Through storytelling, the teacher helps transmit the literary heritage. In addition, oral stories told in many cultures throughout the world have not been retold in written form. What better way to celebrate these stories than to invite members of the children's families and communities to come to school for storytelling time.

Storytelling provides for intimate contact and rapport with the children. No book separates the teacher from the audience. The story may be modified to fit group needs. A difficult word or phrase can be explained in context. Stories can be personalized for very young children by substituting their names for those of the characters. Such a phrase as "and, David, if you had been there you would have seen the biggest Billy Goat Gruff . . ." will redirect the child whose interest has wandered. The pace of the story can be adapted to the children's interests and age levels.

Folktales like "The Three Billy Goats Gruff," "The Little Red Hen," and "Cinderella" are particular favorites of younger children. The repetitive pattern of these tales makes them easy to tell. Originally passed down from generation to generation by word of mouth, these tales were polished and embellished with each retelling. Six-, 7-, and 8-year-olds enjoy hearing longer folktales such as Ashley Bryan's *The Cat's Purr*. They also enjoy some of the tall tales about American folk heroes such as Paul Bunyan, Pecos Bill, and John Henry. Incidents from biographies and chapters from longer books may be told as a way of interesting children in reading them.

Book Talks

Librarians and teachers frequently use a book talk to introduce books to children. The primary purpose of a book talk is to interest children in reading the book themselves. Rather than reveal the whole story, the book talk tells just enough about the book to entice others to read it. A book talk may be about one title; it may be about several unrelated books that would have wide appeal; or it may revolve around several books with a similar theme, such as "getting along in the family" or "courage" or "survival stories." The book talk should begin with the recounting of an amusing episode or exciting moment in the book. The narrator might want to assume the role of a character in a book, such as Julie in *Julie of the Wolves* by Jean George, and tell of her experience of being lost without food or a compass on the North Slope of Alaska. The speaker should stop before the crisis is over or the mystery is solved. Details should be specific. It is better to let the story stand on its own than to characterize it as a "terribly funny" story or the "most exciting" book you've ever read. The speaker's enthusiasm for the book will convey itself. This is one reason why book talks should be given only about stories the speaker genuinely likes. Children will then come to trust this evaluation. It is best if the book is on hand as it is discussed, so that the children can check it out as soon as the book talk is finished.

Providing Time to Read Books

One of the primary purposes of giving book talks, telling stories, and reading aloud to children is to motivate them to read. A major goal of every school should be to develop children who *can* read but also *do* read—who love reading and will become lifetime readers. To become fluent readers, children need to practice reading from real books that capture their interest and imagination. No one could become a competent swimmer or tennis player by practicing four minutes a day. Schools have little influence on the out-of-school life of their students, but they do control the curriculum in school. If we want children to become readers, we must reorder our priorities and provide time for children to read books of their own choosing every day.

Recognizing this need, many teachers have initiated a sustained silent reading (SSR) time. Teachers have used other names, such as "recreational reading," "free reading," or even the acronym DEAR (Drop Everything and Read) used by the teacher in *Ramona Quimby, Age 8* by Beverly Cleary. Whatever the name, however, this is a time when everyone in the class (in some instances, the entire school) reads, including the teacher. SSR times have been successfully established in kindergarten through middle schools. Usually, the reading period is lengthened gradually from ten minutes a day to twenty, thirty, or, in some upper-grade classes, forty-five minutes per day. Recognizing the importance of social interaction among readers, teachers often allow children to read in pairs. In classrooms that use real books for teaching reading and studying themes that cut across the curriculum, children are reading and writing throughout the day. Teachers still have a special time each day for children to read the books they have chosen to read for pleasure.

Providing Time to Talk About Books

Equally important as time for wide reading is time to talk about the books children are reading. When adults discuss books, we have good conversations about the ones we like, but we seldom quiz each other about character development, themes, or setting of the story. As teachers, we want to show this same respect for children as they share their thoughts about books. A good time for informal talk about books is after children have had time to read by themselves. In pairs, small groups, or as a class, children may be invited to tell something about a book, show a picture and tell what is happening, read an interesting or powerful paragraph, and so forth. In such discussions, teachers can learn much about what children are reading and how they talk about books.[4]

Maryann Eeds and Deborah Wells showed how well fifth and sixth graders explored the meaning of novels they were reading through nondirective response groups.[5] The literature discussion groups met two days a week, thirty minutes a day, for four to five weeks. The leaders were undergraduate education students who were instructed to let meaning emerge from the group rather than solicit it. The results of this study showed that the groups collaborated and built meaning that was deeper and richer than what they attained in their solitary reading. The authors concluded, "Talk helps to confirm, extend, and modify individual interpretations and creates a better understanding of the text."

As teachers listen carefully to children's responses in book discussion groups, they can identify teaching possibilities, plan future conversations, or make use of a teachable moment to make a point. When the teacher is an active participant rather than the director of a group, children more readily collaborate to fill their own gaps in understanding and make meaning together. More structured discussion may occur with the books a teacher chooses to read aloud or to read with small groups. The teacher can play an important role in engendering fruitful discussions by demonstrating the types of responses she hopes children will make. When the teacher introduces the story, she might invite children to recognize the author or illustrator, to notice the dedication, or to speculate on the book's content as they look at the cover. As she gives children time to look at the illustrations in picturebooks, she asks, "How do these pictures make you feel?" "What are you thinking about as you look at these illustrations?" As she reads a chapter book, she asks what might happen next or why a character acts as he does. She might introduce Mollie Hunter's *A Stranger Came Ashore* by reading Susan Cooper's *Selkie Girl* and discussing selkie lore with the class. She might pause at a chapter's end and ask children how Hunter makes the reader feel that something dreadful is about to happen. She might ask what clues suggest that Finn Learson is not who he pretends to be. She might introduce the term *foreshadowing* and ask the children to listen for other examples as she reads. At first the teacher calls attention to aspects such as a well-written passage, an apt chapter heading, or a key moment when a character faces a choice. Later, children will begin noticing the kinds of things the teacher has brought out in these discussions. In this way a teacher models reader behaviors that mature readers practice.

Providing Time for the In-Depth Study of Books

If children are to have an opportunity to read and discuss widely, this activity should be balanced with a time for studying books deeply. When children work with books in ways that are meaningful to them—through talk, art making, writing, or drama

A third- and fourth-grade group heard Byrd Baylor's story *I'm in Charge of Celebrations* and wrote about special days they wanted to remember. Mangere Bridge School, Auckland, New Zealand. Colleen Fleming, teacher.

and music—many things happen. Children have greater satisfaction with, and clarify personal meanings about, what they have read. These activities allow many books to be visible in the classroom.

One child's work with a book can dramatically influence another child's willingness to read it. Children working on projects use various skills, exercise more choices, develop planning abilities, and experiment with a variety of learning experiences. In addition, these activities can allow children the opportunity to think more deeply about books and to return to them to explore responses in ways that deepen their understandings.

Teachers who know the children in their classes well recognize the diversity of learning styles this sort of active learning accommodates. They plan diverse activities that enhance children's delight in books, make them want to continue reading more and better books, and cause them to think both more widely and more specifically about what they have read. They know that many options should be open to children and do not expect all children to choose the same book or have the same type of response to a book. They consult with children about possibilities for projects and do not assign all children to do the same project; neither do they expect children to do an activity for every book that they read. The activities suggested here are planned to increase children's enjoyment and understanding of books.

Children's Writing and Children's Books

Children's written work should grow out of their own rich experiences, whether with people, places, and things; research and observation; or literature. Children's writing about books can take many forms. Children should have many opportunities to write about the books they are reading. They should also be encouraged to use books as models for their own writing.

Real possibilities for writing are all around us in the classroom; however, it is literature that gives children a sense of how the written word sounds and looks. Literature has made a tremendous impact on reading programs, and so too has the writing process approach. Few teachers would consider teaching reading without including writing, because learning in one area means learning in the other. Literature informs both processes. As children become authors, they look at professional authors to see how a book works and sounds. They borrow and improvise on the language, patterns, and format of published books.[6] Writing and reading go on all day in a classroom where language arts and reading are intertwined and literature is at the heart of the curriculum.

Helping Children Write About Books In most schools, children are no longer required to write book reports, a particularly inert kind of writing. However, many teachers ask children to write about their reading in other ways. This writing resembles talk, in that a child shares ideas and someone responds to those ideas. Teachers find this is a time-saving idea and can set aside a weekly or biweekly time to react in writing to children's written responses. Some teachers demonstrate supportive responses and let pairs of children react to each other's written work as well. There are various ways a teacher can help children write about their reading.

A *reading log* is a simple record of the title and author of each book a child has read. Needless to say, this is a burden for young children, but it is a source of pride for second graders and older children who like to recall their reading and measure their progress. Teachers might give children six-by-eight-inch cards and let them fill in one side. Then the teacher and child can use these records for generalizing as they talk together about a child's reading. If a child takes her most recent card to the library, librarians might better help her find a book by seeing what she has enjoyed so far.

In a *response journal* children record their comments as they read a novel. Children respond freely as they think about their reading and write about the things that concern or interest them. A *double-entry draft* is a two-sided journal entry in which the reader copies or paraphrases a quote from the book on the left half of the paper. On the right, the reader comments on the quote. Teachers react to both of these journals and engage in a written dialogue with the reader (thereby creating a *dialogue journal*). Whatever we call them, children's written responses to the books they read provide teachers with another window into understanding how readers teach themselves to read.

Writing about books in the same way every day becomes tedious. Teachers may want to vary the way children can respond. They might invite children to keep a sketchbook/journal, where visual art serves as a preface to writing.[7] A single dialogue journal might be kept by a group reading the same book and children can take turns responding. Children might ask their own questions and consider which ones are more interesting to write about. Media-savvy children might be motivated to keep journal entries in the form of a blog or to submit commentary on books to bulletin boards or sites such as Amazon.com or Barnesandnoble.com.

What teachers need to avoid, however, is overusing written response or using a journal as a place in which children answer numbers of questions posed by the teacher. The primary power of journals is that the child owns the ideas, not the teacher. The child is director of the reading, and the child reflects on matters of interest to herself. When children write about their reading, they follow certain patterns, such as retelling, questioning particular words, clarifying meanings, reacting with like or dislike to a particular part of the story, relating a part of the story to their own lives, or otherwise reflecting.

Books That Support Children's Writing When children have a chance to become writers themselves, they begin to notice how other authors work. Literature suggests the many forms that stories, information, or poetry can take; as children experiment with the model, they begin to develop a sensitivity to the conventions of the form. This awareness in turn allows them to bring a wider frame of reference to the reading and writing that follow. Children in elementary classrooms should have an opportunity to experience a variety of well-written fiction, poetry, and nonfiction. At the same time, they can be encouraged to develop an appreciation of language and form through writing. In this way, children develop a sensitivity to language, an increasing control over the power of words, and a diverse writing repertoire.

Ideas for writing can come from the child's own life and from the classroom curriculum. They can also be inspired by books. Teachers can read aloud and then display individual books that serve as springboards or provocative formats for children's writing. Virginia Wright-Frierson's *A North American Rain Forest Scrapbook*, Margaret Wise Brown's *The Important Book*, or Vera B. Williams's *Three Days on a River in a Red Canoe* could serve as possible models for children to use. Many reading and writing connections have been explored in previous chapters. **Teaching Feature 10.3: Books That Serve as Writing Models** suggests stories that teachers might share as examples and incentives for children's own writing.

Exploring Literature Through the Visual Arts

Young children communicate through visual symbols as easily as they communicate through language, yet by the middle grades many children feel very insecure about making art. Children of all ages who have the opportunity to transform their responses to books through visual means are learning to be confident creators. In addition, their familiarity with art can increase their visual literacy and their aesthetic understanding.

Too often children are given a box of crayons and a small space at the top of some lined newsprint paper and told to "make a picture" of the story. How much better

teaching feature 10.3

Books That Serve as Writing Models

Title	Author	Grade Level	Type of Writing
Extra Extra! Fairy Tale News from the Hidden Forest	Ada	2 and up	Newspaper
The Jolly Postman, or Other People's Letters	Ahlberg and Ahlberg	1 and up	Letters from one folktale character to another
Gilda Joyce, Psychic Investigator	Allison	4–7	Letters, stories, journal entries
The Nutty News	Barrett	All ages	Parody of tabloid newspaper
Peeled	Bauer	6 and up	School newspaper
A Gathering of Days: A New England Girl's Journal, 1830–1832	Blos	5 and up	Historical fiction in journal form
Air Is All Around You	Branley	All ages	Expository nonfiction
The Burning Questions of Bingo Brown	Byars	5–8	Journal of interesting questions
Dear Annie	Caseley	1–4	Letters between a girl and her grandfather
Dear Mr. Henshaw	Cleary	5–7	Story told in letters and journal entries
Strider	Cleary	6 and up	Journal entries
Catherine Called Birdy	Cushman	5 and up	Journal entries
My Side of the Mountain	George	4–7	Journal
Spiders	Gibbons	All ages	Expository nonfiction
The Secret Blog of Raisin Rodriguez	Goldschmidt	6 and up	Blog entries

it is to work with children who are "filled to over-flowing" with knowledge about a book or theme. How much more lively artwork might be if the teacher provided many materials from which to choose instead of the usual crayons and thin news-print. Chalk, paints, markers, colored tissue papers, yarn, steel wool, cotton, material scraps, wires—anything that might be useful in depicting characters and scenes should be readily accessible. Teachers might provide more interesting paper such as wallpaper samples, construction paper, hand-painted papers, and remainders from printers. Then when children are asked to make pictures of their favorite part of a story, of a character doing something in the book they have read, or illustrations for their own stories, the results are more exciting.

Paintings, murals, sculptures, crafts, constructions, assemblages, collages, mobiles and stabiles, stitchery and multimedia creations are among the possibilities for visual expression in the classroom. Children's work should mirror the same range of artistic

teaching feature 10.3

Title	Author	Grade Level	Type of Writing
Jazmin's Notebook	Grimes	5–8	Notebook entries and poems
Trial by Journal	Klise	5–7	Journal and scrapbook
Writing Magic: Creating Stories That Fly	Levine	5 and up	How-to about fiction writing
Hey World, Here I Am!	Little	4–7	Poetry and journal entries
Operation Red Jericho	Mowll	6 and up	Letters, maps, diagrams, photographs, and other supporting materials
Autobiography of My Dead Brother	Myers	6 and up	Sketches, comic strips, and text
TTYL	Myracle	6 and up	Instant messaging (IM) transcripts
Call Me María	Ortiz Cofer	6 and up	Poems, letters, and prose
Pictures from Our Vacation	Perkins	2 and up	Journal in words and pictures
Libby on Wednesday	Snyder	5–8	Writing group
Cherries and Cherry Pits	Williams	1 and up	Pictures that serve as prewriting for a child's story
Stringbean's Trip to the Shining Sea	Williams	2 and up	Story in postcard form
Three Days on a River in a Red Canoe	Williams	2 and up	Journal in words and pictures
Adam Canfield: Watch Your Back!	Winerip	5–8	School newspaper
You Have to Write	Wong	2–5	A poem about developing writing ideas
An Island Scrapbook: Dawn to Dusk on a Barrier Island	Wright-Frierson	2 and up	Naturalist's sketchbook/diary

After reading Kathy Jakobsen's *My New York*, fourth graders created a map of the city that showed their own favorite places in the city. PS124, New York, New York. Mary S. Gallivan, teacher.

expression found in the world of visual art outside the classroom. The teacher's role is to design a rich environment for creativity by providing materials, challenging children's thinking, and honoring children's work.

Displays of children's responses can be assembled and mounted carefully. They can be placed alongside a book or books that inspired the work or arranged as a summary of a thematic study. Often a study of a book or genre is extensive enough to warrant a museum exhibit. Explanations written by children help clarify for parents and other classroom observers how the work was created.

A teacher can also make use of a child's desire to replicate an illustrator's way of working by encouraging children to explore various media. Kindergarten children save their finger-painting pictures, cut them up, and use them to create their own story illustrated in the collage style of Eric Carle's

Illustrator Eric Carle's bright collages inspire a kindergartner to experiment with forms. Martin Luther King, Jr., Laboratory School, Evanston Public Schools, Evanston, Illinois. Barbara Friedberg, teacher.

stories such as *The Very Hungry Caterpillar.* Older children use dampened rice paper, ink, and watercolor to try to capture the look of traditional Japanese artwork used by Meilo So in *Pale Male: Citizen Hawk of New York City* by Janet Schulman. These children are answering for themselves the question "How did the illustrator make the pictures?"

Techniques that easily translate to the elementary classroom include collage, scratchboard, marbleized paper, many varieties of painting and printing, and stencil prints. By making these materials and processes readily available for children, teachers can extend the ways in which they visualize their world as well as their appreciation for illustrators' works. **Teaching Feature 10.4: Exploring Artists' Media** provides an overview of illustrators who work in some of these media and a list of materials that will allow children to explore these techniques.

A fourth grader carefully examined Suekichi Akaba's illustrations for *The Crane Wife* by Sumiko Yagawa before trying out his own watercolor response. Barrington Elementary School, Upper Arlington, Ohio. Marlene Harbert, teacher.

Exploring Artists' Media

teaching feature 10.4

Materials Needed	Books That Use Similar Techniques
Printmaking	
Styrofoam trays	*My Beastie Book of ABC* by David Frampton
	Why the Sky Is Far Away by Mary-Joan Gerson, illustrated by Carla Golembe
Ballpoint pen or other blunt instrument	*At Jerusalem's Gate* by Nikki Grimes, illustrated by David Frampton
	Snowflake Bentley by Jaqueline Briggs Martin illustrated by Mary Azarian
	One Potato: A Counting Book of Potato Prints by Diana Pomeroy
Soft cutting blocks (available from art supply houses)	
Linoleum block cutters	
Potatoes	
Water-based printing inks or acrylic paints in tubes	

(continued)

teaching feature 10.4

Materials Needed	Books That Use Similar Techniques
Scratchboard and Crayon Resist	
Construction paper or poster board	*Giants in the Land* by Diana Appelbaum, illustrated by Michael McCurdy
	A Creepy Countdown by Charlotte Huck, illustrated by Jos. A. Smith
	The Hidden Folk by Lise Lunge-Larsen, illustrated by Beth Krommes
Crayons	*The House in the Night* by Susan Marie Swanson, illustrated by Beth Krommes
	In the Time of the Drums by Kim Siegelson, illustrated by Brian Pinkney
Black tempera paint or India ink	*Mammoths on the Move* by Lisa Wheeler, illustrated by Kurt Cyrus
Incising tools or blunt instrument	
Commercial scratchboard and tools	
Collage and Cut Paper	
Wallpapers, wrapping papers	*To Be a Drum* by Evelyn Coleman, illustrated by Aminah Brenda Lynne Robinson
	Leaf Man by Lois Ehlert
String, marbleized papers, construction paper, painted papers, paste papers	*The Top of the World: Climbing Mount Everest* by Steve Jenkins
	One Horse Waiting for Me by Patricia Mullins
	Kogi's Mysterious Journey by Elizabeth Partridge, illustrated by Aki Sogabe
	The Subway Mouse by Barbara Reid
	Pumpkin Day by Nancy Elizabeth Wallace
	The Sons of the Dragon King by Ed Young
Airbrush Technique and Stencils	
Old file folders or stencil paper	*Why Mosquitoes Buzz in People's Ears* by Verna Aardema, illustrated by Leo Dillon and Diane Dillon
Pastel chalks or paint	*The Pot That Juan Built* by Nancy Andrews-Goebel, illustrated by David Diaz
	Sail Away by Donald Crews
Sponges, bristle brush, or toothbrush	*All of You Was Singing* by Richard Lewis, illustrated by Ed Young

Music and Movement in the Classroom

Children often enjoy singing to picturebook versions of well-known songs. They can also interpret literature by composing music or creating a dance. These activities help them think more carefully about the mood of a story or poem and consider their emotional responses to books more thoroughly. In recent years there have been numerous fine picturebook interpretations of well-known songs, including *Yankee Doodle* by Mary Ann Hoberman, *The Farmer in the Dell* by Alexandra Wallner, and *A-Hunting We Will Go* by Steven Kellogg. To children who already know the song, the text of these books presents easy and enjoyable reading.

Many familiar folk songs have been researched and presented in authentic historic detail by such authors as Peter Spier and Woody Guthrie. Spier presents *The Star-Spangled Banner* with historical background so that the songs almost become an informational book, too. These various editions are a good way to make American history come alive as children are introduced to many folk songs that are a part of the American folk tradition.

In addition to the classroom extensions suggested, children might enjoy making their own book versions of other traditional songs like "Home on the Range," "Where Have All the Flowers Gone," or "Old Dan Tucker." Scott R. Sanders has invented details and told his own stories for twenty folk songs in *Hear the Wind Blow: American Folk Songs Retold*. Some of these long and often funny stories would inspire fifth and sixth graders' imaginations.

Matching Music and Literature The process of identifying appropriate music to accompany prose and poetry selections helps children appreciate mood and tone in both literature and music. Second graders discussed the kind of music that could accompany the action of Maurice Sendak's *Where the Wild Things Are*. They recognized and created music with increasing tempo and volume, followed by a quiet conclusion of the story. Older children might enjoy reading one of Jack Prelutsky's *Nightmares* poems to music of their own choosing. Alternatively, a teacher might let children listen to Edvard Grieg's "In the Hall of the Mountain King" or Richard Wagner's "Valkyries' Ride" and ask children which of Prelutsky's poems best suit these pieces. Many themes of subjects featured in literature have counterparts in music. For instance, the quiet awakening of the day in *Dawn* by Uri Shulevitz might be compared to the "Sunrise" movement from the *Grand Canyon Suite* by Ferde Grofé or to Cat Stevens's rendition of Eleanor Farjeon's poem "Morning Has Broken." Teachers can encourage older students to develop their sensitivity to recurring themes in art by juxtaposing literature and music.

Composing Music Poetry can be set to music as children create melody and identify the rhythmical elements. One group of talented 7-year-olds composed music to accompany their own sad tale of a princess who was captured during a battle and taken from her palace. Her knight-in-arms wandered the lonely countryside in search of her, while the poor princess grieved for him in her prison tower. The children made up a musical theme for each of the main characters, which they repeated during the various movements of their composition. The story was first told to their classmates, and then the song was played on the autoharp and glockenspiel. Older students composed a three-movement rhythmical symphony for Ged in Ursula K. Le Guin's *A Wizard of Earthsea*. A recorder repeated Ged's theme in appropriate places in this percussion piece. When literature provides the inspiration for children's musical compositions, children's appreciation for both literature and music will be enriched. Computer programs such as Apple's GarageBand not only make the creation of musical compositions to interpret literature and accompany projects possible but also motivate children to undertake such activities.

Movement and Literature Increasing attention has been given to children's control of their own body movements. The relationship between thought and movement has received much attention, particularly in England. Basic rhythmical movements might be introduced through Mother Goose rhymes. For example, children could walk to "Tommy Snooks and Bessie Brooks," gallop to "Ride a Cock Horse," jump to "Jack Be Nimble," and run to "Wee Willie Winkie." Nursery rhymes could also motivate dramatic action with such verses as "Hickory Dickory Dock," "Three Blind Mice," and "Jack and Jill." A favorite poem for young children to move to is "Holding Hands" by Lenore M. Link, which describes the ponderous way in which elephants walk. By way of contrast, Evelyn Beyer's poem "Jump or Jiggle" details the walk of frogs, caterpillars, worms, bugs, rabbits, and horses. It provides a wonderful opportunity for children to develop diverse movements. Both poems can be found in Jack Prelutsky's *Read-Aloud Rhymes for the Very Young.* In Jean Marzollo's *Pretend You're a Cat*, a longer poem that Jerry Pinkney illustrates as a picturebook, Pinkney's watercolors portray twelve animals and, on the facing pages, children pretending to walk, wiggle, or jump like those particular animals.

As children learn basic movements, they can use them in different areas of space, at different levels, and at different tempos. Swinging, bending, stretching, twisting, bouncing, and shaking are the kinds of body movements that can be made by standing tall, at a middle position, or by stooping low. Other poetry that suggests movement includes "Stop, Go" by Dorothy Baruch, "The African Dance" by Langston Hughes, and "The Potatoes' Dance" by Vachel Lindsay. All of these poems can be found in *Favorite Poems Old and New*, compiled by Helen Ferris.

Extending Literature Through Drama

Books become more real to children as they identify with the characters through creative drama. Young children begin this identification with others through *dramatic play*. A 5-year-old engaged in impromptu play might become an airplane zooming to an airport built of blocks; another assumes the role of mother in the playhouse. Sometimes children of this age will play a very familiar story without adult direction. For example, "The Three Billy Goats Gruff" and "The Three Bears" are often favorites. Dramatic play represents this free response of children as they interpret experience. In schools, this type of natural response can find an outlet in activities that are part of a creative drama program. Creative drama is structured and cooperatively planned playmaking, an approach to learning that focuses on processes rather than production. While occasionally a play developed creatively will be shared with others, the value of creative drama lies in the process of playing and does not require an audience. Creative drama activities exist on a continuum from interpretation to improvisation and can include pantomime, story dramatization, improvisation, readers' theater, and puppetry. All of these activities provide important ways for children to reenter the world of a book, to consider the characters, events, problems, and themes that are central in good literature. Such engagement brings children joy and zest in learning and living while broadening their understandings of both literature and life.

Dramatizing Stories Very young children aged 3 through 5 will become involved in dramatic play, but they usually do not have the sustained attention to act out a complete story. They might play a part of a favorite folktale (for example, crossing the bridge as in "The Three Billy Goats Gruff"), but they seldom will complete a whole story. And no one should expect them to. Primary-grade children enjoy playing simple stories such as the funny tale *Nine-in-One Grr! Grr!* by Blia Xiong or *The Little Red Hen* by Harriet Ziefert. Folktales are also a rich source of dramatization. They are usually short and have plenty of action, a quick plot, and interesting characters.

Stories from myths, such as "Pandora's Box" or "King Midas' Touch," are fine material for 9- to 11-year-olds to dramatize. Middle-grade children also enjoy presenting parts of books to each other in the form of debates, interviews, or discussions or television talk shows. A group of students played the roles of various characters in Natalie Babbitt's *Tuck Everlasting* and were interviewed by another student who took the role of a television talk-show host. They told about their own roles in the events that had taken place and voiced advantages and disadvantages of Winnie's living forever if she chose to drink water from a magic spring. Teachers can help children focus on important and complex issues that characters face in literature by providing these opportunities to explore ideas. This exploration is often a precursor of children's developing the ability to discover themes in literature or factors that influence characters to change.

Readers' Theater Teachers who are hesitant to try drama in their classroom might well begin with *readers' theater*, which involves a group of children in reading a play, a story, or a poem. Children are assigned to read particular parts. After reading through their parts silently, children read the text orally. Children thoroughly enjoy participating in readers' theater. Even though they do not create the dialogue, as they do in improvisation or drama, they do interpret the character's personalities and the mood of the story. They also interact with each other in a kind of play form. The story provides the script, which makes it easy to try in the classroom.

In adapting a story for readers' theater, teachers or students must edit the text to omit phrases like *he said* and *she replied*. A child narrator needs to read the connecting prose between dialogue. Older children can write their own introductions

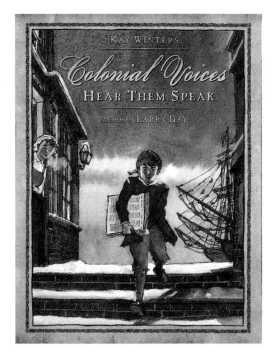

Colonial Voices: Hear Them Speak by Kay Winters is ready-made for a readers' theater presentation and fits in with studies of the American Revolution. Cover of *Colonial Voices: Hear Them Speak* by Kay Winters and illustrated by Larry Day, copyright © 2008 by Kay Winters and Larry Day. Used by permission of Dutton Children's Books, a Division of Penguin Young Readers Group, a Member of Penguin Group (USA) Inc., 345 Hudson Street, New York, NY 10014. All rights reserved.

and decide whether to leave out long descriptive passages or summarize them. Many teachers have found it useful to duplicate the parts of the story that children will read. This way, children can highlight their own parts and cross out unnecessary words. The most effective readers' theater selections contain a lot of dialogue. Folktales are easily adapted for primary children. Some good choices would be Steven Kellogg's *Chicken Little*, Paul Galdone's *The Little Red Hen*, or Carol Jones's *The Gingerbread Man*. At first the teacher might read the narrator's part and let children take the different roles. When children become more capable readers and have had practice with readers' theater, they can take over the role of narrator. A variant of readers' theater best suited to younger children is a form of pantomime called *story theater*. Here a narrator reads a story aloud while children take the role of characters and act out the unfolding tale. Books that have a lot of action or emotional reaction make the best candidates for story theater. The teacher or librarian might read aloud Aleksei Tolstoy's *The Gigantic Turnip* while six children pantomime being the old man, the old woman, the little granddaughter, the dog, the calico cat, and the mouse. As the children gain confidence with this kind of drama, the teacher can stop at appropriate points when the old man calls to his wife and invite the designated child to create the dialogue. Moving from pantomime to extemporaneous dialogue is an easy transition to more complex forms of story reenactment.

Puppetry Many children will lose themselves in the characterization of a puppet while hidden behind a puppet stage even though they might hesitate to express ideas and feelings in front of the class. Through puppetry, children learn to project their voices and develop facility in varying their voice quality to portray different characters. For example, a rather quiet, shy child might use a booming voice as he becomes the giant in "Jack and the Beanstalk." Puppetry also facilitates the development of skills in arts and crafts. Problems of stage construction, backdrops for scenery, and the modeling of characters provide opportunities for the development of creative thinking. A well-played puppet show extends children's appreciation and interpretation of stories and makes literature a more memorable experience for them. Beginning in kindergarten with the construction of paper-bag or simple stick figures, children can gain pleasure from their involvement with puppetry. Materials and types of puppets will range from the simple to the complex, depending on age and the child.

The teaching techniques used in creative drama should be followed, as puppet plays are created cooperatively by children and teachers. It is highly recommended that children "play out" stories before using their puppets. Written scripts are not necessary and can prove very limiting. Playing the story creatively allows the child to identify with the characters before becoming involved with the creation and mechanical manipulation of the puppet.

Connecting Literature and Life

Children sometimes have difficulty picturing life in other times or places or understanding historical time. They can experience books more completely through making maps and time lines and by compiling special collections. Children who thus ask questions about the details and events in literature are also introduced to methods of inquiry and research.

Creating Graphic Organizers

A graphic organizer is a visual representation of an idea. Semantic maps, attribute webs, or word webs often are used to help children group similar ideas into categories following a brainstorming session and display them to others. In these graphic organizers, a word or idea is placed at the center of a chart with spokes radiating toward related words, attributes, or other examples. One group listed "Outsiders in Literature" at the center of a semantic map and drew lines out to the various characters from novels who seem different from their peers. At the chart's center were clustered words describing insiders. Word webs or semantic maps are also useful synthesizing aids for children who are organizing material from a variety of books and sources prior to writing a report.

Venn diagrams and comparison charts have been used as tools for organizing talk and thought, too. One teacher asked a group of children who had read many novels by Betsy Byars to discuss how they are similar. Midway through the conversation children had raised such points as "The parents are never around," "The main character is usually about our age," and "Some big problem is always there." The teacher then helped children generate a chart with the titles of Byars's books, such as *The Night Swimmers, Cracker Jackson,* and *The Pinballs,* placed top-to-bottom on the left side of a large sheet of paper. Across the top of the chart, the children generated categories, such as "Where the Parents Are," "About the Main Character," "Big Problems," and "Who Helps and How." Now that the conversation was well under way, the graphic organizer helped children focus and continue the discussion while they filled in the grid they had created on the chart. Later, other Byars books were added, such as *The Summer of the Swans* and *The House of Wings,* which children also read to see how they fit the pattern. Children created artwork that represented some of the categories and wrote about how the books were alike and different. These were matted and hung next to the comparison chart. This activity helped the children analyze particular stories, synthesize several stories, and evaluate later readings. From the chart, they were able to generalize about books by one author, a sophisticated skill for 10- and 11-year-olds.

Nonfiction books are full of different types of graphic organizers that children learn to identify at a very young age. Kindergarteners may notice labeled drawings and cross-sections in books such as Gail Gibbons's *The Honeymakers* or *Tell Me Tree,* and first and second graders who have experience with nonfiction books readily incorporate such graphic organizers in their own nonfiction writing. Author Steve Moline argues that graphics such as flow charts, tables, picture glossaries, cut-aways, and cross-sections aide children in deepening concepts and ideas from their all content-area learning.[8]

Fifth and sixth graders made a type of sociogram to identify the "outsiders" in various stories. Personality traits that would make you an "insider" were written in the inner circle. Ridgemont Elementary School, Mt. Victory, Ohio. Sheryl Reed and Peggy Harrison, teachers.

Artifacts and Collections

Items or artifacts mentioned in books often seem strange to children, even if explained in context. A child who reads that Ma Ingalls cooked prairie dinners in a spider would be puzzled until she could see this three-legged pan in a reference such as *Colonial Life* by Bobbie Kalman. Hefting a modern-day cast-iron replica would give a child a sense of the endurance of these utensils. This object, although a small part of the story, nonetheless connects reader experience with a part of the real world. A class collection could involve children in assembling book-related artifacts on a large scale. Second graders studying pioneers, for example, could make and collect items that pioneers might have taken west with them: such as a wooden spoon, a cornhusk doll, a flour sack, and a wagon wheel. As the teacher reads aloud *Trouble for Lucy* by Carla Stevens, children add to the display their facsimiles of the wagon master's log, a bouquet of wildflowers gathered by those who walked beside the moving wagons, and a "letter" from Marcus Whitman detailing his experiences with the wagon train. Labels can be made for each article as it is added to the display.

Maps and Time Lines

Often authors of books with historical settings include a geographical map to help the reader locate the story setting. In *Araminta's Paint Box* by Karen Ackerman, a map shows two routes—the route a pioneer girl took to California, and the route her paint box took after she lost it. Other stories make sufficient reference to actual places so that children can infer a story location by carefully comparing the story and a contemporary map. One group of fourth graders found on a road map the probable route Ann Hamilton took in the 1780s when she walked across Pennsylvania in Jean Fritz's *The Cabin Faced West*. The movement of the Wilder family in the Little House books by Laura Ingalls Wilder can be followed on a map. Many fictional and biographical accounts of immigrants can be traced on world maps. As with many of the previous activities or projects in this chapter, maps, too, can help children look across a genre. The sources of folktales might be identified on a world map. The domains of tall-tale heroes and monsters might be located on a U.S. map. African folktales, fiction, and nonfiction might be located on a map of Africa as a way of differentiating features and regions of that continent. Children need many encounters with maps and their working parts (key, symbols, scale, direction) before they become skilled users of all that a map can reveal.

Older children often enjoy making detailed maps of imaginary "countries of the mind," such as that in Lloyd Alexander's *The Remarkable Journey of Prince Jen* or his Prydain in *The Book of Three*, Ursula K. Le Guin's archipelagos in *A Wizard of Earthsea*, or Brian Jacques's Mossflower Woods surrounding *Redwall*. While fantasy provides ample opportunities for children to design their own maps imaginatively, other genres of books can be mapped as well.

The concept of time is difficult for children to grasp until sometime near the end of the concrete operational stage of thinking or the beginning of formal operations (ages 11 to 12). Prior to this period, time lines may help students organize events in a person's life as represented in a book. Time lines also allow children to represent a synthesis of events in several books. A time line from Jean Fritz's *And Then What Happened, Paul Revere?* might include the date of Paul Revere's birth, the date he took over his father's business, the summer he spent in the army, his famous ride, and his death in 1818. Events in the lives of Revere's contemporaries, such as Benjamin Franklin or George Washington, might be more easily compared if they were placed on a time line of the same scale as Revere's.

Placing book events in the world's time challenges even sophisticated readers to select relevant events in both the book and human history. A three-strand time line allows children to separate groups or types of events from others. While *Friedrich*, Hans Peter Richter's story of a Jewish boy caught in pre–World War II Germany, contains a "chronology" of dates in a reference at the back of the book, students might represent selected governmental decrees on one stratum of a time line. A second stratum might represent the number of Jews living in the Third Reich according to yearly censuses. A third stratum might list important events in Friedrich's life. In this way children could see more clearly the political events against which Friedrich's tragic life was played out.

In making time lines, children need to agree on a scale so that events can be clearly shown—by year or by decade, for instance. Time lines can be made of string from which markers for events and years are hung. If children make time lines on a long roll of paper, entries can be written on cards or Post-it notes and placed temporarily along the line. In this way, corrections or realignments can be made easily.

Jackdaws

The term *jackdaw* comes from the British name for a relative of the crow that picks up brightly colored objects and carries them off to its nest. Commercially prepared jackdaw collections are sometimes available from museums and historical sites. These collections, based on an historical event or period, often include facsimile copies of diaries, letters, newspaper articles, advertisements, and other evidence from the time.

Teachers of elementary school children have modified this concept to suit activities and discussion with younger children. These teacher-made collections assemble resource materials that the teacher and children can handle in discussion, in dis-

play, or in actual construction and use. A jackdaw for Yoshiko Uchida's *Journey to Topaz*, for example, might include maps of the western United States on which children could locate the camps in which this Japanese American family was imprisoned in World War II. The jackdaw might also include photocopies of newspaper headlines of the time, relevant articles from that period from magazines such as *Time* and *Colliers*, a facsimile copy of one of the exclusion orders families were handed, and information about the author. Articles and documents that could accompany Laurence Yep's *Dragonwings* include reproductions of photographs of turn-of-the-century San Francisco's Chinatown, photographs of contemporary newspaper accounts of Chinese-built airplanes, a kite like the one Moon Shadow flew, and some green tea. Often sources for the factual material on which an historical fiction title is based are given in an author's note. Some jackdaws can then include copies of these actual

This jackdaw was assembled to help children understand the many themes and historical events in Graham Salisbury's *Under the Blood-Red Sun*.

figure 10.1   Making a Jackdaw

Each book will suggest its own specific items or references to collect. Here is a general list of things that might be included.

- Recipes from the book's time (a typical dinner, a menu for a celebration)
- Price lists of commonly purchased goods then and now (milk, shoes, a dozen eggs, a car)
- A time line of the book's events
- A time line of the period surrounding the book's events
- A map, actual or imagined, of the setting
- A letter, diary, log, or news article that could have been written by or about a book character
- A photocopy of a book-related news article or document
- Artwork from the period (painting, architecture, sculpture)
- Songs, music, or dances from the book's setting (sheet music or lyrics, tapes)
- Clothes of characters of the period (paper dolls, catalog format, collage)
- Something about the author of the book

source materials, or "facsimiles" can be created by the children. All materials can be placed in an appropriately decorated portfolio or box. **Figure 10.1** suggests some of the items that might be included in a jackdaw. Individual book titles will suggest other artifacts that children could include.

Helping children make connections between literature and their own experiences is an important teacher role. However, teachers need to recognize when enough is enough. After a six-week study of Laura Ingalls Wilder's *Farmer Boy*, one fifth grader said, "I hate this book." If teachers' first priority is to foster children's love of reading, they will be less likely to overburden children with factual inquiry. Teachers who appreciate the child's desire to know as a prior condition of learning can appreciate Louise Rosenblatt's criterion for the usefulness of background information: "It will have value only when the student feels the need of it and when it is assimilated into the student's experience of particular literary works."[9]

The School and the Community

To be successful, a classroom literature program needs an enthusiastic teacher, a good book collection, and students who are eager to read. However, to create a true community of readers, each teacher must also involve other teachers, students, administrators, librarians, and parents in discovering the delights of good books.

The Whole-School Program
Children learn what they live. Increasingly, educators are concerned that the quality of living in a school be equal to the quality of learning in that school. The physical

environment of the school provides the context of that learning, but it is only one aspect of it. What teachers really believe in and want for their students will usually be taught. All teachers and librarians must have a strong commitment to literature. Few children discover books by themselves; in most instances, a parent, teacher, or librarian has served as the catalyst for bringing books and children together. As children grow up seeing significant adults as readers, they become readers. Find a teacher who is enthusiastic about children's books, and you will find a class of children who enjoy reading. Invariably, the teacher who reads, who knows books, and who shares this enthusiasm with students will inspire a love of reading. Many schools have made the development of readers their top priority. As a total school faculty they have met and planned certain activities to promote children's interest in reading.

Involving Administrators

No literature program can be successful without the support of the principal. More and more principals and curriculum coordinators are taking time to read aloud to children. One curriculum coordinator makes it a point to read aloud in one of the classrooms in his school district every day.[10] Children look forward to his coming, and he anticipates their response to his choice of books. Another principal has developed a two-tiered reading program called The Principal's Reading Club. Children from kindergarten through second grade make appointments to read with the principal for fifteen minutes from a book of their choice. Students in grades 3 to 6 select a book from a provided list and after three weeks return to discuss it with the principal. The participants receive a reading certificate, button, and pencil that has "I Read to the Principal" on it. More important, children see the principal as someone interested in them and their reading, and it's a wonderful way for the principal to get to know children and their reading abilities and preferences.

The School Library Media Center

Every school needs a trained librarian and a school library media center. While the name has changed over the years to reflect the inclusion of nonprint materials such as films, videos, tapes, slides, computers, and software as well as books, the purpose of the center is to provide the best services and materials to facilitate learning for children. The library media center should be open all day, every day, to serve students in its unique way. Flexible scheduling of story hours or lessons on library research may be directed by the librarian in a special area, leaving the rest of the resources free for others to use. Children can learn without the constant presence of a teacher or librarian. A trained aide can help children find relevant books, films, videos, and DVDs. Parents have served most effectively as volunteers in the school media center. Children increase in their ability to do independent study by using a variety of sources. An abundance of materials should be readily and freely available.

Increasingly, new school library media centers have become the focal point of many schools, with classrooms radiating out from them. The space should be as flexible and fluid as possible to allow for growth and change. The environment should encourage free access to materials at all times. Children flow in and out, doing projects, finding resources, making their own books, producing films. As the library media center becomes more closely identified with the total instructional program, it becomes more integrated into the total school environment.

The Library Media Specialist

The library media specialist plays a very important role in the quality of learning and living that takes place in the library media center, the school, and the community. Serving as a full-time contributing faculty member, the librarian works with children, teachers, parents, and volunteer and professional aides. Specialized training provides background knowledge of children's books and all media for instruction, library media procedures, knowledge of children's development and behavior, understanding of various teaching methods, and knowledge of school curriculum needs and organization. Increasingly, the library media specialist is called on to give leadership, not only in providing the materials for instruction, but in shaping the curriculum itself. The library media program should be an integral part of the total school program. Working with teachers, the media specialist needs to be responsive to the curricular and instructional needs of the school. What units of study are the teachers planning to initiate this year? Books, films, and tapes on these subjects should be gathered together for the teachers' and children's use. Bibliographies of print and nonprint materials based on units of work should be developed cooperatively with teachers. Book lists and curriculum resources should be shared. The function of the school library media center is to provide an information-rich environment where teachers and students become effective users of print and nonprint materials.

Teachers and library media specialists become partners as they work together to help students learn to use information, to be critical of what they read and see, to make judgments about what is authentic and accurate, and to discover meaning. As students share their findings, they learn to question, compare, and combine information. Only such educated students can become contributing citizens to a democratic society.

Selecting Materials

With the increase of both numbers of books published and objections to the selection of certain books, it is essential that schools develop a selection policy. All professional library groups, and other professional organizations like the International Reading Association and the National Council of Teachers of English, strongly recommend that each school district develop a written statement that governs its selection of material. This policy statement should be approved by the school board and subsequently supported by its members if challenged. Factors to be considered in such a policy would include the following: who selects the materials, the quality of materials, appropriate content, needs and interests of special children, school curriculum needs, providing for balance in the collection, and procedures to follow for censorship and challenged material.

Because the subject matter of contemporary children's books is changing, the need for written criteria of selection has increased. Realism in children's books and young-adult novels reflects the same range of topics that can be seen on TV, at the movies, and in current bestsellers. It makes no sense to "protect" children from well-written or well-presented materials on such controversial subjects as abortion, narcotics, or sexual orientation when they see stories on the same subjects on TV. Increased sensitivity to sexism, racism, and bias in books and nonbook materials is another area of recent concern that points up the need for a clear statement on selection policies. Here are some general guidelines to consider when developing policies for book selection:

1. **Who Selects the Materials?** Teachers, students, and parents might recommend particular titles, but the final selection of materials for the school library should be determined by professionally trained personnel. Reliable reviews of children's books play an important part in the selection of books. Four well-known review journals are *Booklist*, the *Bulletin of the Center for Children's Books*, *Horn Book Magazine*, and the *School Library Journal*. Other sources for reviews are listed in Appendix B.

2. **Quality of Materials.** Criteria for evaluation and selection of all types of instructional materials should be established and should be available in written form. Books for the collection should meet the criteria of good literature described in preceding chapters. There may need to be a balance between popular demand and quality literature, but this is a decision that must be made by individual librarians, based on their knowledge of the reading abilities and interests of the children they serve and their own basic philosophy of book selection. A written policy statement of the criteria to be used when purchasing books will help solve this dilemma.

3. **Appropriate Content.** The content of the materials to be selected should be evaluated in terms of the quality of the writing or presentation. Almost any subject can be written about for children, depending on the honesty and sensitivity of its treatment by the author. We should not deliberately shock or frighten children before they have developed the maturity and inner strength to face the tragedies of life. However, literature is one way to experience life, if only vicariously. In the process, a reader can be fortified and educated.

4. **Children's Needs and Interests.** Materials should be purchased with the children who will be using them in mind. This includes materials for children with special needs and books that represent a wide diversity of multicultural experiences. Children from a particular culture should have opportunities to see themselves reflected in books. In a pluralistic society, however, all children should have an opportunity to read about children of different racial, religious, and ethnic backgrounds. Regardless of a child's background, a good selection policy should give children books that provide insight into their own lives but also take them out of those lives to help them see the world in its many dimensions.

5. **School Curriculum Needs.** Librarians should consider the particular needs of the school curriculum when ordering materials. Particular units in social studies or intensive study of the local region will require additional copies of books about the particular state, industries, and people of the region. The function of the school library media center is to provide a wide range of materials specially chosen to meet the demands of the school curriculum.

6. **Balance in the Collection.** Every school library needs to maintain a balanced collection. Keeping in mind the total needs of the school, the librarian should consider the following balances: book and nonbook material (including videotapes, audiotapes, films, CDs, DVDs, and other materials), hardback and paperback books, reference books, and trade books, fiction and nonfiction, poetry and prose, classics (both old and "new"), realistic and fanciful stories, books for younger and older children, books for poor and superior readers at each grade level, books for teachers to read to students and use for enrichment purposes, and professional books for teachers and parents.

Selection Versus Censorship There is a fine line between careful selection of books for children and censorship. The goal of selection is to *include* a book on the basis of its quality of writing and total impact; the goal of censorship is to *exclude* a book in which the content (or even one part) is considered objectionable. Selection policies recommend a balanced collection representative of the various beliefs held by a pluralistic society; censors would impose their privately held beliefs on all. The American Library Association's "Library Bill of Rights" contains six policies relating to censorship of books and the right of free access to the library for all individuals or groups. (Go to <www.ala.org>. and search "Library Bill of Rights.") This statement has been endorsed by the American Association of School Librarians and provides a firm foundation for schools to develop their own policies. Also see *Information Power: Guidelines for School Library Media Programs* (Chicago: American Library Association, 1998).

Dealing with Censorship If there is a demand for censorship, how should it be handled? The first rule is to recognize that anyone has the right to question specific selections. The second rule is to be prepared—have an accepted response process. A written selection policy statement should contain a standardized procedure to follow when materials are challenged and should be part of district policy. The National Council of Teachers of English provides one in its booklet *The Students' Right to Know*.[11] The American Library Association suggests two items to include: (1) "What brought this title to your attention?" (2) "Please comment on the resource as a whole, as well as being specific about those matters that concern you."[12] The major consideration, then, is to have a form available when you need it and to make it specific to the book itself and simple enough to fill out.

Generally, if parents or other citizens feel their voices have been heard and that they have been dealt with fairly, they will abide by the decision of the book selection committee. If, however, they represent a group that is determined to impose its values on the schools, they will continue their pressure. This is why it is essential that every library have a selection policy supported by the board and administration. Librarians and teachers also need to be aware of the support they can obtain from organizations like the Office for Intellectual Freedom of the American Library Association, the Freedom to Read Foundation of ALA, the National Council of Teachers of English, the International Reading Association, the American Civil Liberties Union, and People for the American Way.

Working with Parents and the Community

Many schools have found that by informing and involving parents in school programs and plans, problems such as censorship are headed off or resolved before they can develop into serious discord. Even more important, parent volunteers can be a particularly rich resource for teachers and librarians. Sometimes these volunteers can be parents of students, sometimes they might be volunteers from a senior citizen center. One first-grade teacher has "grandmothers" from a senior citizen center who come once a week for the whole morning. They read stories to small groups of children, even individuals. They help make big books that the teacher uses. Whatever is needed, there is an extra pair of hands to do it. Parents can also serve as resource persons, depending upon their background of experience. One parent who is an Egyptologist became a tremendous resource for third-grade children who were studying mummies. In preparation for this parent's visit, the teacher read aloud *Mummies Made in Egypt* by

Aliki, and the children prepared questions to ask him. He brought Egyptian artifacts and pictures to share with them. Another group of first-grade students were studying about families. They wanted to interview the oldest member of their family about his or her childhood. One grandfather was invited to the class, and children learned how to conduct an interview with him. Wherever possible, teachers should draw on the expertise of the community.

To help their students become part of a community of readers, teachers will want to plan time to communicate with them regularly about their reading. Parents, too, are an integral part of this community, and they will appreciate being informed about the literacy program and their child's progress.

Students can also reciprocate by contributing to the community themselves. Junior high school students in the Bronx so loved Katherine Paterson's *Bridge to Terabithia* that they wanted to share it with others. A literature group went out to the local senior citizens' residence and read it aloud to these new friends. Those seniors were invited to keep reading logs and join in the book discussions.

In one school the parents and children created the Book Nook, a tiny paperback bookstore literally made from a broom closet. They decorated it with Maurice Sendak posters and a charming hanging lamp and even turned the old sink into a "trading pot" where children could place a "used" paperback and exchange it for another. The whole school takes justifiable pride in this paperback bookstore. In another school the parents made a large wooden case on wheels that can be opened to create a bookstore anywhere in the building. Closed, it can be pushed flat against a wall. Parents will need help in getting such bookstores started and assuming responsibility for their operation. The librarian, a teacher who knows books, parents, and one or two children could serve as the selection committee to order new books. If teachers and parents support the store in the beginning, it will sustain itself once children know its regular hours and can find the books they want to buy and read.

With good planning, the community can be a wonderful resource for schools. The more a community participates, the more the people in that community will begin to take ownership and pride in their schools.

Evaluating the Literature Program

It is as easy to identify a school in which literature is an integral part of the curriculum as it is to recognize a home where books are loved and valued. Because we have not recommended any body of content that all children must learn, but rather have suggested that each school should plan its own literature program to include certain categories of experiences with literature, the **Guidelines: Evaluating a Literature Program** on page 306 could serve in two ways. First, they suggest to schools in the planning stages of a literature program what experiences ought to be offered to children. Second, they suggest measures for assessing a literature program already in place in an elementary or middle school. The first goal of all literature programs should be to develop lifetime readers. Since we know children are reading less and less in their free time at home, the school becomes their last best hope, not only for learning how to read, but also for *becoming readers*. Everything we do with books in schools should be measured against these criteria: Will this help children enjoy books? Will this help children become lifetime readers?

We know that children's reading for pleasure drops off when they are faced with the added homework and demands of middle school and high school. But if children have learned to love reading before that time, they will continue to read and increase their reading once they leave college. If they have not discovered the joys of reading before high school, they probably never will.

Evaluating a Literature Program

Guidelines

 Go to www.mhhe.com/kieferbrief1e *to access an expanded version of this evaluation form.*

Consider the following when evaluating a literature program:

Availability of Books and Other Media

- Is there a school library media center in each elementary school building?
- Does it meet American Library Association standards for books and other media?
- Is there a professionally trained librarian and adequate support staff in each building?
- Does every classroom contain several hundred paperbacks and a changing collection of hardbacks?
- Are reference books easily accessible to each classroom?
- May children purchase books in a school-run paperback bookstore?
- Do teachers encourage children to order books through various school book clubs?
- May children take books home?
- Are children made aware of the programs of the public library?

Time for Literature

- Do all children have time to read books of their own choosing every day?
- Do all teachers read to the children once or twice a day?
- Do children have time to discuss their books with an interested adult or with other children every day?
- Are children allowed time to interpret books through art, drama, music, or writing?
- Do children seem attentive and involved as they listen to stories?

- Do they ask to have favorites reread?
- Is literature a part of all areas, across the curriculum?

Motivating Interest

- Do teachers show their enthusiasm for books by sharing new ones with children, reading parts of their favorite children's books, discussing them, and so on?
- Do classroom and library displays call attention to particular books?
- Are children encouraged to set up book displays in the media center, the halls, and their classrooms?
- Does the media specialist plan special events—such as story hours, book talks, sharing films, and working with book clubs?
- Do teachers and librarians work with parents to stimulate children's reading?
- Are special bibliographies prepared by the librarians or groups of children on topics of special interest—mysteries, animal stories, science fiction, fantasy, and so on?
- Are opportunities planned for contacts with authors and illustrators to kindle interest and enthusiasm for reading?

Balance in the Curriculum

- Do teachers and librarians try to introduce children to a wide variety of genres and to different authors when reading aloud?
- Do teachers share poetry as frequently as prose?
- Do children read both fiction and nonfiction?
- Are children exposed to new books and contemporary poems as frequently as some of the old favorites of both prose and poetry?

(continued)

- Do children have a balance of wide reading experiences with small-group, in-depth discussion of books?

Evaluating Children's Growth as Readers

- Do children keep reading logs or records of their free reading?
- Do older students (grade 3 and up) keep a response journal of their reading?
- Do teachers record examples of children's growth and understanding of literature as revealed in their play, talk, art, or writing?
- Do students and teachers together create an assessment portfolio with samples of children's best work?
- Are children allowed to respond to books in a variety of ways (art, drama, writing), rather than by required book reports?
- Is depth of understanding emphasized, rather than the number of books read?
- Are children responding to a greater range and complexity of work?
- What percentage of the children can be described as active readers? Has this percentage increased?
- Are some children beginning to see literature as a source of lifelong pleasure?

Guidelines

Evaluating Teachers' Professional Growth

- Are teachers increasing their knowledge of children's literature?
- What percentage of the staff have taken a course in children's literature in the past five years?
- Are some staff meetings devoted to ways of improving the use of literature in the curriculum?
- Do teachers attend professional meetings that feature programs on children's literature?
- Are in-service programs in literature made available on a regular basis?
- Are in-service programs, such as administering the running record or the Miscue Analysis, given regularly?
- Are such professional journals as *New Advocate*, *Horn Book Magazine*, *Book Links*, and *School Library Journal* available to teachers and librarians?
- Are professional books on children's literature available?
- Have the teachers and librarians had a share in planning their literature programs?
- Do teachers feel responsible not only for teaching children to read but also for helping children find joy in reading?

Notes

1. Based on children's comments recorded by Susan Hepler in *Patterns of Response to Literature: A One-Year Study of a Fifth and Sixth Grade Classroom*, Ph.D. dissertation, Ohio State University, 1982.
2. See Christine C. Pappas, Barbara Z. Kiefer, and Linda L. S. Levstik, *An Integrated Language Perspective in the Elementary Classroom*, 4th ed. (Boston: Pearson Education, 2006).
3. Lesley M. Morrow, "The Impact of a Literature-Based Program on Literacy Achievement, Use of Literature, and Attitudes of Children from Minority Backgrounds," *Reading Research Quarterly* 27 (1992): 251–75.
4. See Taffy E. Raphael and Susan I. McMahon, "Book Club: An Alternative Framework for Reading Instruction," *Reading Teacher* 48.22 (1994): 102–116.
5. Maryann Eeds and Deborah Wells, "Grand Conversations: An Exploration of Meaning Construction in Literature Study Groups," *Research in the Teaching of English* 23.1 (1989): 4–29.
6. See Frederick R. Burton, "Writing What They Read: Reflections on Literature and Child Writers," in *Stories to Grow On*, ed. Julie M. Jensen (Portsmouth, N.H.: Heinemann, 1989), pp. 97–105.
7. See Karen Ernst, *Picturing Learning* (Portsmouth, N.H.: Heinemann, 1994).

8. Steve Moline, *I See What You Mean: Children at Work with Visual Information* (York, Me.: Stenhouse, 1995).
9. Louise Rosenblatt, *Literature as Exploration* (New York: Noble & Noble, 1976), p. 123.
10. James Mitchell, "Sound Bytes, Hamburgers and Billy Joel: Celebrating the Year of the Lifetime Reader," *Reading Today* 9 (August/September 1991): 29.
11. *The Students' Right to Know* (Urbana, Ill.: National Council of Teachers of English, 1982) <www.ncte.org/censorship>.
12. "Statement of Concern About Library/Media Center Resources," in *Intellectual Freedom Manual*, rev. ed. (Chicago: American Library Association, 1996), p. 167 <www.ala.org/alaorg/oif>.

Children's Literature

Go to **www.mhhe.com/kiefer1e** *to access the Children's Literature Database, which includes information on thousands of children's books. Following are some of the titles you will find in the database.*

Titles in blue = multicultural titles

Aardema, Verna. *Why Mosquitoes Buzz in People's Ears*. Illustrated by Leo Dillon and Diane Dillon. Dial, 1975.

Ackerman, Karen. *Araminta's Paint Box*. Illustrated by Betsy Lewin. Atheneum, 1990.

Ada, Alma Flor. *Daniel's Mystery Egg*. Illustrated by G. Brian Karas. Harcourt, 2001.

——. *Extra Extra! Fairy Tale News from the Hidden Forest*. Illustrated by Leslie Tryon. Atheneum, 2007.

——. *My Name Is María Isabel*. Illustrated by K. Dyble Thompson. Atheneum, 1993.

Ahlberg, Janet, and Allan Ahlberg. *The Jolly Postman, or Other People's Letters*. Little, 1986.

Alexander, Lloyd. *The Book of Three*. Holt, 1964.

——. *The Remarkable Journey of Prince Jen*. Dutton, 1991.

Aliki [Aliki Brandenberg]. *Mummies Made in Egypt*. Harper, 1985.

Allison, Jennifer. *Gilda Joyce, Psychic Investigator*. Dutton, 2005.

Anaya, Rudolfo. *The First Tortilla: A Bilingual Story*. Illustrated by Amy Córdova. U New Mexico P, 2007.

Appelbaum, Diana. *Giants in the Land*. Illustrated by Michael McCurdy. Houghton, 1993.

Aston, Dianna. *An Egg Is Quiet*. Illustrated by Sylvia Long. Chronicle, 2006.

Aveni, Anthony. *The First Americans: The Story of Where They Came From and Who They Became*. Illustrated by S. D. Nelson. Scholastic, 2005.

Ayres, Katherine. *North by Night: A Story of the Underground Railroad*. Delacorte, 1998.

Babbitt, Natalie. *Tuck Everlasting*. Farrar, 1975.

Barrett, Ron. *The Nutty News*. Knopf, 2005.

Bartoletti, Susan Campbell. *Hitler Youth: Growing Up in Hitler's Shadow*. Scholastic, 2005.

Bauer, Joan. *Peeled*. Putnam, 2008.

Beard, Darleen Bailey. *Twister*. Illustrated by Nancy Carpenter. Farrar, 1999.

Beatty, Patricia. *Jayhawker*. Morrow, 1991.

Bernard, Robin. *Insects*. National Geographic, 2001.

Bernhard, Emery. *Ladybug*. Illustrated by Durga Bernhard. Holiday, 1992.

Bernhard, Emery, and Durga Bernhard. *The Tree That Rains: The Flood Myth of the Huichol Indians of Mexico*. Holiday, 1994.

Berry, James. *Ajeemah and His Son*. HarperCollins, 1992.

Blos, Joan. *A Gathering of Days: A New England Girl's Journal, 1830–1832*. Scribner's, 1979.

Borden, Louise. *The Journey That Saved Curious George: The True Wartime Escape of Margaret and H. A. Ray*. Illustrated by Allan Drummond. Houghton, 2005.

Branley, Franklyn M. *Air Is All Around You*. Illustrated by Holly Keller. HarperCollins, 1986.

——. *Down Comes the Rain*. Illustrated by James Graham Hale. HarperCollins, 1997.

——. *Flash, Crash, Rumble and Roll*. Illustrated by Barbara and Ed Emberley. Rev. ed. Crowell, 1985.

Brown, Margaret Wise. *The Important Book*. Illustrated by Leonard Weisgard. Harper, 1949.

Bunting, Eve. *Dandelions*. Illustrated by Greg Shed. Harcourt, 1995.

——. *How Many Days to America? A Thanksgiving Story*. Illustrated by Beth Peck. Houghton, 1988.

Byars, Betsy. *The Burning Questions of Bingo Brown*. Viking Penguin, 1988.

——. *Goodbye, Chicken Little*. Harper, 1979.

——. *The Pinballs*. Harper, 1977.

——. *The Summer of the Swans*. Viking, 1970.

Cameron, Ann. *Colibrí*. Farrar, 2003.

Carbone, Elisa. *Night Running: How James Escaped with the Help of His Faithful Dog*. Illustrated by E. B. Lewis. Knopf, 2008.

——. *Stealing Freedom*. Knopf, 1999.

Carle, Eric. *The Very Hungry Caterpillar*. Putnam, 1989 [1969].

Carson, Mary Kay. *The Underground Railroad for Kids: From Slavery to Freedom with 21 Activities*. Chicago Review, 2005.

Caseley, Judith. *Dear Annie*. Greenwillow, 1991.

Chambers, Veronica. *Amistad Rising: The Story of Freedom.* Illustrated by Paul Lee. Harcourt, 1998.

Cheaney, J. B. *My Friend the Enemy.* Knopf, 2005.

Choi, Sook Nyul. *Year of Impossible Goodbyes.* Houghton, 1991.

Chotjewitz, David. *Daniel Half Human and the Good Nazi.* Translated by Doris Orgel. Atheneum, 2004.

Cleary, Beverly. *Dear Mr. Henshaw.* Morrow, 1983.

——. *Ramona Forever.* Illustrated by Alan Tiegreen. Morrow, 1984.

——. *Ramona Quimby, Age 8.* Illustrated by Alan Tiegreen. Morrow, 1981.

——. *Strider.* Illustrated by Paul O. Zelinsky. Morrow, 1991.

Clinton, Catherine. *I, Too, Sing America: Three Centuries of African American Poetry.* Illustrated by Stephen Alcorn. Houghton, 1998.

Cofer, Judith Ortiz. See Ortiz Cofer, Judith.

Collard, Sneed B., III. *The Prairie Builders: Reconstructing America's Grasslands.* Houghton, 2005.

Collier, James Lincoln, and Christopher Collier. *With Every Drop of Blood.* Delacorte, 1994.

Conrad, Pam. *My Daniel.* HarperCollins, 1989.

——. *Prairie Songs.* Illustrated by Darryl Zudeck. HarperCollins, 1985.

Cooper, Susan. *The Selkie Girl.* Illustrated by Warwick Hutton. McElderry, 1986.

Crews, Donald. *Sail Away.* Greenwillow, 1995.

Cummings, Pat. *Ananse and the Lizard: A West African Tale.* Holt, 2002.

Cushman, Karen. *Catherine Called Birdy.* Clarion, 1994.

Dahl, Roald. *James and the Giant Peach.* Illustrated by Nancy Ekholm Burkert. Knopf, 1961.

Danticat, Edwidge. *Behind the Mountains.* Scholastic, 2002.

de Maupassant, Guy. *When Chickens Grow Teeth.* Illustrated by Wendy Anderson Halperin. Orchard, 1996.

Deneberg, Barry. *Shadow Life: A Portrait of Anne Frank and Her Family.* Scholastic, 2005.

Edwards, Michelle. *Chicken Man.* Lothrop, 1991.

Ehlert, Lois. *Leaf Man.* Harcourt, 2005.

Erdrich, Louise. *The Birchbark House.* Hyperion, 1999.

——. *The Game of Silence.* HarperCollins, 2005.

——. *The Porcupine Year.* HarperCollins, 2008.

Facklam, Margery. *The Big Bug Book.* Illustrated by Paul Facklam. Little, 1994.

Feelings, Tom. *The Middle Passage.* Dial, 1995.

Ferris, Helen, comp. *Favorite Poems Old and New.* Illustrated by Leonard Weisgard. Doubleday, 1957.

Fleischman, Paul. *Joyful Noise: Poems for Two Voices.* Illustrated by Eric Beddows. Harper, 1988.

Fox, Paula. *The Slave Dancer.* Bradbury, 1973.

Freedman, Russell. *Buffalo Hunt.* Holiday, 1988.

——. *Children of the Wild West.* Clarion, 1983.

——. *Indian Chiefs.* Holiday, 1987.

——. *An Indian Winter.* Illustrated by Karl Bodmer. Holiday, 1992.

——. *Lincoln: A Photobiography.* Clarion, 1987.

Friend, Catherine. *The Perfect Nest.* Illustrated by John Manders. Candlewick, 2007.

Fritz, Jean. *The Cabin Faced West.* Putnam, 1958.

——. *And Then What Happened, Paul Revere?.* Illustrated by Margo Tomes. Coward-McCann, 1973.

Froman, Nan. *What's That Bug?* Illustrated by Julian Mulock. Little, 2001.

Galdone, Paul. *The Little Red Hen.* Houghton, 1979 [1973].

Gardner, Robert. *Wild Science Projects About Earth's Weather.* Illustrated by Tom Labaff. Enslow, 2007.

Garelick, May. *Where Does the Butterfly Go When It Rains?.* Illustrated by Nicholas Wilton. Mondo, 1997.

George, Jean Craighead. *Julie of the Wolves.* Harper, 1972.

——. *My Side of the Mountain.* Dutton, 1988 [1959].

Gibbons, Gail. *Chicks and Chickens.* Holiday, 2003.

——. *From Seed to Plant.* Holiday, 1991.

——. *Monarch Butterfly.* Holiday, 1989.

Glatshteyn, Yankev. *Emil and Karl.* Translated by Jeffrey Shandler. Roaring Brook, 2006.

Goble, Paul. *The Lost Children.* Simon, 1993.

Greenberg, David T. *Bugs!* Illustrated by Lynn Munsinger. Little, 1997.

Greenberg, Keith Elliott. *A Haitian Family.* Lerner, 1997.

Greenfeld, Howard. *The Hidden Children.* Ticknor, 1993.

Hamilton, Virginia. *The House of Dies Drear.* Illustrated by Eros Keith. Macmillan, 1968.

Hansen, Joyce. *The Captive.* Scholastic, 1994.

——. *I Thought My Soul Would Rise and Fly: The Diary of Patsy, a Freed Girl.* Scholastic, 1997.

Harrison, David L. *Bugs: Poems About Creeping Things.* Boyds, 2007.

Harvey, Brett. *My Prairie Christmas.* Illustrated by Deborah Kogan Ray. Holiday, 1990.

Hautzig, Esther. *The Endless Steppe: Growing Up in Siberia.* Crowell, 1968.

Hathorn, Libby. *Sky Sash So Blue.* Illustrated by Benny Andrews. Simon, 1998.

Hesse, Karen. *The Cats in Krasinski Square.* Illustrated by Wendy Watson. Scholastic, 2004.

Hest, Amy. *In the Rain with Baby Duck.* Illustrated by Jill Barton. Candlewick, 1995.

Hiçyilmaz, Gaye. *The Frozen Waterfall.* Farrar, 1994.

Himelblau, Linda. *The Trouble Begins.* Delacorte, 2005.

Hoberman, Mary Ann. *Yankee Doodle.* Illustrated by Nadine Bernard Westcott. Little, 2004.

Horvath, Polly. *The Pepins and Their Problems.* Farrar, 2004.

Huck, Charlotte. *A Creepy Countdown*. Illustrated by Jos. A. Smith. Greenwillow, 1998.

Hunter, Mollie. *A Stranger Came Ashore*. Harper, 1975.

Innocenti, Roberto, and Christophe Gallaz. *Rose Blanche*. Illustrated by Roberto Innocenti. Creative, 1985.

Jacques, Brian. *Redwall*. Philomel, 1986.

Jenkins, Priscilla Belz. *A Nestful of Eggs*. Illustrated by Lizzy Rockwell. HarperCollins, 1995.

Jenkins, Steve. *The Top of the World: Climbing Mount Everest*. Houghton, 1999.

Jones, Carol. *The Gingerbread Man*. Houghton, 2002.

Kalman, Bobbie. *Colonial Life*. Crabtree, 1992.

Kaplan, William. *One More Border: The True Story of One Family's Escape from War-Torn Europe*. Illustrated by Shelley Tanaka. Groundwood, 1998.

Kellogg, Steven. *A-Hunting We Will Go*. Morrow, 1998.

——. *Chicken Little*. Morrow, 1985.

Kelly, Irene. *It's a Butterfly's Life*. Holiday, 2007.

Krinitz, Esther Nisenthal, and Bernice Steinhardt. *Memories of Survival*. Hyperion, 2005.

Laird, Elizabeth. *Kiss the Dust*. Dutton, 1992.

——. *The Garbage King*. Barrons, 2003.

Le Guin, Ursula K. *A Wizard of Earthsea*. Illustrated by Ruth Robbins. Parnassus, 1968.

Lehman, Barbara. *Rainstorm*. Houghton, 2007.

Lester, Julius. *Days of Tears: A Novel in Dialogue*. Hyperion, 2005.

——. *From Slave Ship to Freedom Road*. Illustrated by Rod Brown. Dial, 1998.

——. *To Be a Slave*. Illustrated by Tom Feelings. Dial, 1968.

Levine, Gail Carson. *Writing Magic: Creating Stories That Fly*. HarperCollins, 2006.

Lewis, J. Patrick. *The Little Buggers: Insect and Spider Poems*. Illustrated by Victoria Chess. Dial, 1998.

Lewis, Richard. *All of You Was Singing*. Illustrated by Ed Young. Macmillan, 1991.

Lionni, Leo. *An Extraordinary Egg*. Knopf, 1994.

Little, Jean. *Hey World, Here I Am!* Illustrated by Sue Truesdell. Harper, 1989.

Lobel, Anita. *No Pretty Pictures: A Child of War*. Greenwillow, 1998.

London, Jonathan. *Hurricane!* Illustrated by Henri Sorensen. HarperCollins, 1998.

Lourie, Peter. *On the Trail of Sacagawea*. Boyds, 2001.

Lowry, Lois. *Number the Stars*. Houghton, 1989.

Lunge-Larsen, Lise. *The Hidden Folk: Stories of Dwarves, Selkies and Other Secret Beings*. Illustrated by Beth Krommes. Houghton, 2004.

Lyon, George Ella. *Come a Tide*. Illustrated by Stephen Gammell. Orchard, 1990.

Lyons, Mary E. *Letters from a Slave Boy: The Story of Joseph Jacobs*. Atheneum, 2007.

——. *Letters from a Slave Girl: The Story of Harriet Jacobs*. Scribner's, 1992.

MacLachlan, Patricia. *Sarah, Plain and Tall*. HarperCollins, 1985.

——. *Three Names*. Illustrated by Alexander Pertzoff. HarperCollins, 1991.

Malone, Michael. R. *A Nicaraguan Family*. Lerner, 1998.

Mankell, Henning. *Secrets in the Fire*. Annick, 2003.

Markle, Sandra. *A Rainy Day*. Illustrated by Cathy Johnson. Orchard, 1993.

Marzollo, Jean. *Pretend You're a Cat*. Illustrated by Jerry Pinkney. Dial, 1990.

Matas, Carol. *Greater Than Angels*. Simon, 1998.

McKissack, Patricia C., and Frederick McKissack. *Christmas in the Big House, Christmas in the Quarters*. Illustrated by John Thompson. Scholastic, 1994.

——. *Days of Jubilee: The End of Slavery in the United States*. Scholastic, 2003.

Medearis, Angela Shelf. *Dancing with the Indians*. Illustrated by Samuel Byrd. Holiday, 1991.

Meltzer, Milton. *Rescue: The Story of How Gentiles Saved Jews in the Holocaust*. HarperCollins, 1988.

Millman, Isaac. *Hidden Child*. Farrar, 2005.

Mochizuki, Ken. *Baseball Saved Us*. Illustrated by Dom Lee. Lee, 1993.

Montgomery, Sy. *Quest for the Tree Kangaroo: An Expedition to the Cloud Forest of New Guinea*. Photographs by Nic Bishop. Houghton, 2006.

——. *The Tarantula Scientist*. Photography by Nic Bishop. Houghton, 2004.

Mosley, Walter. *47*. Little, 2005.

Mowll, Joshua. *Operation Red Jericho*. Candlewick, 2005.

Mullins, Patricia. *One Horse Waiting for Me*. Simon, 1998.

Myers, Walter Dean. *Autobiography of My Dead Brother*. Illustrated by Christopher Meyers. HarperCollins, 2005.

Myracle, Lauren. *TTYL*. Abrams, 2005.

Newbery Linda. *At the Firefly Gate*. Random, 2007.

O'Malley, Kevin. *Captain Raptor and the Moon Mystery*. Illustrated by Patrick O'Brien. Walker, 2005.

Oppenheim, Shulamith Levy. *The Lily Cupboard: A Story of the Holocaust*. Illustrated by Ronald Himler. HarperCollins, 1992.

Orlev, Uri. *The Man from the Other Side*. Houghton, 1991.

Ormerod. Jan. *When an Elephant Comes to School*. Orchard, 2005.

Ortiz Cofer, Judith. *Call Me María*. Orchard, 2004.

Park, Frances, and Ginger Park. *My Freedom Trip*. Illustrated by Debra Reid Jenkins. Boyds, 1998.

Park, Linda Sue. *When My Name Was Keoko*. Clarion, 2002.

Partridge, Elizabeth. *Kogi's Mysterious Journey*. Illustrated by Aki Sogabe. Dutton, 2003.

Patent, Dorothy Hinshaw. *Prairies*. Holiday, 1996.

Paterson, Katherine. *Bridge to Terabithia*. Illustrated by Donna Diamond. Crowell, 1977.

———. *Jip: His Story*. Lodestar, 1996.

Paulsen, Gary. *Nightjohn*. Delacorte, 1993.

———. *Sarny*. Delacorte, 1997.

Peréz, Amada Irma. *Nana's Big Surprise / Nana, ¡Que sorprésa!*. Children's, 2007.

Perkins, Lynne Rae. *Pictures from Our Vacation*. Greenwillow, 2007

Philip, Neil. *War and the Pity of War*. Illustrated by Michael McCurdy. Clarion, 1998.

Pinkney, Andrea Davis. *Silent Thunder*. Hyperion, 1999.

Polacco, Patricia. *Just Plain Fancy*. Bantam/Doubleday, 1990.

———. *Pink and Say*. Philomel, 1994.

Posada, Mia. *Guess What Is Growing Inside This Egg?* Millbrook, 2007.

Powell, Jillian. *From Chick to Chicken*. Raintree, 2001.

Prelutsky, Jack. *Nightmares: Poems to Trouble Your Sleep*. Illustrated by Arnold Lobel. Greenwillow, 1976.

———, ed. *Read-Aloud Rhymes for the Very Young*. Illustrated by Marc Brown. Knopf, 1986.

———. *The Wizard*. Illustrated by Brandon Dorman. Greenwillow, 2007.

Rappaport, Doreen. *Escape from Slavery: Five Journeys to Freedom*. Illustrated by Charles Lilly. HarperCollins, 1991.

Robinett, Harriette Gillem. *Forty Acres and Maybe a Mule*. Atheneum, 1998.

Rockwell, Anne. *Bugs Are Insects*. Illustrated by Steve Jenkins. HarperCollins, 2001.

———. *Honey in a Hive*. Illustrated by S. D. Schindler. HarperCollins, 2005.

Rodanas, Kristina. *Follow the Stars*. Cavendish, 1998.

Rounds, Glen. *Sod Houses on the Great Plains*. Holiday, 1995.

Ruby, Lois. *Steal Away Home*. Macmillan, 1994.

Salisbury, Graham. *Under the Blood-Red Sun*. Delacorte, 1994.

San Souci, Robert D. *Sootface: An Ojibwa Cinderella*. Illustrated by Daniel San Souci. Doubleday, 1994.

Schrier, Jeffrey. *On the Wings of Eagles: An Ethiopian Boy's Story*. Millbrook, 1998.

Schulman, Janet. *Pale Male: Citizen Hawk of New York City*. Illustrated by Meilo So. Knopf, 2008.

Scieszka, Jon. *Seen Art?* Illustrated by Lane Smith. Viking, 2005.

Sendak, Maurice. *Where the Wild Things Are*. HarperCollins, 1963.

Serfozo, Mary. *Rain Talk*. Illustrated by Keiko Narahashi. McElderry, 1990.

Shulevitz, Uri. *Dawn*. Farrar, 1974.

Siegelson, Kim L. *In the Time of the Drums*. Illustrated by Brian Pinkney. Hyperion, 1999.

Sierra, Judy. *Tasty Baby Belly Buttons*. Illustrated by Meilo So. Knopf, 1999.

Simon, Seymour. *Big Bugs*. Chronicle, 2005.

———. *Storms*. Morrow, 1989.

Sipiera, Paul P., and Diane M. Sipiera. *Thunderstorms*. Children's Press, 1998.

Sklansky, Amy E. *Where Do Chicks Come From?* Illustrated by Pam Paparone. HarperCollins, 2005.

Sneve, Virginia Driving Hawk. *Lana's Lakota Moons*. Nebraska, 2007.

Snyder, Zilpha Keatley. *Libby on Wednesday*. Delacorte, 1990.

Spier, Peter. *Peter Spier's Rain*. Doubleday, 1982.

———. *The Star-Spangled Banner*. Doubleday, 1973.

Spinelli, Jerry. *Milkweed*. Knopf, 2003.

Stanley, Jerry. *I Am an American: A True Story of the Japanese Internment*. Crown, 1994.

Staples, Suzanne Fisher. *Under the Persimmon Tree*. Farrar, 2005.

Stevens, Carla. *Trouble for Lucy*. Illustrated by Ronald Himler. Clarion, 1979.

Stevens, Janet, and Susan Crummel Stevens. *Cook-a-Doodle-Doo!* Harcourt, 1999.

Swanson, Susan Marie. *The House in the Night*. Illustrated by Beth Krommes. Houghton, 2008.

Taylor, Peter Lane, and Christos Nicola. *The Secret of Priest's Grotto: A Holocaust Survival* Story. Kar-Ben, 2007.

Temple, Frances. *Grab Hands and Run*. Orchard, 1993.

———. *Tonight, by Sea*. Orchard, 1995.

Tillage, Leon. *Leon's Story*. Illustrated by Susan L. Roth. Farrar, 1997.

Toksvig, Sandi. *Hitler's Canary*. Roaring Brooks, 2007.

Tolstoy, Aleksei. *The Gigantic Turnip*. Illustrated by Niamh Sharkey. Barefoot, 1999.

Trottier, Maxine. *Prairie Willow*. Illustrated by Laura Fernandez and Rick Jacobson. Stoddart, 1998.

Turner, Ann. *Dakota Dugout*. Illustrated by Ronald Himler. Macmillan, 1985.

———. *Nettie's Trip South*. Illustrated by Ronald Himler. Simon, 1987.

Uchida, Yoshiko. *The Bracelet*. Illustrated by Joanna Yardley. Philomel, 1993.

———. *Journey to Topaz*. Illustrated by Donald Carrick. Creative Arts, 1985 [1971].

Van Camp, Richard. *What Is the Most Beautiful Thing You Know About Horses?* Illustrated by George Littlechild. Children's, 2003.

Van Laan, Nancy. *The Magic Bean Tree*. Illustrated by Beatriz Vidal. Houghton, 1998.

———. *Shingebiss: An Ojibwe Legend*. Illustrated by Betsy Bowen. Houghton, 1997.

Veciana-Suarez, Ana. *Flight to Freedom*. Scholastic, 2002.

Walgren, Judy. *The Lost Boys of Natinga: A School for Sudan's Young Refugees*. Houghton, 1998.

Wallace, Nancy Elizabeth. *Pumpkin Day!* Cavendish, 2002.

Wallner, Alexandra. *The Farmer in the Dell*. Holiday, 1998.

Walter, Mildred Pitts. *Alec's Primer*. Illustrated by Larry Johnson. Vermont Folklife Center, 2004.

Warren, Andrea. *Escape from Saigon: How a Vietnam War Orphan Became an American*. Farrar, 2004.

———. *Pioneer Girl: Growing Up on the Prairie*. Morrow, 1998.

———. *Surviving Hitler: A Boy in the Nazi Death Camps*. HarperCollins, 2001.

Watkins, Yoko Kawashima *So Far from the Bamboo Grove*. Lothrop, 1986.

Wheeler, Lisa. *Mammoths on the Move*. Illustrated by Kurt Cyrus. Harcourt, 2006.

Whelan, Gloria. *Goodbye Vietnam*. Knopf, 1992.

White, E. B. *Charlotte's Web*. Harper, 1952.

Wilder, Laura Ingalls. *Farmer Boy*. Illustrated by Garth Williams. Harper, 1953.

Williams, Vera B. *Stringbean's Trip to the Shining Sea*. Illustrated by Vera B. Williams and Jennifer Williams. Greenwillow, 1988.

———. *Three Days on a River in a Red Canoe*. Greenwillow, 1981.

———. *Cherries and Cherry Pits*. Greenwillow, 1986.

Wilson, Karma. *Bear Wants More*. Illustrated by Jane Chapman. McElderry, 2003.

Winerip, Michael. *Adam Canfield: Watch Your Back!* Candlewick, 2007.

Wong, Janet. *You Have to Write*. Illustrated by Teresa Flavin. McElderry, 2002.

Wormell, Mary. *Hilda Hen's Search*. Harcourt, 1994.

Wright-Frierson, Virginia. *An Island Scrapbook: Dawn to Dusk on a Barrier Island*. Simon, 1998.

———. *A North American Rain Forest Scrapbook*. Walker, 1999.

Xiong, Blia. *Nine-in-One Grr! Grr!* Adapted by Cathy Spagnoli. Illustrated by Nancy Hom. Children's, 1989.

Yagawa, Sumiko. *The Crane Wife*. Translated by Katherine Paterson. Illustrated by Suekichi Akaba. Morrow, 1981.

Yep, Laurence. *Dragonwings*. HarperCollins, 1975.

Young, Ed. *The Sons of the Dragon King*. Atheneum, 2004.

Ziefert, Harriet. *The Little Red Hen*. Illustrated by Emily Bolam. Viking, 1995.

Appendix A

Children's Book Awards

Following are descriptions of some of the major awards in children's literature. We have included winners beginning with 1990. For a complete list of award winners, go to the text's Web site at **www.mhhe.com/ kieferbrief1e.**

John Newbery Medal

The John Newbery Medal is named in honor of John Newbery, a British publisher and bookseller of the eighteenth century. He has frequently been called the father of children's literature because he was the first to conceive the idea of publishing books expressly for children.

The award is presented each year to "the author of the most distinguished contribution to American literature for children." Only books published in the preceding year are eligible, and the author must be an American citizen or a permanent resident of the United States. The selection of the winner is made by a committee of the Association for Library Service to Children (ALSC) of the American Library Association. There are now fifteen members on this committee. The winning author is presented with a bronze medal designed by René Paul Chambellan and donated by Frederick G. Melcher. The announcement is made in January or early February. Later, at the summer conference of the American Library Association, a banquet is given in honor of the award winners.

In the following list, for each year the Medal winner is listed first (in boldface italic type), followed by the Honor Books for that year. The date is the year in which the award was conferred. All books were published the preceding year.

1990 *Number the Stars* by Lois Lowry. Houghton.
Afternoon of the Elves by Janet Taylor Lisle. Jackson/Orchard.
Shabanu: Daughter of the Wind by Suzanne Fisher Staples. Knopf.
The Winter Room by Gary Paulsen. Jackson/Orchard.

1991 *Maniac Magee* by Jerry Spinelli. Little.
The True Confessions of Charlotte Doyle by Avi. Jackson/Orchard.

1992 *Shiloh* by Phyllis Reynolds Naylor. Atheneum.
Nothing but the Truth by Avi. Jackson/Orchard.
The Wright Brothers by Russell Freedman. Holiday.

1993 *Missing May* by Cynthia Rylant. Jackson/Orchard.
The Dark-Thirty: Southern Tales of the Supernatural by Patricia C. McKissack. Knopf.
Somewhere in the Darkness by Walter Dean Myers. Scholastic.
What Hearts by Bruce Brooks. HarperCollins.

1994 *The Giver* by Lois Lowry. Houghton.
Crazy Lady by Jane Leslie Conly. HarperCollins.
Dragon's Gate by Laurence Yep. HarperCollins.
Eleanor Roosevelt: A Life of Discovery by Russell Freedman. Clarion.

1995 *Walk Two Moons* by Sharon Creech. HarperCollins.
Catherine, Called Birdy by Karen Cushman. Clarion.
The Ear, the Eye, and the Arm by Nancy Farmer. Jackson/Orchard.

1996 *The Midwife's Apprentice* by Karen Cushman. Clarion.
What Jamie Saw by Carolyn Coman. Front Street.
The Watsons Go to Birmingham: 1963 by Christopher Paul Curtis. Delacorte.
Yolonda's Genius by Carol Fenner. McElderry.
The Great Fire by Jim Murphy. Scholastic.

1997 *The View from Saturday* by E. L. Konigsburg. Atheneum.
A Girl Named Disaster by Nancy Farmer. Jackson/ Orchard.
The Moorchild by Eloise McGraw. Simon.
The Thief by Megan Whalen Turner. Greenwillow.
Belle Prater's Boy by Ruth White. Farrar.

1998 *Out of the Dust* by Karen Hesse. Scholastic.
Ella Enchanted by Gail Carson Levine. HarperCollins.
Lily's Crossing by Patricia Reilly Giff. Delacorte.
Wringer by Jerry Spinelli. HarperCollins.

1999 *Holes* by Louis Sachar. Foster.
A Long Way from Chicago by Richard Peck. Dial.

2000 *Bud, Not Buddy* by Christopher Paul Curtis. Delacorte.
Getting Near to Baby by Audrey Couloumbis. Putnam.
Our Only May Amelia by Jennifer L. Holm. HarperCollins.
26 Fairmount Avenue by Tomie dePaola. Putnam.

2001 *A Year Down Yonder* by Richard Peck. Dial.
Because of Winn-Dixie by Kate DiCamillo. Candlewick.
Hope Was Here by Joan Bauer. Putnam.
Joey Pigza Loses Control by Jack Gantos. Farrar.
The Wanderer by Sharon Creech. HarperCollins.

2002 ***A Single Shard*** by Linda Sue Park. Clarion/
Houghton.

Everything on a Waffle by Polly Horvath. Farrar.

Carver: A Life in Poems by Marilyn Nelson. Front
Street.

2003 ***Crispin: The Cross of Lead*** by Avi. Hyperion.

The House of the Scorpion by Nancy Farmer.
Atheneum.

Pictures of Hollis Woods by Patricia Reilly Giff.
Random.

Hoot by Carl Hiaasen. Knopf.

A Corner of the Universe by Ann M. Martin. Scholastic.

Surviving the Applewhites by Stephanie S. Tolan.
HarperCollins.

2004 ***The Tale of Despereaux: Being the Story of a***
Mouse, a Princess, Some Soup, and a Spool of
Thread by Kate DiCamillo. Illustrated by Timothy
Basil Ering. Candlewick.

Olive's Ocean by Kevin Henkes. Greenwillow.

*An American Plague: The True and Terrifying Story of
the Yellow Fever Epidemic of 1793* by Jim Murphy.
Clarion.

2005 ***Kira-Kira*** by Cynthia Kadohata. Atheneum/Simon.

Al Capone Does My Shirts by Gennifer Choldenko.
Putnam.

*The Voice That Challenged a Nation: Marian Anderson
and the Struggle for Equal Rights* by Russell Freedman.
Clarion/Houghton.

Lizzie Bright and the Buckminster Boy by Gary D.
Schmidt. Clarion/Houghton.

2006 ***Criss Cross*** by Lynne Rae Perkins. Greenwillow.

Whittington by Alan Armstrong. Illustrated by S. D.
Schindler. Random.

Hitler Youth: Growing Up in Hitler's Shadow by Susan
Campbell Bartoletti. Scholastic.

Princess Academy by Shannon Hale. Bloomsbury.

Show Way by Jacqueline Woodson. Illustrated by
Hudson Talbott. Putnam.

2007 ***The Higher Power of Lucky*** by Susan Patron.
Illustrated by Matt Phelan. Simon.

Penny from Heaven by Jennifer L. Holm. Random.

Hattie Big Sky by Kirby Larson. Delacorte Press.

Rules by Cynthia Lord. Scholastic.

2008 ***Good Masters! Sweet Ladies! Voices from***
a Medieval Village by Laura Amy Schlitz.
Candlewick.

Elijah of Buxton by Christopher Paul Curtis.
Scholastic.

The Wednesday Wars by Gary D. Schmidt. Clarion.

Feathers by Jacqueline Woodson. Putnam.

Caldecott Medal

The Caldecott Medal is named in honor of Randolph Caldecott, a prominent English illustrator of children's books during the nineteenth century. This award, presented each year by an awards committee of the Association for Library Service to Children (ALSC) of the American Library Association, is given to "the artist of the most distinguished American picture book for children." In the following list, for each year the Medal winner is listed first (in boldface italic type), followed by the Honor Books for that year. If an illustrator's name is not cited, the author illustrated the book.

1990 ***Lon Po Po: A Red-Riding Hood Story from***
China. Adapted and illustrated by Ed Young.
Philomel.

Bill Peet: An Autobiography by Bill Peet. Houghton.

Color Zoo by Lois Ehlert. Lippincott.

Herschel and the Hanukkah Goblins by Eric Kimmel.
Illustrated by Trina Schart Hyman. Holiday.

The Talking Eggs by Robert D. San Souci. Illustrated
by Jerry Pinkney. Dial.

1991 ***Black and White*** by David Macaulay. Houghton.

Puss in Boots by Charles Perrault. Translated by
Malcolm Arthur. Illustrated by Fred Marcelino.
di Capua/Farrar.

"More More More," Said the Baby by Vera B. Williams.
Greenwillow.

1992 ***Tuesday*** by David Wiesner. Clarion.

Tar Beach by Faith Ringgold. Crown.

1993 ***Mirette on the High Wire*** by Emily Arnold
McCully. Putnam.

Seven Blind Mice by Ed Young. Philomel.

The Stinky Cheese Man and Other Fairly Stupid Tales
by Jon Scieszka. Illustrated by Lane Smith. Viking.

Working Cotton by Sherley Anne Williams.
Illustrated by Carole Byard. Harcourt.

1994 ***Grandfather's Journey*** by Allen Say. Houghton.

Peppe the Lamplighter by Elisa Bartone. Illustrated by
Ted Lewin. Lothrop.

In the Small, Small Pond by Denise Fleming. Holt.

Owen by Kevin Henkes. Greenwillow.

Raven: A Trickster Tale from the Pacific Northwest by
Gerald McDermott. Harcourt.

Yo! Yes? by Chris Raschka. Jackson/Orchard.

1995 ***Smoky Night*** by Eve Bunting. Illustrated by David
Diaz. Harcourt.

Swamp Angel by Paul O. Zelinsky. Dutton.

John Henry by Julius Lester. Illustrated by Jerry
Pinkney. Dial.

Time Flies by Eric Rohmann. Crown.

1996 ***Officer Buckle and Gloria*** by Peggy Rathman.
Putnam.

Alphabet City by Stephen T. Johnson. Viking.

Zin! Zin! Zin! a Violin by Lloyd Moss. Illustrated by Marjorie Priceman. Simon.

The Faithful Friend by Robert D. San Souci. Illustrated by Brian Pinkney. Simon.

Tops and Bottoms by Janet Stephens. Harcourt.

1997 ***Golem*** by David Wisniewski. Clarion.

Hush! A Thai Lullaby by Minfong Ho. Illustrated by Holly Meade. Kroupa/Orchard.

The Graphic Alphabet by David Pelletier. Orchard.

The Paperboy by Dav Pilkey. Orchard.

Starry Messenger by Peter Sis. Foster/Farrar.

1998 ***Rapunzel*** by Paul O. Zelinsky. Dutton.

The Gardener by Sarah Stewart. Illustrated by David Small. Farrar.

Harlem by Walter Dean Myers. Illustrated by Christopher Myers. Scholastic.

There Was an Old Lady Who Swallowed a Fly by Simms Taback. Viking.

1999 ***Snowflake Bentley*** by Jacqueline Briggs Martin. Illustrated by Mary Azarian. Houghton.

Duke Ellington: The Piano Prince and His Orchestra by Andrea Pinkney. Illustrated by Brian Pinkney. Hyperion.

No, David! by David Shannon. Scholastic.

Snow by Uri Shulevitz. Farrar.

Tibet Through the Red Box by Peter Sis. Foster.

2000 ***Joseph Had a Little Overcoat*** by Simms Taback. Viking.

A Child's Calendar by John Updike. Illustrated by Trina Schart Hyman. Holiday.

Sector 7 by David Wiesner. Clarion.

The Ugly Duckling by Hans Christian Andersen. Illustrated by Jerry Pinkney. Morrow.

When Sophie Gets Angry—Really, Really Angry . . . . by Molly Bang. Scholastic.

2001 ***So You Want to Be President?*** by Judith St. George. Illustrated by David Small. Philomel.

Casey at the Bat by Earnest Lawrence Thayer. Illustrated by Christopher Bing. Handprint.

Click, Clack, Moo: Cows That Type by Doreen Cronin. Illustrated by Betsy Lewin. Simon.

Olivia by Ian Falconer. Atheneum.

2002 ***The Three Pigs*** by David Wiesner. Clarion.

The Dinosaurs of Waterhouse Hawkins by Barbara Kerley. Illustrated by Brian Selznick. Scholastic.

Martin's Big Words by Doreen Rappaport. Illustrated by Brian Collier. Hyperion.

The Stray Dog by Marc Simont. HarperCollins.

2003 ***My Friend Rabbit*** by Eric Rohman. Roaring Brook.

The Spider and the Fly by Mary Howitt. Illustrated by Tony DiTerlizzi. Simon.

Hondo and Fabian by Peter McCarty. Holt.

Noah's Ark by Jerry Pinkney. Sea Star.

2004 ***The Man Who Walked Between the Towers*** by Mordicai Gerstein. Roaring Brook.

Ella Sarah Gets Dressed by Margaret Chodos-Irvine. Harcourt.

What Do You Do with a Tail like This? by Steve Jenkins and Robin Page. Houghton.

Don't Let the Pigeon Drive the Bus by Mo Willems. Hyperion.

2005 ***Kitten's First Full Moon*** by Kevin Henkes. Greenwillow.

The Red Book by Barbara Lehman. Houghton.

Coming on Home Soon by Jacqueline Woodson. Illustrated by E. B. Lewis. Putnam.

Knuffle Bunny: A Cautionary Tale by Mo Willems. Hyperion.

2006 ***The Hello, Goodbye Window*** by Norton Juster. Illustrated by Chris Raschka. di Capua/Hyperion.

Rosa by Nikki Giovanni. Illustrated by Bryan Collier. Holt.

Zen Shorts by Jon J. Muth. Scholastic.

Hot Air: The (Mostly) True Story of the First Hot-Air Balloon Ride by Marjorie Priceman. Schwartz/Atheneum/Simon.

Song of the Water Boatman and Other Pond Poems by Joyce Sidman. Illustrated by Beckie Prange. Houghton.

2007 ***Flotsam*** by David Wiesner. Clarion.

Gone Wild: An Endangered Animal Alphabet by David McLimans. Walker.

Moses: When Harriet Tubman Led Her People to Freedom by Carole Boston Weatherford. Illustrated by Kadir Nelson. Hyperion.

2008 ***The Invention of Hugo Cabret*** by Brian Selnick. Scholastic.

Henry's Freedom Box: A True Story from the Underground Railroad by Ellen Levine. Illustrated by Kadir Nelson. Scholastic.

First the Egg by Laura Vaccaro Seeger. Brook/Porter.

The Wall: Growing Up Behind the Iron Curtain by Peter Sis. Farrar/Foster.

Knuffle Bunny Too: A Case of Mistaken Identity by Mo Willems. Hyperion.

Batchelder Award

The Batchelder Award, established in 1966, is given by the Association of Library Service to Children (ALSC) of the American Library Association to the publisher of the most outstanding book of the year that is a translation, published in the United States, of a book that was first published in another country. In 1990, Honor Books were added to this award. The original country of publication is given in parentheses.

1990 *Buster's World* by Bjarne Reuter, translated by Anthea Bell. Dutton. (Denmark)

1991 *A Hand Full of Stars* by Rafik Schami, translated by Rika Lesser. Dutton. (Germany)

1992 *The Man from the Other Side* by Uri Orlev, translated by Hillel Halkin. Houghton. (Israel)

1993 No award

1994 *The Apprentice* by Molina Llorente, translated by Robin Longshaw. Farrar. (Spain)

1995 *The Boys from St. Petri* by Bjarne Reuter, translated by Anthea Bell. Dutton. (Denmark)

1996 *The Lady with the Hat* by Uri Orlev, translated by Hillel Halkin. Houghton. (Israel)

1997 *The Friends* by Kazumi Yumoto, translated by Cathy Hirano. Farrar. (Japan)

1998 *The Robber and Me* by Josef Holub, translated by Elizabeth C. Crawford. Holt. (Germany)

1999 *Thanks to My Mother* by Schoschana Rabinovici, translated by James Skofield. Dial. (Germany)

2000 *The Baboon King* by Anton Quintana, translated by John Nieuwenhuizen. Walker. (Netherlands)

2001 *Samir and Yonatan* by Daniella Carmi, translated by Yael Lotan. Scholastic. (Israel)

2002 *How I Became an American* by Karin Gündisch, translated by James Skofield. Cricket. (Germany)

2003 *The Thief Lord* by Cornelia Funke, translated by Oliver Latsch. Scholastic. (Germany)

2004 *Run, Boy, Run* by Uri Orlev, translated by Hillel Halkin. Lorraine. (Israel)

2005 *The Shadows of Ghadames* by Joëlle Stolz, translated by Catherine Temerson. Delacorte/Random. (France)

2006 *An Innocent Soldier* by Josef Holub, translated by Michael Hofmann. Levine/Scholastic. (Germany)

2007 *The Pull of the Ocean* by Jean-Claude Mourlevat, translated by Y. Maudet. Delacorte Press. (France)

The Killer's Tears by Anne-Laure Bondoux, translated by Y. Maudet. Delacorte Press. (France)

The Last Dragon by Silvana De Mari, translated by Shaun Whiteside. Hyperion/Miramax. (Italy)

2008 *Brave Story* by Miyuki Miyabe, translated by Alexander O. Smith. VIZ Media. (Japan)

The Cat: Or, How I Lost Eternity by Jutta Richter, translated by Anna Brailovsky, with illustrations by Rotraut Susanne Berner. Milkweed. (Germany)

Nicholas and the Gang by Rene Goscinny, translated by Anthea Bell, illustrated by Jean-Jacques Sempe. Phaidon Press. (France)

Laura Ingalls Wilder Award

The Laura Ingalls Wilder Award is given to an author or illustrator whose books (published in the United States) have made a substantial and lasting contribution to literature for children. Established in 1954, this medal was given every five years through 1980. As of 1983, it is given every three years by the Association of Library Service to Children (ALSC) of the American Library Association. The following are the award winners since 1990.

1992 Marcia Brown

1995 Virginia Hamilton

1998 Russell Freedman

2001 Milton Meltzer

2003 Eric Carle

2005 Laurence Yep

2007 James Marshall

Hans Christian Andersen Prize

The Hans Christian Andersen Prize, the first international children's book award, was established in 1956 by the International Board on Books for Young People. Given every two years, the award was expanded in 1966 to honor an illustrator as well as an author. A committee composed of members from different countries judges the selections recommended by the board or library associations in each country. The following have won the Hans Christian Andersen Prize since 1990.

1990 Tormod Haugen (author). Norway.
Lisbeth Zwerger (illustrator). Austria.

1992 Virginia Hamilton (author). United States.
Kveta Pacovská (illustrator). Czechoslovakia.

1994 Michio Mado (author). Japan.
Jörg Müller (illustrator). Switzerland.

1996 Uri Orlev (author). Israel.
Klaus Ensikat (illustrator). Germany.

1998 Katherine Paterson (author). United States.
Tomi Ungerer (illustrator). France.

2000 Anna Maria Machado (author). Brazil.
Anthony Browne (illustrator). United Kingdom.

2002 Aidan Chambers (author). United Kingdom.
Quentin Blake (illustrator). United Kingdom.

2004 Martin Waddell (author). Ireland.
Max Velthuijs (illustrator). Netherlands.

2006 Margaret Mahy (author). New Zealand.
Wolf Erbruch (illustrator). Germany.

2008 Jürg Schubiger (author). Switzerland.
Roberto Innocenti (illustrator). Italy.

General Awards

Boston Globe–Horn Book Awards *Horn Book Magazine,* 56 Roland St., Suite 200, Boston, MA 02129. Currently given for outstanding fiction or poetry, outstanding nonfiction, and outstanding illustration. <www.hbook.com/magazine>.

Golden Kite Award Society of Children's Book Writers, 8271 Beverly Blvd., Los Angeles, CA 90048. Presented annually by the Society of Children's Book Writers to members whose books of fiction, nonfiction, and picture illustration best exhibit excellence and genuinely appeal to interests and concerns of children. <www.scbwi.org>.

International Reading Association Children's Book Award International Reading Association, 800 Barksdale Rd., P.O. Box 8139, Newark, DE 19714-8139. An annual award for a first or second book to an author from any country who shows unusual promise in the children's book field. Since 1987, the award has been presented to both a picturebook and a novel. <www.reading.org>.

New York Times Choice of Best Illustrated Children's Books of the Year New York Times, 229 W. 43rd St., New York, NY 10036. Books are selected for excellence in illustration by a panel of judges.

Awards Based on Special Content

Jane Addams Book Award Jane Addams Peace Association, 777 United Nations Plaza, 6th Floor, New York, NY 10017. For a book with literary merit stressing themes of dignity, equality, peace, and social justice. <www.janeaddamspeace.org>.

Association of Jewish Libraries Awards Foundation for Jewish Culture, 122 E. 42nd St., Room 1512, New York, NY 10168. Given to one or two titles that have made the most outstanding contribution to the field of Jewish literature for children and young people. The Sydney Taylor Body of Work Award, established in 1981, is given for an author's body of work. <www.jewishculture.org>.

Catholic Book Awards Catholic Press Association of the United States and Canada, 205 W. Monroe St., Suite 470, Chicago, IL 60606. Honors selected in five categories and awarded to books with sound Christian and psychological values. <www.catholicpress.org>.

Child Study Children's Book Committee at Bank Street College Award Bank Street College of Education, 610 W. 112th St., New York, NY 10025. For a distinguished book for children or young people that deals honestly and courageously with problems in the world. <www.bnkst.edu>.

Christopher Awards The Christophers, 5 Hanover Square, 11th Floor, New York, NY 10004. Given to works of artistic excellence affirming the highest values of the human spirit. <www.christophers.org>.

Eva L. Gordon Award for Children's Science Literature Helen Ross Russell, Chairman of Publications Committee, ANSS, 44 College Dr., Jersey City, NJ 07305. Given by the American Nature Study Society to an author or illustrator whose body of work in science trade books is accurate, inviting, and timely.

Jefferson Cup Award Children's and Young Adult Roundtable of the Virginia Library Association, P.O. Box 8277, Norfolk, VA 23503-0277. Presented for a distinguished book in American history, historical fiction, or biography. <www.vla.org>.

Ezra Jack Keats Awards Given biennially to a promising new artist and a promising writer. The recipients receive a monetary award and a medallion from the Ezra Jack Keats Foundation, 450 14th Street, Brooklyn, NY 11215-5702. <www.ezra-jack-keats.org>.

Coretta Scott King Awards Social Responsibilities Round Table of the American Library Association, 50 E. Huron St., Chicago, IL 60611. Given to an African American author and an African American illustrator for outstanding inspirational and educational contributions to literature for children. <www.ala.org>.

National Council of Teachers of English Award for Excellence in Poetry for Children National Council of Teachers of English, 1111 Kenyon Rd., Urbana, IL 61801. Given formerly annually and presently every three years to a living American poet for total body of work for children ages 3 to 13. <www.ncte.org>.

National Jewish Book Awards JWB Jewish Book Council, 45 E. 33rd Street, New York, NY 10016. Various awards are given for work or body of work that makes a contribution to Jewish juvenile literature. <www.jcca.org>.

New York Academy of Sciences Children's Science Books Awards The New York Academy of Sciences, 7 World Trade Center, 250 Greenwich St., 40th Floor, New York, NY 10007. For books of high quality in the field of science for children, three awards are given: Younger Children, Older Children, and the Montroll Award for a book that provides unusual historical data or background on a scientific subject. <www.nyas.org>.

Scott O'Dell Award for Historical Fiction Zena Sutherland, 5429 Eastview Park, Chicago, IL 60615. Honors a distinguished work of historical fiction set in the New World. <www.scottodell.com>.

Orbis Pictus Award for Outstanding Nonfiction for Children 1111 W. Kenyon Rd., Urbana, IL 61801. Presented annually by the National Council of Teachers of English to the outstanding nonfiction book of the previous year. <www.ncte.org>.

Phoenix Award Given to the author of a book published for children twenty years before that has not received a major children's book award. Sponsored by the Children's Literature Association. <www.phoenixawards.org>.

Edgar Allan Poe Awards Mystery Writers of America, 17 E. 47th Street, 6th Floor, New York, NY 10017. For best juvenile mystery. <www.mysterywriters.org>.

Michael J. Printz Award Given to a book that exemplifies literary excellence in young-adult literature. Sponsored by the Young Adult Library Services Association of the American Library Association. <www.ala.org>.

Robert F. Sibert Informational Book Award Honors the author whose work of nonfiction has made a significant contribution to the field of children's literature in a given year. Sponsored by the Association of Library Services to Children. <www.ala.org>.

Washington Post/Children's Book Guild Nonfiction Award Washington Post, 1150 15th St. NW, Washington, DC 20071. Given to an author or illustrator for a body of work in juvenile informational books.

Western Writers of America Spur Award Western Writers of America, Inc., 508 Senter Pl., Selah, WA 98942. For the best western juvenile work in two categories, fiction and nonfiction. <www.westernwriters.org>.

Carter G. Woodson Book Award National Council for the Social Studies, 8555 16th Street, Suite 500, Silver Spring, Maryland 20910. Presented to outstanding social science books for young readers that treat sensitively and accurately topics related to ethnic minorities. <www.ncss.org>.

Awards for Lasting Contributions or Service to Children's Literature

Arbuthnot Award International Reading Association, 800 Barksdale Rd., P.O. Box 8139, Newark, DE 19714. Named after May Hill Arbuthnot, an authority on literature for children, this award is given annually to an outstanding teacher of children's literature. <www.reading.org>.

Arbuthnot Honor Lecture The Association of Library Service to Children (ALSC) of the American Library Association, 50 E. Huron St., Chicago, IL 60611. This free public lecture is presented annually by a distinguished author, critic, librarian, historian, or teacher of children's literature. Both the lecturer and the site for the lecture are chosen by an ALSC committee. <www.ala.org>.

Grolier Foundation Award American Library Association Awards Committee, 50 E. Huron St., Chicago, IL 60611. Given to a community librarian or a school librarian who has made an unusual contribution to the stimulation and guidance of reading by children and young people. <www.ala.org>.

Landau Award Salt Lake County Library System, 2197 E. 7000 St., Salt Lake City, UT 84121. Co-sponsored by the Department of Education of the University of Utah and Salt Lake County Library System. The award is given biennially to a teacher of children's literature who has most inspired students to pursue a knowledge of the field. <www.slco.lib.ut.us>.

Lucile Micheels Pannell Award Awards in the "general store" category and in the "children's specialty bookstore" category are presented annually by the Women's National Book Association to the owners of two bookstores whose innovative programs encourage children's reading.

Regina Medal Catholic Library Association, 100 North St., Suite 224, Pittsfield, MA 01201-510. For "continued distinguished contribution to children's literature." <www.cathla.org>.

University of Southern Mississippi Children's Collection Medallion University of Southern Mississippi Book Festival, USM Library, Hattiesburg, MS 39401. For a writer or an illustrator who has made an "outstanding contribution to the field of children's literature." <www.usm.edu>.

For more information about these and other awards, including lists of all prize winners, see *Children's Books: Awards & Prizes,* published and revised periodically by the Children's Book Council, 12 West 37th St., 2nd Floor, New York, NY 10018. Beginning in 1990, each year's *Books in Print* also publishes a listing of the current winners of various prizes. <www.cbcbooks.org>.

Appendix B

Note: Publishers' addresses may change. For complete and up-to-date information, see the current edition of *Literary Market Place* or *Children's Books in Print*.

Comprehensive Lists and Directories

Children's Books in Print. **Greenwood Publishing Group, 88 Post Rd. W., Westport, CT 06881. Annual.** A comprehensive listing of children's books currently in print. Includes titles for grades K–12. Titles are arranged alphabetically by author, title, and illustrator. A list of publisher addresses is provided. Also includes children's book awards for the previous ten years.

Children's Media Market Place, **4th ed. Barbara Stein. Neal-Schuman Publishers, 23 Leonard St., New York, NY 10013. 1995. 275 pp.** Annotated list of publishers of books and producers and distributors of nonprint materials, indexed by format, subject, and special interest. Includes a directory of wholesalers, bookstores, book clubs, and children's television sources.

Educational Media and Technology Yearbook. **Libraries Unlimited, P.O. Box 6633, Englewood, CO 80155. Annual.** Includes articles, surveys, and research on various aspects of media administration, creation, and use. Lists organizations, foundations, and funding agencies for media as well as information on graduate programs. Includes an annotated mediography of basic resources for library media specialists.

Guide to Reference Books for School Media Centers, **5th ed. Barbara Ripp Safford. Libraries Unlimited, P.O. Box 6633, Englewood, CO 80155. 1998. 407 pp.** Includes annotations and evaluations for 2,000 useful reference tools for school media centers. Materials are arranged in order by subject. Also includes a list of sources and selection aids for print and nonprint materials.

Magazines for Children: A Guide for Parents, Teachers, and Librarians, **2nd ed. Selma K. Richardson. American Library Association, 50 E. Huron St., Chicago, IL 60611. 1991. 139 pp., paper.** An annotated list of magazines designed especially for children ages 2–14; includes descriptions of the publications, age levels of users, and evaluative comments.

Reference Books for Children. **Carolyn Sue Peterson and Ann D. Fenton. Scarecrow Press, 4501 Forbes Blvd., Lanham, MD 20706. 1992. 414 pp.** Contains annotated entries over a broad range of curriculum areas, collection needs, interests, and reading levels of children. Books are classified by subject. Annotations provide some guidance in making selections for school collections.

Subject Guide to Children's Books in Print. **Greenwood Publishing Group, 88 Post Rd. W., Westport, CT 06881. Annual.** A companion volume to *Children's Books in Print.* Arranges all children's titles currently in print using over 6,000 subject headings. Particularly useful for finding and ordering titles on specific subjects; however, titles are not annotated.

General Selection Aids

Adventuring with Books: A Booklist for Pre-K–Grade 6, **13th ed. Amy McClure and Jan Kristo, eds. National Council of Teachers of English, 1111 Kenyon Rd., Urbana, IL 61601. 2002. 536 pp., paper.** Annotates about 1,800 children's titles published from 1996 to 1998. Annotations include summary, age, and interest levels. Contents are arranged by genre, broad subject, and theme. Author, title, and subject indexes.

Award-Winning Books for Children and Young Adults. **Betty L. Criscoe. Scarecrow Press, 4501 Forbes Blvd., Lanham, MD 20706. Annual.** Lists books that won awards during the previous year. Includes descriptions of the awards, criteria used for selection, plot synopses of winners, grade levels, and genres.

Best Books for Children: Pre-school through Grade 6. **John T. Gillespie. Greenwood Publishing Group, 88 Post Rd. W., Westport, CT 06881. 2005. 1,500 pp.**

Best Books for Middle School and Junior High Readers: Grades 6–9, **2nd ed. John T. Gillespie and Catherine Barr. Greenwood Publishing Group, 88 Post Rd. W., Westport, CT 06881. 2008. 1,192 pp.** Annotated listings of books that are selected to satisfy recreational needs, curricular needs, and interests of school children through grade 9. Books are arranged by broad age groups, subdivided by types of books. Each contains author, title, illustrator, and subject indexes.

Children's Books from Other Countries. **Carl M. Tomlinson, ed. Scarecrow Press, 4501 Forbes Blvd., Lanham, MD 20706. 1998. 304 pp.** Sponsored by the United States Board on Books for Young People, which also awards the Hans Christian Andersen Medal, the book lists 724 titles published in English, with some translated into English, between 1950 and 1995. Twenty-nine countries are represented. Each book is annotated, and age range and country of origin are given.

Children's Catalog, **18th ed. H. W. Wilson Co., 950 University Ave., Bronx, NY 10452. 2005. 1,346 pp.** A classified (Dewey Decimal System) catalog of about 6,000 recent "best" children's books, including publishing information, grade level, and a brief summary of each title. Also includes alphabetical author, title, subject, and analytical indexes. Contains a list of publishers with addresses. A new edition is issued every five years, with annual supplements in other years.

Choosing Books for Children. Betsy Hearne. University of Illinois Press, 1325 S. Oak St., Champaign, IL 61820. 2000. 250 pp., paper. Contains general selection advice for parents, teachers, and librarians, combined with bibliographies.

The Elementary School Library Collection: A Guide to Books and Other Media, 22nd ed. Linda L. Holms, ed. Brodart Co., 500 Arch St., Williamsport, PA 17705. 1998. 1,150 pp. A basic bibliography of materials, both print and nonprint, for elementary school media center collections. Materials are interfiled and arranged by subject classification (Dewey Decimal System). All entries include bibliographic information, age level, and a brief annotation. Contains author, title, and subject indexes.

The Horn Book Guide to Children's and Young Adult Books. Horn Book, Inc., 56 Roland St., Suite 200, Boston, MA 02129. Semiannual. Provides short reviews of children's and young-adult books published in the United States during the prior publishing season with references to longer reviews in *Horn Book Magazine*. Books are given a numerical evaluation from 1 to 6.

New York Times Parents' Guide to the Best Books for Children. Eden Ross Lipson. Times Books/Random House, 201 E. 50th St., New York, NY 10022. 2000. 421 pp. Indexes books by age appropriateness, listening level, author, title, illustrator, and subject. Books are arranged in broad categories, such as wordless books and picture storybooks.

The World Through Children's Books. Susan Stans, ed. Scarecrow Press, 4501 Forbes Blvd., Lanham, MD 20706. 2002. 324 pp., paper. Companion volume to Children's Books in Other Countries, this book annotates nearly 700 titles written in, or translated into, English and representing approximately 70 countries.

Booklists for Various Levels of Readers

Beyond Picture Books: A Guide to First Readers. Barbara Barstow and Judith Riggle. Greenwood Publishing Group, 88 Post Rd. W., Westport, CT 06881. 1995. 501 pp. Annotates over 1,600 first readers for ages 4–7, with a plot summary, brief evaluation, and bibliographic information. Indexes by title, illustrator, readability, series, and subject.

Books for the Gifted Child. Paula Hauser and Gail Nelson. 1988. 244 pp. Greenwood Publishing Group, 88 Post Rd. W., Westport, CT 06881. This volume critically annotates about 150 titles that would be useful in working with gifted children, ages preschool through 12. They are arranged in alphabetical order with bibliographic information and reading level included. Several chapters on the gifted child are included in the book.

Choices: A Core Collection for Young Reluctant Readers, Vol. 5. Beverley Fahey and Maureen Whalen, eds. John Gordon Burke, Publisher, P.O. Box 1492, Evanston, IL 60204-1492. 2006. 272 pp. Annotates books for second through sixth graders reading below grade level, published between 1983 and 1988, with plot summary, interest level, and reading level. Contains author and subject indexes.

Gifted Books, Gifted Readers. Nancy Polette. Libraries Unlimited, P.O. Box 6633, Englewood, CO 80155.

2000. 282 pp. Provides suggested units with activities and lists of books for four primary elements of literature (style, theme, character, setting). Books that stress these elements, or can be used to motivate thinking about them, are included in the lists.

More Rip-Roaring Reads for Reluctant Teen Readers. Bette D. Ammon and Gale W. Sherman. Libraries Unlimited, P.O. Box 6633, Englewood, CO 80155. 1998. 161 pp., paper. Lists books of high literary quality for reluctant readers in grades 3–12. Has brief annotations, reading and interest levels, and popular subject headings.

Booklists and Indexes for Particular Subjects
Picture Books and Concept Books

A to Zoo: Subject Access to Children's Picture Books, 7th ed. Carolyn W. Lima. Greenwood Publishing Group, 88 Post Rd. W., Westport, CT 06881. 2008. 1,800 pp. Provides subject access to over 8,000 picture books through 600 subject headings with cross-references and full bibliographic citations. Most titles are useful for children from preschool through second grade. Includes author, illustrator, and title lists.

Alphabet: A Handbook of ABC Books and Book Extensions for the Elementary Classroom, 2nd ed. Patricia L. Roberts. Scarecrow Press, 4501 Forbes Blvd., Lanham, MD 20706. 1994. 278 pp. Reviews over 200 alphabet books and provides about 80 activities to use with children from preschool to grade 6.

Alphabet Books as a Key to Language Patterns: An Annotated Action Bibliography. Patricia L. Roberts. Shoe String Press, 2 Linsley St., North Haven, CT 06473. 1987. 263 pp. Lists over 500 alphabet books that can be used in aiding language development under categories such as alliteration, rhymes and verses, and wordless books.

Counting Books Are More Than Numbers: An Annotated Action Bibliography. Patricia L. Roberts. Shoe String Press, 2 Linsley St., North Haven, CT 06473. 1990. 264 pp. Describes 350 books for preschool through second grade that can be used to encourage early understanding of mathematical concepts.

Informational Picture Books for Children. Patricia Jean Cianciolo. American Library Association, 50 E. Huron St., Chicago, IL 60611. 1999. 205 pp., paper. An annotated listing of nonfiction books, divided into major subject areas such as "The Natural World" and "Numbers and Arithmetic." Annotations include age levels and brief synopses.

Popular Series Fiction for K–6 Readers. Rebecca Thomas and Catherine Barr. Greenwood Publishing Group, 88 Post Rd. W., Westport, CT 06881. 2004. 816 pp. This annotated guide is organized alphabetically by series titles and includes information about the author, genre, and appropriate audience. Appendixes include series books for reluctant readers and ESL students.

Folklore, Storytelling, and Reading Aloud

Caroline Feller Bauer's New Handbook for Storytellers. Caroline Feller Bauer. American Library Association, 50 E. Huron St., Chicago, IL 60611. 1993. 550 pp., paper. A thorough guide to telling stories, this book includes ideas for creating puppets, story media, and using music and film in storytelling.

***Index to Fairy Tales, 1987–1992: Including 310 Collections of Fairytales, Folklore, Legends and Myths,* 6th supp. Joseph W. Sprug, comp. Scarecrow Press, 4501 Forbes Blvd., Lanham, MD 20706. 1994. 602 pp.** Indexes a broad range of collections of folktales and other folk literature by author, compiler, subject of tale (including characters, countries, and so on), and titles of tale. Various editions cover different collections, so the total coverage is quite broad.

***More Books Kids Will Sit Still For: The Complete Read-Aloud Guide,* 2nd ed. Judy Freeman. Greenwood Publishing Group, 88 Post Rd. W., Westport, CT 06881. 1995. 869 pp.** Lists over 2,000 titles recommended for reading aloud, and includes plot summaries, extension ideas, and related titles.

***The Read-Aloud Handbook,* 6th ed. Jim Trelease. Penguin Books, 375 Hudson St., New York, NY 10014. 2006. 387 pp., paper.** Contains a rationale for reading aloud, tips for good presentations, and an annotated list of books recommended for reading aloud.

***Stories: A List of Stories to Tell and Read Aloud,* 3rd ed. Marilyn B. Iarusso, ed. New York Public Library Publications Office, Fifth Ave. and 42nd St., New York, NY 10018. 1990. 104 pp.** Suggests proven stories to tell and read aloud to children. Includes poetry. Entries are briefly annotated.

***Storyteller's Sourcebook. 1983–1999.* Margaret Read MacDonald, ed. Gale Research, 835 Penobscot Bldg., Detroit, MI 48226-4094. 2001. 712 pp.** Provides access to folktales and folk literature in 700 collections. Tales are indexed by subject, motif, and title. Index is particularly useful in locating variants of tales.

***Storytelling with Puppets,* 2nd ed. Connie Champlin. American Library Association, 50 E. Huron St., Chicago, IL 60611. 1997. 264 pp.** Techniques for storytelling to younger audiences include open box theater, sound and action stories, and story aprons. Attention is given to multicultural themes and literature-based instruction.

***The Storytime Sourcebook II: A Compendium of Ideas and Resources for Storytellers.* Carolyn M. Cullum. Neal-Schuman Publishers, 23 Leonard St., New York, NY 10013. 2007. 325 pp.** Arranged by themes, lists plans for story-hour programs including books, films, filmstrips, videocassettes, and toys. Includes activities for 3- to 7-year-olds. Print and nonprint indexes.

Historical Fiction, History, and Biography

***From Biography to History: Best Books for Children's Entertainment and Education.* Catherine Barr. Greenwood Publishing Group, 88 Post Rd. W., Westport, CT 06881. 1998. 550 pp.** Indexes biographies in collections by individuals' names and by subject. Biographies are suitable for elementary school through junior high school.

***Literature Connections to World History: K–6 Resources to Enhance and Entice.* Lynda G. Adamson. Libraries Unlimited, P.O. Box 263, Littleton, CO 80160. 1998. 326 pp.** Lists and annotates books and media for younger readers about world history by time period and subject. Includes fiction and nonfiction.

***Literature Connections to World History: 7–12 Resources to Enhance and Entice.* Lynda G. Adamson. Libraries Unlimited, P.O. Box 263, Littleton, CO 80160. 1998. 326 pp.** Lists and annotates books and media for adolescents about world history by time period and subject. Includes fiction and nonfiction.

***Peoples of the American West: Historical Perspectives through Children's Literature.* Mary Hurlbut Cordier. Scarecrow Press, 4501 Forbes Blvd., Lanham, MD 20706. 1989. 230 pp.** Contains an analysis of historical fiction of the West as a genre and an annotated list of 100 books separated into grades K–3 and 4–9.

Cultural and Sexual Identity

***Against Borders: Promoting Books for a Multicultural World.* Hazel Rochman. American Library Association, 50 E. Huron St., Chicago, IL 60611. 1993. 288 pp., paper.** Essays and annotated book lists focus on specific ethnic groups and issues that tie world cultures together through themes.

***American Indian Reference Books for Children and Young Adults.* Barbara J. Kuipers. Libraries Unlimited, P.O. Box 263, Littleton, CO 80160. 1995. 260 pp.** Lists over 200 nonfiction sources of material on Native Americans for grades 3–12. Includes strengths and weaknesses of each book as well as curriculum uses. A section of the book deals with general selection criteria to use for these subjects.

***The Black American in Books for Children: Readings in Racism,* 2nd ed. Donnarae MacCann and Gloria Woodward. Scarecrow Press, 4501 Forbes Blvd., Lanham, MD 20706. 1985. 310 pp.** Collections of articles in which the issue of racism in children's books is considered from a variety of points of view. Includes many citations to books of both good and poor quality that reflect positive and negative values.

***Books in Spanish for Children and Young Adults: An Annotated Guide,* series 3. Isabel Schon. Scarecrow Press, 4501 Forbes Blvd., Lanham, MD 20706. 1993. 305 pp.** Contains listings of books for preschool through high school that have been published since 1982. The listed books represent diverse Hispanic cultures, including Mexico and Central and South America.

***Connecting Cultures: A Guide to Multicultural Literature for Children.* Rebecca L. Thomas. Greenwood Publishing Group, 88 Post Rd. W., Westport, CT 06881. 1996. 689 pp.** Annotated lists for grades K–6 include fiction, folktales, poetry, and songbooks about diverse cultural groups.

***The Coretta Scott King Awards: 1970–2004.* Henrietta M. Smith. American Library Association, 50 E. Huron St., Chicago, IL 60611. 2004. 115 pp.** Lists and annotates award winners and honor books.

***A Guide to Non-Sexist Children's Books: Volume 2, 1976–1985.* Denise Wilms and Ilene Cooper, eds. Academy Publisher, 213 W. Institute Pl., Chicago, IL 60610. 1987. 240 pp., paper.** Lists over 600 books in sections by grade level, through twelfth grade, subdivided into fiction and nonfiction. Indexes by author, title, fiction, and nonfiction subjects. Volume 1, which covered books up to 1976, is also available.

A Latino Heritage: A Guide to Juvenile Books About Latino Peoples and Cultures, **Volume 5. Isabel Schon. Scarecrow Press, 4501 Forbes Blvd., Lanham, MD 20706. 1995. 210 pp.** An annotated subject bibliography of works about the people, history, culture, and politics in the Latino countries as well as works about Latino people in the United States. The author indicates in the annotations the passages in which cultural bias and stereotyping might appear. Covers grades K–12. Volumes 2 (1985) and 3 (1988) are also available.

Kaleidoscope—A Multicultural Booklist for Grades K–8, **4th ed. Nancy Hansen-Krening, ed. National Council of Teachers of English, 1111 W. Kenyon Road, Urbana, IL 61801-1096. 2001. 248 pp.** Celebrating cultural diversity with annotations of nearly 400 books, covers a range from poetry to arts to biographies, folktales, and picture books, focusing especially on people of color.

Other Social Issues

The Bookfinder, Volume 5: When Kids Need Books. **Sharon Spredemann Dreyer. American Guidance Service, Publishers' Building, 4201 Woodland Rd., Circle Pines, MN 55014-1796. 1994. 519 pp., paper.** Subject, author, and title indexes are provided on the top half of the publication, and lengthy reviews that include subject cross-references, age levels, and specific information about the content of the book are on the bottom half. Both fiction and nonfiction are included. The books focus on problems children may experience, feelings, and relationships.

Books to Help Children to Cope with Separation and Loss, **4th ed. Masha K. Rudman, comp. Greenwood Publishing Group, 88 Post Rd. W., Westport, CT 06881. 1994. 514 pp.** Includes several chapters on bibliotherapy plus annotated lists of titles in such categories as death, divorce, adoption, and foster children, and loss of mental or physical functions. About 600 books are arranged by topic with an annotation, evaluation, and recommendations for use with children. Age levels from 3 to 16, interest, and reading level are included in each annotation.

Portraying Persons with Disabilities: An Annotated Bibliography of Fiction for Children. **Debra Robertson. Greenwood Publishing Group, 88 Post Rd. W., Westport, CT 06881. 1992. 482 pp.** Updates *Notes from a Different Drummer* and *More Notes from a Different Drummer,* books that provide annotated lists of titles that portray those with disabilities in fiction. Includes titles that promote better understanding and acceptance of the disabled.

Portraying Persons with Disabilities: An Annotated Bibliography of Nonfiction for Children. **Joan Brest Friedberg, June B. Mullins, and Adelaide Weir Sukiennik. Greenwood Publishing Group, 88 Post Rd. W., Westport, CT 06881. 1992. 400 pp.** Updates *Accept Me as I Am,* listing over 350 nonfiction titles about those with disabilities. Includes introductory essays about the portrayal of disabilities in literature for children.

Curriculum Areas and Genres of Literature

Anatomy of Wonder: A Critical Guide to Science Fiction. **Neil Barron, ed. Greenwood Publishing Group, 88 Post Rd. W., Westport, CT 06881. 2004. 1,016 pp.** Includes a chapter that annotates titles for children and young adults, as well as 3,000 additional titles that would appeal to readers of the genre. Includes discussion of sci-fi poetry, film connections, and a chapter on classroom aids.

Celebrations: Read-Aloud Holiday and Theme Book Programs. **Caroline Feller Bauer. H. W. Wilson Co., 950 University Ave., Bronx, NY 10452. 1985. 301 pp.** Includes readings and plans for holiday activities for both well-known and Bauer's invented holiday occasions.

Fantasy Literature for Children and Young Adults: An Annotated Bibliography, **5th ed. Ruth Nadelman Lyn. Greenwood Publishing Group, 88 Post Rd. W., Westport, CT 06881. 2005. 1,208 pp.** Annotates about 4,800 fantasy novels for 8- to 17-year-olds in ten chapters arranged by topics. Includes specific subject indexes.

Index to Children's Songs: A Title, First Line, and Subject Index. **Carolyn Sue Peterson and Ann D. Fento. H. W. Wilson Co., 950 University Ave., Bronx, NY 10452. 1979. 318 pp.** Indexes over 5,000 songs in 298 children's songbooks, both single titles and collections. Songs are indexed by title and first line as well as by 1,000 subject headings and cross-references.

Index to Poetry for Children and Young People, 1993–1997. **G. Meredith Blackburn, et al. H. W. Wilson Co., 950 University Ave., Bronx, NY 10452. 1999. 400 pp.** The latest in a series of volumes that index collections of poetry by author, title, first line, and subject. Different collections are indexed in each volume. Classifies poems under a wide variety of subjects, making for easy access to poems by their topics.

The Literature of Delight: A Critical Guide to Humorous Books for Children. **Kimberly Olson Fakih. Greenwood Publishing Group, 88 Post Rd. W., Westport, CT 06881. 1993. 269 pp.** Lists 1,000 fiction and nonfiction books with humorous presentations. Chapters include books of nonsense, books of satire and parody, poetry, and so on.

Information About Authors and Illustrators

Bookpeople: A Second Album. **1990. 200 pp., paper.**

Bookpeople: A Multicultural Album. **1992. 170 pp., paper. Both by Sharon L. McElmeel. Libraries Unlimited, P.O. Box 263, Littleton, CO 80160.** Each volume introduces authors and illustrators of picture books for grades 3–9. Brief biographies include highlights of life and career and selected bibliographies of their work.

Children's Book Illustration and Design II. **Julie Cummins, ed. PBC International, One School St., Glen Cove, NY 11542. 1997. 240 pp., hardcover.** This beautifully designed and printed volume includes a sample of picturebook illustrators, brief biographies, and information about the illustrators' media and techniques.

The Essential Guide to Children's Books and Their Creators. **Anita Silvey, ed. Houghton Mifflin, 222 Berkeley St., Boston, MA 02116. 2002. 800 pp.** This handsomely designed book includes biographical descriptions of and first-person reflections by important twentieth-century authors and illustrators and critical essays on a range of topics central to the study of children's literature.

The Illustrator's Notebook. **Lee Kingman, ed. Horn Book, 11 Beacon St., Boston, MA 02108. 1978. 168 pp.** Contains excerpts from articles by artists and illustrators that have appeared in the *Horn Book Magazine.* Articles discuss philosophy of illustration, history, illustration's place in the arts, and illustrators' experiences with various techniques of illustration.

Illustrators of Children's Books 1967–1976. **Lee Kingman, Grace Allen Hogarth, and Harriet Quimbly, eds. Horn Book, 11 Beacon St., Boston, MA 02108. 1978. 290 pp.** Contains brief biographical and career sketches of artists and illustrators for children who were actively at work in this field during the period. Articles discuss techniques, philosophy, and trends in illustration during the period. Bibliographies are included for each illustrator, as are selected bibliographies covering art and illustration of the period.

The Marble in the Water: Essays on Contemporary Writers of Fiction for Children and Young Adults. **David Rees. Horn Book, 11 Beacon St., Boston, MA 02108. 1980. 224 pp., paper.** Essays on 18 British and American authors, including Beverly Cleary, Paula Fox, Judy Blume, and Paul Zindel.

Meet the Authors and Illustrators: 60 Creators of Favorite Children's Books Talk About Their Work. **Deborah Kovacs and James Preller. Scholastic Inc., 730 Broadway, New York, NY 10003. 2001. 142 pp.** Two children's book authors have collected information on favorite authors and illustrators from around the world. Each two-page highlight includes information about the author or illustrator, selected titles, pictures, and a "do-it-yourself" activity suggested for children.

Newbery Medal Books: 1922–1955. **Bertha Mahoney Miller and Elinor Whitney Field, eds. 1955. 458 pp.**

Caldecott Medal Books: 1938–1957. **Bertha Mahoney Miller and Elinor Whitney Field, eds. 1957. 239 pp.**

Newbery and Caldecott Medal Books: 1956–1965. **Lee Kingman, ed. 1965. 300 pp.**

Newbery and Caldecott Medal Books: 1966–1975. **Lee Kingman, ed. 1975. 321 pp.**

Newbery and Caldecott Medal Books: 1976–1985. **Lee Kingman, ed. 1986. 321 pp. All published by Horn Book, 11 Beacon St., Boston, MA 02108.** Each volume contains biographical sketches and texts of the award winners' acceptance speeches as well as general observations of trends in the awards.

Ninth Book of Junior Authors and Illustrators. **Connie Rockman, ed. 2005. 600 pp. Latest in a series published by H. W. Wilson Co., 950 University Ave., Bronx, NY 10452.** These volumes provide readable biographies of popular authors for young people that include, generally, a biographical statement by the author or illustrator, a photograph, a brief biography, and a list of that person's works.

Pauses: Autobiographical Reflections of 101 Creators of Children's Books. **Lee Bennett Hopkins. Harper-Collins, 10 E. 53rd St., New York, NY 10022. 1995. 233 pp.** A collection of personal reflections taken from interviews with noted authors and illustrators.

A Sense of Story: Essays on Contemporary Writers for Children. **John Rowe Townsend. Horn Book, 56 Roland St., Ste. 200, Beacon St., Boston, MA 02129. 1973. 216 pp.** Includes essays on 19 English-language authors for children, including brief biographies, notes on their books, critical remarks, and lists of their books. Essays reflect the critical position of the author.

Something About the Author. **Anne Commaire. Gale Research, 835 Penobscot Bldg., Detroit, MI 48226-4094. There are over 186 volumes in print, added to periodically.** Clear and sizable essays on contemporary authors and illustrators. Updating allows more-recent authors to be included. Contains photographs as well as reproductions from works of the illustrators. Suitable for middle-grade children to use for gathering biographical information.

A Sounding of Storytellers: New and Revised Essays on Contemporary Writers for Children. **John Rowe Townsend. Harper & Row, 10 E. 53rd St., New York, NY 10022. 1979. 218 pp.** Townsend reevaluates seven of the authors included in his earlier *A Sense of Story,* including the new ground they have covered in more-recent works. Several American authors are included in the new selections, including Vera Cleaver and Bill Cleaver, Virginia Hamilton, and E. L. Konigsburg.

Periodicals

Appraisal: Science Books for Young People. **Children's Science Book Review Committee, Northeastern University, 54 Lake Hall, Boston, MA 02115. Quarterly.** Each issue contains reviews of about 75 children's and young-adult science and technology books. Gives age levels and ratings of quality.

Bookbird. **IBBY, The International Board on Books for Young People, University of Toronto Press, 5201 Dufferin St., North York, Ontario M3H 5T8, Canada. Quarterly.** This excellent journal reflects the international character of children's literature through articles and profiles of authors and illustrators from member countries. Themed issues have included "Children's Poetry," "Southeast Asia," "Girls and Women," and "Philosophy for Children."

Book Links. **American Library Association, 50 E. Huron St., Chicago, IL 60611. Six times/year.** This publication connects books, libraries, and classrooms. Special features include "book strategies" or guides for teaching a particular book, interviews with authors and illustrators to discover their personal story behind the book, book themes, poetry, and "just for fun," books for children to read and enjoy.

Booklist. **American Library Association, 50 E. Huron St., Chicago, IL 60611. Twice/month.** Reviews both adult and children's titles, including both print and nonprint materials. Reviews are annotated and graded by age levels and grades. Includes reviews of new selection tools. Often contains subject lists of good books in particular fields. Lists prize-winning books annually.

Book Review Digest. H. W. Wilson Co., 950 University Ave., Bronx, NY 10452. **Ten times/year. Service basis rates quoted on request.** Evaluates about 4,000 adult and children's books per year. For those books included, provides citations from several reviews that have appeared in other review periodicals.

Book World. c/o Washington Post, 1150 15th St. NW, **Washington, DC 20071. Weekly.** A weekly supplement to the *Post* and several other newspapers. Reviews children's books regularly. Issues large special children's book editions in fall and spring.

The Bulletin of the Center for Children's Books. Johns **Hopkins University Press, 2715 N. Charles St., Baltimore, MD 21218. 11 issues.** Reviews about 75 current children's books in each issue with negative as well as favorable reviews. Each entry is graded. Annotations stress curricular use, values, and literary merit.

Canadian Children's Literature. CC Press, P.O. Box 335, **University of Guelph, Guelph, Ontario N1G ZW1, Canada. Quarterly.** Literary analysis, criticism, and reviews of Canadian children's literature. A thematic approach for each issue. Predominantly written in English, but some articles are in French or in French and English.

CBC Magazine. Children's Book Council, 12 W. 37th **St., New York, NY 10018. <www.cbcbooks.org/ cbcmagazine>.** A Web site about children's books, including information about special events, free and inexpensive materials from publishers, and lists of prizewinners, as well as discussion of new books.

Childhood Education. Association for Childhood **Education International, 17904 Georgia Ave., Suite 215, Olney, MD 20902. Six times/year.** Includes a column on children's books that contains annotated reviews on about 25 books.

Children and Libraries. Association for Library Services to Children and Young Adult Services Division, American Library Association, 50 E. Huron **St., Chicago, IL 60611. Quarterly.** Provides articles on issues in children's literature and children's librarianship, international news, texts of speeches, and lists of upcoming events of interest in the field. Articles are often annotated bibliographies on subjects of current interest.

Children's Literature in Education. c/o Agathon Press, **233 Spring St., New York, NY 10013. Quarterly.** Publishes longer articles on English and American children's literature, including criticism, history, and biographical essays.

Cricket Magazine. Marianne Carus, ed. Carus Corp., **315 Fifth St., Box 300, Peru, IL 61354. Monthly.** A literary magazine for children of elementary school age. Includes new stories and poems by well-known children's authors as well as excerpts and serializations of older pieces of literature. Includes children's reviews of books, interviews with authors, and children's writing.

Five Owls. Five Owls, 2000 Aldrich Ave. S., Minneapolis, MN 55405. **Four issues/year.** Each online issue provides an article on a theme or topic and bibliographies that enhance or support it. Includes a signed review section.

Horn Book Magazine. Horn Book, Inc., 56 Roland St., **Ste. 200, Boston, MA 02129. Bimonthly. <www .hbook.com>.** Includes detailed reviews of children's books judged by the editorial staff to be the best in children's literature. Contains articles about the literature, interviews with authors, and text of important speeches in the field of literature (Newbery and Caldecott acceptance speeches are published in the August issue each year). October issue lists the outstanding books of the previous year.

Journal of Children's Literature. Children's Literature **Assembly of the National Council of Teachers of English. <www.childrensliteratureassembly.org>. Two issues/year.** The journal comes with membership in the Children's Literature Assembly and features articles, book reviews, and classroom ideas that focus on children's literature.

Knowledge Quest (formerly School Library Media Quarterly). American Association of School Librarians, American Library Association, 50 E. Huron **St., Chicago, IL 60611. Quarterly.** Official journal of the AASL. Includes articles on book evaluations, censorship, library services, standards of service, and so on.

Language Arts. National Council of Teachers of English, 1111 Kenyon Rd., Urbana, IL 61801. **Monthly September to May.** "Books for Children" section features regular reviews of new books. Several issues focus on literature and reading, containing articles on authors, using literature in the classroom, and so on.

The Lion and the Unicorn. Johns Hopkins University **Press, P.O. Box 19966, Baltimore, MD 21211. Three issues/year.** Literary criticism, book reviews, and interviews with authors of children's literature. Each issue presents a particular theme or genre around which articles are centered.

The New York Times Book Review. New York Times **Co., 229 W. 43rd St., New York, NY 10036. Weekly.** Weekly column entitled "For Younger Readers" reviews a few children's books. Two issues in fall and spring are devoted to children's books exclusively. Before Christmas, a list of outstanding books is included.

Publisher's Weekly. R.R. Bowker, 121 Chanlon Rd., **New Providence, NJ 07974. Weekly.** Twice a year, in spring and fall, a "Children's Book Number" is published that includes new titles from all major publishers, as well as reviews. Negative reviews are included. Occasionally includes feature articles on children's books and publishing for children.

School Library Journal. P.O. Box 16388, North Hollywood, CA 91615. **Monthly.** Reviews most children's books, using librarians, teachers, and critics from around the country as reviewers. Includes both positive and negative reviews. Categorizes reviews by age levels. Also includes feature articles on children's literature, children's library services, technology, and nonprint materials. December issue includes a "Best Books" section.

Science Books and Films. American Association for **the Advancement of Science, 1200 New York Ave. NW., Washington, DC 20005. Bimonthly.** Reviews trade, text, and reference books for students in all grades in both pure and applied sciences. Includes nonprint materials. Indicates level of expertise required to use a piece of material. Books are reviewed by specialists in the field.

Science and Children. National Science Teachers Association, 1840 Wilson Blvd., Arlington, VA 22201. Eight times/year. Includes a monthly column that reviews books and nonprint materials.

Selected Professional Web Sites

American Association of School Librarians
<www.ala.org/aasl>.
The American Association of School Librarians is a division of the American Library Association responsible for planning, improving, and extending library media services for children and young people. Its Web site offers Kids Connect, a question answering and referral service to help K–12 students with research or personal interests.

Association of Library Services to Children
<www.ala.org/alsc>.
The Association of Library Services to Children is the division of the American Library Association that oversees the Caldecott and Newbery awards and provides many other activities relating to children and books.

Children's Book Council
<www.cbcbooks.org>.
The Children's Book Council is the trade association of U.S. publishers of children's books. The Council promotes the use and enjoyment of trade books and related materials for young people and disseminates information about

children's trade book publishing. This site provides links to author Web sites and provides bibliographies such as Notable Social Studies Trade Books for Children and Outstanding Science Books for Children.

Cooperative Children's Book Center (CCBC)
<www.soemadison.wisc.edu/ccbc/index.htm>.
The Cooperative Children's Book Center at the University of Wisconsin is a noncirculating examination study and research library for adults with an interest in children's and young-adult literature. CCBC-Net is an electronic forum to discuss books for children and young adults.

International Reading Association
<www.reading.org>.
The International Reading Association seeks to promote literacy by improving the quality of reading instruction, serving as a clearinghouse for reading research, and promoting life-long reading habits.

National Council of Teachers of English
<www.ncte.org>.
NCTE is a professional organization of educators in English Studies, Literacy, and the Language Arts. NCTE-talk provides a monthly forum on special interests such as assessment.

Young Adult Library Services Association of the American Library Association
<www.ala.org/yalsa>.
The Young Adult Library Services Association is the division of the American Library Association that oversees the Printz Award and provides many other activities relating to young adults.

Author, Illustrator, Title Index

Maruki, Toshi, 75, 214
Marvelous Math, 175
Marzollo, Jean, 294
Masterpiece, 128
Matas, Carol, 7
Matthews, L. S., 31
Maudie and Me and the Dirty Book, 191
Max, 75
McCaughrean, Geraldine, 110, 112
McClosky, Robert, 26, 48, 63
McCord, David, 161, 167
McCully, Emily Arnold, 253
McKay, Hilary, 188
McKissack, Patricia C., 280
McPhail, David, 33
McSwigan, Marie, 217
Meet the Austins, 4, 188
Meltzer, Milton, 241
Mermaid Summer, 6
Mermaids and Monsters, 112
Merriam, Eve, 168, 169, 177
Meyer, Louis A., 216
Meyers, Christopher, 61, 65
Michelson, Richard, 63
Midnight Horse, The, 134
Miles, Betty, 191
Miller, Margaret, 255
Millions, 10, 33
Millions of Cats, 63
Mills, Claudia, 205
Milne, A. A., 3, 126, 128, 159
Milway, Katie Smith, 84
Miraculous Journey of Edward Tulane, The, 128–129
Miss Mary Mack and Other Street Rhymes, 156
Miss Polly Has a Dolly, 7
Mitten, Tony, 158
M.L.K.: Journey of a King, 240
Moe, Jørgen Engebretsen
Mohammed, Khadra, 84
Mojave, 161
Moline, Steve, 297
Mommy Laid an Egg, 259
Monarch Butterfly, 256
Monkey and Me, 7
Monkey Island, 280
Montgomery, Sy, 239, 240, 259, 280
Moon, Have You Met My Mother?, 167, 174
"Moon's the North Wind's Cooky, The," 160
Morales, Yuyi, 13
"Morning Has Broken," 293
Morris, Ann, 255
Morris, Gerald, 138
Morrison, Lillian, 168
Moser, Barry, 98, 109
Moses, 64
Moses, Sheila P., 219, 220
Mosley, Walter, 217, 220

Mosque, 257
Mosquito Bite, 239, 253–254
Most Beautiful Place in the World, The, 188, 193
Mother Goose; Numbers on the Loose, 156
Mother's Journey, A, 247
Mound, Lawrence, 250
Mourlevat, Jean Claude, 7
Mowll, Joshua, 216
Mr. Chickee's Funny Money, 32
Mr. Popper's Penguins, 129
Mr. Rabbit and the Lovely Present, 69
"Mrs. Peck-Pigeon," 157
Mufaro's Beautiful Daughter, 104, 105
Mummies Made in Egypt, 258, 304
"Mummy Slept Late and Daddy Fixed Breakfast," 166
Murawski, Diane, 239
Murdock, Catherine Gilbert, 138
Murphy, Jim, 240, 251, 254
Muth, John, 63
My America: A Poetry Atlas of the United States, 175
My America series, 213
My Bonny Light Horseman, 216
My Brother Sam Is Dead, 214
My Dog May Be a Genius, 158
My Heart Is on the Ground: The Diary of Nannie Little Rose, 219
My Mother Is the Most Beautiful Woman in the World, 4
My Name Is Celia/Me llamo Celia, 250
My New York, 290
My One Hundred Adventures, 200
My Side of the Mountain, 6
My Very First Mother Goose, 156
Myers, Walter Dean, 188
Mysterious Universe, The, 6
Mystery of the Mammoth Bones, The: And How It Was Solved, 251

N

Nancy Drew books, 199
Narnia series, 126, 189
Natarella, Margaret, 167
National Geographic Our World: A Child's First Picture Atlas, 259
Naylor, Phyllis Reynolds, 201
Nelson, Kadir, 64, 214
Nelson, Marilyn, 163
Nelson, Scott Reynolds, 239, 240, 251

Neuman, Susan B., 8
Nevius, Carol, 64
Newbery, John, 60
Night of the Howling Dogs, 189
Night Swimmers, The, 297
Nightingale, The, 125
Nightmares, 293
Nine-in-One Grr! Grr!, 295
Noah's Ark, 114
North American Rain Forest Scrapbook, A, 287
Norton, Mary, 131, 143
Nory Ryan's Song, 214
Not a Stick, 6
Number the Stars, 7, 187, 215
Nye, Naomi Shihab, 169

O

O'Connor, Jane, 7
Odyssey, The, 112
Oh, the Places You'll Go!, 4
Old Woman and Her Pig, The: An Appalachian Folk Tale, 97–98
Oliver Finds His Way, 34, 35
Olive's Ocean, 12
O'Mally, Kevin, 281
On My Honor, 33, 192
On Reading Books to Children: Parents and Teachers, 8
Once Upon a Poem, 164
One at a Time, 161
One-Eyed Giant, The, 112
One Hen, 84
1, 2, Buckle My Shoe, 67
O'Neill, Alexis, 75–76
Operation Red Jericho, 216
Operation Typhoon Shore, 216
Opie, Iona, 156
Orgel, Doris, 68
Ormerod, Jan, 280
Osborne, Mary Pope, 112
Out of the Dust, 10
Over in the Pink House, 156
Oxford Illustrated Book of American Children's Poems, 168

P

Pale Male: Citizen Hawk of New York City, 291
Panchatantra, 108
"Pandora's Box," 295
Parish, Peggy, 26
Park, Barbara, 11
Park, Linda Sue, 12, 191, 229
Parker, Nancy Winslow, 255–256
Park's Quest, 217
Paschkis, Julie, 76

Paterson, Katherine, 6, 12, 188, 194, 217, 220–221, 305
Paulsen, Gary, 189
"Peach," 160
Pearce, Philippa, 136, 143
Pearsall, Shelley, 220
Pearson, Mary E., 141
Peck, Richard, 216
Pelly D, The Diary of, 141
Pepins and Their Problems, The, 280
Peppe the Lamplighter, 214
Percy Jackson series, 126
Perkins, Lynne Rae, 7, 188
Permanent Rose, 188
Perrault, Charles, 98, 106
Persephone, 110
Peter Pan, 126
Phantom Tollbooth, The, 32
"Pickety Fence, The," 167
Pictures from Our Vacation, 7
Pierce, Tamora, 138
Pinballs, The, 194, 270, 271, 297
Pinkney, Jerry, 72, 73, 98, 108, 114, 125, 294
Piping Down the Valleys Wide, 159
Pippi Goes on Board, 129
Pippi in the South Seas, 129
Pippi Longstocking, 129
Place My Words are Looking for, The, 169
Poems for the Very Young, 168
Pogany, Willy, 112
Polacco, Patricia, 73
Polar Express, The, 63
Poole, Amy Lowry, 109
Poppy, 7
Porcupine Year, The, 215, 217, 219
Portis, Antoinette, 6
Potter, Beatrix, 35, 60, 73–74, 127, 144
Prairie Songs, 221
Prehistoric Actual Size, 256, 258
Prelutsky, Jack, 158, 161, 168, 169, 174, 175, 176, 280, 293, 294
Pretend You're a Cat, 294
Pretty Salma; A Red Riding Hood Story from Africa, 105
Princess Ben, 138
Princess Furball, 104
Prineas, Sarah, 134
Pringle, Laurence, 241
Probuduti, 63
Project Mulberry, 12, 191
Pryor, Bonnie, 215
Psst!, 64–65
Pterosaurs, 253
Pull of the Ocean, The, 7

Subject Index

folktales *(continued)*
    themes in, 103–104
    types of, 97–99, 100
    versions of, 105
foreshadowing, 285
formal operational stage, 141
format
    of nonfiction books, 258
    of picturebooks, 72–73
free verse, 165
Froebel, Friedrich, 156

G
gender, reading choices and, 27
gender stereotyping, 75
generous person/greedy person, 108
Gilligan, Carol, 32
Gothic art, 70
graphic organizers, 297–300
Great Depression, historical fiction about, 228

H
haiku, 165
Hans Christian Andersen Medal, 13, 15
helpful companions, 107
hero myths, 110
hierarchy of needs, 33–34
high fantasy, 138–140
historical fiction, 213–214
    challenging perspectives in, 230–231
    chronological approach to, 224–229
    classroom approaches to, 222, 223
    curriculum standards and, 233–234
    evaluating, 218–222
    ten-point model for teaching controversial issues, 232–233
    thematic approach to, 223
    types of, 215–218
    value of, 214–215
how-to books, 248
human behavior, insights into given in children's literature, 6–7
humor
    in picturebooks, 82–83
    in poetry, 172–173
    in realistic fiction, 201–202

I
identification books, 249
illustration
    artistic conventions in, 69
    artist's personal style, 71
    color in, 63

composition in, 64–65
line and shape in, 61
media used for, 65–68
perspective in, 64
space in, 63
value in, 63
imagery, in poetry, 159–160
imaginary realms, 137–138
imagination, developed by children's literature, 6, 141, 145
immigrants, historical fiction about, 227–228
Impressionism, 69, 70
informational books. *See* nonfiction
intelligence, development of, 30–31
International Board on Books for Young People, 13, 15
intuition, 141

J
jackdaws, 299–300
Japanese prints, 71
Jones, Susan, 18
journals, for children's writing, 287
"journey-novel," 101

K
King, Dr. Martin Luther, Jr., 17, 18
Kohlberg, Lawrence, 32

L
language
    authenticity of, 220
    figurative, 160–161, 220–221
    in picturebooks, 73–75
    uses of, 45
    vividness of in nonfiction, 254
language development, reading response and, 31–32
learning theory, 30–31
library media specialists, 302
life-cycle books, 249
limericks, 165
line and shape, in illustration, 61
literary fairy tales, 126–127
literature-based curriculum
    book talks, 283
    books that serve as writing models, 288–289
    components of, 278–279
    drama in, 294–296
    evaluation of, 305–307
    graphic organizers, 297–300

music and movement used with, 293–294
purposes of, 272–273
reading aloud, 279–282
reading books, 284
selecting materials, 302–304
storytelling, 283
talking about books, 284–285
using fiction and nonfiction books together, 273–278
visual arts for exploring literature, 288–291
whole-school program, 300–304
working with parents and the community, 304–305
lyrical poetry, 165

M
magical gifts, 105–106, 107
magical powers, fantasy about, 134–135
maps, 298–299
Maslow, Abraham, 33–34
media, in illustration, 65–68, 257–258, 291–292
media center, 301
metaphor, 160
Middle Ages, historical fiction about, 224
middle school children
    books for, 43–44
    reader response of, 47–49
Mildred L. Batchelder Award, 15
mixed media, 66
moral development, reading response and, 32–33
Mother Goose rhymes, 156
motifs, 105–108
movement, in the classroom, 294
multicultural experiences, poetry about, 173–174
music, in the classroom., 293–294
mysteries, in realistic fiction, 203–204
myths, 109
    creation myths, 109–110
    editions, 110–111
    hero myths, 110
    nature myths, 110

N
naming, 107
narrative poetry, 164
National Association for the Education of Young Children, 205

National Council of Teachers of English (CTE), 240, 259
National Literacy Trust, 27
Native Americans
    historical fiction about, 224–225, 274–275
    nonfiction about, 274–275
nature and seasons, poetry about, 171
nature myths, 110
NCTE/IRA Standards for the English Language Arts, 90
Near Eastern art, 70
Newbery Medal, 13, 15, 191, 201, 229, 239–240
nonfiction, 239
    accuracy and authenticity in, 241–247
    adequacy of coverage in, 251
    audience for, 250–251
    avoidance of stereotypes in, 245
    awards for, 239–241
    challenging perspectives on, 259–260
    content and perspective in, 247, 250–252
    curriculum standards and, 262–263
    defined, 239
    evaluating, 242
    illustrations and format, 256–258
    inclusion of all significant facts in, 243–244
    scientific inquiry demonstrated in, 251–252
    style in, 253–254
    types of, 248–249
    up-to-dateness of, 243
    use of facts to support generalizations, 245–246
nonfictions, avoidance of anthropomorphism in, 246–247
nostalgia, 4
nursery rhymes, 155–156

O
onomatopoeia, 158
operational stage, 141
Orbis Pictus Award for Outstanding Nonfiction for Children, 15, 240, 259
organization, in nonfiction books, 254–256

P
painting, 66
participant role in language use, 45

peer recommendations, reading choices and, 28
pen and ink, for illustration, 66
performance poetry, 178
personal values, in children's literature, 5–7
personality development, reading response and, 33–35
personification, 160
perspective, 64
photographic essays, 249
photographs, in nonfiction books, 257–258
physical development, reading response and, 29–30
Piaget, Jean, 30–31, 32, 145
picturebooks
    alphabet and counting, 77
    animals as people in, 81
    artistic conventions in, 69
    artist's personal style in, 71
    awards for, 16–17
    children around the world in, 80
    choice of media for, 65–68
    color in, 85–87
    content of, 75–76
    cultural referents in, 85, 87
    curriculum standards and, 90
    defined, 59–61
    elements of design, 61–65
    evaluating, 74
    familiar experiences in, 79–80
    family depicted in, 78–79
    fantasy in, 83
    format of, 72–73
    history of, 60
    humorous, 82–83
    language of, 73–75
    modern folktale style in, 82
    nonfiction, 229
    social and environmental concerns in, 81
    stereotypes in, 16
    ten-point model for teaching controversial issues, 88–89
    wordless books, 77–78
plot, 10, 101–102, 105
poetry, 155
    about animals, 172
    challenging perspectives on, 177–179
    children's preferences in, 166–167
    choral reading of, 176–177
    curriculum standards and, 181–182
    early forms, 155–156

evaluating, 162–163
of everyday experience, 170–171
figurative language in, 160–161
forms of for children, 164–165
humorous, 172
imagery in, 159–160
impact of, 162
including in classroom day, 174–175
multicultural collections, 173–174
of nature and seasons, 171
performance poetry, 178
poetry books for children, 167–174
reading to children, 175–176
rhyme and sound in, 158–159
rhythm in, 156–157
shape in, 161–162
spoken word, 178
ten-point model for teaching controversial issues, 180–181
poetry slams, 178
point of view, 12
porquoi (why) tales, 98, 100
preoperational stage, 141
preposterous situations, fantasy about, 129–130
preschool children, response of to literature, 46–47
preschoolers, books for, 35–37
primary age children
    books for, 37–43
    reader response of, 46–47
printmaking, 66
puppetry, 296
Pura Belpré Medal, 13, 15, 17

R

race, of author, 192–193
reader response theory, 45–46
reader's theater, 295–296
reading aloud, 279–282
reading log, 286–287
reading preferences, 25–26
    age and gender differences, 26–27
    other determinants, 27–28
    understanding children's choices, 28
realism, defining, 189–191
realistic fiction, 187–189
    author's background, 192–193

categorizing for appropriateness, 194
challenging perspectives on, 204–205
curriculum standards and, 208
defining realism in, 189–191
evaluating, 193
popular types of, 199–204
sampling of, 195–198
ten-point model for teaching controversial issues, 206–207
realistic tales, 99, 100
reference aids, in nonfiction books, 255–256
refugees, fiction and nonfiction about, 278
Renaissance, the
    art of, 69, 70
    historical fiction about, 225
repetition
    as plot element, 102
    in poetry, 159
reproduction, factual treatment of, 243–244
response journal, 287
rhyme, in poetry, 158
rhythm, in poetry, 156–157
Robert F. Sibert Informational Book Medal, 13, 15, 240
Rococo art, 70
Romanticism, in art, 70

S

school library, 301
school stories, 203
Science Content Standards, 119–120, 181–182, 263
science fiction, 140–142
scientific inquiry, in nonfiction books, 251–252
sensorimotor stage, 145
setting, 10
sex, factual treatment of, 243–244
shape, in poetry, 161–162
sijo, 165
simile, 160
slavery
    historical fiction about, 226–227, 275–276
    nonfiction about, 275–276
social concerns, depicted in picturebooks, 81
social influences on reading choices, 27–28
Social Studies Standards, 148–149, 233–234
sound, in poetry, 158
space, in illustration, 63

spectator role in language use, 45
spoken word poetry, 178
sports, in realistic fiction, 202–203
stereotypes, 16
    cultural, 75–76
    gender, 75
    in nonfiction, 245
    in realistic fiction, 191–192
stitchery and cloth, for illustration, 66
story theater, 296
storytelling, 283
structure, in nonfiction books, 255
style, 11–12
    in folktales, 103
    in nonfiction, 253–254
supernatural, the, 135–136
Surrealism, 70
survey books, 249
suspense, 135–136

T

Ten-Point Model for teaching controversial issues, 12, 17–21
    for historical fiction, 232–233
    for language choices in poetry, 180–181
    for modern fantasy, 146–147
    for nonfiction, 261–262
    for picturebooks, 88–89
    for realistic fiction, 206–207
    for traditional literature, 117–118
theme, 10–11, 103–104
time-shift fantasy, 136–137
timelines, 298–299
title page, of picturebook, 72
toys, fantasy about, 128
traditional literature, 96–97
    the Bible as literature, 114–115
    challenging perspectives on, 115–116, 118
    curriculum standards and, 119–120
    epic and legendary heroes, 111–113
    evaluating, 101
    fables, 108–109
    folktales, 97–107
    myths, 109–111
    ten-point model for teaching controversial issues in, 117–118
type design, in picturebooks, 73